HOLIDAY FUN
IN PLASTIC CANVAS

Making the holidays special for your family and friends is easy with Holiday Fun in Plastic Canvas. The handy holiday guide contains more than 75 projects that capture the spirit of special days, from Valentine's Day through Christmas. You'll find a variety of door decorations to greet your guests and tissue boxes to tickle your fancy, as well as a host of home accents that double as great gifts. It's never been easier — or more fun — to decorate your home for the holidays!

LEISURE ARTS, INC.
and
OXMOOR HOUSE, INC.

HOLIDAY FUN IN PLASTIC CANVAS

EDITORIAL STAFF

Vice President and Editor-in-Chief:
Anne Van Wagner Childs
Executive Director: Sandra Graham Case
Editorial Director: Susan Frantz Wiles
Publications Director: Carla Bentley
Creative Art Director: Gloria Bearden
Production Art Director: Melinda Stout

PRODUCTION
Managing Editor: Lisa Truxton Curton
Senior Editors: Donna Brown Hill and
Catherine Hubmann
Senior Project Coordinator: Susan McManus
Johnson
Project Coordinators: Alice Crowder,
Michelle Sass Goodrich, Sherry James, and
Rhonda Goerke Lombardo
Project Assistants: Kandi Ashford and JoAnn Forrest

DESIGN
Design Director: Patricia Wallenfang Sowers

EDITORIAL
Managing Editor: Linda L. Trimble
Associate Editor: Darla Burdette Kelsay
Assistant Editors: Tammi Williamson Bradley,
Terri Leming Davidson, and Robyn Sheffield-Edwards
Copy Editor: Laura Lee Weland

ART
Crafts Art Director: Rhonda Hodge Shelby
Senior Production Artist: Katie Murphy
Production Artists: Jonathan M. Flaxman,
Sonya McFatrich, Brent Miller, Dana Vaughn,
Mary Ellen Wilhelm, Karen L. Wilson, and
Dianna K. Winters
Photography Stylists: Sondra Daniel, Karen Hall,
Aurora Huston, Zaneta Senger, and Alaina Sokora

BUSINESS STAFF

Publisher: Bruce Akin
Vice President, Finance: Tom Siebenmorgen
Vice President, Retail Sales: Thomas L. Carlisle
Retail Sales Director: Richard Tignor
Vice President, Retail Marketing: Pam Stebbins
Retail Marketing Director: Margaret Sweetin
Retail Customer Service Manager: Carolyn Pruss

General Merchandise Manager: Russ Barnett
Distribution Director: Ed M. Strackbein
Executive Director of Marketing and Circulation:
Guy A. Crossley
Circulation Manager: Byron L. Taylor
Print Production Manager: Laura Lockhart
Print Production Coordinator: Nancy Reddick Baker

HOLIDAY FUN IN PLASTIC CANVAS
from the *Plastic Canvas Creations* series
Published by Leisure Arts, Inc., and Oxmoor House, Inc.

Library of Congress Catalog Number 96-76636
Hardcover ISBN 0-8487-1555-1
Softcover ISBN 1-57486-052-6

TABLE OF CONTENTS

Holiday Welcome

It's fun to ring in holidays all through the year with our cheery welcome sign! Stitched on 7 mesh plastic canvas, the sign features interchangeable motifs for several special occasions. We've included eye-catching designs for Valentine's Day, St. Patrick's Day, Easter, the Fourth of July, Halloween, Thanksgiving, and Christmas. We also used the motifs to create a variety of coordinating projects, which are shown throughout the book. Celebrating has never been easier!

Holiday Welcome Sign, page 8

You can celebrate lots of special days with this sweet messenger! Stitched on 7 mesh plastic canvas, the radiant angel holds a welcome sign when she's not heralding a holiday. Our collection of interchangeable motifs covers all the major holidays, and we've even included some pretty hair accessories for dressing her in the spirit of each occasion. What a heavenly way to celebrate!

Holiday Angel, page 12

HOLIDAY WELCOME SIGN
(Shown on pages 4 and 5.)

Skill Level: Intermediate
Sign Size: 18"w x 6³/₄"h
Approx Motif Size: 2¹/₂"w x 3¹/₂"h each
Supplies: Worsted weight yarn or Needloft® Plastic Canvas Yarn (refer to color keys), DMC Embroidery Floss (refer to color key), two 12" x 18" sheets of 7 mesh plastic canvas, three 10¹/₂" x 13¹/₂" sheets of 7 mesh plastic canvas, one 10¹/₂" x 13¹/₂" sheet of 10 mesh plastic canvas, #16 and #20 tapestry needles, sewing needle, nylon thread, sixteen 16" lengths of jute, three ⁵/₈" dia blue shank buttons, sawtooth hanger, and clear-drying craft glue
Stitches Used: Backstitch, Cross Stitch, French Knot, Gobelin Stitch, Lazy Daisy Stitch, Mosaic Stitch, Overcast Stitch, Tent Stitch, and Turkey Loop Stitch
Instructions: Photo models were stitched using worsted weight yarn and embroidery floss. Use #16 tapestry needle when working on 7 mesh canvas. Use #20 tapestry needle when working on 10 mesh canvas. Follow chart to cut Witch Star from 10 mesh plastic canvas. Follow chart and use required stitches to work Witch Star. Use dk yellow embroidery floss to cover unworked edges of Witch Star with Overcast Stitches. Follow chart to cut two

Sign pieces, 121 x 45 threads each, from 12" x 18" sheets of 7 mesh plastic canvas. Sign is worked through two thicknesses of plastic canvas. Follow chart and use required stitches to work Left Section of Sign. Follow chart and use required stitches to begin stitching Right Section on the next unworked thread of the stitched piece. Cut all remaining pieces from 7 mesh plastic canvas. Follow charts and use required stitches to work remaining pieces. Work stitches indicated by double lines on chart by inserting needle in same holes twice for complete coverage. Refer to photos for yarn color to cover unworked edges with Overcast Stitches. Use nylon thread and sewing needle to sew buttons to Sign at ◆'s. Use six strands of dk yellow embroidery floss to tack Witch Star to Witch at ▲'s. Glue Pumpkin Leaf to Pumpkin. Glue Ghost Bow to Ghost. Glue Cat Bow to Cat. Refer to photo for placement and glue motifs to desired lengths of folded jute. Tie remaining jute length into a bow around jute on Firecrackers. Use sewing needle and nylon thread to tack sawtooth hanger to wrong side of Sign.

NL	COLOR	
✎	00	black - 12 yds
✎*		black
✎	02	red - 20 yds
⬭	07	pink - 5 yds
⬭	08	lt flesh - 5 yds
⬭	20	yellow - 4 yds
⬭	26	lt green - 6 yds
✎	27	green - 8 yds
✎	33	dk blue - 56 yds
⬭	35	blue - 5 yds
⬭	39	ecru - 66 yds
✎*		ecru
✎	45	lavender - 4 yds
⬭	52	dk orange - 5 yds
⬭	57	dk yellow - 12 yds
○	52	dk orange Turkey Loop
O*		black Lazy Daisy

*Use 2-ply yarn.

Leprechaun (20 x 31 threads)

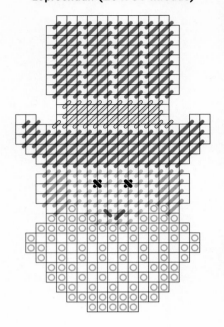

Valentine (23 x 29 threads)

Sign (121 x 45 threads) (Cut 2)
Left Section

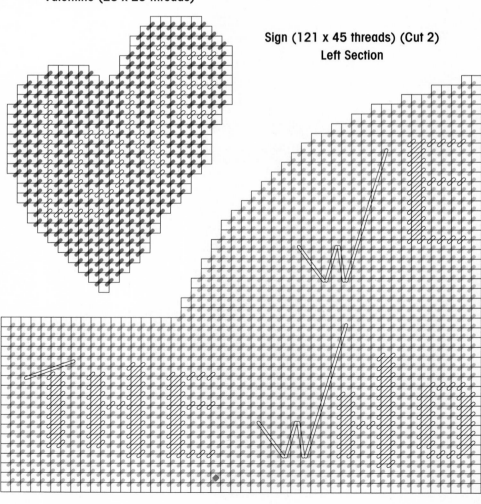

8

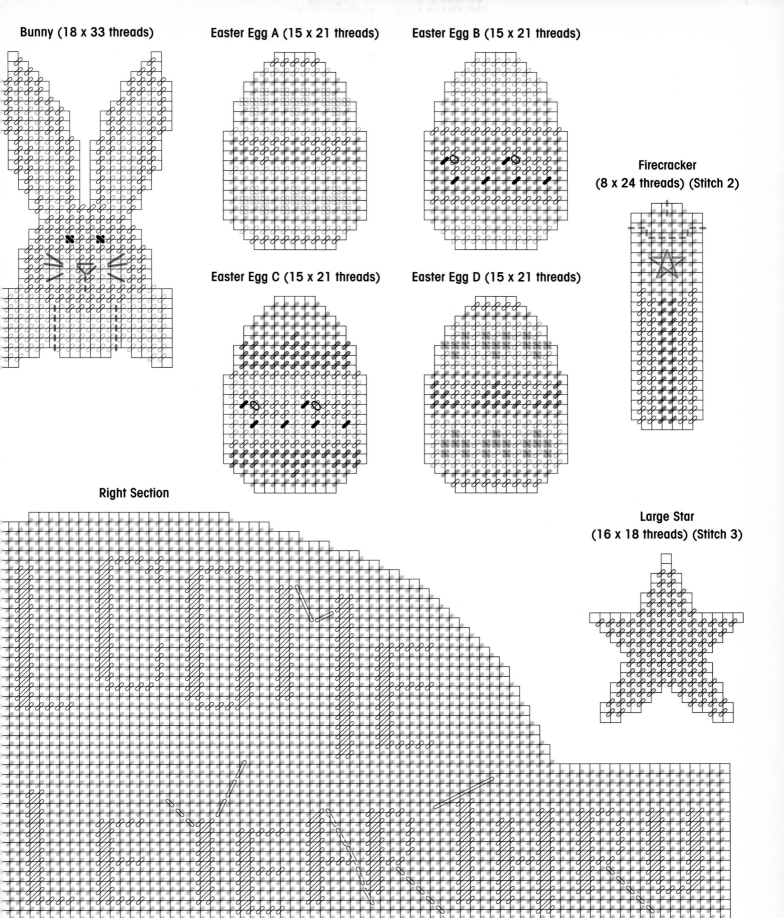

Bunny (18 x 33 threads)

Easter Egg A (15 x 21 threads)

Easter Egg B (15 x 21 threads)

Firecracker (8 x 24 threads) (Stitch 2)

Easter Egg C (15 x 21 threads)

Easter Egg D (15 x 21 threads)

Right Section

Large Star (16 x 18 threads) (Stitch 3)

Continued on page 10.

9

NL	COLOR		NL	COLOR
00	black		57	dk yellow
02	red		58	orange - 6 yds
08	lt flesh		00	black Fr. Knot
11	lt orange - 4 yds		33	dk blue Fr. Knot
14	brown - 1 yd		47	flesh Fr. Knot
17	gold - 2 yds		58	orange Turkey Loop
23	yellow green - 1 yd		17	gold Turkey Loop
27	green			
33	dk blue			

*Use 2-ply yarn.

DMC	COLOR
726 †	dk yellow - 1 yd

†Use 12 strands of floss.

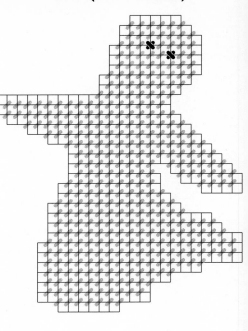

39	ecru
*	ecru
47	flesh - 4 yds
52	dk orange

Uncle Sam (16 x 43 threads)

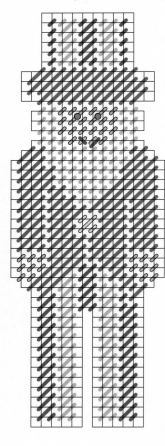

Flag (24 x 23 threads)

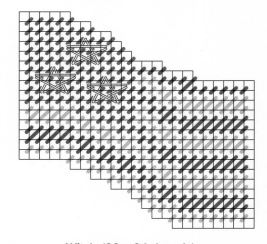

Ghost Bow (11 x 6 threads)

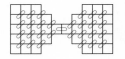

Cat Bow (7 x 7 threads)

Witch (28 x 34 threads)

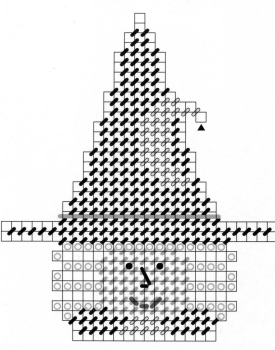

Cat (20 x 29 threads)

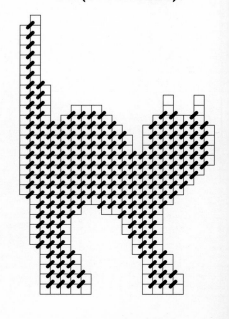

Witch Star
(6 x 7 threads) 10 mesh

Candy Corn (17 x 22 threads)

Pumpkin Leaf (6 x 7 threads)

Candy Cane (15 x 34 threads)

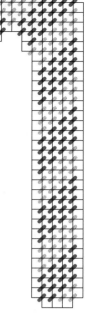

Pumpkin (20 x 33 threads)

Santa (26 x 43 threads)

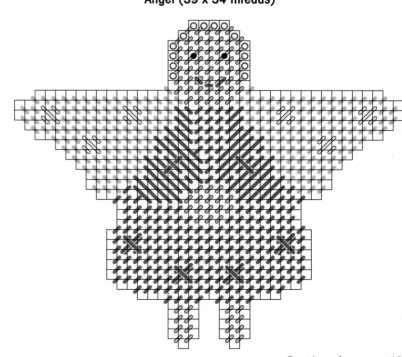

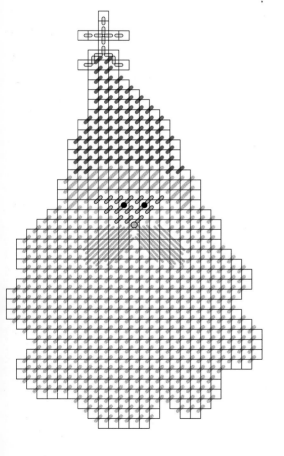

Angel (39 x 34 threads)

Continued on page 12.

NL	COLOR	
✏	00	black
✏	02	red
✏	27	green
✏	39	ecru
✏	52	dk orange
●	00	black

Snowflake (22 x 22 threads)

Snowman (27 x 39 threads)

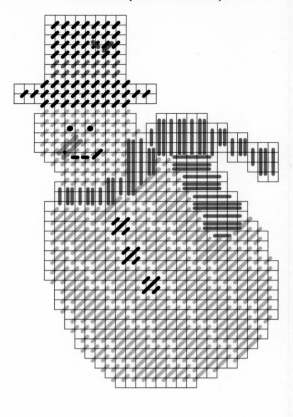

HOLIDAY ANGEL
(Shown on pages 6 and 7.)
Skill Level: Intermediate
Angel Size: 7³/₄"w x 9"h x 7"d
Supplies: Needloft® Plastic Canvas Yarn or worsted weight yarn (refer to color keys), DMC Embroidery Floss (refer to color keys), one 12" x 18" sheet of 7 mesh plastic canvas, one 10¹/₂" x 13¹/₂" sheet of 7 mesh plastic canvas, one 10¹/₂" x 13¹/₂" sheet of 10 mesh plastic canvas, #16 tapestry needle (for working with 7 mesh plastic canvas), and #20 tapestry needle (for working with 10 mesh plastic canvas), sewing needle, nylon thread, Velcro® brand fastener, and 1³/₈"l quilting pins
Stitches Used: Backstitch, Cross Stitch, French Knot, Mosaic Stitch, Overcast Stitch, Tent Stitch, and Turkey Loop Stitch
Instructions: Photo model was stitched using Needloft® Plastic Canvas Yarn and embroidery Floss. Cut Body from 12" x 18" sheet of 7 mesh canvas. Cut Wings Front, Wings Back, and Arms from 7 mesh plastic canvas. Cut all remaining pieces from 10 mesh plastic canvas. Use 3 strands of floss for Backstitch and French Knots and 12 strands of floss for all other stitches when working 10 mesh pieces. Follow charts and use required stitches to

work Holiday Angel pieces, leaving stitches in shaded areas unworked. Before adding Backstitch, complete background with dk blue Tent Stitches as indicated on Body chart. Matching ■'s and ★'s, work stitches in shaded areas to join back of Body, forming a cone. Refer to photo for placement and bend Arms around Body. Use red yarn and match ▲'s to tack Arms together. Use white yarn to join Wings Front to Wings Back. Use white yarn to tack Wings to Arms and Body. Use sewing needle and nylon thread to tack one ¹/₂" square of loop (soft) Velcro® to wrong side of each Sign. Tack one ¹/₂" square of hook (hard) Velcro® to right side of Arms. Insert one quilting pin under stitches on wrong side of each Bow, Star, and Heart Adornment.

Holiday Angel design by Maryanne Moreck.

Valentine's Day Sign
(22 x 19 threads) 10 mesh

Heart Adornment
(12 x 10 threads)
10 mesh

Red Bow (22 x 9 threads) 10 mesh

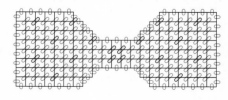

DMC	COLOR		DMC	COLOR
blanc	white - 16 yds		910	green - 3 yds
310	black - 10 yds		946	orange - 1 yd
321	red - 9 yds		3755	lt blue - 7 yds
414	grey - 1 yd		3818	dk green - 12 yds
415	lt grey - 1 yd		3826	rust - 2 yds
498	dk red - 7 yds		310	black Fr. Knot
677	gold - 29 yds		321	red Fr. Knot
760	pink - 1 yd		498	dk red Fr. Knot
823	dk blue - 9 yds		677	gold Fr. Knot
838	dk brown - 5 yds		838	dk brown Fr. Knot
869	brown - 7 yds		906	yellow green Fr. Knot - 1 yd
890	vy dk green - 3 yds		3818	dk green Fr. Knot

Christmas Sign (23 x 23 threads)
10 mesh

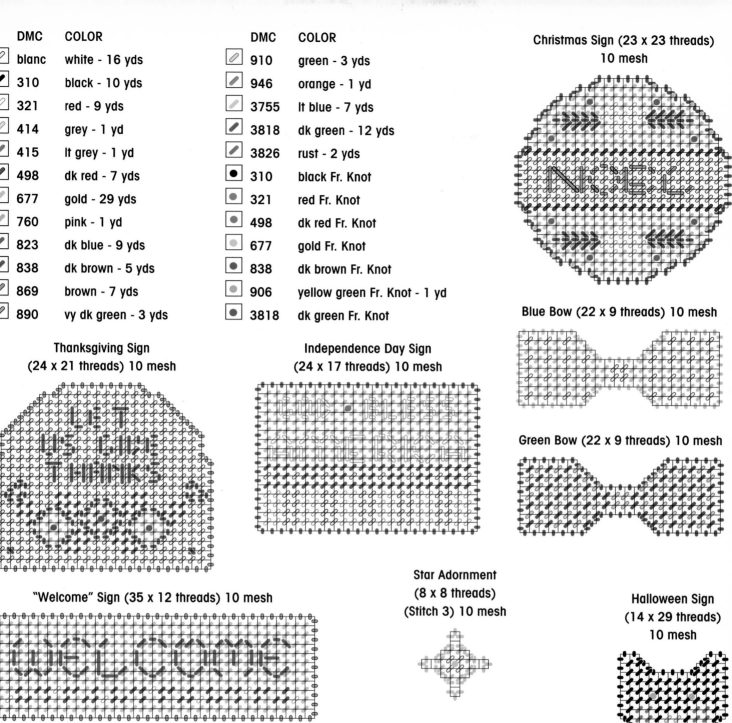

Thanksgiving Sign
(24 x 21 threads) 10 mesh

Independence Day Sign
(24 x 17 threads) 10 mesh

Blue Bow (22 x 9 threads) 10 mesh

Green Bow (22 x 9 threads) 10 mesh

"Welcome" Sign (35 x 12 threads) 10 mesh

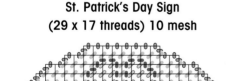

Star Adornment
(8 x 8 threads)
(Stitch 3) 10 mesh

Halloween Sign
(14 x 29 threads)
10 mesh

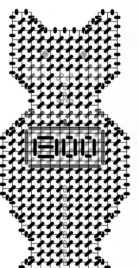

St. Patrick's Day Sign
(29 x 17 threads) 10 mesh

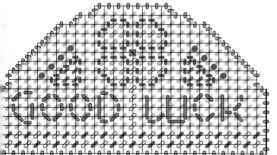

Easter Sign
(29 x 18 threads) 10 mesh

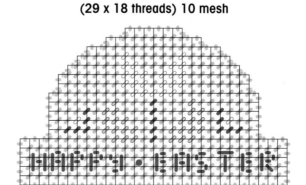

Continued on page 14.

13

Wings Front (52 x 20 threads) 7 mesh

Wings Back (52 x 20 threads) 7 mesh

Arms (66 x 23 threads) 7 mesh

NL	COLOR
00	black - 2 yds
01	red - 15 yds
02	lt red - 12 yds
07	pink - 1 yd
14	brown - 10 yds
16	tan - 8 yds
28	green - 6 yds

NL	COLOR
31	dk blue - 23 yds
35	blue - 6 yds
40	lt gold - 16 yds
41	white - 24 yds
56	flesh - 6 yds
14	brown Turkey Loop

DMC	COLOR
*321	red

*Use 6 strands of floss.

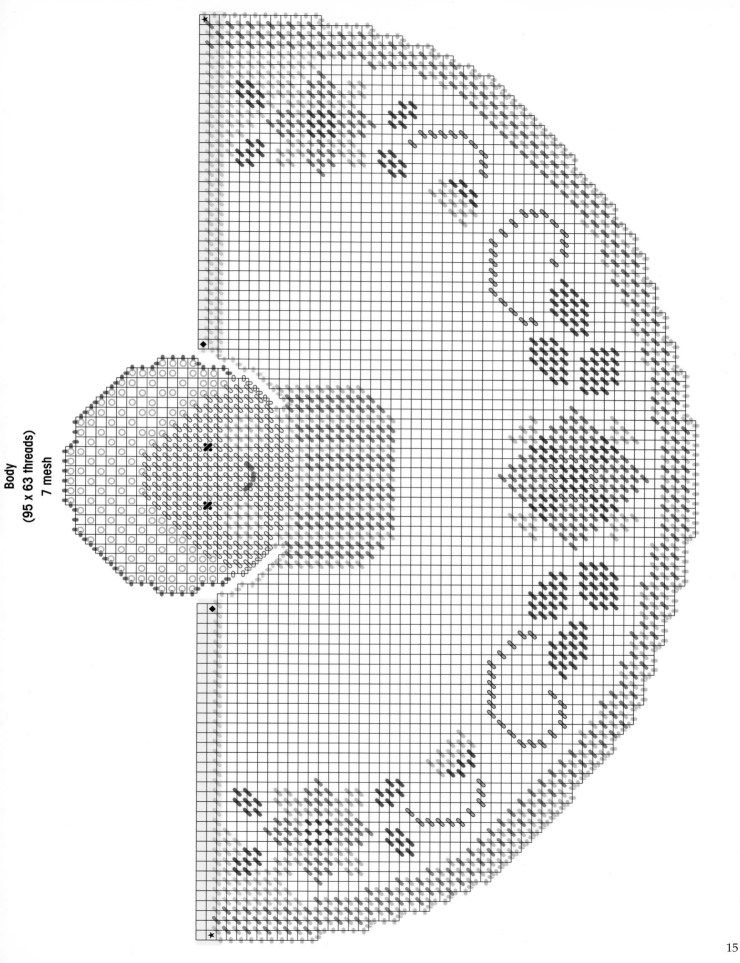

Body
(95 x 63 threads)
7 mesh

Valentine's Day

Brimming with sweet sentiments, this collection captures the charm of a Valentine's Day favorite — candy conversation hearts. A dainty lapel pin (right) guarantees plenty of hugs on Valentine's Day, and the fanciful heart box (below) offers a precious way to deliver tender messages of love. (Opposite) Convey your heartfelt feelings to a special sweetheart with our magnet and coaster set. The tissue box cover makes a darling accent for your home or office.

VALENTINE SET

Skill Level: Intermediate
Supplies For The Entire Set: Worsted weight yarn or Needloft® Plastic Canvas Yarn (refer to color key and photo), DMC Embroidery Floss (refer to color key), four 10½" x 13½" sheets of 7 mesh plastic canvas, one 10½" x 13½" sheet of 10 mesh plastic canvas, #16 tapestry needle (for use with 7 mesh canvas), #20 tapestry needle (for use with 10 mesh canvas), two 6" lengths each of ¼"w pink, purple, yellow, and green satin ribbon, magnetic strip, one 1½" pin back, cork or felt (optional), and clear-drying craft glue
Stitches Used: Backstitch, Cross Stitch, French Knot, Gobelin Stitch, Mosaic Stitch, Overcast Stitch, Scotch Stitch, and Tent Stitch

MAGNET

Size: 2¼"w x 2"h
Instructions: Photo model was stitched using embroidery floss. Use twelve strands for Cross Stitch and Overcast Stitch. Use six strands for Backstitch and French Knots. Cut Magnet from 10 mesh canvas. Follow chart and use required stitches to work Magnet. Glue magnetic strip to wrong side of completed stitched piece.

COASTERS

Size: 3½"w x 3½"h each
Instructions: Photo models were stitched using worsted weight yarn. Cut Coasters from 7 mesh canvas. Follow chart and use required stitches to work desired Coaster. If backing is desired, cut cork or felt slightly smaller than stitched piece. Glue cork or felt to wrong side of Coaster.

CANDY BOX

Size: 6"w x 5"h x 2"d
Instructions: Photo model was stitched using worsted weight yarn. Cut pieces from 7 mesh canvas. Follow charts and use required stitches to work Candy Box pieces. For Top Sides, cut two pieces of canvas 55 x 4 threads each. (**Note:** Top Sides are not worked.) For Bottom Sides, cut two pieces of canvas 57 x 12 threads each. Work Bottom Sides using white Scotch Stitches over five threads. Use white yarn for all joining and tacking. Join Bottom Sides along short edges. Match joined edges of Bottom Sides to ▲'s on right side of Bottom. Tack Bottom Sides to Bottom. Join Top Sides along short edges. Match joined edges of Top Sides to ■'s on wrong side of Top. Tack Top Sides to Top. Refer to photo for placement and tack Small Hearts to Bottom Sides. Tie each ribbon length into a bow and trim ends. Glue bows to Small Hearts.

TISSUE BOX COVER

Size: 4¾"w x 5¾"h x 4¾"d
(**Note:** Fits a 4¼"w x 5¼"h x 4¼"d boutique tissue box.)
Instructions: Photo model was stitched using worsted weight yarn. Cut pieces from 7 mesh canvas. Follow charts and use required stitches to work Tissue Box Cover pieces. Use white yarn for all joining. Join Sides along long edges. Join Top to Sides.

LAPEL PIN

Size: 2"w x 1½"h
Instructions: Photo model was stitched using embroidery floss. Use twelve strands for Cross Stitch and Overcast Stitch. Use six strands for Backstitch and French Knots. Cut Lapel Pin from 10 mesh canvas. Follow chart and use required stitches to work Lapel Pin. Glue pin back to wrong side of completed stitched piece.

Valentine Set designs by Maryanne Moreck.

Magnet (24 x 19 threads) 10 mesh

Tissue Box Cover Side
(32 x 38 threads) (Stitch 4) 7 mesh

Tissue Box Cover Top (32 x 32 threads) 7 mesh

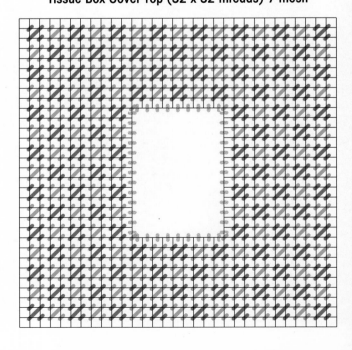

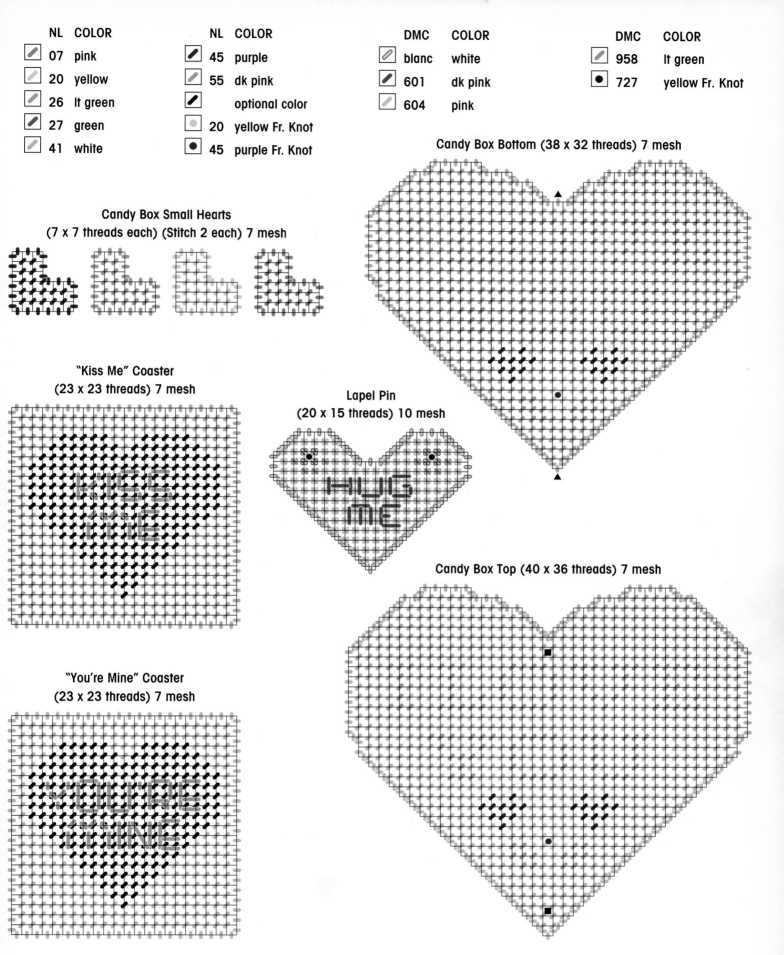

NL	COLOR		NL	COLOR
07	pink		45	purple
20	yellow		55	dk pink
26	lt green			optional color
27	green		20	yellow Fr. Knot
41	white		45	purple Fr. Knot

DMC	COLOR		DMC	COLOR
blanc	white		958	lt green
601	dk pink		727	yellow Fr. Knot
604	pink			

Candy Box Bottom (38 x 32 threads) 7 mesh

Candy Box Small Hearts
(7 x 7 threads each) (Stitch 2 each) 7 mesh

"Kiss Me" Coaster
(23 x 23 threads) 7 mesh

Lapel Pin
(20 x 15 threads) 10 mesh

HUG
ME

KISS
ME

"You're Mine" Coaster
(23 x 23 threads) 7 mesh

YOU'RE
MINE

Candy Box Top (40 x 36 threads) 7 mesh

ST. PATRICK'S DAY

Don't be caught without a touch of green on St. Patrick's Day — wear our lucky shamrock pin (right) *on your lapel! Not only does the pin honor the patron saint of Ireland, who is credited for establishing the shamrock on the Emerald Isle, but it will also keep you from being pinched! Dressed in traditional green, this folksy couple* (below) *will bring you the luck of the Irish.* (Opposite) *Our "beary" cute leprechaun, with his boldly lettered sign, offers a fun way to let everyone know you're proud of your heritage.*

IRISH SHELF SITTERS

Skill Level: Intermediate
Girl Size: 2½"w x 9½"h x 1¾"d
Boy Size: 2½"w x 10½"h x 1¾"d
Supplies: Worsted weight yarn or Needloft® Plastic Canvas Yarn (refer to color key), one 10½" x 13½" sheet of 7 mesh plastic canvas, #16 tapestry needle, three 8" lengths of ⅛"w white satin ribbon, and clear-drying craft glue
Stitches Used: Backstitch, French Knot, Gobelin Stitch, Lazy Daisy Stitch, Overcast Stitch, and Tent Stitch

Instructions: Photo models were stitched using worsted weight yarn. Follow charts and use required stitches to work Irish Shelf Sitter pieces.

Body Instructions: (**Note:** Words in parentheses refer to Boy.) Cut thirty-six 12" lengths of peach (green) yarn. Place nine lengths together and tie a knot near one end. With knot on wrong side of Body, thread loose ends through one opening in upper Body. To form elbow, tie a knot 1" from Body. Tie a third knot 1¾" from elbow and trim ends. Refer to photo to place third knot between one Hand A and one Hand B. Use peach yarn to join Hand pieces together. Repeat for remaining upper opening in Body. Place nine lengths of peach (green) yarn together and tie a knot near one end. With knot on wrong side of Body, thread loose ends through one opening in lower Body. To form knee, tie a knot 2" from Body. Tie a third knot 2½" from knee and trim ends. Refer to photo to place third knot between one Shoe Front (Boot Front) and one Shoe Back (Boot Back). Use green (black) yarn to join Shoe (Boot) pieces together. Repeat for remaining lower opening in Body. Use green yarn for remainder of joining. Match ▲'s to join ends of Body together. Join Bottom to Body.

For Girl only, refer to photo for placement and thread four 6" lengths of orange yarn through Body on each side of head. Fold yarn lengths in half matching ends. Tie one ribbon length into a bow around yarn on each side of head and trim ends. Tie remaining ribbon length into a bow and trim ends. Glue bow to Body.

Irish Shelf Sitter designs by Linda Huffman.

NL	COLOR		NL	COLOR
✎	00 black		✎	57 yellow
✎*	black		✎*	pink
✎	28 green		●	00 black Fr. Knot
✎	41 white		●	35 blue Fr. Knot
✎	52 orange		✎	28 green Lazy Daisy
✎	56 peach		*Use 2-ply yarn.	

Shoe Front
(8 x 9 threads)
(Stitch 2)

Shoe Back
(8 x 9 threads)
(Stitch 2)

Bottom
(17 x 11 threads)
(Stitch 2)

Boot Front
(8 x 8 threads)
(Stitch 2)

Boot Back
(8 x 8 threads)
(Stitch 2)

Girl's Body (28 x 28 threads)

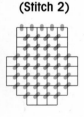

Hand A
(7 x 7 threads)
(Stitch 4)

Hand B
(7 x 7 threads)
(Stitch 4)

Boy's Body (31 x 31 threads)

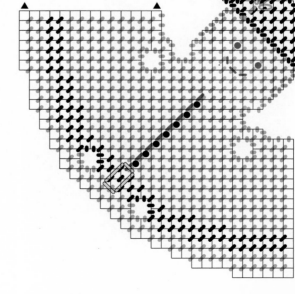

"I'M IRISH" SIGN

Skill Level: Intermediate
Size: 9½"w x 5¾"h
Supplies: Worsted weight yarn or Needloft® Plastic Canvas Yarn (refer to color key and photo), metallic gold yarn, one 10½" x 13½" sheet of 7 mesh plastic canvas, one 10½" x 13½" sheet of 10 mesh plastic canvas, #16 and #20 tapestry needles, 18" length of ⅝"w white grosgrain ribbon, and clear-drying craft glue
Stitches Used: Backstitch, Gobelin Stitch, Overcast Stitch, and Tent Stitch
Instructions: "I'm Irish" Sign was stitched using worsted weight yarn. Shamrocks were stitched using metallic gold yarn. Cut "I'm Irish" Sign from 7 mesh plastic canvas. Cut two Shamrocks from 10 mesh plastic canvas. Use #16 tapestry needle when stitching on 7 mesh plastic canvas and #20 tapestry needle when stitching on 10 mesh plastic canvas. Follow charts and use required stitches to work "I'm Irish" Sign pieces. Refer to photo for placement and glue Shamrocks to "I'm Irish" Sign. Glue ribbon ends to wrong side of completed stitched piece.

SHAMROCK LAPEL PIN

Skill Level: Beginner
Lapel Pin Size: 1¾"w x 1¾"h
Supplies: Worsted weight yarn or Needloft® Plastic Canvas Yarn (refer to color key and photo), one 10½" x 13½" sheet of 7 mesh plastic canvas, #16 tapestry needle, one 1" long pin back, and clear-drying craft glue
Stitches Used: Overcast Stitch and Tent Stitch
Instructions: Photo model was stitched using green worsted weight yarn. Follow chart and use required stitches to work Shamrock. Glue pin back to wrong side of completed stitched piece.

SHAMROCK HAT DECORATION

Skill Level: Intermediate
Shamrock Size: 1¼"w x 1¼"h
Supplies: Metallic gold yarn (refer to photo), one 10½" x 13½" sheet of 10 mesh plastic canvas, #20 tapestry needle, desired hat, and clear-drying craft glue
Stitches Used: Overcast Stitch and Tent Stitch
Instructions: Photo model was stitched using metallic gold yarn. Follow chart and use required stitches to work Shamrock. Glue completed stitched piece to hat.

NL	COLOR
✎ 27	green
✎ 41	white
✎	optional color

Shamrock (12 x 12 threads)

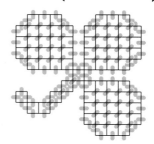

"I'm Irish" Sign (64 x 39 threads)

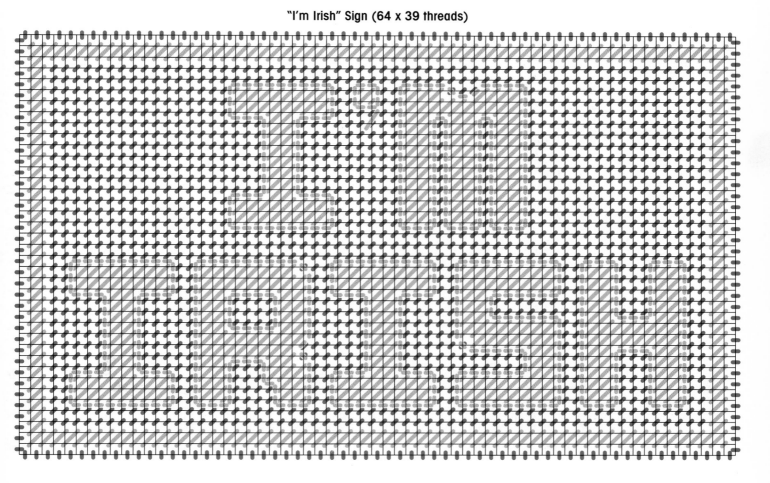

EASTER

Wearing their spring bonnets with all the frills, these darling little lambs will be the hit of your Easter celebration! "Ewe" will love our sweet little plant poke (right) and photo frame (below). (Opposite) Your guests are sure to flock to our charming centerpiece. The sweet lamb lifts off its bed of colorful flowers to reveal a secret candy dish.

LAMB PHOTO FRAME

Skill Level: Intermediate

Size: 6"w x 9"h x 3"d

(**Note:** Frame opening is approximately 3"w x 2½"h.)

Supplies: Worsted weight yarn or Needloft® Plastic Canvas Yarn (refer to color key), one 10½" x 13½" sheet of 7 mesh plastic canvas, #16 tapestry needle, and clear-drying craft glue

Stitches Used: Backstitch, French Knot, Gobelin Stitch, Mosaic Stitch, Overcast Stitch, Scotch Stitch, Tent Stitch, and Turkey Loop Stitch

Instructions: Photo model was stitched using worsted weight yarn. Follow charts and use required stitches to work Lamb Photo Frame pieces. Follow Front chart to cut Back from plastic canvas, omitting opening. Use white yarn to join Stands to Back between ✚'s. Use yarn color to match closest stitching area for all tacking. Referring to photo for placement, tack Flower A, Flower B, and one Flower C to Leaf Cluster. Tack Leaf Cluster to Front. Tack Ear and remaining Flower C to Front. Cut two 10" lengths of purple yarn. Bring yarn ends up at ▲'s on Front and tie yarn ends into a bow. Knot and trim yarn ends. Glue edges of desired photo to wrong side of Front. Refer to photo for yarn color used to join Front to Back along all edges.

Lamb Photo Frame design by Dick Martin.

NL	COLOR		NL	COLOR
00	black - 2 yds		40	lt gold - 5 yds
*	black		41	white - 7 yds
07	pink - 2 yds		45	purple - 3 yds
08	lt pink - 1 yd		20	yellow Fr. Knot
20	yellow - 1 yd		45	purple Fr. Knot
25	green - 3 yds		41	white Turkey Loop
26	lt green - 1 yd			*Use 2-ply yarn.

Photo Frame Front (40 x 59 threads)

Photo Frame Stand
(20 x 34 threads) (Cut 2)

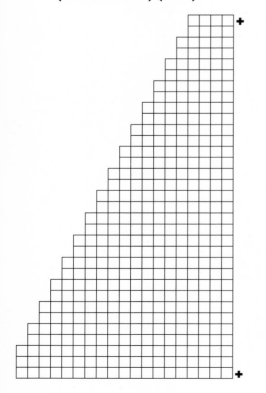

Photo Frame Flower A
(6 x 6 threads)

Photo Frame Flower B
(6 x 6 threads)

Photo Frame Flower C
(4 x 4 threads)
(Stitch 2)

Photo Frame Ear
(10 x 10 threads)

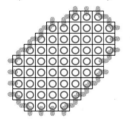

Photo Frame Leaf Cluster
(10 x 13 threads)

LAMB PLANT POKE
Skill Level: Beginner
Size: 4$\frac{1}{2}$"w x 4$\frac{1}{2}$"h x $\frac{1}{2}$"d
Supplies: Worsted weight yarn or Needloft® Plastic Canvas Yarn (refer to color key), one 10$\frac{1}{2}$" x 13$\frac{1}{2}$" sheet of 7 mesh plastic canvas, #16 tapestry needle, one wooden skewer, and clear-drying craft glue
Stitches Used: Backstitch, French Knot, Gobelin Stitch, Mosaic Stitch, Overcast Stitch, Tent Stitch, and Turkey Loop Stitch
Instructions: Photo model was stitched using worsted weight yarn. Follow charts and use required stitches to work Lamb Plant Poke pieces. Use yarn color to match closest stitching area for all tacking. Referring to photo for placement, tack one Flower A and Flower B to Leaf Cluster. Tack Leaf Cluster to Lamb. Tack Ear, Leaf, and remaining Flower A to Lamb. Tie a 10" length of purple yarn into a bow around Lamb's neck. Knot and trim yarn ends. Glue wooden skewer to wrong side of completed stitched piece.

Lamb Plant Poke design by Dick Martin.

NL	COLOR	
00	black - 1 yd	
*	black	
07	pink - 1 yd	
08	lt pink - 1 yd	
25	green - 2 yds	
26	lt green - 1 yd	
40	lt gold - 3 yds	
41	white - 6 yds	
45	purple - 3 yds	
20	yellow Fr. Knot - 1 yd	
45	purple Fr. Knot	
41	white Turkey Loop	

*Use 2-ply yarn.

Plant Poke Flower A
(4 x 4 threads)
(Stitch 2)

Plant Poke Flower B
(4 x 4 threads)

Plant Poke Leaf Cluster
(8 x 8 threads)

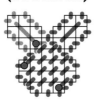

Plant Poke Leaf
(4 x 4 threads)

Plant Poke Ear
(7 x 7 threads)

Plant Poke Lamb (29 x 30 threads)

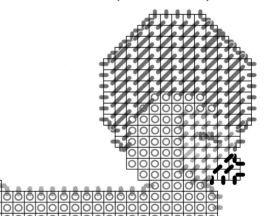

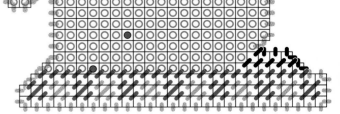

LAMB CENTERPIECE

Skill Level: Advanced

Size: 9¹/₂"w x 9"h x 9¹/₂"d

Supplies: Worsted weight yarn or Needloft® Plastic Canvas Yarn (refer to color keys), four 10¹/₂" x 13¹/₂" sheets of 7 mesh plastic canvas, and #16 tapestry needle

Stitches Used: Backstitch, French Knot, Gobelin Stitch, Mosaic Stitch, Overcast Stitch, Scotch Stitch, Tent Stitch, and Turkey Loop Stitch

Instructions: Photo model was stitched using worsted weight yarn. Follow charts and use required stitches to work Lamb Centerpiece pieces, leaving stitches in shaded areas unworked. Match ★'s and work stitches in shaded areas to join short ends of Dish Side, forming a cylinder. Refer to photo for placement to assemble Lamb Centerpiece. Place Dish Side over unworked canvas in center of Base Top, forming an oval. Use It green yarn to join unworked edges of Dish Side to Base Top. Match ▲'s and use yarn color to match closest stitching area to join Eggs to Base Top. Use yellow yarn to tack Flower D pieces to Base Top. Use white yarn to tack one Flower A to each Egg and Base Top. Use white yarn to join Base Bottom to Base Top.

Use white yarn and match ◆'s to tack one Ear to each Head Side. Matching like symbols, bend Head Top and place along edges of one Head Side. Beginning at ❤'s and ending at ✪'s, use yarn color to match closest stitching area to join Head Side to Head Top. Repeat to join remaining Head Side to Head Top. Unless otherwise indicated, use white yarn for remainder of joining and tacking. Matching ♣'s, fold and join edges of Body as indicated by arrow. Matching ■'s, fold and join edges of Body as indicated by arrow. Bend canvas and match ❖'s and ✳'s to join edges of Body between ❖'s and ✳'s. Place Support under shaded areas of Body. Work stitches in shaded area of Body through Body and Support. Match ✚'s and ▲'s to join Head Sides and Head Top to Body. Join Tail pieces together. Tack Tail to Body. Match ☽'s and use black yarn to join Leg Backs to Leg Fronts. Use black yarn to tack Legs to Body.

Use yarn color to match closest stitching area to tack remaining Flowers to Leaves. Use green yarn to tack Leaves to Bonnet. Cut two 18" lengths of purple yarn. Thread one yarn length through Bonnet at each ❤. Fold each yarn length in half, matching ends. Tie yarn lengths into a bow around Lamb's neck. Knot and trim yarn ends.

Lamb Centerpiece design by Dick Martin.

NL	COLOR	
07	pink - 6 yds	
08	It pink - 10 yds	
20	yellow - 5 yds	
25	green - 13 yds	
26	It green - 28 yds	
41	white - 115 yds	
45	purple - 14 yds	
● 20	yellow Fr. Knot	
● 45	purple Fr. Knot	

Dish Side (18 x 86 threads)

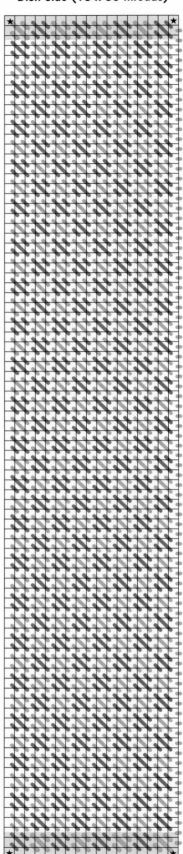

Egg A (12 x 12 threads)

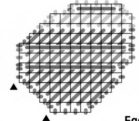

Egg B (12 x 12 threads)

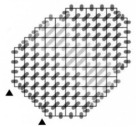

Egg C (12 x 12 threads)

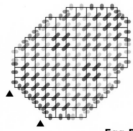

Egg D (12 x 12 threads)

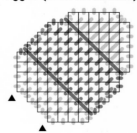

Flower A
(6 x 6 threads) (Stitch 5)

Flower B
(8 x 8 threads)

Flower C
(8 x 8 threads)

Leaves (15 x 15 threads)

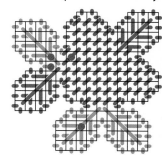

Flower D (10 x 10 threads)
(Stitch 4)

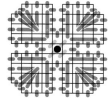

Base Top/Bottom (64 x 64 threads) (Cut 2, Stitch 1)

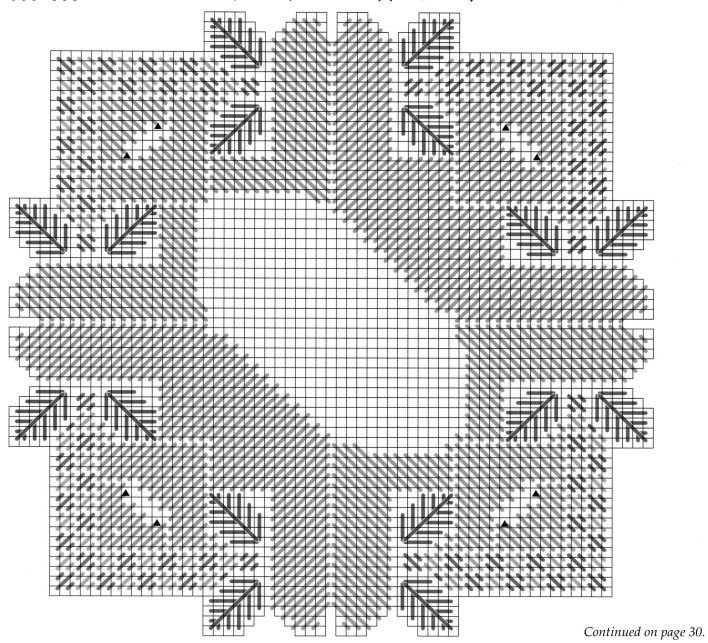

Continued on page 30.

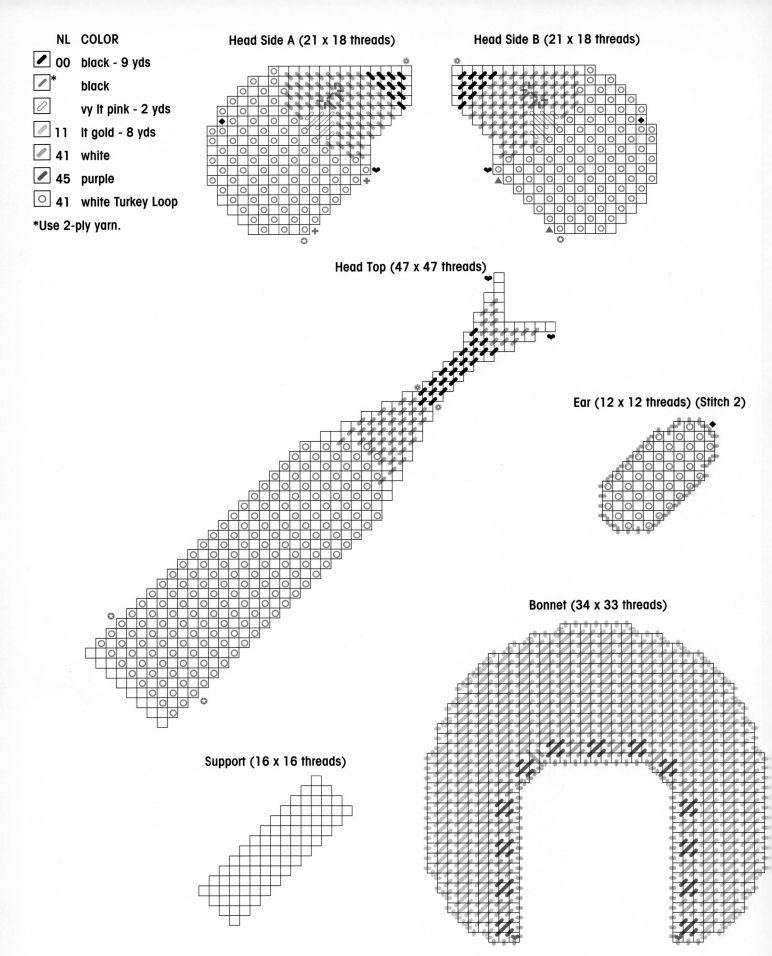

NL COLOR

00 black - 9 yds

* black

vy lt pink - 2 yds

11 lt gold - 8 yds

41 white

45 purple

41 white Turkey Loop

*Use 2-ply yarn.

Head Side A (21 x 18 threads)

Head Side B (21 x 18 threads)

Head Top (47 x 47 threads)

Ear (12 x 12 threads) (Stitch 2)

Bonnet (34 x 33 threads)

Support (16 x 16 threads)

Tail Side A (15 x 12 threads)

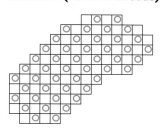

Tail Side B (15 x 12 threads)

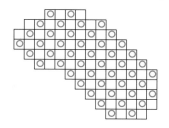

Leg Back (13 x 13 threads) (Stitch 2)

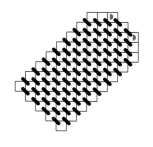

Body (69 x 69 threads)

Leg Front A (16 x 13 threads)

Leg Front B (16 x 13 threads)

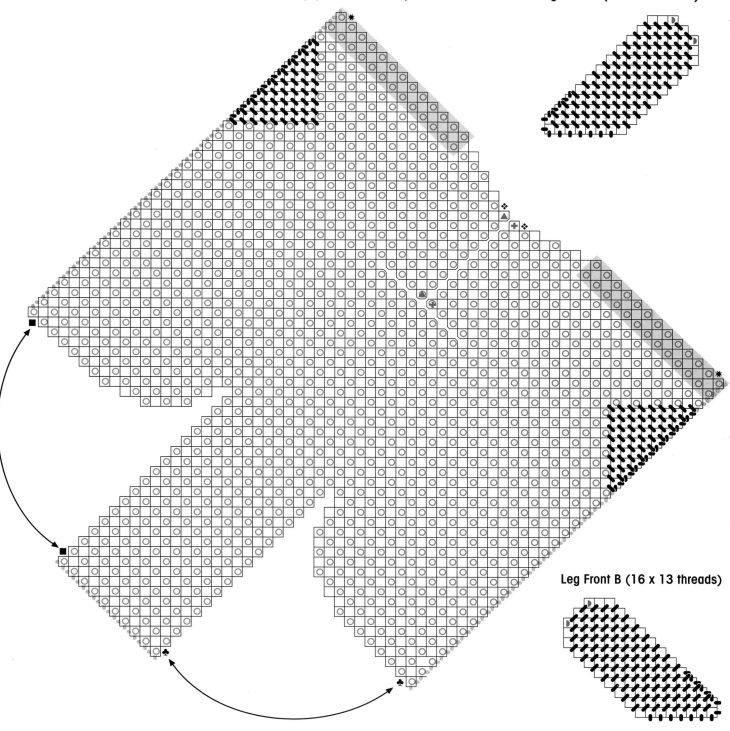

Patriotic Days

Symbols of our great country, eagles have long been associated with power, courage, and freedom. The mighty birds soar in this collection to help you celebrate our nation's patriotic days. Great for posting memos, an eagle magnet (right) captures the American spirit. The flag-waving holder (below) is home to coasters embellished with images of the stately bird, as well as that grand lady, the Statue of Liberty. (Opposite) Our eagle door decoration honors the good old U.S.A. It's an ideal accent for Independence Day!

Eagle Magnet, page 43

Patriotic Coaster Set, page 40

Eagle Door Banner, page 37

33

Patriotic Sampler, page 36
Eagle Candle Band, page 43

Eagle Candy Cup, page 43

Americana abounds in this admirable assortment! (Opposite) *A sampler featuring the United States' famous motto,* In God We Trust, *is designed to fit in a standard frame. The eagle candle band adds a regal touch to a candle and coordinates with the magnet shown on page 32. Our eagle candy cup* (left) *makes a patriotic party favor. Worked on 5 mesh plastic canvas, the star-spangled rug* (below) *resembles a spectacular spray of fireworks.*

Star Rug, page 42

PATRIOTIC SAMPLER

(Shown on page 34.)
Skill Level: Beginner
Size: 10"w x 8"h
Supplies: Worsted weight yarn or Needloft® Plastic Canvas Yarn (refer to color key), one 10½" x 13½" sheet of 7 mesh plastic canvas, #16 tapestry needle, and purchased frame with an 8" x 10" opening
Stitch Used: Tent Stitch

Instructions: Photo model was stitched using worsted weight yarn. Follow chart and use Tent Stitches to work Patriotic Sampler. Complete background with ecru Tent Stitches as indicated on chart. Insert completed stitched piece into frame.

Patriotic Sampler design by Polly Carbonari.

NL	COLOR
01	red - 15 yds
17	gold - 5 yds
32	blue - 12 yds
39	ecru - 35 yds

Patriotic Sampler (67 x 54 threads)

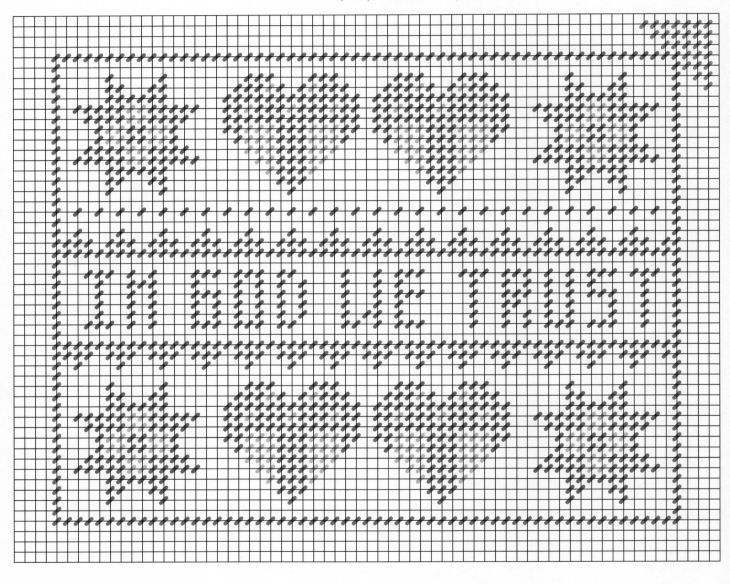

EAGLE DOOR BANNER

(Shown on page 33.)

Skill Level: Advanced

Size: 18"w x 15¼"h x ½"d

Supplies: Worsted weight yarn or Needloft® Plastic Canvas Yarn (refer to color keys), metallic gold yarn, one 12" x 18" sheet of 7 mesh plastic canvas, one 10½" x 13½" sheet of 7 mesh plastic canvas, #16 tapestry needle, nine 6" lengths of metallic gold cord, metallic gold foil cutting paper, sawtooth hanger, and clear-drying craft glue

Stitches Used: Backstitch, Cross Stitch, French Knot, Gobelin Stitch, Overcast Stitch, and Tent Stitch

Instructions: Photo model was stitched using worsted weight yarn and metallic gold yarn. Both Sections of Banner are stitched on one 12" x 18" sheet of canvas. Follow chart and use required stitches to work Top Section. Follow chart and use required stitches work first row of Bottom Section on the first unworked thread below the Top Section. Follow charts and use required stitches to work remaining Eagle Door Banner pieces, leaving stitches in shaded areas unworked. Bring two cord lengths up through Banner at one ★, leaving 1" of cord ends on wrong side. Glue short ends on wrong side of Banner. Twist lengths loosely together and take lengths back down at second ★. Glue remaining ends to wrong side of Banner. Match ■'s to place Head on Banner. Work stitches in shaded area of Head to join Head to Banner. Match like symbols to place Wings on Banner. Work stitches in shaded areas of Wings to join Wings to Banner. Thread one end of one cord length through each **1** on Banner. Glue ends of cord to wrong side of Banner. Repeat for remaining numbers, adding each cord length in numerical order. For vines, bring two cord lengths up through Banner at ▲, leaving 1" of cord ends on wrong side. Glue short ends on wrong side of Banner. Refer to photo and twist cord lengths together. Glue remaining ends to right side of Banner. Match like symbols and use metallic gold yarn to tack Feet to Banner. Follow Patterns to cut out five arrowheads, seven leaves, and three dots from metallic gold foil cutting paper. Fold arrowheads and leaves as indicated by broken lines on Patterns. Glue paper pieces to Eagle Door Banner. For hanger, use white yarn to tack sawtooth hanger to wrong side of Banner.

Eagle Door Banner design by Dick Martin.

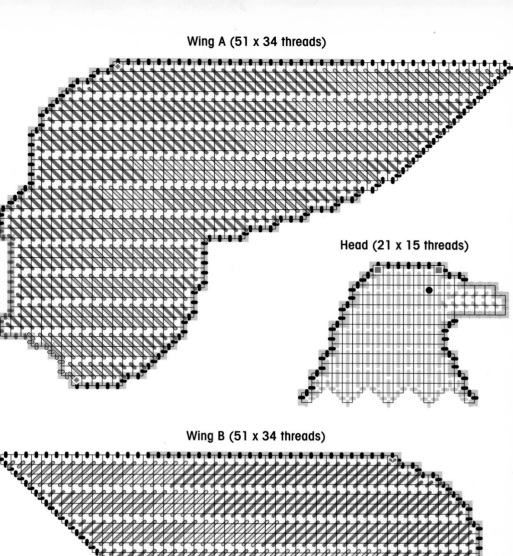

Wing A (51 x 34 threads)

Head (21 x 15 threads)

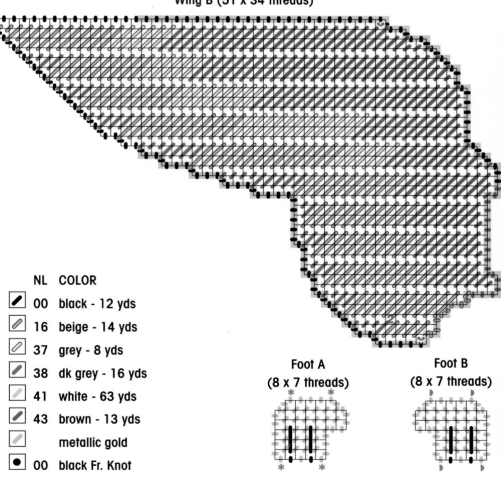

Wing B (51 x 34 threads)

NL	COLOR
00	black - 12 yds
16	beige - 14 yds
37	grey - 8 yds
38	dk grey - 16 yds
41	white - 63 yds
43	brown - 13 yds
	metallic gold
00	black Fr. Knot

Foot A
(8 x 7 threads)

Foot B
(8 x 7 threads)

Continued on page 38.

NL	COLOR
00	black
01	red - 14 yds
17	gold -1 yd

NL	COLOR
37	grey
38	dk grey
41	white

NL	COLOR
43	brown
48	blue - 14 yds
	metallic gold - 6 yds

Patterns

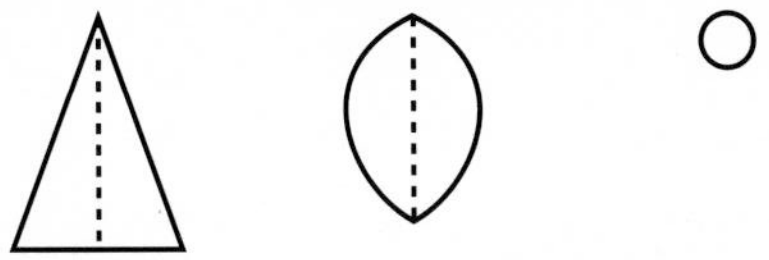

Banner (90 x 101 threads)

Top Section

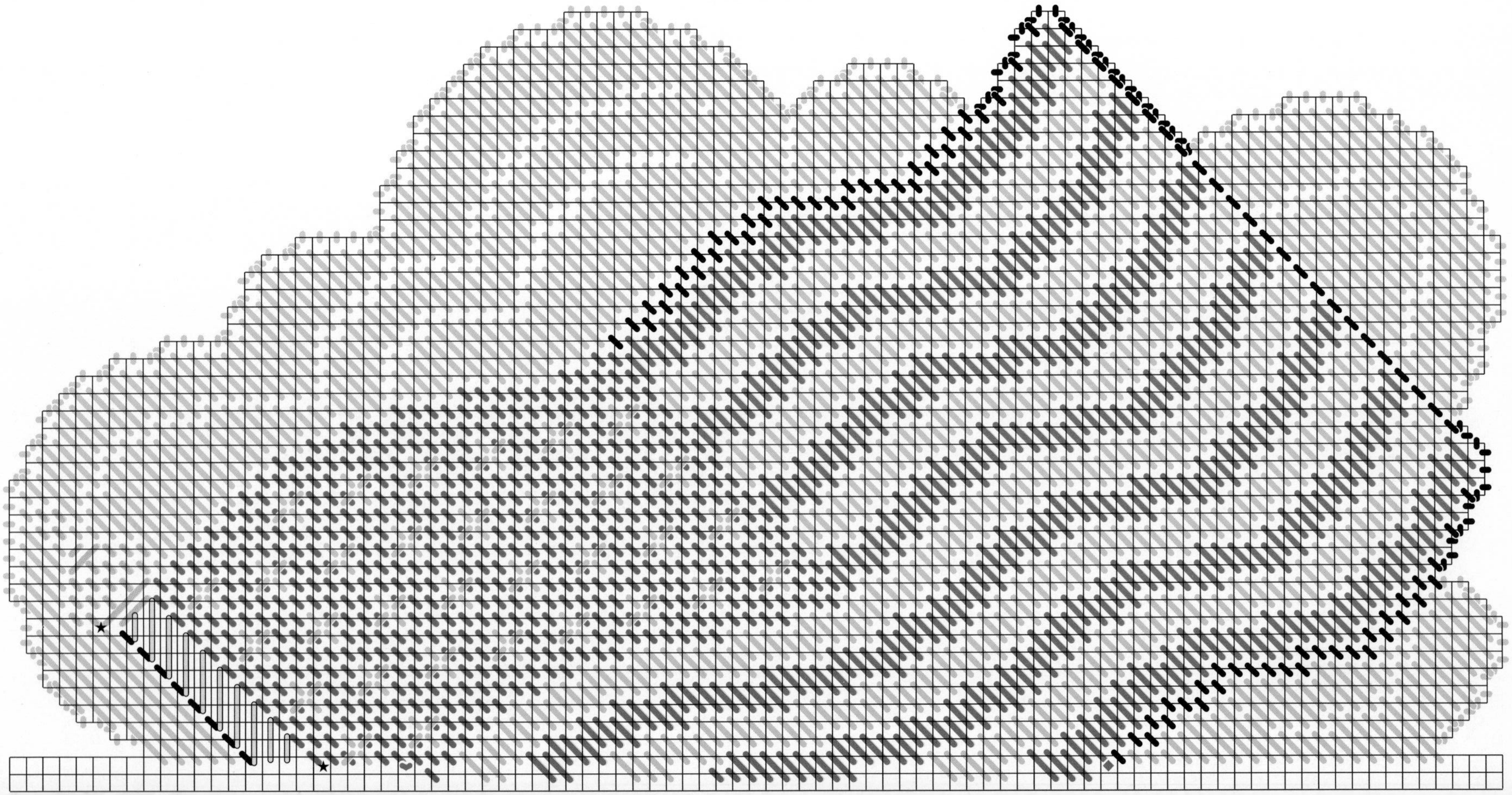

Bottom Section

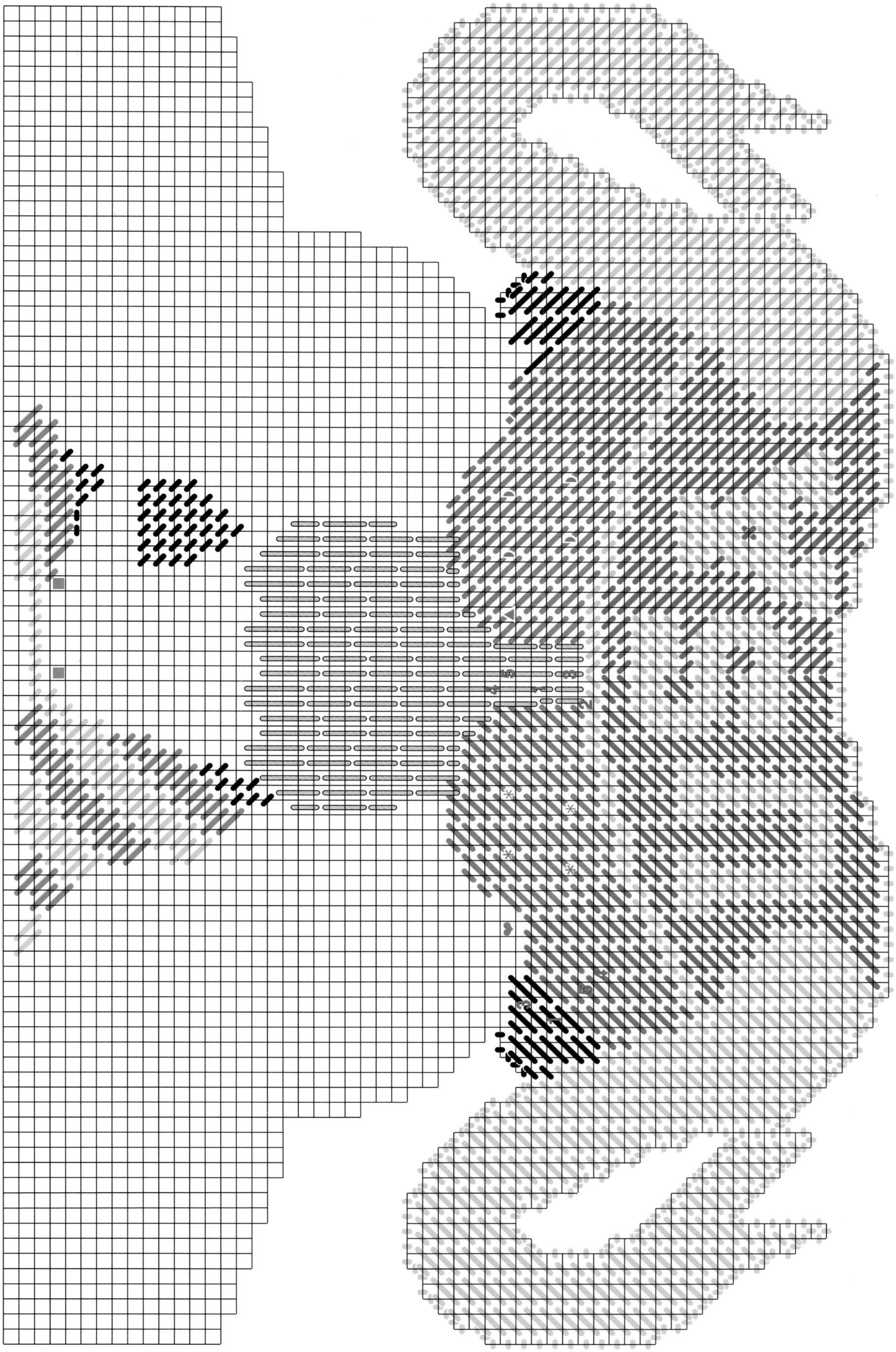

PATRIOTIC COASTER SET

(Shown on page 32.)

Skill Level: Intermediate

Coaster Size: 3³/₄"w x 3³/₄"h each

Holder Size: 4¹/₄"w x 4"h x 1¹/₂"d

Supplies: Sport weight yarn (refer to color key), DMC Embroidery Floss (refer to color key), two 10¹/₂" x 13¹/₂" sheets of 10 mesh plastic canvas, #20 tapestry needle, cork or felt (optional), and clear-drying craft glue

Stitches Used: Alternating Scotch Stitch, Backstitch, Overcast Stitch, and Tent Stitch

Instructions: Photo model was stitched using sport weight yarn and embroidery floss. Follow charts and use required stitches to work Patriotic Coaster Set pieces. Before adding Backstitch, complete backgrounds with Tent Stitches as indicated on charts. For Bottom, cut a piece of plastic canvas 41 x 14 threads. (**Note:** Bottom is not worked.) Use dk blue yarn for all joining. Join Sides to Back. Join Bottom to Sides and Back. Join Sides and Bottom to unworked edges of Front. If backing for Coasters is desired, cut cork or felt slightly smaller than stitched piece. Glue cork or felt to wrong side of Coaster.

Patriotic Coaster Set design by Mary Perry.

 white - 23 yds

 gold - 3 yds

red - 4 yds

dk red - 1 yd

lt blue - 18 yds

blue - 27 yds

dk blue - 60 yds

brown - 3 yds

grey - 9 yds

dk grey - 7 yds

black - 1 yd

DMC	COLOR	
*blanc	white - 2 yds	
*310	black - 2 yds	

*Use 3 strands of floss.

Eagle Coaster (37 x 37 threads) (Stitch 3)

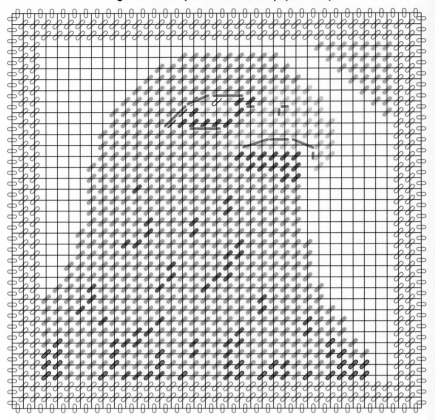

Statue Of Liberty Coaster (37 x 37 threads) (Stitch 3)

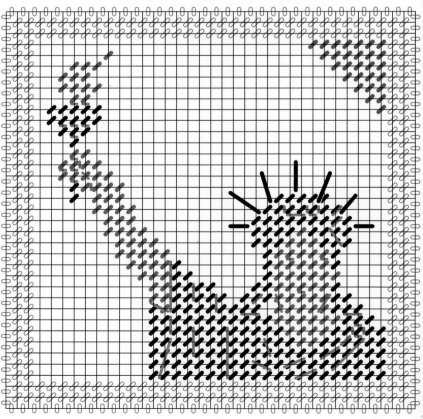

Front (41 x 39 threads)

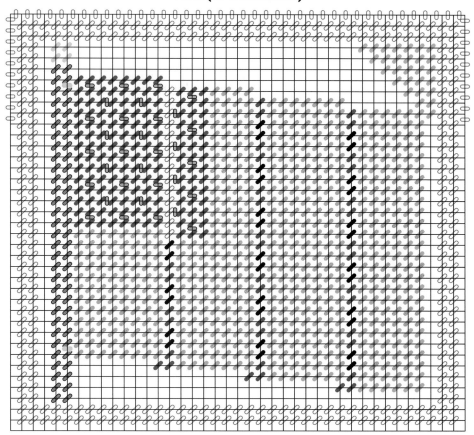

Side (14 x 29 threads) (Stitch 2)

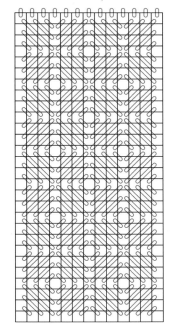

Back (41 x 29 threads)

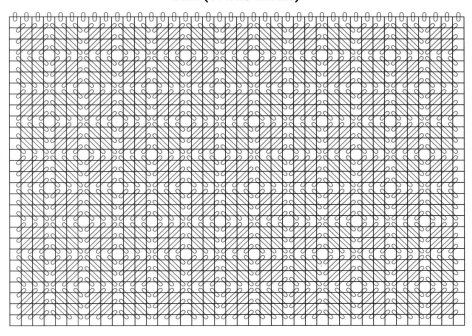

STAR RUG

(Shown on page 35.)
Skill Level: Beginner
Size: 23$\frac{1}{2}$"w x 17$\frac{3}{4}$"h
Supplies: Worsted weight yarn or Needloft® Plastic Canvas Yarn (refer to color key), two 13$\frac{5}{8}$" x 21$\frac{5}{8}$" sheets of 5 mesh plastic canvas, #16 tapestry needle, non-skid rug backing (optional), and Scotchgard™ brand fabric protector (optional)
Stitches Used: Gobelin Stitch, Overcast Stitch, Scotch Stitch, and Tent Stitch
Instructions: Photo model was stitched using two strands of worsted weight yarn. Follow charts and use required stitches to work Rug pieces. Use red yarn and refer to Rug Diagram to join Blocks. Use red Overcast Stitches to cover unworked edges. Follow manufacturer's directions to apply non-skid rug backing and Scotchgard™ brand fabric protector to completed stitched piece.

Star Rug design by Michele Wilcox.

NL	COLOR
01	red - 140 yds
17	gold - 30 yds
32	blue - 95 yds
39	ecru - 90 yds

Rug Diagram

Block A	Block B	Block A	Block B
Block B	Block A	Block B	Block A
Block A	Block B	Block A	Block B

Block A (30 x 30 threads) (Stitch 6)

Block B (30 x 30 threads) (Stitch 6)

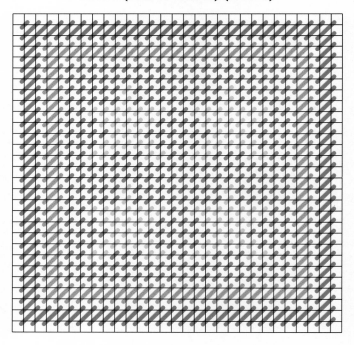

EAGLE CANDLE BAND

(Shown on page 34.)
Skill Level: Intermediate
Band Size: 1"h x 1" dia
Supplies: Sport weight yarn (refer to color key), DMC Embroidery Floss (refer to color key), one 10½" x 13½" sheet of 10 mesh plastic canvas, and #20 tapestry needle
Stitches Used: Backstitch, Overcast Stitch, Scotch Stitch, and Tent Stitch
Instructions: Photo model was stitched using sport weight yarn and embroidery floss. Follow charts and use required stitches to work Eagle and Candle Band. Use yarn color to match closest stitching area to join short ends of Candle Band. Use tan yarn to tack Eagle to Candle Band.

EAGLE MAGNET

(Shown on page 32.)
Skill Level: Intermediate
Size: 2¼"w x 3"h
Supplies: Sport weight yarn (refer to color key), DMC Embroidery Floss (refer to color key), one 10½" x 13½" sheet of 10 mesh plastic canvas, #20 tapestry needle, magnetic strip, and clear-drying craft glue
Stitches Used: Backstitch, Overcast Stitch, and Tent Stitch
Instructions: Photo model was stitched using sport weight yarn and embroidery floss. Follow chart and use required stitches to work Eagle. Glue magnetic strip to wrong side of completed stitched piece.

Eagle Candle Band and Eagle Magnet designs by Mary Perry.

EAGLE CANDY CUP

(Shown on page 35.)
Skill Level: Beginner
Size: 3"w x 3¼"h x 1¾"d
Supplies: Worsted weight yarn or Needloft® Plastic Canvas Yarn (refer to color key), DMC Embroidery Floss (refer to color key), one 10½" x 13½" sheet of white 7 mesh plastic canvas, and #16 tapestry needle
Stitches Used: Backstitch, Overcast Stitch, Scotch Stitch, and Tent Stitch
Instructions: Photo model was stitched using worsted weight yarn and embroidery floss. Follow charts and use required stitches to work Eagle Candy Cup pieces. Use yarn color to match closest stitching area to join Sides to Back. Use white yarn to join remaining edges of Sides to Back. Use blue yarn to join Sides to Front. Cut a piece of plastic canvas 11 x 20 threads for Bottom. (**Note:** Bottom is not worked.) Use brown yarn to join Bottom to Front. Use white yarn to join Bottom to Back and Sides.

Eagle Candy Cup design by Mary Perry.

COLOR	
	white
	gold
	red
	blue
	tan

DMC	COLOR
*300	brown
*310	black
*414	grey

*Use 6 strands of floss.

Candle Band
(11 x 29 threads)

Eagle (23 x 30 threads)

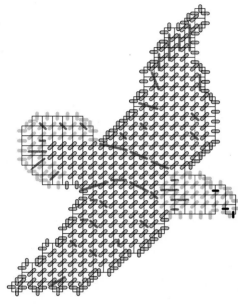

NL	COLOR
00	black - 1 yd
01	red - 2 yds
14	brown - 1 yd
17	gold - 1 yd
32	blue - 3 yds
38	grey - 2 yds
41	white - 6 yds

DMC	COLOR
*310	black - 1 yd

*Use 3 strands of floss.

Front (20 x 22 threads)

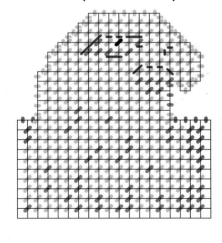

Back (20 x 11 threads)

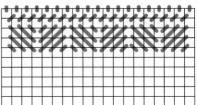

Side (11 x 11 threads)
(Stitch 2)

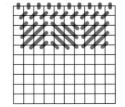

HALLOWEEN

Expecting an invasion of ghosts and goblins on Halloween night? Liven up the party with a host of Halloween goodies! Our candy corn magnet (right) and jack-o'-lantern tissue box cover (below) will add a tantalizing touch to the celebration. (Opposite) Keep snack foods frightfully fresh with our bewitching bag clips and jar lid, and when it's time to trick the neighbors for a treat, our terrifying totes, stitched on black plastic canvas, will have your goodies in the bag!

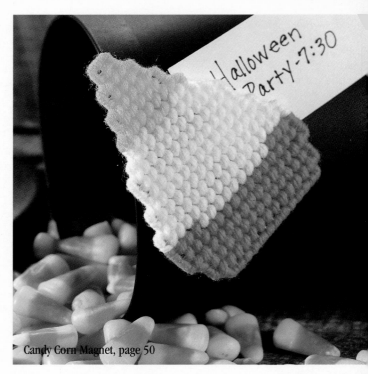

Candy Corn Magnet, page 50

Jack-O'-Lantern Tissue Box Cover, page 55

44

Jolt your guests into the holiday spirit with our Frankenstein door sign (below). Decked out in our All Hallows' Eve accessories (right) — which include a set of spooky button covers, earrings, a lapel pin, and matching necklaces — you'll scare up a batch of catchy compliments. (Opposite) The wacky witch tote can double as a spellbinding table accent or door decoration.

Halloween Jewelry, page 58

Monster Door Hanger, page 50

Witch Tote, page 52

A hodgepodge of Halloween motifs transforms a plain grapevine wreath (right) into a haunting display. Worked on squares of 5 mesh plastic canvas, our harvesttime rug (below) will attract the trick-or-treaters, and the matching wall hanging (opposite) will greet the little visitors with a jovial "Boo!"

Halloween Wreath, page 50

Jack-O'-Lantern Rug, page 54

48

Jack-O'-Lantern Wall Hanging, page 51

HALLOWEEN BAG CLIPS

(Shown on page 45.)
Skill Level: Beginner
Approx Size: 3¼"w x 4½"h each
Supplies For Two Bag Clips: Worsted weight yarn or Needloft® Plastic Canvas Yarn (refer to photo), one 10½" x 13½" sheet of 7 mesh plastic canvas, #16 tapestry needle, two wooden clothespins, and clear-drying craft glue
Stitches Used: Backstitch, Cross Stitch, Overcast Stitch, and Tent Stitch
Instructions: Photo models were stitched using worsted weight yarn. Follow charts, page 10, to work Cat, Cat Bow, Ghost, and Ghost Bow pieces. Use yarn color to match closest stitching area to cover unworked edges. Refer to photo for placement to glue pieces together. Glue clothespins to wrong sides of completed stitched pieces.

HALLOWEEN WREATH

(Shown on page 48.)
Skill Level: Beginner
Size: 18" dia
Supplies: Needloft® Plastic Canvas Yarn or worsted weight yarn (refer to color key, page 10), two 10½" x 13½" sheets of 7 mesh plastic canvas, one 10½" x 13½" sheet of 10 mesh plastic canvas, #16 and #20 tapestry needles, one 18" dia grapevine wreath, raffia, desired floral decorations, and hot glue gun and glue sticks
Stitches Used: Backstitch, Cross Stitch, French Knot, Gobelin Stitch, Overcast Stitch, Tent Stitch, and Turkey Loop Stitch
Instructions: Photo models were stitched using Needloft® Plastic Canvas Yarn. Follow charts, pages 10 and 11, to work Ghost, Ghost Bow, Witch, Witch Star, Cat, Cat Bow, Pumpkin, Pumpkin Leaf, and Candy Corn pieces. Refer to photo for yarn colors used to cover unworked edges. Use yellow yarn to tack Witch Star to Witch at ▲'s. Tie raffia into a bow. Refer to photo for placement to glue pieces together and assemble wreath.

CANDY CORN MAGNET

(Shown on page 44.)
Skill Level: Beginner
Size: 2½"w x 3¼"h
Supplies: Worsted weight yarn or Needloft® Plastic Canvas Yarn (refer to photo), one 10½" x 13½" sheet of 7 mesh plastic canvas, #16 tapestry needle, magnetic strip, and clear-drying craft glue
Stitches Used: Overcast Stitch and Tent Stitch

Instructions: Photo model was stitched using worsted weight yarn. Follow chart, page 11, to work Candy Corn. Use yarn color to match closest stitching area to cover unworked edges. Glue magnetic strip to wrong side of completed stitched piece.

"BOO" JAR LID

(Shown on page 45.)
Skill Level: Beginner
Size: 2½"w x 2½"h
Supplies: Worsted weight yarn or Needloft® Plastic Canvas Yarn (refer to color key), one 10½" x 13½" sheet of 7 mesh plastic canvas, #16 tapestry needle, one small-mouth jar lid ring, two each of 3mm, 5mm, and 7mm moving eyes, and clear-drying craft glue
Stitch Used: Tent Stitch
Instructions: Photo model was stitched using worsted weight yarn. Follow chart and use Tent Stitches to work "Boo" Jar Lid. Refer to photo for placement to glue moving eyes to stitched piece. Glue completed stitched piece into jar lid ring.

MONSTER DOOR HANGER

(Shown on page 46.)
Skill Level: Beginner
Size: 3¼"w x 9½"h
Supplies: Worsted weight yarn or Needloft® Plastic Canvas Yarn (refer to color key), one 10½" x 13½" sheet of 7 mesh plastic canvas, and #16 tapestry needle
Stitches Used: Backstitch, Cross Stitch, Gobelin Stitch, Overcast Stitch, and Tent Stitch
Instructions: Photo model was stitched using worsted weight yarn. Follow chart and use required stitches to work Monster Door Hanger.

"Boo" Jar Lid design by Debra Scheblein.

Monster Door Hanger design by Jack Peatman for LuvLee.

"Boo" Jar Lid (18 x 18 threads)

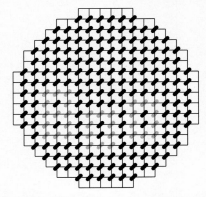

Monster Door Hanger (21 x 64 threads)

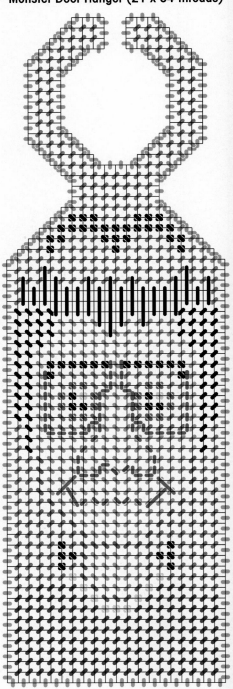

NL	COLOR		NL	COLOR
✎ 00	black		✎ 45	lt purple
✎ 02	red		✎ 57	yellow
✎ 28	green		✎ 58	orange
✎ 37	grey		✎ 61	lt green
✎ 41	white		✎ 64	purple

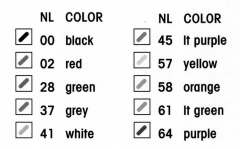

JACK-O'-LANTERN WALL HANGING
(Shown on page 49.)
Skill Level: Beginner
Size: 8"w x 10"h
Supplies: Needloft® Plastic Canvas Yarn or worsted weight yarn (refer to color key), one 10½" x 13½" sheet of 7 mesh plastic canvas, #16 tapestry needle, sewing needle and thread, and sawtooth hanger
Stitches Used: Mosaic Stitch, Overcast Stitch, and Tent Stitch

Instructions: Photo model was stitched using Needloft® Plastic Canvas Yarn. Follow chart and use required stitches to work Jack-O'-Lantern Wall Hanging. Use black Overcast Stitches to cover edges of stitched piece. Use sewing needle and thread to tack sawtooth hanger to wrong side of Wall Hanging.

Jack-O'-Lantern Wall Hanging by Polly Carbonari.

NL	COLOR
00	black - 18 yds
10	orange - 16 yds
12	lt orange - 16 yds
14	brown - 2 yds
30	green - 14 yds
39	ecru - 23 yds

Jack-O'-Lantern Wall Hanging (54 x 68 threads)

WITCH TOTE

(Shown on page 47.)

Skill Level: Advanced

Size: 9¹/₂"w x 18"h x 3¹/₂"d

Supplies: Worsted weight yarn or Needloft® Plastic Canvas Yarn (refer to color keys), DMC Embroidery Floss (refer to color keys), four 10¹/₂" x 13¹/₂" sheets of 7 mesh plastic canvas, #16 tapestry needle, Velcro® brand fastener, sewing needle, and nylon thread

Stitches Used: Backstitch, Gobelin Stitch, Overcast Stitch, Tent Stitch, and Turkey Loop Stitch

Instructions: Photo model was stitched using worsted weight yarn and embroidery floss. Follow charts and use required stitches to work Witch Tote Bag pieces, leaving stitches in shaded areas unworked. Unless otherwise indicated, use black for all joining. For Sides, match ◗'s and ✚'s to join one Fold C to one Fold A and one Fold B. Repeat to join remaining Fold pieces. Match ■'s to join one Upper Side to each Fold A and Fold B piece. Join each pair of Upper Sides along adjacent long edges. Match ♥'s to join Lower Back to Upper Back. Join Sides to Front, Lower Back, and Upper Back, leaving stitches in shaded areas unworked. Use yarn color to match closest stitching area to join Face to Back. Join Shoulder A pieces to Shoulder B pieces, leaving shaded areas unworked. Join Arm A pieces to Arm B pieces, leaving top edges unworked. Matching shaded areas, work stitches in shaded areas of Back to join Shoulders to Back and Side through four thicknesses of plastic canvas. Refer to photo for placement to join Arms to Shoulders through four thicknesses of plastic canvas. Use green yarn to tack Arms together at ♠'s. Join Bottom to Front, Back, and Sides. Using orange yarn, join two Leg pieces together along long edges. Repeat with remaining Leg pieces. Join Foot A and Foot B pieces together. Join Feet to Legs. Match ❖'s to tack Legs to Front and Bottom through four thicknesses. Use pink yarn and match ▲'s to tack Tongue to Front. Use sewing needle and thread to tack a 1" piece of hook (hard) Velcro® to wrong side of Front at top edge. Tack a 1" piece of loop (soft) Velcro® to wrong side of Back. Refer to photo for placement and thread 10" lengths of white floss through Feet. Tie each length into a bow and trim ends.

Witch Tote design by Debbie Tabor.

Tongue (7 x 9 threads)

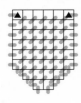

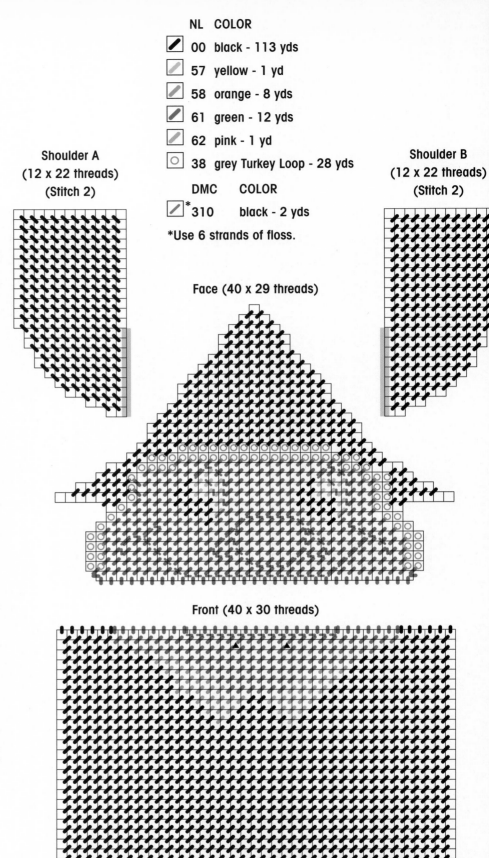

NL	COLOR	
00	black	- 113 yds
57	yellow	- 1 yd
58	orange	- 8 yds
61	green	- 12 yds
62	pink	- 1 yd
38	grey Turkey Loop	- 28 yds

DMC	COLOR	
*310	black	- 2 yds

*Use 6 strands of floss.

Shoulder A
(12 x 22 threads)
(Stitch 2)

Shoulder B
(12 x 22 threads)
(Stitch 2)

Face (40 x 29 threads)

Front (40 x 30 threads)

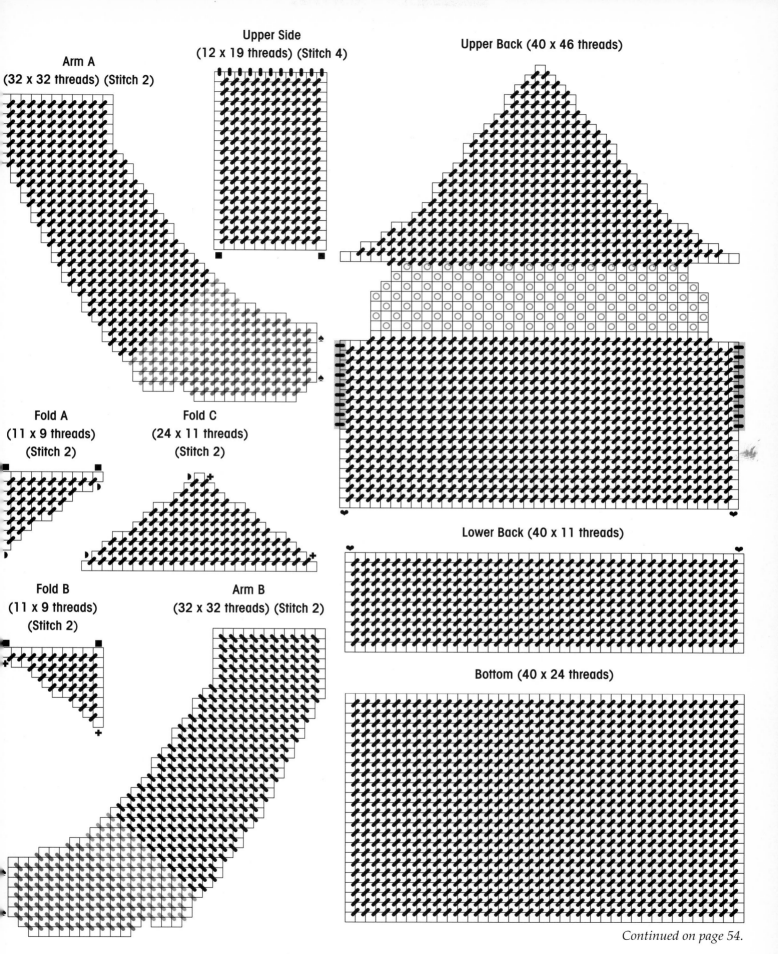

Arm A
(32 x 32 threads) (Stitch 2)

Upper Side
(12 x 19 threads) (Stitch 4)

Upper Back (40 x 46 threads)

Fold A
(11 x 9 threads)
(Stitch 2)

Fold C
(24 x 11 threads)
(Stitch 2)

Lower Back (40 x 11 threads)

Fold B
(11 x 9 threads)
(Stitch 2)

Arm B
(32 x 32 threads) (Stitch 2)

Bottom (40 x 24 threads)

Continued on page 54.

NL COLOR

✏ 00 black

✏ 58 orange

DMC COLOR

✏ *blanc white

*Use 6 strands of floss.

Foot A (20 x 24 threads)
(Stitch 2)

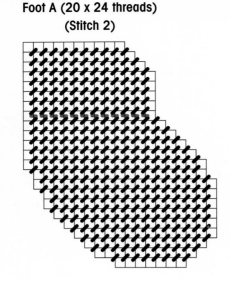

Leg (11 x 21 threads)
(Stitch 4)

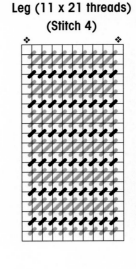

Foot B (20 x 24 threads)
(Stitch 2)

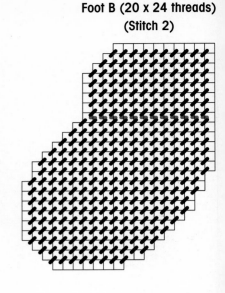

JACK-O'-LANTERN RUG

(Shown on page 48.)
Skill Level: Beginner
Size: 23½"w x 17¾"h
Supplies: Needloft® Plastic Canvas Yarn or worsted weight yarn (refer to color key), two 13⅝" x 21⅝" sheets of 5 mesh plastic canvas, #16 tapestry needle, non-skid rug backing (optional), and Scotchgard™ brand fabric protector (optional)
Stitches Used: Gobelin Stitch, Overcast Stitch, Scotch Stitch, and Tent Stitch

Instructions: Photo model was stitched using two strands of Needloft® Plastic Canvas Yarn. Follow charts and use required stitches to work Rug pieces. Refer to Rug Diagram, page 42, and join Blocks using green yarn. Cover unworked edges using green Overcast Stitches. Follow manufacturer's directions to apply non-skid rug backing and Scotchgard™ brand fabric protector to completed stitched piece.

Jack-O'-Lantern Rug design by Michele Wilcox.

NL COLOR

✏ 00 black - 17 yds

✏ 12 orange - 129 yds

✏ 30 green - 132 yds

✏ 39 ecru - 37 yds

Block A (30 x 30 threads) (Stitch 6)

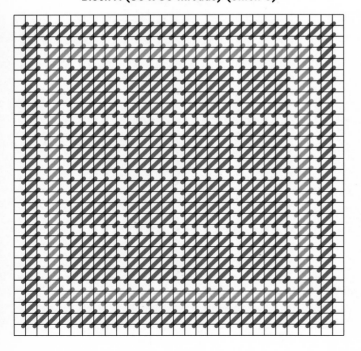

Block B (30 x 30 threads) (Stitch 6)

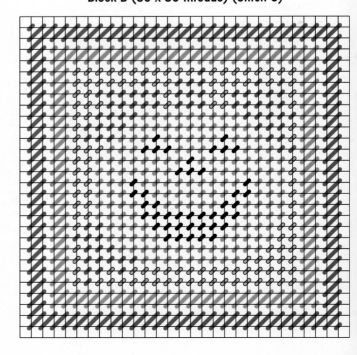

JACK-O'-LANTERN TISSUE BOX COVER

(Shown on page 44.)

Skill Level: Beginner

Size: 5"w x 7½"h x 5"d

(Note: Fits a 4¼"w x 5¼"h x 4¼"d boutique tissue box.)

Supplies: Worsted weight yarn or Needloft® Plastic Canvas Yarn (refer to color key), two 10½" x 13½" sheets of 7 mesh plastic canvas, and #16 tapestry needle

Stitches Used: Gobelin Stitch, Overcast Stitch, Scotch Stitch, and Tent Stitch

Instructions: Photo model was stitched using worsted weight yarn. Follow charts and use required stitches to work Jack-O'-Lantern Tissue Box Cover pieces. Refer to photo for placement to assemble pieces. Use brown yarn to join Stem pieces together along side edges. With wrong sides together, use green yarn to join Leaf Front to Leaf Back along all edges. Use brown yarn to tack Leaf to Stem. Use brown yarn to join Stem to Top. Use orange yarn for remainder of joining. Join Sides along long edges. Join Top to Sides.

Jack-O'-Lantern Tissue Box Cover design by Kimberley Irvin.

NL	COLOR
14	brown - 5 yds
17	yellow - 7 yds
29	green - 3 yds
52	orange - 50 yds

Stem
(10 x 10 threads)
(Stitch 4)

Leaf Front
(13 x 11 threads)

Leaf Back
(13 x 11 threads)

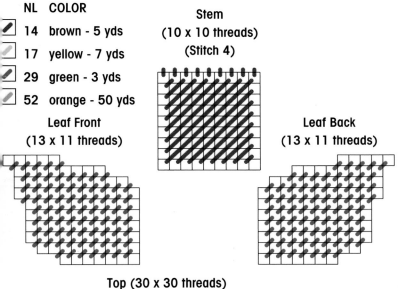

Top (30 x 30 threads)

Side A (30 x 38 threads)

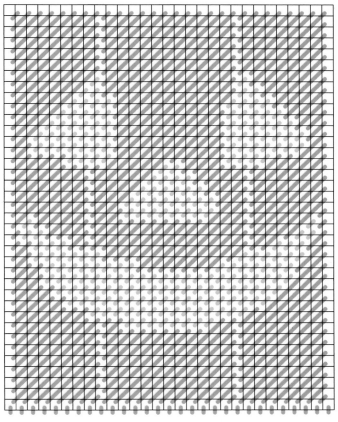

Side B (30 x 38 threads) (Stitch 3)

55

HALLOWEEN TOTE BAGS

(Shown on page 45.)
Skill Level: Beginner
Size: 8½"w x 15"h x 2½"d each
Supplies For One Tote Bag: Worsted weight yarn or Needloft® Plastic Canvas Yarn (refer to color key), three 10½" x 13½" sheets of black 7 mesh plastic canvas, and #16 tapestry needle
Stitches Used: Backstitch, Cross Stitch, Overcast Stitch, and Tent Stitch

Instructions: Photo models were stitched using worsted weight yarn. Follow chart and use required stitches to work desired Front, leaving stitches in shaded areas unworked. For Bottom, cut one piece of plastic canvas 57 x 17 threads. For Sides, cut two pieces of plastic canvas 17 x 63 threads each. For Handles, cut two pieces of plastic canvas 91 x 8 threads each. (**Note:** Back, Bottom, Sides, and Handles are not worked.) Use orange for all joining.

Join Front and Back to Sides along long edges. Join Bottom to Front, Back, and Sides. Match corners of Handle to ◆'s on wrong side of Front. Work stitches in shaded areas to join Handle to Front. Repeat with remaining Handle and Back. Use orange Overcast Stitches to cover unworked edges.

Halloween Tote Bag designs by Judy Hill.

"Monster Stash" Front/Back (57 x 63 threads) (Cut 2, Stitch 1)

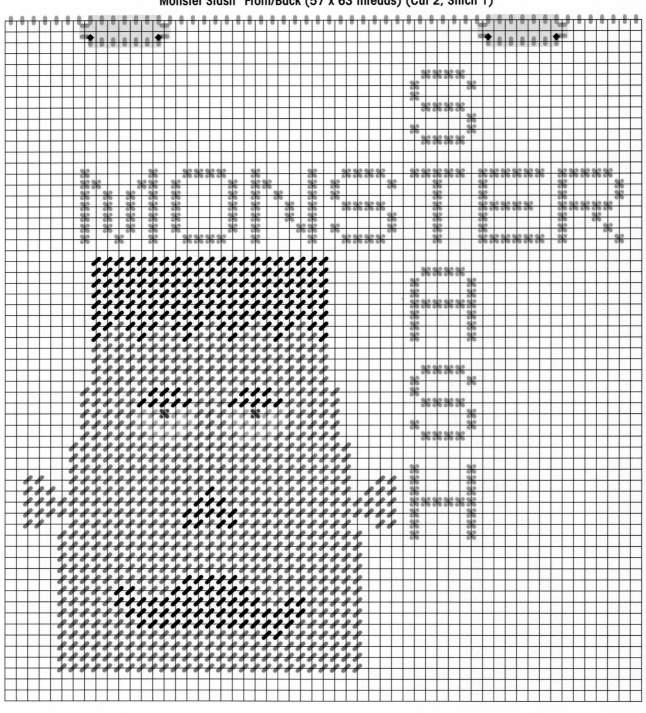

NL	COLOR		NL	COLOR
00	black		41	white
14	brown		43	tan
37	grey		52	orange
38	dk grey			

"Trick Or Treat" Front/Back (57 x 63 threads) (Cut 2, Stitch 1)

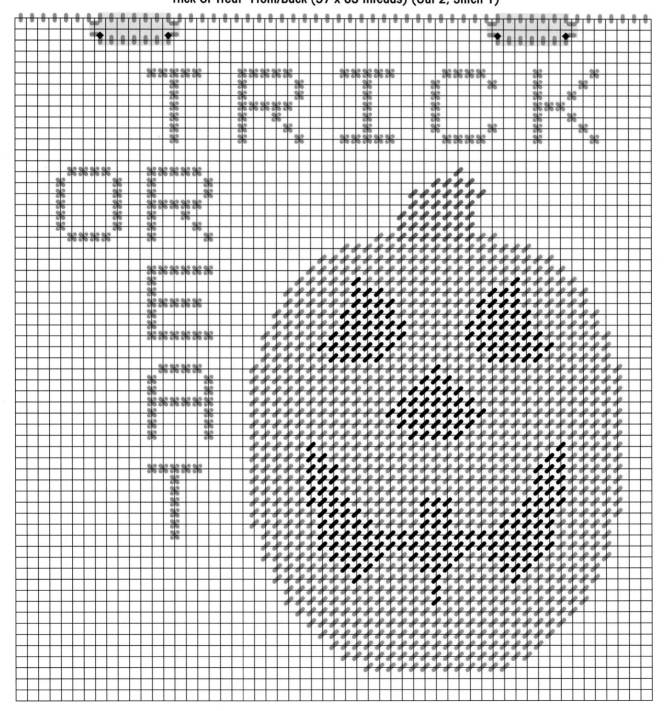

HALLOWEEN JEWELRY

(Shown on page 46.)
Skill Level: Intermediate
Stitches Used: Backstitch, French Knot, Fringe Stitch, Gobelin Stitch, Overcast Stitch, and Tent Stitch

SPOOKY BUTTON COVERS

Approx Size: 1¼"w x 1½"h each
Supplies: DMC Embroidery Floss (refer to color key), one 10½" x 13½" sheet of 10 mesh plastic canvas, and #20 tapestry needle

Instructions: Photo models were stitched using 12 strands of embroidery floss for Overcast Stitches and Tent Stitches. Use six strands of embroidery floss for Backstitches and French Knots. Follow charts and use required stitches to work desired Fronts. Use floss colors to match closest stitching areas to join Backs to Fronts.

JACK-O'-LANTERN EARRINGS

Size: 1"w x 1"h each
Supplies: DMC Embroidery Floss (refer to color key), one 10½" x 13½" sheet of 10 mesh plastic canvas, #20 tapestry needle, two 4mm flat post earring backs, and clear-drying craft glue

Instructions: Photo models were stitched using 12 strands of embroidery floss for Overcast Stitches and Tent Stitches. Use six strands of embroidery floss for Backstitches. Follow chart and use required stitches to work two Jack-O'-Lantern Fronts. Use floss colors to match closest stitching area to cover unworked edges with Overcast Stitches. Glue posts to wrong side of completed stitched pieces.

WITCH LAPEL PIN

Size: 1½"w x 2½"h
Supplies: DMC Embroidery Floss (refer to color key and instructions), one 8" x 11" sheet of 14 mesh plastic canvas, #24 tapestry needle, one 1" long pin back, and clear-drying craft glue

Instructions: Photo model was stitched using six strands of embroidery floss for Gobelin Stitches, Overcast Stitches, and Tent Stitches. Use three strands of floss for all other stitches. (**Note:** For different face colors, we substituted 738 tan in place of 906 green on two Witches and 3072 grey in place of 906 green on one Witch. For different hat color, we substituted 333 purple in place of 310 black on one Witch.) Follow charts and use required stitches to work Lapel Pin pieces. Work one each of Witch B, Witch D, and Witch E. Work two of Witch C. Work three of Witch A. Use floss color to match closest stitching area to cover unworked edges with Overcast Stitches. Refer to photo for placement to glue Witches together. Glue pin back to Witches.

WITCH NECKLACE

Size: 28" long
Supplies: DMC Embroidery Floss (refer to color key and instructions), one 10½" x 13½" sheet of 10 mesh plastic canvas, #20 tapestry needle, 1 yard of white dental floss, one silver clasp, seven 7mm silver jump rings, assorted beads (refer to photo), needle nose pliers, eight 6" lengths of ⅛"w black satin ribbon, two 2" lengths of ⅛"w black satin ribbon, and clear-drying craft glue

Instructions: Photo model was stitched using 12 strands of embroidery floss for Gobelin Stitches, Overcast Stitches, and Tent Stitches. Use six strands of floss for all other stitches. (**Note:** For different face colors, we substituted 738 tan in place of 906 green on two Witches and 3072 grey in place of 906 green on one Witch. For different hat color, we substituted 333 purple in place of 310 black on one Witch.) Follow charts and use required stitches to work three each of Witches A, B, and C. Work two each of Witches D and E. Use floss color to match closest stitching area to cover unworked edges with Overcast Stitches. Use pliers to place jump rings through tops of seven Witches. Refer to photo for placement to assemble Necklace. Tie one end of dental floss onto clasp. Thread beads and jump rings onto dental floss. Tie loose end of dental floss onto clasp ring. Fold four 8" ribbon lengths around Necklace. Glue ends of each ribbon length to wrong side of one Witch. Tie remaining 8" ribbon lengths into bows around folded ribbons and trim ends. Glue end of one 2" length of ribbon to wrong side of each remaining Witch. Glue loose end of each ribbon to one Witch on Necklace.

HALLOWEEN NECKLACE

Size: 27" long
Supplies: DMC Embroidery Floss (refer to color key), one 10½" x 13½" sheet of 10 mesh plastic canvas, #20 tapestry needle, 1 yard of white dental floss, one silver clasp, six 7mm silver jump rings, assorted beads (refer to photo), needle nose pliers, thirteen 8" lengths of ⅛"w orange satin ribbon, and clear-drying craft glue

Instructions: Photo model was stitched using 12 strands of embroidery floss for Tent Stitches and Overcast Stitches. Use six strands of embroidery floss for Backstitches and French Knots. Follow charts and use required stitches to work six Candy Corn Fronts, three Ghost Fronts, three Jack-O'-Lantern Fronts, and two Cat Fronts. Use floss color to match closest stitching area to cover unworked edges with Overcast Stitches. Use pliers to place one jump ring through top of each Candy Corn. Refer to photo for placement to assemble Necklace. Tie one end of dental floss onto clasp. Thread beads and jump rings onto dental floss. Tie loose end of dental floss onto clasp ring. Thread one length of ribbon through top of one Jack-O'-Lantern. Fold ribbon over center of Necklace. Glue ends of ribbon to wrong side of one Ghost. Thread one length of ribbon through each remaining stitched piece. Fold ribbon lengths around Necklace. Glue ends of each ribbon length to wrong side of each stitched piece. Tie remaining ribbon lengths into bows around folded ribbons and trim ends.

Halloween Jewelry designs by Becky Dill.

DMC	COLOR
blanc	white
310	black
321	red
608	orange
645	dk grey
738	tan
906	green
973	yellow
310	black Fr. Knot
433	brown Fr. Knot
906	green Fr. Knot
3072	grey Fr. Knot
433	brown Fringe

Witch A
(11 x 11 threads)

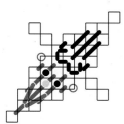

Witch B
(9 x 9 threads)

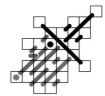
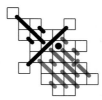

Witch C
(9 x 9 threads)

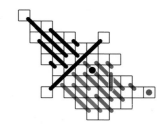

Witch D
(13 x 11 threads)

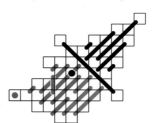

Witch E
(13 x 11 threads)

Cat Front
(16 x 19 threads)

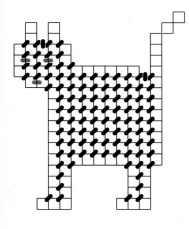

Jack-O'-Lantern Front
(11 x 12 threads)

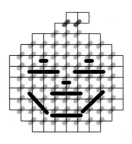

Candy Corn Front
(11 x 13 threads)

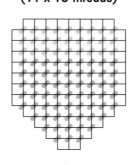

Ghost Front
(12 x 14 threads)

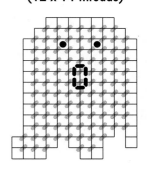

Cat Back
(16 x 19 threads)

Jack-O'-Lantern Back
(11 x 12 threads)

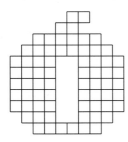

Candy Corn Back
(11 x 13 threads)

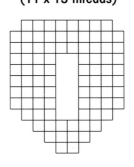

Ghost Back
(12 x 14 threads)

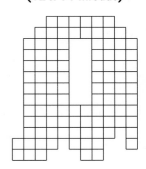

THANKSGIVING

A thankful spirit shines through in this autumn collection! Steeped in the tradition of the first New England Thanksgiving, the projects will enhance your holiday. Native American magnets (right) pay homage to those who shared the day with the early Colonists, and our ornamental corn (below) symbolizes the bountiful harvest they enjoyed. Wild turkeys could be found at the heart of the celebration, so we used the grand bird to create a dazzling basket centerpiece (opposite).

Native American and Feather Magnets, page 64

Ornamental Corn Bundle, page 64

Turkey Centerpiece, page 66

Turkey Door Banner, page 66

Sporting handsome plumage, our turkey door decoration (opposite), stitched on 7 mesh plastic canvas, will invite everyone to come in and join the festivities. Designed to coordinate with the centerpiece shown on page 61, it nests above a string of colorful autumn leaves. Decorative headbands and beads dress up a pair of Native American figures (left) outfitted in worsted weight "deerskins." The ornamental corn napkin ring (below) serves as a reminder of that first joyous celebration and our many blessings as Americans.

Ornamental Corn Napkin Ring, page 64

Native American Candlestick Figures, page 65

ORNAMENTAL CORN BUNDLE AND ORNAMENTAL CORN NAPKIN RING

(Corn Bundle shown on page 60.)
(Corn Napkin Ring shown on page 63.)
Skill Level: Beginner
Corn Bundle Size: 6"w x 8 1/2"h x 2"d
Corn Napkin Ring Size: 1 1/4"w x 6"h
Supplies: Tan, lt gold, gold, yellow, dk yellow, rust, brown, dk brown, orange, and beige worsted weight yarn (refer to photo), one 10 1/2" x 13 1/2" sheet of .7 mesh plastic canvas, #16 tapestry needle, 4" x 4" squares of tan paper twist, rubber band, raffia, napkin, polyester fiberfill, and clear-drying craft glue
Stitches Used: Overcast Stitch and Tent Stitch

Instructions For Corn Bundle: Photo model was stitched using worsted weight yarn. Follow charts and use desired yarn colors to work four Front #1 pieces, four Front #2 pieces, and eight Backs. Use optional color 1 for all joining. Match A to B and C to D to fold down sections of Fronts. Join sections of Front indicated by heavy black lines. Match ▲'s to join Fronts to Backs while lightly stuffing with polyester fiberfill. Refer to photo for placement and glue a square of paper twist around stitched area of each Back. To form husk, clip ends of paper. Stack ears of Corn into a bundle. Use rubber band around papers to hold stitched pieces in place. Tie 18" lengths of raffia into a bow around Corn Bundle and trim ends.

Instructions For Corn Napkin Ring: Photo model was stitched using worsted weight yarn. Follow Corn Bundle Instructions to stitch, join, and stuff one Front and one Back. Refer to photo for placement to glue a square of paper twist around stitched area of Back. To form husk, clip ends of paper. Tie 14" lengths of raffia into a bow around paper. Glue center of 12" lengths of raffia to back of completed stitched piece. Use 12" lengths of raffia to tie Corn Napkin Ring to napkin.

Ornamental Corn Bundle and Ornamental Corn Napkin Ring designs by Virginia Hockenbury.

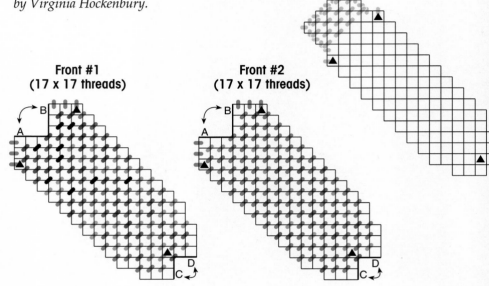

☑ tan
☑ optional color 1
☑ optional color 2
☑ optional color 3
☑ optional color 4
☑ optional color 5
☑ optional color 6

Back (18 x 18 threads)

Front #1 (17 x 17 threads)

Front #2 (17 x 17 threads)

NATIVE AMERICAN MAGNET AND FEATHER MAGNET

(Shown on page 60.)
Skill Level: Beginner
Native American Size: 2"w x 4 1/2"h
Feather Size: 1 1/4"w x 4 1/2"h
Supplies: Worsted weight yarn or Needloft® Plastic Canvas Yarn (refer to color key), one 10 1/2" x 13 1/2" sheet of 7 mesh plastic canvas, #16 tapestry needle, magnetic strip, and clear-drying craft glue
Stitches Used: Backstitch, French Knot, Gobelin Stitch, Overcast Stitch, Smyrna Cross Stitch, and Tent Stitch
Instructions: Photo models were stitched using worsted weight yarn. Follow chart and use required stitches to work desired magnet. Glue magnetic strip to wrong side of completed stitched piece.

Native American Magnet and Feather Magnet designs by Dick Martin.

NL	COLOR		NL	COLOR
☑ 00	black		☑ 54	turquoise
☑ 13	tan		● 00	black Fr. Knot
☑ 52	orange			

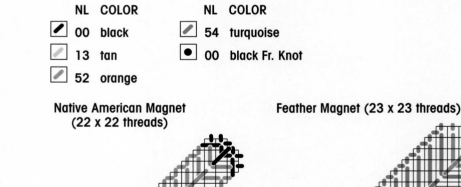

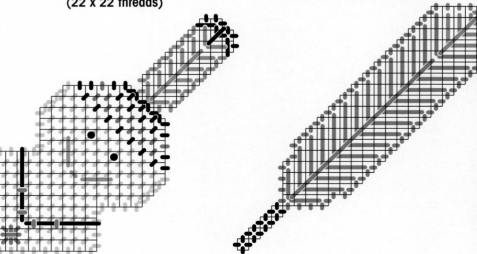

Native American Magnet (22 x 22 threads)

Feather Magnet (23 x 23 threads)

NATIVE AMERICAN CANDLESTICK FIGURES

(Shown on page 63.)
Skill Level: Advanced
Approx Size: 11"h x ³/₄" dia each
Supplies: Worsted weight yarn or Needloft® Plastic Canvas Yarn (refer to color key and instructions), DMC Embroidery Floss (refer to color key and instructions), one 12" x 18" sheet of Darice® Super Soft® 7 mesh plastic canvas, one 8" x 11" sheet of 14 mesh plastic canvas, #16 and #24 tapestry needles, beading needle, 54 turquoise seed beads, and 56 multi-colored 3mm glass beads
Stitches Used: Backstitch, Beaded Loop Stitch, French Knot, Gobelin Stitch, Overcast Stitch, Tent Stitch, and Turkey Loop Stitch Variation

Instructions For Man: Photo model was stitched using worsted weight yarn and embroidery floss. Cut Badge from 14 mesh canvas. Cut Man, Arms, and Feathers from 7 mesh canvas. Follow charts and use required stitches to work pieces. Use 975 brown floss to work Turkey Loop Stitch Variation (Fig. 25, page 94) in pink shaded areas. For necklace, refer to photo for placement and thread 24 seed beads and Badge onto one 18" strand of black floss. Secure ends on wrong side of Man at ■'s. Use yarn color to match closest stitching area to join Man along long edges. Use brown yarn and match ★'s to tack Arms to Man. Use dk brown yarn to tack Feathers to Man. For headband, cut one 8" length each of lt turquoise, turquoise, and rust yarn. Braid yarn lengths together for 3". Tie headband around Man and trim ends.

Instructions For Woman: Photo model was stitched using worsted weight yarn and embroidery floss. Cut Woman and Arms from 7 mesh canvas. Follow charts and use required stitches to work Woman and Arms. For necklace, refer to photo for placement and thread 30 seed beads onto one 18" strand of black floss. Secure ends on wrong side of Woman at ✚'s. For beaded fringe, cut six strands of 975 brown floss 28" long. Refer to Beaded Loop Stitch (Fig. 9, page 93) and use 3mm beads to work 14 beaded loops across blue shaded area. For each hair braid, cut three 6" lengths of black yarn. Refer to photo for placement and thread yarn ends through Woman. With ends even, braid yarn lengths together. Tie each braid end with a 6" length of turquoise yarn and trim ends. Use yarn color to match closest stitching area to join Woman along long edges. Use brown yarn and match ★'s to tack Arms to Woman. For headband, cut one 8" length each of lt turquoise, turquoise, and rust yarn. Braid yarn lengths together for 3". Tie headband around Woman and trim ends.

Native American Candlestick Figure designs by Becky Dill.

NL	COLOR
00	black - 5 yds
08	pink - 1 yd
13	brown - 19 yds
14	dk brown - 5 yds
18	flesh - 2 yds
39	ecru - 1 yd
00	black Fr. Knot

DMC	COLOR
*ecru	ecru - 1 yd
†310	black - 1 yd
*321	red - 2 yds
*726	yellow - 2 yds
*996	blue - 2 yds

*Use 6 strands of floss.

†Use 1 strand of floss.

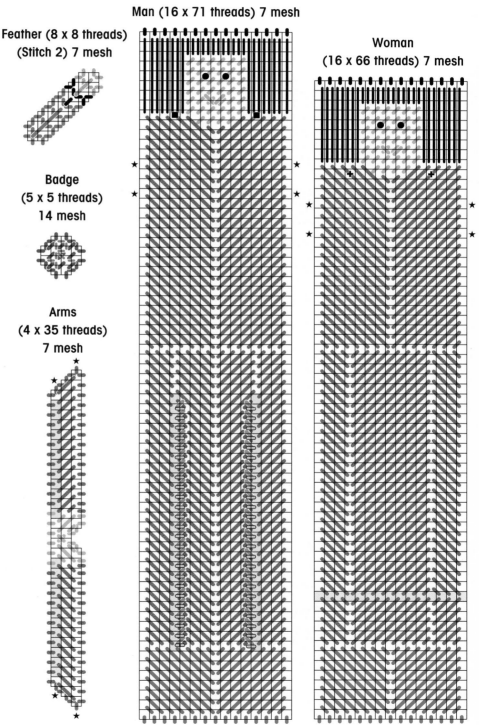

Feather (8 x 8 threads)
(Stitch 2) 7 mesh

Badge
(5 x 5 threads)
14 mesh

Arms
(4 x 35 threads)
7 mesh

Man (16 x 71 threads) 7 mesh

Woman
(16 x 66 threads) 7 mesh

TURKEY DOOR BANNER

(Shown on page 62.)

Skill Level: Advanced

Size: 13½"w x 28"h x 7½"d

Supplies: Worsted weight yarn or Needloft® Plastic Canvas Yarn (refer to color keys), four 10½" x 13½" sheets of 7 mesh plastic canvas, #16 tapestry needle, sawtooth hanger, sewing needle and thread, and clear-drying craft glue

Stitches Used: Backstitch, French Knot, Gobelin Stitch, Overcast Stitch, and Tent Stitch

Instructions: Photo model was stitched using worsted weight yarn. Follow charts and use required stitches to work Turkey Door Banner pieces, leaving stitches in shaded areas unworked. Work stitches indicated by double lines on chart for Front by inserting needle in same hole twice for complete coverage. Turn Tail over so that wrong side is facing up and work stitches in shaded areas. Refer to photo for yarn colors to work one additional piece each of Leaf A, Leaf B, Leaf C, and Leaf D. For Bottom, follow chart to cut an extra Middle

Section. (**Note:** Bottom is not worked.) Match ■'s to tack Beak to Front using orange yarn. Matching ▲'s, fold sections of Front together. Use tan yarn to join sections along unworked edges on top of head. Refer to photo for placement and use yarn color to match closest stitching area to tack Tail Feathers and Tail Center to Tail. Use black yarn to join lower edge of Front to curved edge of Bottom. Match ✛'s and ★'s and use brown yarn to join Front to Tail. Use black yarn to join Bottom to Tail. Refer to photo and use black yarn to join Wing A and Wing B to remaining unworked edges of Front and Tail. Use black yarn to tack Wing Tops and Wing Middles to Wings and Front through four thicknesses of canvas. Use black yarn to tack Middle Section to Bottom and Tail through three thicknesses of canvas. Use brown yarn and match ✪'s to join Leaf Strip to Middle Section. Refer to photo for placement and glue Leaves to Middle Section and Leaf Strip. Use sewing needle and thread to tack sawtooth hanger to wrong side of completed stitched piece.

TURKEY CENTERPIECE

(Shown on page 61.)

Skill Level: Advanced

Size: 13½"w x 10½"h x 7½"d

Supplies: Worsted weight yarn or Needloft® Plastic Canvas Yarn (refer to color keys), three 10½" x 13½" sheets of 7 mesh plastic canvas, and #16 tapestry needle

Stitches Used: French Knot, Gobelin Stitch, Overcast Stitch, and Tent Stitch

Instructions: Photo model was stitched using worsted weight yarn. Follow charts and Turkey Door Banner Instructions to work Beak, Front, Tail, Tail Center, Tail Feathers, Wings, Wing Tops, and Wing Middles. Follow Turkey Door Banner Instructions to assemble Turkey Centerpiece, omitting instructions for Middle Section, Leaf Strip, and Leaves.

Turkey Door Banner and Turkey Centerpiece designs by Dick Martin.

Leaf A (14 x 14 threads)

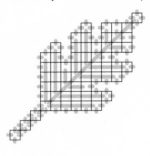

Leaf B (17 x 17 threads)

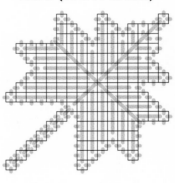

Wing Top (17 x 17 threads)
(Stitch 2)

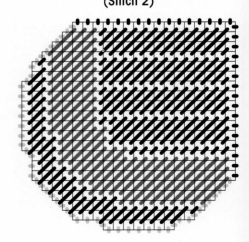

Leaf C (24 x 24 threads)

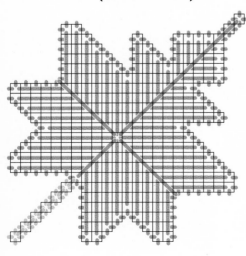

Leaf D (23 x 23 threads)

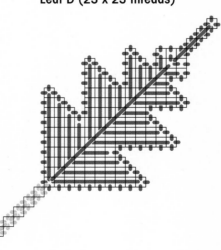

Wing Middle (22 x 22 threads)
(Stitch 2)

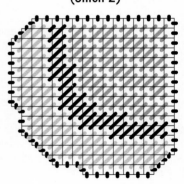

NL	COLOR		NL	COLOR
00	black - 22 yds		14	brown - 67 yds
12	lt orange - 10 yds		39	ecru - 8 yds
13	gold - 54 yds		40	lt gold - 25 yds

Tail Feathers (56 x 33 threads)

Tail Center (40 x 25 threads)

Middle Section (60 x 30 threads)

Leaf Strip
(8 x 71 threads)

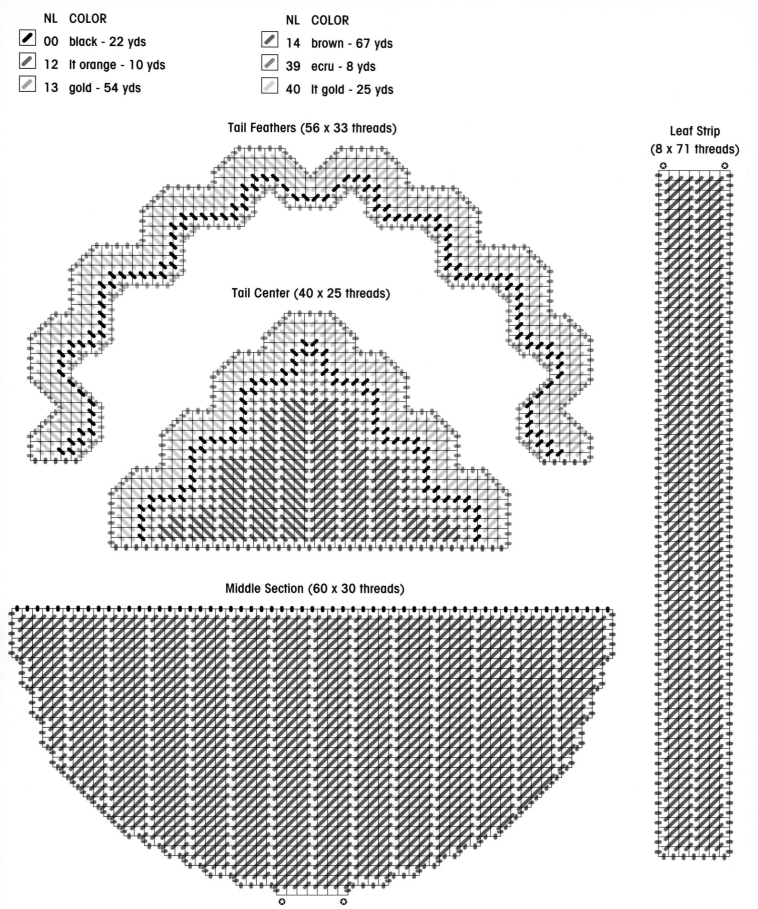

Continued on page 68.

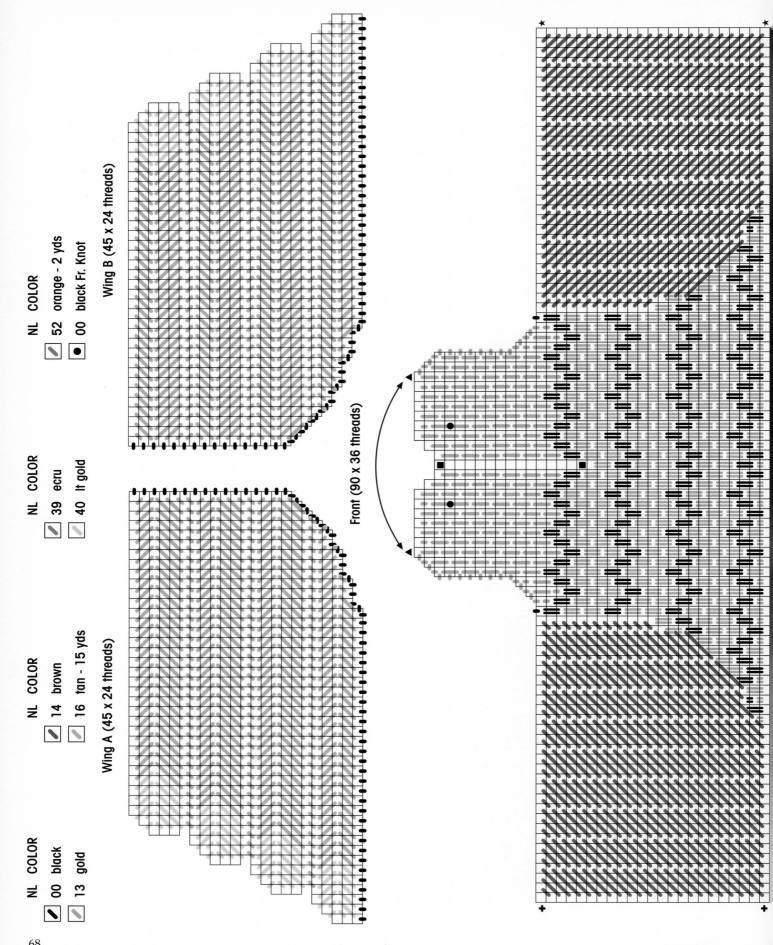

NL COLOR
▨ 00 black
▨ 13 gold

NL COLOR
▨ 14 brown
▨ 16 tan - 15 yds

Wing A (45 x 24 threads)

NL COLOR
▨ 39 ecru
▨ 40 lt gold

NL COLOR
▨ 52 orange - 2 yds
● 00 black Fr. Knot

Wing B (45 x 24 threads)

Front (90 x 36 threads)

Beak
(14 x 12 threads)

Tail (90 x 68 threads)

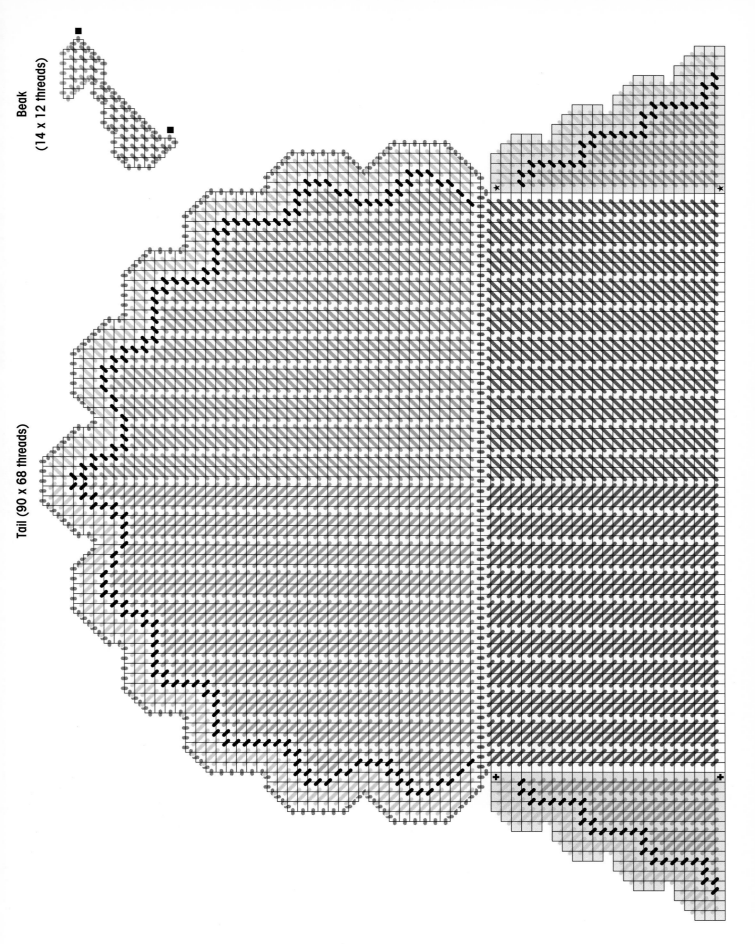

CHRISTMAS

The spirit of Christmas shines brightly in this delightful collection, which begins with a star-shaped ornament (right) constructed from miniature triangles. Carrying a lantern to light her way, a heavenly helper hastens across a starry night sky on a boutique tissue box cover (below). (Opposite) The Nativity is beautifully portrayed in a three-dimensional setting accented with metallic threads.

Star Ornament, page 91

Angel Tissue Box Cover, page 91

70

"Oh Holy Night" Door Banner, page 76

Santa Ornament, page 89

This merry Santa ornament (right)
wishes everyone a merry "Ho-Ho-Ho!"
Our friendly snowman holds a set of
wintry snowball coasters (below).

Snowman Coaster Set, page 84

Warm up your winter fun with one of these festive mugs (left) filled with your favorite hot beverage. Worked on clear and brown plastic canvas, a gingerbread train (below) rolls along on peppermint "wheels." The open car can be filled with candy or other treats.

Gingerbread Train, page 80

73

Fashioned using super-soft 7 mesh canvas, our merry Yuletide carolers (right) offer a joyous note to the holidays. A cheery winter landscape, complete with an evergreen decked with red bead "ornaments," graces the door sign (below).

Christmas Door Hanger, page 90

Christmas Caroler Candlestick Figures, page 88

Church Ornament, page 85

The simple church ornament (left) is a testament to the true meaning of Christmas. Trimmed with a checkered border, our Santa pillow (below) depicts the kindly gift-giver and one of his elves sharing a special moment.

Santa Pillow, page 86

"OH HOLY NIGHT" DOOR BANNER

(Shown on page 71.)
Skill Level: Advanced
Size: 11¼"w x 15½"h x 1¼"d
Supplies: Worsted weight yarn (refer to color key), sport weight yarn (refer to color key), metallic gold braid, metallic silver braid, two 10½" x 13½" sheets of 7 mesh plastic canvas, one 10½" x 13½" sheet of 10 mesh plastic canvas, #16 and #20 tapestry needles, sawtooth hanger, and glue gun and glue sticks
Stitches Used: Alicia Lace Stitch, Backstitch, Cross Stitch, Gobelin Stitch, Mosaic Stitch, Overcast Stitch, Scotch Stitch, Tent Stitch, and Turkey Loop Stitch
Stable Instructions: Photo model was stitched on 7 mesh plastic canvas using worsted weight yarn and metallic braid. Use #16 tapestry needle when working with 7 mesh canvas. Follow charts and use required stitches to work Stable pieces. Use dk brown yarn for all joining and tacking. With right sides together, join one long edge of Base Top to unworked edge of Stable. Join Base Sides to Base Top along short edges. Join Base Bottom to Base Sides. Join Base Front to Base Top, Base Bottom, and Base Sides. Join Base Back to Base Bottom and Base Sides. Tack Base Back to Stable along unworked edge of Base Back.

Instructions for Wise Men, Baby Jesus, and Star: Photo models were stitched on 10 mesh plastic canvas using sport weight yarn. Use #20 tapestry needle when working with 10 mesh canvas. Follow charts and use required stitches to work Wise Men, Baby Jesus, and Star. For Wise Men Supports, cut three pieces of 7 mesh canvas 7 x 20 threads each. Join each Wise Men Support along short edges, forming three cylinders. Cover unworked edges with dk brown Overcast Stitches. For Baby Jesus Supports, cut one piece of 7 mesh canvas 5 x 20 threads and one piece of 7 mesh canvas 5 x 16 threads. Join each Baby Jesus Support along short edges, forming two cylinders. Cover unworked edges with dk brown Overcast Stitches. Refer to photo for placement and glue Star and Wise Man #1 to Stable. Glue one stitched edge of each Baby Jesus Support to wrong side of Baby Jesus. Glue Baby Jesus Supports to Stable. Glue one stitched edge of each Wise Men Support to wrong side of Wise Men #2 & #3. Glue Wise Men Supports to Stable. Use dk brown yarn to tack sawtooth hanger to wrong side of Stable.

"Oh Holy Night" Door Banner design by Jack Peatman for LuvLee.

NL	COLOR	
✎	00	black - 24 yds
✎	06	brown - 38 yds
✎	11	yellow - 1 yd
✎	15	dk brown - 76 yds
✎	18	beige - 5 yds
✎	32	dk blue - 14 yds
✎	39	ecru - 9 yds
✎	40	tan - 1 yd
✎		metallic silver braid - 12 yds
✎		metallic gold braid - 38 yds

Stable Base Side (9 x 11 threads)
(Stitch 2) 7 mesh

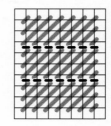

Stable Base Top/Bottom
(69 x 9 threads) (Stitch 2) 7 mesh

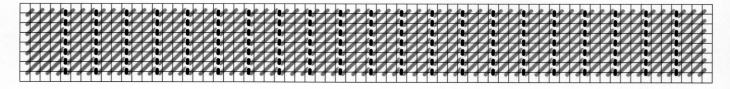

Stable Base Front/Back
(69 x 11 threads) (Cut 2, Stitch 1) 7 mesh

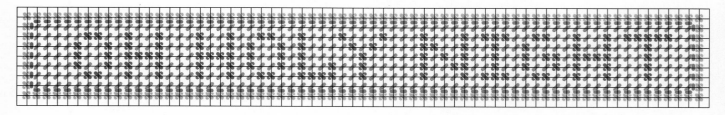

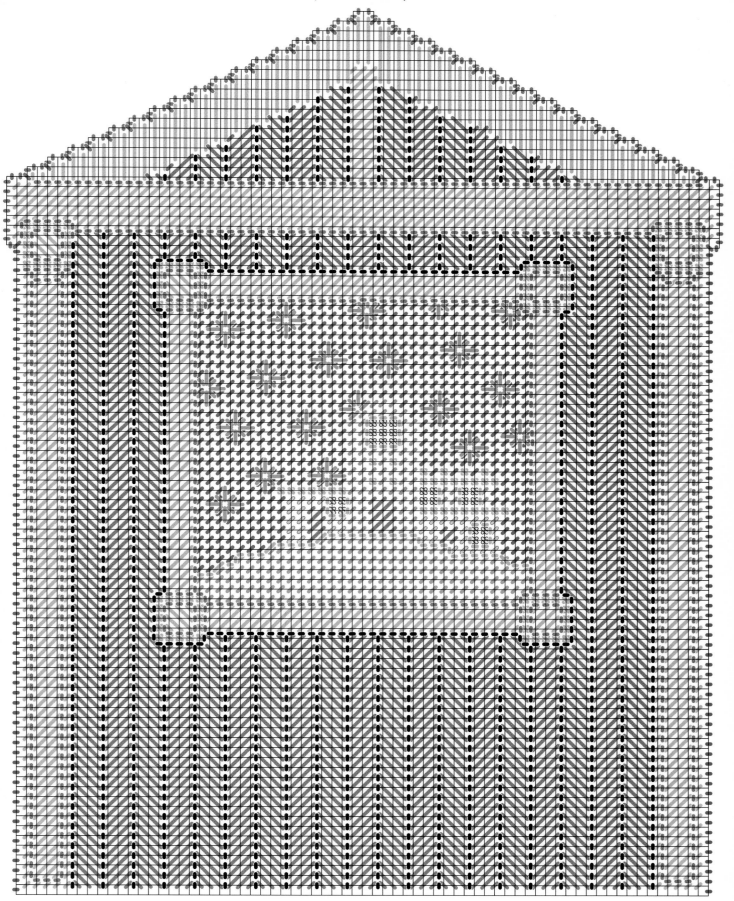

Continued on page 78.

COLOR

- white - 5 yds
- flesh - 5 yds
- dk pink - 9 yds
- red - 3 yds
- dk red - 2 yds
- lt purple - 6 yds
- purple - 8 yds
- dk purple - 6 yds
- lt blue - 7 yds
- blue - 2 yds
- dk blue - 3 yds
- lt grey blue - 3 yds
- grey blue - 3 yds
- lt green - 4 yds

COLOR

- green - 3 yds
- dk green - 2 yds
- lt turquoise - 8 yds
- turquoise - 3 yds
- brown - 5 yds
- rust - 2 yds
- dk brown - 4 yds
- grey - 4 yds
- black - 5 yds
- metallic gold braid
- *metallic silver braid
- white Turkey Loop
- grey Turkey Loop
- black Turkey Loop

*Use 2 strands of braid.

Wise Man #1
(30 x 82 threads) 10 mesh

Baby Jesus (32 x 29 threads) 10 mesh

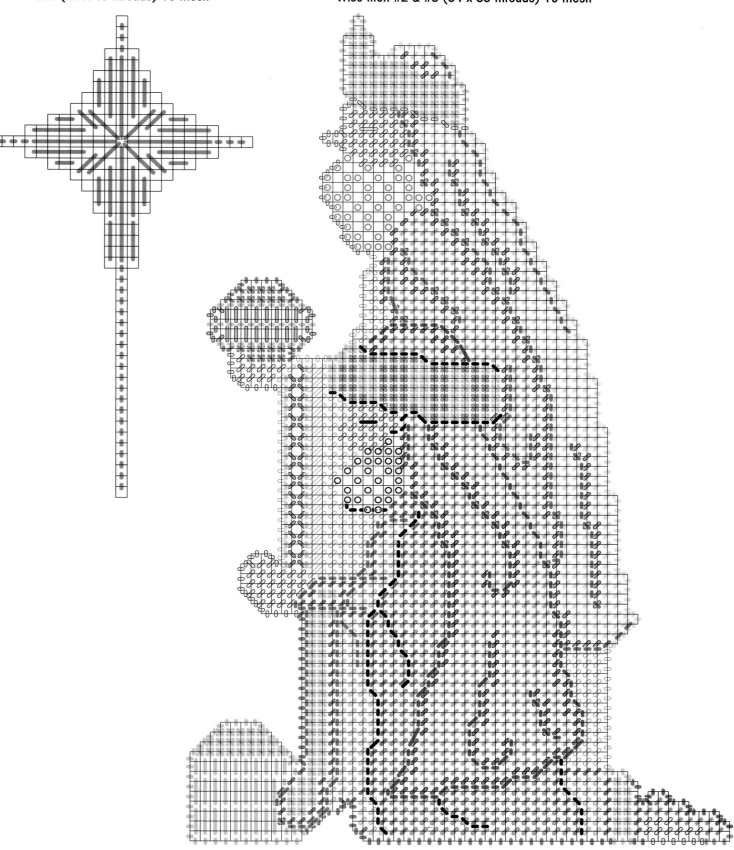

GINGERBREAD TRAIN

(Shown on page 73.)

Skill Level: Intermediate

Supplies: Worsted weight yarn or Needloft® Plastic Canvas Yarn (refer to color keys), one 10½" x 13½" sheet of clear 7 mesh plastic canvas, three 10½" x 13½" sheets of brown 7 mesh plastic canvas, #16 tapestry needle, one ½" gold liberty bell, and clear-drying craft glue or hot glue gun and glue sticks

Stitches Used: Backstitch, Cross Stitch, Gobelin Stitch, Overcast Stitch, Scotch Stitch, Tent Stitch, and Turkey Loop Stitch

Instructions: Photo model was stitched using worsted weight yarn. Follow charts to cut Smokestack, Candy Cane, Large Wheel pieces and Small Wheel pieces from clear plastic canvas. Cut remaining pieces from brown plastic canvas. Follow charts and use required stitches to work Wheel pieces, leaving red Backstitches unworked. Use white yarn to join Wheel Fronts to Wheel Backs. Work red Backstitches through two thicknesses of plastic canvas. Follow charts and use required stitches to work remaining Gingerbread Train pieces, leaving stitches in shaded areas unworked. To attach completed Train pieces, refer to photo to tie 6" lengths of green yarn between Bottoms of stitched pieces.

Engine Size: 6"w x 5¼"h x 2¾"d

Engine Instructions: Matching ■'s, join Cow Catcher to Front between ■'s using red yarn. Use yarn color to match stitching area to join ends of Smokestack, forming a cylinder. Use white yarn for remainder of joining. Matching like symbols, join Front and Back to Sides. Matching ◗'s and ♣'s, join Front Window to Sides. Join long edges of Boiler Top to Sides. Join Boiler Top to Front Window and Front. Join Bottom to Front, Back, and Sides. Join unworked edges of Engine Top to Sides and Front Window. Refer to photo for placement and use red yarn to tack liberty bell to Front Window. Thread an 8" length of green yarn through one Large Wheel and two Small Wheels. Glue threaded Wheels to one Side. Repeat to thread and glue three more Wheels to remaining Side. Glue Smokestack to Boiler Top. Glue Candy Cane to Back.

Car Size: 4¼"w x 2½"h x 2¾"d

Car Instructions: Use white for all joining. Refer to photo for placement to join Front and Back to Sides. Join Bottom to Front, Back, and Sides. Glue two Small Wheels to each Side.

Caboose Size: 5½"w x 4"h x 2¾"d

Caboose Instructions: Use blue yarn and match ▲'s to join Door to Back. Use white yarn for remainder of joining. Matching ✿'s and ❤'s, join Front to Sides. Matching ◇'s and working stitches in shaded areas, join Back to Sides. Refer to photo for placement and join Short Railings to Long Railing. Matching ✚'s, join Short Railings to Back and Sides through three thicknesses of plastic canvas. Join Bottom to Front, Back, Sides, and Railings. Join Top to Front, Back, and Sides. Glue two Small Wheels to each Side. Cut a 6" length of red yarn. Tie yarn into a bow and trim ends. Glue bow to wreath on Front.

Gingerbread Train design by Pam MacIver.

NL	COLOR
02	red - 15 yds
28	green - 5 yds
32	blue - 4 yds
41	white - 43 yds
57	yellow - 3 yds
58	orange - 3 yds

Engine Front Window
(14 x 18 threads)

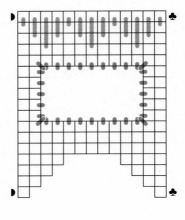

Smokestack (21 x 6 threads)

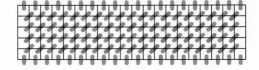

Small Wheel
Front/Back
(8 x 8 threads)
(Cut 24)

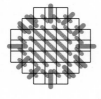

Large Wheel
Front/Back
(12 x 12 threads)
(Cut 4)

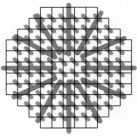

Engine Side A
(33 x 32 threads)

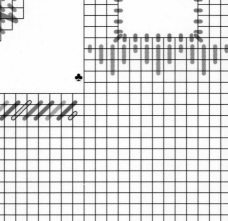

Candy Cane
(5 x 10 threads)

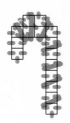

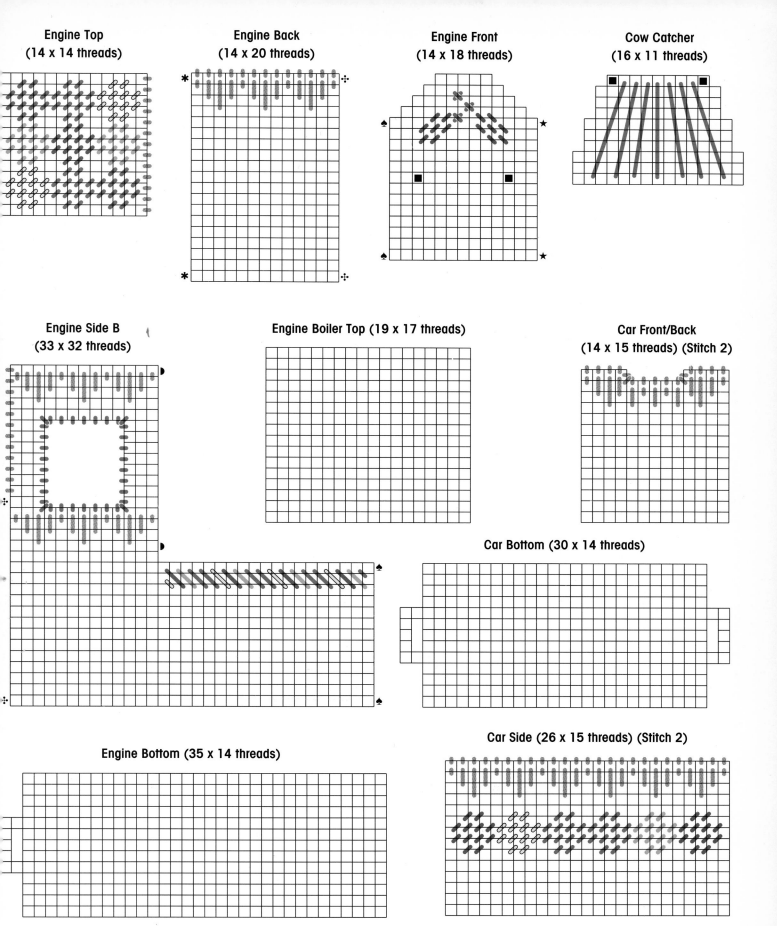

Engine Top
(14 x 14 threads)

Engine Back
(14 x 20 threads)

Engine Front
(14 x 18 threads)

Cow Catcher
(16 x 11 threads)

Engine Side B
(33 x 32 threads)

Engine Boiler Top (19 x 17 threads)

Car Front/Back
(14 x 15 threads) (Stitch 2)

Car Bottom (30 x 14 threads)

Engine Bottom (35 x 14 threads)

Car Side (26 x 15 threads) (Stitch 2)

Continued on page 82.

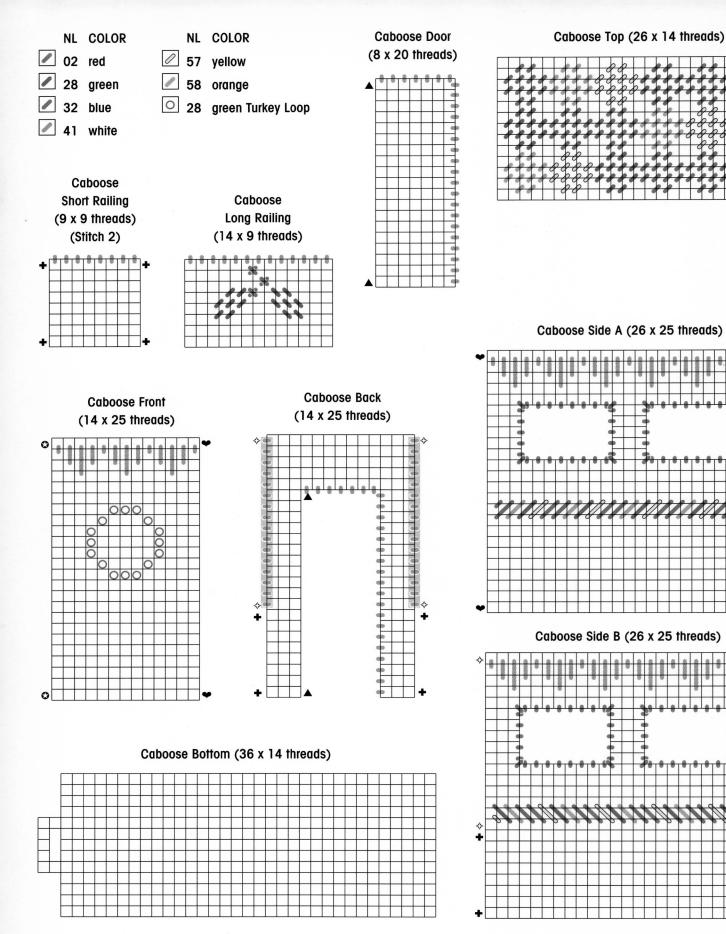

NL	COLOR		NL	COLOR
02	red		57	yellow
28	green		58	orange
32	blue		28	green Turkey Loop
41	white			

Caboose Door
(8 x 20 threads)

Caboose Top (26 x 14 threads)

**Caboose
Short Railing
(9 x 9 threads)
(Stitch 2)**

**Caboose
Long Railing
(14 x 9 threads)**

Caboose Side A (26 x 25 threads)

**Caboose Front
(14 x 25 threads)**

**Caboose Back
(14 x 25 threads)**

Caboose Side B (26 x 25 threads)

Caboose Bottom (36 x 14 threads)

"HO HO HO" MUG INSERT AND SNOWFLAKE MUG INSERT

(Shown on page 73.)

Skill Level: Beginner

Approx Insert Size: 3½"h x 3¼" dia each

Supplies For Both Inserts: Worsted weight yarn or Needloft® Plastic Canvas Yarn (refer to color key), one 10½" x 13½" sheet of 7 mesh plastic canvas, #16 tapestry needle, one red Crafter's Pride® Mugs Your Way™ mug, and one white Crafter's Pride® Mugs Your Way™ mug

Stitches Used: Backstitch, French Knot, Overcast Stitch, and Tent Stitch

Instructions: Photo models were stitched using worsted weight yarn. Follow chart and use required stitches to work desired Mug Insert. Use yarn color to match closest stitching area to join ends of Mug Insert, forming a cylinder. Place Insert inside mug, aligning joined edges with Mug handle. Remove stitched piece before washing mug.

"Ho Ho Ho" Mug Insert and Snowflake Mug Insert designs by Studio M.

NL	COLOR
02	red
28	green
32	blue
41	white
41	white Fr. Knot

"Ho Ho Ho" Mug Insert
(65 x 24 threads)

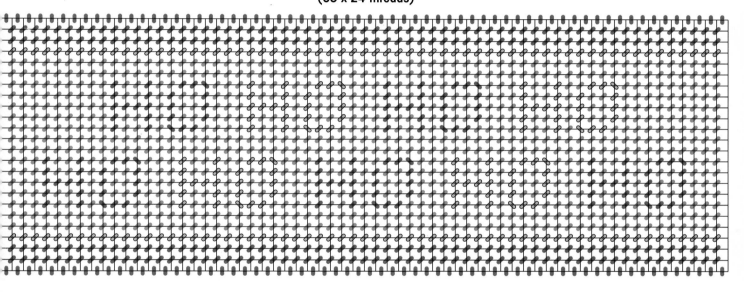

Snowflake Mug Insert
(64 x 24 threads)

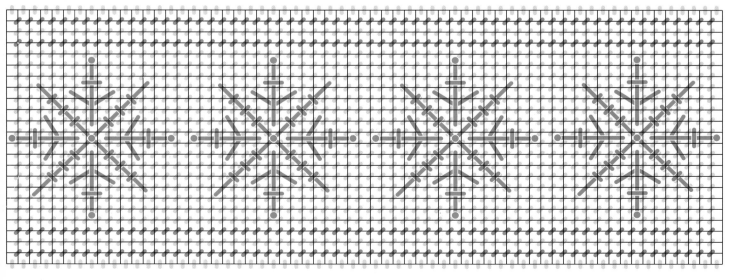

SNOWMAN COASTER SET
(Shown on page 72.)
Skill Level: Intermediate
Coaster Size: 4"w x 4"h
Holder Size: 6³/4"w x 9"h x 2"d
Supplies: Worsted weight yarn or Needloft® Plastic Canvas Yarn (refer to color key), two 10¹/2" x 13¹/2" sheets of 7 mesh plastic canvas, #16 tapestry needle, 12" length of ¹/2"w blue satin ribbon, one ³/4" dia gold liberty bell, cork or felt (optional), and clear-drying craft glue
Stitches Used: Backstitch, Cross Stitch, Fringe Stitch, Gobelin Stitch, Overcast Stitch, and Tent Stitch
Instructions: Photo model was stitched using worsted weight yarn. Follow chart and use required stitches to work Snowman through two thicknesses of canvas. Use two plies each of green yarn and white yarn to work Fringe Stitches. Trim Fringe Stitches to ³/4". Follow charts and use required stitches to work remaining Snowman Coaster Set pieces. For Holder Bottom, cut a piece of plastic canvas 29 x 12 threads. (**Note:** Bottom is not worked.)

Use white yarn for all joining and tacking, unless otherwise indicated. Tack Arm to Snowman at ♦'s. Matching ★'s and ▲'s, join Sides to Front. Match ■'s and join Side A to Snowman. Match ♥'s and join Side B to Snowman. Join Bottom to Front, Sides, and Snowman. Refer to photo for placement and tack bell to Front using blue yarn. Tie ribbon into a bow and trim ends. Glue bow to Front. If backing for Coasters is desired, cut cork or felt slightly smaller than Coaster and glue to wrong side of completed stitched piece.

Snowman Coaster Set design by Jack Peatman for LuvLee.

NL	COLOR	
☑	00	black - 1 yd
☑	28	green - 4 yds
☑	32	blue - 6 yds
☑	36	lt blue - 10 yds
☑	41	white - 65 yds
☑	58	orange - 1 yd
○	*	Fringe

*Use 2 plies each of green yarn and white yarn.

Snowman (45 x 60 threads) (Cut 2)

Coaster (26 x 26 threads) (Stitch 6)

Arm (15 x 17 threads)

Front (29 x 16 threads)

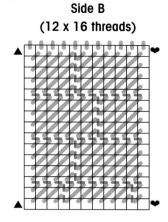

Side A
(12 x 16 threads)

Side B
(12 x 16 threads)

CHURCH ORNAMENT
(Shown on page 75.)
Skill Level: Beginner
Size: 2"w x 3½"h x 2¾"d
Supplies: Worsted weight yarn or Needloft® Plastic Canvas Yarn (refer to color key), one 10½" x 13½" sheet of 7 mesh plastic canvas, #16 tapestry needle, nylon thread, and clear-drying craft glue
Stitches Used: Backstitch, French Knot, Overcast Stitch, and Tent Stitch
Instructions: Photo model was stitched using worsted weight yarn. Follow charts and use required stitches to work Church Ornament pieces. For Bottom, cut a piece of plastic canvas 10 x 16 threads. Work Bottom using white Tent Stitches. Use black yarn to join Roof pieces along unworked edges. Refer to photo to assemble Ornament. Use white yarn for remainder of joining. Join Church Sides to Church Front and Church Back. Join Church Front, Back, and Sides to Bottom. Join Steeple Sides to Steeple Front and Steeple Back. Glue Roof to Church Front, Back, and Sides. Glue Steeple to Roof. For hanger, thread an 8" length of nylon thread through Roof. Tie thread into a knot 3" from Roof and trim thread ends.

Church Ornament design by Kathy Martel.

NL	COLOR
✎ 00	black - 7 yds
✎ 02	red - 1 yd
✎ 27	green - 1 yd
✎ 41	white - 15 yds
✎ 57	yellow - 1 yd
● 00	black Fr. Knot

Steeple Side
(4 x 9 threads)
(Stitch 2)

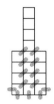

Steeple
Front/Back
(4 x 8 threads)
(Stitch 2)

Roof (19 x 10 threads) (Stitch 2)

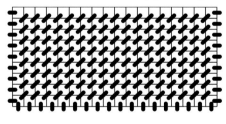

Church Front
(10 x 14 threads)

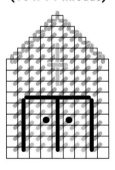

Church Back
(10 x 14 threads)

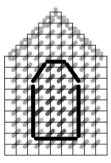

Church Side
(16 x 10 threads) (Stitch 2)

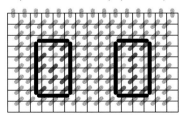

SANTA PILLOW

(Shown on page 75.)

Skill Level: Intermediate

Approx Size: 16½"w x 12½"h x 2½"d

Supplies: Worsted weight yarn or Needloft® Plastic Canvas Yarn (refer to color key), two 12" x 18" sheets of Darice® 7 mesh Super Soft® plastic canvas, #16 tapestry needle, and polyester fiberfill

Stitches Used: Backstitch, French Knot, Overcast Stitch, and Tent Stitch

Instructions: Photo model was stitched using worsted weight yarn. Both Sections are stitched on one piece of canvas. For Front, cut a piece of plastic canvas 108 x 81 threads. Follow chart and use required stitches to work Left Section. Follow chart and use required stitches to begin stitching Right Section on the next unworked thread of the stitched piece. Before adding Backstitches, complete background with white Tent Stitches as indicated on chart. For Back, cut a piece of plastic canvas 108 x 81 threads. Work Back with green Tent Stitches. With wrong sides together, use green to join Front to Back while stuffing with polyester fiberfill.

Santa Pillow design by Jack Peatman for LuvLee.

NL	COLOR	NL	COLOR
00	black - 5 yds	34	lt blue - 3 yds
01	red - 11 yds	36	vy lt blue - 5 yds
*	red	37	lt grey - 3 yds
02	lt red - 5 yds	38	grey - 5 yds
03	dk red - 6 yds	*	grey
07	pink - 1 yd	40	lt tan - 1 yd
13	brown - 4 yds	41	white - 96 yds
*	brown	43	lt brown - 3 yds
14	dk brown - 4 yds	*	lt brown
18	tan - 3 yds	48	dk blue - 1 yd
28	lt green - 9 yds	56	flesh - 3 yds
29	green - 172 yds	57	yellow - 1 yd
32	blue - 2 yds	● 48	dk blue Fr. Knot

*Use 2-ply yarn.

Santa Pillow Front
(108 x 81 threads)   **Left Section**

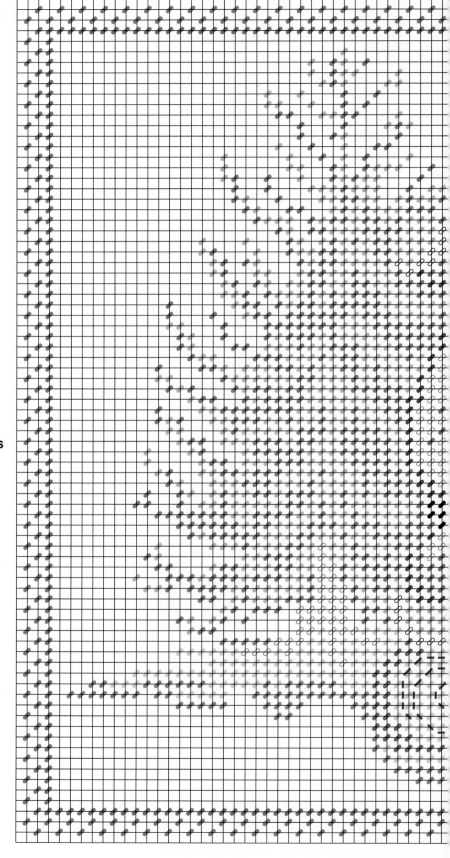

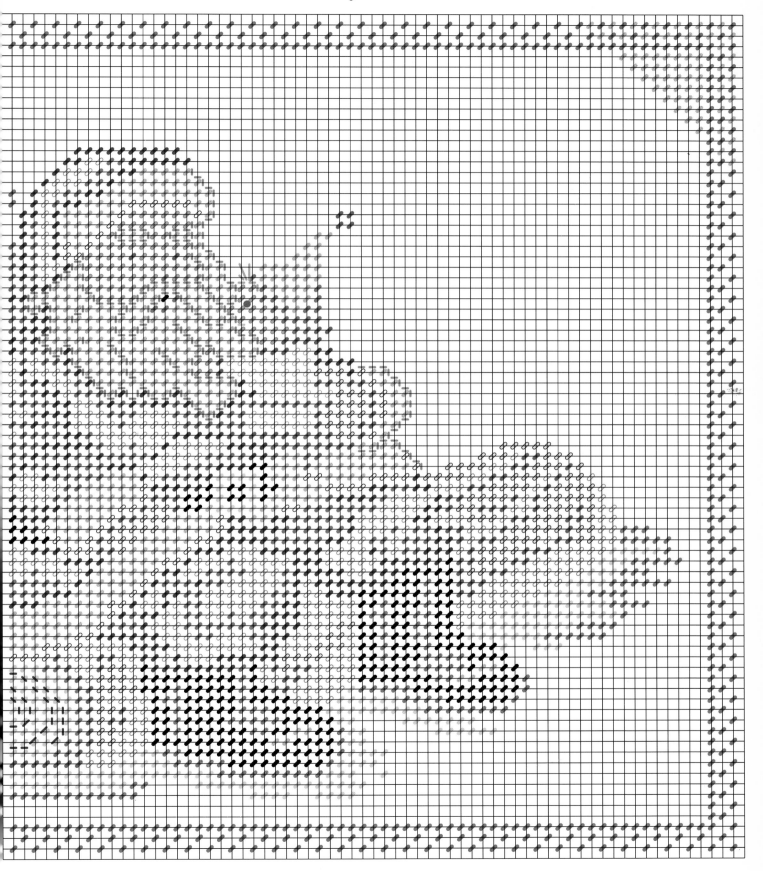

CHRISTMAS CAROLER CANDLESTICK FIGURES

(Shown on page 74.)

Skill Level: Intermediate

Supplies: Worsted weight yarn or Needloft® Plastic Canvas Yarn (refer to color key), one 12" x 18" sheet of Darice® Super Soft® 7 mesh plastic canvas, one 10½" x 13½" sheet of 10 mesh plastic canvas, #16 tapestry needle (for working with 7 mesh plastic canvas), # 20 tapestry needle (for working with 10 mesh plastic canvas), and clear-drying craft glue

Stitches Used: Backstitch, French Knot, Fringe Stitch, Gobelin Stitch, Mosaic Stitch, Overcast Stitch, Scotch Stitch, and Tent Stitch

LADY CAROLER

Size: 9½"h x ¾" dia

Instructions: Photo model was stitched using worsted weight yarn. Follow charts and use required stitches to work Lady Caroler pieces and one Hymnal. Use yarn color to match closest stitching area for all joining and tacking. Refer to photo for placement to tack Bonnet to Lady. Join Lady along long edges. Match ★'s and tack Lady's Arms to Lady. Tack Hymnal to Lady's Arms. Join sections of Skirt indicated by heavy black lines. Join Skirt along short edges, forming a cylinder. Slide Skirt onto Lady.

GENTLEMAN CAROLER

Size: 10½"h x ¾" dia

Instructions: Photo model was stitched using worsted weight yarn. Cut Scarf, Scarf End A, and Scarf End B from 10 mesh canvas. Cut remaining Gentleman pieces and one Hymnal from 7 mesh canvas. Follow charts and use required stitches to work pieces. Use yarn color to match closest stitching area for all joining and tacking. Join Gentleman along long edges. Join Scarf along unworked edges, forming a cylinder. Refer to photo for placement to tack Scarf Ends to Scarf. Slide Scarf onto Gentleman. Match ★'s and tack Gentleman's Arms to Gentleman. Tack Hymnal to Gentleman's Arms. Match ▲'s and tack Coattail to Gentleman. Slide Hat Brim onto Gentleman. Tie a 6" length of green yarn into a bow and trim ends. Glue bow to Gentleman above Hat Brim.

Christmas Caroler Candlestick Figure designs by Becky Dill.

NL	COLOR	
00	black - 9 yds	
01	red - 17 yds	
08	flesh - 2 yds	
14	brown - 5 yds	
27	green - 1 yd	
38	grey - 6 yds	
40	tan - 2 yds	
41	white - 2 yds	
	pink - 1 yd	*
14	brown Fr. Knot	
35	blue Fr. Knot - 1yd	
41	white Fr. Knot	
57	yellow Fr. Knot - 1yd	
01	red Fringe	

*Use 2-ply yarn.

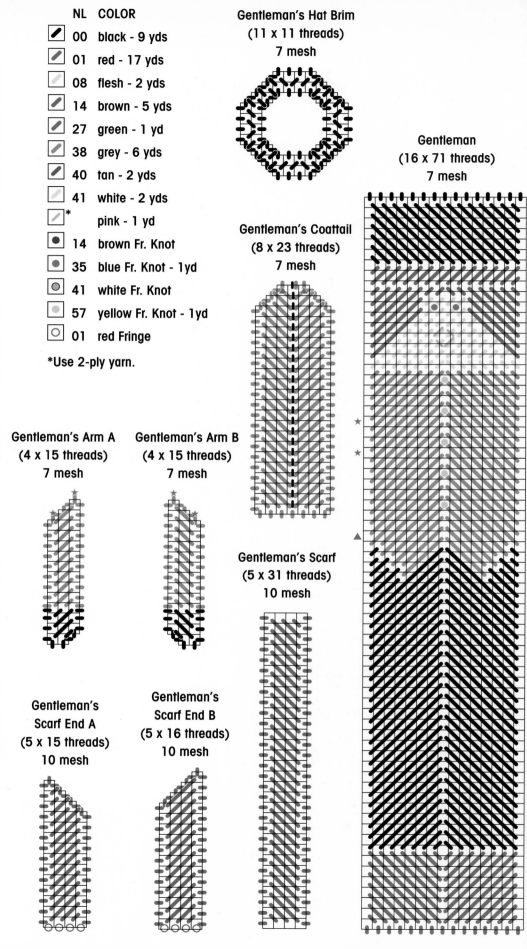

Gentleman's Hat Brim
(11 x 11 threads)
7 mesh

Gentleman
(16 x 71 threads)
7 mesh

Gentleman's Coattail
(8 x 23 threads)
7 mesh

Gentleman's Arm A
(4 x 15 threads)
7 mesh

Gentleman's Arm B
(4 x 15 threads)
7 mesh

Gentleman's Scarf
(5 x 31 threads)
10 mesh

Gentleman's Scarf End A
(5 x 15 threads)
10 mesh

Gentleman's Scarf End B
(5 x 16 threads)
10 mesh

Lady's Bonnet (21 x 8 threads) 7 mesh

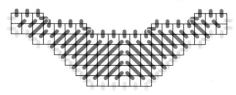

Lady's Skirt (22 x 6 threads) 7 mesh

Hymnal (6 x 8 threads) 7 mesh

Lady (16 x 64 threads) 7 mesh

Lady's Arm A (4 x 18 threads) 7 mesh

Lady's Arm B (4 x 18 threads) 7 mesh

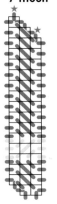

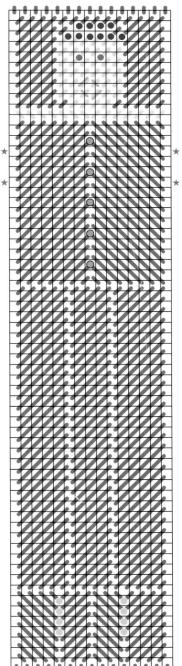

SANTA ORNAMENT

(Shown on page 72.)
Skill Level: Beginner
Size: 3¼"w x 6½"h
Supplies: Worsted weight yarn or Needloft® Plastic Canvas Yarn (refer to color key), one 10½" x 13½" sheet of 7 mesh plastic canvas, #16 tapestry needle, 6" length of ¹/₁₆"w green satin ribbon, nylon thread, and clear-drying craft glue
Stitches Used: Backstitch, Gobelin Stitch, Overcast Stitch, Scotch Stitch, Tent Stitch, and Turkey Loop Stitch
Instructions: Photo model was stitched using worsted weight yarn. Follow chart and use required stitches to work Santa Ornament. Work stitches indicated by double lines on chart by inserting needle in same holes twice for complete coverage. Tie ribbon into a bow and trim ends. Refer to photo for placement and glue bow to Santa Ornament. For hanger, thread an 8" length of nylon thread through top of Ornament. Tie nylon thread into a knot 3" from stitched piece and trim ends.

Santa Ornament design by Peggy Astle.

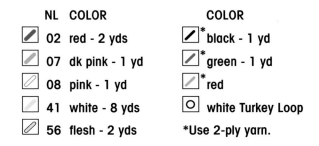

NL	COLOR		COLOR
02	red - 2 yds		*black - 1 yd
07	dk pink - 1 yd		*green - 1 yd
08	pink - 1 yd		*red
41	white - 8 yds	⊙	white Turkey Loop
56	flesh - 2 yds		*Use 2-ply yarn.

Santa Ornament (32 x 32 threads)

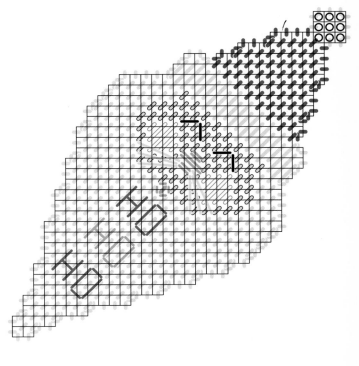

CHRISTMAS DOOR HANGER
(Shown on page 74.)
Skill Level: Intermediate
Size: 3 1/4"w x 9 3/4"h
Supplies: Worsted weight yarn or Needloft® Plastic Canvas Yarn (refer to color key), one 10 1/2" x 13 1/2" sheet of 7 mesh plastic canvas, #16 tapestry needle, sewing needle, nylon thread, sixteen 5mm red wood beads, 12" length of 1/4"w white satin ribbon, and clear-drying craft glue
Stitches Used: Backstitch, Gobelin Stitch, Overcast Stitch, and Tent Stitch
Instructions: Photo model was stitched using worsted weight yarn. Follow chart and use required stitches to work Christmas Door Hanger. Using sewing needle and nylon thread, refer to photo for placement to attach beads to stitched piece. Tie ribbon into a bow and trim ends. Glue bow to completed stitched piece.

Christmas Door Hanger design by Karen Simmons.

NL	COLOR
01	red - 1 yd
13	rust - 4 yds
15	brown - 1 yd
16	tan - 1 yd
27	green - 6 yds
37	lt grey - 1 yd
38	grey - 1 yd
41	white - 6 yds
48	blue - 7 yds
*	black - 1 yd

*Use 2-ply yarn.

Christmas Door Hanger
(21 x 64 threads)

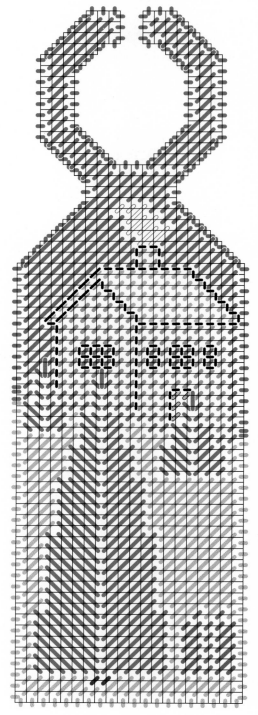

STAR ORNAMENT
(Shown on page 70.)
Skill Level: Intermediate
Size: 3³/₄"w x 3³/₄"h x 1³/₄"d
Supplies: Metallic gold yarn, one 10¹/₂" x 13¹/₂" sheet of 7 mesh plastic canvas, #16 tapestry needle, and nylon thread
Stitches Used: Gobelin Stitch, Overcast Stitch, and Tent Stitch
Instructions: Photo model was stitched using metallic gold yarn. Follow chart and use required stitches to work Star Ornament Sections. Match ■'s to join two Sections along straight edges, forming a diamond shape. Repeat to join remaining Sections.

Refer to photo for placement and join five diamond shapes, forming front of Ornament. (**Note:** Pieces will fold as they are joined.) Repeat to form back of Ornament. Use metallic gold Overcast Stitches to cover unworked edges. Place front and back with wrong sides together. Use metallic gold yarn to tack front and back pieces together at each of the five inner corners. For hanger, thread an 8" length of nylon thread through front and back of Ornament. Tie thread into a knot 3" above Ornament and trim thread ends.

Star Ornament design by Marion Peairs.

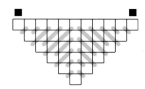

metallic gold - 24 yds

Section (12 x 7 threads)
(Stitch 20)

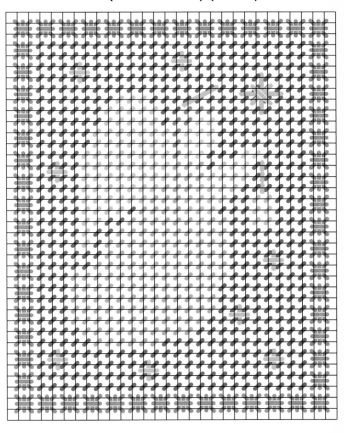

ANGEL TISSUE BOX COVER
(Shown on page 70.)
Skill Level: Intermediate
Size: 4³/₄"w x 5³/₄"h x 4³/₄"d
(**Note:** Fits a 4¹/₄"w x 5¹/₄"h x 4¹/₄"d boutique tissue box.)
Supplies: Worsted weight yarn or Needloft® Plastic Canvas Yarn (refer to color key and photo), metallic gold yarn, one 10¹/₂" x 13¹/₂" sheet of 7 mesh plastic canvas, and #16 tapestry needle
Stitches Used: Backstitch, Braided Cross Stitch Variation, Double Cross Stitch, Smyrna Cross Stitch, Tent Stitch, and Upright Cross Stitch
Instructions: Photo model was stitched using worsted weight yarn and metallic gold yarn. Follow charts and use required stitches to work Angel Tissue Box Cover pieces. Use white Braided Cross Stitch Variation to cover unworked edges of opening in Top. Use white Braided Cross Stitch Variation for all joining. Join Sides along long edges. Join Top to Sides. Use white Braided Cross Stitch Variation to cover unworked edges of Sides.

Angel Tissue Box Cover design by Nancy Dorman.

NL	COLOR		COLOR
08	flesh - 2 yds		dress color - 14 yds
14	brown - 2 yds		sleeve color - 3 yds
31	dk blue - 44 yds		metallic gold - 20 yds
41	white - 28 yds		

Top (30 x 30 threads)

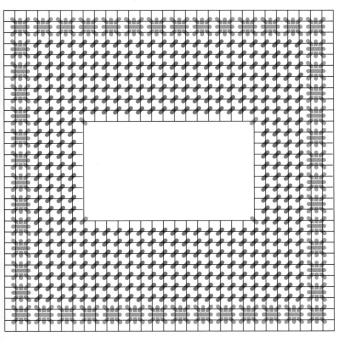

Side (30 x 38 threads) (Stitch 4)

91

GENERAL INSTRUCTIONS
WORKING WITH YARN

To help you select colors for your projects, we have included numbers for Needloft® Plastic Canvas Yarn and DMC Embroidery Floss in our color keys. The headings in the color key are for Needloft® Yarn (**NL**), DMC Embroidery Floss (**DMC**), and the descriptive color name (**COLOR**). Needloft® Yarn is 100% nylon and is suitable only for 7 mesh plastic canvas.

Worsted weight yarn is used for most of the projects in this issue. Worsted weight yarn has four plies that are twisted together to form one strand. When the instructions indicate 2-ply yarn, separate the strand of yarn and stitch using only two of the four plies.

Needloft® Yarn will not easily separate. When the instructions call for "2-ply" yarn, we recommend that you substitute with six strands of embroidery floss.

WORKING WITH PLASTIC CANVAS

Throughout this leaflet, the lines of the canvas will be referred to as threads. However, they are not actually "threads" since the canvas is nonwoven. To cut plastic canvas pieces accurately, count **threads** (not **holes**) as shown in **Fig. 1**.

Fig. 1

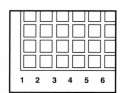

The charts may show slits in the plastic canvas **(Fig. 2)**. To make slits, use a craft knife to cut exactly through the center of an intersection of plastic canvas threads **(Fig. 3)**. Repeat for number of intersections needed. When working piece, be careful not to carry yarn across slits.

Fig. 2

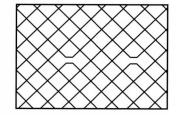

Fig. 3

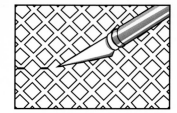

WASHING INSTRUCTIONS

If you used washable yarn for all of your stitches, you may hand wash plastic canvas projects in warm water with a mild soap. Do not rub or scrub stitches; this will cause the yarn to fuzz. Allow your stitched piece to air dry. Do not put stitched pieces in a clothes dryer. The plastic canvas could melt in the heat of a dryer. Do not dry-clean your plastic canvas. The chemicals used in dry cleaning could dissolve the plastic canvas. When piece is dry, you may need to trim the fuzz from your project with a small pair of sharp scissors.

GENERAL INFORMATION

1. **Fig. 1** shows how to count threads accurately. Follow charts to cut out plastic canvas pieces.
2. Backstitches used for detail **(Fig. 7)**, French Knots **(Fig. 13, page 93)**, and Lazy Daisy Stitches **(Fig.16, page 93)**, are worked over completed stitches.
3. Unless otherwise indicated, Overcast Stitches **(Fig. 18, page 94)** are used to cover edges of pieces and to join pieces.

STITCH DIAGRAMS

> **Unless otherwise indicated, bring threaded needle up at 1 and all odd numbers and down at 2 and all even numbers.**

ALICIA LACE STITCH

This series of stitches is worked in diagonal rows and forms a lacy pattern. Follow **Fig. 4** and work in one direction to cover every other diagonal row of intersections. Then work in the other direction **(Fig. 5)** to cover the remaining intersections.

Fig. 4

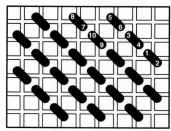

Fig. 5

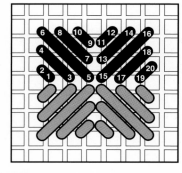

ALTERNATING SCOTCH STITCH

This Scotch Stitch variation is worked over three or more threads, forming alternating blocks **(Fig. 6)**.

Fig. 6

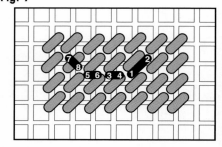

BACKSTITCH

This stitch is worked over completed stitches to outline or define **(Fig. 7)**. It is sometimes worked over more than one thread. Backstitch may also be used to cover canvas as shown in **Fig. 8**.

Fig. 7

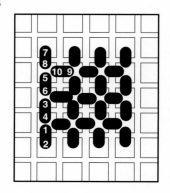

Fig. 8

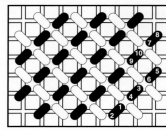

BEADED LOOP STITCH

This stitch is used to form "drops" of beads. Bring needle up at 1. Thread four beads onto floss. Skipping last bead, bring needle through first three beads and go down at 2 as shown in **Fig. 9**.

Fig. 9

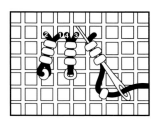

BRAIDED CROSS STITCH VARIATION

This stitch is used to cover the edge of the canvas and to join pieces of canvas. Begin by working stitches 1 through 3 as shown in **Fig. 10a**. Starting with 4, proceed as shown in **Figs. 10b** and **10c**, working forward over three threads and back over two threads. It may be necessary to make extra stitches at the corners for better coverage.

Fig. 10a

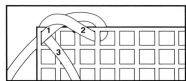

Fig. 10b

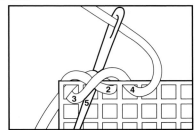

Fig. 10c

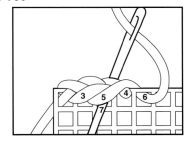

CROSS STITCH

This stitch is composed of two stitches **(Fig. 11)**. The top stitch of each cross must always be made in the same direction. The number of intersections may vary according to the chart.

Fig. 11

DOUBLE CROSS STITCH VARIATION

This stitch is composed of four stitches **(Fig. 12)**. The top stitch of each cross must always be made in the same direction.

Fig. 12

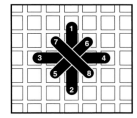

FRENCH KNOT

Bring needle up through hole. Wrap yarn once around needle and insert needle in same hole, holding end of yarn with non-stitching fingers **(Fig. 13)**. Tighten knot, then pull needle through canvas, holding yarn until it must be released.

Fig. 13

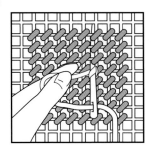

FRINGE STITCH

Fold an 8" length of yarn or floss in half. Thread needle with loose ends of yarn. Take needle down at 1, leaving a 1" loop on top of the canvas. Come up at 2, bring needle through loop, and pull tightly **(Fig. 14)**. Trim Fringe Stitch as desired.

Fig. 14

GOBELIN STITCH

This basic straight stitch is worked over two or more threads or intersections. The number of threads or intersections may vary according to the chart **(Fig. 15)**.

Fig. 15

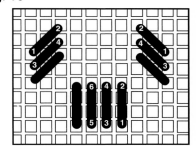

LAZY DAISY STITCH

Bring needle up at 1, make a loop and go down at 1 again **(Fig. 16)**. Come up at 2, keeping yarn below needle's point. Pull needle through and secure loop by bringing yarn over loop and going down at 2.

Fig. 16

Continued on page 94.

MOSAIC STITCH

This three-stitch pattern forms small squares **(Fig. 17)**.

Fig. 17

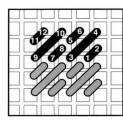

OVERCAST STITCH

This stitch covers the edge of the canvas and joins pieces of canvas **(Fig. 18)**. It may be necessary to go through the same hole more than once to get an even coverage on the edge, especially at the corners.

Fig. 18

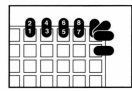

SCOTCH STITCH

This stitch forms a square. It may be worked over three or more horizontal threads by three or more vertical threads. **Fig. 19** shows it worked over three threads.

Fig. 19

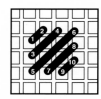

SMYRNA CROSS STITCH

This stitch is worked over two threads as a decorative stitch. Each stitch is worked completely before going on to the next **(Fig. 20)**.

Fig. 20

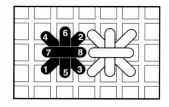

TENT STITCH

This stitch is worked in vertical or horizontal rows over one intersection as shown in **Fig. 21**. Follow **Fig. 22** to work the **Reversed Tent Stitch**. Sometimes when you are working Tent Stitches, the last stitch on the row will look "pulled" on the front of your piece when you are changing directions. To avoid this problem, leave a loop of yarn on the wrong side of the stitched piece after making the last stitch in the row. When making the first stitch in the next row, run your needle through the loop **(Fig. 23)**. Gently pull yarn until all stitches are even.

Fig. 21

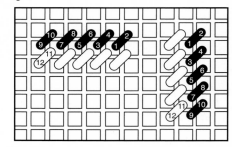

Fig. 22

Fig. 23

TURKEY LOOP STITCH

This stitch is composed of locked loops. Bring needle up through hole and back down through same hole, forming a loop on top of the canvas. A locking stitch is then made across the thread directly below or to either side of loop as shown in **Fig. 24**.

Fig. 24

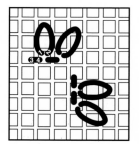

TURKEY LOOP STITCH VARIATION

This stitch forms wider loops than the Turkey Loop Stitch. Bring needle up through hole and back down through next hole, forming a loop on top of the canvas. A locking stitch is then made by bringing needle up and down in same holes as shown in **Fig. 25**.

Fig. 25

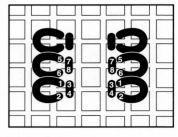

UPRIGHT CROSS STITCH

This stitch is worked over two threads as shown in **Fig. 26**. The top stitch of each cross must always be made in the same direction.

Fig. 26

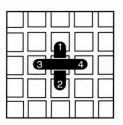

Instructions tested and photography items made by Kandi Ashford, Toni Bowden, Kathleen Boyd, Virginia Cates, JoAnn Forrest, Janice Gordon, Wanda Hopkins, Joanne McCallum, Sadie Wilson, and Janie Wright.

INDEX

INDEX (Continued)

ANCIENT
EGYPT

ANCIENT
EGYPT

THE DEFINITIVE VISUAL HISTORY

STEVEN SNAPE

DK London

Senior Editor	Angela Wilkes
Senior Art Editor	Gadi Farfour
Editors	Daniel Byrne, Alison Sturgeon, Andrew Szudek
US Editor	Kayla Dugger
Designer	Daksheeta Pattni
CGI coordinator	Phil Gamble
Senior Managing Art Editor	Lee Griffiths
Managing Editor	Gareth Jones
Production Editor	George Nimmo
Senior Production Controller	Rachel Ng
Picture Researcher	Sarah Smithies
Jacket Design Development Manager	Sophia M.T.T.
Associate Publishing Director	Liz Wheeler
Art Director	Karen Self
Publishing Director	Jonathan Metcalf

DK Delhi

Senior Art Editors	Ira Sharma, Chhaya Sajwan
Project Art Editor	Sourabh Challariya
Art Editor	Anukriti Arora
Assistant Art Editor	Ankita Das
Senior Editor	Janashree Singha
Editor	Rishi Bryan
Managing Editor	Soma B. Chowdhury
Senior Managing Art Editor	Arunesh Talapatra
Senior Cartographer	Mohammad Hassan
Senior Jacket Designer	Suhita Dharamjit
Senior DTP Designer	Harish Aggarwal
DTP Designers	Bimlesh Tiwary, Mohammad Rizwan
Picture Research Manager	Taiyaba Khatoon
Pre-production Manager	Balwant Singh
Production Manager	Pankaj Sharma
Editorial Head	Glenda Fernandes
Design Head	Malavika Talukder

First American Edition, 2021
Published in the United States by DK Publishing
1450 Broadway, Suite 801, New York, NY 10018

A catalog record for this book
is available from the Library of Congress.
ISBN 978-0-7440-2924-6

Printed in UAE

For the curious

www.dk.com

contents

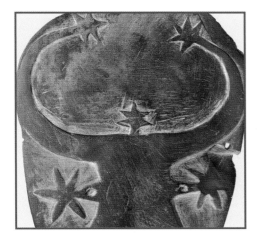

1 Early Egypt
c.4400–2686 BCE

2 The Old Kingdom
c.2686–2055 BCE

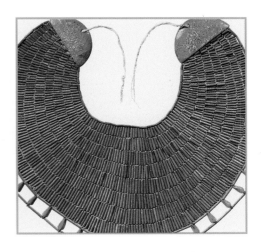

3 The Middle Kingdom
c.2055–1550 BCE

4 The Early New Kingdom
c.1550–1295 BCE

5 The Late New Kingdom
c.1295–1069 BCE

6 The Late Period
c.1069–332 BCE

7 The Greco-Roman Period c.332 BCE–395 CE

AUTHOR

Steven Snape

Steven Snape is Reader in Egyptian Archaeology at the University of Liverpool, where he has also been Director of the Garstang Museum of Archaeology. He has directed archaeological fieldwork in Egypt in Sinai, the Eastern Delta, Abydos, and Thebes and is currently Director of the excavations at the Ramesside fortress-town of Zawiyet Umm el-Rakham. His main research interests are settlement archaeology, the Ramesside Period, and sacred landscapes in ancient Egypt. He has published widely on topics connected to the archaeology of Egypt, including the books *Ancient Egyptian Tombs: The Culture of Life and Death* (Wiley-Blackwell, 2011) and *The Complete Towns and Cities of Ancient Egypt* (Thames & Hudson, 2014).

CONSULTANT

Joyce Tyldesley

Joyce Tyldesley is Professor of Egyptology at the University of Manchester, where she teaches Egyptology online to students around the world. She is also an Honorary Research Associate of the Manchester Museum and President of Bolton Archaeology and Egyptology Society. Her research focuses on the lives of the women of ancient Egypt. She has extensive excavation experience in both Egypt and Europe and is the author of more than 20 best-selling books on ancient Egypt, including *Nefertiti's Face: The Creation of an Icon* (Profile Books, 2018) and *Cleopatra: Last Queen of Egypt* (Profile Books 2008), which was a BBC Radio 4 Book of the Week.

CONTRIBUTOR (DIRECTORY)

Andrew Humphreys

Andrew Humphreys is a journalist, author, and travel writer who specializes in Egypt. He is the author of *National Geographic Egypt*, as well as *On the Nile* (American University in Cairo Press). He has written and contributed to guidebooks on Egypt for DK and Lonely Planet. He is also the main contributing author for *Journey: An Illustrated History of Travel* (DK).

△ **A pilgrimage to Abydos**
This wall painting from the tomb of Sennefer depicts a
pilgrimage to the holy city of Abydos, where Osiris—
the god of the afterlife—was believed to be buried.

Introduction

No ancient civilization is more intriguing and exciting than the Egypt of the pharaohs. Its art, monuments, and gods are all still recognized today, but they are only part of its long and captivating story. Surviving documentary evidence shows that the ancient Egyptians, from kings to carpenters, were all part of a vibrant culture—one that continues to fascinate thousands of years later.

Ancient Egypt is one of the most famous, and yet most mysterious, of ancient civilizations. It is also one of the longest, covering a vast passage of time. When Cleopatra VII died in 30 BCE, for instance, more than 2,000 years ago, the Great Pyramid was already 2,500 years old and hieroglyphs had been in use for 600 years before that.

This long period was filled with achievements that are still very visible today. The monuments of ancient Egypt—its huge royal pyramids and vast temples, in particular—are some of the greatest of human architectural triumphs and seem even more astonishing when we take into account the simple tools that were used to build them.

A lasting legacy

The kings and queens of ancient Egypt were determined to create a legacy that would last for ever, and we still know their names today—names such as Tutankhamen, Ramesses, Hatshepsut, and Cleopatra. But the legacy of ancient Egypt is not only to be found in the enormous buildings constructed by its rulers, but also in the exquisite objects that they created. These artifacts expressed the religious devotion and hopes for the afterlife of many thousands of Egyptians, and they are among the most popular museum exhibits around the world.

These museum treasures, however, are not just limited to spectacular and famous objects, such as the gold mask of Tutankhamen or the Rosetta Stone. They also include archaeological discoveries that remind us that the ancient Egyptians were very much real people who lived lives that were in some ways different, but in many ways similar, to our own lives today.

We know about these lives lived thousands of years ago from the archaeological evidence that is available. Crucially, this includes documents written by the ancient Egyptians themselves—inscriptions on the walls of temples that were carved and painted for both future generations and the gods to read, as well as official records needed to run the Egyptian state; reports of legal cases; and personal letters addressed to friends, neighbors, and enemies.

The Egyptian civilization

Using meticulous maps and detailed images of hundreds of the most amazing objects and buildings created by the Egyptians, this book investigates the many facets of their civilization. We see how, from its humble beginnings as a series of simple farming communities, Egypt became a unified country and went on to be a superpower that dominated much of northeast Africa, western Asia, and the eastern Mediterranean for 3,000 years.

The history of Egypt was not, however, one of continuous stability, and the book traces the fluctuating fortunes of the Egyptian state as it competed with fierce regional rivals, such as Nubia, the Hittites, and later Rome. It also delves into the lives and reigns of individual kings and queens to find out how they altered the course of Egyptian history and culture: from Narmer, who first united Egypt, to Cleopatra VII, after whose reign Egypt ceased to be an independent country.

We explore the religion of the ancient Egyptians—the gods that they worshipped and how they worshipped them. We visit the tombs of both royal and nonroyal Egyptians, seeing how carefully they were prepared for their owners, with wall paintings, texts, and the huge range of the everyday objects needed for the afterlife. We also examine the breathtaking works of art created for tombs and temples. Perhaps most revealing of all, we visit the houses of ordinary Egyptians to see what life was really like for the people who lived near the banks of the River Nile, from the food they ate to the hairstyles they wore, and from the games they played to the decorated coffins in which they were finally laid to rest.

Chronology of dynasties

The chronology of ancient Egypt is based on the reigns of individual kings, grouped into dynasties, and further grouped into longer periods of time. Egyptologists know the names and sequence of most of the kings of Egypt from 3000 BCE onward.

Predynastic Period	Early Dynastic Period	Old Kingdom	First Intermediate Period	Middle Kingdom
c.4400–3000 BCE	c.3000–2686 BCE	c.2686–2160 BCE	c.2160–2055 BCE	c.2055–1650 BCE

Predynastic Period — c.4400–3000 BCE

The Badarian Period (c.4400–4000 BCE)

Naqada I/Amratian Period (c.4000–3500 BCE)

Naqada II/Gerzean Period (c.3500–3200 BCE)

Naqada III/Dynasty 0 (c.3200–3000 BCE)
Narmer

Early Dynastic Period — c.3000–2686 BCE

1st Dynasty (c.3000–2890 BCE)
Aha
Djer
Djet
Den
Queen Merneith
Anedjib
Semerkhet
Qa'a

2nd Dynasty (2890–2686 BCE)
Hotepsekhemwy
Raneb
Nynetjer
Weneg
Sened
Peribsen
Khasekhemwy

Old Kingdom — c.2686–2160 BCE

3rd Dynasty (2686–2613 BCE)
Nebka
Djoser
Sekhemkhet
Khaba
Sanakht
Huni

4th Dynasty (2613–2494 BCE)
Snefru
Khufu (Cheops)
Djedefre
Khaefre (Chephren)
Menkaure (Mycerinus)
Shepseskaf

5th Dynasty (2494–2345 BCE)
Userkaf
Sahure
Neferirkare
Shepseskare
Neferefre
Niuserre
Menkauhor
Djedkare Isesi
Unas

6th Dynasty (2345–2181 BCE)
Teti
Userkara
Pepi I
Merenre
Pepi II
Nitiqret

7th & 8th Dynasties (2181–2160 BCE)
Numerous short-lived kings

First Intermediate Period — c.2160–2055 BCE

9th and 10th Dynasty (2160–2025 BCE)
Khety I
Khety II
Khety III
Merikare

11th Dynasty Thebes only (2125–2055 BCE)
Montuhotep I
Intef I
Intef II
Intef III

Middle Kingdom — c.2055–1650 BCE

11th Dynasty (2055–1985 BCE)
Montuhotep II
Montuhotep III
Montuhotep IV

12th Dynasty (1985–1773 BCE)
Amenemhat I
Senwosret I
Amenemhat II
Senwosret II
Senwosret III
Amenemhat III
Amenemhat IV
Sobekneferu

13th Dynasty (1773–AFTER 1650 BCE)
Wegaf
Sobekhotep II
Iykhernefert Neferhotep
Ameny-intef-Amenemhat
Hor
Khendjer
Sobekhotep III
Neferhotep I
Sahthor
Sobekhotep IV
Sobekhotep V
Ay

14th Dynasty (1773–1650 BCE)
Minor rulers, starting with Nehesy, probably contemporary with 13th or 15th Dynasty

---

NAMING CONVENTIONS

For most of the Dynastic Period, Egyptian kings had a series of five names. The two most important names were the Birth Name and the Throne Name, which were both written in cartouches (oval loops that encircle a royal name). The Egyptians distinguished kings with similar Birth Names by their Throne Names, as they did not use regnal numbers. The king we call Ramesses II was known to the Egyptians as Ramesses Usermaatre-Setepenre (but some letters refer to him more familiarly as "Sese").

Greek and Roman historians also knew some kings by variants of their names. For example, Khufu became known as Cheops. Some of these Classical versions of names are still used today. While most Egyptologists use the name Senwosret for some 12th Dynasty kings, others prefer the Classical version, Sesostris.

△ The north wall of Tutankhamen's tomb showing the king at his funeral (right) and embracing Osiris, god of the underworld (left)

Second Intermediate Period	New Kingdom	Third Intermediate Period	Late Period	Greco-Roman Period
c.1650–1550 BCE	c.1550–1069 BCE	c.1069–664 BCE	c.664–332 BCE	c.332 BCE–395 CE

15th Dynasty
(1650–1550 BCE)
Salitis
Khyan
Apepi
Khamudi

16th Dynasty
(1650–1580 BCE)
Theban early rulers
contemporary with
the 15th Dynasty

17th Dynasty
(c.1580–1550 BCE)
Rahotep
Sobekemsaf I
Intef VI
Intef VII
Intef VIII
Sobekemsaf II
Seqenenre Ta'a
Kamose

18th Dynasty
(1550–1295 BCE)
Ahmose
Amenhotep I
Tuthmosis I
Tuthmosis II
Tuthmosis III
Hatshepsut
Amenhotep II
Tuthmosis IV
Amenhotep III
Akhenaten/Amenhotep IV
Smenkhkare
Tutankhamen
Ay
Horemheb

19th Dynasty
(1295–1186 BCE)
Ramesses I
Seti I
Ramesses II
Merenptah
Amenmesse
Seti II
Siptah
Twosret

20th Dynasty
(1186–1069 BCE)
Sethnakht
Ramesses III
Ramesses IV
Ramesses V
Ramesses VI
Ramesses VII
Ramesses VIII
Ramesses IX
Ramesses X
Ramesses XI

21st Dynasty
(1069–945 BCE)
Smendes
Amenemnisu
Psusennes I
Amenemope
Osorkon the Elder
Siamun
Psusennes II

22nd Dynasty (945–715 BCE)
Sheshonq
Osorkon I
Sheshonq II
Takelot I
Osorkon II
Takelot II
Sheshonq III
Pimay
Sheshonq V
Osorkon IV

23rd Dynasty (818–715 BCE)
Pedubastis I
Iuput I
Sheshonq IV
Osorkon III
Takelot III
Rudamon
Peftjauawybast
Iuput II

24th Dynasty (727–715 BCE)
Tefnakht
Bakenrenef

25th Dynasty (747–656 BCE)
Piankhy
Shabaqo
Shabitqo
Taharqa
Tantamani

26th Dynasty
(664–525 BCE)
Necho I
Psamtek I
Necho II
Psamtek II
Apries
Ahmose II
Psamtek III

27th Dynasty
(525–404 BCE)
Cambyses
Darius I
Xerxes I
Artaxerxes I
Darius II
Artaxerxes II

28th Dynasty
(404–399 BCE)
Amyrtaios

29th Dynasty
(399–380 BCE)
Nepherites I
Hakor
Nepherites II

30th Dynasty
(380–343 BCE)
Nectanebo I
Teos
Nectanebo II

31st Dynasty
(399–380 BCE)
Artaxerxes III
Arses
Darius III

Macedonian Dynasty
(332–310 BCE)
Alexander the Great
Philip Arrhidaeus
Alexander IV

Ptolemaic Dynasty
(305–30 BCE)
Ptolemy I Soter I
Ptolemy II Philadelphus
Berenike II
Ptolemy III Euergetes I
Ptolemy IV Philopator
Ptolemy V Epiphanes
Ptolemy VI Philometor
Ptolemy VII Neos Philopator
Ptolemy VIII Euergetes II
Ptolemy IX Soter II
Ptolemy X Alexander I
Ptolemy IX Soter II
(restored)
Ptolemy XI Alexander II
Ptolemy XII Neos Dionysos
Cleopatra VII Philopator
Ptolemy XIII
Ptolemy XIV
Ptolemy XV Caesarion

Roman Period
(30 BCE–395 CE)

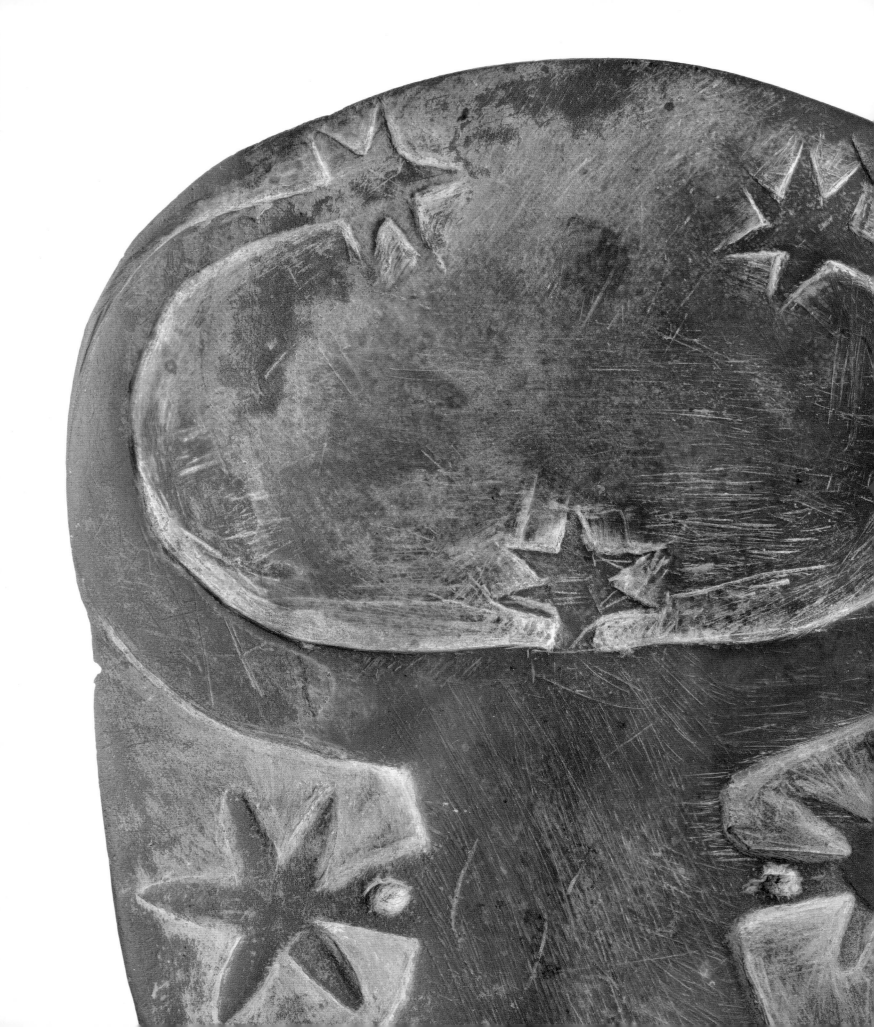

◁ **The Gerzeh Slate**
This schist palette from
the Naqada II Period
shows that religious belief
was developing during the
Predynastic Period. It depicts
the head and horns of a cow
goddess (possibly Hathor)
surrounded by stars.

1
Early
Egypt
C.4000–2686 BCE

Early Egypt

In the period between 500,000 and 9000 BCE, the northeast of Africa was occupied by groups of hunter-gatherers. For much of this time, the climate was wetter than it is today and these groups were able to roam across what is now the Sahara Desert, hunting large mammals. A dry period put an end to that way of life, and when the climate became wetter again, in around 9000 BCE, people adopted a different way of life. During the Saharan Neolithic period (8800–6800 BCE), humans began to live in more permanent settlements, herd cattle, and make pottery. By 5000 BCE, similar communities had appeared in the Nile Valley and Delta, and by 4400 BCE, their way of life was becoming culturally more sophisticated.

The Predynastic Period

Archaeological sites in southern Egypt are better preserved than those in the Delta, and many traces of an increasingly sophisticated culture have been found at sites in Upper Egypt, especially cemeteries. The artifacts discovered there suggest that the people who lived in the Predynastic Period were skilled at producing ceramics and objects made of stone and metal. The evolution of such artifacts has made it possible to identify different phases of this period, which lasted from 4400 to 3000 BCE.

The most important site in southern Egypt was Hierakonpolis. This settlement grew in importance to become a city with a developed administrative system headed by a ruler. The rulers of such towns began to depict themselves in art as powerful kings who defeated their enemies. This was probably a time of conflict between different warring factions in southern Egypt, all of which wished to extend their territories. Artifacts recovered from Hierakonpolis include some bearing the names of people claiming to be kings. The best known of these kings was Narmer, who may have defeated both his southern rivals and northern Egypt to unify Egypt as a single state.

The Early Dynastic Period

The unification of Egypt had several consequences, one of which was the founding of Memphis as the country's capital. It was strategically located close to where the Nile Valley meets the Delta, so it was an ideal place from which to govern all of Egypt. The political structure of the new nation was based on the idea of a divine kingship, which was ideally passed down from father to son. From this point on, Egypt was dynastic, and the Early Dynastic Period that followed the unification was made up of the first two dynasties.

Much of what is known about the kings of these dynasties comes from the Umm el-Qa'ab cemetery at Abydos in southern Egypt. For reasons that are not known, most of the kings of the 1st and 2nd Dynasties chose this as the royal necropolis, just as late Predynastic rulers such as Narmer had done. Over time, the tombs that were built in this cemetery became larger and more elaborate and were used to celebrate the lives of their royal owners. This interest in using funerary monuments to immortalize the power of kings was to reach its peak in the following Old Kingdom.

◁ **Naqadan figurine**

c.4400 BCE Beginning of the Badarian Period in Upper Egypt

c.4000 BCE Beginning of the Naqada I Period in Upper Egypt

c.5000 BCE Settlement of Merimde Beni Salama, in Lower Egypt

c.4200 BCE First signs of the Maadi culture in Lower Egypt

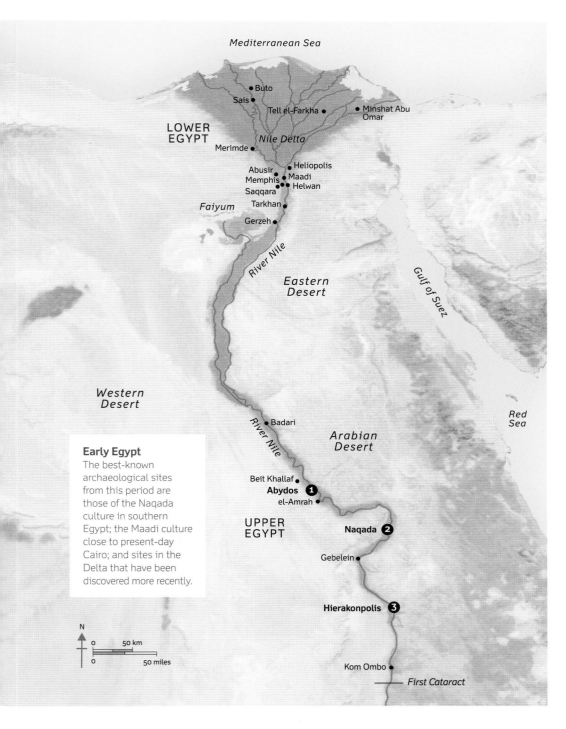

Mediterranean Sea

• Buto
Sais •
Tell el-Farkha • • Minshat Abu
Omar

LOWER
EGYPT   Nile Delta

Merimde •

Abusir •   • Heliopolis
Memphis • • Maadi
Saqqara • • Helwan
Faiyum   Tarkhan •
Gerzeh •

River Nile

Eastern
Desert

Gulf of Suez

Western
Desert

• Badari

Arabian
Desert

Red
Sea

River Nile

Early Egypt
The best-known
archaeological sites
from this period are
those of the Naqada
culture in southern
Egypt; the Maadi culture
close to present-day
Cairo; and sites in the
Delta that have been
discovered more recently.

Beit Khallaf •
Abydos • ❶
el-Amrah •

UPPER
EGYPT

Naqada • ❷

Gebelein •

Hierakonpolis • ❸

N

0   50 km
0   50 miles

Kom Ombo •
—— First Cataract

❶ The Umm el-Qa'ab necropolis, Abydos

❷ Pot from Naqada depicting a boat burial

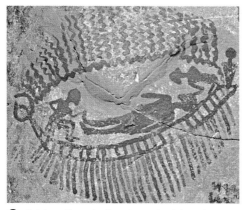

❸ Tomb painting, Hierakonpolis

c.**3300** BCE Hierakonpolis
becomes the dominant
city in Upper Egypt

c.**3200** BCE Beginning
of the Naqada III Period

c.**2890** BCE Beginning
of the 2nd Dynasty

c.**2686** BCE End of the
2nd Dynasty and the
Early Dynastic Period

c.**3500** BCE Beginning
of the Naqada II Period
in Upper Egypt

c.**3250** BCE Writing is
first used in Egypt

c.**3000** BCE Narmer unites
Egypt. Aha becomes the
first king of the 1st Dynasty

c.**2690** BCE Khasekhemwy
builds the largest Early
Dynastic tomb at Abydos

King Seti I burns incense to honor his ancestors

Prince Ramesses reads the offering ritual from a roll of papyrus

Name of Menes, the legendary first king of Egypt

Chronology and kings

King lists and the history of ancient Egypt

Carved onto temple walls or copied into histories of Egypt, lists of royal names known as king lists are an important source of information about the chronology—the historical sequence—of the ancient Egyptian civilization.

Between 290 and 260 BCE, an Egyptian priest named Manetho wrote a history of Egypt that he called *Aegyptiaca*. It was probably written as part of an attempt by the Ptolemaic kings, the Greek monarchs of the Hellenistic Period (c.332–30 BCE), to gather knowledge about the history of the country that they now ruled and about which they knew very little.

The *Aegyptiaca* itself has not survived, but later authors copied Manetho's lists of ancient kings, which were organized into ruling families known as dynasties. These king lists now inform our basic understanding of ancient Egyptian chronology. Manetho probably drew his information from documents that he found in temple archives, but most of these have been lost. The best surviving example is the Turin Canon (so called because of its present location in the Egyptian Museum in Turin, Italy). A fragmentary papyrus from the Ramesside Period (c.1295–1069 BCE), it lists the names of kings, mainly in their correct chronological order.

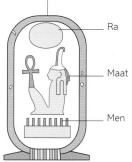

Ra

Maat

Men

△ **The name of a king**
A cartouche is an oval frame surrounding the birth name or throne name of an Egyptian king—two of the king's five official "great names." This cartouche refers to Seti I by his throne name, *Men-Maat-Ra*.

Name of Montuhotep II, the founder of the Middle Kingdom

Name of Khufu, the builder of the Great Pyramid at Giza

Name of Ahmose, the founder of the New Kingdom

Name of Amenhotep III, the ninth king of the 18th Dynasty

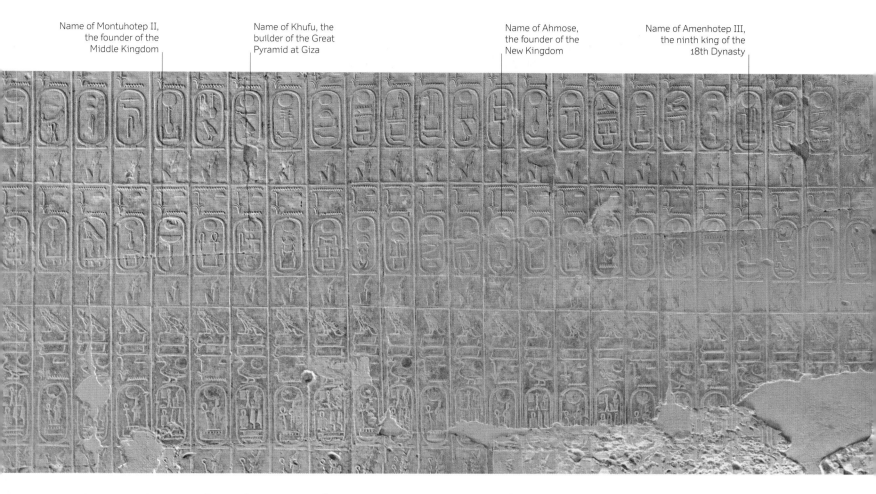

△ **Abydos king list**
This "official" list of kings, both real and mythical, recognized by Seti I, was carved on the walls of his temple at Abydos, c. 1280 BCE. It does not include the names of the female king Hatshepsut or the rulers of the Amarna Period (1352–1323 BCE).

King lists were not always accurate, partly because they were sometimes used as royal propaganda. A good example is the list carved on the walls of the Temple of Seti I at Abydos (above). Here, the king selectively named those he claimed as his royal ancestors in order to confirm his own right to rule. Other king lists exist, such as that of Tuthmosis III in the Karnak temple complex, but these are less helpful, because they do not list the kings in chronological order.

Dating by reigns

For literate Egyptians, the identity of the current king and the length of his or her reign were important in other ways. The Egyptians did not have a universal calendar that numbered years from a specific date in the past: they counted time using the name of the king; the year of his reign; and the day, month, and season. The date on a document, a letter, or even a wine label might therefore read: "Year 3, 2nd month of Summer, Day 5, under the Majesty of the king of Upper and Lower Egypt, *Neb-Maat-Re* [Amenhotep III]."

With this system, it was important to know both the name of the current king and how long he had reigned. If a scribe wanted to refer to events in the past, he had to know the order and length of the reigns of earlier kings. However, dating time in this way was only of interest to the upper, literate level of the population, and most Egyptians probably had only a vague idea of who the current king was, let alone how long he had been on the throne.

THE PALERMO STONE

The largest of seven surviving fragments of a double-sided basalt stela about 6 ft 6 in (2 m) high, the Palermo Stone is kept in the Archaeological Museum in Palermo, Sicily. Its provenance is not fully known. In addition to providing a list of royal names, the stela also provides details of events that took place during the lives of the kings listed. The original document from which it was copied dated to the later part of the Old Kingdom (c. 2686–2181 BCE).

The River Nile

The lifeblood of ancient Egypt

The Greek historian Herodotus described Egypt as the gift of the River Nile. Without the Nile, ancient Egypt would never have developed from a collection of small early settlements into a powerful and vibrant civilization.

Apart from a tiny number of people who lived in the desert, every ancient Egyptian lived close to the Nile or the canals that led from it. The river was vital to life—without it, Egypt would have been restricted to the fringes of the Mediterranean Sea, where limited rainfall provided the only source of fresh water. Ancient Egypt was blessed by the river, and even today, it is the only area of North Africa able to sustain a settled population of any size away from the coast.

Mighty river

The Nile is the longest river in the world. Around 4,200 miles (6,800 kilometers) long, it is mainly fed by the Blue Nile, which originates from rainfall in the highlands of Ethiopia, and the White Nile, which comes from the run-off from a series of East African lakes. These two rivers meet just to the north of Khartoum, the modern capital of Sudan, and continue north toward the Mediterranean. The Nile runs through most of Egypt as a single, wide

river, but just after it passes through modern Cairo, it splits into a series of branches, creating a fan-shaped delta, before flowing into the Mediterranean. Along its course, the river crosses a series of rapids formed by bands of hard stone—known as the cataracts of the Nile—which make river travel hazardous.

The Egyptians divided ancient Egypt into two parts, based on the geography of the Nile. The term Lower Egypt refers to the Nile Delta, while Upper Egypt refers to the Nile Valley south of the Delta, as far as the first cataract at Aswan—the source of the river in ancient Egyptian mythology. The king of Egypt usually took the title "King of Upper and Lower Egypt" or "Lord of the Two Lands," reflecting this dual aspect of the kingdom.

Settlements and inundation

Both the Valley and the Delta were prime areas for settlement. Prehistoric villages were established alongside the river, where people could water their animals and grow their crops. The river provided enough resources for the population to grow: villages became towns, and some eventually grew into cities.

Regular flooding, or inundation, was one of the most important features of the Nile. The rainfall that fed the Blue Nile was seasonal, so the river rose and

▷ **Fowling**
In this tomb painting, the New Kingdom official Nebamun and his family hunt birds in the marshes of the Nile. Many Egyptians used the river for hunting, fishing, and boating.

◁ **The source of the Nile**
This relief from the temple of Isis at Philae shows Hapy, the god of the river, guarded by a great snake, pouring the waters of the Nile from two jars.

▷ **Blue hippo**
This glazed blue faience figure made during the Middle Kingdom depicts a hippopotamus—a feared threat to boatmen on the Nile.

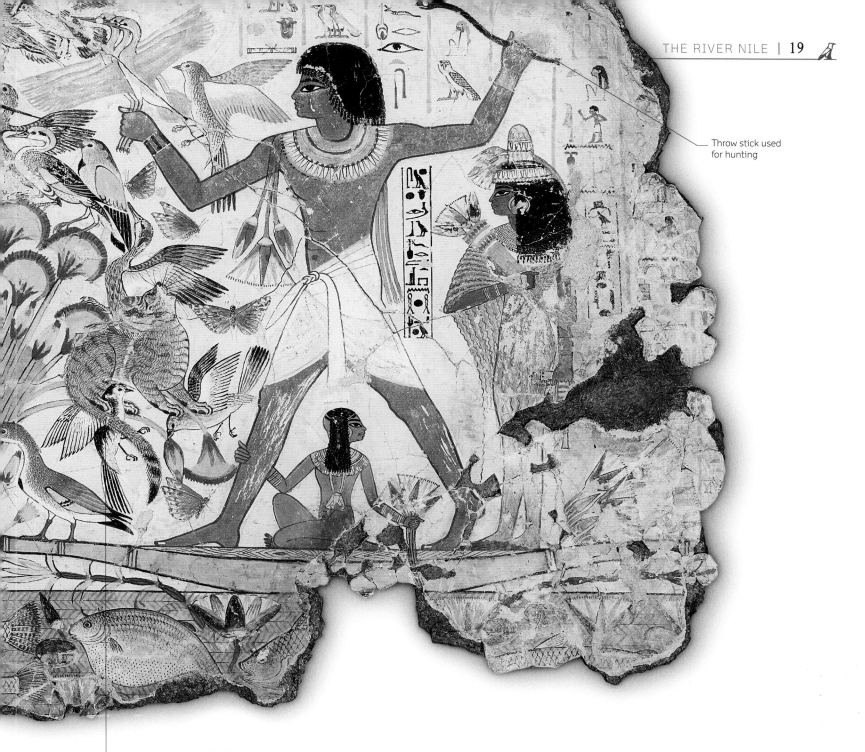

Throw stick used
for hunting

Nebamun's
agile cat
catches a bird

fell during the course of each year. At its highest level, in late summer, the river would breach its banks and flood the adjoining countryside before gradually receding to its normal course.

Although a particularly high inundation might temporarily flood nearby villages and towns, the overall effect was beneficial. The inundation provided a natural form of irrigation, and the water could be trapped in large basins specially made for that purpose. The waters that washed from the Ethiopian uplands were also full of silt, which provided a natural fertilizer for the crops sown after the floods.

The ancient Egyptians based the three seasons of their year on the cycle of the inundation: *akhet* (the inundation season), *peret* (the season of "coming forth" of the crops on the land), and *shemu* (summer). For the agricultural workers who made up the vast majority of the population, the year was a mixture of intense activity during the growing season and periods of relative inactivity that lasted for much of the summer and during the inundation itself. When they were not busy farming, these workers could be co-opted to help with other projects—such as building tombs and pyramids.

The Nile

As the River Nile flows north past the island of Elephantine (shown here on the left) and the modern city of Aswan, it is immediately clear why it was such a vital resource for the ancient Egyptians. The mighty river has created narrow strips of rich, fertile land along each bank—in stark contrast to the dry, sandy cliffs of the desert beyond—which made it possible for them to cultivate crops. The sailboats on the river are a visual reminder that the Nile was also the main thoroughfare for transporting both people and cargo, such as the granite that they used in famous monuments.

Farming the Black Land

Agriculture in ancient Egypt

The River Nile made Egypt a fertile land able to produce an astonishing abundance of crops. This fertility, more than gold, precious stones, or any other raw material, was the basis of Egypt's wealth and power in the ancient world.

The Nile's annual flood cycle (see pp.18–19) brought major natural benefits to Egypt by irrigating the land along the river and enriching it with silt, a natural fertilizer. This created the perfect conditions for farming and enabled the population to grow, helping make Egypt a powerful state.

Growing food

The river effectively made farming much easier: farmers just had to plant their crops in the moist, rich, black soil and then wait for them to germinate and flourish during the warm growing season. As long as the floodwaters reached the right level, there would be a rich harvest. A low level of inundation, however, would fail to irrigate enough farmland, leading to poorer yields and possible famine.

Bread and beer were the staples of the Egyptian diet. Both were made from cereals—wheat and barley—so these were the most important crops grown in the Nile Valley and Delta. Farmers also grew vegetables, including cucumbers, onions, and lettuce,

◁ **Sickle of Amenemhat**
This model sickle, which is only 9 in (23 cm) long, was made for the "Fieldworker of Amen, Amenemhat." It was probably for use in the afterlife.

and in many parts of Egypt, they also cultivated date palms. The milder climate in the Delta made it possible to grow vines there and produce wine. Ducks and geese were an important source of protein, as were sheep and goats. Archaeological evidence suggests that villagers also often kept pigs, but they rarely feature in the depictions of animals in tomb scenes. Egyptians prized cattle for their meat, but they rarely ate beef, because it was costly to produce.

The Red Land and Black Land

The dramatic, contrasting landscapes of Egypt had a profound effect on how the ancient Egyptians perceived the world. For them, the difference between what they called the Red Land and the Black Land was obvious. The Red Land was their name for the rocky, red ocher–colored desert where nothing could grow and where they buried their dead. The Black Land, on the other hand, signified the dark, fertile land on either side of the River Nile in which all their crops could be grown.

The Egyptians therefore often used red in their paintings as a negative color—one that they associated with death. On the other hand, they regarded black and green as positive colors associated with life, growth, and resurrection after death.

◁ **Lush fields and red desert**
In many parts of the Nile Valley, as here at Thebes, the contrast between the fertile black soil and the barren red desert is a striking feature of the landscape.

Sennedjem pulls flax, a plant used to make linen

Orchard of fruit trees

▷ **Watering a garden**
This detail from a painting in the tomb of Ipuy at Deir el-Medina (c.1250 BCE) shows a gardener raising a bucket of water using a pulleylike device called a *shaduf.*

It is easy to imagine ancient Egypt as being full of grand stone buildings in cities populated by pharaohs and their retinues, but in fact the vast majority of the population lived in small villages and spent their lives working in the fields—usually as tenant farmers. The importance of agricultural work in ancient Egypt was reflected in people's ideas about the afterlife. They believed, for example, that all of the dead would have to work for the god Osiris in an afterlife known as the Field of Reeds (see pp.262–263). Paintings of this afterlife, and farming in general, are often seen on the walls of the tombs of high-ranking people and provide vital evidence about how people worked the land throughout ancient Egyptian history.

▽ **The Field of Reeds**
In this painting in their New Kingdom tomb at Deir el-Medina, an artisan named Sennedjem and his wife Iyneferti carry out various agricultural tasks in the Field of Reeds—all while wearing their finest white linen garments.

Sennedjem reaps wheat with a sickle

Iyneferti sows seeds for the next harvest

Sailing on the Nile

Boats and river transportation

Many scenes painted on the walls of Egyptian tombs and temples show gods, kings, and ordinary people sailing on the river. The importance of the Nile as a natural highway through the land cannot be overemphasized.

While the water provided by the River Nile was vital to the survival of people and their crops and animals in ancient Egypt, it was also the main sewage and waste-disposal system for the villages and towns along its banks. But the river helped define the civilization in other ways, too.

Traveling overland in ancient Egypt was difficult. Other than tracks across the desert, there were no roads, partly because the annual floods (see pp.18–19) would have washed them away. People had to walk everywhere, and if they wanted to transport small quantities of goods, they would use donkeys as pack animals. (Camels were unknown until late in Egyptian history.) Apart from a few chariots used by the military and the elite, wheeled transportation was extremely rare because of the lack of roads.

The Nile, however, provided an easy and accessible way to travel, whether in a small boat made of papyrus stems or in a state barge built from the finest timber imported from Lebanon. During the flood season, boats were the only feasible way to travel from one village to another. Sailing was especially easy: the prevailing winds blew from north to south, making it easy to sail south, and the natural flow of the river from south to north carried boats along with it. The hieroglyphic sign for the word "to travel south" depicts a boat in full sail, while the word meaning "to travel north" shows a boat with the sail furled.

Transporting stone

Boats were used for a multitude of purposes: as funeral barges, for pilgrimages to holy sites, and for moving large quantities of grain around the land. One aspect of river travel in particular, however, had an important impact on the development of ancient Egyptian culture: the transportation of huge stone monuments. It would have been impossible to drag ancient Egypt's colossal statues and obelisks—some weighing up to 1,102 tons (1,000 tonnes)—over land for the vast distances between the quarries and the temples. Instead, they could be floated up or down the river on barges from the granite quarries at Aswan, for example, to the Nile Valley or as far as the Nile Delta at the end of the river.

△ **Modern felucca**
Despite the advent of the motorboat, traditional sailboats called feluccas still travel the Nile today.

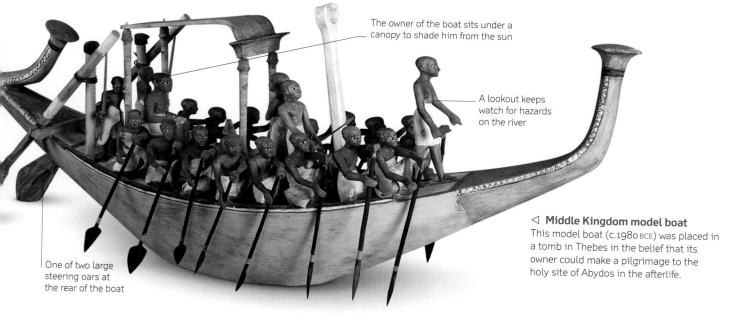

The owner of the boat sits under a canopy to shade him from the sun

A lookout keeps watch for hazards on the river

One of two large steering oars at the rear of the boat

◁ **Middle Kingdom model boat**
This model boat (c.1980 BCE) was placed in a tomb in Thebes in the belief that its owner could make a pilgrimage to the holy site of Abydos in the afterlife.

Isis, the
mother
of Horus

Horus, wearing the
double crown of Upper
and Lower Egypt

▽ **Horus at Edfu**
In this carved scene from the Temple of Horus at Edfu,
the god Horus, standing on his boat, harpoons a tiny
hippopotamus representing his enemy, Seth.

Seth, depicted as
a hippopotamus

Local government

Regions, nomes, and towns

Ancient Egypt was a large, complex country that needed to be overseen by both central government and local officials. It was therefore divided into a series of geographical regions with different levels of administrative responsibility.

To Egyptians, their country was made up of two parts, Lower and Upper Egypt, and this was reflected in the way in which it was governed. In the New Kingdom, there were two separate civil administrations. The northern capital was usually the city of Memphis, and the southern capital was Thebes. The head of each administration was a *Tjaty* (Vizier), who reported directly to the king, the "Lord of Two Lands."

Earlier, in the Old Kingdom, governance had been simpler. The national center of power was Memphis, and nearly all senior government officials were based there. However, some type of local government was needed even then, if only to organize collecting taxes for the state. The "nome" was the most enduring form of local government, lasting throughout Dynastic

Egypt. The term comes from *nomos*, the Greek version of the Egyptian word *sepat*, meaning a district with a town as its local capital. Although the size, boundaries, and number of nomes varied over time, there were usually 42 altogether.

Creating the nomes

No one knows the origin of the nomes and their boundaries, although most were centered around a significant town. They seem to have been created by central government rather than based on regions of Egypt that already existed. Smaller nomes were often in more fertile parts of the Nile Valley than larger ones, which suggests that they were all meant to have roughly the same economic status. Each nome had its

The nomes of Egypt map showing Mediterranean Sea, LOWER EGYPT, UPPER EGYPT, Gulf of Suez, River Nile, and nome numbers.

△ **The nomes of Egypt**
The classic divisions of Egypt into its 42 nomes (22 for Upper Egypt and 20 for Lower Egypt), each with a nome capital which acted as a central administrative hub.

KEY
1–20 Lower Egypt nome numbers
1–22 Upper Egypt nome numbers

▷ **Regional gods**
This scene on a wall of the temple of Ramesses II at Abydos (c.1279–1213 BCE) shows a procession of regional deities personifying the nomes of Egypt, bringing offerings to the main god of the temple.

Symbol of the town of
Gbytyw (Coptos)

own distinctive symbol, which also acted as its name. Together, they symbolized the whole of Egypt, and they appear in "nome lists" on the walls of temples right up until the Greco-Roman Period. Today, however, nomes are usually referred to by the name of their capitals: the Coptite nome in Upper Egypt, for example, is named after the city of Coptos.

The power of the nomarchs

The most important official of each nome, the nomarch or "Great Overlord of the *Sepat*," was in theory appointed by the king. In fact, this role often became hereditary, leading to powerful local "dynasties" of officials. These dynasties gained even more power during the First Intermediate Period (the time between the Old Kingdom and the Middle Kingdom), when there was no king.

The most obvious archaeological legacy of the nome capitals is not the settlements themselves, but the splendid cemeteries that many nomarchs built for themselves as a statement of their regional prestige. The walls of these splendid tombs often depict a vital aspect of the nomarchs' role: collecting taxes (in the form of agricultural surpluses) on behalf of the king or the state.

Double-falcon symbol of the Coptite Nome

◁ **A king and his nome god**
In this Old Kingdom statue, King Sahure of the 5th Dynasty (right) sits beside a "nome god" (left), an Egyptian deity that personified a nome. This particular god represents the Coptite nome.

After the Old Kingdom, individual towns (usually called *Niwt*) or new royal estates (often called *Hwt*) became centers of economic and political power that were just as important as nomes. By the Ramesside Period, documents such as the Wilbour Papyrus (an ancient tax assessment) suggest that some nomes were thriving districts with important urban centers, whereas others were little more than grazing land.

Symbol of the estate of *Hwt-sat-Aset*

Symbol of the town of *Iunet* (Dendera)

Symbol of the town of *Nebutet*

Predynastic Egypt

The first settlements and their legacy

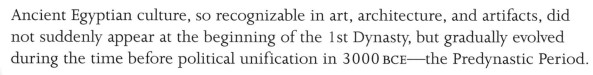

Ancient Egyptian culture, so recognizable in art, architecture, and artifacts, did not suddenly appear at the beginning of the 1st Dynasty, but gradually evolved during the time before political unification in 3000 BCE—the Predynastic Period.

△ **Ostrich palette**
This large siltstone palette was not just functional, but is decorated in relief with a line of ostriches—common animals in the desert.

The later Neolithic Period in the Nile Valley is often referred to as the Predynastic Period, because it predated the dynasties of kings who ruled Egypt from around 3000 BCE. During this time, people began to settle in one place and farm the land; they developed complex new skills; and the first political centers formed around villages, which then grew into towns.

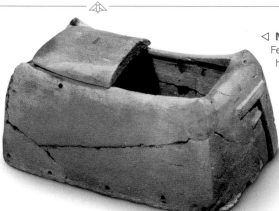

◁ **Model house**
Few mud-brick buildings have survived the passage of time, making this clay model of a house a rare find. It dates from the Naqada II phase and shows what houses of the time might have looked like.

Tracing the past
Much of the archaeological evidence for the Predynastic Period comes from burial sites, which have survived better than settlements. Sophisticated artifacts appear to have first emerged in Middle Egypt (the northern part of Upper Egypt), especially at Badari, Matmar, and Mostagedda. Soon afterward, they appeared farther south, at sites such as Mahasna, el-Amrah, Naqada, and Hu. At the northern end of the Nile Valley, particularly at el-Gerzeh, the objects found in graves show increasing levels of skill and artistry.

The artifacts found at the different sites differed over time—especially the pottery vessels, enabling archaeologists to date them. Based on these variations, the Predynastic Period is divided into four phases: The Badarian Period, c.4400–4000 BCE; Naqada I (or the Amratian Period), c.4000–3500 BCE; Naqada II (or the Gerzean Period), c.3500–3200 BCE; and Naqada III (or Dynasty 0), c.3200–3000BCE.

The most characteristic pottery from the first two periods is polished, black-topped red ware of various shapes (see pp.32–33). During the later two periods, there was a preference for buff-colored pots, often painted with stylized landscapes and scenes of life along the river, including boats and human figures.

The Naqada culture
Ceramic pots are the most striking objects of the Naqada culture, but they were not the only form of craftsmanship. Other high-quality objects have been found that indicate the growth of wealth and social hierarchies in Predynastic communities. Stoneworkers created exquisitely flaked flint knives, as well as vessels made from decorative hard stones such as breccia, diorite, and granite. They also made maceheads from hard stones, suggesting warlike activity (maces played a central role both during

" … the **adoption** of a **herding lifestyle** was associated over the **long term** with the spread of **new ritual practices**."

DAVID WENGROW, *THE ARCHAEOLOGY OF EARLY EGYPT*, 2006

and after the Unification Period). Dark siltstone was the main stone used to make small palettes for crushing and preparing pigments for cosmetics (see far left).

Metalworking developed throughout the Predynastic Period, as seen in many copper objects, including large tools and weapons. Another metal, which was to become crucial in the development of some sites in southern Egypt, also made its appearance—gold.

Animals feature in all forms of Predynastic art. The mixture of wild creatures from the desert and river valley (notably the hippopotamus) and farm animals such as cattle suggests an economy that was in the process of evolving from hunting to cultivation.

The Maadi culture

In Lower Egypt, archaeological evidence from the Predynastic Period is best preserved in a few sites on the edges of the Delta or in the region close to modern Cairo, especially Maadi. This gives its name to the Maadi Cultural Complex, the site of a culture that lasted from c.4000 to 3200 BCE. This produced fewer artifacts than the roughly contemporary Naqada culture (or did not place them in graves), but it did appear to have an active copper industry. During the Naqada II phase, artifacts from the Naqada culture became common in northern sites, including Minshat Abu Omar in the eastern Delta. This suggests that the Naqada culture was dominant in the north before the unification of Egypt.

PREDYNASTIC TRADE

Archaeologists have found bone and ivory figurines in several Predynastic sites. This one (of unknown origin, but probably dating to Naqada I) depicts a naked woman. The figurine is fairly typical, apart from its eyes, which are made of lapis lazuli. A striking blue stone, lapis was highly valued throughout Egyptian history and appears on other Predynastic artifacts. The closest known source of lapis to Egypt, however, was in quarries at Badakhshan, in northeast Afghanistan. This suggests that even before the unification of Egypt, the Nile Valley was already part of an extensive trade network and that valuable materials were transported huge distances, both by land and sea. Such journeys would have required complex planning and a series of trading posts set up along an established route.

IVORY FIGURINE WITH LAPIS LAZULI EYES

▷ **Model of cattle**
This small, painted clay model of four horned cows grazing was placed in a grave in el-Amrah, c.3500 BCE. This shows how important cattle were to their owners. Taming wild cattle and managing herds was a key development of the Predynastic Period.

The mud mixture
is carried to the
brickmaker

The brickmaker uses
a mold to produce
rows of bricks

Kneading the
mud-brick mixture

△ **Brickmakers at work**
This mural from the tomb of Rekhmire, a vizier and governor
of Thebes during the 18th Dynasty, contains the most
detailed known image of brickmaking known from ancient
Egypt. It is part of a series that depicts the different
industries and workshops that Rekhmire was in charge of.

Cities of mud

Building with mud brick

Mud bricks were the principal building material of ancient Egypt, and their importance cannot be overstated. Their widespread use made it possible to construct everything—from huts to cities—quickly and easily.

The buildings and monuments that have survived from ancient Egypt create the impression that the main building material was stone. Certainly, the most impressive monuments built to last for eternity, such as temples and tombs, were often built from stone, but the vast majority of buildings in Egyptian villages, towns, and cities were made from mud brick.

Making bricks

Mud brick had several advantages over stone or other materials. Mud was easy to find along the banks of the Nile or local canals, so it was available to most people. The method for making mud bricks was also extremely simple and cheap. Mud was mixed with sand and straw to create a mixture of the right consistency, then pressed into a rectangular mold to form a brick. The mold was then immediately removed, ready to use for the next brick.

Mud bricks were not fired like most modern clay bricks, but left to dry for about three days, then turned over to dry the other side. The mortar used to bond the bricks together was the same type of mud mixture from which the bricks themselves were made. With very little effort, just about anyone could produce large quantities of mud brick, which was useful if, for example, someone wanted to rebuild part of their house after an unusually high inundation. There was a fundamental problem with the bricks, however. As they were not fired, any lengthy exposure to water turned them back into mud—with the inevitable consequences. This is the main reason why so few mud-brick buildings have survived.

Grand buildings

Bricks were not just the simple building material of the peasant farmer, however; they were also used extensively for royal buildings. Modern studies have shown that a team of four brickmakers could produce about 6,000 bricks a day. Far more brickmakers would have been required to produce bricks for the largest state projects. The interior of Senwosret III's pyramid at Dahshur, for example, is built from around 24.5 million bricks, and Buhen Fort, in present-day Sudan, is made of around 4.6 million. It would have been far more expensive and difficult to build these massive structures from stone and would have required a much more specialized workforce. The rapid construction of cities such as Amarna (see pp.182–183) and Pr-Ramesses (see pp.220–221) was only made possible by the extensive use of the modest mud brick.

△ **Stamped mud brick**
The mud bricks for major projects were often stamped with the name of the king to indicate their owner. This brick bears the joint names of Tuthmosis I and Hatshepsut, who both ruled during the 18th Dynasty.

The brickmaker mixes mud, sand, and straw

Brick mold

◁ **Model of brickmaking**
Wooden models were a key part of the burial goods of many Middle Kingdom tombs. The owner of this model believed that it would provide him with an eternal supply of mud bricks.

Predynastic pottery

Ceramic art from prehistoric Egypt

The ancient Egyptians produced some of their most sophisticated and striking pottery during the Predynastic Period. Even before they had kings, hieroglyphs, or stone buildings, the inhabitants of the Nile Valley crafted beautiful pots, including their earliest attempts at creating two- and three-dimensional art.

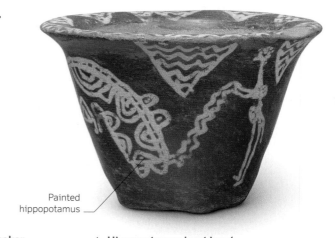

Painted hippopotamus

△ **Hippopotamus hunt bowl**
Hunting scenes featured on Predynastic pottery. This bowl from Naqada I–II depicts a man harpooning a hippopotamus—a scene that may represent man's control over nature.

Shiny surface created by polishing

Narrow rim with lip

▽ **Black-topped beaker**
Another example of black-topped red ware from Naqada I, this simple beaker may have been either molded from slabs of clay or made from coils.

△ **Polished Badarian pot**
The earliest form of black-topped red ware can be seen in this vessel from the Badarian Period (the first part of the Predynastic Period).

△ **Carrot-shaped vessel**
Black-topped red ware, such as this, dates from the Naqada I Period and is one of the most recognizable types of pottery from early Egypt. This vessel has an unusual carrot shape.

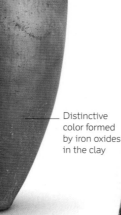

Polished red ware body without black top

Distinctive color formed by iron oxides in the clay

Flat rim

◁ **Vessel painted to imitate stone**
It took hours of labor to carve vessels out of stone. This ceramic pot from Naqada II, imitating the shape and surface of a stone vessel with two handles, was a less costly alternative.

Surface painted to look like stone

Geometric pattern painted in white

▷ **Red ware with geometric patterns**
In the Naqada I Period, this red polished ware with white painted decoration was a popular and decorative variant of red ware.

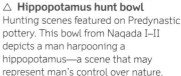

Dark red painted line

△ **Vessel with netting decoration**
This cylindrical pot has incised, wavy decoration near its rim. The painted lines may imitate the net bags that were used to carry such vessels.

Sculpted human foot

△ **Bowl with human feet**
Here, a Naqada I–II vessel combines a bowl with sculptural details. It may represent the hieroglyph "*in*," meaning "to bring."

MAKING POTS

The ancient Egyptians used two types of clay for their pots. The first type was the alluvial silt that they found on the banks of the Nile. It was easy to work, but usually produced vessels that were rough and porous. The second type was better-quality marl clay that they dug up from deposits at the edges of the desert in southern Egypt. This required rigorous treatment to make it malleable, and it had to be fired at high temperatures. The finished pots, however, were hard, smooth, and white or buff in color.

Model of potter forming a bowl on a potter's wheel

▷ **Decorated ware with human figures**
This decorated ware pot from Naqada II depicts a boat with a cabin containing human or divine figures. Such themes became more important in art after the unification of Egypt.

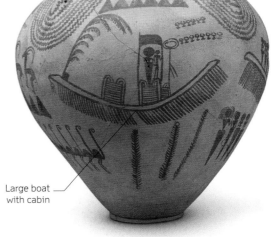

Large boat with cabin

Complex painted tree

◁ **Decorated ware with nature scene**
This jar is a good example of a Naqada II decorated ware vessel: buff-colored pottery with darker painted decoration. It shows a scene from the natural world, with a large, detailed tree and a flock of flamingos.

▽ **Bowl in the form of a bird**
The Egyptians of the Predynastic Period loved vessels shaped like animals, both in stone and ceramic. This fine example is modeled on the body of a bird.

Simplified head

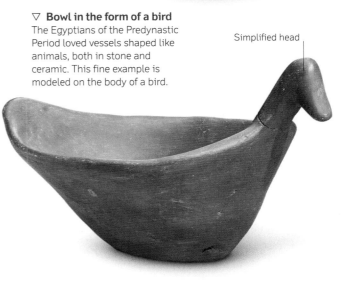

△ **Master of the animals**
This motif of a human seizing two wild beasts was common in Mesopotamian art at the time. It may symbolize control over nature.

◁ **Smiting prisoners**
A figure advances with a mace raised over its head, ready to slay defeated enemies. A common way of depicting the victorious Egyptian king, such images continued in art until the Greco-Roman Period.

▷ **Human conflict**
Scenes of battle suggest that warfare was an important feature of the late Predynastic Period. A range of weaponry, including spears, shields, bows, and maces, was being developed at this time.

Hierakonpolis

The first known city of ancient Egypt

The most important archaeological site from the Late Predynastic or Unification Period is Hierakonpolis in southern Egypt. For over a century, excavations there have provided fascinating evidence about the earliest cities in the Nile Valley.

The ancient city of Nekhen is best known today as the archaeological site of Hierakonpolis. It is situated in the southern part of the Nile Valley, between Thebes and Aswan—a significant area for the Naqada culture (see pp.28–29). Hierakonpolis rose to prominence some time during the late Naqada II and III phases of the Predynastic Period. It seems to have been a local center of power—its rulers were extremely ambitious and wanted to extend their authority over as much of the surrounding area as possible.

Hierakonpolis had several characteristics that made it a city rather than simply a large town. It was obviously larger than a town, and more people lived there, but it also controlled the land all around it so that it was able to commandeer its resources (especially the food grown there) for its residents. Cities also favor the development of specialized industries, particularly those involving skilled labor or new technologies. Social hierarchies also evolve over a period of time, as indicated in ancient Egypt by

Large, banana-shaped boat of a type often found in late Predynastic art

Boats may have belonged to local rulers, and appear here as symbols of power

tombs of varying size and splendor and a political system that holds sway well beyond the city boundary. Grand architecture in the form of monuments or a ceremonial area is also a characteristic of a city. Hierakonpolis can be considered a true city in all of these regards. No other site has shown evidence of each one of these factors, so Hierakonpolis is usually referred to as Egypt's first city.

Life in the city

The inhabitants of Hierakonpolis used sophisticated technology. Crafts and industries that had emerged in other Predynastic sites, such as metalwork, pottery, stonework, and boat building, were developed further at Hierakonpolis. The population's food and drink were, at least in part, supplied by central production facilities, as shown by a large brewery complex unearthed there.

◁ **Lapis figurine**
This extraordinary lapis-lazuli figure excavated at Hierakonpolis is in keeping with previous figurines. It may represent a goddess. The head and the body were found by different archaeological expeditions and fitted together.

The location of Hierakonpolis was also favorable. It was close to the Wadi Abbad corridor leading through Egypt's gold-rich Eastern Desert to the Red Sea. The gold from this area seems to have attracted traders from as far away as Mesopotamia, in southwest Asia. Aspects of early cities in Mesopotamia may have influenced the development of Hierakonpolis, and Egypt in general, during unification.

Appetite for conflict

Extensive excavations at Hierakonpolis have uncovered a great number of objects depicting scenes of warfare and enemies being slaughtered, particularly in "Tomb 100" (see above) and the later Narmer Palette (see pp.44–45). These artifacts provide compelling evidence of the growing power of the city's rulers and their desire to win new territory.

△ **Wall painting from Hierakonpolis "Tomb 100"**
The tomb that contained this painting was discovered at Hierakonpolis in 1899, but its location has since been lost. It is the first Egyptian tomb known to have had painted walls, and it may have belonged to a local ruler. The paintings illustrate the important themes of conflict and warfare.

MAP OF THE **ANCIENT CITY**

By the end of the Predynastic Period, Hierakonpolis occupied much of the area around the Wadi Abu Suffian, a depression at the edge of the desert. The ancient city was not a single urban center, but a cluster of settlements, cemeteries, industrial complexes (especially for making pottery), and ceremonial centers, often quite far apart. During the 2nd Dynasty, King Khasekhemwy built a huge sacred enclosure known as the "Fort." After Egypt was unified, however, people abandoned much of early Hierakonpolis and settled on what is now the Kom el-Ahmar mound in the flood plain of the Nile.

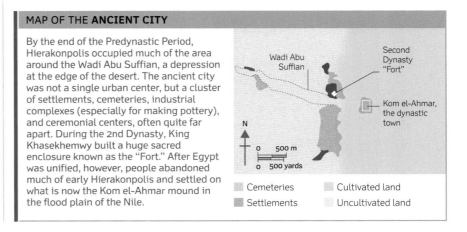

Wadi Abu Suffian

Second Dynasty "Fort"

Kom el-Ahmar, the dynastic town

N

0   500 m
0   500 yards

Cemeteries

Settlements

Cultivated land

Uncultivated land

Early temples and deities

Religion in the Predynastic Period

One of the core elements of ancient Egyptian religion—the worship of a variety of gods and goddesses in specially built temples—developed during the Late Predynastic and Early Dynastic Periods.

No one knows exactly when the Egyptians started to build temples for their gods, nor do they know exactly which gods the Egyptians worshipped during the Predynastic Period. There is, however, plenty of evidence to suggest that by the Unification Period, and into the 1st and 2nd Dynasties, a number of important sites for worshipping gods (known as cult centers) had emerged in both the Nile Valley and the Delta. At these cult centers, groups of people had developed ritual practices relating to a god or gods. The evidence for the identities of these gods comes partly from the surviving images of different deities that appear on Predynastic pottery, for instance. However, the Egyptians also created three-dimensional representations—varying in size from small figurines to colossal statues—which may have acted as cult images of the gods themselves.

Cult images

The worship of gods in ancient Egypt was based upon the idea that a god or goddess could reside within (but not be limited by) a divine image, such as a statue. Worshippers could regard that statue as the physical embodiment of a god and respect it accordingly. Divine service was modeled on the way that a servant would treat their master or mistress. A person's servant would bring them food and drink, wash them, and dress them. In a similar fashion, a god's priests would offer food and drink to the statue of the god. They would also wash it and change its clothes. When the Egyptians referred to a priest as a hm ntr (god's servant), they meant servant in the most literal sense.

◁ **Tell el-Farkha figurine**
This gold-covered statuette is similar in shape to other divine male figures from the late Predynastic and early Dynastic Periods. It was found at Tell el-Farkha in the Nile Delta, where excavations have uncovered an important cache of religious objects.

The god's house

Because ritual activities involved a personal relationship between the deity and its servants, they could not just be carried out anywhere. The Egyptians believed that a god, like a human being, required a house in which to spend time privately among his or her servants. They referred to the temple itself as the pr ntr (god's house), and they meant this literally. The relationship between humans and gods was based on the actions of human beings, especially servants and masters, and on the places where humans interacted.

THE TEMPLE OF **NEITH**

The clearest image of an early Egyptian temple is roughly sketched on a simple label from the 1st Dynasty that shows King Aha carrying out a series of mostly obscure activities. However, one section shows a simple temple possibly made from a few wooden uprights supporting walls of reed matting, as suggested in the reconstruction below.

The temple belonged to the goddess Neith, who is identified by her standard in the "courtyard" of the temple. Neith is especially associated with Sais in the western Delta, and the label may record a royal visit there.

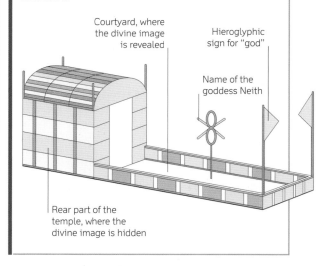

Courtyard, where the divine image is revealed

Hieroglyphic sign for "god"

Name of the goddess Neith

Rear part of the temple, where the divine image is hidden

Arms raised like
the horns of a cow

Small head with
a beaklike face

Stylized
long neck

Slender waist

White skirt

The first temples

Despite their similarities, ordinary houses and
temples were different in a number of important
ways. This is most apparent in the great stone temples
of the New Kingdom—their form and scale make
them look completely different from houses, although
the underlying concept behind them is basically the
same. In the Predynastic and Early Dynastic Periods,
temples were not built from stone, but from materials
that were easier to come by, such as mud brick, reed
matting, and small amounts of wood. These simple,
perishable components would not have lasted for long
in the floodplain of the Nile Valley and Delta, so very
few traces of these early temples have survived.
Historians have had to rely on a small number of
illustrations to work out what they might have looked
like (see box, left).

The architecture of later stone temples borrowed
decorative elements from these early buildings, which
were constructed of simple materials. For instance,
the walls of Greco-Roman temples were designed with
borders that mimicked the fringes of reed matting.
These ornaments were intended to bring to mind the
primitive nature of the ancient structures, which they
were trying to emulate as homes for the gods.

Houses for gods

The very first temples included not only rooms at
their rear (where the image of the god could be kept
and served by priests), but also more open areas, such
as courtyards. These open areas were semipublic
places where the god could appear to a greater
number of people. This is the origin of the typical
Egyptian form of temple, which developed throughout
the Dynastic Period.

The Egyptians seem to have built temples either in
response to orders from the king or as part of local
initiatives to make simple temples for local gods. The
second reason seems to have been more common at
this time in ancient Egypt.

◁ **Terracotta female figure**
This mysterious statue
from around 3500–3400 BCE
depicts a female figure with
a simplified lower body and
raised arms. It seems to be
celebrating a ritual and may
represent a mother goddess.
Similar figures often appear
in Predynastic art, both as
figurines and on pots.

Gods and goddesses

The major Egyptian deities

Most Egyptian gods had distinct identities expressed by their different names and roles. They also often had a personal appearance and symbolic attributes that made them instantly recognizable in art. Some were associated with specific cities or regions of Egypt, and many formed family groups with other gods.

Double crown of Upper and Lower Egypt

▷ Mut
The wife of Amen, Mut had her own temple in the Karnak complex in Thebes. The mother of the moon god Khonsu, she is usually depicted as a woman wearing the double crown of Upper and Lower Egypt.

Was scepter, a symbol of royal authority

▷ Atum
The most important of the creator gods, Atum was the ancestor of four generations of gods who ruled Egypt. People worshipped him alongside Ra at Heliopolis, near modern Cairo.

▷ Isis and Horus
The sister and wife of Osiris, Isis had a crucial role as the ideal divine mother, protecting her son Horus from Seth. In the Late Period, her cult was especially important at sites such as Philae.

Vulture head covering, worn only by queens and goddesses

Curved animal head

▷ Horus
Originally a sky god (as indicated by his falcon form), Horus came to embody divine kingship. He was usually shown wearing the double crown of Upper and Lower Egypt.

Two-feather crown, part of Amen's iconography

Bright blue glazed faience

△ Seth
The brother of Osiris, whom he murdered, Seth also competed with his nephew, Horus, for the throne of Egypt. He had a human body but the head of a strange animal.

Figure of a king, protected by the falcon god

▷ Amen
Originally a local god at Thebes, Amen (who later merged with the sun god Ra) became the most important deity of the New Kingdom. His main "home" was the massive temple complex at Karnak in Thebes.

◁ Sekhmet

Represented as a lioness wearing a sun disk, Sekhmet was the ferocious daughter of the sun god Ra. She was also the wife of Ptah and, like him, popular at Memphis.

Golden sun disk

Head of an ibis (a sacred bird)

▷ Thoth

Depicted as an ibis, an ibis-headed man, or a baboon, Thoth was associated with writing and knowledge. His main cult center was at Hermopolis Magna in Middle Egypt.

▷ Ptah

The husband of Sekhmet and the father of Nefertum, Ptah was a creator god and the patron of craftsmen. His cult at Memphis was one of the most important in dynastic Egypt.

Statue made from lapis lazuli, a semiprecious stone

The sun disk signifies her relationship to the sun god Ra

Platform represents hieroglyph for universal order

◁ Hathor

A goddess with a number of different roles, Hathor was the daughter of Ra. Female priests often served her cult. She was usually depicted as either a cow or a woman wearing a sun disk between two curved horns.

Wings of the goddess Isis wrap around his lower body

◁ Osiris

The king of Egypt, Osiris went on to rule in the afterlife after being murdered by his brother, Seth. His iconography (a mummy with the crown, crook, and flail of royal authority) reflects this.

◁ Ra

The most important sun god and chief royal god of the Old Kingdom, Ra was said to cross the sky every day in his boat. He was usually depicted as a falcon or a falcon-headed man wearing a sun disk.

Relief of Ra as a falcon

Small pyramid capstone from a private tomb

The unification of Egypt

Competing rulers and the dawn of the kingdom

The most important moment of Egypt's history was in around 3000 BCE, when it became a single unified state. The unification was the result of competition and conflict between local rulers, as well as economic factors.

During the Late Predynastic Period, Hierakonpolis developed into a large and prosperous city in southern Egypt (see pp.34–35). It might also have become the capital of a larger region, as its rulers extended their control over more of the land around the city. Their ambition for expansion probably brought them into conflict with the rulers of other mini-kingdoms that were developing both to the north and, to a lesser extent, to the south.

This period of rivalry between different rulers is now known as the Unification Period, because the winner went on to become the first king of a united Egypt. Many historians think that rulers from Hierakonpolis were probably the victors in this power struggle and that they eventually controlled territory that stretched northward along the Nile Valley and into the Delta.

Ceremonial objects

The most revealing sources of evidence about the events of the Unification Period are the regal objects that were commissioned by regional rulers—high-ranking individuals with political and economic power. They used these artifacts to record their successes—especially military successes, because warfare was becoming a key aspect of their authority.

Conflict is the central theme of the paintings in Hierakonpolis Tomb 100, but that tomb is unusual in depicting such themes on wall paintings—most of the artifacts celebrating war were things that were much more portable. They took the form of ordinary items such as knife handles, maceheads, and cosmetic palettes, but they were much larger than their everyday counterparts and were decorated with elaborate, carved reliefs. Many of these objects have an uncertain provenance—no one knows exactly

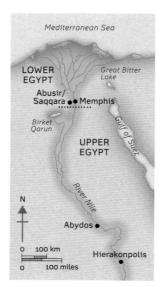

◁ **Upper and Lower Egypt**
This map shows the areas of Upper and Lower Egypt before unification, when the country was united under the rule of the first "King of the Two Kingdoms."

where they originally came from before they fell into the hands of dealers in antiquities.

Fortunately, the most important group of items comes from an archaeological excavation, the so-called "Main Deposit" in the temple area at Hierakonpolis. This collection of extraordinary objects seems to have been ceremonial in nature. They may have been gifts to the god of the temple (possibly Horus) that were presented by individuals who were both offering thanks to the deity and celebrating their own achievements. These individuals can be called kings, as they are shown wearing the same crowns and other regalia that symbolized Egyptian royalty for the next 3,000 years.

SCORPION MACEHEAD

This huge limestone macehead is from Hierakonpolis, c.3100–3000 BCE. Its carved reliefs record the actions of a king whose name is written with the hieroglyph of a scorpion. It is unusual among the ornate ceremonial objects from this period, because its primary concern is not military achievement. Instead, the king—holding a mattock (a tool for digging)—appears to be inaugurating a canal or irrigation project. This suggests that the king played a part in economic activity at the time when Egypt was becoming unified.

King "Scorpion," mattock in hand, wearing the white crown of Upper Egypt

"Ideology emerges with the state: a body of thought to complement a political entity."

BARRY KEMP, *ANCIENT EGYPT: ANATOMY OF A CIVILIZATION*, 2009

Some of these kings' names are recorded, although hieroglyphs from the period are notoriously difficult to decipher. Perhaps the most striking features of the carved reliefs used to decorate these artifacts are the detailed depictions of savage and powerful beasts, such as lions and bulls, which are shown trampling on their enemies or ripping them apart. These animals may represent kings defeating their foes in battle, which suggests that the king who commissioned the reliefs wanted to be seen as something more than human.

Although it is difficult to write a detailed history of the period based on these objects, it is clear that the concept of royal power, and how it was enshrined in art, developed at around the same time as the birth of the unified Egyptian state. Royal power found its greatest expression in the Narmer Palette (see pp.44–45) and was only able to flourish because, during the same period, the Egyptians invented a system of writing, which meant that they were able to record their own history.

▽ **Detail of handle**
This "Master of the Animals" figure also appears in art of the period from Mesopotamia.

Figure grasps an animal in each hand

Ivory handle

Ripple-flaked flint blade

△ **Gebel el-Araq knife**
The scenes of conflict on the carved handle of this knife (c.3500–3200 BCE) are typical of the Unification Period.

The rampaging lion may represent the superhuman power of the ruler, as sphinxes do later

A scavenging bird picks at the feet of a corpse

◁ **Battlefield Palette**
This segment of a stone palette from c.3100 BCE depicts the aftermath of a battle. The slain enemies are strewn on the battlefield at the bottom. At the top, banners representing the victorious army lead away the prisoners of war.

The invention of writing

Egyptian hieroglyphs

The kingdom of Egypt could not have existed without writing. It is no coincidence that three key events—the unification of Egypt, the emergence of kings, and the development of writing—all appeared at roughly the same time.

The development of writing was crucial for most ancient cultures, especially those that were evolving and expanding. Writing was essential for a state to function—to send out messages and royal decrees, record accounts, and collect taxes. Although writing seems to have appeared before unification, the kings of the newly unified Egypt would have depended on it to rule the Valley and Delta regions.

Different systems of writing developed around the Near East. Egypt's form of writing was distinctive—a hieroglyphic script based on recognizable images of things. The script was used to represent the language that had been spoken in what was now Egypt for centuries. Hieroglyphs first appeared both on labels and on objects such as the palettes and maceheads of the Unification Period. As the hieroglyphic script of this time was purely pictorial, it is often hard to know whether the symbols stand for text or should be interpreted as depictions of actual things.

ANKH **KA**

△ **Ankh-*Ka* vessel**
In this vessel, probably used to provide offerings for the soul of its owner, the two hieroglyphs for "ankh" (life) and "*ka*" (soul) are intertwined as a play on images and words.

From the Early Dynastic Period onward, hieroglyphs were used in a more sophisticated way. The signs began to represent sounds or groups of sounds (similar to letters or groups of letters), and their appearance lost any obvious relationship with their form—a door bolt represented the sound "s," a foot the sound "b," and a horned viper the sound "f." The appearance of some other signs was important, however, as they determined the meaning of a word. Verbs denoting types of travel, for instance, might use a boat or a pair of legs to make the meaning clear.

A swifter script

The problem with the hieroglyphic script was its very pictorial nature. It takes a considerable amount of time to write even a short piece of text using hieroglyphs, because each sign, if written properly, is a small drawing rather than a concise pattern of lines as in most alphabetic scripts. Recognizing this, the Egyptians invented an abbreviated, cursive form of the script, now known as hieratic. This is the script that they wrote on papyrus for letters and administrative documents.

For grand public inscriptions on tombs and temples, however, nothing could replace the authority of the hieroglyphic script, which the Egyptians referred to as "God's words."

The name "Den" in a *serekh*   King Den, sitting on a raised throne

△ **Label of King Den**
Ivory and wooden labels once attached to containers are often found in early royal tombs. More complex labels include events from the reign of a king—in this case, of King Den.

Part of the name of
Ramesses II, written
within a cartouche

The hieroglyphs
for "King of Upper
and Lower Egypt"

This rectangular
hieroglyph stands
for the word "house"

This elaborately carved owl
stands for the sound "m" or, as
here, the word "in."

△ **Monumental hieroglyphs at the Ramesseum**
Hieroglyphs, rather than the hieratic script, were used
for royal monuments throughout ancient Egyptian
history. Here, a dedication of Ramesses II describes
parts of the building on which it was carved.

The white crown of
Upper Egypt

The name of the
king, *Nar-Mer*

Falcon possibly
representing Horus

The red crown
of Lower Egypt

The king's
sandal bearer

A bull (the
king) tramples its
enemies underfoot

◁ **Front of the palette**
King Narmer is the focal point of this
side of the palette. He is shown as
the triumphant king, subjugating his
lowly enemies. His crown and mace
emphasize his power and authority.

Image of the cow goddess Bat

The Narmer Palette

A statement of kingship

One of the most important objects ever excavated in Egypt, the Narmer Palette was found in the so-called "Main Deposit" at Hierakonpolis. Made of siltstone and 25¼ in (64 cm) high, it is perhaps the most spectacularly oversized ceremonial object found from this period. Based on the shape of a cosmetic palette used to crush pigments for face paint, it is more like a tablet and might have been a gift from Narmer, the first king of unified Egypt, to a god, probably Horus (who appears as a falcon on the front). The palette is carved on both sides, each of which depicts symbolic aspects of Narmer's military victories and power.

Triumphant ruler

The main image, which dominates the front of the palette, shows Narmer in a typical pose associated with Egyptian kings, standing with his mace raised over a subjugated enemy, ready to smite him. This image is notable not just because it portrays what the king represented to the populace, but also because the depiction of the king himself is typical of two-dimensional art in ancient Egypt. In fact, some scholars refer to the palette as the first piece of Egyptian art, or art of the Dynastic Period. The king is shown with his head in profile, his chest facing forward, and each arm and leg clearly visible. The palette also follows other conventions of Egyptian art. The king, the main subject of the scene, is shown on a much

◁ **Back of the palette**
Mythical beasts dominate here. The leopards with entwined serpentine necks might represent the joining of Upper and Lower Egypt.

larger scale than the other figures. His enemies are smaller than him and his servant, the sandal bearer, is tiny.

Mythical beasts

On the back of the palette, the space is evenly divided into a series of horizontal scenes, similar to present-day cartoon strips. At the top, Narmer (on the left) leads his victorious troops to survey the headless corpses of his enemies lined up on the ground.

The larger central scene is composed around a shallow central hollow, which would have been used to ground pigments in a normal palette. This is defined by the entwined necks of two mythical creatures that combine the features of a giraffe and a leopard or lion. These beasts may symbolize the unification of Upper and Lower Egypt.

Some scholars believe that the Narmer Palette celebrates Narmer's unification of Egypt by military means. The scenes of conflict and victory, the mythical beasts, and the fact that Narmer is shown wearing the crown of Upper Egypt on the front of the palette and that of Lower Egypt on the back support this idea. Although this interpretation of the unification might be simplistic, the Narmer Palette was clearly intended to be, above all, a clear visual statement of the military prowess and royal power of someone who definitely regarded himself as king.

△ **The tomb of King Djer**
The only parts of the tombs at Abydos to have survived are those underground, as here, which have numerous chambers where objects for the king's afterlife were stored. There is no trace of the buildings above ground.

Royal tombs at Abydos

The necropolis of Egypt's earliest kings

The cemetery of the 1st and 2nd Dynasty kings at Abydos provides the earliest evidence of what would later become a defining feature of kingship in ancient Egypt—the monumental tomb.

The necropolis at Abydos was one of the most important burial sites in Egypt. At different periods throughout Egyptian history, Abydos was closely associated with the concept of the afterlife, primarily because it was regarded as the burial place of Osiris, the divine king of the afterlife. This association often overshadows the role of Abydos as the most important royal cemetery of the kings of the 1st and 2nd Dynasties.

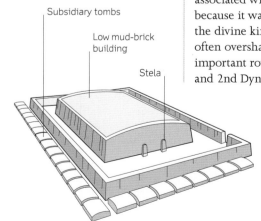

Subsidiary tombs

Low mud-brick building

Stela

◁ **1st Dynasty tomb**
This reconstruction shows what the building above a 1st Dynasty royal tomb at Abydos might have looked like. The main tomb was surrounded by a series of smaller subsidiary tombs.

No one knows why Abydos rose to prominence as an early royal necropolis. It is not likely to have been due to its proximity to the town of Thinis, which was powerful during the Unification Period. In fact, kings who one would expect to have been buried at Hierakonpolis have tombs at Abydos—notably Narmer (Dynasty 0) and his successor, Aha (1st Dynasty).

Abydos was certainly used for large important burials well before the Unification Period. Even after Memphis became the capital of the newly unified Egypt, it was Abydos, many miles away to the south, which seems to have been chosen as the national royal cemetery. The royal cemetery was gradually relocated to Saqqara, closer to the state capital at Memphis during the 2nd Dynasty, and most of the Egyptian kings were buried there by the 3rd Dynasty.

▷ **Stela of King Djet**
Each tomb was identified by a tall stone stela with the name of the king carved on it. Here, the name of King Djet is inscribed within a *serekh* panel, on top of which stands a falcon representing the god Horus.

The 1st and 2nd Dynasty royal tombs were located a short distance into the desert at Abydos, at a site that has become known in modern times as the Umm el-Qa'ab (Mother of Pots), because the ground is strewn with broken pottery left behind by pilgrims bearing offerings to Osiris. Most of the kings of the 1st and 2nd Dynasties were buried here, within quite a limited area, clustered together in relatively small tombs made largely of mud bricks.

Disputed tombs

Some archaeologists questioned whether these tombs belonged to the kings and thought that Saqqara, the burial ground for Memphis, was also the royal burial ground of the Early Dynastic Period. They identified the structures at Abydos as cenotaphs—monuments built to honor the kings—rather than actual tombs. This view has been discounted now, partly because the Umm el-Qa'ab tombs were not the only parts of the mortuary landscape created by these kings.

> " ... the remains which have **survived** the **lust of gold,** the **fury of fanaticism** and the **greed of speculators** ... "
>
> FLINDERS PETRIE, 1900

As well as the tombs, which might have been small simply because of the lack of space in this sacred site, the Early Dynastic kings also built huge, rectangular mud-brick enclosures closer to the edge of Abydos, in an area now known as the North Cemetery.

The only one of these enclosures still standing above ground today is the Shunet el-Zebib (Storeroom of Raisins), built by Khasekhemwy, the last king of the 2nd Dynasty (see below). No one knows how these enclosures were used in the funerary rites of the kings, but some of them were surrounded by life-size wooden models of boats, probably the predecessors of the boat burials found close to some of the Old Kingdom pyramids at a later date.

Shunet el-Zebib enclosure

Buried model boats

◁ **Enclosure and boats**
The vast Shunet el-Zebib enclosure, seen in the background here, measures 410 x 19½ ft (125 x 65 m). In the foreground are the remains of a series of life-size model boats, part of the king's burial goods, which would have been useful to him in the afterlife.

The first kings of Egypt

Rulers of the 1st and 2nd Dynasties

During the Early Dynastic Period, the unification of Egypt was strengthened by central rule. By the end of the 2nd Dynasty, around 350 years later, the key characteristics of the ancient Egyptian civilization were already firmly established.

The role of the king was possibly the defining feature of ancient Egyptian culture. The ceremonial objects of the Unification Period show the king as a powerful ruler and suggest that he had superhuman powers. This idea grew and developed over time. Part of the king's power was thought to come from the gods, because he was regarded as the intermediary between the deities and the people.

The king demonstrated his absolute authority and control over Egypt's resources by building grand royal monuments, such as the tombs at Abydos. His power may even have extended to ordering the sacrificial burials of attendants to accompany him in the afterlife. Massive royal monuments, temples, and tombs are an obvious characteristic of ancient Egypt. The most striking examples were the huge stone pyramids that were built in the following Old Kingdom.

Establishing territory

The territorial boundaries of Egypt became more clearly established during this period. The southern border was defined as the First Cataract (shallow, rapid sections) of the Nile, and Elephantine became Egypt's most southern town. The eastern and western edges of the Delta probably also came to represent the boundaries of what was now Egypt. The ruling dynasties and families of Upper and Lower Egypt appear to have made marriages of convenience among themselves to extend their power and influence.

△ **Kingly aggression**
This ivory label for King Den's sandals shows the king in typically aggressive pose, smiting a foreign enemy. The hieroglyphs on the far right may read "First time [of smiting] the East".

This is suggested by the number of royal women whose names refer to the goddess Neith, who was traditionally connected with the western Delta town of Sais.

"White Walls," which later became the city of Memphis, was founded close to the point where the Nile divides into the streams of the Delta. This was a strategic location for ruling over the newly integrated Egypt. The court officials who were based at Memphis were buried in nearby cemeteries, notably at Saqqara, where they would eventually be joined by their kings.

◁ **Khasekhemwy**
This limestone statue of Khasekhemwy shows him on his throne, wearing the white crown of Upper Egypt.

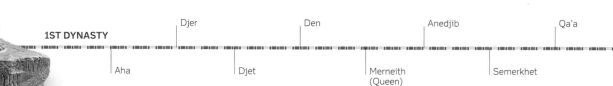

1ST DYNASTY

	Djer		Den		Anedjib		Qa'a
Aha		Djet		Merneith (Queen)		Semerkhet	

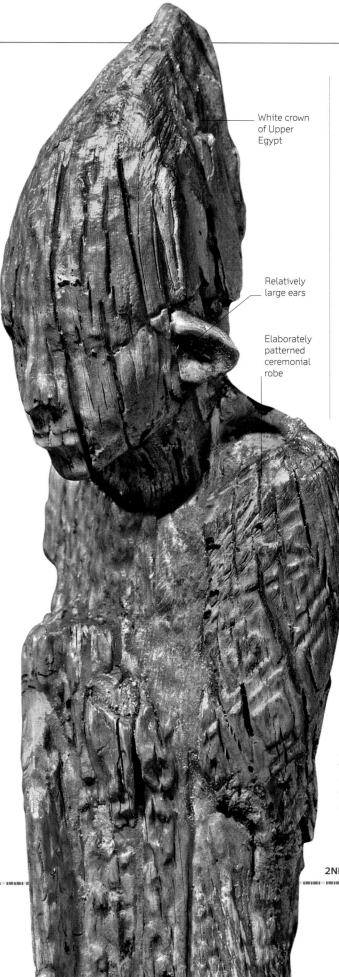

White crown of Upper Egypt

Relatively large ears

Elaborately patterned ceremonial robe

OBJECTS FOR **ETERNITY**

The royal tombs at Abydos had been thoroughly looted well before they were excavated by archaeologists at the end of the 19th century. This looting may have taken place as early as the First Intermediate Period. However, the tomb robbers missed enough precious items to show that even though the tombs themselves might be small, they were full of treasures.

This stone vessel is typical of the fine materials that were available to the king. It is made from dolomite, a stone that is hard and difficult to obtain. It is sealed with a lid of gold foil and gold thread, secured with small clay seals.

STONE VESSEL WITH GOLD FOIL LID

Early Egyptian politics

In terms of foreign affairs, Egyptian policy, as at every period, was to destabilize its southern neighbor, Nubia. The Egyptians established trade routes along the coast of northern Sinai toward the cities of southern Palestine, but images of the king of Egypt smiting "Easterners," and specifically nomadic groups in the Eastern Desert and Sinai, suggest that they adopted a more aggressive approach.

Internal politics are more difficult to fathom. Only one royal woman—Merneith—has a large tomb at the Umm el-Qa'ab, suggesting that she may have ruled as king. It is also not clear why the first kings of the 2nd Dynasty seem to have been buried at Saqqara and later kings back at the royal necropolis at Abydos. Very little is known about most of the 2nd Dynasty kings, but Khasekhemwy, the last of them, built the largest tomb to date at Abydos, as well as the great enclosure of Shunet el-Zebib and a similar one at Hierakonpolis. He set a high standard for monument making at the end of the 2nd Dynasty— one that the 3rd Dynasty kings, especially Djoser, tried their best to surpass.

◁ **King in jubilee robe**
This small ivory figure of an elderly, unnamed king wears the robe associated with celebrating the *Sed* festival. Traditionally, this marked the successful completion of 30 years on the throne.

2ND DYNASTY

Raneb | Weneg | Peribsen

Hotepsekhemwy | Nynetjer | Sened | Khasekhemwy

Private tombs

Feeding the dead for eternity

The development of the nonroyal tomb was an important feature of the Early Dynastic Period. The inspiration for this development was centered on the requirements of the spiritual form called the "ka."

The evidence from the Early Dynastic royal tombs at Abydos and the later royal tombs at Saqqara and other cemeteries close to Memphis shows that kings expected a unique afterlife. Although no one knows exactly what these kings thought would happen to them after death, it is obvious that they expected something that was unavailable to ordinary people. Egyptologists believe it probably involved an afterlife with the gods.

Ordinary people, or everyone apart from the king, had rather different expectations regarding the afterlife. The Egyptians did not have just one idea about what happened to a person's spiritual essence, their "soul," after death, but various fluid ideas that changed a great deal in the First Intermediate Period and the New Kingdom.

Early Dynastic private tombs show the development of beliefs that were later clearly expressed in Old Kingdom tombs. Simple graves in the desert give away little about the religious beliefs of those buried there, but larger and more complex tombs are more revealing.

The ka

The ancient Egyptians believed that everyone had a spiritual life force called the "ka" that existed within them while they were alive. After death, the ka carried on living in this world and had similar needs to those of a living human, but it needed a physical host, which was provided by the dead body itself. Perhaps coming across bodies buried in the desert sands had made the Egyptians think that preserving the body was vital in order for the ka to survive. The body and ka together needed a home, the tomb, but this was not simply a resting place for the ka-filled body; it also needed to provide the ka with food and drink.

Offerings

Ideally, people who were still alive would supply food and drink on an ongoing basis, in the form of offerings at the tomb. Alternatively, people could prepare their own tombs with magic models, images, and texts (preferably to be read out loud by the living) that would summon the food that the ka needed. A tomb, therefore, had a dual purpose: to protect the body and to provide a place where the living

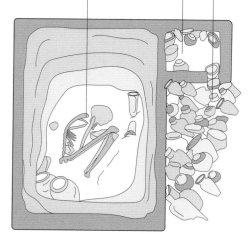

Pots of offerings left in and around the offering chapel

Burial

Offering chapel

△ **Tarkhan tomb 1845**
This is a typical tomb. The body is buried within a mud-brick enclosure that has an offering chapel attached to it. The ancient Egyptians believed that the ka was able to travel between the two parts of the tomb.

◁ **Gaming disk**
This disk was found in the tomb of Hemaka, a high official, at Saqqara. Games were provided in some tombs for the ka to entertain itself.

"A thousand loaves of bread, **a thousand jars** of beer **for the ka** of ..."

EXTRACT FROM THE "OFFERING PRAYER"

Decorative edge

could bring offerings for the *ka*. They were therefore built with two parts. The first was where the dead person was buried, to keep the body safe. The second was an offering chapel, where people could bring things to feed the *ka*. The *ka* living in the tomb did not only have to be fed, but also had to be able to amuse itself for eternity, so games of different kinds were often provided for it in the larger tombs of wealthy people.

Egyptian private tombs developed architecturally over time, depending on their location, the wealth of their owners, and new ideas about the afterlife. The two-part structure incorporating a burial chamber and offering chapel was, however, fundamental to all of them, because the concept of the *ka* and its requirements formed a recurring theme throughout ancient Egyptian history.

△ **Boat of death**
The corpse in this late Predynastic ceramic model boat is shown in the fetal position, the most common pose for the body in simple burials at the time.

The deceased eats from a table of offerings

◁ **Offering stela of Satka**
Decorated stelae (stone slabs) within tombs indicated where offerings could be made to feed the *ka*. They depicted the tomb owner eating and also acted as magical substitutes for offerings.

2
The Old Kingdom
c.2686–2055 BCE

The Old Kingdom

Pyramid building is the main thing that everyone associates with the Old Kingdom (3rd–6th Dynasties). This was probably how the kings of the period saw it, too, because their motivation for expending such vast resources on these very visible monuments was partly to immortalize their own memory. There were other reasons, however, for building pyramids. They played a key role in the growing importance of sun worship and were also places where the kings could be provided for in the afterlife, in cult services held at the mortuary temple attached to each pyramid.

The pyramids of the Old Kingdom were the largest structures ever built in Egypt, so constructing them required an enormous amount of resources, not only in terms of stone and equipment, but also in terms of labor. This was only possible because Egypt was both politically and economically centralized in the Old Kingdom.

The royal cemeteries at Memphis

The first pyramid was built by Djoser early in the 3rd Dynasty at Saqqara. Building the pyramid at Saqqara was significant, as the area to the west of Memphis, which was the capital of the Old Kingdom kings, became an extended royal necropolis for the kings, replacing the Early Dynastic royal cemetery at Abydos. Saqqara was the heart of the Memphite necropolis, but pyramids were also built to the south of it, at sites such as Dahshur and Meidum, and north of it, at Abusir and Abu Roash. The most famous cluster of pyramids was at Giza, where the largest single pyramid, that of Khufu, was built in the 4th Dynasty. Unlike Djoser's original pyramid, which had stepped sides, these later pyramids had steep, straight sides.

Court and regional cemeteries

The tombs of the kings' relatives and important court officials were built close to the pyramids. These were often substantial structures made of stone, with extensively decorated walls, and they became larger and more elaborate during the course of the Old Kingdom. The royal pyramids, on the other hand, became smaller after the 4th Dynasty.

The archaeology of Old Kingdom Egypt is less well-documented away from the area around Memphis, but a few regional cemeteries have provided some important information about the period. These include the tombs of expedition leaders, which were built on Egypt's southern border with Nubia.

The First Intermediate Period

The collapse of royal authority at the end of the Old Kingdom left Egypt politically fragmented, and power was seized by people who aspired to become kings of Egypt. The most prominent of these warlords were initially based at Herakleopolis Magna (the 9th and 10th Dynasties), but the ultimate victors in the competition to reunite Egypt under a single king were the kings of the 11th Dynasty. This family came from a city that would go on to play a leading role in Egypt's immediate future—Thebes.

◁ **Statue of Kai and his children**

c.**2667** BCE Djoser becomes king. Step Pyramid built at Saqqara

c.**2613** BCE Snefru, the first king of the 4th Dynasty, becomes king

c.**2487** BCE Sahure becomes king. Abusir becomes a royal necropolis

c.**2686** BCE Beginning of the 3rd Dynasty and the Old Kingdom

c.**2613** BCE Death of Huni, the last king of the 3rd Dynasty

c.**2589** BCE Khufu becomes king. The Great Pyramid is built at Giza

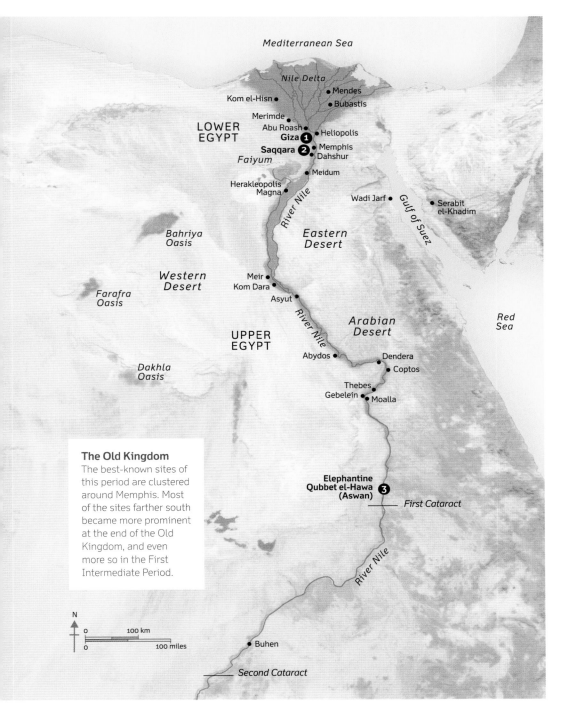

Mediterranean Sea

Nile Delta

Kom el-Hisn •
• Mendes
• Bubastis

Merimde •
Abu Roash •
Giza ❶
Heliopolis •

LOWER
EGYPT

Saqqara ❷
Memphis •
Dahshur •

Faiyum

• Meidum

Herakleopolis
Magna •

Wadi Jarf •
• Serabit
el-Khadim

River Nile

Gulf of Suez

Bahriya
Oasis

Eastern
Desert

Western
Desert

Meir •
Kom Dara •

Farafra
Oasis

Asyut •

River Nile

Arabian
Desert

Red
Sea

UPPER
EGYPT

Dakhla
Oasis

Abydos •
Dendera •
• Coptos

Thebes •
Gebelein •
• Moalla

**Elephantine
Qubbet el-Hawa
(Aswan)** ❸

First Cataract

River Nile

The Old Kingdom
The best-known sites of
this period are clustered
around Memphis. Most
of the sites farther south
became more prominent
at the end of the Old
Kingdom, and even
more so in the First
Intermediate Period.

N

0   100 km
0   100 miles

• Buhen

Second Cataract

❶ The Giza pyramid complex

❷ Pyramid texts from the Pyramid of Pepi, Saqqara

❸ The tombs of Qubbet el-Hawa, Aswan

c.2345 BCE Teti
becomes the first king
of the 6th Dynasty

c.2184 BCE The death
of Pepi II and the end of
the Old Kingdom

c.2125 BCE Thebans
rule southern Egypt

c.2375 BCE Unas becomes
king. The earliest Pyramid
Texts are written

c.2278 BCE Pepi II
becomes king

c.2160–2025 BCE
Herakleopolitans rule
northern Egypt

c.2055 BCE
Montuhotep II
reunifies Egypt

Djoser's Step Pyramid

The rise of the pyramid

In terms of historical significance, architectural invention, and technological innovation, no building from ancient Egypt is as important as the Step Pyramid of King Djoser at Saqqara, built around 2750 BCE.

The Step Pyramid of King Djoser (also known as Netjerikhet) was a landmark building in many ways. Not only was it the first Egyptian pyramid, it also broke the tradition of royal burial at Abydos by being built at Saqqara—near the Egyptian capital of Memphis. Previously, royal tombs had been low, square structures called mastabas (from the Arabic for "bench"). The most imposing parts of these tomb complexes had been the huge mud-brick enclosures built a short distance away from the actual tombs, as

at Shunet ez-Zebib (see pp.46–47). Djoser's pyramid, however, was visually striking and recognizably a royal monument. It was built just to the west of Memphis, on the edge of the desert plateau overlooking the Nile Valley. This meant that it could be seen from many miles away in Memphis set against the *akhet* (the western horizon), which was increasingly regarded as the portal to the afterlife. After Djoser, all of the 3rd to 6th Dynasty royal tombs were built there.

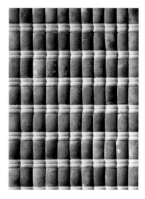

△ **Wall tiles**
The underground rooms of the pyramid complex were decorated with turquoise tiles that imitated the reed matting covering the walls of the king's palace.

Heb Sed Court   Mortuary temple

Imitation chapels   Step Pyramid

△ **The funerary complex**
The pyramid itself was just one part of a complex of buildings designed to help the king on his way to a beneficial afterlife.

Apex, uniting the heavens and the Earth

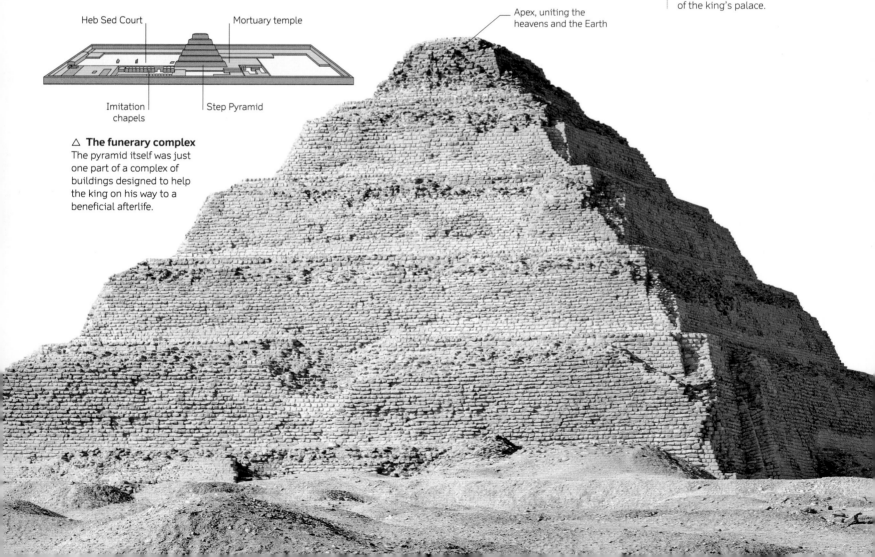

▷ **The Famine Stela at Sehel**
Very little is known about Djoser or the events of his reign. He was remembered in later times as a good king; the Ptolemaic Famine Stela on the island of Sehel, near Aswan, describes how the actions of Djoser (and Imhotep) saved Egypt from a seven-year drought.

The first pyramid

Djoser's tomb was built in stages. Initially, it seems to have followed the traditional model of a mastaba set within a walled funerary enclosure, but it developed into something far more ambitious. To increase the height of the tomb, three more "mastabas" of gradually diminishing sizes were built on top of it, creating a monument of four "steps." An additional two layers were then added to the top, creating a six-step, pointed building—the very first Egyptian pyramid.

The sheer scale of the pyramid immortalized Djoser, but its stepped form may also have had a religious significance. As mentioned in the Pyramid Texts (see pp.70–71), it created a symbolic stairway to the heavens, thereby uniting heaven and Earth. It was a form that was later adapted to make the "true" straight-sided pyramids at the end of the 3rd Dynasty and the beginning of the 4th Dynasty.

The Step Pyramid was not only innovative from an architectural point of view—it also represented a huge step forward in technology because it was built of stone. Earlier royal tombs had a few stone elements within them, but they were mainly built of mud brick. This was the first time that an entire building had been constructed from stone—it is the oldest monumental stone building in the world.

Venerating the king

The Step Pyramid was the centerpiece of a whole complex of buildings. The burial chamber itself was situated directly beneath the pyramid and was surrounded by underground galleries where burial goods needed for the afterlife were stored. Above the ground, a tall enclosure wall formed the perimeter of a rectangle containing the pyramid and a series of other buildings. The mortuary temple built against the side of the pyramid seems to have been where people

◁ **Step Pyramid**
The Step Pyramid of Djoser is one of the most immediately recognizable monuments from the ancient world. It was the tomb and funerary monument of King Djoser, who became known as the "Discoverer of Stoneworking."

came to make offerings to the dead king. Nearby was a small stone chamber, known by the Arabic word serdab (cellar). This contained a life-size statue of the king—a feature that was to become common in the private mastaba tombs of the Old Kingdom.

It is not known for certain what many of the other buildings within the complex were for, but some of them may represent full-size stone models of temples from different parts of Egypt. The entire southern part of the enclosure was taken up by the so-called Heb Sed Court. This was provided specifically for the dead king so that, in the afterlife, he could enact a ritual that he had performed during his lifetime and thereby demonstrate his kingly prowess.

IMHOTEP

Imhotep was a high official during Djoser's reign and is traditionally credited by many Egyptologists as being the architect of the Step Pyramid. He had the rare distinction of being a nonroyal Egyptian who was later venerated as a god. He was associated with a similar range of scribal activity and learning as that of the god Thoth, and in the Late Period and Ptolemaic Period, he was especially connected to medicine and healing. The quantity of Imhotep-related cult objects from this period, including this bronze statuette, demonstrates the popularity of his cult at the time. It is widely believed that Imhotep was buried at Saqqara—but, despite several attempts to locate his tomb, it has never been found.

BRONZE STATUETTE OF IMHOTEP

Working with stone

The building blocks of Egyptian culture

One of the defining features of ancient Egyptian culture is its enormous monuments—temples, tombs, and colossal statues. None of this would have been possible without an accessible source of good-quality stone.

One of the great natural resources of ancient Egypt was stone—specifically, stone that could be used for buildings and for objects such as statues, stelae, obelisks, and altars. It was the material chosen to build monuments that were to last forever, such as tombs and temples. Everyday buildings, such as houses and palaces, were mostly made from mud brick.

The most widely available stone for building was limestone, found at the edges of the desert along most of the Nile Valley. Its easy accessibility made it invaluable for projects that required huge amounts of

stone, such as the Old Kingdom pyramids. Limestone varied greatly in quality from one quarry to another. When the finest-quality stone was required, specific quarries were exploited, such as the Tura quarries across the river from Memphis, which supplied the fine white stone used for the exterior casing of many of the pyramids.

In the south of Egypt, the local building stone was sandstone. More regular in quality than limestone but less fine-grained, it was widely used to build temples in the New Kingdom at Thebes, and for many of the great temples of the Greco-Roman period.

Harder stones and specialists

Limestone and sandstone are relatively soft, and so they are fairly easy to quarry and work. For very special buildings, harder stones were required, and Egypt also had access to such material: granite at Aswan; basalt in the Western Desert; quartzite in the Eastern Desert; and travertine (Egyptian alabaster) from quarries in the desert close to Amarna.

These stones were more difficult to quarry and transport, and only specialists equipped with appropriate tools could work on them. Access to such craftsmen and the stone itself was restricted to royalty throughout most of ancient Egyptian history. The difficulty of completing a project such as quarrying and transporting a monolithic granite obelisk from Aswan to Thebes was itself an achievement worth celebrating as a special gift from the king to the gods.

△ **Mallet and chisel**
Egyptian masons used stone tools to remove blocks of stone from the quarries. To carve reliefs and statues, however, they used wooden mallets and chisels made of expensive copper.

THE DIARY OF MERER

This remarkable papyrus document was found at the site of Wadi el-Jarf, on Egypt's Red Sea coast. It is a work diary describing the activities of an official called Merer, who may have been at Wadi el-Jarf to oversee expeditions to Sinai, probably to find copper to make tools. The main subject of the diary is the work that Merer undertook on a related royal project, organizing the transport of limestone from the Tura quarries across the river to Giza. This stone was probably used in the fine casing of the exterior of the Great Pyramid of Khufu (see pp.66–67).

▷ **Sandstone**
The Gebel Silsila sandstone quarries in southern Egypt were especially important for building in the New Kingdom. They were situated close to the riverbank, making it easier to move the cut stone onto barges.

▽ **Stone sculpture**
Scenes on the walls of Old Kingdom private tombs often show craftsmen creating the features of the tomb. Here, sculptors are at work on a statue of the tomb owner. As a potential substitute for the dead body and receiver of offerings, the statue had to be suitably durable—made of stone.

Skilled sculptor trained in fine carving

Copper chisel set in a wooden shaft

The 4th & 5th Dynasties

The first pharaohs of the sun

The central period of the Old Kingdom, the 4th and 5th Dynasties, was a high point for the power of the king and the growing importance of solar religion, both demonstrated by building more royal pyramids.

Egyptian history is easier to understand from the 4th Dynasty, when it is fairly clear who the kings were, who followed whom, and how they were related to each other. More is also known about the wider royal family at this time, as several royal pyramids were surrounded by the mastaba tombs of courtiers and relations. However, all we know about most of these kings is that they built pyramids for themselves. Other events during their reigns are something of a mystery.

Two dynasties

The founder of the 4th Dynasty was Snefru, whose successor was Khufu (also known as Cheops). Khufu was succeeded by two of his sons, first Djedefre (whose tomb at Abu Roash is the northernmost major pyramid) and then Khaefre (also known as Chephren), who chose to build his pyramid close to that of his father. Khaefre's son Menkaure (also

known as Mycerinus) built a pyramid that completed the Giza group. Menkaure was himself succeeded by Shepseskaf, who may have been his son, but who broke with tradition by building a huge mastaba-style tomb rather than a pyramid at Saqqara.

The first king of the 5th Dynasty, Userkaf, may have been related to the 4th Dynasty royal family. He chose Saqqara as the site for his pyramid, very close to the pyramid complex of Djoser, possibly signaling a desire to be associated with his illustrious royal ancestor. The next two kings, Sahure and Neferirkare, may both have been Userkaf's sons, whereas the following two, Neferefre and Niuserre, were the sons of Neferirkare. These four kings form a clear group, as they were all buried at Abusir. Their royal names also all incorporate the name of the sun god, Ra, indicating his growing importance at the time. The main cult center of Ra was at Heliopolis,

△ **King Neferefre**
This statuette of Neferefre comes from the king's mortuary temple at Abusir. He is protected by the god Horus, who was often depicted as a falcon.

The eyes of the goddess and the king were later gouged out

As his divine mother, Sekhmet suckles Niuserre

◁ **Niuserre suckled by Sekhmet**
Old Kingdom rulers often depicted themselves in the company of gods. This relief fragment from a mortuary temple at Abusir shows King Niuserre with the goddess Sekhmet, his divine mother.

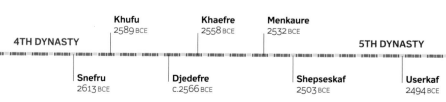

	Khufu 2589 BCE		Khaefre 2558 BCE		Menkaure 2532 BCE		
4TH DYNASTY						**5TH DYNASTY**	
	Snefru 2613 BCE		Djedefre c.2566 BCE			Shepseskaf 2503 BCE	Userkaf 2494 BCE

A royal nemes headdress worn by the king

▷ **Menkaure and Hathor**
The Menkaure pyramid complex contains a series of sculptures showing the king with various gods. Here, Menkaure is supported by a figure depicting either his mother or wife. She may be associated with the goddess Hathor.

just across the river from Memphis, and additional smaller sun temples were built by the first six kings of this dynasty. Shepseskare was probably also one of the "Abusir kings," but no evidence of his monuments has ever been found.

The relationship between the last three kings of the 5th Dynasty—Menkauhor, Djedkare Isesi, and Unas—is not known. The latter two were buried in pyramids at Saqqara, and the Pyramid of Unas is of particular interest because it was the first pyramid in which the Pyramid Texts were inscribed (see pp.70–71).

Growing influence

The success of pyramid building at this time suggests that Egypt was a strong, centralized state during the 4th and 5th Dynasties. Its influence on its immediate neighbors seems to have gradually expanded: kings sent frequent expeditions to Sinai and into the Western Desert in search of minerals, and trading centers were established in Nubia, notably in the town of Buhen. Egyptian artifacts have also been found in the Near East, especially the coastal city of Byblos, providing early evidence of a long-term relationship between Egypt and a port that gave it good access to the fine timber produced in Lebanon.

There is scant evidence of activity within Egypt itself during this period, other than in the area around Memphis. One development worth noting in the cemeteries of high officials, however, is that their tombs were becoming larger, especially at Saqqara. This trend, both in the capital and later, more significantly, in the provinces, foreshadowed key political developments in the 6th Dynasty.

Sahure
2487 BCE

Shepseskare
2455 BCE

Niuserre
2445 BCE

Djedkare Isesi
2414 BCE

Neferirkare
2475 BCE

Neferefre
2448 BCE

Menkauhor
2421 BCE

Unas
2375 BCE

The true pyramid

The evolution of an iconic building

During the 3rd and 4th Dynasties, the pyramid developed rapidly as a royal tomb in several ways. The most obvious change was a dramatic increase in size. At 100 ft (60 m) high, Djoser's Step Pyramid was already impressive enough, but it is dwarfed by the largest pyramid of all, that of Khufu (see pp.66–67), built less than 100 years later, which was originally 481 ft (147 m) in height. The other great change was the transition from the stepped pyramid to one that had straight sides—the "true" pyramid. Old Kingdom pyramids decreased in size after Khufu's reign, so the century from Djoser to Khufu was a golden age of pyramid building—but it was not without problems.

Trial and error

These problems can be seen in the pyramid at Meidum. There is much debate as to who built it, but it was probably Snefru, the first king of the 4th Dynasty; or Snefru may have completed a pyramid started by his predecessor, Huni. In any case, the pyramid was a failure, because a part of it collapsed. This might have been due to structural weaknesses caused by trying to convert a step pyramid into a straight-sided one by giving it a heavy, new outer skin of masonry, or it may simply have been built at too steep an angle. The switch from a tall, pointed pyramid to one that was more squat can be seen in the change of shape of the so-called Bent Pyramid of Snefru at Dahshur.

The most prolific of pyramid builders, Snefru built a second pyramid at Dahshur, the Red Pyramid. His son, Khufu, meanwhile, moved the royal necropolis to Giza, where he started work on possibly the most famous set of royal tombs in the world—those of Khufu, Khaefre, and Menkaure.

Other innovations followed the adoption of the straight-sided pyramid. The most important of these was the layout of the pyramid complex—a group of buildings of which the pyramid was only one part. The rectangular enclosure that surrounded the Step

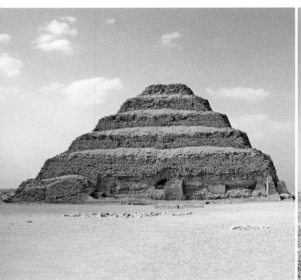

△ **The Step Pyramid**
Although it was substantially smaller than its immediate successors, Djoser's pyramid, at 100 ft (60 m) in height, was still an impressive monument. It was taller than the later pyramids of the 5th and 6th Dynasties and dominated the necropolis at Saqqara.

△ **The Meidum Pyramid**
Built by Snefru and possibly started by his predecessor, Huni, the Meidum Pyramid was structurally weak, and a part of it collapsed. It was originally built as a stepped pyramid, but then more stone was added to its sides to convert it into a straight-sided pyramid. When finished, it was 302 ft (92 m) in height.

△ **The Bent Pyramid**
Originally called the Southern Shining Pyramid, this was Snefru's second pyramid. The angle of its sides was reduced during construction, possibly due to concerns that it, too, might collapse. It stands at 344 ft (105 m) in height.

"Man fears time, but time fears the pyramids."

ARAB PROVERB OF UNCERTAIN ORIGIN

Pyramid was replaced by a standardized set of buildings: a mortuary temple built against the east face of the pyramid; a long causeway running down from the temple on the desert plateau toward the valley; and a so-called valley building that acted as a terminus for the causeway. The exact functions of these buildings are not clear, but they played an important role in the king's funeral ceremonies and in ensuring the continuation of offerings to him.

Another significant development was the building of rooms inside the pyramid. Djoser's pyramid was a solid mass of masonry that rose above an underground burial chamber. Later pyramids, however, had interiors. The Great Pyramid of Khufu, for example, is honeycombed with rooms and corridors.

Logistical challenges

All the pyramids were built of local limestone. For Djoser's pyramid, the limestone was cut into relatively small blocks, similar in size to the mud bricks used in the Early Dynastic monuments. The later pyramids, however, were built from huge blocks of stone, which gave them a much more solid form but were difficult to transport and use on site. Sophisticated systems of construction and administration therefore had to be put in place to run the vast projects, and seasonal workers were imported to the building sites from all over Egypt. The ancient Egyptians transported granite down the Nile from Aswan and brought copper from Sinai. The pyramid was, to a large degree, the supreme demonstration of the power of the Egyptian state in the early Old Kingdom.

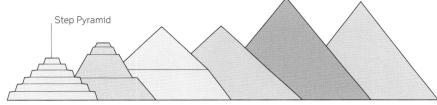

Step Pyramid

THE COMPARATIVE SCALE OF PYRAMIDS FROM DJOSER TO KHAEFRE

△ **The Red Pyramid**
The sides of Snefru's third pyramid have shallow slopes, like the Bent Pyramid. The Red Pyramid was made of sandstone and originally encased in white Tura limestone. It is 344 ft (105 m) tall and is the largest pyramid of the Dahshur necropolis.

△ **The Great Pyramid**
At 481 ft (147 m) in height, the so-called Horizon of Khufu is the tallest pyramid ever built. It took some 20 years to build, and for most of history, it was the tallest human-made structure in the world. It was the ultimate symbol of the ancient Egyptian kings' ability to direct Egypt's resources to a single royal project.

△ **The Khaefre Pyramid**
Only slightly smaller than the pyramid of his father, Khufu, Khaefre's pyramid is 472 ft (144 m) in height and was known, appropriately, as "Great is Khaefre." Its blocks diminish in size as they get higher, and the top part of the pyramid retains its limestone outer casing.

The pyramids of Giza

The mountains of pharaoh

Instantly recognizable and the epitome of royal power, the pyramids of Giza are for many people the most iconic monuments of ancient Egypt. They are also profoundly mysterious buildings.

During the Old Kingdom, the kings of Egypt chose to build their tombs—usually pyramids—in various locations on the west bank of the Nile. All of these places were close to the city of Memphis, and many of them were in sight of Heliopolis, the main cult center of the solar god Ra, across the river.

Within these general parameters, each king chose the specific site for his tomb, taking certain factors into consideration. For the site to be suitable, the underlying stone had to be strong enough to bear the great weight of the tomb. The king also had to decide whether he wished to be buried alongside previous monarchs or in a completely new location, free from any associations with the past. Most

kings wanted be buried with their predecessors, so important clusters of pyramids can be seen at the sites of Abusir; Saqqara; Dahshur; and, most famously, Giza.

Khufu's pyramid
The most famous group of pyramids is at Giza. The first pyramid to be built there was that of Khufu, who did not follow his father Snefru to Dahshur, but chose this more northerly site. The most obvious feature of

▷ **Khufu statue**
The only complete statue to bear the name of King Khufu is this tiny, 3 in (7.5 cm) tall ivory statuette that was excavated from a temple at Abydos.

KHUFU'S **SOLAR BOAT**

The Giza pyramids are some of the most extensively explored monuments in the world, but a discovery in 1954 showed that there was more to find. Several pyramids have large boat pits near them, but two unexcavated pits close to Khufu's pyramid were found to be still intact, and one of them was opened. It contained a full-sized boat, complete with oars and a spacious cabin. No one knows what the purpose of the boat was. It shows signs of having been in water, so it may have been used to carry Khufu's body to Giza during his funeral ceremonies. Or it might have been for Khufu's use after death, possibly to carry him across the sky with the sun god Ra. Now reconstructed, the 143 ft (44 m) long vessel is one of the oldest boats in the world.

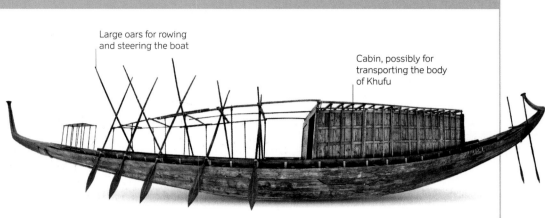

Large oars for rowing and steering the boat

Cabin, possibly for transporting the body of Khufu

Khufu's pyramid is its size—it is the largest of the royal pyramids. The pyramid itself was just one part of Khufu's funerary complex, however. Next to the pyramid, he built a small mortuary temple connected by a causeway to another building in the valley. The causeway is now in poor condition, and the valley building is buried beneath farmland. On either side of the pyramid, Khufu also built huge cemeteries of mastaba tombs, which were laid out in neat, regular rows. These were for his family and courtiers so that they could be buried beside him for eternity.

Khaefre and Menkaure

Khufu's son, Khaefre, chose to build his pyramid close to his father's. Although it is smaller, it was built on higher ground and has steeper sides, which makes it look taller. In many ways, it is a better example of an Old Kingdom pyramid complex than Khufu's. It has a large mortuary temple, and its valley building, which is made of huge blocks of red granite, is one of the best-preserved pieces of Old Kingdom architecture. The pyramid of Khaefre's own son, Menkaure, is the smallest of the Giza group. It was still unfinished when Menkaure died, but it, too, has the classic features of an Old Kingdom pyramid complex.

> ## "The whole is of **stone polished** and **fitted together** in the **most exact** manner."

THE GREEK HISTORIAN HERODOTUS DESCRIBES KHUFU'S PYRAMID

Orientation

Khufu's pyramid was laid out so that two of its sides aligned to true north with impressive precision. It was also built close to the edge of the desert plateau, overlooking the valley. When his successors built pyramids at Giza, they did so with their predecessors' monuments in mind. Khaefre's pyramid was laid out to match his father's, but his causeway was positioned so that his valley building stood right next to a small temple that stood in front of the Great Sphinx.

Menkaure, building his pyramid with the two earlier pyramids in mind, chose a spot so that a straight line could be drawn linking the southwest corners of all three of the Giza pyramids. The reasoning behind these and other alignments is not clear. Some writers have argued that the Giza pyramids were designed to mirror constellations of stars, especially that of Orion, but few scholars have been convinced by this idea.

▽ **Plan of Giza**
The relationship between the different parts of the Giza complex is best appreciated from above. Khufu's pyramid is aligned with true north, and the south side of Khaefre's pyramid is roughly aligned with the Sphinx to the east.

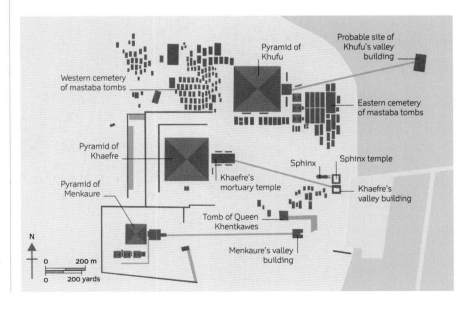

Probable site of Khufu's valley building

Pyramid of Khufu

Western cemetery of mastaba tombs

Eastern cemetery of mastaba tombs

Pyramid of Khaefre

Sphinx

Sphinx temple

Pyramid of Menkaure

Khaefre's mortuary temple

Khaefre's valley building

Tomb of Queen Khentkawes

Menkaure's valley building

N

0   200 m

0   200 yards

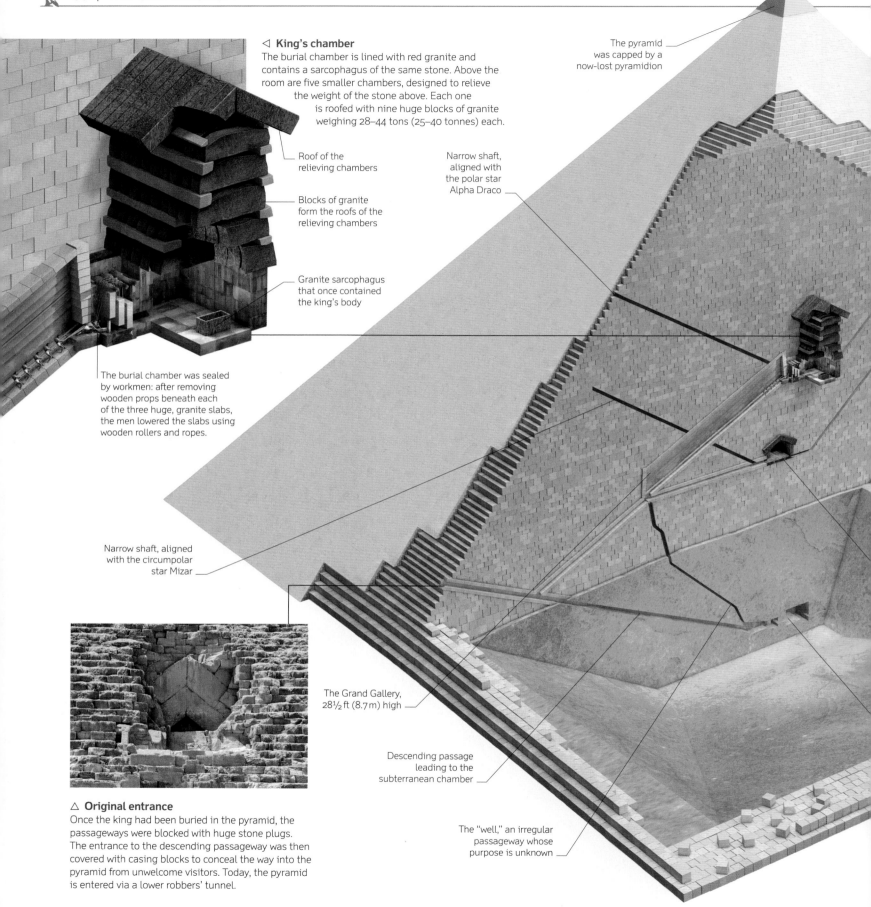

◁ **King's chamber**
The burial chamber is lined with red granite and contains a sarcophagus of the same stone. Above the room are five smaller chambers, designed to relieve the weight of the stone above. Each one is roofed with nine huge blocks of granite weighing 28–44 tons (25–40 tonnes) each.

Roof of the relieving chambers

Blocks of granite form the roofs of the relieving chambers

Granite sarcophagus that once contained the king's body

The burial chamber was sealed by workmen: after removing wooden props beneath each of the three huge, granite slabs, the men lowered the slabs using wooden rollers and ropes.

Narrow shaft, aligned with the circumpolar star Mizar

△ **Original entrance**
Once the king had been buried in the pyramid, the passageways were blocked with huge stone plugs. The entrance to the descending passageway was then covered with casing blocks to conceal the way into the pyramid from unwelcome visitors. Today, the pyramid is entered via a lower robbers' tunnel.

The pyramid was capped by a now-lost pyramidion

Narrow shaft, aligned with the polar star Alpha Draco

The Grand Gallery, 28½ ft (8.7 m) high

Descending passage leading to the subterranean chamber

The "well," an irregular passageway whose purpose is unknown

△ A mountain of stone
Estimates based on the visible parts of the pyramid suggest that it was made of 2.3 million blocks of stone, which may have weighed around 2.8 tons (2.5 tonnes) each.

Narrow shaft oriented toward the constellation of Orion

Narrow shaft oriented toward the star Sirius

Khufu's pyramid
"The horizon of Khufu"

The pyramid built by King Khufu at Giza is not only the largest of the royal pyramids of Egypt, it is also one of the most intriguing. Compared to almost all other pyramids, it has a very complicated internal structure, with a series of interconnected rooms and passages—some of which, such as the Grand Gallery, are unique. Although the purpose of some of these internal features seems obvious, especially the king's chamber, the function of others is less clear. They may have been incorporated when plans changed during the construction of the pyramid, or they may have served purposes that modern scholars are unaware of.

◁ Outer casing
The exterior of the pyramid was finished with a casing of the finest white limestone, which came from the Tura quarries on the other side of the Nile. This high-quality stone was later stripped from the pyramid and reused for buildings during the later dynastic periods and in medieval Cairo.

Wedge-shaped blocks of limestone create a smooth surface

Outer casing of fine, white limestone from the Tura quarries

◁ Survival of the pyramid
The pyramid of Khufu has long been emptied of its burial equipment and robbed of much of its stone, but it is still an impressive monument. It is the only one of the Seven Wonders of the Ancient World that has remained largely intact, and it has been a constant source of fascination for both visitors and scholars.

So-called queen's chamber, possibly for a *ka* statue of the king

Incomplete subterranean chamber, whose use is unknown

BUILDING THE **PYRAMID**

The secret to building a large pyramid was good organization—the right number of workmen and the right amount of stone in the right place. A series of ramps was probably used, with gangs of workmen dragging the stone blocks into place. At first, simple, linear ramps on each side of the pyramid would have maximized the amount of stone that could be moved. As the pyramid grew taller, the ramps would have been made longer to avoid too steep an angle of ascent. At this point, the linear ramps may have been replaced by a spiral one running around the upper parts of the pyramid.

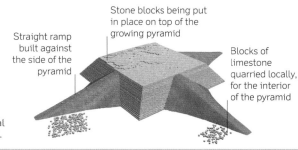

Straight ramp built against the side of the pyramid

Stone blocks being put in place on top of the growing pyramid

Blocks of limestone quarried locally, for the interior of the pyramid

▷ **Ear stela**
Visitors to the Sphinx in the New Kingdom often left dedicatory stelae. Many of these featured an ear, symbolizing their hopes that the god would hear their prayers.

The Great Sphinx

The "Father of Terror"

A colossal statue, the Great Sphinx at Giza is one of the most instantly recognizable images of ancient Egypt and rivals the pyramids as an expression of royal power in the Old Kingdom. The ceremonial slate palettes of the late Predynastic and Early Dynastic Periods first introduced images of the king as an animal, such as a lion or bull. Later, images of hybrid human/animal creatures emphasized the special nature of the royal person they represented. With the body of a lion and the head of a man, the sphinx is a supernatural creature representing the godlike power of the king. The word "sphinx" is believed to come from a Greek version of an Egyptian term for a statue, especially a statue of a king: *shesep-ankh*, which means "living image."

Mysterious origin

Many images depicting kings as sphinxes survive from ancient Egypt, but the Sphinx at Giza is by far the most famous. It was built on a solid knoll of rock in the limestone quarries that supplied stone for the Giza pyramids. Scholars agree that it represents one of the 4th Dynasty kings—probably Khaefre or his father, Khufu. It sits close to Khaefre's Valley

▽ **A stone colossus**
At 248 ft (75.5 m) long and 65 ft (20 m) high, the Great Sphinx at Giza is one of the largest statues ever built. No statue in Egypt could match it until that of Amenhotep III, more than 1,000 years later.

SIDE VIEW

Building, in an area where stone was quarried in Khufu's time. A temple for worshipping the king was built in front of the Sphinx.

Exactly why such a grand statue of the king was built in the Old Kingdom is a mystery, but as a major part of the landscape at Giza, it attracted the attention of many Egyptians for the rest of dynastic history. By the New Kingdom, it was regarded as a statue of the god Horemakhet and was worshipped as such by kings and commoners alike.

A prince's dream

According to his own account, an 18th Dynasty prince called Tuthmosis fell asleep in the shade of the Sphinx while hunting. In a dream, the god Horemakhet prophesied that he would become king if he cleared the sand covering much of the statue. The prince carried out the request, became Tuthmosis IV, and recorded the incident on a stela, which he set on the ground, probably below an existing statue of his father, Amenhotep II. Other New Kingdom additions to the Sphinx included a false beard and new cladding on parts of the worn statue.

During the Middle Ages, the Sphinx's nose was hacked off. By this time, the Sphinx had acquired a new name: *Abu'l-Hol*, meaning "the Father of Terror."

◁ **The face of the Sphinx**
Although the Great Sphinx was revered, it was not left alone by later generations. Its head and chest were subjected to several additions (including a false beard), and it has been altered and mutilated throughout its 4,500-year history.

Nose damaged in the Middle Ages

Position of New Kingdom false beard (later removed)

Position of a statue of the New Kingdom king Amenhotep II

"Dream stela" of Tuthmosis IV

The Pyramid Texts

A handbook for the royal afterlife

Although they are extremely impressive, the great pyramids of the early Old Kingdom are completely devoid of texts describing what the king expected to happen to him after death. All that changed at the end of the 5th Dynasty.

Little is known about the expectations of the kings of the 4th, 5th, and 6th Dynasties regarding the afterlife. From the end of the 5th Dynasty onward, however, religious texts about the royal afterlife were inscribed on the walls of the chambers within pyramids. These are known as the Pyramid Texts. They first appeared in the Pyramid of Unas and then in the pyramids of the 6th Dynasty kings Teti, Pepi I, Merenre, and Pepi II. They also exist in the pyramids of three queens of Pepi II and in the 8th Dynasty Pyramid of Ibi.

Spells and rituals

The Pyramid Texts are a selection of protective spells, rituals, and a wide variety of sometimes contradictory ideas about the afterlife drawn from a much more extensive body of literature. They were designed to be read out loud, possibly as part of the funeral ritual. Unas's pyramid, for example, contains 236 spells, but the complete Pyramid Texts include more than a thousand different spells. No one knows why certain spells were chosen over others, just that they were carefully inscribed on the walls of the king's burial chamber, the antechamber to the burial chamber, and the corridor leading to the pyramid entrance.

The texts cover several different themes. Some refer to the offerings that should be made to the dead king, similar to those made to the *ka* spirit (the person's soul) in private tombs. Others are protective spells designed to shield the king's body in its sarcophagus from any harm. The king was not, however, an ordinary mortal, and his afterlife was therefore different from anyone else's.

Joining the gods

A particularly important set of spells summoned the king to rise from his sarcophagus and join the gods. His journey was a version of the journey of the sun god, Ra, who travels through the darkness of the *Duat* (underworld) to emerge reborn into the light of day.

These spells connect the king with the sun and place great emphasis on a solar afterlife, in which the king will travel alongside Ra. This solar afterlife might also be reflected in the very shape of the pyramid itself, as the Pyramid Texts describe the rays of the sun being "made firm" so that the king can walk on them to heaven. Perhaps the sloping sides of the pyramid could be seen as solidified rays of the sun.

◁ **The Pyramid of Pepi I**
This small fragment of an interior wall from the Pyramid of Pepi I has hieroglyphs that are filled with blue paint for emphasis. The ownership of this text is clear, because the name Pepi, in its oval cartouche, appears four times.

◁ **The Pyramid of Unas**
Beneath a ceiling carved with a starry sky, the walls
of the internal chambers of the Pyramid of Unas are
covered with vertical columns of the Pyramid Texts.
Here, the antechamber opens into the burial
chamber containing the royal sarcophagus.

Other spells refer to a stellar afterlife, in which the
king will join the "undying stars" of the northern sky.
Osiris, a major afterlife deity, is also invoked, pointing
to the great importance that he had from the end of
the Old Kingdom onward. The power of the king as a
god in his own right is expressed in the so-called
"Cannibal Hymn," in which the king eats the gods
in order to absorb their power.

The Pyramid Texts can also be seen as the first in a
series of religious texts about the afterlife that evolved
into the Coffin Texts in the Middle Kingdom (see
below). These in turn gave rise to the various New
Kingdom books concerning the afterlife that were
used by both kings and private individuals, including
the Book of the Dead (see pp.208–209).

COFFIN **TEXTS**

From the end of the Old Kingdom, religious texts
describing an afterlife were also used by people who
were not royal. Inscribed on the interiors of coffins,
these are known as the Coffin Texts. Much of the
material from the Pyramid Texts was reused in these
guides to the afterlife, but they were adapted to suit their
owners. The most important of these texts was the *Book
of Two Ways*, which was sometimes accompanied by a
painted plan of the underworld to help the deceased find
their way.

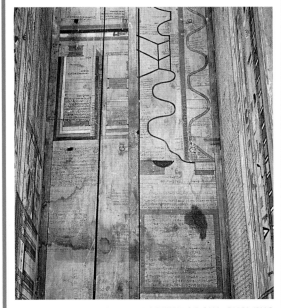

BOOK OF TWO WAYS **IN THE COFFIN OF GUA, SHOWING
A PAINTED PLAN OF THE UNDERWORLD**

Mastaba tombs

Tombs for the royal courtiers

During the Old Kingdom, it was not only the king who needed a magnificent tomb. Members of the royal court also required a suitably visible eternal resting place. Their tombs usually took the form of a mastaba.

Old Kingdom tombs, or rather the parts of them above the ground, evolved from the squat, solid mud-brick mastabas used by kings and their high officials during the Early Dynastic Period. The largest tombs belonging to court officials of the 1st and 2nd Dynasties were located at Saqqara, on the edge of the desert, overlooking the valley. They were huge buildings, and they needed to be, because they were essentially storerooms for vast quantities of goods, especially food, that the deceased would need in the afterlife. The mastaba of the high official Hemaka, for example, is 187 ft (57 m) long and 75 ft (23 m) wide. However, from the beginning of the Old Kingdom, the purpose of elite mastabas changed. Instead of simply being storerooms, they became places where people could make offerings to the ka (or soul) of the deceased.

Gifts of the king

In the 4th Dynasty, mastabas became standardized in both form and size, largely because they were built in the court cemeteries that formed part of the royal pyramid-building project. Rows and rows of regularly sized mastabas can be found around the complex of King Khufu, for instance, and the size of a mastaba

and its proximity to the pyramid reflected the status of its owner at the royal court. Because they were built as royal projects, these tombs were direct gifts of the king.

The standard mastaba was a solid, rectangular building with gently sloping limestone exterior walls. The interior was filled with rubble, apart from a vertical shaft that ran through it to the small burial chamber underground. The offering chapel was also modest in size—just two or three rooms built around a false door fixed to the southern end of the mastaba's eastern wall (see pp.74–75).

The growth of the mastaba

During the 5th and 6th Dynasties, mastabas developed in two important ways. First, they became larger and more complex. Rather than being a solid mass, they were given an increasing number of rooms with specific purposes. Some rooms were used to store offerings or the equipment used in the offering ceremonies. Other semisealed rooms known as serdabs were used as safes to house the statues of the

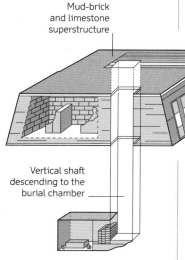

Mud-brick and limestone superstructure

Vertical shaft descending to the burial chamber

△ **Mastaba tomb**
The superstructure of mastaba tombs became larger and more complex. However, the burial chamber, accessed by a vertical shaft, remained small and, in most cases, undecorated.

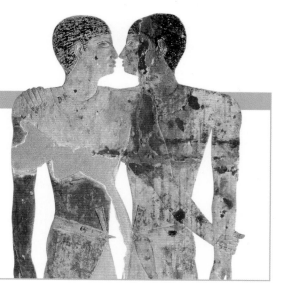

TWO **BROTHERS?**

The formalistic style of imagery in Old Kingdom tombs makes it difficult to work out how the people depicted on their walls were related in real life. Conventional labels, such as "his father," "her daughter," or "his sister," only provide a very basic idea of how the different individuals were connected.

The unusual image of two men, Khnumhotep and Niankhkhnum, embracing appears on the walls of the mastaba tomb that they shared at Saqqara. The tomb is known as the Tomb of the Two Brothers, but the painting might also be a rare, undisguised representation of a same-sex relationship between two men from ancient Egypt. Frustratingly, the texts written on the walls of the tomb do nothing to clarify the relationship.

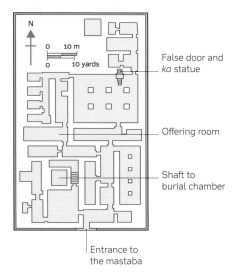

▽ **Mereruka's tomb floor plan**
In the 5th and 6th Dynasties, the interiors of the largest mastabas were filled with rooms. These were used for making offerings, storing the ritual equipment used in offering ceremonies, and to provide wall space for the increasingly extensive scenes of daily life.

False door and *ka* statue

Offering room

Shaft to burial chamber

Entrance to the mastaba

▽ **Limestone head**
During the reigns of Khufu and Khaefre, there was a short-lived and unexplained fashion for placing limestone heads in courtiers' tombs. They are so individual in style that they are likely to be portrait heads of the tomb owners.

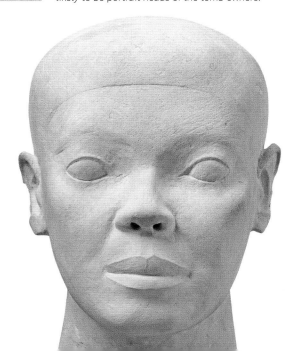

△ **Mereruka**
In this remarkable combination of a false door and a life-size *ka* statue, the Vizier Mereruka appears to be entering the offering chapel. The altar, on which offerings would have been placed, stands at his feet, at the top of a flight of steps.

tomb owners that were becoming common in such tombs. At the heart of the mastaba, there was a false door, where the offering ritual took place. The walls of all the rooms were covered with scenes designed to help the *ka* in its afterlife—not just pictures of food offerings, but also images of Egypt, which the *ka* would be able to enjoy forever.

The second development was that high officials' mastabas were no longer always built close to the pyramids of their royal masters. This suggests that court officials were becoming more independent and often paid for their tombs. However, royal gifts (such as stone sarcophagi) were always appreciated and were mentioned in the tomb autobiographies inscribed on the walls of these mastabas, which had become longer and more detailed.

▷ **The false door of Neferiu**
This large and complex false door belongs to the Royal Seal Bearer Neferiu. Dating from the end of the Old Kingdom or the beginning of the First Intermediate Period, it describes Neferiu's good deeds in life. An outstanding monument, it shows all the different elements of the classic false door.

False door

The portal of the *ka* spirit

During the Old Kingdom, the idea that the tomb was a home for the *ka* spirit (or soul) of the deceased developed, so the tombs of courtiers and officials became increasingly complex. The false door, or false door stela, was a key feature of tombs, because it formed the portal between the part of the tomb where the *ka* should remain undisturbed (the burial chamber) and the part provided for visitors bearing offerings (the offering chapel).

A magic threshold

Most false doors were made of solid slabs of stone, so they were "false" in the sense that living people could not pass through them. The *ka*, however, was able to pass through solid objects, especially those designed to look like everyday things.

False doors became increasingly elaborate, as they provided a place where texts and images beneficial to the tomb owner could be carved and painted. The false door had first and foremost to be a realistic depiction of a doorway, but it also identified the tomb owner, so the details of his name and title were very important. These details gradually expanded and included statements about the virtues of the deceased, providing visitors with additional reasons to make offerings to him (or less commonly, her). Over time, it became traditional for people to provide their tombs with detailed autobiographies. Pictures of the tomb owner often appear on false doors—usually in a large rectangular panel above the carving of the doorway. The standard image depicts the owner sitting in front of a large table of food offerings. This showed visitors what they were expected to do inside the offering chapel—namely, leave food offerings in front of the false door for the *ka* to "eat." It also, however, served as a magical substitute for real food, if offerings from visitors were scarce. The pictures of food could then become real victuals for the *ka* and would be able to prevent it from being hungry for eternity.

Prayers for offerings were also carved on false doors. These too had magical powers. Ideally, they would be read out loud by a living visitor to the tomb in order to generate the "thousand loaves of bread, thousand jars of beer, meat and fowl, and every good thing" that the *ka* required. If, however, the prayers were not read out loud, the fact that they were written on the false door in hieroglyphs gave them magic powers and ensured that the things they described became real.

Although false doors were most commonly used during the Old Kingdom, they remained an important feature of tombs throughout the Dynastic Period. They were also used by kings as portals to the afterlife in their mortuary temples, which were royal versions of ordinary people's offering chapels.

▽ **Eyes for the *ka***
The doorway at the center of the false door is carved with false bolts and handles. It also has two eyes so that the tomb owner is able to see into the offering chapel from the burial chamber. These eyes are similar in appearance to the protective Eye of Horus amulet.

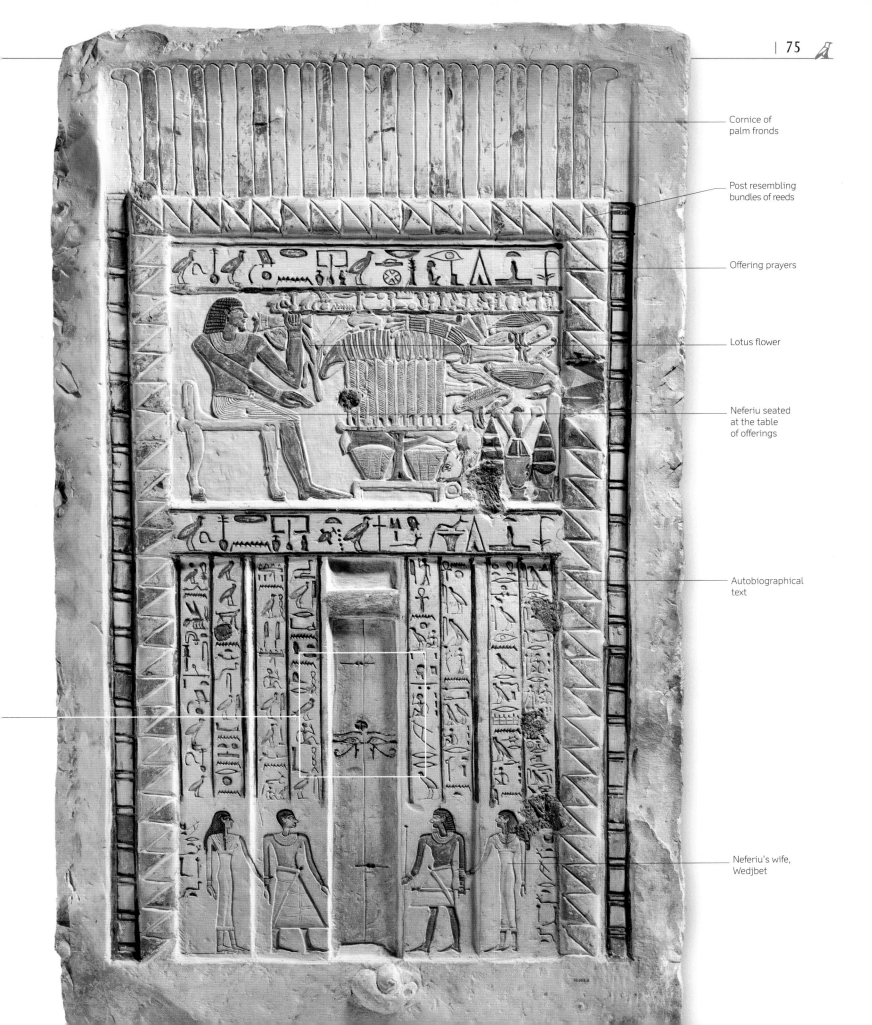

Cornice of
palm fronds

Post resembling
bundles of reeds

Offering prayers

Lotus flower

Neferiu seated
at the table
of offerings

Autobiographical
text

Neferiu's wife,
Wedjbet

Painting techniques
Art and craft

The ancient Egyptians left behind a wealth of images that once covered the walls of their temples and tombs. The techniques used by the artists who painted them make them instantly recognizable as Egyptian.

△ **Tomb painting**
This painting simply shows the hieroglyphs for the sounds "k" and "a." The artist who painted this basket and vulture did so with exquisite detail.

Many paintings from Egyptian monuments have survived for thousands of years, both on relief carvings and flat surfaces. The painted walls of underground tombs in the desert are especially well preserved, but some open-air temples have also kept traces of their original decoration. This is partly because the Egyptians used mineral pigments, which not only made their paintings glow with vibrant color, but which were remarkably permanent.

Most of these mineral pigments could be sourced locally, but some, such as lapis lazuli, came from neighboring lands. As a result, artists had a wide variety of pigments at their disposal—ocher (clay) for red and yellow, soot for black, copper compounds for green, and lapis for deep blue. In the New Kingdom, artists added more colors to the palette, including orpiment (a mineral related to arsenic) for bright yellow and cobalt for a lighter shade of blue.

The human figure
Not only is its color palette distinctive—Egyptian painting is also instantly recognizable because of the rather stilted look of the human figures. This stylized approach was deliberate, as the Egyptians rarely aimed for perspective or naturalism in their art. It was more important to them that any object, including the human body, was shown as "complete" as possible.

This search for "completeness" meant that bodies were broken down into different parts, each drawn in its most recognizable form, then reassembled. Heads were almost always shown in profile, but with the eye drawn as if it was seen front-on. Arms were painted hanging away from the body to make them clear to see, and in standing figures, legs were shown one behind the other. Chests were depicted front-on, while waists were shown from the side. This method of depicting the human figure served the Egyptians well, as it changed remarkably little for 3,000 years.

Rules of proportion
The ancient Egyptians also tried to bring order and regularity to their paintings by establishing a "canon of proportion"—a set of rules governing the relative proportions of different parts of the human body. These ensured that a painting of a king, for example, would look the same, regardless of the scale on which it was drawn. Professional painters and sculptors had to follow these rules, which gave them little scope for imagination or development. Today, they might be considered artisans rather than artists. Even though they worked within rigid guidelines, they were still able to demonstrate their skills, however, in the fine details of a painting or by the inventive way in which they interpreted a traditional theme.

▽ **Palette and paintbrushes**
Pigments were kept in small clay pots or, as in this example bearing the cartouche of Amenhotep III, in the recesses of palettes that both artists and scribes used. Rough brushes were made from bundles of reeds and fine-nibbed brushes and pens from single reeds.

Empty hollow for a small pigment "cake"

Brush made from a bundle of reeds and rushes

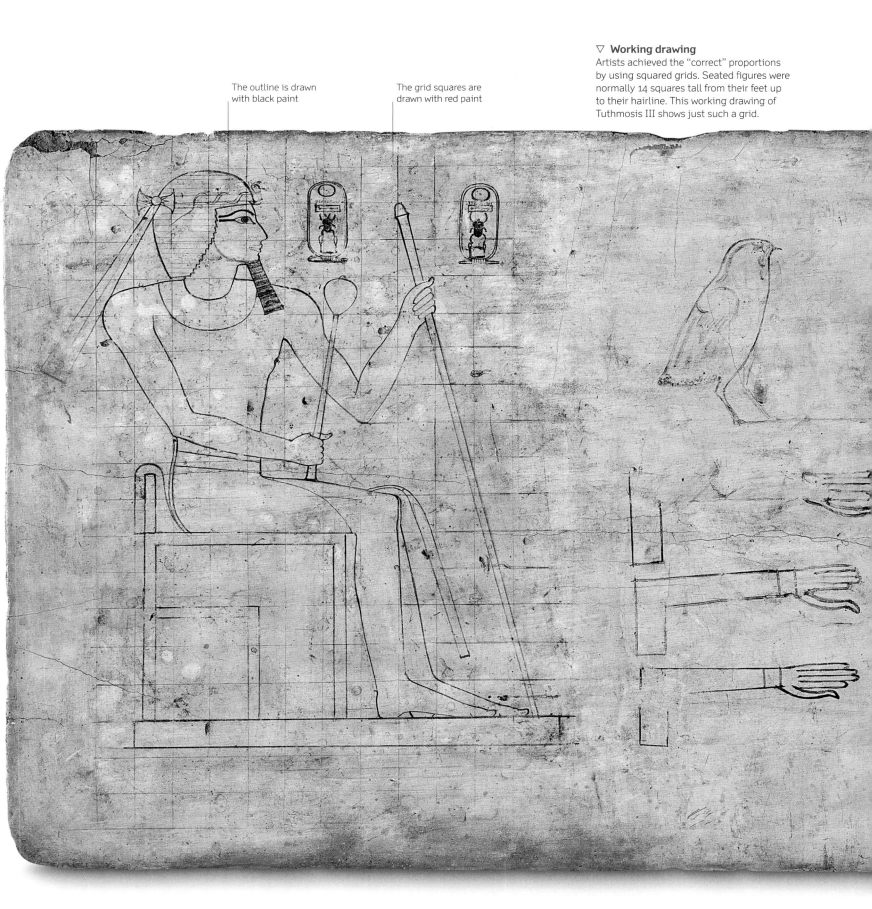

The outline is drawn with black paint

The grid squares are drawn with red paint

▽ **Working drawing**
Artists achieved the "correct" proportions by using squared grids. Seated figures were normally 14 squares tall from their feet up to their hairline. This working drawing of Tuthmosis III shows just such a grid.

The Meidum Geese

These geese formed part of a scene painted on the north wall of the early 4th Dynasty tomb chapel of Atet, the wife of the Vizier Nefermaat, at Meidum, close to the pyramid of Snefru. It was set below a scene of fowling on the marshes. As in many elite tombs of all periods, the artists who decorated it paid great attention to detail when depicting the natural world so that the tomb owner would be able to enjoy it for eternity. These boldly painted red-breasted geese were painted to look as lifelike as possible, yet they are still positioned according to artistic convention.

Fashion in the Old Kingdom

Elegance for eternity

The images of upper-class Egyptians found in Old Kingdom tombs provide an insight into how the ancient Egyptians dressed, but they are highly idealized, because in the afterlife, it was important to look one's best.

The purpose of the pictures and statues found in Egyptian tombs was to show the tomb owners and their families as they wanted to appear for eternity, not how they actually looked in real life. For both men and women, this meant having an ideal body—being young, slim, and physically fit, even though most tomb owners would have been quite mature when they died. Where images of older people with fuller figures do appear in statues or on tomb walls, it was not an attempt at realistic portraiture, but to indicate their high social status.

There were also conventions regarding skin color. High-status men were usually shown with reddish-brown skin, possibly to signal the active, outdoor lives that even rich Egyptians lived. Women were fashionably pale, maybe to show that they did not need to leave the house to work in the fields like peasants.

Dressing to impress

The clothes worn by both men and women were usually made of fine white linen. Produced from flax, this was the staple fabric of ancient Egypt. Wool was occasionally used for clothes, but cotton was not imported until the 1st century BCE, and silk only arrived six centuries later. Jewelry was usually only worn by women in the Old Kingdom, although later, in the New Kingdom, men also wore it. The most popular forms of jewelry were broad, multicolored

◁ **Beaded dress**
Unusual beaded dresses such as this have been found in some tombs. It is not known if they were worn in real life or if they were intended for the afterlife only.

necklaces or collars. Men and women also wore perfume, described as "sweet oils" in the offering texts of the time.

Rahotep and Nofret

The statues of Rahotep and Nofret on the right are typical of how an upper-class couple might be shown in the Old Kingdom. Rahotep is wearing a short kilt, which shows off his muscular torso and legs; it is unlikely that he dressed so scantily in real life. Nofret's costume is possibly truer to life—a close-fitting, ankle-length sheath dress with broad shoulder straps and a shawl around her shoulders.

The couple's hairstyles are fashionable for the period. Rahotep has short, cropped hair, and Nofret sports a full bob, held in place by a broad band decorated with flowers. Rahotep also has a mustache, which was popular in the early 4th Dynasty. It was a short-lived fashion: elite Egyptian men are rarely shown with facial hair.

▽ **Princess Nofretiabet**
Although elite Egyptians usually dressed in white linen, there were exceptions. This image of Princess Nofretiabet wearing a single-shouldered leopardskin dress is a striking example.

"May he be given **clothing from the two treasuries** and **merhet-oil** from the two chambers."

OFFERING TEXT OF THE OLD KINGDOM

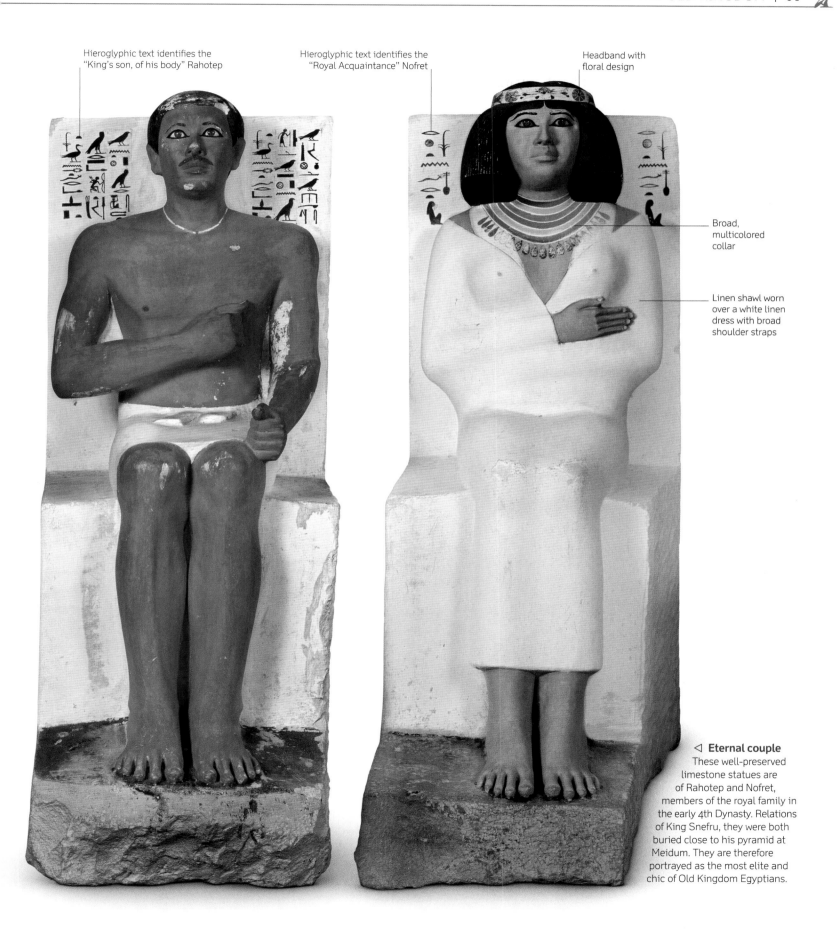

Hieroglyphic text identifies the "King's son, of his body" Rahotep

Hieroglyphic text identifies the "Royal Acquaintance" Nofret

Headband with floral design

Broad, multicolored collar

Linen shawl worn over a white linen dress with broad shoulder straps

◁ **Eternal couple**
These well-preserved limestone statues are of Rahotep and Nofret, members of the royal family in the early 4th Dynasty. Relations of King Snefru, they were both buried close to his pyramid at Meidum. They are therefore portrayed as the most elite and chic of Old Kingdom Egyptians.

Royal mortuary temples

Offerings for the pyramid owner

Although less spectacular than the pyramid itself, the other buildings of the pyramid complex, especially the mortuary temple, played a crucial role in ensuring that the king enjoyed a good afterlife within his tomb.

A pyramid could be seen from miles around, but it was just part of a group of connected buildings that made up the pyramid complex. All of these buildings were needed to create a suitable environment for the king's funeral, the resting place of his body, and the rituals that continued after his burial.

Approaching the pyramid complex, the funeral cortege would first come to the valley building. Here, it disembarked at the side of a canal before traveling along a paved, and often covered, causeway to the mortuary temple. Usually built against the eastern side of the pyramid, the mortuary temple was a more complex version of the offering chapels that were linked to private tombs. A small subsidiary pyramid, whose purpose is not fully clear, was the final part of the complex.

The Pyramid Texts (see pp.70–71) describe the afterlife that the king enjoyed beyond the tomb, but he had other needs, too, because he had several *kas*,

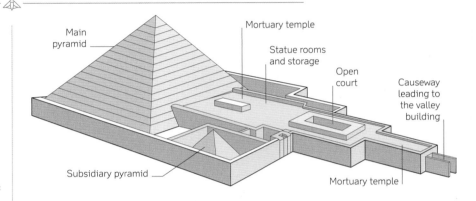

Main pyramid

Mortuary temple

Statue rooms and storage

Open court

Causeway leading to the valley building

Subsidiary pyramid

Mortuary temple

each of which had to be treated in a different way. The mortuary temple was where offerings were made to these different spiritual forms of the king.

Preparing for eternity

Unlike other people, kings did not rely on their families, friends, or passersby to provide them with food, drink, or prayers after death. Instead, they used their wealth to finance preparations for a constant supply of whatever their *kas* might need. Royal estates from all over Egypt were gifted to a king's pyramid so that their produce would "belong" to the dead king and provide food for the mortuary temple. Income from these estates also paid the priests and officials who collected the food, transported it, and offered it in the temple. In the Old Kingdom, each royal pyramid had its own administrative system that required a large staff. This included priests who

△ **Sahure reconstruction**
Although his pyramid is less impressive than some earlier examples, the pyramid complex of King Sahure, of the 5th Dynasty, is an excellent example of how the different elements of the complex fitted together to form an architectural whole.

△ **The mortuary temple of Sahure**
Although now all but destroyed, the mortuary temple next to the Pyramid of Sahure at Abusir has retained some of its original architectural features. The granite columns and the basalt floor were built to last forever.

> "As the **god is provided** with a god's offering, so **Unas** is **provided** with this **his bread**."

OFFERING RITUAL FROM THE PYRAMID OF UNAS

A flint knife cuts off the
foreleg of an oryx

A butcher carries away a
choice cut of meat

△ **Sahure relief**
The meat offerings to King
Sahure included beef and
venison. This relief from his
mortuary temple shows men
butchering animals at the
pyramid complex, where
the meats were presented as
an offering to the king's *ka*.

not only carried out the daily rituals within
the mortuary temple, but also took care of the
equipment used in them.

Built to last

The buildings of the pyramid complex were meant
to last forever, so they had to stand the test of time.
Mortuary temples in particular were built with great
care using durable materials that could withstand
the footsteps of endless generations of priests and
worshippers. Hard, black basalt was generally used
for the floors, its color possibly mimicking the black
land of the fertile Nile Valley. Red granite was used
for other parts of the temple, especially the columns
supporting the roof.

The Great Pyramid has a simple mortuary
temple, but from the reign of Khaefre onward,
mortuary temples became more complex. For the
rest of the Old Kingdom, they had five separate
rooms devoted to different aspects of the king, each
containing a statue of him that was used as a focus
for offerings.

THE ABUSIR **PAPYRI**

Three groups of papyri associated with the Pyramid of
Neferirkare at Abusir provide details of the activities
of the priestly staff at an Old Kingdom mortuary temple.
These documents list rosters of priests who were on duty
as part of the offerings and at special festivals. The
papyri also list the ritual equipment that was used
on these occasions, as well as the different foods and
other products that were received by the temple staff,
especially from the estates belonging to the pyramid.

Music and dance

Funerals and festivities

One of the liveliest themes depicted in the wall paintings of ancient Egyptian tombs throughout all periods was music and dance. Sometimes music was connected with religious rituals, and dances with important ceremonies such as funerals, but they were often simply portrayed as a form of entertainment.

Music

Singing was the most common form of music making in Egypt. Some women were called "singers," but they were usually priestesses who sang hymns to worship a particular god or goddess in a temple as part of a religious ceremony. Although no one knows what ancient Egyptian music actually sounded like, the words of some of the songs that were sung by harpists have been found in hieroglyphic texts in tombs. Not surprisingly, given the context, a common theme of these songs is the brevity of life.

A wide variety of musical instruments is shown in tomb scenes, and some actual instruments have been found in burials. The Egyptians used percussion, stringed instruments, and wind instruments. At its simplest, percussion took the form of clapping and using simple instruments called clappers, often made of bone or ivory. Drums did not appear in tomb paintings until the Middle Kingdom.

The most common stringed instrument throughout all periods of ancient Egyptian history was the harp. Lyres and lutes were first introduced during the New Kingdom and were usually played by women. Wind

△ **A lady shakes her sistrum**
The sistrum was a rattle usually made of bronze and often incorporating the face of the goddess Hathor. Its ancient name, *sesheshet*, suggests the sound that it made. Associated with religious ceremonies, it was considered suitable for upper-class women.

△ **Lute player and young dancer**
In the New Kingdom, there was an increasing number of images of professional musicians and dancers who entertained clients on festive occasions. This scene shows a woman playing a lute. She is accompanied by a young dancing girl, who may have been an apprentice with this particular troupe.

△ **A harpist entertains Inherkau**
This scene from the tomb of Inkerkau at Deir el-Medina shows a harpist playing for the tomb owner and his family. Harpists were often depicted as male and blind, and shown kneeling on the ground to play a harp to accompany their songs.

"Follow your … **happiness**, do **the things on Earth** which **your heart** commands."

HARPER'S SONG FROM THE MIDDLE KINGDOM

instruments were made from hollow reeds and came in various forms. Although the trumpets found in the tomb of Tutankhamen were made of silver and bronze, most military trumpets were made of reeds.

Dance

Wall paintings from private tombs suggest that dancing also took place in two quite contrasting settings. Like music, dancing often formed an integral part of religious ceremonies, and groups of dancers— always of the same sex—performed ritual dances, especially at funerals. These were closely associated with local traditions, and the best known groups were the male *mww* dancers who took part in funerals at Thebes during the New Kingdom.

People also danced to entertain, however, and there is evidence for this from early on, as seen in the "pygmy of the god's dances" brought back from Nubia as a gift for the king in the Old Kingdom tomb of Harkhuf (see pp.86–87). By the New Kingdom, dancing as a form of entertainment seemed to involve mixed groups of musicians and scantily clad dancing girls performing at upper-class banquets.

Upper-class Egyptians did not seem to dance for pleasure. However, as all that is known about Egyptian dancing is based on the formalized depictions on the walls of elite private tombs, it may be that there is simply no record of any tradition of the informal dancing that took place in villages—especially at times of celebration, such as harvests or childbirth.

△ **Shoulder harp**
This arched harp, with its individually pegged strings and large sound box, is a real-life example of the type of harp often depicted in tomb scenes.

△ **New Kingdom instruments**
Pictures of musicians in the New Kingdom showed an increasing range of musical instruments. The woman above is playing a long double pipe made from two reeds. A stringed instrument known as a "thin lyre" is also visible on the right.

△ **Dancers in the tomb of Antefoker**
This rather stylized painting of a group of female dancers and priestesses comes from a Middle Kingdom private tomb at Thebes. It is fairly typical of many images of dancers that predate the New Kingdom, as they were usually associated with religious ceremonies and rituals, such as funerals.

△ **Dancers at a banquet**
In this famous scene of a banquet from the New Kingdom tomb of a wealthy official named Nebamun, these dancing girls are shown moving sinuously in a dance that is clearly meant to be erotic. Tomb scenes tended to present an idealized vision of life.

Southern expeditions

Egypt in Nubia during the Old Kingdom

Set on an island at the First Cataract of the Nile, the town of Elephantine was on ancient Egypt's southern border. It was also the starting point for trading and other expeditions into Nubia.

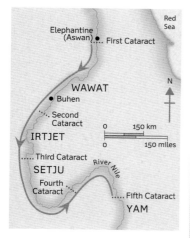

△ **Harkhuf's journeys**
No one knows exactly where the regions Harkhuf visited are, but they were a long way to the south of Egypt's frontier at Elephantine. This map shows where some of these regions may have been.

During the Old Kingdom, the island of Elephantine was important both strategically, as Egypt's border with Nubia, and economically, as a transfer point for cargo being shipped along the Nile. Formed of the granite boulders that make up the First Cataract of the Nile, it remained Egypt's southern border throughout the Dynastic Period. Given its strategic position, it had a special status and is one of the few places in Egypt where settlements can be traced from the Early Dynastic Period to the Greco-Roman Period. Today, it is part of the southern city of Aswan.

Tomb autobiographies

At a time when political and economic power was concentrated in and around the city of Memphis, Elephantine was unusual because it was the base of a series of high officials who had important royal duties. Not only was Elephantine on a border that had to be fiercely guarded, but it was also the starting point for trading expeditions southward along the Nile into Nubia and beyond. The ancient name for Elephantine, *Abu*, is related to the Egyptian word for elephant, possibly signifying the value of the ivory trade between Nubia and Egypt.

A great deal is known about the activities of these high officials from the autobiographies inscribed on the walls of the impressive tombs carved out of the rock. These tombs lie on the west bank of the Nile, overlooking Elephantine at a site that is now known as Qubbet el-Hawa. The main theme of these autobiographies is the extent of royal favors granted to the tomb owners as reward for their impressive deeds, especially in Nubia. The reports of these activities provide a detailed account of Egypt's relations with Nubia during the Old Kingdom, especially in its later years.

Harkhuf

Historically, the most important autobiography is that of an official named Harkhuf. The inscription reveals that Harkhuf enjoyed many titles, some of which suggest that he oversaw southern Egypt for Kings Merenre and Pepi II. He also led four expeditions into Nubia, visiting the regions of Wawat, Setju, and Irtjet. It is difficult to specify exactly where these regions were, and scholars debate how far into Lower or Upper Nubia Harkhuf traveled. He did, however, report one ominous development. During Harkhuf's

▽ **Qubbet el-Hawa**
Standing high above the Nile, the Old and Middle Kingdom tombs cut out of the rock at Qubbet el-Hawa overlook the island town of Elephantine. Long causeways lead from the river to the tombs.

Terraces of Old and Middle Kingdom tombs

▷ **Harkhuf's titles**
In his tomb inscription, Harkhuf is introduced by many titles: The Count, Sole Companion, Lector-Priest, Chamberlain, Warden of Nekhen, Major of Nekheb, Royal Seal Bearer, Chief of Scouts, Royal Councilor of all the affairs of Upper Egypt, and the favorite of his, Lord Harkhuf.

△ **Pygmy toy**
Dancing dwarves and ivory were two of the most desirable products to be brought back to Egypt from Nubia. Here, they are combined in a single toy.

first expedition, Wawat, Setju, and Irtjet were each governed by a different Nubian leader, but by the time of his last expedition, the three regions had united under a single ruler. This unification of Nubia signified potential trouble on Egypt's southern border.

Harkhuf's autobiography also includes the text of a letter that he received from Pepi II, in which the young king expressed delight at one of the things that Harkhuf had brought back for him—a "pygmy of the god's dances from the land of the horizon dwellers."

Sabni and Pepinakht
The dangers of these expeditions are stressed on the tomb that Sabni shared with his father, Mekhu. Sabni's autobiography describes how he set off on an expedition (served by 100 donkeys) to bring back the body of his father, who had died in Nubia. Sabni buried his father at Qubbet el-Hawa and then continued north to Memphis, where the king praised him for his heroic actions and for the goods that he had brought back from Nubia.

The most famous of the tomb owners buried at Elephantine was Pepinakht, also known as Hekaib. He was held in such high regard that he was later venerated as a sort of local saint during the Middle Kingdom, and shrines were erected in his honor at Elephantine. Pepinakht considered the Nubians a threat to Egypt, and he was happy to reduce their numbers. The autobiography on his tomb recounts that the king "sent me to devastate the land of Wawat and Irtjet. I did what pleases my Lord and killed a great many there."

The collapse of the Old Kingdom brought Egypt's dominance of Nubia to a temporary halt, and in the Middle Kingdom, a different relationship developed between Egypt and its southern neighbor.

"I returned with **300 donkeys** loaded with **incense**, ebony, **panther-skins**, **elephant tusks** ..."

AUTOBIOGRAPHY OF HARKHUF

End of the Old Kingdom

The collapse of the Pyramid Age

One of the puzzles of ancient Egypt is why the Old Kingdom came to an end. There are many different theories that might explain why central royal authority collapsed in Egypt at the end of the 6th Dynasty.

There was probably no single reason for the collapse of the Old Kingdom. It was probably the result of a combination of related factors that began to emerge during the 5th and 6th Dynasties. One way to measure the extent of royal power in the Old Kingdom is to look at the size of the pyramids. Many scholars maintain that the larger the pyramid, the richer the state and, more importantly, the greater the king's control over state resources.

Pyramids and power

Looked at it in this way, the kings of the early 4th Dynasty would have been the most powerful kings of the Old Kingdom. The pyramids of the 5th and 6th Dynasties were certainly smaller than those of the 4th Dynasty, but they do not show a constant pattern of decline. On average, the 6th Dynasty pyramids were no smaller than those of the 5th Dynasty, and the regularity of their sizes (the pyramids of Teti, Pepi I, Merenre, and Pepi II were all planned to be 172 ft/52.5 m high) suggests consistency rather than decline. Also, the kings were paying more attention at the time to other parts of the pyramid complex apart from just the pyramid itself (see pp.82–83).

◁ **Ankhnesmeryre and Pepi II**
This alabaster statuette shows Queen Ankhnesmeryra holding her son, Pepi II, who became king at the age of 6.

◁ **Teti's sistrum**
A sistrum was a rattle used in religious ceremonies. This alabaster example has an inscription that describes Teti as "Beloved of the goddess Hathor, Lady of Dendera."

Local rulers

However, the 6th Dynasty kings also made substantial donations to temples in different parts of Egypt away from the capital, including those at Bubastis, Abydos, Dendera, and Elephantine. These towns were the homes of local officials who were becoming increasingly influential, and this weakened the power of the king. Pepi I, for instance, married two sisters, both of them named Ankhnesmeryra, whose father, Khui, was an important official at Abydos.

The increasing power of these local officials, who went on to become regional rulers, was a contributing factor in the collapse of both the Old Kingdom and the First Intermediate Period that followed it. This might, however, have been the result rather than the cause of the collapse of the kings' authority, as local "rulers" stepped in to fill the gap created by weak leadership.

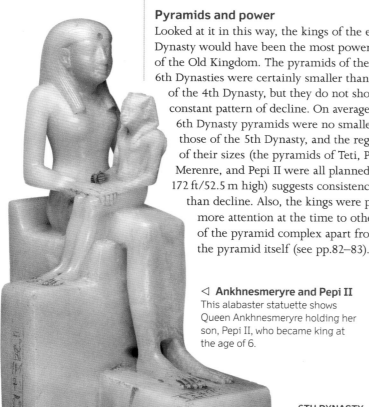

6TH DYNASTY

Pepi I
2323 BCE

Pepi II
2278 BCE

Teti
2345 BCE

Merenre
2321 BCE

CLIMATE **CHANGE**

Drought was a major problem during the Late Old Kingdom. Rainfall was declining, and it was becoming drier. As a result, the water levels of the River Nile dropped, reducing how much food people could grow. Also, the nearby savannah lands, which had been used by seminomadic people for grazing, gradually turned into a desert. The nomads were then forced into the Nile Valley and Delta, where food was already scarce. These starving nomadic groups are depicted on the walls of Unas's pyramid complex.

**RELIEF CARVING DEPICTING
A STARVING NOMAD**

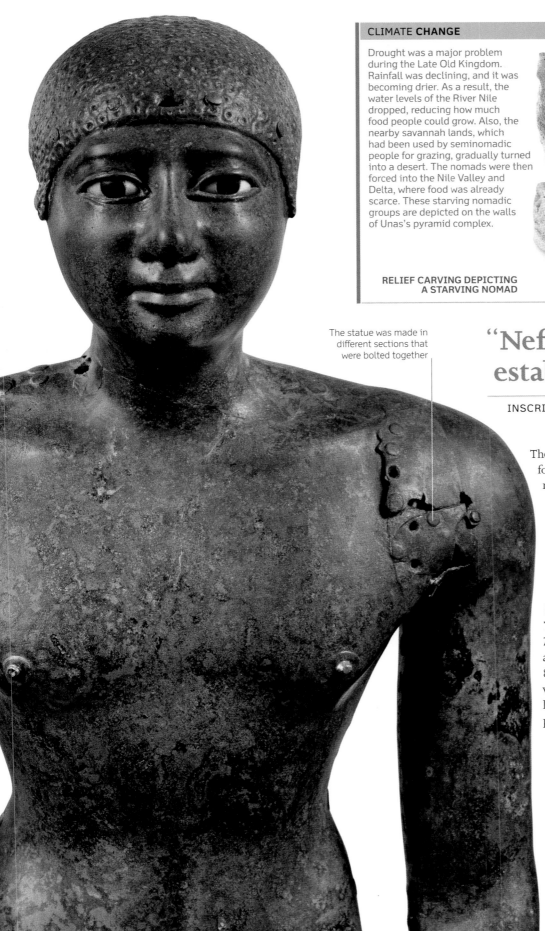

The statue was made in different sections that were bolted together

"**Neferkare** (Pepi II) is **established** and **living**."

INSCRIPTION ON THE LAST OLD KINGDOM PYRAMID

The last king of the 6th Dynasty, Pepi II, reigned for a very long time—possibly 94 years. This might have led to instability, because by the time he was laid to rest in his pyramid, his sons and heirs had already died, and it may not have been clear who the next king was. Pepi II might have been followed by the short-lived female ruler later known as Nitocris, an unusual king for unusual times.

Period of chaos

The Egyptian historian Manetho describes the 7th Dynasty as "70 kings in 70 days," which is another way of saying a period of chaos. The 8th Dynasty seems to have consisted of kings who were based in Memphis. They had very little power in Egypt beyond the capital and, possibly, parts of the Delta.

◁ **Royal copper statue**
Most metal statues from ancient Egypt were melted down, and the metal was reused. This rare surviving example from the reign of Pepi I (or possibly his son, Merenre) suggests, however, that copper was still being imported from the Sinai mines during the 6th Dynasty.

First Intermediate Period

A time of chaos

The collapse of royal authority at the end of the Old Kingdom created a crisis for Egypt. After more than 800 years as a strong, centralized state focused on royal rule, Egypt faced an unprecedented future without a king.

In later times, the First Intermediate Period was regarded as an era of great calamity. With no king on the throne, the established order was turned on its head, and chaos reigned. Wealthy people were left poor and homeless; foreigners flooded into Egypt, bringing their cattle to graze on Egyptian land; and the royal cemeteries were ransacked.

However, much of our information about the chaotic nature of the First Intermediate Period comes from much later sources, and in particular from educational texts aimed partly at drilling into students that an Egypt without a king was an Egypt without order or stability. In fact, the situation was far more complicated than that. An analysis of grave goods from this period suggests that away from the capital, Memphis, most people were just as wealthy as they had been during the Old Kingdom.

Tombs for local rulers

Nevertheless, the collapse of centralized royal authority at the end of the Old Kingdom meant that the regions were now left to fend for themselves. In fact, the transition to local rule seems to have begun in the 6th Dynasty, when the control of Egypt's regions, or nomes, transferred to local rulers, who passed on power from father to son with little royal interference. One of the most obvious effects of this transition was the emergence of regional cemeteries of elite tombs in

◁ **Stela of Djemi**
In his tomb autobiography, a local ruler called Djemi, the "Troop Commander and Overseer of Mercenaries," claimed to have successfully campaigned in Upper Egypt and Lower Nubia.

the provinces. These tombs must have been built close to the capitals of the nomes, where the local rulers lived, but almost every trace of these towns and cities built in the floodplain of the Nile has now vanished. The large, elaborate, and highly decorated tombs built for the elite (the local rulers) are especially noticeable in Middle and Upper Egypt, where they were cut into the rock face of the cliffs overlooking the Nile Valley.

Building local tombs continued well into the Middle Kingdom, a visible indication that regional independence was not completely crushed at the end of the First Intermediate Period. Stone stelae celebrating the lives of the deceased also started to appear in cemeteries, continuing the tradition of autobiographies on tombs that had begun during the Old Kingdom (see pp.92–93). Local officials wrote on these stelae, describing all the good things that they had done for their local region, such as feeding the hungry and clothing the naked—tasks that had previously been the king's responsibility.

◁ **Statue of Nakhti**
During the First Intermediate Period, the city of Asyut became an ally of the Herakleopolitans. Its rulers were buried in tombs containing the finest artifacts, such as this statue belonging to Nakhti, the "Overseer of the Seal."

> "**Men** will take up **weapons of war** and the **land** will live in **turmoil**."
>
> FROM THE *PROPHECY OF NEFERTI*

A Nubian archer and an Egyptian greet each other with a gesture of friendship

△ **Archers' stela**
Soldiers began to appear on stelae in southern Egypt, indicating the militarized nature of society in the First Intermediate Period. Many Nubian mercenaries, including archers, were enlisted by southern warlords and were buried in expensive tombs.

The 9th and 10th Dynasties

It was only a matter of time before local rulers tried to extend their influence beyond their own nomes and to compete with each other for a greater share of Egypt. The earliest successful attempt at carrying out such a power grab was made by the family of the nomarchs based at Herakleopolis Magna, a city in a strategic position to the south of Memphis.

The Herakleopolitan rulers, who began to refer to themselves as kings, seem to have taken control of much of the Nile Valley and possibly the Delta, too. Although they failed to unify the whole of Egypt under their control, they were influential enough to later appear as kings in king lists and to form Manetho's 9th and 10th Dynasties. Other powerful regional families either allied themselves with them or became their vassals. The most important of these

were the rulers at Asyut, a city in a strategic position on a bend of the Nile. Its ideal position meant that the Herakleopolitans could easily fend off any competition from southern Egypt.

◁ **Scene of butchery**
Regional tombs in the First Intermediate Period were often decorated in a manner based on that of the elite mastabas of the Old Kingdom. This scene of butchery from the tomb of Iti, at Gebelein, revives a common Old Kingdom motif in a simple, naive style.

▷ **Relief of Ankhtify**
This image of Ankhtify from the entrance of his tomb chapel shows him as a conventional upper-class Egyptian of the Old Kingdom. It contrasts with the exceptional role he gives himself in his biography. At some point, the face was vandalized, possibly by Ankhtify's victorious and vengeful Theban enemies.

Long staff

Short scepter is a traditional emblem of authority

Traditional Old Kingdom kilt

Ankhtify and the Intefs

Warlords in the south

While the Herakleopolitans and their allies were in control of northern Egypt, there was a struggle for the leadership of the south between Ankhtify of Moalla, a remarkable local ruler, and his enemies, the Thebans.

The tomb of Ankhtify in southern Egypt is a unique monument. Other rock-cut tombs were built in the provinces during the First Intermediate Period, but Ankhtify's tomb has multiple parts and was set on the side of a hill that looks like a natural pyramid.

Ankhtify was not a king but a nomarch—one of several influential local rulers who competed for power after the collapse of the Old Kingdom. Based in the town of Hefat, in the third Upper Egyptian nome, Ankhtify gradually extended his rule to the south, over the first and second nomes. He also had ambitions to push northward, which brought him into conflict with the local rulers of the Theban and Coptite nomes.

Competing warlords

Traditionally, the autobiographies written on tombs recounted the favors of the king enjoyed by the tomb owner, but as there was no king during this period, people wrote about their own achievements instead. Ankhtify went further. In the text that covers the pillars of his offering chapel, he describes how he was summoned by the god Horus to take command of his region of Egypt.

Although he did not claim to be a king, Ankhtify made himself sound royal, saying that he fed the hungry and that none of the people he ruled were short on food. In fact, he claimed that people had begun to eat their children. This was probably an exaggeration, but there was certainly a problem transporting food to some parts of Egypt during the early First Intermediate Period, and this led to famine.

The rise of Thebes

There is no suggestion in the text on Ankhtify's tomb that he was ever defeated in battle, but it is telling that he never mentions a final victory over the Thebans and their Coptite allies. Nor is there any evidence that he founded a local dynasty that survived after his death. Recent excavations suggest that his tomb was pillaged soon after he was buried, possibly by victorious Thebans eager to desecrate the tomb of a hated enemy.

It was the Thebans who ultimately gained control of the south of Egypt and went on to compete with the Herakleopolitans for the throne of a reunited Egypt. Their leaders, a family called Intef, or Montuhotep, were later known as the 11th Dynasty.

△ **Stela of Intef II**
This stela of Wahankh Intef II of Thebes features two hymns—one to the god Ra and one to the goddess Hathor. Intef's name is written in a cartouche, which was a royal privilege.

◁ **Ankhtify's tale**
The pillars of the offering chapel of Ankhtify's tomb are carved with Ankhtify's extensive autobiography. The text is a key source of information about events in southern Egypt during the First Intermediate Period.

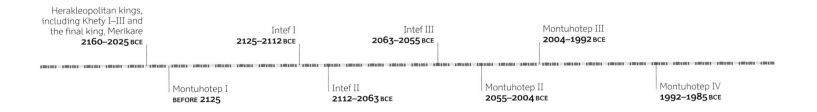

Herakleopolitan kings, including Khety I–III and the final king, Merikare
2160–2025 BCE

Intef I
2125–2112 BCE

Intef III
2063–2055 BCE

Montuhotep III
2004–1992 BCE

Montuhotep I
BEFORE 2125

Intef II
2112–2063 BCE

Montuhotep II
2055–2004 BCE

Montuhotep IV
1992–1985 BCE

Montuhotep II

Egypt reunited

The military successes of the Thebans against their Herakleopolitan enemies paved the way for the political integration of Egypt as a unified state under a single king. That king was Nebhepetre Montuhotep II.

Evidence suggests that a victory over Ankhtify gave the Thebans control of the southern nomes of Egypt, but the Herakleopolitans (see pp.92–93) challenged their rule. For several generations, but especially during the reigns of Intefs I–III, military conflict flared up between these two powers, mainly for control of the stretch of the Nile between Abydos and Asyut. Although the details of the conflict are unclear, both the Thebans and the Herakleopolitans seem to have regarded themselves as the legitimate kings of Egypt and conferred themselves with royal titles.

Man of destiny

The most important member of the Theban 11th Dynasty was Nebhepetre Montuhotep II. For the first 14 years of his 50-year reign, he ruled over the territories in the south of Egypt, which he had inherited from his father, Intef III. The rest of his reign was spent locked in an intermittent war with the Herakleopolitans. The two main events of this war were the Theban's capture of Asyut (the strongest of the enemy allies) and the death of the last major Herakleopolitan king, Merikare.

A remarkable piece of evidence for this conflict is the Tomb of the Warriors, which was built close to Montuhotep's tomb at Thebes. This mass grave contains the bodies of 60 soldiers who appear to have died fighting the Herakleopolitans. In honor of their loyalty, they were buried close to their king.

▷ **Royal statue**
Montuhotep II's temple-tomb contained a life-size statue of the king associating him with the god Osiris. He is shown dressed in a white jubilee robe and wearing the red crown of Lower Egypt.

Reuniting Egypt

After his victory, Montuhotep reviewed the leaders of the Egyptian nomes. Rulers who had opposed him, such as the nomarch of Asyut, were removed from power, whereas those who had supported him, or who had at least remained neutral, stayed in their hereditary posts. For this reason, cities such as Beni Hasan and Hermopolis Magna in Middle Egypt were able to maintain stable local government throughout the First Intermediate Period and well into the Middle Kingdom.

To emphasize that he was now in control of the whole of Egypt, Montuhotep initiated an ambitious building program that included constructing several new temples. Most of these were later demolished to make room for larger buildings, but their remains show that he built temples at some of the principal sites in Upper Egypt, including Elephantine, Dendera, and Abydos.

The rise of Thebes

Montuhotep II continued to rule from Thebes after the reunification of Egypt. He based his national government there and showed no interest in reinstating the region around Memphis either for the royal court or for royal burials. Instead, he concentrated his efforts on transforming Thebes into a suitably impressive capital city.

The local patron god of the Thebans was Amen, who was primarily worshipped at Karnak, in the northern part of Thebes. Under the Intefs and Montuhotep I, Karnak had grown as a place of worship because Amen was now an important state god thanks to royal patronage. Thebes also had more grand monuments, being the site of the grand tombs of the 11th Dynasty

△ **Royal regalia**
This relief carving from Deir el-Bahri shows Montuhotep in the regalia of a king, including the white crown of Upper Egypt, the false beard, and the uraeus (royal cobra) on his brow.

▷ **Grand design**
The temple-tomb of Montuhotep II at Deir el-Bahri represented a return to royal monument building after a century of political crisis. It is radically innovative yet shows a respect for tradition.

"**Respect** the nobles, **support** your people, **fortify** your borders."

ROYAL ADVICE FROM THE *INSTRUCTION FOR MERIKARE*

△ **Expansion abroad**
As well as unifying Egypt, Montuhotep began to extend the boundaries of his kingdom, both to the south and east. This relief from his tomb seems to show Asiatic enemies being slain.

rulers. These tombs were built on the west side of the Nile, to mirror the Temple of Karnak on the east side of the river.

Like his Intef ancestors, Montuhotep II was buried at Thebes, but he was the king of all Egypt, so his tomb had to reflect his importance. His architects therefore designed a unique temple-tomb in the desert bay of Deir el-Bahri, close to the Theban mountain.

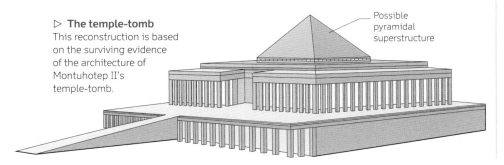

▷ **The temple-tomb**
This reconstruction is based on the surviving evidence of the architecture of Montuhotep II's temple-tomb.

Possible pyramidal superstructure

Both the choice of site and the prominence given to Amen in the decoration reflected Montuhotep's Theban roots. The addition of a pyramid-shaped structure on top of the main building may also have paid tribute to an earlier royal tradition.

Montuhotep II reigned for half a century, but his two successors did not live for long. When Montuhotep IV died, the throne passed to a new family, the 12th Dynasty, which focused on aggressively extending Egypt's borders.

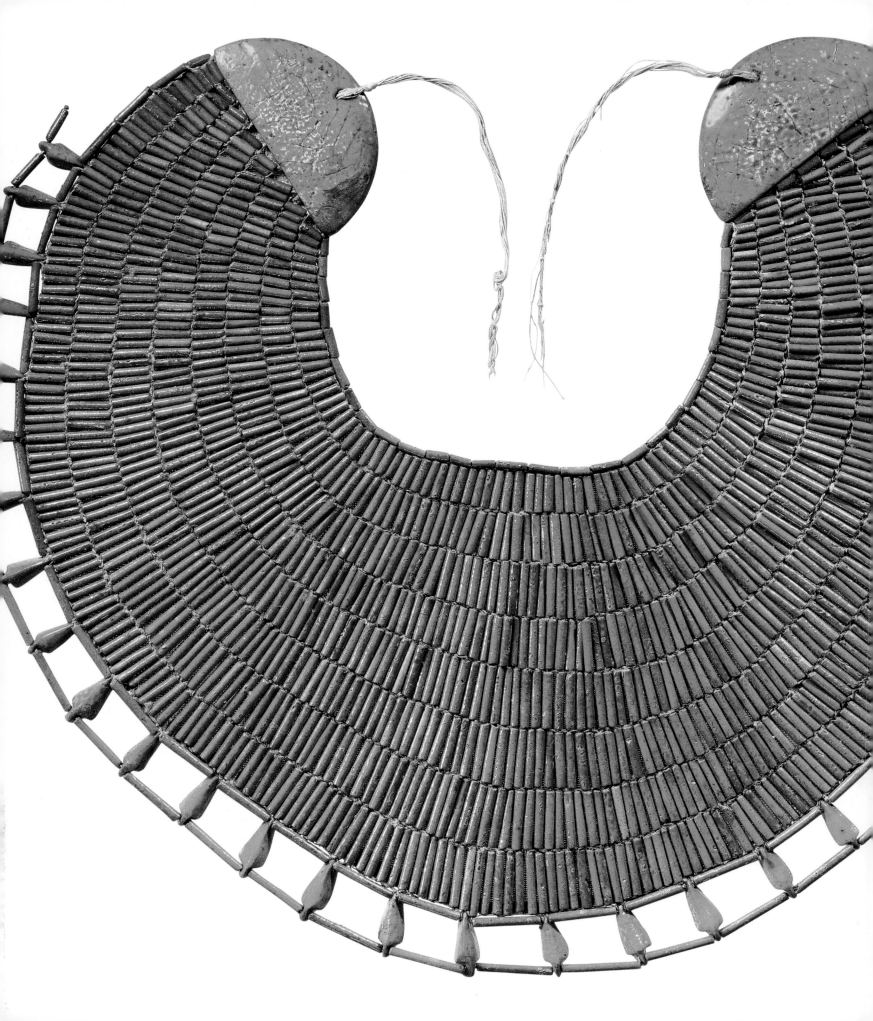

3

The Middle Kingdom

C.2055–1550 BCE

The Middle Kingdom

The First Intermediate Period came to an end when the Theban forces of Montuhotep II defeated the Herakleopolitans and reunified Egypt. This began a new period of Egyptian history, known as the Middle Kingdom, which was both similar to and different from the Old Kingdom. The most obvious similarity was royal authority and some of the ways in which the kings expressed it. One of the differences was that a considerable amount of political power now lay in the provinces, as a legacy of the First Intermediate Period. Another difference was that the kings of the Middle Kingdom took far more interest in the world beyond Egypt's borders.

The primacy of Thebes

As the rulers of the 11th Dynasty were based at Thebes, it is not surprising that after the unification they built most of their monuments in their own city. The main beneficiary of this was the god Amen, who had a temple at Karnak, but other Theban gods, such as Montu, were also given new temples. Building temples at Thebes was continued by the kings of the 12th and 13th Dynasties.

Pyramids and provincial tombs

The ultimate expression of royal power in the Old Kingdom was the pyramid. Middle Kingdom kings wished to follow this example, and every ruler with the resources to do so built a pyramid. However, even the largest of their pyramids did not come close in size or sophistication to the greatest pyramids of the 4th Dynasty, although they did bear comparison to those of the 5th and 6th Dynasties. Most of these pyramids were built farther south than those of the Old Kingdom, at sites such as Lisht (which was close to the new capital of Itj-Tawy) or at Kahun and Hawara, near the mouth of the Faiyum.

Another difference in the Middle Kingdom pyramids was that few of them had extensive cemeteries for court officials built next to them, as in the Old Kingdom. Nonroyal elite tombs tended to be built in the provinces instead, near the regional administrative centers of local officials. The best tombs were dug into the faces of cliffs high above the Nile Valley. These were located at sites such as Beni Hasan, el-Bersheh, and Asyut, where regional governors were more important than they had been in the Old Kingdom.

Nubia and the Hyksos

During the Middle Kingdom, the Egyptians began to build an empire that conquered and held large amounts of territory. A series of invasions, followed by the construction of an impressive series of fortresses, brought Lower Nubia under direct Egyptian control. This had the double advantage of giving the Egyptians access to the trade routes farther south and of partly neutralizing any threat that the Nubians might pose. However, at the end of the Middle Kingdom, the threat to Egypt did not come from the south, but from the east. At the close of the 12th Dynasty, a dynasty of Canaanites, the Hyksos, established themselves in the eastern Delta, from where they extended their rule into Middle Egypt. The Thebans in the south stood alone once again, but this time against an enemy that threatened the survival of Egypt itself.

◁ **Model of a servant girl**

1985 BCE Amenemhat I becomes the first king of the 12th Dynasty

1870 BCE Senwosret III becomes king. Fortresses built in Nubia

2055 BCE Montuhotep II becomes king at Thebes and reunifies Egypt

2004 BCE Death of Montuhotep II

1877 BCE Senwosret II becomes king. Foundation of Kahun

1831 BCE Amenemhat III becomes king and starts building two pyramids

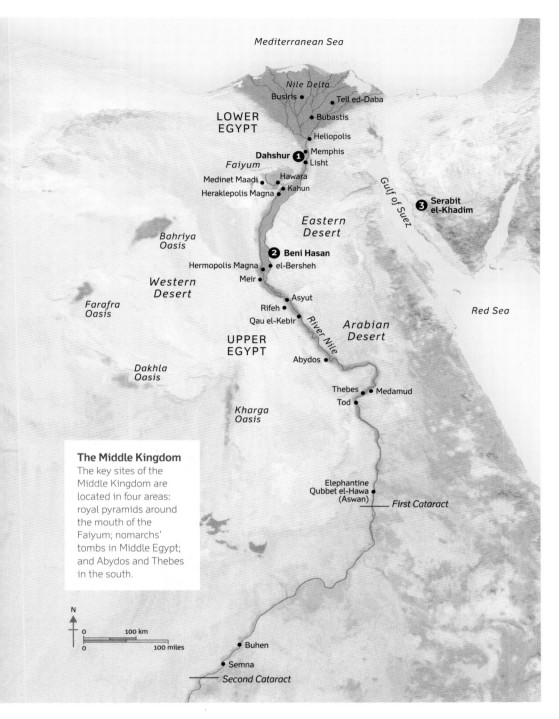

Mediterranean Sea

Nile Delta

Busiris • • Tell ed-Daba

**LOWER
EGYPT**

• Bubastis

• Heliopolis

Dahshur ❶ • Memphis
• Lisht

Faiyum

Medinet Maadi • Hawara
• • Kahun

Heraklepolis Magna •

Gulf of Suez

❸ **Serabit
el-Khadim**

*Eastern
Desert*

*Bahriya
Oasis*

❷ **Beni Hasan**

Hermopolis Magna • • el-Bersheh

Meir •

*Western
Desert*

*Farafra
Oasis*

Rifeh • • Asyut

Qau el-Kebir •

**UPPER
EGYPT**

River Nile

*Arabian
Desert*

Red Sea

*Dakhla
Oasis*

Abydos •

Thebes • • Medamud
Tod •

*Kharga
Oasis*

Elephantine
Qubbet el-Hawa
(Aswan) • —— *First Cataract*

The Middle Kingdom
The key sites of the
Middle Kingdom are
located in four areas:
royal pyramids around
the mouth of the
Faiyum; nomarchs'
tombs in Middle Egypt;
and Abydos and Thebes
in the south.

N

0   100 km

0   100 miles

• Buhen

• Semna

—— *Second Cataract*

❶ Pyramid of Amenemhat III, Dahshur

❷ Nomarchs' tombs, Beni Hasan

❸ Stela Temple, Serabit el-Khadim

1777 BCE Sobekneferu
becomes king

1750 BCE The 13th
Dynasty kings
active at Abydos

1580 BCE The 17th
Dynasty established
at Thebes

1773 BCE End of
the 12th Dynasty

1650 BCE Hyksos rulers take
over the eastern Delta

1555 BCE Kamose
becomes king at Thebes

Kings of the 12th Dynasty

Egypt's classical age

The Middle Kingdom includes the later part of the 11th Dynasty and some of the 13th Dynasty before it merged into the Second Intermediate Period. At its core were the two centuries during which Egypt was ruled by the family known as the 12th Dynasty.

It is not known how or why the 12th Dynasty succeeded the 11th. Perhaps Montuhotep IV (the last 11th Dynasty king) had no obvious successor and Amenemhat I, who may have been a high-ranking Theban court official, stepped in to fill the gap. It was certainly a period of instability: there is evidence to suggest that Amenemhat I himself was later assassinated as part of a coup at court, but even if this were the case, the throne passed safely to Amenemhat's son, Senwosret I.

The 12th Dynasty was one of the most successful ruling families in Egyptian history. Not only did it hold on to the throne for generations, but it also reigned at a time when Egypt flourished in many ways.

A stable dynasty

The stability of the 12th Dynasty was partly due to the long reigns of the individual kings—apart from Senwosret II, they all ruled for three decades or more until the end of the dynasty. The succession of the throne from father to son was also more or less guaranteed by a practice known as co-regency, in which the king appointed his successor to rule alongside him as a junior partner. This meant that when the king died, his heir was already in place.

△ **Amenemhat I**
1985–1956 BCE
The first king of the 12th Dynasty, Amenemhat I was possibly the Vizier Amenemhat of the 11th Dynasty. He made Itj-Tawy the center of government and revived the art of pyramid building.

△ **Senwosret I**
1956–1911 BCE
The son of Amenemhat I, Senwosret I followed his father's example by building a pyramid at Lisht. He was a prolific builder, especially at Thebes. He was also a warrior and pushed southward to begin creating an Egyptian empire in Nubia.

△ **Senwosret III**
1870–1831 BCE
Possibly the most powerful king of the 12th Dynasty, Senwosret III reigned for nearly 40 years. He built some of Egypt's greatest monuments and established an Egyptian empire (see pp.110–111).

"A king shall come from the south, Ameny, the justified, by name."

FROM THE *PROPHECY OF NEFERTI*

A new capital

Amenemhat I abandoned Thebes as the capital of Egypt and chose a new site close to the junction between the Valley and the Delta, but not at Memphis. The new capital was at a place called *Amenemhat-Itj-Tawy*, which means "Amenemhat seizes the Two Lands." The exact location of Itj-Tawy, as it is usually called, is not known, but it was probably somewhere close to Lisht, where both Amenemhat I and Senwosret I were buried, reviving the custom of burying kings in the north.

The new capital was not a great city, like Memphis or Thebes, but a relatively small and possibly fortified royal residence that was used mainly for government purposes and little else. From there, the 12th Dynasty kings pursued aggressive policies against their neighbors, especially Nubia, which set the scene for large-scale martial activity in the New Kingdom. The building projects of the 12th Dynasty kings were far more extensive than those of the Old Kingdom, and local officials continued to build impressive tombs for themselves in the provinces.

The 12th Dynasty was not just a period of political transition, but also a time of cultural change. Some Old Kingdom traditions were revived, such as building pyramids, but literature also flourished. Up until then, writing had been used mainly for accounts, keeping records, and inscriptions on tombs. Now, however, people began to write imaginative works of fiction, such as *The Story of Sinuhe*.

△ **Amenemhat III**
1831–1786 BCE
The son of Senwosret III, Amenemhat III continued his father's policies. Like Senwosret II, he developed the area around the Faiyum Oasis and sent expeditions to the mines of Sinai.

△ **Amenemhat IV**
1786–1777 BCE
Amenemhat IV only reigned for around nine years. He sent expeditions into Sinai, Upper Egypt, and the Land of Punt, looking for minerals and precious stones. When he died, the throne passed to Sobekneferu, who was probably his sister-wife.

△ **Sobekneferu**
1777–1773 BCE
Sobekneferu's short reign, the last of the 12th Dynasty, was followed by a time of instability in the land. Women rarely ruled ancient Egypt, and usually only did so when a king died without leaving an heir.

Royal building projects

The return of the pyramid

During the Middle Kingdom, the kings of Egypt had two main architectural ambitions—to resume building pyramids as royal tombs and to erect and restore temples throughout the land.

Wishing to emulate their Old Kingdom predecessors, the 12th Dynasty kings built tombs in the shape of pyramids, but these Middle Kingdom pyramids were different from those that came before them in several ways. They were often built more cheaply, and the interiors were filled with rubble or mud brick instead of blocks of stone. This might explain why most of them are in such poor condition today.

The first 12th Dynasty pyramids were built at Lisht, close to the new capital, Itj-Tawy, for Amenemhat I and Senwosret I. Both of these kings used simplified versions of the 6th Dynasty pyramid complexes, such as that of Pepi II, as their model. Some of the later pyramids were built in the region around Memphis, notably at Dahshur, where the two Old Kingdom pyramids built by Snefru were joined by those of

Amenemhat II, Senwosret III, and Amenemhat III (see pp.62–63). Nearby, at Mazghuna, two pyramids now in ruins may have been built by Amenemhat IV and Sobekneferu. Senwosret II favored sites near the mouth of the Faiyum, with his pyramid at Kahun, while Amenemhat III built a second pyramid at Hawara.

Temples in the provinces

The kings of the Middle Kingdom found Egypt full of temples made of mud brick and left them standing with some stone additions. They did this partly to restore damage caused during the First Intermediate Period, but also to put their royal stamp on buildings that had, up until then, been made entirely from local materials by local people. The kings made generous donations of stone elements to these local places of worship—a limestone gateway, an obelisk, or maybe even an entire stone temple—but these gifts were certain to show the god being worshipped by the king and by him alone. They benefited him by strengthening and publicly demonstrating his personal connection with the god.

In some areas, especially the Faiyum, well-preserved Middle Kingdom temples have survived to this day, but most of them were wholly or partly destroyed by work on later buildings. At Medamud, north of Thebes, for instance, a temple built by Senwosret I (itself on top of an earlier Old Kingdom building) has more or less disappeared beneath the New Kingdom and Greco-Roman temples that were later built on the same spot.

Similarly, at Hermopolis Magna, in Middle Egypt, a single monumental gateway is all that remains of a temple precinct built by Amenemhat II—it was later filled with temples built by successive generations of kings from the New Kingdom onward.

Heliopolis and Thebes

The Middle Kingdom kings also built temples at the most important royal centers, such as Heliopolis, one of the major temple sites of the Old Kingdom. Here, Senwosret I built a grand temple for the god Atum, the partner of the god Ra. All that is left of this important building today is a single granite obelisk.

The place that seems to have attracted the most attention in terms of building during the Middle Kingdom was Thebes, where the precinct of the god Amen (a minor, obscure god during the Old Kingdom) was expanded when Amen became the divine patron of the Middle Kingdom kings.

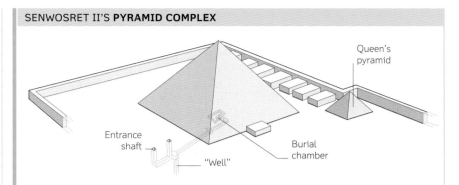

SENWOSRET II'S PYRAMID COMPLEX

Queen's pyramid

Entrance shaft

"Well"

Burial chamber

The pyramids of the 12th Dynasty kings are, with few exceptions, unimpressive when compared to those of the Old Kingdom, both in size and the quality of materials used. The interiors of the pyramids of Senwosret II and Amenemhat III, however, are remarkably complex due to concern about the security of the royal burial chamber. Senwosret II's pyramid at Kahun was especially confusing for robbers looking for an entrance—instead of being on the side of the pyramid, it was accessed via a vertical shaft to the south of the pyramid. This branched into a complicated set of corridors and chambers (including a "well," the bottom of which has never been reached), which finally led to the burial chamber itself.

Amen was just as important to the New Kingdom kings, and yet many of the buildings constructed during the Middle Kingdom were later swept away or destroyed by the vast construction projects of the 18th Dynasty. The best-known example of this was the so-called White Chapel of Senwosret I at Karnak, which was built as part of a festival complex to commemorate the jubilee celebrating the 30th year of his reign.

The White Chapel was later demolished, and the stone was used as rubble fill for a pylon of Amenhotep III. Fortunately, modern archaeologists recovered its remains and were able to reconstruct the entire building (see below).

▽ **The White Chapel**
The elegant White Chapel of Senwosret I at Karnak is a rare survival of what must have been an impressive set of buildings created for Amen during the reign of Senwosret I.

SENWOSRET I EMBRACES THE GOD AMEN

Provincial cemeteries

Local tombs for local officials

Some of the most impressive buildings to have survived from the Middle Kingdom are the large, well-decorated tombs of local dynasties of regional officials, hewn out of the cliffs overlooking the Nile Valley.

In the Middle Kingdom, there were essentially four types of cemetery. The most lavish were the royal tombs—pyramids—and the court cemeteries associated with them. The least lavish were those of the vast majority of the peasant population of Egypt—simple graves containing a few grave goods. As well as these two contrasting forms of cemetery, there were two other types of tombs in the provincial cemeteries of the Middle Kingdom.

△ **Tombs at Beni Hasan**
The nomarchs' tombs in the cliffs at Beni Hasan have grand, elaborate entrances. They were designed to look like the pillared portals of their owners' houses.

Nomarchs' tombs

During the First Intermediate Period, Egypt's regions enjoyed an autonomy that they had not known in the highly centralized Old Kingdom, and the reunification of Egypt at the beginning of the Middle Kingdom did not put a complete end to this (see pp.94–95). Local nomarchs (rulers) and administrators carried on building large, elaborate tombs for themselves, which they funded from their resources, thus retaining a measure of independence from the king. This autonomy was limited, but it was sufficient for the nomarchs to continue this tradition and to build several important provincial cemeteries.

Grand monuments

The elite regional tombs that have survived the best are found on the edge of the desert, high above the floodplain of the Nile, in places where it was possible to cut into the cliffs. In some locations, such as at Beni Hasan, el-Bersheh, Meir, Asyut, and Rifeh, several generations of local rulers excavated tombs for themselves alongside those of their ancestors, creating rows of rock-cut tombs looking out over the Nile Valley, which can be seen from far away. These tombs often appear to be huge caves, but many of them have splendid entrances with pillars, carved to look like the grand doorways of the large houses that their owners had while they were alive.

Honoring the dead

As in the mastabas of the Old Kingdom, the largest part of these tombs was the offering chapel. The burial chamber itself was quite modest—usually a space just big enough for a coffin, set at the bottom of a vertical shaft that opened up either in the offering chapel itself or in the courtyard in front of it.

Beautifully carved hand

◁ **Statue of Nemtyhotep**
This impressive quartzite statue from the Asyut region depicts the steward Nemtyhotep. With its simple, cloaked body and finely modeled head, it is a typical example of a Middle Kingdom private statue.

> "He made it as **his monument** ... adorning **his city** and perpetuating his **name**."

KHNUMHOTEP II ON HIS TOMB AT BENI HASAN

The walls of these tombs were covered with texts and pictures chosen to guarantee the afterlife of their owners. The range of images was very similar to that of the multiroomed mastaba tombs of the Late Old Kingdom. Many of them depicted scenes of everyday life, especially of people producing food and other goods for the tomb owner. Others showed the owner and his family enjoying themselves out in the country, hunting, boating, or catching birds.

These Middle Kingdom tombs also had another purpose, however—to celebrate a tomb owner's accomplishments by recording outstanding things that he had achieved during his lifetime. This was partly intended to win the king's approval, as was traditional, but some of the successes were beyond the sphere of royal authority, indicating a degree of independence.

Middle-class cemeteries

The fourth type of tomb belonged to people who might be called the middle class, although the term does not apply to ancient Egypt. These people were soldiers, doctors, and minor officials who could afford something better than a desert grave, but not as expensive as the rock-cut tombs built by the nomarchs. The best example of this type of cemetery is at Beni Hasan, where archaeologist John Garstang excavated 888 shaft tombs on the rocky slope beneath the nomarchs' tombs from 1902 to 1904.

These middle-class tombs were essentially the same as the burial shafts of the elite tombs. They were cut vertically into the rock, between 6–13 ft (2–4 m) deep, and at the bottom of the shaft, one or more tiny chambers were carved out to make room for a box coffin. This was usually surrounded by a few grave goods, such as wooden models of the servants needed for the afterlife.

Although these tombs were far more modest than the nomarchs' tombs in the cliffside above them, they mark an important point in Egyptian social history. Up until that point, only the high elite of Egyptian society would have been able to spend so much money building and equipping a tomb.

△ **The tomb of Khnumhotep II**
In a scene reminiscent of Old Kingdom mastabas, the nomarch Khnumhotep II and his family are shown enjoying the aristocratic pursuits of hunting, fishing, and fowling on the walls of his tomb at Beni Hasan.

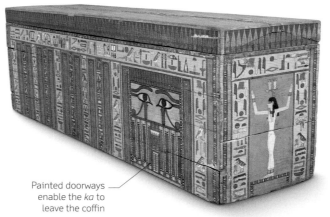

◁ **Protective goddesses**
Like many Late Middle Kingdom examples, Khnumnakht's coffin was protected at each end by images of goddesses. This emphasized the link with Osiris, whose body was also defended by them.

Vertical bands enlist the protection of various deities, especially those connected to Osiris

Painted doorways enable the *ka* to leave the coffin

Large eyes make it possible for the *ka* to see out of the coffin

The Offering Formula ensures eternal offerings for the *ka*

Coffin of Khnumnakht

"Chests of life"

One effect of the First Intermediate Period was that ideas about the afterlife, which had previously been limited to the king, became common among a much wider range of people. The belief that the *ka* or spirit within a tomb had to be fed and housed for eternity continued. Now, however, people also believed that a person had several spiritual forms, each of which had specific needs of its own after the body had died. These included an afterlife beyond the tomb. The kings' expectations expressed in the Pyramid Texts (see pp.70–71) included afterlives with the sun, the stars, and Osiris himself. Nonroyal Egyptians seized upon this idea of an afterlife with Osiris and were concerned about how to enter his kingdom and be accepted there.

Spells and images

The only way to achieve the Osirian afterlife was to own the texts, spells, and magical images needed to take you there. The main places to display these were the surfaces of rectangular wooden "box" coffins, found in large numbers in cemeteries throughout

◁ **Khnumnakht's coffin**
The exact location of Khnumnakht's tomb is not known, but the heavily decorated style of his coffin suggests that it came from one of the provincial cemeteries of Middle Egypt.

Egypt from this period. These coffins appealed to an ancient Egyptian middle class, who could not afford large decorated tombs and for whom the coffin became, in effect, a miniature tomb. The interior of a box coffin contained lists and images of everything that the deceased might need in the afterlife, and the floor often depicted a map of the underworld, taken from texts known as the *Book of Two Ways*, which described routes through the afterlife.

But the box coffin did not just serve the idea of an Osirian afterlife; it also helped the *ka*. The texts, prayers, and spells on the exterior were therefore just as concerned with offerings for the *ka* as they were about the afterlife with Osiris. How the coffins were decorated varied from region to region, but in some parts of Egypt, the texts and images covered every surface of the coffin, both inside and out.

Joined with Osiris

The body inside the box was often enclosed within a tight-fitting inner coffin that looked like a wrapped mummy whose head was exposed. This was meant to represent the body of Osiris, emphasizing the close connection between the deceased person and the god. The inner coffin was turned on its side inside the box coffin so that its face lined up with the eyes painted on the outside. This enabled the *ka* to see out of the coffin into the world beyond.

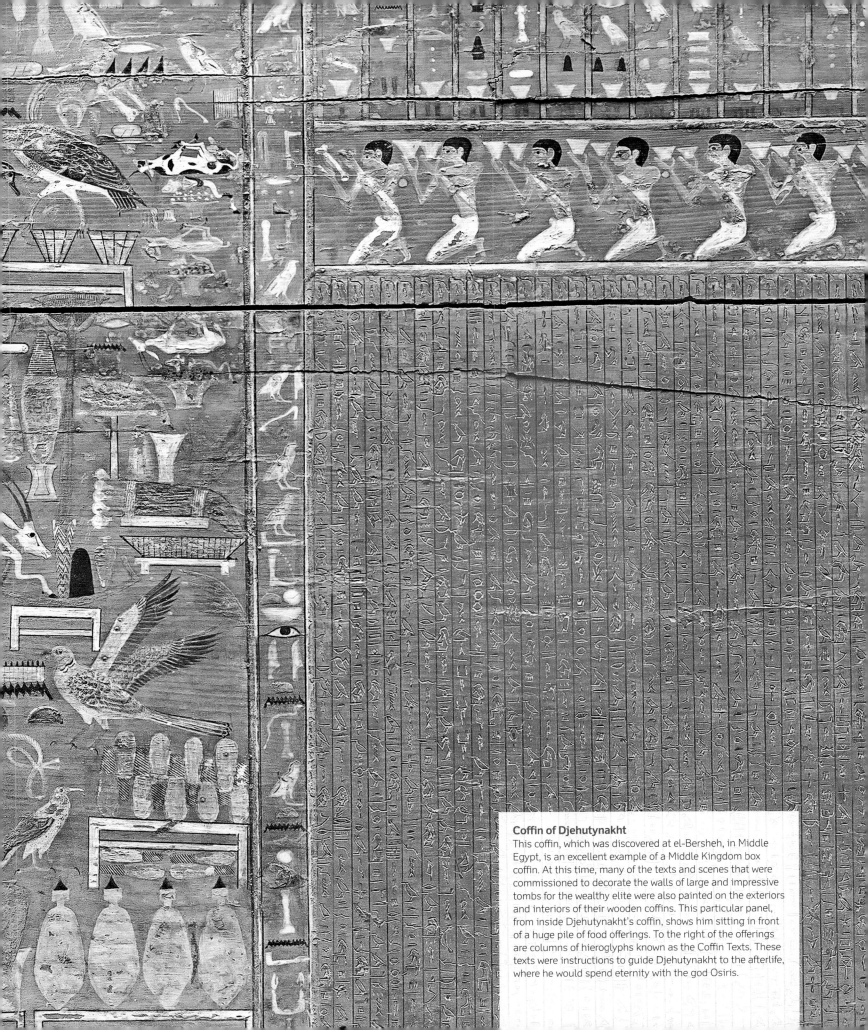

Coffin of Djehutynakht

This coffin, which was discovered at el-Bersheh, in Middle Egypt, is an excellent example of a Middle Kingdom box coffin. At this time, many of the texts and scenes that were commissioned to decorate the walls of large and impressive tombs for the wealthy elite were also painted on the exteriors and interiors of their wooden coffins. This particular panel, from inside Djehutynakht's coffin, shows him sitting in front of a huge pile of food offerings. To the right of the offerings are columns of hieroglyphs known as the Coffin Texts. These texts were instructions to guide Djehutynakht to the afterlife, where he would spend eternity with the god Osiris.

Senwosret III

The 12th Dynasty's greatest king

Senwosret III was the most powerful king of the Middle Kingdom. He preserved established royal traditions, but he was also an important innovator in art, religion, and politics.

Under Senwosret III, the power of both Egypt and its king increased significantly. By hia reign, the regional influence of the local nomarchs had diminished, and a more limited form of government had passed to local town-mayors. This strengthened the authority of the royal court, and Senwosret took full advantage of it to consolidate the conquests that his predecessor, Senwosret I, had made in Nubia. He built a series of fortresses on or near the Second Cataract of the Nile, bringing Lower Nubia under Egyptian control and creating a barrier against the Nubians who lived farther south. He became so important in the area that the Egyptians who settled in Nubia later worshipped him as a god during the New Kingdom.

Immortalized in stone

Senwosret III was a prolific builder throughout Egypt. An inscription in the Wadi Hammamat, for example, refers to an expedition that he sent there to quarry basalt for the now-lost temple of the god Herishef in Herakleopolis Magna. However, it was the site of Abydos that he singled out for special attention. During the Middle Kingdom, Abydos had become an important place of pilgrimage because it was regarded as the burial place of the god Osiris. In the 19th year of his reign, Senwosret sent an official named Ikhernofret to carry out renovation work in the area and to organize a festival known as the Mysteries of Osiris.

Also, although Senwosret III built a pyramid complex for himself at Dahshur, it seems that only his family was buried there and that he himself was buried in a huge underground tomb that he had excavated at Abydos. Partly for this reason, the site became even more popular with visitors, who left hundreds of stelae and statues there during his reign.

Like his predecessors, Senwosret III sometimes depicted himself as superhuman, but on many of his statues, his face looks careworn. There has been much debate about what this means, but the images were probably not intended to be realistic, but rather to send a message. Perhaps the king wanted to show that he, too, was human and listened to the concerns of his people. This might also explain the large ears that feature on his statues.

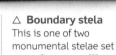

△ **Boundary stela**
This is one of two monumental stelae set up by Senwosret III at the Second Cataract frontier. It proclaims the supremacy of Egypt and demands that future kings maintain this border against the Nubians to the south.

The body of a fierce and powerful lion

▷ **Senwosret III sphinx**
Like many Egyptian kings, Senwosret used art to project an image of himself as a superhuman. The sphinx was a hybrid creature often used to symbolize the strength and otherworldly nature of the Middle Kingdom kings.

▷ **Careworn face**
The lined face, heavy eyelids, downturned mouth, and prominent ears make the statues of Senwosret III some of the most distinctive of any Egyptian king. No one knows why he chose to be depicted in this way.

1870 BCE Senwosret III takes the throne after the death of his father, Senwosret II

1862 BCE Sets up the first stela on the border with Nubia

1856 BCE Sends a quarrying expedition to Wadi Hammamat

1854 BCE Erects the second stela on the border with Nubia

1851 BCE Sends Ikhernofret to renovate the site of Abydos

1840 BCE Celebrates his 30-year jubilee

1831 BCE Dies and is succeeded by his son, Amenemhat III

The cobra is a symbol of kingship

Towns and houses

Homes for communities

Archaeological excavation and study of Middle Kingdom towns and villages has provided a fascinating insight into how the Egyptian state planned and built towns and villages for its workers and their families.

△ **House and garden**
This large and elaborate wooden model from the Middle Kingdom tomb of Meketre shows part of a wealthy residence built for leisure—an open courtyard containing a central pool surrounded by trees.

Detailed information about settlements is scarce for every period of Egyptian history, but there is more archaeological evidence of towns and villages from the Middle Kingdom than from the Old Kingdom. Although no "ordinary" towns or villages still exist, some types of settlement have survived because the Egyptian state created them for special circumstances. Realistic models of residential and industrial buildings found in tombs have provided additional information about houses and homes.

Town planning

The Egyptian state could build villages, towns, and even cities on very short notice. The best examples of this state control in the Middle Kingdom are the fortress-towns in Nubia (see pp.132–133). Within Egypt itself, some projects required housing for the people working on them. The town at Qasr es-Sagha, north of the lush oasis called the Faiyum, for example, provided accommodation for quarry workers. As the work gangs were probably made up of young men who were only employed on a seasonal basis, the accommodation looked like barracks—the basic sleeping quarters were divided into housing units for each work team. Towns such as Qasr es-Sagha were the descendants of the pyramid-building towns of the Old Kingdom but on a more modest scale.

Another type of settlement first built during the Old Kingdom was the town for priests. These towns were built close to royal and elite tombs to house the large numbers of priests needed to make regular offerings to the deceased. Unlike Qasr es-Sagha, priests' towns were in use all year round, but they seem to have been occupied by rotating staffs of priests who worked there temporarily for a certain number of days a year.

Kahun

A similar but more complex example of a priests' town is Kahun. Senwosret II founded it to provide accommodation for the priests who would make daily offerings on his behalf at his

---

PLAN OF **KAHUN**

Kahun is a typical example of a town planned by a central government during the Middle Kingdom. This map of the parts that have been excavated illustrates an important feature that has been found in other similar settlements. The houses are laid out according to a strict grid system within an enclosure wall that defines the exterior of the town. The map also indicates that the layout of Kahun is divided along social lines, with a large dividing wall between the two sectors of the town. On the right, wealthy community leaders managed large "mansions" that ran along the main street from the entrance of the town. Most of the population of Kahun, however, were likely to have been agricultural workers and would have occupied the rows of back-to-back terraces on the left side. This was a town designed for generations of residents who would have raised their families there and regarded Kahun as their home.

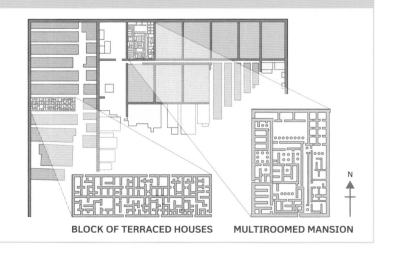

BLOCK OF TERRACED HOUSES   **MULTIROOMED MANSION**

N

pyramid complex (see pp.102–103) near the Faiyum. Because it was so far away from any existing town, Kahun was probably meant to provide homes not only for the priests, but also for their families on a permanent basis. It therefore needed a more complex infrastructure.

The size of Kahun and the number of houses there suggest that it had a population of many thousands (5,000 is a low estimate), which is well above the number needed solely for the king's offering cult. In light of this, Senwosret II may have built Kahun with a second aim in mind—namely to act as a major new agricultural center in the fertile Faiyum, an area

▷ **Soul house**
These clay models, known as soul houses, gave poor people an alternative to the expensive offering chapels in some of the Middle Kingdom cemeteries. This example seems to have been modeled on a rather grand residence.

developed during the 12th Dynasty. The town was divided into residential areas for the poor and the wealthy. Although the vast majority of the population lived in small houses, the community leaders had large mansions in which food was produced and stored for the whole community.

Workers empty buckets of grain into a silo

◁ **Model of a granary**
Places for storing food (especially the grain for bread and beer) were an important part of towns, both as separate buildings and as part of mansions. Egyptians put models of granaries in tombs to ensure that the deceased would have food for eternity.

Scribes note the amounts of grain received and given out

The model is color-coded. Brown is used for the wooden doorway and white for the limestone threshold

Sports and games

Playing in ancient Egypt

Archaeological evidence suggests that throughout their history, the ancient Egyptians were not very interested in athletic pursuits, apart from possibly wrestling. They did, however, greatly enjoy board games.

One of the big differences between a city in ancient Egypt and an ancient Greek or Roman one was the lack of places where organized sports could take place. There are plenty of examples of Egyptian kings describing their prowess at chariot riding, archery, and hunting—all activities that showed off the skills vital for a warrior. But there is little evidence of Egyptians taking part in team sports or athletic competitions of any kind, which suggests that they only played sports at a very local level.

Outdoor sports
There are some rare exceptions, mostly found in private tombs. At the necropolis of Beni Hasan, some of the Middle Kingdom nomarchs' tombs contain images of gymnastic displays and sports, including a primitive form of hockey. Even more remarkable are the extensive scenes of wrestlers in several of these tombs. The wall painting at the tomb of Khety, for example (far right), shows either 122 pairs of wrestlers or possibly a single pair of competitors practicing a wide variety of different holds and throws.

Indoor games
The ancient Egyptians seem to have preferred leisure activities that were less physical, such as board games, which were extremely popular. Several different types of board game have been identified from surviving examples of the boards themselves, but as no copies of the rules have been found, reconstructing exactly how each game was played is largely guesswork.

The best known of these games was Senet, which was played on a board of 30 squares. It seems to have been a little like backgammon, as two players competed by moving their pieces around the board to the finish. In another game, Mehen (below right), the board looked like a coiled serpent and players presumably moved their small spherical playing pieces from slot to slot, from the outer edge of the board to the center. Unlike Senet, Mehen did not have a set number of slots, which could range in number from 30 to 300.

Possibly the most visually appealing board game was one known as Hounds and Jackals, in which two players also raced their pieces to an end point. In this case, the pieces were tall pins that fit into 58 holes on top of the board. Although the original name and the rules are not known, the end point may have been the *shen* (protection) symbol at the top of the board. Each player had five tall pins with heads carved to look like hounds and jackals.

△ **Senet board**
Board games and their playing pieces were often made from precious or decorative materials, like this senet board made of blue faience. The pieces could be stored in the drawer under the board.

Hound-headed playing piece

Jackal-headed playing piece

Container for the pieces

◁ **Hounds and Jackals**
This elegant ivory Hounds and Jackals set is from a Middle Kingdom private tomb at Deir el-Bahri. It shows that gaming boards were regarded as miniature works of art, as well as prized personal possessions.

The central eye is probably where the game ended

△ **Mehen**
This circular stone Mehen board comes from a tomb from the 1st Dynasty, when Egyptians often played the game. It had ceased to be popular by the First Intermediate Period.

△ **Wrestling scene**
The tomb of Khety at Beni Hasan contains some of the most detailed illustrations of the popular sport of wrestling. The many figures shown are probably meant to be "read" as a series of wrestling moves, similar to a present-day comic strip.

This wrestler is breaking a hold

One wrestler lifts the other off the ground

A healthy diet

Eating and drinking in ancient Egypt

Thanks to Egypt's warm climate and the rich, fertile land created by the Nile's annual floods, the Egyptians had a wide variety of food and drink available to them. This ranged from bread and beer to poultry, game, and salad vegetables.

◁ **Sharing a drink**
The social aspect of eating and drinking is celebrated in this relief from the Middle Kingdom. It shows a group of men enjoying a drink together using the typical hemispherical cups of the period.

and local brewers. Most Egyptian beer was probably quite low in alcohol content, and it seems to have been drunk in large quantities.

Animals

The most coveted foods were the more expensive forms of animal protein, such as beef, but cattle needed special grazing pastures and were usually kept in large herds that were owned by institutions.

The ancient Egyptians left a wealth of evidence about what they liked to eat and drink. Tomb paintings and models, lists of offerings, animal bones, and storage vessels are just some of the things that reveal which types of food and drink they had at their disposal.

For every Egyptian, whether rich or poor, bread was the staple diet and seems to have been eaten at every meal. It was made from Egypt's abundant supply of emmer wheat and sometimes barley. State workers were often paid in bread and sometimes in grain, which suggests that bread was not just made by official bakers, but also by ordinary people in their homes.

Beer, which was made from the same basic ingredients as bread, was also widely available. It was produced by both large-scale specialists

◁ **Butchery**
Elite tombs were often decorated with scenes of butchery or contained models of a butcher in action. This was to ensure that the tomb owner had a continuous supply of the best meat for eternity.

Sifting flour

"If you have eaten **three loaves** of **bread** and **drunk two jugs** of **beer** and your belly is still hungry, **restrain it**!"

ANCIENT EGYPTIAN WISDOM TEXT

Sheep and goats were more common, but they were probably prized for their milk more than for their meat. The same may be true of ducks and geese, which were valued for their eggs, as well as their meat (although eggs never feature in the lists of food offerings in tombs). Chickens were bred for the same reason, but they were only brought to Egypt in the Late Period.

Archaeological work at sites such as the workmen's village at Amarna has shown that people kept and ate pigs, although they are rarely mentioned as food in either the written or visual records. Similarly, although Greek writers claimed that the Egyptians had a taboo about eating fish, there is plenty of evidence that fish from both the Nile and the sea were caught to eat. These were either consumed right away or split, gutted, and sun-dried to eat later.

WINE MAKING

The Nile Delta and the oases had climates that were suitable for cultivating grapes, so they became centers of wine production. Wine was a luxury item, and wine making was often depicted in the tombs of wealthy people. It was bottled in large jars, called amphorae, which were often marked with details about the vintage. These included the estate on which it was produced; the year in which it was bottled; and references to its quality, which ranged from "good" to "very, very good."

MURAL OF WINE MAKING IN THEBES

Hunting game was another way of supplementing the diet, especially in the earlier periods of Egyptian history, when the Nile Valley was surrounded by savannah lands rather than desert. Different types of antelope were caught for their meat, and some were even successfully bred in captivity.

Vegetables and fruits

The onion was the most common vegetable in Egypt. Garlic and leeks were also in good supply, as were salad vegetables, particularly lettuces and cucumbers. Few Egyptians had a regular source of meat, so most people obtained their protein from legumes, such as lentils, peas, beans, and chickpeas. The range of fruits available was limited compared to modern Egypt, but figs, and especially dates, were popular.

Cooking

The Egyptians' cooking techniques included roasting, baking, and grilling. There is no evidence that they used sauces or combined different types of food to make complicated dishes. The food that they ate was cooked simply and served plain.

Grinding grain with a quern

Mixing flour and water

◁ **Tomb model of a bakery**
Huge quantities of bread were needed to feed the population of Egypt. This tomb model shows a team of bakers at work—in this case, to produce bread for the afterlife.

Medicine

Sickness and health in ancient Egypt

Egyptian doctors were esteemed in the ancient world for their advanced medical skills. Many sources, including some of the earliest medical texts, show that the ancient Egyptians were extremely interested in tackling ill health and disease.

△ **Figure vessel**
The external appearance of a vessel might indicate its magical and/or medical function. This elaborate vase shaped like a kneeling woman might have been made to contain milk to give to a child.

Professional doctors (swnw) appear early in Egyptian history and include senior medical staff, as well as specialists such as ophthalmologists and dentists.

There was a certain overlap between the role of a doctor and that of a priest, because medical training was mainly carried out in temple settings. Although most doctors were men, there were a few female doctors. In fact, unofficially, at a local level, more women might have been involved in areas such as childbirth, where magic and medicine traditionally merged (see pp.120–121).

By the Late Period, embalmers were also listed as doctors, and it is possible that the ancient Egyptians learned about the internal workings of the body from mummifying corpses, although historians may have overestimated the importance of this.

Modern research on the dead bodies of ancient Egyptians has provided fascinating insights into some of the illnesses from which they suffered, especially parasitic infestations and dental disease. Some mummies have even been found with prosthetic toes, showing that the Egyptians made attempts to replace parts of lost limbs.

Medical textbooks

The most advanced forms of medical knowledge are found in some papyri relating to medical matters that have survived. The Kahun Medical Papyrus from the Middle Kingdom is the earliest of these and contains medical advice on matters ranging from veterinary matters to treatment for gynecological problems. Most

◁ **Juniper berries**
Egyptian medical texts often refer to plants to use as medicine when treating illness. Only a small percentage of these, including juniper berries, have been identified with species that are known today.

of the latter are attributed to the problems associated with a "detached and wandering" uterus.

The Edwin Smith Surgical Papyrus from the early New Kingdom was a physician's guide to treating external trauma. It provided a list of symptoms to aid diagnosis and a recommendation of which conditions doctors should "treat," "not treat," or "contend with." The most common recommendation was to allow a patient to recuperate in bed without any form of invasive treatment. The papyrus also advised doctors to treat external wounds with compounds of honey and copper, which had a positive antibacterial effect.

◁ **Tools of the trade**
Hesy-Re was a high official of the 3rd Dynasty who owned a tomb at Saqqara. It contained a series of wooden panels depicting him and lists his titles, one of which reads "Great One of the Dentists."

THE EBERS **MEDICAL PAPYRUS**

Dating from the early New Kingdom, this is an important document in the history of medicine, because it refers to liquids circulating around the body and recognizes the central role played by the heart. The Egyptians thought that, as well as pumping blood and water around the body, the heart also moved a corruptive substance called *wekhdu*. An excess of *wekhdu*, which might present as boils filled with pus, was believed to cause disease and eventually kill a patient. Although this might seem primitive, it was an early attempt to understand the nature of disease.

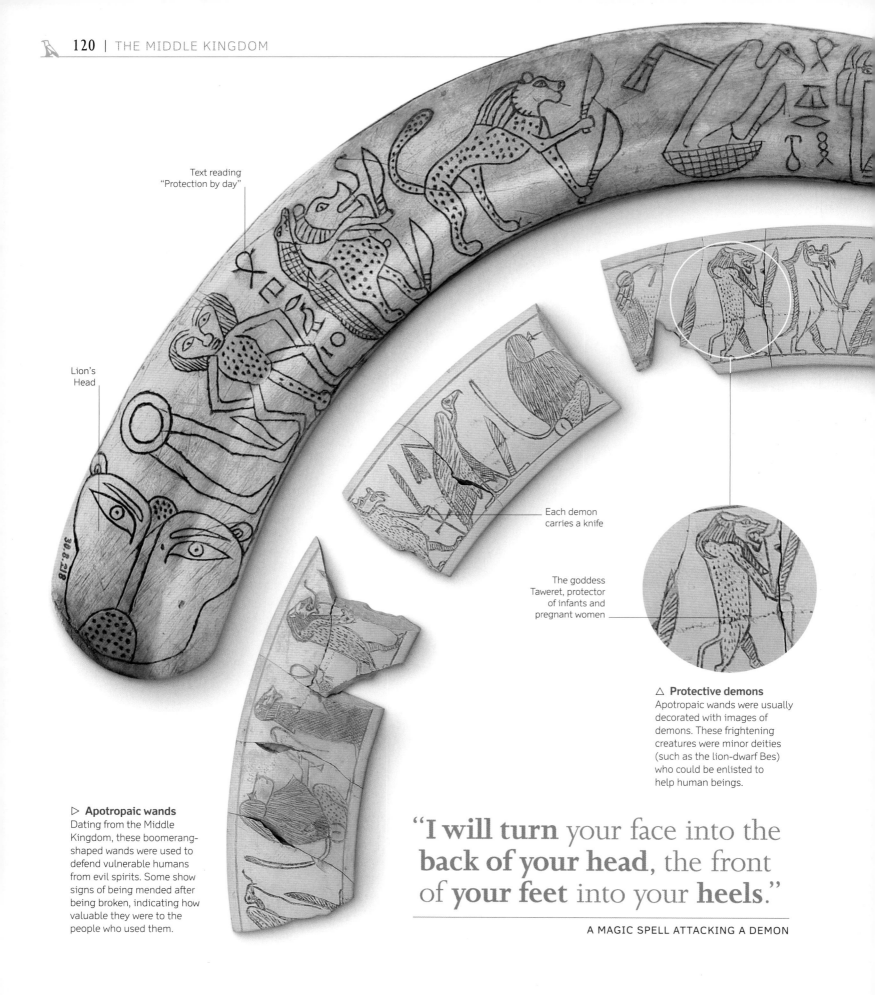

Text reading "Protection by day"

Lion's Head

Each demon carries a knife

The goddess Taweret, protector of infants and pregnant women

△ **Protective demons**
Apotropaic wands were usually decorated with images of demons. These frightening creatures were minor deities (such as the lion-dwarf Bes) who could be enlisted to help human beings.

▷ **Apotropaic wands**
Dating from the Middle Kingdom, these boomerang-shaped wands were used to defend vulnerable humans from evil spirits. Some show signs of being mended after being broken, indicating how valuable they were to the people who used them.

"**I will turn** your face into the **back of your head**, the front of **your feet** into your **heels**."

A MAGIC SPELL ATTACKING A DEMON

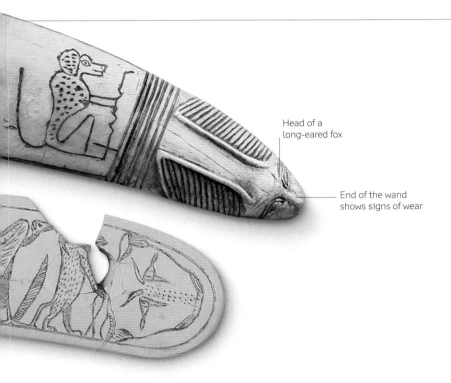

Head of a
long-eared fox

End of the wand
shows signs of wear

Magic wands

Controlling the supernatural world

Thanks to the many texts and images that have survived on temple walls, papyri, and stelae, there is a good deal of information about the official religion of ancient Egypt. Far less is known, however, about the religious practices of ordinary Egyptians, which seem to have been a mixture of religion, magic, superstition, and folk medicine.

Priests and magicians

The highest-ranking magicians of ancient Egypt were Lector Priests, who read out the books of ritual during temple ceremonies. In Egyptian fiction, these men are often depicted as characters who could perform miracles. The priests of Sekhmet, the goddess of healing, were held in particularly high regard for their abilities to cure the sick, as Sekhmet was connected to pestilence and plague.

Texts from Deir el-Medina also refer to local people who acted as "wise women" or "scorpion charmers" in the New Kingdom. Their role seems to have been to protect villagers from evil spirits thought to torment the living with problems ranging from sickness and sudden death to bad luck and being attacked by poisonous creatures.

A remarkable set of objects from the Middle Kingdom provides an insight into how this magic was used. The so-called Magician's Tomb, discovered near the Ramesseum in Thebes, yielded a wooden box that proved to be a treasure trove of magical artifacts of various dates. These included papyri inscribed with magical spells, a wooden statuette of a woman wearing a lion mask and holding two snakes, and a bronze snake-headed wand.

The Magician's Tomb box also contained a group of flat, boomerang-shaped objects made from hippopotamus tusks. Decorated with images of protective demons (many of which carried knives), these wands were probably used to scare off malicious spirits that were intent on doing harm. Exactly how they were used is not known, but they were certainly apotropaic (meant to ward off evil). One of the wands depicts a group of protective demons. The reverse side bears the inscription: "We have come so that we may extend our protection around the healthy child Minhotep."

▽ **Snake wand**
This bronze serpent staff from the Magician's Tomb may represent the goddess Weret-Hekau (meaning "great of magic"). It recalls the staves of the Egyptian magicians in the biblical *Book of Exodus*, which turned into snakes.

Foreign expeditions
New horizons

During the Middle Kingdom, Egypt increasingly looked beyond the Nile Valley and Delta for the resources it needed. Military-style expeditions were sent to quarry and mine, to trade with strong neighbors, and to raid weaker ones.

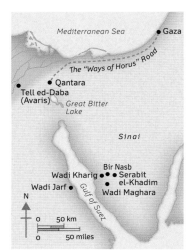

△ **Map of Sinai**
This map of Sinai shows the sites of Egyptian expeditions during the Middle Kingdom. The Egyptians used the north of Sinai as a route into the Levant and beyond, while they exploited the southwest for its mineral resources.

From its very foundation as a state, Egypt had been interested in its neighbors. There is evidence of it suppressing the Nubians and fighting "Easterners" from the 1st Dynasty onward. There are, however, also indications that Egypt's economic interests extended beyond its borders during the Old Kingdom: it traded with Nubia, bought timber from Lebanon, and sent expeditions to quarry stone in the Western Desert. The Egyptians also established sources of valuable or important metals, developing gold mines in the Eastern Desert and copper mines in southern Sinai.

Records show that meanwhile, Egypt was also engaged in military action with various, mostly nomadic groups of people who lived in areas of particular interest to them, such as Sinai and southern Palestine. These people, usually referred to by scholars as "Asiatics," were known to the Egyptians as "Aamu" or "Retenu."

In the Middle Kingdom, Egypt's interest in its neighbors grew. Its conquest of Lower Nubia (see pp.130–131) was an obvious example of this, but there were other areas on which it also set its sights.

Mines and quarries
Egypt stepped up its ambitious mining and quarrying projects throughout the Middle Kingdom. The town of Qasr es-Sagha, north of the Faiyum, was used for quarrying basalt and the Wadi Hammamat, in the Eastern Desert, became an important center of gold production. The copper mines of southern

▷ **Semiprecious stones**
This pectoral (chest ornament) of Princess Sithathoriunut incorporates garnet and carnelian from the Eastern Desert, gold from the Eastern Desert or Nubia, turquoise from Sinai, and dark blue lapis lazuli from Afghanistan.

Sinai probably also reached their peak of production during this period, yielding vast quantities of copper that were shipped back to Egypt. Turquoise, which the Egyptians used to make decorative objects such as jewelry, was also mined there.

The work in Sinai was organized along military lines. At first, expeditions were sent to work at the mines there for a specified time before returning to Egypt, and temporary campsites were set up to house the seasonal workers. An important mountain-top temple built for the goddess Hathor, "Mistress of Turquoise," at the site of Serabit el-Khadim indicates, however, that the Egyptian occupation of Sinai became more permanent.

The Levant
Having expanded into Nubia and successfully exploited Sinai, Egypt took a greater interest in the Levant (an area in the present-day Middle East). It continued to foster its long-term relationship with the Lebanese port city of Byblos, which was a source of good-quality timber, but several sources suggest that the Egyptians also had political interests in the region. Although the *Story of Sinuhe* is fictional, the amount of

background detail in it shows that the Egyptians knew a great deal about the political and economic situation of the Levant (see pp.134–135). The stela of a soldier named Khusobek also reveals that Egypt embarked on several military campaigns in the southern Levant during the 12th Dynasty.

Perhaps the most intriguing evidence of these campaigns is a large block of granite that was used as the base of a statue in Ramesses II's building works at Memphis. The block was covered with an inscription indicating that it was originally part of a 12th Dynasty building. Now known as the Annals of Amenemhat II, this inscription records a series of events that took place during the reign of Amenemhat II.

Among references to visitors from Kush and turquoise arriving from Sinai, it refers to expeditions setting off to and returning from foreign lands. The locations of these lands are not known, but they were probably in the Levant, and the expeditions may have been raiding parties of Egyptian soldiers. Some scholars suggest that these raids went as far north as Syria and possibly even to Cyprus. The main aim of these expeditions may have been to bring back foreign goods, but they were also the precursor to Egypt's far more ambitious imperialist actions in the region at the beginning of the New Kingdom.

MULTICULTURAL **INFLUENCES**

Not all of the people who served on Egypt's mining expeditions were Egyptian. Asiatics based in Egypt were enrolled as guides to the Sinai region, and the mining gangs included local Sinai people who may or may not have worked voluntarily. One remarkable artifact that shows the multicultural nature of these expeditions is a small stone sphinx that was found at the site of Serabit el-Khadim. The sphinx bears two short inscriptions. One is written in Egyptian hieroglyphs, and the other is in Proto-Sinaitic—a lettering system that would later evolve into the first alphabet scripts.

Egyptian hieroglyphs

Proto-Sinaitic script

SANDSTONE SPHINX FROM SERABIT EL-KHADIM

△ **Serabit el-Khadim**
Several kings of the Middle Kingdom, and later those of the New Kingdom, added to the temple of Serabit el-Khadim in southern Sinai. The temple is notable for the stelae erected by both kings and expedition leaders.

Jewelry

Personal ornaments

The Egyptians did not have precious gemstones, such as diamonds, rubies, sapphires, and emeralds, until the Greco-Roman Period. However, they did have access to gold, silver, and semiprecious stones, such as turquoise, lapis lazuli, amethyst, carnelian, and garnet. Colored faience was a cheaper and popular option for jewelry.

◁ **Middle Kingdom anklet**
Claw-shaped pendants made from semiprecious stones such as carnelian are often found in amulets. This gold pendant is set on an anklet of amethyst beads, which were typical of the period.

Amethyst beads

Gold claw

◁ **Broad collar**
Most broad collars were not made of precious materials, but of cheap faience beads. This one from the Middle Kingdom was found in the tomb of a man buried at Thebes.

Sun disk made of carnelian

△ **Scarab ornament**
This unusual ornament shows a scarab beetle in flight. It has elements that can be read as the name of Senwosret II, for whom it may have been made.

Cartouche of King Khyan

▷ **Scarab ring**
Seals shaped like a scarab were often used as a decorative part of jewelry. This one, which shows the base of the scarab, has been set within a gold ring.

◁ **Gold broad collar**
Royal broad collars were more elaborate and were made of gold and beads of semiprecious stones. This falcon-headed broad collar belonged to a 12th Dynasty woman named Senebtisi, who was buried with her jewelry collection at Lisht.

▽ **Gold clasp**
Clasps in the shape of an intricate double knot were popular with the Middle Kingdom upper classes. This particular clasp belonged to the same Senebtisi who was buried wearing the royal broad collar shown below.

Gold head of a falcon

Double-knot clasp

Tear-shaped gold beads

▷ **Gazelle-head diadem**
This unusual diadem, made of gold, carnelian, and colored glass, was found in the tomb of Tuthmosis III's three foreign wives.

Gold gazelle heads

Carnelian and glass rosette

△ **Ring of Nefertiti**
This gold ring bears the name of Nefertiti, but its real owner is not known. It is said to be part of a hoard of jewels found at Amarna.

△ **Wedjat-eye ring**
Most ancient Egyptians wore inexpensive jewelry made of faience. This blue faience ring with a wedjat eye would also have been used as a protective amulet.

▷ **Hinged cuff bracelet**
Wide, cuff-shaped bracelets were popular among elite women of the New Kingdom. This example, made of gold with colored panels, had hinges so that it would fit tightly.

△ **Butterfly bracelets**
Silver was less common than gold in Egypt, so silver jewelry was rare. These silver bracelets inlaid with semiprecious stones belonged to Hetepheres, the mother of Khufu.

Inlaid butterfly

Earring posts for attachment to earlobes

▽ **Faience necklace with *menat***
Some of the necklaces worn by Egyptians were so heavy that they required a *menat*, or counterweight. These were often as decorative as the necklaces themselves.

△ **Ribbed hoop earrings**
Gold earrings with this distinctive ribbed design were popular in the New Kingdom. This pair belonged to one of Tuthmosis III's wives.

Medium-sized faience beads

△ **Decorative earplugs**
Glass was more widely available in the New Kingdom and was used in many different ways. These striking earplugs are made of blue and green glass.

Menat counterweight

Multiple strands of tiny, colored faience beads

The Myth of Osiris

King of Egypt, king of the dead

No god was more important to the Egyptians than Osiris, who became king of the dead. The series of connected stories that make up his myth relate exactly how this came to be.

The ancient Egyptians did not have one core religious text that explained the relationship between humans and the divine. What they had instead was a series of myths in which the gods played the leading roles. These myths explained the world and how people were supposed to behave in it.

One of the most notable aspects of these myths is that the gods are often guilty of bad behavior and have the vices, as well as the virtues, of human beings. Taken as a whole, the myths do not form a coherent narrative. They are often contradictory and sometimes give different versions of the same events. The most important myths of all are those that are associated with the god Osiris.

Creating the world

The story of Osiris begins with a tale about the creation of the world. In the beginning, an island rose

△ **Judging the dead**
As king of the Field of Reeds, Osiris sat in judgment over the dead, who sought to live with him for eternity. Depictions of this process, and its successful outcome (a good afterlife), were often drawn on papyri. The papyrus shown above depicts the judgment of Hunefer, a scribe.

◁ **Seth stela**
Although the god Seth, depicted on the left of this stela, is an aggressive character in the Osiris myth, he was not portrayed as wholly evil. He was also shown as a powerful god who could be worshipped like any other.

"Hail to thee **Osiris**, **Lord of Eternity** and **King** of **Gods**."

FROM THE *GREAT HYMN TO OSIRIS*

thought that he was the rightful heir to the throne. In the ensuing dispute between Horus and Seth, Isis protected Horus until he was old enough to meet his uncle in combat. When he did so, he defeated Seth and finally gained the throne of Egypt.

This myth told the Egyptians many things—how the world was created, how the gods came into being, and why kingship was important to Egypt. It also showed how royal succession should pass from father to son and the importance of being a supportive wife and mother. For most Egyptians, however, the most important aspect of the story was its promise of an afterlife in a kingdom ruled by Osiris—a dead god and also god of the dead.

The kingdom of Osiris

This idea of an afterlife rose from the close association between Osiris and the king. When a king died, he joined with Osiris (became "an Osiris"), while his successor inherited "the Horus-Throne of the Living." The living king was regarded as an embodiment of Horus, so he was divine in nature, but he was also human and formed a link between the gods and humans. An afterlife in the kingdom of Osiris, the Field of Reeds, was also possible for ordinary Egyptians, and they actively prepared for this. For this reason, Osirian beliefs can be found inscribed on Middle Kingdom coffins (see pp.106–107) and in the literature now known as the Book of the Dead (see pp.208–209).

Much of ancient Egyptian burial culture stemmed from this belief in an afterlife. Egyptians decorated their coffins with images of Isis and Nephthys, who protected the body of Osiris and so could protect ordinary people, too. Speculation about the afterlife also led to the creation of shabti figurines. These miniature helpers were buried with the dead to carry out work for them in the underworld (see pp.262–263).

▽ **Osiris and Isis**
This Late Period statue shows the goddess Isis standing behind the smaller figure of her husband, Osiris. Her wings are spread around him to protect him.

from the great sea of chaos, and on it the primeval god Atum appeared. On his own, Atum generated the gods Shu and Tefnut, a brother-and-sister couple, who produced the siblings Geb and Nut. The four children of Geb and Nut were the brothers Osiris and Seth and the sisters Isis and Nephthys. In the next part of the story, Osiris is married to Isis, and Seth is married to Nephthys.

Osiris was the divine king of Egypt, but his popularity attracted the jealousy of Seth, who trapped his brother in an elaborate chest and threw him into the Nile. Isis then tracked down the body of Osiris, only for Seth to dismember and scatter it around Egypt. Isis (aided by Nephthys) recovered the body of her husband and, by magic, put it back together again and revived Osiris enough to become pregnant by him. Osiris then left Egypt and became the god of the dead. Horus, the son of Isis and Osiris, then became the rightful king of Egypt. However, Osiris's brother, Seth, also

▷ **The goddess Nephthys**
Wooden statuettes and other depictions of Isis and Nephthys are often found in tombs from the Middle Kingdom and later. Their purpose was to protect the body of the tomb owner, just as Isis and Nephthys had protected the body of Osiris.

Abydos

Pilgrims at the tomb of Osiris

By the Middle Kingdom, Abydos was regarded as the burial site of Osiris, the god of the afterlife. From then onward, it was an important pilgrimage site for kings and commoners alike.

The growing importance of Osiris as a god of the dead for the whole of Egypt had a dramatic impact on the site of Abydos in the Middle Kingdom. The Msyth of Osiris (see pp.126–127) described the death, dismemberment, and burial of the god, and Abydos was regarded as the place where he was buried. The exact spot was thought to be the 1st Dynasty royal tomb of King Djer, at the Umm el-Qa'ab cemetery. Perhaps, by the Middle Kingdom, vague memories of early royal burial at Abydos had combined with the idea of a mythic time when gods ruled Egypt to create a sense of a special location.

The festival of Osiris

The main center of worship for Osiris was his cult temple in the town of Abydos. Between the temple and the tomb at the Umm el-Qa'ab (known in the Middle Kingdom as Peker), there was a valley between two low plateaus now known as the North and Middle cemeteries. The North Cemetery was where the Early Dynastic kings had built huge funerary enclosures, one of which, the Shunet ez-Zebib, was still visible in the Middle Kingdom (see pp.46–47).

A processional route 1 mile (2 km) long ran along the valley floor between the Osiris Temple and Peker. This was used during an annual festival, now known as the Mysteries of Osiris, that was similar in character to a medieval passion play. The idea behind the festival was to transport the dead Osiris from his temple to his tomb, where he remained

◁ **Sihathor statue**
This block statue of an official named Sihathor was found among a range of monuments in a mahat-chapel. He is shown in the patient pose of a pilgrim, squatting on the ground, with his cloak wrapped around him.

overnight. He was then brought back to life and taken back to his temple. Most of what is known about these events comes from a stela left at Abydos by an official named Ikhernofret. He was sent to Abydos by Senwosret III (who also had a tomb built for himself there) to renovate the temple and, especially, the sacred boat in which Osiris was carried, and to reorganize the sacred drama of the Osiris festival.

Many Egyptians wished to visit Abydos during the festival as pilgrims witnessing the miraculous rebirth of Osiris. By doing this, they hoped to receive favors from the god for their afterlives. They also wanted to be present at Abydos forever, so, like Ikhernofret, they erected stone stelae there, which listed their names and possibly those of their families. To make sure that these stelae (and sometimes statues) could be seen by Osiris during his procession, they placed them in small mud-brick structures called mahat-chapels, overlooking the processional route. The largest chapels contained collections of stelae and statues belonging to several generations of the same family.

The slope of the North Cemetery, which was considered a very desirable position to have a

Amenysonb raises his arms in prayer

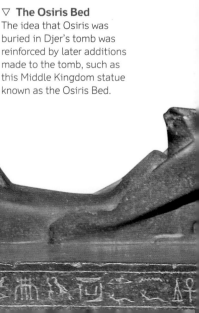

▽ **The Osiris Bed**
The idea that Osiris was buried in Djer's tomb was reinforced by later additions made to the tomb, such as this Middle Kingdom statue known as the Osiris Bed.

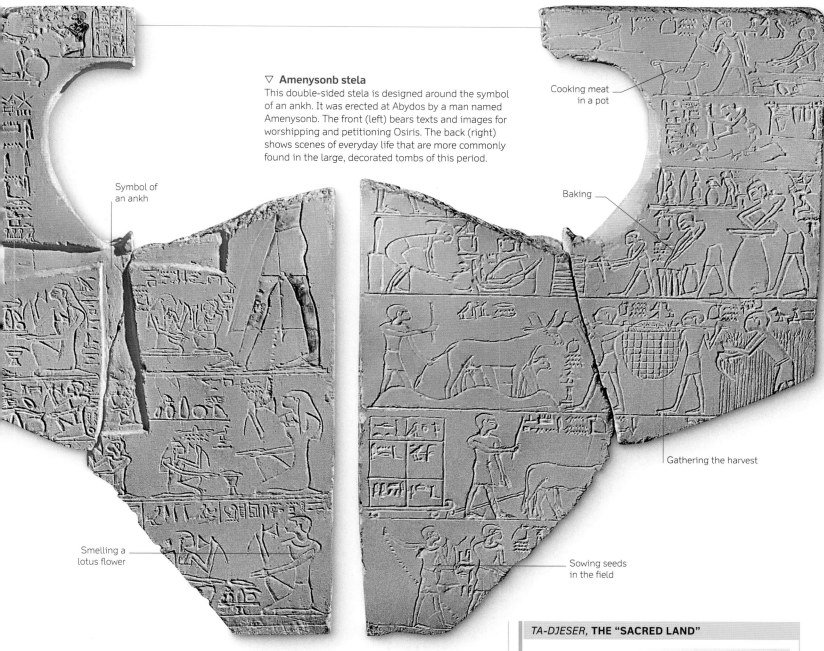

▽ **Amenysonb stela**
This double-sided stela is designed around the symbol of an ankh. It was erected at Abydos by a man named Amenysonb. The front (left) bears texts and images for worshipping and petitioning Osiris. The back (right) shows scenes of everyday life that are more commonly found in the large, decorated tombs of this period.

Cooking meat in a pot

Symbol of an ankh

Baking

Gathering the harvest

Smelling a lotus flower

Sowing seeds in the field

mahat-chapel, was called the Terrace of the Great God. There, both robbers and archaeologists have recovered thousands of stelae, whose inscriptions have provided the most important evidence of the genealogy and religious customs of ordinary people during the Middle Kingdom.

"I made my **mahat-chapel** upon the Terrace of the Great God **to see the god every day**."

DECLARATION ON A MIDDLE KINGDOM STELA FROM ABYDOS

TA-DJESER, THE "SACRED LAND"

The necropolis at Abydos was one of the most important burial sites in ancient Egypt because of the presence of the Tomb of Osiris at the Umm el-Qa'ab. In the Middle Kingdom, the northern part of the site was dominated by the Terrace of the Great God (referring to Osiris) with its hundreds of tombs and mud-brick mahat-chapels. In the New Kingdom, the so-called "Portal Temple" of Ramesses II was built (above) close to the main temple of Osiris, giving access to the Terrace.

Egypt and Nubia

The first Egyptian empire

Egypt's most important neighbor was Nubia, which had considerable mineral wealth. In the Middle Kingdom, Egypt moved to conquer Lower Nubia, thereby creating an empire, and built forts to defend its new territory.

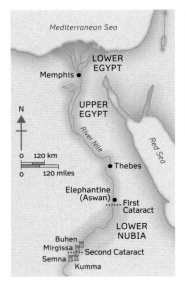

△ **Map of Nubia**
This map roughly shows the extent of Lower Nubia. Egyptian control of Lower Nubia in the Middle Kingdom was based on a system of fortresses built close to the Second Cataract of the Nile.

Egypt's relationship with Nubia was governed by two major factors: opportunity and threat. With extensive natural resources, including gold, and trade routes leading farther south into Africa, Nubia offered riches that contributed to the wealth of Egypt. However, left to itself, Nubia could develop into a powerful kingdom, like Egypt itself. For these reasons, from the Early Dynastic period onward, Egypt tried to control or destabilize Nubia by any means possible, including by military force.

During the Old Kingdom, Egypt was relatively successful in controlling Nubia, exploiting quarries in Nubia's Western Desert and establishing a trading center at Buhen, near the Second Cataract of the Nile. It was only during the Middle Kingdom, however, that Egypt tried to conquer and hold territory in Nubia, creating the first Egyptian empire.

The conquest of Nubia

Although Montuhotep II's greatest achievement was to reunify Egypt by defeating his Herakleopolitan rivals, he also carried out a series of military campaigns farther south as part of a policy that would be continued by his successors. The aim of this policy seemed to be to reduce the power of the Nubians, who had been encroaching on Egypt's traditional southern boundary during the First Intermediate Period, but this largely punitive action in

Lower Nubia soon developed into something that went far beyond the ambitions of the Old Kingdom kings, even at the height of their power.

Amenemhat I claimed to have conquered Lower Nubia (Wawat) by the 29th year of his reign. His son, Senwosret I, then started to build fortresses in the region, notably at Buhen, which became the greatest fortress-town of Middle Kingdom Nubia. Under Senwosret III, many more fortresses were built, especially around the natural frontier of the Second Cataract. These fortresses were constructed on rocky outcrops overlooking the Nile, such as Semna and Kumma, or on islands in the river, such as Uronarti. Buhen and Mirgissa meanwhile became heavily defended trading posts. As a result of all this building, Lower Nubia was brought firmly under Egyptian

Remnants of black paint

▷ **Egyptian soldiers**
This model of Egyptian soldiers was found in the tomb of an 11th Dynasty Egyptian nomarch named Meshety next to a model of Nubian archers. In Middle Kingdom Egypt, the military included both Egyptian soldiers and Nubian mercenaries.

◁ **Nubian tribute bearers**
This scene from an Egyptian private tomb of the New Kingdom shows Nubians bearing large quantities of gold in tribute. The Nubian gold mines were far more productive than those in Egypt's Eastern Desert and were the main reason for Egypt's interest in annexing Nubia.

Basket of gold nuggets

Large gold chains

control, and Egypt was able to defend its new southern border against attack from the Upper Nubians who lived farther south.

Semna and Kush

Semna Fort played a strategic role in Egypt's defense plans. A set of stelae erected by Senwosret III proclaim that Semna was to act as a checkpoint to prevent Nubians from the south—primarily economic migrants—entering the territory controlled by Egypt unless they were coming to carry out closely controlled trading at Mirgissa.

Various reports sent from Semna to the southern administration at Thebes have also survived and describe what happened at Semna. Written on papyrus, these Semna Dispatches, as they are

known, describe Egyptian patrols scouting around Semna in search of unwelcome Nubians and the Medjay people who lived in the desert.

Although Lower Nubia was now firmly under Egyptian control, the huge area to the south of the Second Cataract that the Egyptians called Kush held onto its independence. During the Middle Kingdom, and particularly during the Second Intermediate Period, Kush saw urban expansion around key sites such as Kerma and Sai. These sites became the basis of an administration that may have been a kingdom itself, although there are no written records from Kush at this time. It was too strong for the Egyptians to defeat in any case, and later, in the Second Intermediate Period, it would go on to become a threat to southern Egypt.

▽ **Bread token**
The administration of the Nubian fortresses included systems for the distribution of food to the soldiers, like this token for loaves of bread.

Buhen Fortress

The nucleus of the Nubian defenses

The fortress-town of Buhen was one of the most impressive feats of military architecture from ancient Egypt. It had been a small trading center in the Old Kingdom, but in the Middle Kingdom, it became the centerpiece of a sophisticated group of fortified settlements and smaller forts around the Second Cataract of the Nile. Buhen was built on the riverbank and consisted of an outer town and an inner citadel. It was designed to be capable of withstanding any attack mounted by the Nubians, but it does not seem to have seen major action. It was abandoned in the Second Intermediate Period, but occupied again in the New Kingdom.

▽ **Buhen reconstructed**
Most of our evidence for Buhen comes from the extensive excavations that took place there between 1957 and 1964. This work was an attempt to excavate and record as much as possible of the site before it was destroyed by Lake Nasser.

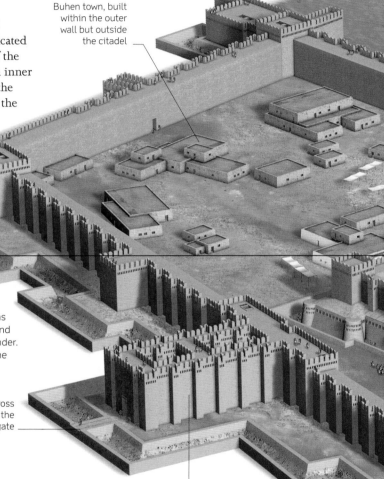

Buhen town, built within the outer wall but outside the citadel

Bridge across the moat into the outer western gate

The weakest part of the outer wall, its entrance, was defended by the huge outer western gate

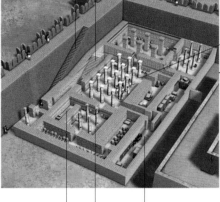

Staircase to ramparts

Staircase to second floor

Columned Hall

Garrison commander's bedroom

Living room

Storage area (possibly for weapons)

◁ **Command center**
A large and distinctive building in the northwest corner of the citadel was probably the garrison headquarters and the residence of the garrison commander. A staircase provided easy access to the ramparts of the citadel.

A FORTRESS OF MUD

The strong, thick walls of Buhen were made of unfired mud brick, which was easily available and quick to build with. It is estimated that over 4.6 million bricks were used in its construction. Unfortunately, after the Aswan High Dam was built, the fortress was submerged by Lake Nasser and its walls turned back into mud.

RUIN OF BUHEN FORTRESS

A drawbridge crossed the ditch here

Two massive towers extended the entrance passage to make it easier to defend

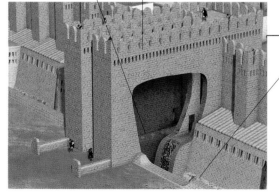

The gateway crossed the inner ditch

◁ **Inner western gate**
The most elaborate defenses at Buhen appear in the inner western gate. Two tall towers flank a passageway that had at least four doors, and a drawbridge, which ran on rollers over the ditch.

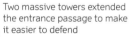

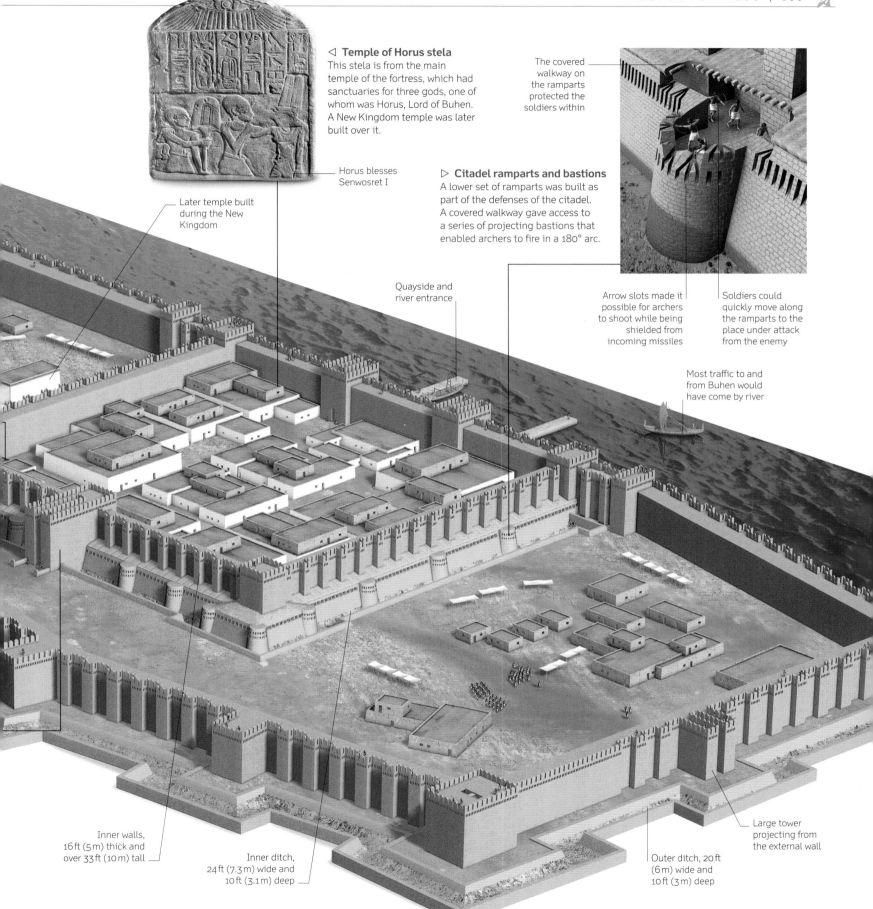

◁ Temple of Horus stela
This stela is from the main temple of the fortress, which had sanctuaries for three gods, one of whom was Horus, Lord of Buhen. A New Kingdom temple was later built over it.

Horus blesses Senwosret I

The covered walkway on the ramparts protected the soldiers within

▷ Citadel ramparts and bastions
A lower set of ramparts was built as part of the defenses of the citadel. A covered walkway gave access to a series of projecting bastions that enabled archers to fire in a 180° arc.

Later temple built during the New Kingdom

Quayside and river entrance

Arrow slots made it possible for archers to shoot while being shielded from incoming missiles

Soldiers could quickly move along the ramparts to the place under attack from the enemy

Most traffic to and from Buhen would have come by river

Inner walls, 16 ft (5 m) thick and over 33 ft (10 m) tall

Inner ditch, 24 ft (7.3 m) wide and 10 ft (3.1 m) deep

Outer ditch, 20 ft (6 m) wide and 10 ft (3 m) deep

Large tower projecting from the external wall

Storytelling

The varied delights of Egyptian literature

The literature of ancient Egypt is a rich treasury of imaginative stories about gods and people, talking animals, magical realism, long journeys, and the eventual triumph of right over wrong.

Ancient Egypt was one of the first civilizations to create fiction. Some of its stories read like fairytales, some are like religious texts about the exploits of the gods, and others reflect the everyday experiences of ordinary Egyptians. It is difficult to assess Egyptian literature as a whole, however, because the only stories to survive are those that were written down, often as training exercises for young scribes. Stories were usually told out loud and passed down from one generation to the next.

Storytelling might have been a common form of entertainment both in villages and palaces, and the stories are a blend of comedy and tragedy, with a moral element. The tradition of Egyptian storytelling seems to have been established in the Middle Kingdom, but it developed later.

Travelers' tales

A common theme in Egyptian stories is travel. The most popular—and most copied—tale is the *Story of Sinuhe*, about a courtier who flees Egypt and makes a new life for himself among the tribes of Lebanon. After many adventures, Sinuhe returns to Egypt to ensure that he has a proper burial. The moral of this story seems to be that there is no place like home. Sinuhe's tale follows the same format as the tomb autobiographies of high-ranking officials in the Middle and New Kingdom Egypt, and this, together with the historical accuracy of the background detail, has made scholars wonder if Sinuhe was a real person.

Another tale in the same tradition is the *Voyage of Wenamun*. Written at the end of the New Kingdom, it tells the story of Wenamun, an official, who also

△ **Uraeus**
The rearing cobra was a symbol of royalty worn by kings and queens. The role of the snake in *Shipwrecked Sailor* reflects the ambiguity that Egyptians felt toward snakes—they were regarded as both good and bad.

◁ **Woman and crocodile**

This illustration shows a woman drinking close to a crocodile—a creature that could represent retribution in Egyptian literature. In one story, a priest creates a crocodile from wax to eat the lover of his adulterous wife.

travels to Lebanon, but this time by ship to find timber for the temple of Amen at Karnak. It is thought by some to be an account of a real trading mission, as the problems that Wenamun encounters with people he meets reflect Egypt's diminished status in the Eastern Mediterranean at that time.

In a less realistic vein, the *Shipwrecked Sailor* tells of a traveler who is cast away on an island inhabited by a huge talking snake. In a story within the story, the snake tells a sad tale of how he came to be alone after his family was killed by a falling star. Unlike the snake, the sailor eventually returns home and is reunited with his family.

Stories with a moral

Another theme of many Egyptian stories is men and gods behaving badly. In the *Destruction of Mankind*, the god Ra, angry with humans for rebelling against him, transforms his daughter Hathor into the ferocious god Sekhmet and sends her to kill every human being. Ra then realizes that he has made a mistake. He is only able to stop Hathor-Sekhmet by mixing a large quantity of beer with a red dye and pouring it over the earth. Convinced that she is drinking the blood of humans, Hathor-Sekhmet becomes drunk and is unable to continue her slaughter.

In many stories, kings are also shown to have human weaknesses. In one of a group of tales, called *Wondrous Tales*, King Snefru devises some

entertainment for himself—being rowed across a lake in a boat by beautiful maidens clad only in fishing nets. The king's idyllic day is spoiled when one of the maidens drops her turquoise fish-shaped pendant into the lake. Fortunately, the famous magician Djadjaemankh is on hand to help and simply rolls back the lake to retrieve the pendant.

The actions of the characters in these stories may have caused a lively debate among Egyptian listeners. There is certainly a strong moral sense in many of the tales. Those who do wrong are usually punished at the conclusion of the story, particularly if they have done something that would have been frowned upon in Egyptian society. Likewise, good actions are rewarded, and shrewdness is shown to be a virtue.

One story that seems to have been deeply rooted in the everyday experience of most Egyptians is *The Eloquent Peasant*. In this tale, a simple man is traveling with a donkey laden with goods to sell. As he travels from place to place, he is beset by problems caused by spiteful, petty bureaucrats, which he tries to solve simply by speaking persuasively. Unlike many Egyptian stories, this one must have struck a chord with listeners, who may have experienced similar struggles with difficult local officials.

△ **Fish pendant**

The piece of jewelry at the heart of the story about Snefru and the pendant may have been inspired by fish pendants such as the one shown.

△ **Sinuhe ostracon**

Judging by the number of copies that have survived, the *Story of Sinuhe* was very popular in ancient Egypt. Versions have been found written on papyrus and, as here, on limestone ostraca.

SCRIBES

Very few people in ancient Egypt were able to read or write, possibly only around 5 percent of the population. Being literate gave people (men) access to careers that were only available to the highest social classes—the government, the priesthood, and the highest ranks of the army. Literacy was a badge of the ruling class in ancient Egypt throughout its entire history, but it was particularly important during the New Kingdom because it enabled a talented, literate scribe from the provinces to rise through the ranks of society to become an important minister of state. Scribes were trained in several different places, including temple schools, but the most important start in life for an educated Egyptian was to have a parent—invariably a father—who was himself literate.

SCRIBES FROM THE TOMB OF HOREMHEB

Time of unrest

The Second Intermediate Period

At the end of the Middle Kingdom, Egypt was threatened by Asiatics from the north and Nubians from the south. The following period of turmoil is known as the Second Intermediate Period. Only the Thebans stood up to the invaders.

The 13th Dynasty was very different from the 12th, when a small number of related kings had enjoyed relatively long reigns. The 13th Dynasty lasted for 123 years and had up to 50 kings, most of whom must have reigned for a very short time. It is unlikely that all of these kings came from the same family. There may have been a system of elective kingship, in which people from important families took turns being king.

As a result, the 13th Dynasty was weak. Two of the kings, Ameny-Qemau and Khendjer, made modest attempts to build pyramids at Dahshur and South Saqqara, and Neferhotep I was active at Abydos, which remained an important destination for pilgrims. However, the 13th Dynasty was essentially a time when the authority of the kings broke down and Egypt fell under the control of foreign rulers.

The Hyksos

During the 12th and 13th Dynasties, large numbers of Asiatics arrived in Egypt. Some were seminomadic people, and others were slaves that Egyptian soldiers

◁ **Wooden statue of King Hor**
This statue of the 13th Dynasty king Hor was designed to house the king's *ka* after his death. The hieroglyph for *ka* was a pair of raised arms, which are seen here attached to the king's head.

had captured on their raids into foreign lands. The Asiatics' wealth of local knowledge made them valuable to the Egyptians, who used them as scouts on their expeditions to Sinai and the Levant (an area in the present-day Middle East).

A large Asiatic community settled and grew in the eastern Delta, at a site later known as the city of Avaris. As central royal authority declined during the 13th Dynasty, Avaris was gradually taken over by Canaanites, who already controlled much of the southern Levant. When the 13th Dynasty finally drew to a close, these Canaanites proclaimed themselves kings based in the eastern Delta, but they harbored ambitions to control the whole of Egypt. At some stage, they controlled great swathes of territory, including the Nile Valley and Delta and areas to the south of Thebes.

△ **Worshipping Montu**
Sobekemsaf II, a 17th Dynasty king, extensively restored the temple of Montu, a Theban warrior god, at Medamud, north of Thebes. In this relief from the temple, the king is shown worshipping Montu, alongside the god Amen.

ASIATICS AT **BENI HASAN**

Excavations carried out at the site of Tell ed-Daba (Avaris) in the eastern Delta have produced the most telling evidence of Asiatics being in Egypt during the Late Middle Kingdom. The immigration of people from the east was not, however, a sudden phenomenon. Small groups of Asiatics had been making their way into Egypt throughout the Middle Kingdom, as this scene from the tomb of Khnumhotep II at Beni Hasan shows. It depicts a band of colorfully dressed Aamu Asiatics, led by a man named Absha. The metalworking equipment strapped to one of the donkeys suggests that they might have been a group of itinerant tinkers.

AN ASIATIC FAMILY IN EGYPT

These Canaanite kings later became known as the Hyksos, a term that comes from an Egyptian word meaning "rulers of foreign lands," and they formed the 15th Dynasty. (Very little is known about the 14th Dynasty.) The Hyksos were probably few in number compared to the native population of Egypt, but they nevertheless ruled for around a century. They presented themselves as kings of Egypt and inscribed their names in royal cartouches in monumental texts, just as the kings before them had, possibly to convince the Egyptians under their control that not much had changed. The best-known Hyksos rulers were Sheshi, Khyan, and Apepi.

The rise of Kush
The 13th Dynasty kings also failed to follow the exhortations of Senwosret III, who commanded on his stelae at Semna that Egypt should maintain its boundaries in Nubia forever. Instead, Egypt gradually lost control over Lower Nubia, especially in the face of aggression from the Kushites, who were now a formidable power in their own right, as shown by the increasing size of Kerma (one of the largest archaeological sites in ancient Nubia). The Kushites took control of the Egyptian fortresses in Nubia and claimed the region for themselves. The danger to Egypt was clear—the Kushites wanted to expand their territory, so southern Egypt was now vulnerable.

The 16th and 17th Dynasties
The Hyksos' domination of northern Egypt led to the end of the 13th Dynasty, and they ruled as the 15th Dynasty. Meanwhile, the 16th Dynasty, the true successors of the 13th, ruled southern Egypt from Thebes, with around 14 kings over a period of 60 or 70 years. This dynasty was followed by the 17th. Founded by Rahotep, a king of unknown origin, this new Theban dynasty also had a rapid succession of kings, but it clearly had a mission: to expel Egypt's foreign rulers and to reunite the country under its leadership. When it eventually achieved this, the 17th Dynasty came to an end and the New Kingdom began.

△ **Scarab of Khyan**
The Hyksos kings announced their presence throughout Egypt by issuing small scarab seals and amulets. These were engraved with hieroglyphs of their names set in cartouches, like those of the kings preceding them.

> ## "Prince Apepi was in Avaris and all the land paid tribute to him."

THE QUARREL OF APEPI AND SEKENENRE

4

The Early New Kingdom

c.1550–1295 BCE

The Early New Kingdom

Although King Ahmose was a member of the Theban 17th Dynasty, he is regarded as the founder of 18th Dynasty, and therefore of the New Kingdom. This is because his reign, which began in 1550 BCE, represented a new beginning for Egypt. By expelling the Hyksos from Avaris (Tell ed-Daba), their east Delta capital, and reunifying Egypt, he ended the political fragmentation of the Second Intermediate Period.

The Egyptian Empire

Ahmose's military exploits set an example for the kings who followed him, as they conquered territories in Nubia and the Levant, bringing them under direct Egyptian control. In Nubia, the conquest was total, as the Egyptian forces fought their way up the Nile until there were no more opponents left. The new territory that they gained was rich in gold and brought Egypt great wealth. In the Levant, Egyptian kings conquered lands as far north as Syria, but this brought them into conflict with the kingdom of Mitanni, and later the Hittites. The shifting balance of power between Egypt and these two kingdoms dominated foreign relations for the rest of the New Kingdom.

Monument makers

The kings of the 18th Dynasty were eager to celebrate their achievements, including their military victories, and to emulate the great buildings of earlier kings. However, these New Kingdom rulers also had ideas of their own, particularly with regard to the form that a royal tomb should take. They abandoned pyramids in favor of tombs cut into the rock of the Valley of the Kings and built conspicuous monuments in the form of huge temples. These were sometimes additions to temples that already existed, especially the Amen-Ra complex at Karnak, but many kings also built new temples for themselves—their mortuary temples. As a result of all this building work, fueled by the kings' desire to be close to Amen-Ra (now the principal god of the Egyptian pantheon), Thebes became the most important site in Egypt in terms of monuments. High-ranking Egyptians continued to be buried in heavily decorated tombs at Thebes, as well as at Saqqara, near Egypt's administrative capital, Memphis.

A time of change

Due to their monuments, which contain extensive summaries of their achievements, far more is known about the individual New Kingdom kings and how they wished to be remembered than about the monarchs of earlier periods. Tuthmosis III, for example, appeared as a great warrior, and Amenhotep III as a king at a time when Egypt was a superpower. Hatshepsut was represented as a successful female king, and Akhenaten as a ruler with a unique religious vision.

Archaeologists have also, however, uncovered other kinds of evidence that reveal some fascinating information about the New Kingdom. These include the ruins of Amarna, one of ancient Egypt's best-known cities; diplomatic correspondence; new types of burial goods; and paintings and artifacts illustrating the lavish lives led by the elite. Most striking of all was the spectacular tomb of Tutankhamen, which was discovered in the Valley of the Kings.

◁ **Gold statuette from the tomb of Tutankhamen**

1492 BCE Tuthmosis I becomes the first king to be buried in the Valley of the Kings

1458 BCE Tuthmosis III becomes sole king, and wins the Battle of Megiddo

1550 BCE Ahmose defeats the Hyksos and reunites Egypt

1504 BCE Tuthmosis I becomes king. He then conquers territory from Syria to Sudan

1473 BCE Hatshepsut, the most successful female king, takes the throne

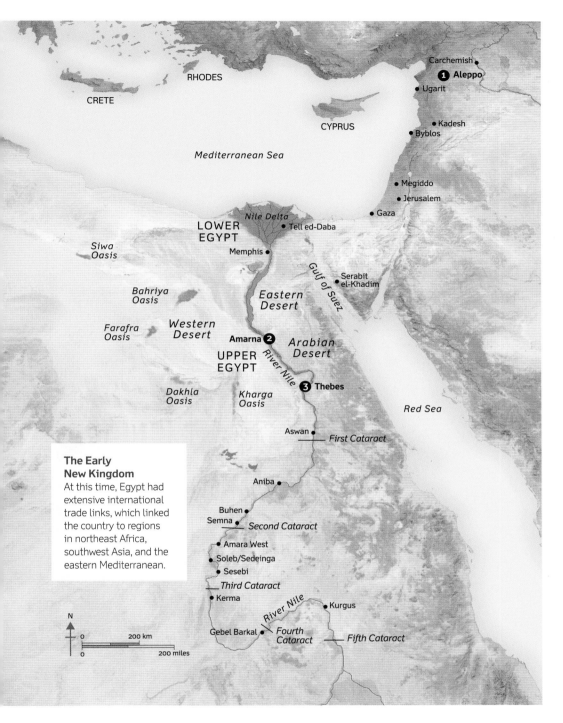

CRETE

RHODES

CYPRUS

Carchemish

1 **Aleppo**

Ugarit

Kadesh

Byblos

Mediterranean Sea

Megiddo

Jerusalem

Gaza

Nile Delta

LOWER EGYPT

Tell ed-Daba

Siwa Oasis

Memphis

Serabit el-Khadim

Gulf of Suez

Eastern Desert

Bahriya Oasis

Farafra Oasis

Western Desert

Amarna **2**

Arabian Desert

UPPER EGYPT

River Nile

Dakhla Oasis

Kharga Oasis

Thebes **3**

Red Sea

Aswan —— *First Cataract*

Aniba

Buhen

Semna —— *Second Cataract*

Amara West

Soleb/Sedeinga

Sesebi

Third Cataract

Kerma

River Nile

Kurgus

Gebel Barkal

Fourth Cataract

Fifth Cataract

The Early New Kingdom

At this time, Egypt had extensive international trade links, which linked the country to regions in northeast Africa, southwest Asia, and the eastern Mediterranean.

N

0 —— 200 km

0 —— 200 miles

1 Syrians bringing horses as tribute

2 Official's house, Amarna

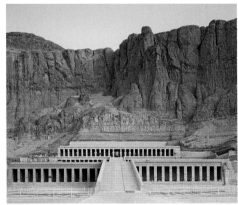

3 Hatshepsut's mortuary temple, Thebes

1390 BCE Amenhotep III becomes king. The peak of Egyptian international power

1336 BCE Tutankhamen becomes king, and abandons Amarna

1427 BCE Amenhotep II becomes king, and makes peace with the Mitanni

1352 BCE Amenhotep IV (Akhenaten) becomes king, and founds the city of Amarna

1295 BCE Death of Horemheb, the last king of the 18th Dynasty

Expelling the Hyksos
Egypt reunified

The Hyksos rulers had to be defeated and their capital at Avaris captured before Egypt could be reunified under an Egyptian king. The experience of that war influenced Egypt's view of the world during the New Kingdom.

The only effective resistance to foreign powers trying to carve up Egypt in the Second Intermediate Period was mounted by the Thebans, who continued to fight both the Hyksos and the Kushites. They also claimed to be the kings of Egypt and are now known as the 17th Dynasty. The state of Egypt at the time is clearly depicted on stelae erected by Kamose, the last of these Theban kings. When describing his wars against the Hyksos, he refers to himself as "sitting joined with an Asiatic and a Nubian, each man having his own share of this Egypt." The military struggle was long, hard, and sporadic for several generations.

One of the most telling and gruesome pieces of evidence for this is the body of Kamose's predecessor, Sekenenre Taa II. His skull was riven with holes that

△ **Kamose dagger**
Distinctively shaped daggers such as this seem to have been prized by high-ranking Egyptian officers during the war with the Hyksos. This dagger was found with the mummy of Kamose.

▷ **Ahmose I ax**
One of the most striking objects in the cache of burial goods from the tomb of Queen Ahhotep was this ceremonial gold ax. It celebrates the victories of her son, Ahmose.

Ahmose I in the form of a sphinx

look as if they were made by a Hyksos battle-ax. Kamose himself did not live to see the ultimate victory over the Hyksos. The Kamose stelae describe one of the strategies adopted by the Thebans against their enemies—they seized control of the Western Desert oases to prevent the Hyksos and the Kushites from communicating, making it effectively impossible for them to coordinate their attacks on the Thebans.

Ahmose the soldier
A dramatic piece of evidence for the Thebans' eventual victory over their Hyksos and Nubian enemies comes not from a royal monument, but from an autobiographical text from a private tomb. Ahmose, son of Ibana, came from the town of el-Kab, south of Thebes, and was a career soldier at a time of intense

AHMOSE, SON OF IBANA

Although it was considered inappropriate to depict scenes of battle in private tombs, there was no reluctance to celebrate a soldier's career in text. An entire wall of the tomb of the career soldier Ahmose, son of Ibana, at el-Kab, is covered with an extensive account of his life spent fighting the enemies of successive Egyptian kings, including the Hyksos, the Nubians, and Egyptian rebels. His successes, which brought him royal rewards and loot taken from his enemies, made his family rich. This made it possible for him to have a large and impressive tomb in which to immortalize his achievements.

"When **Avaris was besieged**, I fought on foot in the presence of **His Majesty**."

AHMOSE AT THE HYKSOS CAPITAL

military activity. His tomb biography describes how he rose through the ranks and was rewarded by successive kings. A wealthy man, he eventually retired to el-Kab, where his grandson built a tomb for him. Ahmose served under Ahmose I, Amenhotep I, and Tuthmosis I, following in the footsteps of his father, who had served under Sekenenre Taa II.

Ahmose saw service mainly as a marine, operating from fighting boats on the Nile. His first posting as a young man was on a ship named *The Wild Bull*, but he also refers to fighting on foot and accompanying the king "when he rode about on his chariot." This shows that new forms of military equipment (chariots only first appeared in Egypt in the Second Intermediate Period) along with combined land/water operations were being employed by the Theban army to defeat a strong and entrenched enemy.

Egypt reunited

The Thebans managed to drive the Hyksos north from the territory that they controlled in Middle Egypt. They then successfully laid siege to the Hyksos capital at Avaris and eventually captured it. Egypt was finally liberated from foreign occupation.

This had several significant consequences. The victorious Thebans were now the kings of a united Egypt, and they established a new dynasty, the 18th Dynasty, which would last for more than 250 years. This dynasty was, however, defined in its early reigns by continued military activity. It was not enough to simply drive the foreigners out of Egypt; they had to be pursued and crushed and their territories brought under the direct control of a new and extensive Egyptian empire.

The wings of Horus, "Lord of the Sky"

▷ **Kamose stela**
This is one of two stelae erected by Kamose at Karnak. They describe details of the war against the Hyksos during his short reign.

In this cartouche, the king refers to himself as Kamose the Brave

Weapons and warfare

Military equipment from ancient Egypt

Until the Second Intermediate Period, the weaponry of the Egyptian army was relatively unsophisticated. That changed when more technologically advanced weaponry, such as the chariot and sharper swords and axes, was needed to combat dangerous enemies such as the Hyksos, the Mitanni, and the Hittites.

Rock-crystal pommel

Wooden handle with bronze studs

▽ Golden dagger sheath

Weapons, especially royal weapons, were sometimes decorated with expensive materials, as this finely embossed gold sheath for Tutankhamen's iron dagger shows.

▷ Bronze dagger

This type of dagger, with its distinctive handle, was typical of the Second Intermediate Period and early New Kingdom. It seems to have been carried by high-status troops and officers.

Bronze blade with reinforced central rib

△ Ceremonial shield

Like many military states, the ancient Egyptians made some weapons not for the battlefield, but for parade and display. This ceremonial shield depicts Tutankhamen as a sphinx crushing his Nubian enemies.

◁ Arrowhead

Egyptian armies relied on archers for much of their firepower on the battlefield. Arrow shafts were usually made from reeds and arrow heads were made from flint; bone; wood; and, more rarely, metal.

◁ Tutankhamen's dagger

Although the elaborate handle immediately attracts attention, an Egyptian would have noticed that the blade was made from a metal even rarer than gold—iron.

△ Chariot of Yuya

Elite chariot regiments in the New Kingdom rode these light, fast vehicles, drawn by two horses. This rare example belonged to Yuya, the chariot officer who was the father of Queen Tiy.

A single shaft connected the carriage to the horses

▽ *Khepesh* sword

The *khepesh*, or "sickle sword," was a weapon used right across the Near East. It was particularly favored by Egyptian kings during the New Kingdom.

Blade and handle made from a single piece of bronze

Shield painted
to look like
cowhide

▽ **Golden flies**
The Egyptians awarded some items
of jewelry as military decorations.
Known as the "Gold of the Brave,"
they might have included these
gold fly amulets.

▷ **Self bow**
Archers were an important
part of the Egyptian army.
Most bows, especially
those for foot archers rather
than charioteers, were self
bows—made from a single
piece of wood.

The symbolism of the
flies is unknown, but
they may have been
associated with war

◁ **Model shield
and spears**
These models from the
Middle Kingdom show some
of the typical weapons of the
period, including the large,
round-topped shield that was
made of cowhide.

Spear case also
made of cowhide

Ax-head attached
to the haft with
binding

Socket for
attachment to
the haft

△ **"Duckbill" ax**
The modern name for this ax-head is
derived from its shape. Originating in
present-day Syria/Palestine, this Hyksos
ax was more efficient than the D-shaped
Egyptian axes.

Carriage for two people:
a driver and a warrior

▷ **Middle Kingdom ax**
An example of the relatively
simple technology of Egyptian
weaponry before the New
Kingdom, this weapon has a
long cutting edge attached to
a handle, but it could not be
swung with much force.

◁ **New Kingdom ax**
This type of ax was a big
improvement on earlier
axes. Its shape, weight,
and curved blade made
it a fierce weapon that
could be swung with real
force on the battlefield.

A family at war

The queens and kings of the 17th and 18th Dynasties

At the end of 17th Dynasty and the beginning of 18th Dynasty, Egypt was ruled by a royal family that produced not only warrior-kings who reunited Egypt, but some of the most remarkable women in Egyptian history.

One of the main assets of the family that reunified and then ruled Egypt in the late 17th and early 18th Dynasties was its women. Royal women feature prominently on the monuments of the period, and this seems to reflect their status. Up until this time, Egyptian royal women had stayed in the background, but now they did more than simply support their husbands and sons and stood alongside them as figures of considerable political importance. They seemed to have taken to heart the role of the goddess Isis and wanted to support their own Osiris and/or Horus, possibly to ensure continuity in the royal family at a time when Egypt was constantly at war and the king was always at risk of being killed.

◁ **Tetisheri stela**
On this stela, King Ahmose makes offerings to Tetisheri, the "mother of his mother, mother of his father." Ahmose erected the stela in a mortuary complex that he built for Tetisheri at Abydos.

the wife of Sekenenre Taa I. Tetisheri was the mother not only of Sekenenre Taa II, but also of his sister-wife, Ahhotep, and possibly Kamose, too.

Sekenenre Taa II fathered 10 or 11 children with Ahhotep and two of her sisters, but his death in battle may have caused a succession crisis. This was because despite having many children, the next male in line for the throne, his son Ahmose, was too young to assume the role of a fighting monarch. The crown therefore seems to have passed to Kamose, who may have been Ahmose's uncle. When Kamose died just three years later, the throne passed to Ahmose, who followed family tradition and married one of his sisters, Ahmose-Nefertari.

Complex line of succession

The woman who was recognized by later generations as the great matriarch of this family was Tetisheri,

Powerful women

Ahmose was particularly eager to honor the female members of his family. He built a mortuary complex for his grandmother, Tetisheri, at Abydos and recorded on a stela there that this was in addition to the tomb that he had already built for her at Thebes. In the 18th year of his reign, he also set up a stela at Karnak, on which he described his mother, Ahhotep, as someone who had controlled the Theban army, expelled rebels, and pacified Upper Egypt. Ahhotep's part in this, unusual for a queen, demonstrates not just her forceful nature, but also the important role that royal women had played in the struggle against the Hyksos (see pp.142–143).

The seven children of Ahmose and Ahmose-Nefertari included the next king, Amenhotep I, and his sister-wife, Merytamen, who may have died

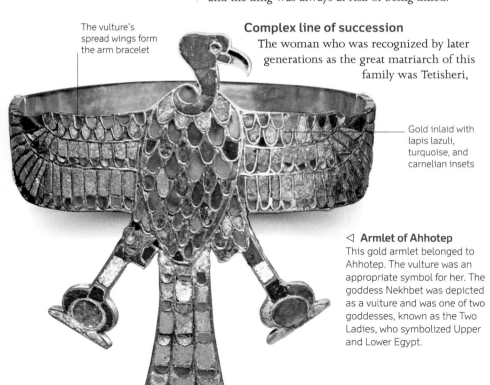

The vulture's spread wings form the arm bracelet

Gold inlaid with lapis lazuli, turquoise, and carnelian insets

◁ **Armlet of Ahhotep**
This gold armlet belonged to Ahhotep. The vulture was an appropriate symbol for her. The goddess Nekhbet was depicted as a vulture and was one of two goddesses, known as the Two Ladies, who symbolized Upper and Lower Egypt.

young. On his monuments, Amenhotep I is often shown alongside his mother, who was still clearly a formidable presence at court. Amenhotep did not remarry, and when he died without an heir, the throne passed to an experienced soldier named Tuthmosis, whose origins are not clear.

Tuthmosis I may have been one of Amenhotep I's trusted courtiers, but he might also have been the grandson of Sekenenre Taa II through one of the lesser princes whom Sekenenre had fathered. Whatever his origins, Tuthmosis' marriage to Mutnofret, another one of Amenhotep I's sisters, gave him a claim to be a member of the royal family of the 18th Dynasty. In fact, he was the first in a long line of kings that would rule Egypt until the death of Tutankhamen more than 170 years later.

AHMOSE-NEFERTARI, QUEEN AND GODDESS

Queen Ahmose-Nefertari appears in many works of art from the Ramesside Period, especially at Thebes, where she was worshipped as a local deity, alongside her son Amenhotep I, as a protectress of the Theban Necropolis. This may have been because Thebes became a royal burial place in the early New Kingdom. Nowhere is the worship of the goddess Ahmose-Nefertari more apparent than at Deir el-Medina, where her image often features on stelae used for private worship. She also appears on the walls of private tombs at Thebes, such as the one below from the tomb of Kynebu. A priest, Kynebu lived during the reign of Ramesses VIII, four centuries after Ahmose-Nefertari's death.

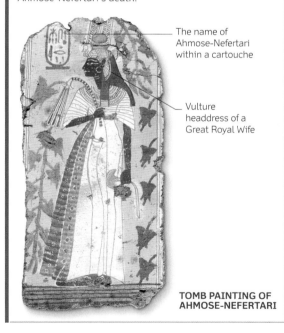

The name of Ahmose-Nefertari within a cartouche

Vulture headdress of a Great Royal Wife

TOMB PAINTING OF AHMOSE-NEFERTARI

◁ **Ahhotep's coffin**
The tomb of Queen Ahhotep was discovered in the Dra Abu el-Naga cemetery at Thebes by Auguste Mariette in 1858. It contained a magnificent collection of objects, including this gilded coffin.

△ **Ramose and Meryptah**
The tomb of Ramose, the Overseer of Horses, from the late 18th
Dynasty is a masterpiece of relief work. It shows how elite men
and women of this period liked to be seen—with elaborate
hairstyles and jewelry and strongly emphasized eyes.

Lotus flower held
by Meryptah

Broad, beaded collar
worn by men and women
at the time

Hair and cosmetics

Keeping young and beautiful

The pictures of men and women on the walls of their tombs, and the range of beauty products and accessories placed within the tombs, show how important it was to the Egyptians to look their best.

Elite Egyptians were not only generally portrayed as being young and physically fit—statues and paintings of them also emphasize that they were the proud owners of the latest hairstyles. Many of these hairstyles, however, were probably wigs, as most men wore their natural hair shortly cropped. Wigs were possibly the best way to reconcile people's wish to have an elaborate and sometimes extremely heavy hairstyle with the intense heat of the Egyptian climate.

Changes in hairstyle

Egyptian art provides a glimpse of the different types of hairstyles that people wore at different periods. In the Old Kingdom, women tended to wear their hair shoulder-length or longer. A popular variation on this was a wig that was divided into three parts: one hung down the woman's back, while the two on either side were brought forward over her shoulders. In the Middle Kingdom, women were shown with thick, wavy hair, whereas in the New Kingdom, long, straight wigs were popular. Example of wigs found in tombs from the latter period are often very large. They would have enveloped the head, apart from the face, and come down to the shoulders.

In the late 18th Dynasty and the Ramesside Period, elite men and women were often shown with long hair. Men's hair fell in wavy strands past their shoulders and women's hair was even longer, but these were just the major trends, and there were considerable innovations and variations in hairstyles throughout every period.

Toiletries and cosmetics

The Egyptians did not wear perfume in the modern sense of an essential oil mixed with alcohol, but used a range of oils and fats that they blended with fragrant floral scents, including lotus and henna. Frankincense and myrrh were also used.

Both men and women wore makeup. Eye makeup was common, especially as it was thought to be good for the eyes. Kohl, usually made from galena (lead) or malachite (copper) ores, was the most popular type of makeup, as shown by the large number of small, kohl-filled cosmetic jars that have been found in Egyptian tombs and by the striking images of dark-rimmed eyes in tomb paintings.

There is less evidence of other kinds of makeup in ancient Egypt, but there is at least one picture of a woman painting her lips. This can be seen in the Turin Erotic Papyrus.

△ **Copper mirror**
Egyptian mirrors were simple disks of metal—usually copper, but occasionally silver—that were polished to provide a good reflection of someone's face. Their handles often took the form of a woman or a female deity.

◁ **Tiy's kohl tube**
The dark kohl used around eyes was kept in various types of vessels. Long tubes with applicators were especially popular, like this decorative example inscribed with the name of Queen Tiy.

◁ **Luxury comb**
Hair accessories and styling implements are often found in tombs. Many of them were decorated with motifs drawn from the natural world, such as this comb featuring a sleeping gazelle.

Empire builders

Warrior kings on the Nile and Euphrates

During the early reigns of the New Kingdom, Egypt conquered vast tracts of land in the Levant and in Nubia. This was largely in response to the insecurity caused by the foreign occupations of Egypt in the Second Intermediate Period.

The accession of King Ahmose, his expulsion of the Hyksos, and the subsequent reunification of Egypt marked the start of a new phase of Egyptian history—the beginning of the 18th Dynasty and the New Kingdom. The new dynasty introduced many innovations, including a new royal burial ground in the Valley of the Kings (see pp.160–161), but other changes had wider implications for both Egypt and its neighbors.

The warrior king

Since Narmer, military power had been considered a key attribute of kingship. Destroying both foreign enemies and domestic rebels was an aspect of *maat*, or cosmic order, that the king needed to carry out for the gods, as well as for his own security and that of Egypt.

In the Old Kingdom, however, military activity seems to have been modest in scale. Although in art the king was constantly shown smiting his enemies, the reality was rather different. Egypt had, for example, neither a permanent army nor a professional officer class, because when troops were

◁ **Statue of Amenhotep I**
Amenhotep I successfully continued Ahmose's empire-building program. He was also the patron of the royal necropolis workers at Deir el-Medina, where this statue was found.

needed for the occasional military or punitive action, they were recruited from the civilian population.

This changed in the Middle Kingdom, because the conquest of Nubia and the maintenance of the fortresses, built to defend Egypt's southern borders, made a professional army necessary. This created careers for men like the soldier Khusobek (see pp.120–121), but the number of professional soldiers was small in relation to the population of Egypt, and the upper echelons of society were unlikely to aspire to a military career. The New Kingdom, by contrast, was much more militaristic. The extensive conquests of the early New Kingdom, and the need to defend those conquests against powerful external enemies, made an official army a necessity. Army service became mandatory for a significant number of Egyptians, and the status of professional officers rose to equal that of priests and civil servants.

The king himself played a leading role in this new, militarized Egypt, and he was depicted not just in the traditional smiting pose, but also using the latest military equipment, such as the chariot. Royal regalia now included the "blue crown," which was based on a military helmet.

Foundations of the empire

For Ahmose and his immediate successors, the capture of Avaris, important though it was, was not the end of the war against the Hyksos. Immediately after the sack of Avaris, Ahmose laid siege to the town

KERMA

The city of Kerma was the most important urban center of Kush. It appears to have been the capital of some powerful rulers during the Second Intermediate Period. The Kushites did not have a written script, so the names of these rulers are not known. The purpose of the ceremonial buildings at Kerma, such as the tall mud-brick structure that is known today as the Western Deffufa, is a mystery. However, an elite cemetery was found at the site. It contains huge tumulus tombs in which servants were buried with their masters.

of Sharuhen for three years. Sharuhen lay in southern Palestine, well beyond the traditional borders of Egypt. Ahmose was clearly taking the fight to other Canaanites in the region and not just to those who had occupied Egypt.

It is not clear why Egypt developed such a large empire in New Kingdom, but it might have been driven by a need for security. It was not enough to crush the Hyksos in Egypt—other Canaanites had to be destroyed to prevent further invasions, and once conquered, their territory had to be held. The same applied in Nubia. The destruction of the Kushite kingdom was a priority during the reigns of Ahmose, Amenhotep I, and Tuthmosis I, but it was only under Hatshepsut/Tuthmosis III that both Lower and Upper Nubia were brought firmly under Egyptian control.

The king's statue is shaded from the sun

Incense is burned to worship the king's statue

◁ **Worshipping the statue of Tuthmosis I**
No king extended Egypt's borders farther than Tuthmosis I. His conquests were marked by two boundary stelae. One stood by the Euphrates at Carchemish (on the border between modern Turkey and Syria). The other was 1,240 miles (2,000 km) away at Kurgus, in Upper Nubia (modern Sudan).

Sled on which the king's statue is being dragged

Hatshepsut

A queen becomes king

One of the most remarkable monarchs in Egyptian history was Hatshepsut, a rare example of a female king of Egypt. During her reign, she consolidated Egyptian imperial power and built many important monuments.

In around 1492 BCE, Tuthmosis I died. His successors had probably been his sons by Queen Mutnofret, Amenmose or Wadjmose, but they had died before their father. The throne then passed to their younger brother, who became Tuthmosis II. Following dynastic precedent, Tuthmosis II married his half-sister, Hatshepsut, who appeared on his monuments standing behind him in a suitably queenly pose. The couple produced a daughter, Neferure, and Tuthmosis II had a son, also called Tuthmosis, by a minor wife. It is not known how long Tuthmosis II's reign was, but it appears to have been short and he seems to have achieved little.

The succession

When Tuthmosis II died, the throne passed to his male heir, who became Tuthmosis III. The new king seems to have been too young to take control as ruler of Egypt, and so Hatshepsut, his aunt/stepmother, became regent to govern until he was old enough to rule by himself. There was nothing unusual in this; their family had included several strong women who supported their husbands and children. What was unusual was that by the 7th year of Tuthmosis III's reign, Hatshepsut had started referring to herself as a king, writing her name within a cartouche, and giving herself the throne name "Maatkare."

△ **Hatshepsut as a man and a sphinx**
These two statues show Hatshepsut in the traditional guises of a strong male king and a powerful sphinx. Hatshepsut commissioned such statues in order to align herself with royal tradition and assert her suitability to be king.

The precedents for female kingship were not encouraging—notably the short reign of Sobekneferu at the end of the 12th Dynasty—but Hatshepsut set about establishing an identity that would coincide with the traditional role of a male king. On royal monuments, therefore, she was increasingly depicted as a conventional, physically fit male king.

Royal fathers

To emphasize her right to rule as king, Hatshepsut went out of her way to associate herself with her father, or rather her two fathers—Tuthmosis I and the god Amen-Ra. Tuthmosis I had been a powerful king, and Hatshepsut used his authority to strengthen her claim to the throne. On the walls of her mortuary temple at Deir el-Bahri, she is shown in a royal coronation scene in which Tuthmosis I presents her

▽ **Offering to Amen-Ra**
On this block of stone from the Red Chapel shrine at Karnak, Hatshepsut (on the left) is shown offering Amen-Ra (on the right) the two colossal granite obelisks that she set up at the site.

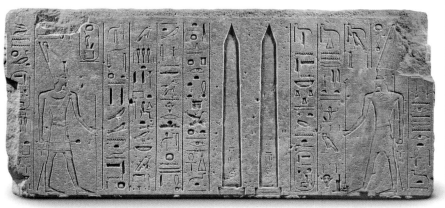

to the court as his successor to the throne. The role of Tuthmosis II in this is not mentioned. Other scenes depict Amen-Ra, whom she referred to as "father" not just in the sense in which kings referred to themselves as the "sons" of various gods, but as her real-life father. These two fathers come together in the so-called Divine Birth scenes on the walls of Deir el-Bahri, where it is explained that Amen-Ra was present within Tuthmosis I when he made Hatshepsut's mother, Ahmose, pregnant with her. This ingenious myth provided all the divine and dynastic justification that Hatshepsut needed to claim the throne.

Hatshepsut at Karnak

Hatshepsut's devotion to Amen-Ra manifested itself in other ways, too. The development of Karnak, the home of Amen-Ra, had been a major part of the building projects of previous rulers of the 18th Dynasty. Hatshepsut made a point of continuing her father's work there, and two of her projects stand out. One was the quarrying, transport, and erection of a series of enormous granite obelisks at Karnak, whose inscriptions clarify that their purpose was to honor Amen-Ra. The second was the construction of a shrine, now known as the Red Chapel, at the heart of Karnak. This was made of red quartzite and black basalt, and it contained the god's image.

These monuments were places where Hatshepsut could proclaim her close relationship with Amen-Ra. An inscription on a statue of herself makes this clear: "My reward from my father is life, stability, and dominion on the Horus-throne of the Living, like Ra, forever."

The uraeus on her brow has been damaged

Striped nemes headdress

▷ **Woman king**
This statue from Hatshepsut's mortuary temple at Deir el-Bahri is one of several that show her as king, but with a female body. Hatshepsut's status is indicated by the striped nemes-headdress that she is wearing and by the royal titles on her throne.

Childhood

Little Egyptians

Everything that is known about children in ancient Egypt comes from the art and literature created by adults. Although it is hard to generalize, these suggest that the ancient Egyptians treasured their children.

The importance of the family in ancient Egyptian society is often stressed in religious texts and maxims. In the school text the *Instruction of Ani*, male students are advised to: "Take a wife while you are young so that she will make a son for you; she should bear for you while you are youthful."

While children were certainly considered a social and economic asset in farming communities, there is also plenty of evidence of deep emotional bonds within families. This might have been partly because they recognized how vulnerable young children, especially newborns, were to illness and death. Ani says: "When death comes, he takes the infant who is in his mother's arms just as one who has reached old age." As a result, protective magic was very much focused on pregnant women and infants (see pp.120–121).

Growing up

Most Egyptian sons learned the same trade as their father, whether he was a peasant farmer or a king. Equally, girls were expected to follow in their mothers' footsteps and grow up to take on domestic tasks.

The only children who went to school were the sons of elite, literate officials, and scribes. At school, they learned how to read and write by using imaginative stories, administrative documents, or wisdom (religious) literature such as the *Instruction of Ani* as models. These not only helped them learn to write, but also taught

◁ **Two girls squabbling**
The artists who painted New Kingdom tombs clearly found the things that children did amusing, as in this small illustration of girls arguing while adults around them gather in the harvest.

them how to be good Egyptians. If a boy was successful at school, he would become the sort of fine young person who was a credit to his parents, and to his father in particular. According to the *Teachings of Ptahhotep*, a father should treat a worthy and upright son well: "Do every good thing for him because he is your son begotten of your very being; do not separate your love from him."

Families in art

The ancient Egyptians recognized that children were different from adults, and the special regard in which they were held is often captured in art. Children are usually shown naked, sometimes with a distinctive hairstyle—the "sidelock of youth"—and possibly with a finger in their mouth. Family groups are often portrayed in statues or on the walls of tombs. These artworks affirm the identities of everyone depicted and often create the impression of happy families.

▽ **Seneb's children**
This statue is famous partly because it depicts Seneb, a high-status dwarf who lived during the Old Kingdom. It also shows his wife and two tiny children, who are standing where Seneb's legs might be in a more conventional group statue of a family.

▷ **Feeder cup**
This remarkable example of a feeder cup is made of blue faience. It is decorated with illustrations of protective creatures that have been enlisted to safeguard the health of children who drink from it.

▽ **Inherkau and his family**
On the walls of his tomb at Deir el-Medina, the craftsman Inherkau is shown surrounded by different generations of his family. He appears to be especially fond of the three grandchildren who are standing and kneeling at his feet.

Distinctive hairstyle typical of a child

The text identifies this girl as Inherkau's grandchild

Hatshepsut's temple

A monument built on history and myth

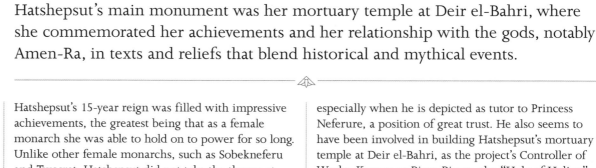

Hatshepsut's main monument was her mortuary temple at Deir el-Bahri, where she commemorated her achievements and her relationship with the gods, notably Amen-Ra, in texts and reliefs that blend historical and mythical events.

△ **Senenmut and Princess Neferure**
Senenmut owned an extraordinary number of statues, often made from expensive stone. These were probably gifts from Hatshepsut and allowed him to show how close he was to the king and her daughter.

Hatshepsut's 15-year reign was filled with impressive achievements, the greatest being that as a female monarch she was able to hold on to power for so long. Unlike other female monarchs, such as Sobekneferu and Twosret, Hatshepsut did not take the throne at the end of a dynasty, but in the middle of the 18th Dynasty. She had the ongoing problem of Tuthmosis III, the "rightful" king, becoming old enough to replace her one day, but her short-term solution was to portray him on her monuments, especially at Karnak, as a partner king. Co-regency between older and younger rulers was fairly common at the time.

Hatshepsut could not rule alone, however, and she depended on the loyalty of high-ranking government officials. The most prominent of these was Senenmut, whose title, "Overseer of the Granaries of Amen," obscures the key role he played at court. His statues portray him as a loyal servant of King Hatshepsut,

especially when he is depicted as tutor to Princess Neferure, a position of great trust. He also seems to have been involved in building Hatshepsut's mortuary temple at Deir el-Bahri, as the project's Controller of Works. Known as *Djeser-Djeseru*, the "Holy of Holies," this magnificent temple was the most important building of Hatshepsut's reign.

Deir el-Bahri

The site that Hatshepsut chose for her temple was unusual but not unique, as it was built alongside the temple-tomb of Nebhepetre Montuhotep II, which may have partly inspired her. Rising in a series of terraces at the foot of the Theban mountain, *Djeser-Djeseru* is one of the most beautiful buildings created by an Egyptian king. It was where Hatshepsut was to be celebrated after her death, but it also had another purpose—to justify her kingship. The building included a chapel dedicated to her father, Tuthmosis I, and chapels linking Hatshepsut with Osiris and Ra.

Most important of all, the central shrine on the highest level of the temple was built to house the barque that carried the statue of Amen-Ra of Karnak to the temples on the west bank during the Beautiful Festival of the Western Valley. Scenes on the walls of the temple's terraces depict key moments of Hatshepsut's life, including her divine birth, obelisks being taken to Karnak, and the expedition to Punt.

The land of Punt

No one knows exactly where the land of Punt was, but it was somewhere to the south of Egypt and could only be reached by sea. It may have been in present-day Eritrea, Somalia, or even southwest Arabia. Punt was famous above all for its trees, which produced the sweet-smelling incense that was such an important part of religious ritual in Egypt.

Previous kings had sent expeditions to Punt, but Hatshepsut's expedition was vitally important to her, because the incense (and the trees that produced it)

INCENSE TREES FROM PUNT

Hatshepsut did not just describe her expedition to Punt on the walls of Deir el-Bahri, she also illustrated it in a series of vivid reliefs. Punt's strangeness was conveyed by images of its unfamiliar flora and fauna, the odd-looking people who lived there, and their houses built on stilts. Most important of all were the pictures of the incense trees. These are shown being placed in baskets and carried to ships to be taken back to Egypt.

taken back to Egypt was destined for rituals dedicated to the worship of Amen-Ra, another example of her close relationship with her divine "father."

Death, burial, and legacy

Hatshepsut was buried in the Valley of the Kings in a tomb with a long, undecorated, curving corridor that led to her burial chamber. She apparently intended to be buried alongside Tuthmosis I in a pair of matching stone sarcophagi. The new king, Tuthmosis III, however, seems to have harbored ill feelings toward the woman who had barred him from active kingship for so long. The body of Tuthmosis I was removed

from the tomb and buried elsewhere, and many images of Hatshepsut—her statues and the paintings of her on the walls of her temple—were destroyed. This destruction is generally attributed to Tuthmosis III, who seems to have tried to erase Hatshepsut's legacy during the later part of his reign.

△ **Deir el-Bahri**
Nestling in a desert bay on the west bank at Thebes, Hatshepsut's mortuary temple rises in a harmonious series of elegant terraces. Its innermost rooms are cut into the Theban mountain itself.

> ## "I have made for him a **Punt** in **his garden** at **Thebes**, just **as he commanded me**."
>
> HATSHEPSUT DESCRIBES THE PLANTING OF INCENSE TREES FOR AMEN-RA

◁ **Hatshepsut and Tuthmosis III**
This relief on the exterior of the Red Chapel at Karnak shows identical images of both Hatshepsut and Tuthmosis III, distinguished only by their names, although one is an older woman and the other a young man.

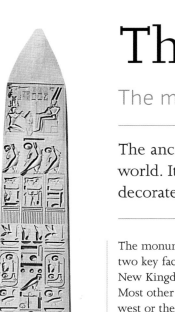

Thebes

The monumental capital of the New Kingdom

The ancient city of Thebes is one of the richest archaeological sites in the world. It is a treasure trove of monuments, which include royal temples, decorated tombs, and even workers' houses.

The monumental landscape at Thebes was shaped by two key factors, especially during its heyday in the New Kingdom. The first of these was its geography. Most other Egyptian cities were built either to the west or the east of the Nile (such as Memphis and Amarna respectively), but Thebes was cut in half by the river and had important monuments on each side. It is often said that the eastern bank belonged to the "land of the living" and the west to the "land of the dead." Although this is partly true, it is a simplification. Amenhotep III, for instance, built an enormous palace complex at Malqata, on the west bank.

The second major factor in Thebes' development was its history. In the Old Kingdom, it had been something of a backwater in the south of Egypt, but during the First Intermediate Period, Theban rulers came to the fore and eventually unified Egypt under the Middle Kingdom. It was Theban kings, too, who reunified Egypt after the Second Intermediate Period to found the New Kingdom. Both of these achievements gave the city a huge amount of prestige, and the Theban kings of both the Middle and New

Kingdoms were keen to enhance their native city by building monuments of national importance there. Chief among these was Karnak, the home of Amen, the Thebans' local—and later Egypt's national—god.

The east bank

Most of the population of Thebes lived on the east bank. The houses that once stood there have mostly gone, but the great monuments that were built around them are still there. The largest of these by far is the Karnak complex, at the northern end of the city. This consisted of the huge temple of Amen (later Amen-Ra), plus a temple for his wife, Mut, and one for the god Montu. Together, these temples formed one of the largest religious complexes in the world.

As Amen-Ra had become the patron god not just of Thebes, but also of the Egyptian empire, vast resources were poured into Karnak and successive kings aimed to equal or surpass the works of their predecessors. Much of the Middle Kingdom temple was removed during enlargements carried out in the New Kingdom, but it is clear that most of the rulers of both periods

▷ **Plan of Thebes**
The distribution of the main archaeological sites at Thebes shows the difference between the monuments on the east and west banks of the Nile. The west side is dominated by tombs and mortuary temples.

◁ **Luxor Temple obelisk**
The Theban kings put an enormous amount of resources into building monuments at Thebes. This gigantic obelisk was raised at Luxor Temple.

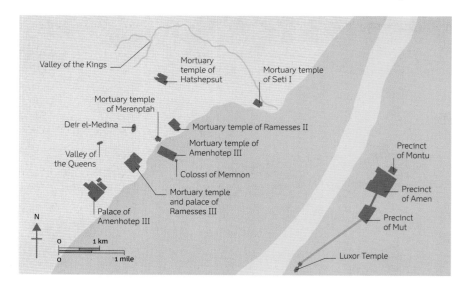

Valley of the Kings
Mortuary temple of Hatshepsut
Mortuary temple of Seti I
Mortuary temple of Merenptah
Deir el-Medina
Mortuary temple of Ramesses II
Valley of the Queens
Mortuary temple of Amenhotep III
Colossi of Memnon
Mortuary temple and palace of Ramesses III
Palace of Amenhotep III
Precinct of Montu
Precinct of Amen
Precinct of Mut
Luxor Temple
N
0   1 km
0   1 mile

△ **View of Luxor**
All of the temples at Thebes have suffered some form of damage, but the sheer scale of the remains has attracted many artists. This view of Luxor was painted by the 19th-century British artist David Roberts.

added to the Karnak complex. To the south of the city stood Luxor Temple, which faced north and served as a subsidiary of the complex. During the annual Opet Festival, the statues of Amen-Ra, Mut, and Khonsu were carried from Karnak to Luxor Temple in a procession visible to all the inhabitants of Thebes.

The west bank
This side of the river was largely devoted to mortuary monuments. These included royal tombs, especially those in the Valley of the Kings, which was where most of the New Kingdom kings were buried. Close to the Valley lay the village of Deir el-Medina, which housed the artisans responsible for decorating the royal tombs (see pp.230–233).

As well as requiring a tomb, each king also needed a mortuary temple where his cult could be celebrated for eternity. These mortuary temples also had an important connection to Karnak. During the Beautiful Festival of the Western Valley, the divine family of Amen-Ra, Mut, and Khonsu would leave Karnak, cross the river, and visit different mortuary temples, celebrating the link between the kings and the gods.

However, the west bank was not only for kings. On the lower slopes of the Theban mountain, behind and around the royal mortuary temples, many hundreds of decorated tombs were built for the kings' high-ranking officials. This ensured that nonroyals could also enjoy an afterlife in the domain of the god Amen-Ra, the ultimate "owner" of Thebes.

Top of the column is shaped like a papyrus bud

▷ **The sun court of Amenhotep III**
Each king was influenced by personal preferences when building at Thebes. Amenhotep III was very interested in solar religion, so he built this open courtyard at Luxor Temple.

The Valley of the Kings

"The Great Place"

Possibly the most famous necropolis in the world, the Valley of the Kings contains the tombs of the kings who ruled Egypt in the New Kingdom, the time of its greatest power. Magnificently decorated, they were once filled with treasure.

In many respects, the rulers of the New Kingdom built similar things to their predecessors in the Middle Kingdom, but they made them much larger and better.

During both periods, Egypt was unified by Theban monarchs who went on to build empires and who regarded Thebes as the home not just of their dynasties, but also of their patron god, Amen. The expansion of Amen's temple at Karnak during the New Kingdom was therefore essentially a continuation of the work that the Middle Kingdom rulers had begun at the site, but it was on a far grander scale. There was, however, one significant way in which

the New Kingdom was different from the Middle Kingdom. Whereas the 12th Dynasty kings had returned to the Old Kingdom practice of building pyramids in the north of Egypt, the kings of the 18th to 20th Dynasties did not, and chose—with very few exceptions—to be buried close to

◁ **Guardian deity**
The dead king needed protection during his dangerous journey to the afterlife. This was provided by guardian deities, such as the one represented by this wooden model found in the tomb of Tuthmosis III.

△ **View of the valley**
By the end of the New Kingdom, the floor of the Valley of the Kings was filled with tombs. Today, partly due to uncertainty about who owned them, these tombs are referred to by their KV (King's Valley) number. KV62, the last royal tomb to be discovered here, belonged to Tutankhamen.

"Drawn with outlines, cut with the chisel, filled with color, and completed."

FROM THE PLAN OF RAMESSES IV'S TOMB

PLAN OF A ROYAL TOMB

This drawing, on a papyrus kept in the Turin Museum in Italy, is the best-preserved plan of a royal tomb from the Valley of the Kings. It shows the tomb of Ramesses IV and is likely to have been drawn when work on the tomb had been completed. The speckled red band represents the rock of the valley into which the tomb was cut, and the white rectangle (bottom center) indicates the king's sarcophagus. The burial chamber is given its ancient Egyptian name, the "House of Gold," and is set within four gold shrines, like those found in the tomb of Tutankhamen (see pp.192–193). The text also lists the measurements of different parts of the tomb.

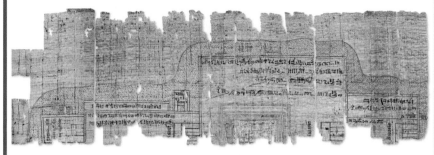

PLAN OF RAMESSES IV'S TOMB

Amen, at Thebes. Also, the New Kingdom royal tombs at Thebes were not like the imposing structures of the past—they were meant to be hidden. One possible reason for this is that the earlier tombs had been broken into and plundered. It seems that neither the thick stone masonry of the Old Kingdom pyramids nor the cunning internal design of the later Middle Kingdom pyramids had been sufficient to keep robbers out and protect the bodies and burial goods of the tomb owners within.

Hidden tombs

The new site for the royal tombs was the Valley of the Kings, which cut through the Theban mountain and was difficult to access. The tombs were dug in unlikely parts of the valley, and once sealed, they were effectively invisible. The words of the official Ineni, architect for Tuthmosis I, testify to this secrecy. In the autobiography inscribed in his tomb, he says that he, "Oversaw the excavation of the tomb of His Majesty, alone, no one hearing, no one seeing."

The location of these tombs could not, however, have been entirely secret. Teams of workers were needed to build them, and they were housed in the village of Deir el-Medina. They referred to their place of work as "The Great Place" or "The Valley."

Decorating royal tombs

The tombs in the Valley of the Kings were in some ways similar to the royal pyramids, with multiple corridors and rooms that eventually led to the king's burial chamber. The internal walls of the rock-cut tombs in the Valley of the Kings were covered with colorful scenes and texts similar to the

Pyramid Texts of the Old Kingdom (see pp.70–71), but the New Kingdom texts provide a much more coherent account of the journey that the dead king had to undertake before he could be reunited with Osiris and Ra.

During the New Kingdom, tombs in the Valley became increasingly large, partly because their walls and ceilings had to provide enough space for the extensive religious texts required. Paradoxically, the smallest tombs tend to belong to powerful 18th Dynasty kings, while some of the largest belong to the weaker rulers of the 20th Dynasty. Ramesside royal tombs also tended to have large, elaborate entrances, which suggests that secrecy was no longer as important in the late New Kingdom.

◁ **Interior of KV11**
The tomb of Ramesses III (KV11) is one of the best examples of a large New Kingdom tomb. This pillared hall is inscribed and painted with colorful scenes showing Ramesses making offerings to the gods of the afterlife, especially Osiris.

The tomb of Ramesses IV
By the 20th Dynasty, Egyptian kings had long abandoned
the idea of building secret royal tombs in the Valley
of the Kings. Instead, they focused on building large and
impressive tombs there. For some of the Late New Kingdom
kings, such as Ramesses IV, it was their only impressive
monument. This is the chamber in which Ramesses IV was
buried. It is richly decorated with scenes and texts to ensure
that the king passed successfully to the next life, but as in
many other tombs in the Valley of the Kings, Ramesses IV's
sarcophagus was smashed and looted by robbers.

Consolidating the empire

Tuthmosis III and Amenhotep II

The reigns of Tuthmosis III and Amenhotep II were vital in the development of Egypt's empire. Through war and diplomacy, these kings crushed the Canaanites, neutralized Mitanni, and brought all of Nubia under the imperial yoke.

Despite the military achievements of the first kings of the 18th Dynasty, the Levant remained a thorn in Egypt's side. Far from being subjugated, the Canaanite cities of the southern Levant (an area in the Middle East) continued to cause trouble for Egypt. Major movements of people during the Second Intermediate Period had also led to the emergence of a new power in the region between the River Euphrates and the River Balikh. This was the kingdom of Mitanni.

Mitanni

During its relatively short history, Mitanni faced numerous problems with its neighbors, including the military ambitions of the first kings of the 18th Dynasty. Tuthmosis I's campaigns in Syria and the erection of his boundary stela on the Mitannian border on the Euphrates were regarded by the Mitannians as a clear provocation and threat. In response, they encouraged the Canaanites who were under Egyptian control to rebel against their masters, which they were more than willing to do.

During the latter part of Hatshepsut's reign, the Mitannian client states of Kadesh and Tunip expanded their areas of control, pushing westward toward Byblos and southward. When Hatshepsut died, the ruler of Kadesh, possibly sensing an opportunity, began to gather a substantial Canaanite coalition at the city of Megiddo (Armageddon). Tuthmosis III took decisive action, leading an Egyptian army against

the Canaanites. He achieved a stunning victory outside the walls of Megiddo, and, after a siege, captured the city and the Canaanite leaders within it.

War and peace with Mitanni

To consolidate his victory at Megiddo, Tuthmosis III carried out a series of campaigns over the following years, culminating in an invasion of Mitanni itself. However, the Mitannians retreated deep into their own territory, leaving Tuthmosis III far from his lines of communication and forcing him to withdraw. In fact, the Egyptian and Mitannian forces never met in battle at all. Instead, the Mitannians continued to stir up insurrection within Egypt's Levantine empire, making it necessary for Tuthmosis III's successor, Amenhotep II, to continue carrying out sporadic punitive military campaigns in the region.

This stand-off between Egypt and Mitanni was resolved during the reign of Amenhotep II, who signed a peace treaty with his enemy. By then, Mitanni was facing more pressing problems,

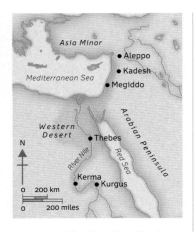

△ **The Egyptian Empire**
By the end of the reign of Tuthmosis III, Egypt had not just conquered vast swathes of neighboring territory but had created an empire that strengthened its security and gave it an invaluable source of revenue.

▷ **Tuthmosis III, warrior-king**
The best sources of information about the campaigns of Tuthmosis III are the accounts that the king inscribed on the walls of the temple of Karnak. Here, he is shown crushing his enemies.

especially from its western neighbors, the Hittites. It was therefore to its advantage to make a quick peace with Egypt. Similarly, the Egyptians were only too happy to negotiate firm borders for their empire, within which they could do as they wished without interference from the Mitannians.

The subjugation of Nubia

During the reigns of Hatshepsut and Tuthmosis III, Nubia seems to have finally been brought under complete Egyptian control. Kerma was captured, Upper Nubia (as far as the Fourth Cataract) was turned into an Egyptian province, and Tuthmosis III set up a boundary stela beside that of his grandfather at Kurgus. The lists of all the tribute-bringing lands that are carved onto the walls of the temple of Karnak provide evidence of this subjugation. In the 31st year of Tuthmosis III's reign, both Wawat (Lower Nubia) and Kush (Upper Nubia) sent tribute to Egypt. By then, an imperial administration—based on that of Upper and Lower Egypt—had been created for Upper and Lower Nubia. The overall responsibility for this jewel in the crown of Egypt's empire was given to an official known as the "King's Son of Kush." With Nubia now firmly under its control, Egypt no longer had any significant enemies on its southern border, freeing it to concentrate its full military attention on the Levant.

△ **Slain enemies**
The destruction of its enemies was a popular subject in Egyptian royal art. This vivid relief, which was reused in a temple built by Ramesses IV, shows Asiatic soldiers being killed in battle with Amenhotep II.

▷ **Ivory wrist guard**
Despite enjoying a generally peaceful reign, Tuthmosis IV still had images made of himself as a mighty warrior. This ivory wrist guard, which was found at Amarna, shows the king in the classic pose of smiting an enemy.

Theban tombs

Portals to the afterlife

The private tombs that were built during the New Kingdom shared some of the features of their Old and Middle Kingdom predecessors. However, they also had their own unique characteristics.

In the Old Kingdom, the largest and best-decorated private tombs belonged to members of the court, so they were built at the Saqqara necropolis, near the capital, Memphis. In the Middle Kingdom, such high-class tombs could also be found in the provinces. This was due to the fact that local governors had gained a measure of independence from the king, so they could afford to build their own tombs. The best examples of these are the rock-cut sepulchers built by the nomarchs of Middle Egypt.

Saqqara and Thebes

In the New Kingdom, Saqqara once again became an important cemetery for Memphis-based officials. However, the best-preserved private tombs, like those of the kings, were built at Thebes. These sepulchers belonged to high-ranking members of the administration—such as civil servants, priests, and military officers—who were often buried in family or occupation-based groups. Most of their tombs retained the traditional two-room format, which

◁ **Cosmetic box from the tomb of Kha**
Although most New Kingdom tombs were robbed in antiquity, some retained their contents until modern times. They demonstrate that people were buried with their most prized everyday possessions.

featured an offering chapel and an adjoining burial chamber. However, local variations of this style also appeared at Thebes and elsewhere.

T-shaped tombs

The style of the earliest tombs of the 18th Dynasty was inspired by that of a small number of Middle Kingdom rock-cut tombs that had been built into the Theban mountain. These tombs are sometimes called saff tombs (from an Arabic word meaning "row") because of their wide, pillared, portico entrances. Behind these very visible parts of the offering chapel, a deep corridor led straight into the rock so that, from above, the tomb looked like an upside-down letter "T." This Middle Kingdom design was adopted by New Kingdom architects, and some of the existing tombs were altered to

△ **Painting from the tomb of Nebamun**
Some of the paintings produced for the Theban tombs are clearly the work of highly skilled artists. The painter of this gaggle of geese at the tomb of Nebamun had an excellent grasp of composition.

Saff tomb

accommodate new owners. A key change in the design was that the spaces between the porticoes were sealed, leaving room for a door, which led into two narrow rooms. These were the broad hall, which stood just beyond the entrance, and the long hall, which contained the shrine. Because of the poor quality of the rock at Thebes, the internal walls of these tombs were usually plastered before they were painted. This gave the painters a smooth, flat surface to work on.

Tomb decoration

The tombs were decorated in a way that was similar to that of traditional Theban offering chapels. The walls of the broad hall were covered with scenes from the deceased person's life. Following Old and Middle Kingdom tradition, these emphasized the tomb owner's career. In the largest tombs, such as that of the Vizier Rekhmire, a wide range of activities is depicted, demonstrating the breadth of the individual's responsibilities. While the broad hall

celebrated the person's life, the long hall was devoted to their death and afterlife. Here, the wall scenes focused on the process of being laid to rest and then being greeted by the gods, especially Osiris.

The burial chamber itself was usually quite modest. Located beneath the long hall, it was undecorated and was just big enough to hold the tomb owner's coffins and burial equipment. It was accessed via a shaft that was dug either in the tomb itself or in the courtyard in front of it.

Ramesside tombs at Thebes

At Thebes, this basic design evolved over the 500 years of the New Kingdom. The T-shape was gradually abandoned in favor of a squarer, sometimes columned format. By the Ramesside Period, the interior decoration had also changed. Scenes of the individual's daily life had been reduced in favor of images of their devotion to the gods and their hope of joining them in the afterlife.

▽ **West bank view**
The hills to the west of Thebes are honeycombed with tombs that were built there for over 500 years. The most visible of these are the saff tombs, which have characteristically pillared porticoes.

Private statues

People in wood and stone

During the New Kingdom, a huge range of statues of people who were not royal was created. Most of them served as stand-ins for their owners either to receive offerings in their tombs or to make offerings in the temples of the gods.

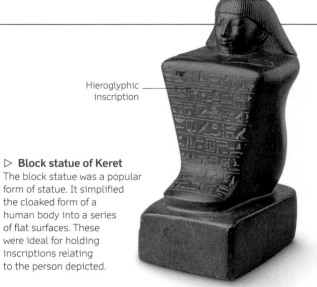

Hieroglyphic inscription

▷ **Block statue of Keret**
The block statue was a popular form of statue. It simplified the cloaked form of a human body into a series of flat surfaces. These were ideal for holding inscriptions relating to the person depicted.

Yellow flesh tones, conventional for elite women

◁ **Idet and Ruiu**
The relationships between individuals depicted in group statues are usually made clear in the texts inscribed on them. This is not the case with this statue of two ladies, whose connection remains a mystery.

Heavy wig, popular in the late New Kingdom

Necklace

△ **Yuny and Renenutet**
This statue of a husband and wife from the city of Asyut shows the pair dressed in the most fashionable clothing, hairstyles, and jewelry of the Ramesside Period.

△ **Nebsen and Nebet-ta**
The inscriptions on this pair statue identify the couple as husband and wife. He was a treasury scribe, and she was a musician at a temple of Isis.

Scribal palette

Pen in hand

▷ **Amenhotep, son of Hapu**
This fine example of a scribal statue shows the famous Amenhotep, son of Hapu. He is sitting on the ground, ready to start writing, with a papyrus spread between his knees.

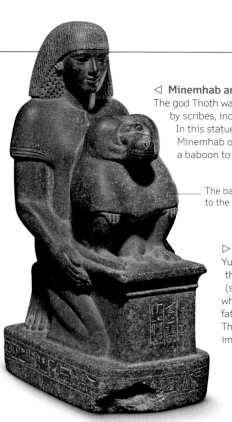

◁ Minemhab and Thoth
The god Thoth was often worshipped by scribes, including high officials. In this statue, a scribe named Minemhab offers an image of a baboon to the god.

The baboon was sacred to the god Thoth

▷ Yuny and Osiris
Yuny from Asyut owned this naophorous (shrine-carrying) statue, which was found in his father's tomb-chapel. The shrine contains the image of the god Osiris.

Naos shrine

Image of Ahmose-Nefertari

▷ Penmernab and ram head
This painted statue from Deir el-Medina depicts a man named Penmernab offering a model of the head of a ram to Amen-Ra.

Staff topped with a seated figure of Amen-Ra

Amulet of the god Bes

Girdle of gold leaf

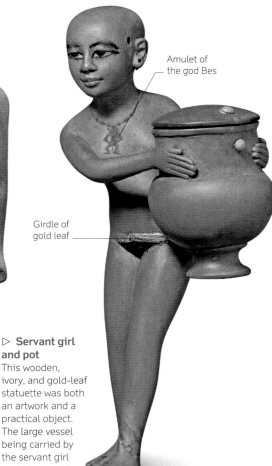

◁ Ramose
On this wooden statue from Deir el-Medina, the scribe Ramose is shown carrying a pole bearing an image of the god Amen-Ra.

△ Hapi
This unusual statue shows a man named Hapi squatting or kneeling on the ground or possibly on a cushion, with one leg tucked up beneath him.

▷ Huwebenef
Made of wood, this small statuette of a child named Huwebenef was one of a pair of child statues found in a woman's coffin.

▷ Servant girl and pot
This wooden, ivory, and gold-leaf statuette was both an artwork and a practical object. The large vessel being carried by the servant girl could be used to store cosmetics.

New Kingdom fashion

Dressing to impress

The New Kingdom elite, men and women alike, wished to be portrayed in art wearing clothes that were both highly fashionable and luxurious. To them, their appearance was mainly a marker of wealth and status.

Archaeologists have recovered surprisingly few actual clothes from the grave goods of the New Kingdom elite, possibly because so many of the tombs were robbed. However, the tomb paintings and private statues that have survived from this period give a good idea of what well-dressed, upper-class Egyptians wished to look like in the 18th to 20th Dynasties.

Love of luxury

Overall, the most obvious difference between the clothes worn during the New Kingdom and those of the previous Kingdoms was a greater sense of extravagant luxury. At the beginning of the 18th Dynasty, the style of dress was relatively restrained, but by the end of the dynasty and the Ramesside Period, it had become sophisticated and more ostentatious. People no longer wore the simple sheath dresses popular in the Old and Middle Kingdoms, but long, loose outfits whose decorative effect was largely created by the pleated linen that they were made of. These were worn by both men and women.

The typical outfit of an upper-class man during the Ramesside Period consisted of a shirt with short, wide sleeves; a long, tightly pleated skirt; and a loose, pleated garment like an apron that was worn over the skirt.

Women showed their taste and status by wearing long, loose, tightly pleated dresses. Color does not seem to have been very important, but both men and women liked to be seen in dazzling white linen, which was difficult to maintain, and therefore a sign of wealth.

▽ **Statue of Akhenaten and Nefertiti**
Images of the royal family often show them in clothing particular to their position, which nonroyals would not have worn. Nefertiti's finely pleated dress below is, however, similar to the fashions of the period.

The pointed front curves upward on some sandals

△ **Nefertari's sandals**
Ancient Egyptian people of all classes mainly wore sandals woven from simple materials such as palm fronds. This pair was found in the tomb of Nefertari, Great Royal Wife of Ramesses II.

People wore their hair longer and in more elaborate hairstyles than previously, and jewelry, especially the colorful broad collars worn by both men and women, were more detailed and opulent.

Occasion dressing

The guests at a banquet depicted in a wall painting in the tomb of Nebamun, a wealthy official (right), show what elite men and women wore on special occasions in the late-18th Dynasty. The women are all dressed almost identically in long, pleated linen dresses; long, curly wigs; large, colorful collars; and enormous gold earrings. The men are dressed in a similar fashion, but without the large earrings, and their hairstyles are not quite as extravagant. Although the guests at the banquet are shown in their best finery, it is noticeable that the serving girls are virtually naked. Their hairstyles and jewelry, however, are very similar to those of the women who they are serving.

One intriguing part of the outfits is the cone that each guest is wearing on their head. There is no consensus about what these were. They might have been cones of perfumed wax that wafted perfume as they melted during the banquet.

A serving girl is offering a couple of guests a drink

This girl is carrying a floral headband and a bowl of wax for the head cones

Each guest is holding fragrant flowers

Broad collar of colored beads

△ **Banquet scene from the tomb of Nebamun**
Scenes of tomb owners and their friends and families, like this wall painting from Nebamun's tomb, are the best source of information about what people wore in the New Kingdom. The images were idealized, however, as they were intended to be for eternity.

Duties of the vizier

The prime minister of Egypt

Although the king was the nominal head of the government in dynastic Egypt, the effective head of state in many periods was an official known as the *Tjaty*, or vizier. Little is known about the viziers of the Old Kingdom, except that they seem to have been relatives of the king. The viziers of the late Middle Kingdom are better known, largely because they provided permanence in government at a time when there were numerous kings. Although viziers were theoretically appointed by the king from the various officials who served him, it was common practice for the office to be passed on from father to son.

The best evidence for the role played by the vizier comes from the New Kingdom, especially the 18th Dynasty. In this period, the vizier's responsibilities were so great that the vizierate was split between two officials, who were responsible for Lower Egypt and Upper Egypt respectively. The power of these viziers was at its greatest during the early New Kingdom, but it waned during the Ramesside Period. By then, other officials had gained prominence, especially the High Priests of Amen at Thebes.

The Vizier Rekhmire

One of the best known of all the viziers is Rekhmire, who served under Tuthmosis III and Amenhotep II. Rekhmire's tomb is one of the largest private tombs at Thebes, and its walls are inscribed with an extensive text that can also be found in the tombs of other viziers of the time. This text has two major segments,

△ **Judgment**
This painting shows Rekhmire sitting in judgment at court. He holds the staff and scepter of authority and wears the long halternecked garment that was typical of New Kingdom viziers. He was ordered to judge all people impartially and fairly.

△ **Tax collection**
Egyptian taxes were paid in the form of agricultural produce. In this scene, a minor official working for Rekhmire organizes the transport of a shipment of jars that probably contain wine or oil. The official is scolding an exhausted porter, who has taken a brief rest from his backbreaking work.

△ **Official warehouses**
The goods that were received as taxes were carefully accounted for and then stored in large warehouses. From there, they were distributed to state employees as wages, while any surplus could be traded for other items.

"See to it that all is done **in accordance** with **the law** and … **done** correctly."

TUTHMOSIS III INSTALLS REKHMIRE AS VIZIER

which are known as the Installation of the Vizier and the Duties of the Vizier sections. These describe how Rekhmire was confirmed in his office by Tuthmosis III and what his responsibilities were.

The Duties of the Vizier section makes it clear that Rekhmire's chief responsibility was to make sure that justice was served on behalf of the king. He was therefore a legal judge who settled disputes and dispensed judgment in court cases, but he was also responsible for the administration of the major state institutions. This involved making sure that taxes were collected and that royal revenues were spent on royal projects. He was also expected to deputize for the king in a variety of situations, such as when foreign officials came to Egypt to pay tribute.

In addition to the Installation and Duties texts, the walls of Rekhmire's tomb are decorated with numerous images and inscriptions of Rekhmire himself discharging his duties. These provide a fascinating pictorial guide to the life of a vizier in the early 18th Dynasty. Needless to say, they inform visitors to the tomb that Rekhmire discharged these duties in an excellent manner and to the great satisfaction of the king.

▷ **Statue of Iuy**
Iuy was one of the viziers of the Second Intermediate Period. His tomb at Thebes contained this remarkable wooden statue, which shows him dressed in the long robe of a high official of the time.

△ **Foreign tribute**
A large part of Rekhmire's tomb is devoted to images of foreigners bringing exotic tribute to Egypt. Here, in the midst of a procession, a Nubian tribute bearer brings a giraffe, which has a monkey on its neck.

△ **Metalworking**
Part of the vizier's job was to oversee work on major projects. In this scene, a group of metalworkers is shown pouring molten metal from a crucible into a large mold in order to cast a pair of huge bronze doors. On the right, a porter provides charcoal for the furnace.

△ **Making statues**
Overseeing the production of statues, especially the royal statues intended for temples, was another responsibility of the vizier. Here, craftsmen climb scaffolding to add polish and final details to a stone statue of the seated king.

Amenhotep III

King of the Golden Age

The reign of Amenhotep III was one of the high points of Egyptian history. It was a period of peace and prosperity in which craftsmen produced some of Egypt's most magnificent works of art.

Amenhotep III came to the throne at a particularly fortunate time. He was the latest of a long-established dynasty of kings, and thanks to the military and diplomatic successes of his predecessors, he inherited a rich and extensive empire and a period of peace with Egypt's most dangerous enemy, Mitanni.

Amenhotep capitalized on this success during his 38-year reign. Egypt's relationship with Mitanni became closer, as is clear from the Amarna Letters (see pp.180–181). These show that there was a strong personal relationship between Amenhotep III and King Tushratta of Mitanni. Amenhotep also strengthened his grip on Nubia by building temples there. Nubia was where the Egyptians experimented with displays of divine kingship, so he built temples at Soleb and Sedeinga, where he and Queen Tiy could be worshipped as gods.

△ **The Luxor Temple**
Known as the Southern Harim, the Luxor Temple was built to provide a resting place for Amen-Ra and his family during the Opet Festival, when the king's *ka* was regenerated.

Egypt's Golden Age

Amenhotep's reign is often referred to as Egypt's Golden Age, partly because of the wealth, peace, and political stability that it enjoyed, but also because of the exquisite works of art that Egyptian craftsmen produced at the time. These included royal and private sculptures in a variety of colorful stones, relief carvings, and paintings of the highest quality in decorated tombs and temples, and exquisite objets d'art and jewelry made from faience, glass, precious metals, and semiprecious stones.

It was also a golden age of Egyptian architecture. Amenhotep III built temples throughout Egypt, and although many of these were damaged, destroyed, or reused by later kings, enough evidence has survived to show the grand scale of his projects. At Memphis, for example, he built a temple for the god Ptah that rivaled the great Amen-Ra temple at Karnak.

◁ **Colossus of Memnon**
This is one of a pair of statues that flanked the entrance to Amenhotep III's mortuary temple. The Colossi of Memnon are so called because they were later attributed to the Ethiopian king who fought with the Greeks at Troy.

SEKHMET STATUES

Very little remains of Amenhotep III's temple at Kom el-Hetan, but many statues have been found at the site, the most numerous being life-sized statues of the goddess Sekhmet. These Sekhmet statues show the goddess either seated or standing, but each one is inscribed with an individual identity, such as Sekhmet the fiery one, or Sekhmet, Lady of Imaut. It is thought that there were originally 730 of these statues (two for each day of the week) and that together they may have been used to invoke Sekhmet's help in fighting plague and pestilence in Egypt.

SCULPTURE OF SEKHMET

"The one who brings plans into existence, abundant in monuments, plentiful in miracles."

AMENHOTEP III ON HIMSELF

He also erected a series of monolithic quartzite statues of the god Thoth in the form of a baboon at Hermopolis Magna, each of which stood at more than 14 ft (4 m) in height. But the main focus of Amenhotep's building ambitions was Thebes. At Karnak, he extended the temple of Amen-Ra and that of his wife, the goddess Mut. He also greatly enlarged the Luxor Temple to make it a suitable place for the reception of Amen-Ra and his family during the Opet festival.

Solar religion

Amenhotep III's afterlife was secured by a huge underground tomb, which he built not in the Valley of the Kings, but in the nearby Western Valley. His mortuary temple at Kom el-Hetan, on the west bank at Thebes, was also built on a grand scale, but little of it remains.

A striking aspect of both the Kom el-Hetan and Luxor temples was the space devoted to large, open courtyards. These expressed a particular aspect of theology that fascinated Amenhotep—the divine significance of the sun. This focus on the sun and sunlight as manifestations of the divine increased during the reign of his son, Amenhotep IV, who renamed himself Akhenaten (see pp.178–179).

Blue crown, originally made of metal disks

▷ **Amenhotep III**
The statues from Amenhotep III's time were very distinctive. The faces of both gods and humans were often stylized, with almond-shaped eyes and pursed lips. In this statue of Amenhotep III, the king is shown wearing the blue crown, which was based on a military helmet.

Pendants from
original crown

**QUEEN TIY WITH
HATHORIC CROWN**

Inlaid eyes
make the
head look
lifelike

▷ **Bust of Tiy**
This wooden bust
of Tiy has silver,
gold, and glass
additions. At some
point, it was adapted
and its original silver,
baglike wig was covered.
This gave prominence to the
tall plumes, sun disk, and
Hathoric horns that
emphasize Tiy's divinity.

Queen Tiy

Amenhotep III's great queen

The leading royal consort of the New Kingdom was not one of the queens of the early 18th Dynasty, nor the famous Nefertiti, but Queen Tiy, Great Royal Wife of Amenhotep III.

Although Tiy became one of the prominent queens in Egyptian history, she was not of royal birth. Her parents came from the town of Akhmim; her father was the chariot commander Yuya, and her mother was his wife Thuyu.

Queen, mother, goddess

By the 2nd year of Amenhotep III's reign, Tiy was not just his wife, but his chief queen. She was the mother of four daughters and at least two sons. Her eldest son, Tuthmosis, died before his father, making Amenhotep IV crown prince. Tiy's importance, despite her humble background, is proclaimed on a series of commemorative scarabs that Amenhotep III produced to celebrate their union: "Royal Wife Tiy, may she live. The name of her father is Yuya. The name of her mother is Thuyu. She is the wife of a strong king." Strikingly, both in this text and elsewhere, Tiy's name is written in a cartouche. She was also given unprecedented prominence in royal monuments. She is shown alongside the king and even portrayed as a

▷ **Commemorative scarab**
Amenhotep III distributed scarabs to announce events that were important to him. These events included his marriage to Queen Tiy, and the creation of a pleasure lake for her.

divine being. A temple was built for her at Sedeinga, in Nubia, where she was worshipped as a form of the goddess Hathor. She was also depicted as a sphinx and as a form of the goddess Taweret.

After the death of Amenhotep III, Tiy continued to be active. Tushratta of Mitanni regarded her as an influential person, writing directly to her to complain about his deteriorating relationship with her son. A stela of Tiy found at Medinet Gurob suggests that she went there some time after her husband's death. Gurob was a major harim palace in the Faiyum, built to house some of the many royal wives and their attendants. Tiy also seems to have visited the city of Amarna, where she is depicted alongside Akhenaten in the tomb of her steward, Huya. Amenhotep III's tomb contained a suite of rooms intended for Tiy's burial with him. A stone sarcophagus was also prepared for her in Akhenaten's tomb at Amarna, and items of her burial equipment were also discovered in the mysterious KV55, in the Valley of the Kings. The current whereabouts of Tiy's body are disputed. Tutankhamen's tomb contains a model coffin housing a lock of her hair, presumably a memento of his beloved grandmother. He may have ordered a burial for her at Thebes.

△ **Faience figure of Tiy**
Images of Tiy often associated her with goddesses. The inscription on this figure refers to the vulture goddess Nekhbet. Her vulture headdress with its triple uraei identifies her as both a royal and a divine mother.

1390 BCE Amenhotep III becomes king

1379 BCE Amenhotep III creates a pleasure lake for Tiy at Akhmim

1342 BCE Tiy possibly visits Amarna

1388 BCE Royal Marriage scarab issued

1352 BCE Amenhotep III dies, and Amenhotep IV becomes king

1340 BCE Likely death of Tiy

Akhenaten

Egypt's heretic king

No king of ancient Egypt had a more dramatic impact on the culture of the country he ruled than Akhenaten. More than three thousand years after his death, he is still the subject of fierce controversy.

Akhenaten did not expect to be king. His elder brother, Tuthmosis, was the heir to Amenhotep III, but when Tuthmosis died before his father, the younger son, Amenhotep, became co-regent. When Amenhotep III died, Amenhotep IV became sole ruler and then changed his name to Akhenaten.

Solar religion and the Aten

Amenhotep III had been interested in solar religion, but Amenhotep IV developed this interest much further than his father. He believed that he had a special bond with Aten, a form of the sun god that appeared as a sun disk whose rays shone down upon the king and his family.

Having a favorite deity was not unusual, but Amenhotep IV worshipped the Aten to the exclusion of all the other gods in the official state religion. In the early years of his reign, he tried to persuade the Thebans to worship the Aten by building temples to him at Karnak, but the religious identity of Thebes was too closely bound up with Amen-Ra, so Amenhotep had to look for another place in which to worship his god.

In the fifth year of his reign, Amenhotep did several extraordinary things. He changed his name from Amenhotep (meaning "Amen is Satisfied") to

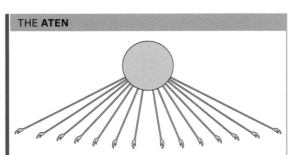

THE ATEN

Akhenaten rejected the pantheon of gods worshipped by the Egyptians. His god, the Aten, came from a tradition of solar deities but without the human characteristics of gods such as Ra. The Aten was depicted as a sun disk with sun rays like arms stretching out to the Earth. Each ray had a hand, often holding out an ankh—representing life—to the royal family. This simple image represented a god who was, in essence, life-giving sunlight.

Akhenaten (meaning "Effective for the Aten"). He also began to move his court to a new capital city that he called Akhetaten ("The Horizon of the Aten"), now known as Amarna. He created the entire city from scratch at a new site in Middle Egypt and carved boundary stelae in the cliffs to the east and west of it. These set out the city's purpose—to build temples for the Aten, residences for the royal family, a new royal cemetery, and tombs for members of the court that Akhenaten took with him to Amarna. Although they are not mentioned on the boundary stelae, there were also villas and small houses for the civilian population of Amarna, and these have been the focus of much of the archaeological work carried out there.

The image of the king

All of this was revolutionary, but Akhenaten also changed another fundamental aspect of Egyptian elite culture—the way in which the king and his family were represented in art. A series of colossal statues found at Karnak show that he made this change early in his reign. Instead of depicting the king with a conventionally powerful physique, images

▽ **Talatat blocks**
Amarna was built quickly, because it was mostly constructed of small blocks of limestone called talatat. These were much easier to transport and use than the large stone blocks that had traditionally been used to build temples. This talatat block depicts Akhenaten sacrificing a duck.

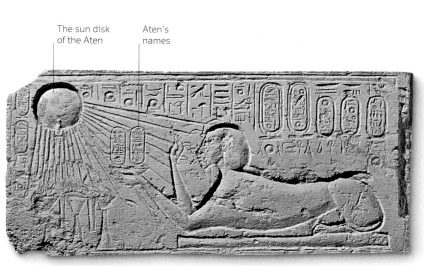

The sun disk of the Aten

Aten's names

△ **Akhenaten as a sphinx**
Not all of the art of Akhenaten's reign was revolutionary.
The king was sometimes shown in the traditional form of
a superhuman. Here, he is depicted as a sphinx offering the
Aten a pair of cartouches containing the god's own name.

of Akhenaten show him as a slim, attenuated figure
with a narrow chest, wide hips, and spindly arms and
legs. He is also given a strangely elongated head, a
prominent chin, and full lips.

There have been many theories about the reasons
for this dramatic change of style in art. Some claim
that it was an unusually accurate depiction of an
acute medical condition that afflicted the king.
Others maintain that it aimed to reflect the theology
of "Atenism" in art—Akhenaten wanted to depict
himself as an androgynous figure in honor of
the Aten, who was essentially neither male nor
female. Whatever the explanation, this extreme
Amarna style of art was not just applied to
images of the king, but also to those of other
members of the royal family.

Akhenaten died in around the 17th year
of his reign (1336 BCE). He may have been
buried in the royal tomb that he had
prepared for himself at Akhetaten, but he
probably did not rest there for very long.
With Akhenaten dead, there seems to
have been little interest among the court,
or even his own family, in continuing the
revolution that he had started.

▷ **Colossal statue of Akhenaten**
The new royal image introduced by Akhenaten
is evident in the statues of him. They retain
the traditional regal emblems of the crown,
flail, and scepter; but the king looks neither
male nor female, but a mixture of the two.

A false beard
elongates
the face

The Amarna Letters

Diplomacy and trade in the 14th century BCE

Sometimes, archaeological discoveries, even illicit ones, completely transform our understanding of the past. The Amarna Letters are just such a discovery. They enable us to read the actual words that ancient kings wrote to each other.

△ **Cretans bearing gifts**
Scenes of foreigners bearing tributes feature in several New Kingdom private tombs. This group of visitors from Crete, which was never part of Egypt's empire, was probably engaged in some form of trade.

In 1886 or 1887, illegal excavations at the site of Amarna uncovered hundreds of hard clay tablets that were covered with strange patterns. These tablets fell into the hands of antiquities dealers, museums, and others and were eventually recognized as letters written in the wedge-shaped cuneiform script of the ancient Near East. Today, 382 examples of these tablets are known and are referred to collectively as the Amarna Letters.

Writing and filing
The Amarna Letters were found in what seems to have been the "Place of the Letters of Pharaoh," where the king's correspondence was filed. They cover the period from the 30th year of Amenhotep III's reign to the first year of Tutankhamen's. The earliest letters were probably "live" correspondence taken to Amarna by Egyptian foreign officials.

Correspondents seem to have written to each other in Babylonian, the diplomatic language of the period, using cuneiform script inscribed on clay tablets. When tablets arrived in Egypt, they were translated into Egyptian and copied onto papyrus. Then, when the king wrote back, this process was reversed. Almost all of the Amarna tablets are letters received by the king, but many of them refer to the king's previous replies, making it possible to reconstruct the replies that were sent from Egypt.

The tablets were left behind when Amarna was abandoned, but the papyrus copies were presumably taken with the government to Memphis or Thebes.

The letters fall into two groups: those written to or from "brother" kings and those to or from Egypt's vassals.

Brothers and vassals
In the 14th century BCE, there was no doubt who the great powers in the Near East and the Eastern Mediterranean were. These were territories whose rulers regarded each other with a grudging diplomatic respect and addressed each other as "brothers" in their correspondence.

Egypt had a special place in these relationships, because it did not feel threatened by its neighbors, as the Mitanni and Hittites did. For this reason, everybody wanted to befriend the Egyptian king, and the main point of their "Brother" letters was to ensure Egypt's continued friendship and to maintain

▽ **"Brother" and "Vassal" states**
The range of states that took part in the "Brother" and "Vassal" correspondences with Egypt shows that Egypt's sphere of influence stretched from Turkey's Aegean coast in the west to the Persian Gulf in the east. Mycenaean Greece remained independent.

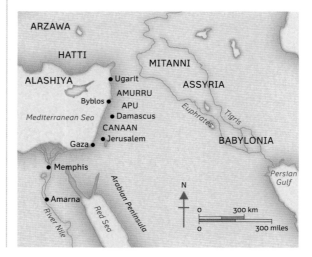

"**May my brother** send to me very **large quantities of gold**."

KING TUSHRATTA WRITES TO AMENHOTEP III

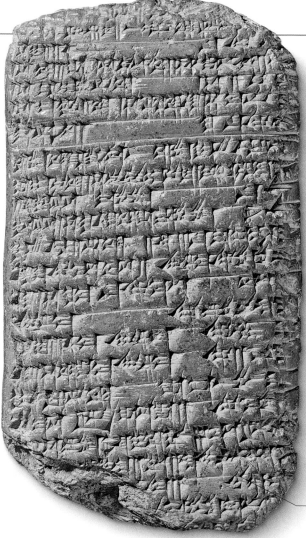

Wedge-shaped
cuneiform text

the diplomatic status quo. In one such letter, for example, Tushratta of Mitanni expresses concern that Amenhotep IV does not seem as committed to Egypt's special relationship with Mitanni as Amenhotep III had been.

The "Brother" letters are full of assurances of respect and sometimes refer to gifts that accompanied the letters. These were often personal presents from one king to another, but some letters intimate trade on a significant scale, most notably the large quantities of copper sent to Egypt from Alashiya, king of Cyprus.

The "Vassal" letters are also full of assurances, this time given by the rulers of the Levantine cities that lay within the three provinces of Egypt's Levantine Empire—Canaan, Apu, and Amurru. These vassals had to express their loyalty in word and deed, as they were expected to put themselves and their cities at the disposal of the Egyptian state—to provide quarters for passing regiments of the Egyptian army, for example. They were also expected to provide resources that the king of Egypt required on demand—technologically sophisticated materials such as glass, for instance.

△ **Longer letters**
These clay tablets are particularly fine examples of some of the longer Amarna Letters. The one on the left was sent from King Burnaburiash of Babylon to Akhenaten; the one on the right was sent from King Tushratta of Mitanni to Queen Tiy.

ULU BURUN

This replica of a ship that sank off Ulu Burun, on the southern coast of Turkey, in around 1300 BCE, gives a good sense of what a Late Bronze Age trading vessel looked like. The original ship provides the best evidence for the existence of international trade during this period and indicates the importance of maritime transport for moving large cargoes around the Mediterranean. It is not known where the ship came from or where it was going, but it contained a variety of goods that were transported around the Eastern Mediterranean at the time. Its most significant cargo in both weight and value was 354 ingots (10 tons/9 tonnes) of raw copper.

**SHIPWRECK CLOSE TO THE
SHORE OF ULU BURUN**

Amarna

The court of the sun king

Akhenaten's devotion to the sun god called the Aten inspired him to build a new city where he could worship his god in a setting that was completely free of associations with any other deities.

Akhenaten decided that Thebes was not the appropriate place for his religious capital, because it was closely associated with the worship of Amen-Ra. His early attempts to build new temples suitable for worshipping the Aten at Karnak were not enough. He wanted to found an entirely new city that would be the exclusive domain of the Aten, just as Thebes was the domain of Amen-Ra.

The site that Akhenaten chose for his new city, supposedly on the advice of the Aten itself, was roughly halfway between Memphis in the north and Thebes in the south. It was a large bay formed by surrounding cliffs on the east side of the Nile, and he selected it mainly because no significant building work had been carried out there before. It was a virgin site, free of connections with any

other gods. Akhenaten named his new city Akhetaten, meaning "The Horizon of the Aten." It is better known today as Amarna.

The temples of Amarna
Akhenaten clearly stated his intentions for Amarna in a series of inscriptions that he carved into the face of the cliffs surrounding the city. On these boundary stelae, he claimed that his primary aim was to build suitable places of worship for the Aten. These were chiefly the House of the Aten and the Mansion of the Aten, which have been identified as the Great Aten Temple and the Smaller Aten Temple, which stood within the Central City. The Great Aten Temple was made up of several linked buildings. The Gempaaten ("[The Place where] the Aten is found") had a

△ **Scepter tip**
During the Amarna Period, artisans made particularly fine objects out of precious materials. This exquisite foot of a gold scepter is inscribed with the name of Princess Meketaten.

◁ **North Palace**
One of the most extensively excavated buildings at Amarna is the North Palace. It contains inscriptions that strongly suggest it was the residence of Akhenaten's eldest royal daughter, Princess Meritaten.

conventional pylon entrance but consisted of open courts filled with more than 700 stone altars for offerings to the Aten. The area next to the Gempaaten was filled with an even greater number of altars, which were made of brick. Behind the Gempaaten stood the Sanctuary, which was probably reserved for the exclusive use of the king and his immediate family. The purpose of the Small Aten Temple is not clear, but it might have been a mortuary temple for Akhenaten. Farther south, the smaller temples of the Kom el-Nana and Meru-Aten were constructed for the Amarna queens.

Palaces and tombs

The main residence of the royal family at Amarna seems to have been the North Riverside Palace. The royal road that cuts through the heart of the Central City probably ran as far north as this palace. The road made it possible for the royal family to travel in chariots to the Central City, passing the North Palace and eventually reaching the Great Palace, which was mainly used for royal ceremonies and displays. A bridge over the road connected the Great Palace to the King's House, which seems to have been a relatively small residence for the king within the Central City.

Akhenaten clearly planned to develop a royal cemetery similar to that of the Valley of the Kings at Thebes. His tomb was in a deep desert valley to the east of Amarna. As at Thebes, the elite were buried in rock-cut tombs in the face of the cliffs overlooking the city (again, similar to those at Thebes), while the lower classes were buried in cemeteries in the desert between the city and the cliffs.

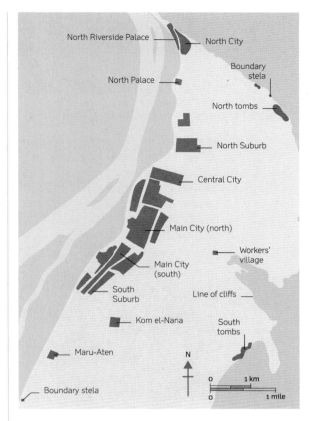

△ **Plan of Amarna**
Amarna ran from north to south, to the east of the Nile and lying roughly parallel to it. The site includes the desert bay and cliffs to the east.

The people of Amarna

The texts on Akhenaten's boundary stelae provide very little information about the houses, workshops, and government offices that made up the majority of the buildings at Amarna. Archaeologists have, however, unearthed traces of extensive living quarters that were used by people of all the different social classes in Amarna. Most of these dwellings were excavated in the Main City and in the North and South Suburbs (see pp.184–185).

▽ **Palace floor**
Much of the interior decoration of the palaces at Amarna was inspired by scenes from the natural world. Plants and animals found along the river were popular and were painted in vivid pigments on plaster.

"I shall make **Akhetaten** for **the Aten**, my **father**, in **this place**."

AKHENATEN ANNOUNCES HIS PLAN FOR AMARNA

House of Ranefer

A typical New Kingdom villa

One of the great archaeological discoveries at Amarna has been the houses of the people who lived there; such evidence of homes rarely occurs elsewhere. The large and complex houses of the elite population, normally referred to as Amarna villas, are particularly important, as they provide detailed information about the buildings in which these families lived and, in some cases, worked. One of the best examples of an Amarna villa, although by no means the largest, is the one that belonged to the chariot officer Ranefer in the southern part of the main city at Amarna.

▽ Bathroom

Amarna villas included well-equipped and comfortable bathrooms. Servants probably carried out tasks such as pouring water over people taking a shower and removing the container of waste from beneath the toilet seat.

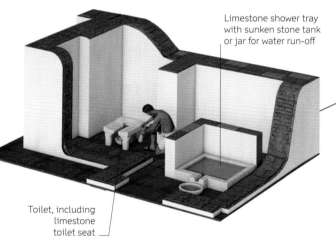

Limestone shower tray with sunken stone tank or jar for water run-off

Toilet, including limestone toilet seat

Beds were often placed on raised platforms

Roof of wooden beams, overlaid with matting and mud plaster

Roofed entrance hall leading to ground floor

Whitewashed mud plaster

Window grilles, made from single pieces of limestone

Second story of several rooms

Double doorway with jambs and lintels bearing name and titles of house owner

RANEFER HOUSE **AND SURROUNDING STRUCTURES**

Although the details of Amarna villas differ, their floorplans have several elements in common, such as a central hall and ancillary rooms. Most of the villas also had facilities outside the main house, which might have included extensive grounds and a chapel. The external facilities attached to Ranefer's villa included granaries, a well, and rooms that were probably used for preparing food. These were vital amenities necessary to produce bread and beer to feed the household.

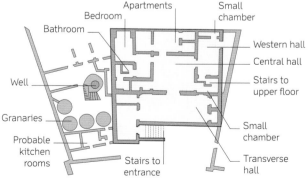

Bedroom

Bathroom

Apartments

Small chamber

Well

Granaries

Probable kitchen rooms

Stairs to entrance

Western hall

Central hall

Stairs to upper floor

Small chamber

Transverse hall

PLAN OF THE RANEFER COMPLEX

△ Survival of Amarna villas

Amarna is the only city in Egypt where large New Kingdom villas still exist in sufficiently good condition to reveal their layout in any detail. Written records show that other cities in Egypt, such as Thebes and Memphis, also had such mansions for elite officials and their families, but these buildings have not survived.

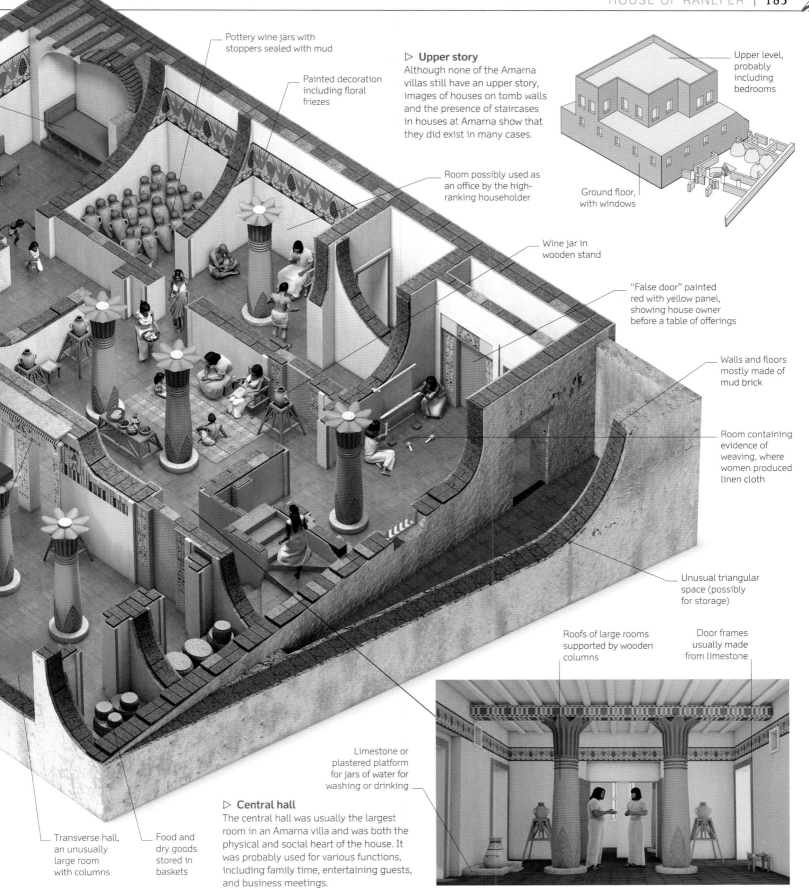

Pottery wine jars with stoppers sealed with mud

Painted decoration including floral friezes

▷ **Upper story**
Although none of the Amarna villas still have an upper story, images of houses on tomb walls and the presence of staircases in houses at Amarna show that they did exist in many cases.

Upper level, probably including bedrooms

Ground floor, with windows

Room possibly used as an office by the high-ranking householder

Wine jar in wooden stand

"False door" painted red with yellow panel, showing house owner before a table of offerings

Walls and floors mostly made of mud brick

Room containing evidence of weaving, where women produced linen cloth

Unusual triangular space (possibly for storage)

Roofs of large rooms supported by wooden columns

Door frames usually made from limestone

Limestone or plastered platform for jars of water for washing or drinking

Transverse hall, an unusually large room with columns

Food and dry goods stored in baskets

▷ **Central hall**
The central hall was usually the largest room in an Amarna villa and was both the physical and social heart of the house. It was probably used for various functions, including family time, entertaining guests, and business meetings.

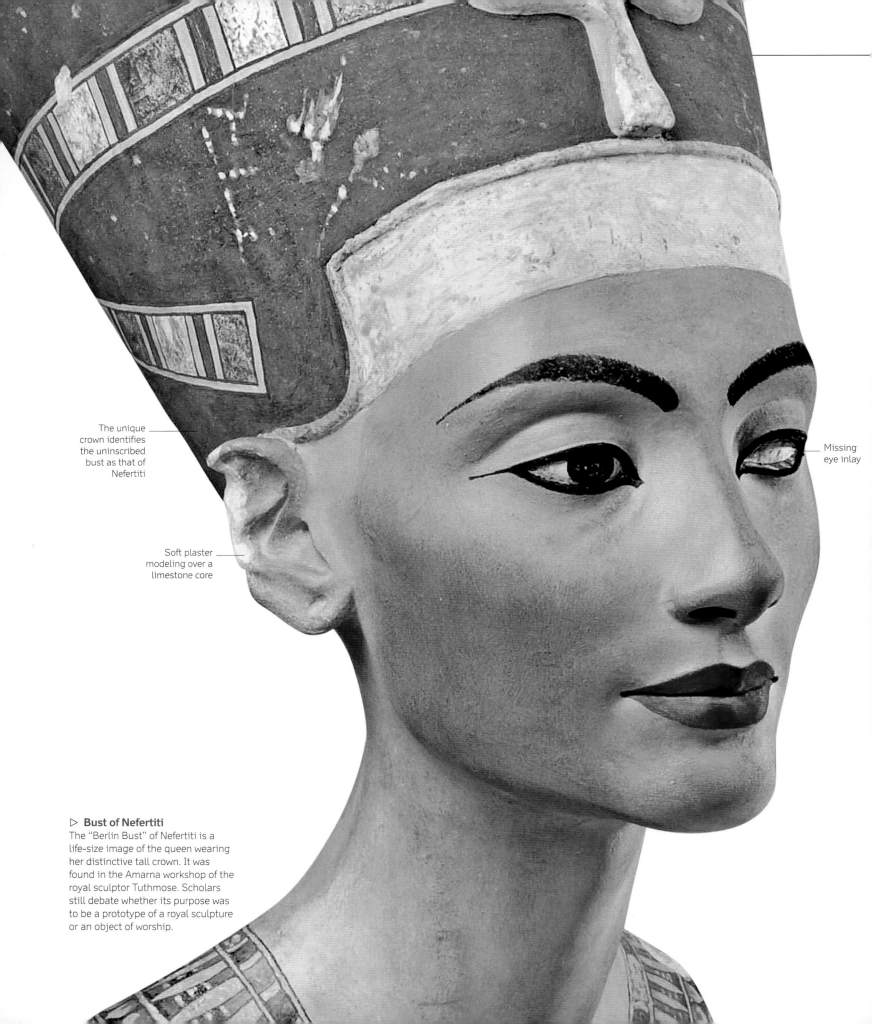

The unique crown identifies the uninscribed bust as that of Nefertiti

Missing eye inlay

Soft plaster modeling over a limestone core

▷ **Bust of Nefertiti**
The "Berlin Bust" of Nefertiti is a life-size image of the queen wearing her distinctive tall crown. It was found in the Amarna workshop of the royal sculptor Tuthmose. Scholars still debate whether its purpose was to be a prototype of a royal sculpture or an object of worship.

Nefertiti

"A Beautiful One Has Come"

Akhenaten may have been the dominant personality behind the major artistic and religious changes of the Amarna Period, but he had an indispensable partner in these changes—the Great Royal Wife Nefertiti.

Today, Nefertiti is one of the most recognizable ancient Egyptians, known through her famous bust in Berlin. It is surprising, therefore, that so little is really known about her. The lack of evidence about her origins, importance, and ultimate demise has only added to her allure as the most mysterious and beautiful queen of ancient Egypt.

Nefertiti's name, meaning "A Beautiful One Has Come," has led to speculation in the past that she was not Egyptian, but possibly a Mitannian princess sent to Egypt as a diplomatic bride. However, most scholars think she was Egyptian and had a sister, Mutnodjmet. Nefertiti may have come from the same well-connected Akhmim family as Queen Tiy, and her father may have been Tiy's brother, Ay.

Nefertiti is best known as Akhenaten's Great Royal Wife and the mother of six daughters. She seems to have been a key figure in the developing theology of the Amarna Period (see pp.178–179). She was one of the few people apart from the king, for example, to whom the god Aten extended his life-giving hands. In fact, art of the Amarna Period often shows Nefertiti as being only slightly less important than the king himself. Religious scenes of the royal family, for instance, depict a divine triad not of god father, goddess mother, and king, as was normal, but of god (Aten), king (Akhenaten), and queen (Nefertiti). Nefertiti's role as a reflection of Akhenaten even extends to artworks showing her with the same distinctive physiognomy as him.

Nefertiti's disappearance from all records after Year 12 of Akhenaten's reign (when Amarna may have been struck by plague) led to speculation about her death, banishment, or transformation into Smenkhkare, Akhenaten's successor. A recently discovered quarry inscription near Amarna shows, however, that she was still alive in Year 16. She was meant to be buried in the royal tomb at Amarna, but her final resting place is unknown.

△ **Amarna princess**
The unique art style of the Amarna Period extended to the royal daughters, who were shown with similar facial features to their father, but also with these strangely elongated heads.

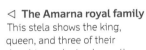

◁ **The Amarna royal family**
This stela shows the king, queen, and three of their daughters relaxing beneath the rays of the Aten. High-ranking members of society were expected to worship the Aten through the royal family.

1352 BCE Amenhotep III dies and is succeeded by Amenhotep IV

1349 BCE Akhenaten and Nefertiti move to Amarna

1341 BCE Princess Meritaten becomes her father's Great Royal Wife

1336 BCE Akhenaten dies and is succeeded by Smenkhkare

1349 BCE Amenhotep IV changes his name to Akhenaten

1342 BCE Nefertiti disappears from all records in Amarna

1338 BCE Nefertiti is still alive

△ **Floor tiles**
The decorative features of a palace often emphasized the king's role as a vanquisher of foreign enemies. These glazed floor tiles depict various enemies who could now be trodden underfoot.

Royal palaces

The dwelling places of the kings

It is easy to imagine that the palaces of the Egyptian kings must have been as grand in scale and impressive as the European royal palaces of the 18th and 19th centuries, but they were in fact relatively modest.

Although the royal tombs and major temples of ancient Egypt were built of the strongest and most durable materials available—usually stone—the royal palaces were not. Much like the houses of ordinary Egyptians, they were constructed from less permanent materials, usually mud brick, with small amounts of stone or wood in places. This means that just like domestic houses, very few palaces have survived. Tombs and temples were built to last so that kings and gods could be worshipped for eternity, but a king may rarely have stayed in one place for long during the course of his lifetime.

◁ **Medinet Habu palace**
As part of the complex of the mortuary temple of Ramesses III, this palace may have been built in Ramesses' lifetime. If so, he may have used it both as his residence at Thebes and also for ceremonies.

king did not need elaborate suites of rooms while he was traveling around the country on business.

Ceremonial palaces
Another type of palace might be called a "ceremonial palace," where different public or semipublic ceremonies were carried out in an appropriately formal setting. These palaces sometimes had a high window, elaborately framed with images of royal power, through which the king could look down on loyal officials and reward them. These so-called Windows of Appearance are often shown in the tombs of officials who had been rewarded in this way. One such window has also been found in the remains of a small palace attached to the mortuary temple of Ramesses III at Medinet Habu. Built alongside the great court of the temple itself, this palace would have been a suitable place for a large crowd to gather before the king.

Temporary and permanent residences
Some of the most interesting information about life in Egyptian palaces comes from administrative documents that talk about how they were run. They refer to "Mooring Places of Pharaoh," the places in which the king and his retinue stayed for short periods of time as they traveled around Egypt. Throughout Egyptian history, the king would be on the move, traveling around the country on tours on inspection, and he needed rest houses in which to stay. This accommodation had to be built quickly, a short time ahead of the king's arrival, so they were not meant to be permanent. The king usually traveled by boat along the Nile, so the rest houses were probably built close to the river. This explains why they were called Mooring Places, and also why they have not survived.

A more permanent form of residence was the so-called "harim-palace," which provided long-term accommodation for the numerous royal women and their children. The best-known example of this is the palace-town of Medinet Gurob in the Faiyum.

Palaces for work
Archaeological remains also indicate that not all palaces were primarily royal residences. The palace of King Merenptah that has been excavated at Memphis, for example, is essentially a large and complex audience hall. Based on the architecture of a temple, its layout meant that a petitioner had to walk through a series of courts and halls before reaching the throne room, where the king made his legal judgments. A few private apartments were attached to this sequence of halls, but they were little more than a small bedroom and a bathroom, which suggests that the

△ **Window of Appearance**
This tomb relief depicts a Window of Appearance. This was an ideal location for the king to reward loyal subjects.

THE NORTH PALACE **AT AMARNA**

Permanent palaces for long-term occupancy are rare in Egypt, but one place that still has remnants of a group of royal palaces is Amarna. Here, several palaces used both as residences and for public ceremonies have survived. One of them, known as the North Palace, seems to have been the residence of a royal woman, possibly Princess Meritaten. The palace is a self-contained complex within its own enclosure wall and combines the attributes of a luxurious home, including a large central swimming pool, with more functional features, such as stalls for cattle and residential quarters for servants.

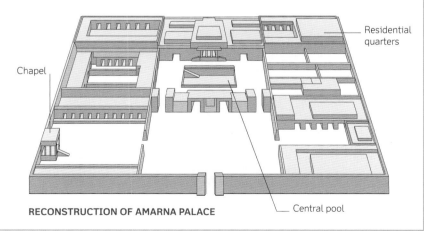

Chapel

Residential quarters

RECONSTRUCTION OF AMARNA PALACE

Central pool

Tutankhamen

The break with Amarna and new beginnings

Although famous for his tomb, which was discovered in 1922, Tutankhamen was also an important, if short-lived, king. It was during his reign that the city of Amarna, and all it stood for, was dramatically abandoned.

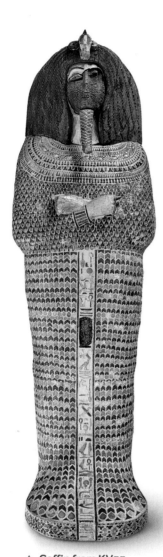

△ **Coffin from KV55**
This coffin may have been used to bury Smenkhkare. Its royal cartouches have been carefully removed and its face roughly ripped off, but it is still an impressive piece of burial equipment.

The events immediately after the death of Akhenaten are hotly debated by Egyptologists, who cannot agree on the existence, gender, or identities of some of the key figures involved. It is likely that Akhenaten was succeeded by Smenkhkare, who was probably his son and who was married to Meritaten, the eldest daughter of Akhenaten and Nefertiti. The similarity of Smenkhkare's throne name, Neferneferuaten, to that of Nefertiti, has led to speculation that they were in fact the same person, but the probable identity of the body found in tomb KV55 (see left) makes that unlikely. Whoever Smenkhkare (1338–1336 BCE) was, he or she ruled for little more than a year before being succeeded by Tutankhaten, who was possibly his/her younger brother.

The reign of Tutankhamen

Two facts suggest that Tutankhaten came to the throne as a child—he only reigned from 1336 to 1327 BCE, and the body in his tomb was that of a teenager. This means that many of the actions ascribed to Tutankhaten were in fact those of his close advisors, most of whom were the same officials who had advised Akhenaten.

It is remarkable how quickly Akhenaten's innovations were overturned. Tutankhaten's name was "de-Atenized" and changed to Tutankhamen, and his queen, Ankhesenpaaten (another daughter of Akhenaten and Nefertiti), became Ankhesenamen. The city of Amarna was abandoned and the court was moved to Memphis. Thebes became the most important religious site in Egypt once again, and Amen was reinstated as the principal Egyptian god. Tutankhamen's agenda was

clearly laid out on the so-called Restoration Stela, which he set up at Karnak. On it, he describes the chaotic state of Egypt when he came to the throne and how he restored all of the ancient gods to their rightful places.

Attempts to restore the damage caused by the Amarna Period—which had included removing the name of Amen from many monuments—began during the reign of Tutankhamen. It is less clear whether actual attacks on Akhenaten's legacy, including the fabric of the city of Amarna itself, began in Tutankhamen's reign or later.

Tombs KV55 and KV62

Part of this restoration may have included the creation of the small tomb in the Valley of the Kings known as KV55. It was badly excavated in 1907, but was found to contain a collection of material that seemed to have come from Amarna. This included objects that may have belonged to the Amarna tomb of Akhenaten's mother, Queen Tiy, and burial goods belonging to his wife, Queen Kiya. The most impressive item was a coffin covered in gold, which was probably made for Kiya and then altered later. It contained the body of a man who was comparatively young at the time of his death. It is tempting to believe that this was the body of Tutankhamen's brother, Smenkhkare, which had been brought from Amarna to be reinterred at Thebes.

◁ **Smenkhkare and Meritaten**
The king and queen on this stela, depicted in the Amarna artistic style, are usually identified as Akhenaten's son and successor, Smenkhkare, and Meritaten, the daughter of Akhenaten and Nefertiti.

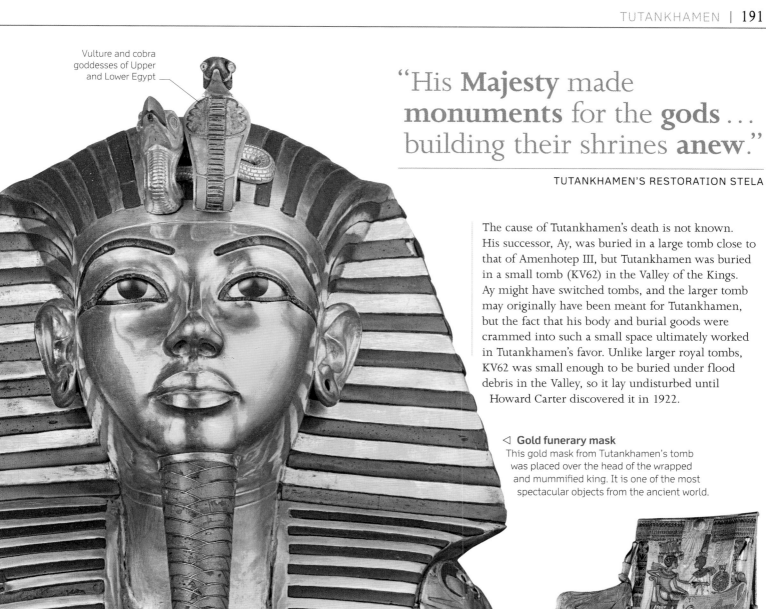

Vulture and cobra goddesses of Upper and Lower Egypt

"His **Majesty** made **monuments** for the **gods** ... building their shrines **anew**."

TUTANKHAMEN'S RESTORATION STELA

The cause of Tutankhamen's death is not known. His successor, Ay, was buried in a large tomb close to that of Amenhotep III, but Tutankhamen was buried in a small tomb (KV62) in the Valley of the Kings. Ay might have switched tombs, and the larger tomb may originally have been meant for Tutankhamen, but the fact that his body and burial goods were crammed into such a small space ultimately worked in Tutankhamen's favor. Unlike larger royal tombs, KV62 was small enough to be buried under flood debris in the Valley, so it lay undisturbed until Howard Carter discovered it in 1922.

◁ **Gold funerary mask**
This gold mask from Tutankhamen's tomb was placed over the head of the wrapped and mummified king. It is one of the most spectacular objects from the ancient world.

△ **Golden throne**
This gold throne was one of the treasures found in Tutankhamen's tomb. The back panel shows the king with his wife, Ankhesenamen. The Aten shines above them, suggesting that the throne was made in Amarna before the royal court moved to Thebes.

ALABASTER **CANOPIC JARS**

Apart from the coffins containing the body of the king, the most important object in the tomb was the gilded canopic shrine, which was the main item in the treasury. Inside the shrine, an alabaster chest held the internal organs of the king, stored in a series of four alabaster jars with lids carved to represent Tutankhamen himself.

Carved stoppers

▽ **Cross-section of tombs**

This cross-section of the tomb of Tutankhamen (KV62) shows how small it was compared to a more conventional royal tomb, that of Ramesses VI (KV9), which lies above it.

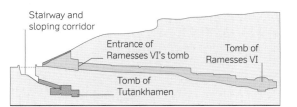

Stairway and sloping corridor

Entrance of Ramesses VI's tomb

Tomb of Ramesses VI

Tomb of Tutankhamen

The tomb of Tutankhamen

Equipped for eternity

Tutankhamen was buried in the small KV62 tomb in the Valley of the Kings rather than the larger tomb being prepared for him, close to that of Amenhotep III in the Western Valley. Ay took over the larger tomb when he became king on Tutankhamen's death, leaving the problem of how to fit Tutankhamen's immense collection of burial equipment in the limited space available. Although the burial chamber is well laid out, the annexe and antechamber in particular were found filled with wonderful objects piled on top of each other. This chaotic distribution of the grave goods was also partly caused by the activities of tomb robbers, who ransacked these rooms, especially boxes and chests, looking for small, valuable objects to steal.

ANNEXE

One of six beds found within the tomb

Pole from a portable pavilion

Woven baskets and pottery jars

Case for throwing sticks and slings

Chest made to contain clothing

One of three couches, decorated with divine hippopotamuses, cows, and lions

Dismantled chariots

Stool of ebony and ivory

Boxes containing preserved joints of meat

Box containing faience vessels and other objects

Sloping corridor (originally filled with rubble)

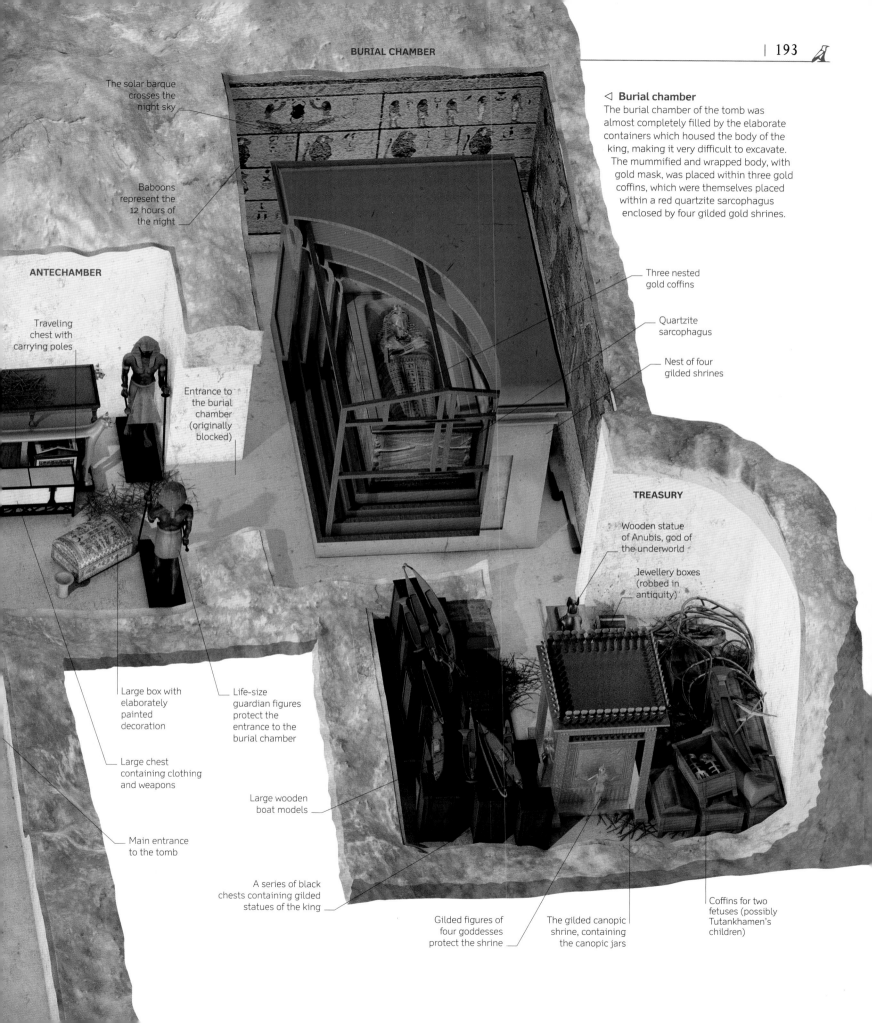

The solar barque crosses the night sky

Baboons represent the 12 hours of the night

ANTECHAMBER

Traveling chest with carrying poles

Entrance to the burial chamber (originally blocked)

◁ Burial chamber
The burial chamber of the tomb was almost completely filled by the elaborate containers which housed the body of the king, making it very difficult to excavate. The mummified and wrapped body, with gold mask, was placed within three gold coffins, which were themselves placed within a red quartzite sarcophagus enclosed by four gilded gold shrines.

Three nested gold coffins

Quartzite sarcophagus

Nest of four gilded shrines

TREASURY

Wooden statue of Anubis, god of the underworld

Jewellery boxes (robbed in antiquity)

Large box with elaborately painted decoration

Life-size guardian figures protect the entrance to the burial chamber

Large chest containing clothing and weapons

Large wooden boat models

Main entrance to the tomb

A series of black chests containing gilded statues of the king

Gilded figures of four goddesses protect the shrine

The gilded canopic shrine, containing the canopic jars

Coffins for two fetuses (possibly Tutankhamen's children)

End of the 18th Dynasty

The struggle for the throne

At the end of the 18th Dynasty, powerful individuals tried to take the throne of Egypt for themselves. It was a time when the royal line had failed, after two centuries of rule by the same family.

△ **Ay in the tomb of Tutankhamen**
In his tomb, Tutankhamen (center) is shown being prepared for the afterlife by Ay (right). The new king is identified by his blue crown, and because his own name is written in a cartouche.

The early death of Tutankhamen, who died without leaving an heir, created a succession crisis of great complexity. There was no other suitable male of the royal family—neither another son of Akhenaten nor one of Amenhotep III. The elder daughter of Akhenaten, Princess Meritaten, had also died.

One possible heir was Tutankhamen's widow, Ankhesenamen, and it seems that she may have tried to secure the throne for herself. A letter addressed to the Hittite king has been found in which an unnamed Egyptian queen, whose husband has just died, invites the king to send a son to marry her and to become king of Egypt. The Hittite king sent a son, but he died on his way to Egypt, which did little to improve the already poor relationship between Egypt and the Hittites.

King Ay

The identity of the king who emerged from this crisis is made clear on the walls of Tutankhamen's tomb. The dead king is shown having his funeral rites performed by a new king named Ay. It is possible that Ay was Nefertiti's father. He was certainly a member of the Amarna court and went on to serve Tutankhamen and then to put himself forward as king. His bid for the throne will have been made easier by the absence of another member of Tutankhamen's court—the ambitious General Horemheb, who may have been campaigning against the Hittites when Tutankhamen died. Ay must have been very old when he became king. He reigned for just three years, after which Horemheb seized the throne.

King Horemheb

Even before he became king, Horemheb had had an impressive tomb built for himself. Like other high-ranking officials of the period who were most active in northern Egypt, especially at Memphis, he intended to be buried at Saqqara. This ancient Memphite burial ground was important again, and the area to the south of the pyramid of Unas started to fill with elite tombs designed to look like temples, with grand pylon gateways, columned halls, and open courts. In his own tomb, Horemheb is depicted as a successful general who took numerous prisoners of war and

Distinctive Nubian hairstyle

"Behold, **Amen** has come to the **palace** ..., to establish his **crown on his head**."

CORONATION PROCLAMATION OF HOREMHEB

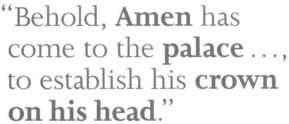

◁ **Nubian prisoners**
Horemheb demonstrated his military successes by decorating the walls of his Memphite tomb with scenes of foreign prisoners being brought to Egypt.

Gold necklaces, a royal
reward for military success

Royal uraeus added after
Horemheb became king

was rewarded by Tutankhamen. When he became king, however, Horemheb started work on a second tomb, in the Valley of the Kings, which was eventually used for his burial. In the meantime, his Memphite tomb was adapted to honor his new royal status and uraeus serpents were carved upon his previously nonroyal brow.

Horemheb and Paramessu

During his reign, Horemheb continued the post-Amarna restoration of Egypt that Tutankhamen had begun (see pp.190–191). Otherwise, he focused mainly on foreign affairs. During the reign of Akhenaten, the Hittites had effectively conquered Mitanni and taken over its Levantine empire. At first, this did not pose a problem for Egypt, as the Hittites were careful not to impinge on Egyptian territory. By the end of the 18th

Dynasty, however, the relationship between the two superpowers had deteriorated into one of hostility and open warfare.

Horemheb had no son and wanted to avert a succession crisis, so he appointed another high-ranking military officer, named Paramessu, as his heir. This was a wise choice. It ensured that the throne passed to a military officer at a time when Egypt was at war with a strong enemy. Also, Paramessu, who became Ramesses I, already had a son and a grandson. This meant that Egypt had a ready-made new royal family, which would become the 19th Dynasty.

◁ **Scribal statue of Paramessu**
Members of Egypt's elite often chose to be depicted as humble scribes. However, as these inscriptions show, their high status was also made abundantly clear.

△ **Horemheb's rewards**
Scenes of being rewarded by the king were common in New Kingdom private tombs. In this fragment of a relief from his tomb at Memphis, Horemheb is shown enjoying the military decorations that Tutankhamen has awarded him. Such decorations were known as "the gold of the brave."

5
The Late
New Kingdom
c.1295–1069 BCE

The Late New Kingdom

The 19th and 20th Dynasties, both of which were roughly 100 years long, constituted The Late New Kingdom. The dominant figure of this era was Ramesses II, who ruled for nearly a third of the entire period.

Ramesside Egypt

Ramesses II continued the work of his father, Seti I, in carrying out building works throughout Egypt and in Nubia. As well as completing Seti I's temple at Abydos, Ramesses II also built one there for himself. Virtually every major town and city in Egypt benefited from his activities, especially Thebes and Memphis, where he built on a colossal scale. In Nubia, he built even more impressive monuments, including the temple of Abu Simbel. He also turned his hometown in the east Delta into an imperial capital city, which he named Pr-Ramesses, after himself.

Another major archaeological site from this period is the village of Deir el-Medina, built for the craftsmen who worked in the Valley of the Kings. It has yielded artifacts that shine an extraordinary light on the domestic lives of ordinary, working Egyptians. Thanks to these finds, Deir el-Medina is now one of the best-known villages of the ancient world.

Foreign friends and foes

For most of the 19th Dynasty, Egypt's foreign policy had been dominated by her relationship with the other major power in the region—the Hittites. But military confrontation between the two powers during Seti I's reign and the early years of Ramesses II was eventually replaced by mutual understanding, confirmed by a treaty that led to four decades of relative peace. When Merenptah became king, however, a problem that had been increasing during the reigns of his predecessors burst upon Egypt—large groups of Libyans from the west attempted to migrate en masse into the Nile Delta. Merenptah's military defeat of these persistent people had to be repeated during Ramesses III's reign, but the settlement of Libyan prisoners of war in the eastern Delta had consequences that became apparent during the Third Intermediate Period.

Perhaps even more challenging for Ramesses III was the Sea-Peoples' attempted invasion of Egypt. This confederation of seafarers had swept everything before them before they were halted at the gateway to Egypt itself.

Problems of the 20th Dynasty

The difficulties faced by the kings of the 20th Dynasty were not confined to foreign invasions, but also encompassed domestic issues. Ramesses III was the most successful king of the dynasty, not just because of his military victories, but because he was the last king who managed to build all three of the Theban monuments that every king wished to build: a tomb in the Valley of the Kings, additions to Karnak, and a large mortuary temple for himself.

After Ramesses III's death, a further eight kings named Ramesses ruled Egypt, but none of them was able to equal their predecessor's achievements. By the reign of Ramesses XI, royal authority had declined and Egypt was beset by numerous troubles—a failing economy, tomb robberies, and the rise of Libyan warlords.

◁ **Mummy mask of Khonsu**

1294 BCE Seti I becomes king. He later builds his temple at Abydos

1274 BCE Ramesses II fights the Hittites at the Battle of Kadesh

1295 BCE Ramesses I becomes the first king of the 19th Dynasty

1279 BCE Ramesses II becomes king. Begins work on Abu Simbel

1259 BCE Peace treaty signed with the Hittites

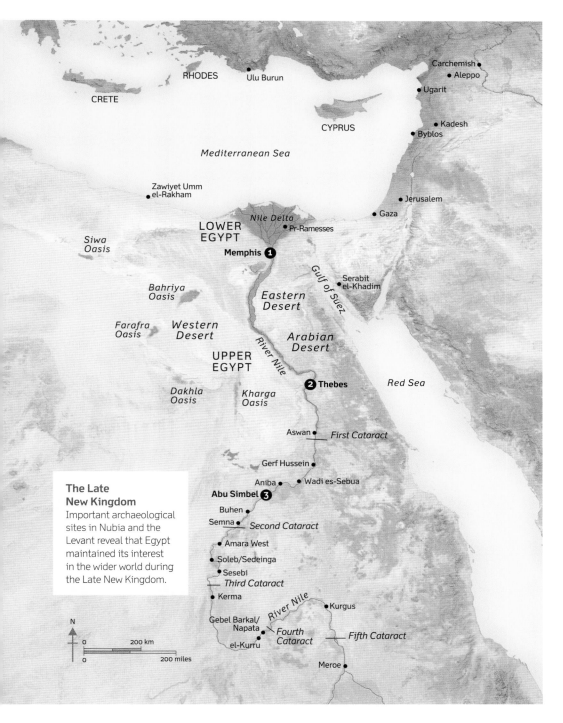

RHODES

Ulu Burun

CRETE

Carchemish
● Aleppo

● Ugarit

CYPRUS

Kadesh
Byblos

Mediterranean Sea

Zawiyet Umm
● el-Rakham

● Jerusalem

Nile Delta

● Gaza

LOWER
EGYPT

● Pr-Ramesses

*Siwa
Oasis*

Memphis **1**

*Bahriya
Oasis*

*Eastern
Desert*

Serabit
● el-Khadim

Gulf of Suez

*Farafra
Oasis*

*Western
Desert*

*Arabian
Desert*

UPPER
EGYPT

River Nile

Red Sea

*Dakhla
Oasis*

*Kharga
Oasis*

2 Thebes

Aswan ● ─── *First Cataract*

Gerf Hussein ●

Aniba ● ● Wadi es-Sebua

Abu Simbel **3**

Buhen

Semna ● ─── *Second Cataract*

● Amara West

● Soleb/Sedeinga

● Sesebi

── *Third Cataract*

● Kerma

Gebel Barkal/
Napata

River Nile

● Kurgus

*Fourth
Cataract*

● el-Kurru

Fifth Cataract

● Meroe

**The Late
New Kingdom**
Important archaeological
sites in Nubia and the
Levant reveal that Egypt
maintained its interest
in the wider world during
the Late New Kingdom.

N

0 ── 200 km
0 ── 200 miles

1 West Hall of Ramesses II, Memphis

2 Luxor Temple, Thebes

3 Great Temple, Abu Simbel

1213 BCE Death of
Ramesses II. Merenptah
becomes king

1184 BCE Ramesses III
becomes king. Wars with
the Libyans and the
Sea Peoples

1099 BCE Ramesses XI
succeeds Ramesses X

1188 BCE Twosret
becomes the last ruler
of the 19th Dynasty

1126 BCE Ramesses VII takes
the throne. Robberies begin
in the Valley of the Kings

1069 BCE Death of Ramesses XI.
The end of the 20th Dynasty and
the New Kingdom

Seti I

Restoring harmony

Seti I's reign was a period of stability after the upheaval of the Amarna Period. Seti I was a king in the traditional mold of New Kingdom monarchs: a soldier and a builder at sites associated with Egypt's gods, especially Thebes and Abydos.

△ **Seti I shabti**
Seti I's burial equipment included hundreds of blue glazed shabtis. Each figure wears the royal nemes headdress and carries the tools needed to work for Osiris in the afterlife.

The death of the elderly Ramesses I after little more than a year on the throne left his son, Seti I, as king of Egypt. After burying Ramesses in one of the smaller tombs in the Valley of the Kings, Seti set about establishing his own legacy.

Order and harmony
Restoration was a common theme in the texts that new kings inscribed on the monuments that they erected—they hoped to distinguish themselves from previous rulers by repairing the damage that they had caused. Seti I wanted to restore Egypt to *maat*, cosmic order, after the chaos wrought by the Amarna Period. His restoration works did include major projects, but he may also have added his name to public buildings simply to make his presence known in places all over Egypt. He was also happy to continue projects that were already in progress, most notably the Great Hypostyle Hall at Karnak.

Seti followed custom in his work at Thebes, not only adding to Karnak, but also building a mortuary temple for himself at Gurna, on the west bank. He was also an innovator, building temples in unusual places, such as at Kanais in the Eastern Desert. This temple, next to a well, was for miners working in the area.

His most impressive monument, however, was the temple that he built at Abydos, the site of Osiris's burial. Following ancient tradition there, Seti I built a massive mahat-temple with seven chapels for the gods worshipped, featuring members of Osiris's family and the divine Seti himself. Behind the temple, he built the so-called Osireion—a false underground tomb made of massive blocks of granite.

Seti the warrior
Right from the start of his reign, Seti was determined to win back the Levantine provinces of the Egyptian empire that had been lost during and just after the

Horus pours libations for his father, Osiris

▷ **Temple of Seti I**
With its delicately carved and painted walls, Seti I's temple at Abydos is one of the most beautiful temples in the whole of Egypt. It was built of the finest grade limestone and is remarkably well preserved.

△ **Making an offering**
Ramesses I built few monuments in his short reign.
The most substantial was a small chapel at Abydos,
which Seti I finished. This relief carving of his father
making an offering to Osiris is on a wall of the chapel.

Amarna Period. In Year 1, he crossed northern Sinai
and recaptured Gaza, the capital of the province of
Canaan. In later campaigns, he pushed farther north
and brought the province of Upe back under Egyptian
control. He also took the third Levantine province,
Amurru, along with the city of Kadesh, although the
Hittites soon reversed these gains.

Seti I's campaigns were commemorated on victory
stelae that he erected in towns such as Beth-Shan and
Damascus. They also feature in the reliefs he carved
on the walls of his temples. An exterior wall of the
hypostyle hall at Karnak displays detailed images of
some of his wars. Seti is shown crossing into Sinai
with his army and crushing his enemies, including
the Bedouin Shasu people. He is also seen winning
victories against the Libyans in the west.

Seti I died in the north of Egypt, after 16 years
on the throne. His body was transported up the Nile
to Thebes, where it was placed in a sarcophagus of
translucent calcite in the tomb that had been prepared
for him. It was the longest and deepest tomb ever built
for a monarch in the Valley of the Kings.

▷ **The king with a goddess**
Seti I commissioned some of the most exquisite royal
monuments. On this plastered, carved, and painted
pillar from his tomb in the Valley of the Kings, he is
depicted with the goddess Hathor.

Karnak temple complex

The home of the Theban gods

In the New Kingdom, the temple complex at Karnak, in the northern part of Thebes, became one of the largest religious centers in the world. At its heart was the great Temple of Amen-Ra, which was added to and amended by a succession of kings over a period of 2,000 years. It was the nucleus of a network of religious buildings, including Luxor Temple and the Valley of the Kings. Immediately to the south of the Amen-Ra enclosure was a smaller complex of buildings for Amen-Ra's wife, the goddess Mut, while to the north was the temple of the Theban god Montu.

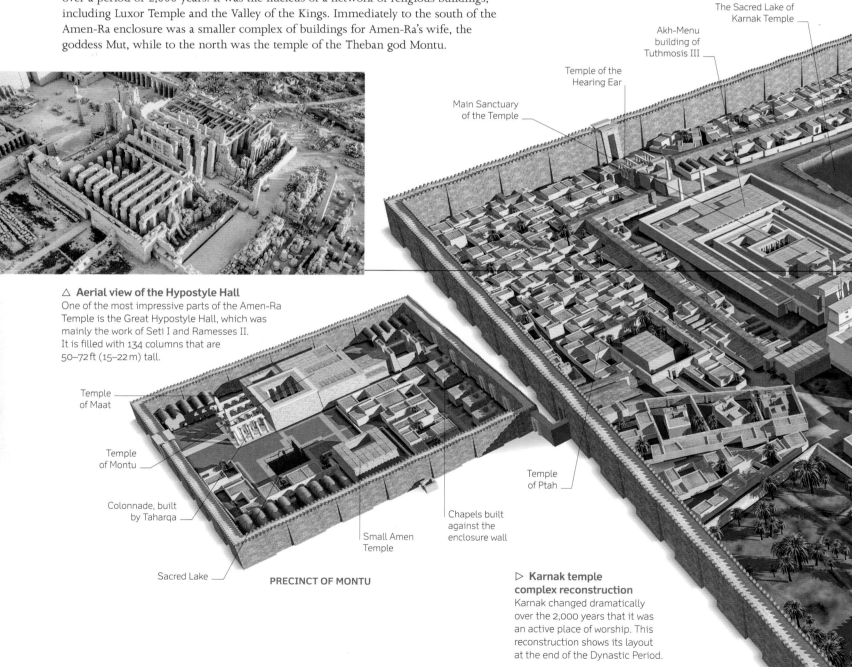

△ **Aerial view of the Hypostyle Hall**
One of the most impressive parts of the Amen-Ra Temple is the Great Hypostyle Hall, which was mainly the work of Seti I and Ramesses II. It is filled with 134 columns that are 50–72 ft (15–22 m) tall.

The Sacred Lake of
Karnak Temple

Akh-Menu
building of
Tuthmosis III

Temple of the
Hearing Ear

Main Sanctuary
of the Temple

Temple
of Maat

Temple
of Montu

Colonnade, built
by Taharqa

Sacred Lake

Small Amen
Temple

Chapels built
against the
enclosure wall

Temple
of Ptah

PRECINCT OF MONTU

▷ **Karnak temple
complex reconstruction**
Karnak changed dramatically over the 2,000 years that it was an active place of worship. This reconstruction shows its layout at the end of the Dynastic Period.

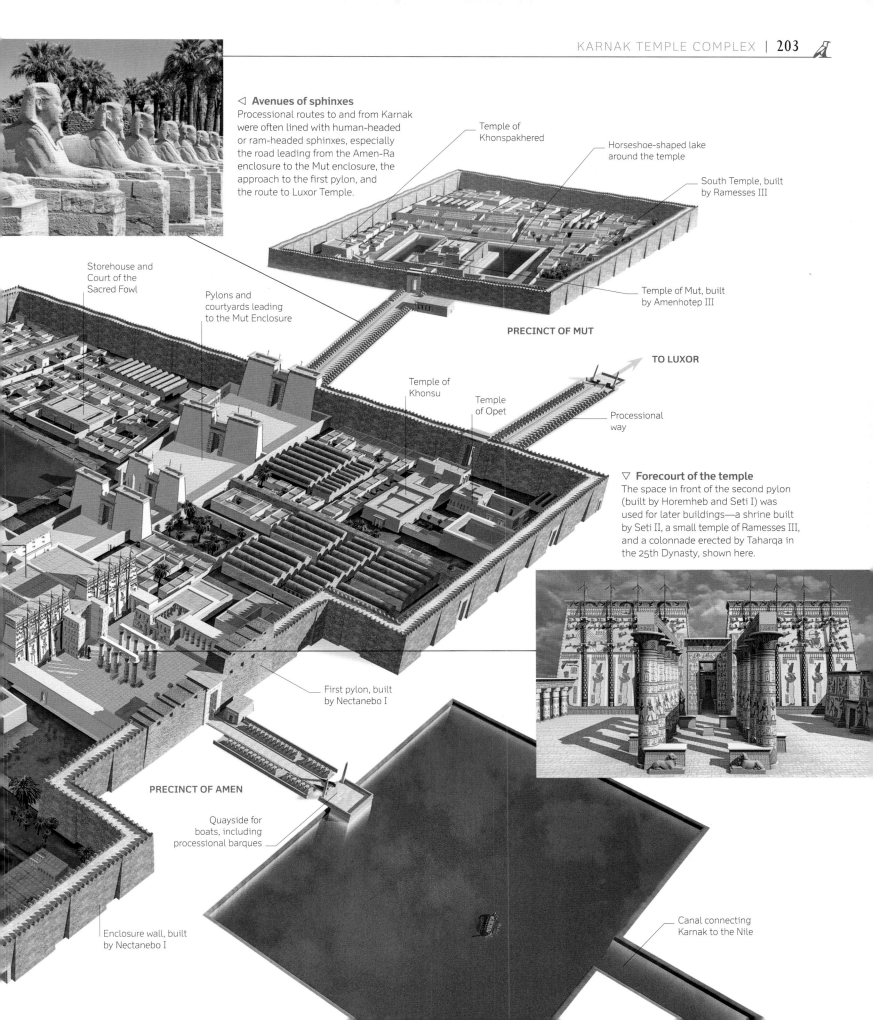

◁ **Avenues of sphinxes**
Processional routes to and from Karnak were often lined with human-headed or ram-headed sphinxes, especially the road leading from the Amen-Ra enclosure to the Mut enclosure, the approach to the first pylon, and the route to Luxor Temple.

Temple of Khonspakhered

Horseshoe-shaped lake around the temple

South Temple, built by Ramesses III

Storehouse and Court of the Sacred Fowl

Pylons and courtyards leading to the Mut Enclosure

Temple of Mut, built by Amenhotep III

PRECINCT OF MUT

TO LUXOR

Temple of Khonsu

Temple of Opet

Processional way

▽ **Forecourt of the temple**
The space in front of the second pylon (built by Horemheb and Seti I) was used for later buildings—a shrine built by Seti II, a small temple of Ramesses III, and a colonnade erected by Taharqa in the 25th Dynasty, shown here.

First pylon, built by Nectanebo I

PRECINCT OF AMEN

Quayside for boats, including processional barques

Enclosure wall, built by Nectanebo I

Canal connecting Karnak to the Nile

△ **The Great Hypostyle Hall in the Amen Temple**
This immense, columned hall is one of the most imposing parts of the Amen Temple. Completed by Ramesses II, it was designed to be an intermediary area between the open court and the hidden sanctuary.

The Precinct of Amen

The house of Amen-Ra, king of the gods

The Amen Temple is one of the most impressive monuments of ancient Egypt, a site of vast scale where visitors feel dwarfed by the giant columns, pylons, obelisks, and statues that surround them.

If pyramids were the defining buildings of the Old Kingdom in terms of monuments, in the New Kingdom, it was temples. Many cities in Egypt had impressive temples, but the Amen Temple at Karnak was the most spectacular of them all.

Building for Amen
The first burst of building activity at Karnak took place in the Middle Kingdom, when rulers of a Theban origin, now kings of a united Egypt, had the resources to create a suitably magnificent home for their patron deity, Amen. Most of this temple, mainly the work of kings of the 12th Dynasty, was swept away during later building work, although some elements, such as the White Chapel built by Senwosret I, have survived. It was the New Kingdom that saw the most dramatic building works at Karnak,

◁ **Central axis of the temple**
As the great doors that once guarded access to the temple are now gone, visitors can look straight from the main entrance to the sanctuary at the very heart of the temple.

as kings competed with their predecessors to construct ever more majestic buildings for Amen, who was now merged with the sun god and called Amen-Ra. Some of the grandest additions are the monolithic granite obelisks erected by Tuthmosis I, Hatshepsut, and Tuthmosis III and the Great Hypostyle Hall completed by Ramesses II. Amenhotep III added several pylon gateways to the temple.

Temple design

Although the pharaohs' additions over 2,000 years make Karnak look complicated, it is actually very simple in concept and followed the same basic blueprint as temples of the Early Dynastic Period (see pp.36–37). A sanctuary contained the image of Amen-Ra, sitting in a barque shrine. This barque

▷ **Colossus of Ramesses II**
Ramesses II erected colossal statues of himself throughout Egypt. This example, which is 50 ft (15 m) tall, stands in front of the second pylon at Karnak.

shrine was taken on procession at different times of the year, and the layout of the Amen Temple reflected this: the building was arranged around central, processional routes that led directly out of the temple, west toward the Nile, or south toward the Mut Temple and Karnak. This arrangement had to be taken into account when planning any later additions to Karnak, so all pylons, courtyards, or pillared halls were built symmetrically, either around the central axis or to one side of it, like the side temple of Ramesses III.

▽ **Temple of Amen-Ra**
Building work had to be planned around the central axis of the Amen Temple, a straight, processional route along which priests carried the barque of Amen. All new elements were therefore built on either side of the central axis, giving the temple a distinctive sense of symmetry.

Akh-Menu (Festival Hall) built by Tuthmosis III

Obelisks of Tuthmosis I, Hatshepsut, and Tuthmosis III

Great Hypostyle Hall

Flagpoles attached to the front of the pylon

Porch added by rulers of the Third Intermediate Period

Courtyard with some remains of the Middle Kingdom Temple

Sanctuary containing the barque shrine of the god Amen-Ra

Second pylon, built by Horemheb and Seti I

Side temple added by Ramesses III

Colonnade added by Taharqa in the 25th Dynasty

First pylon, built by Nectanebo I in the 30th Dynasty

Outer walls that enclosed the entire Precinct of Amen

Theban mortuary temples

"Mansions of Millions of Years"

▽ **Medinet Habu pylon**
The huge pylon gateways
of mortuary temples were
often used as billboards for
images of the king. Here,
Ramesses III is shown
defeating his enemies.

In the New Kingdom, the Valley of the Kings was chosen as the new site for royal burials. As a consequence, it was no longer possible to build mortuary temples adjacent to the kings' tombs.

From at least the beginning of the Old Kingdom, a royal tomb was more than simply a place where a king was buried; it was also a place that served the dead king's cult for eternity. As expressed in the Pyramid Texts, when a king died, he joined the gods in the afterlife, but his *ka*, or *kas*, remained in the tomb to receive food offerings from his people (see pp.70–71).

For this reason, a mortuary temple was built beside the king's pyramid. This was often a large and impressive structure made of the most durable materials and set within a complex of related buildings (see pp.82–83). When kings began to build pyramids again in the Middle Kingdom, mortuary temples were therefore built next to them.

In the New Kingdom, a new tradition was established. At the beginning of the 18th Dynasty, kings started to be buried in secret tombs in the

Valley of the Kings (see pp.160–161). Because these tombs were meant to be hidden, it was no longer possible to build mortuary temples beside them. Not only would doing so reveal the location of the tomb, but the topography of the valley made it unsuitable for large buildings. The valley was also difficult to reach, and the king's cult required that his temple be visited regularly.

A new architecture

The solution to this problem was to separate the mortuary temple from the tomb. One stage of this development can be seen in Hatshepsut's mortuary temple at Deir el-Bahri, which was built against the side of the Theban mountain. The rock of the mountain physically connected her temple to her tomb, which was cut into the Valley of the Kings on the far side of a high ridge. However, most mortuary temples of this period were built at the edge of the desert, close to the inhabited areas of the west bank at Thebes, so they were even further removed from their tombs. This extreme separation of the temple from its tomb was inspired by a new form of architecture that was already in use for conventional cult temples.

All of these temples had certain characteristics in common, namely pylon gateways, open courts, and hypostyle halls. Externally, there was no obvious difference between the Medinet Habu mortuary temple of Ramesses III, for example, and any of the major cult temples. The king's temple, however, was referred to differently, and was called a "Mansion of Millions of Years"—a phrase that celebrated the enduring legacy of the now-divine king.

Decoration and function

Hatshepsut's mortuary temple was also influential in other ways. Broadly speaking, the external parts of her temple celebrated her achievements as king. This theme was picked up by later kings, although their achievements tended to be more military in nature. The inner parts of her temple were more directly connected to her relationship

△ **Medinet Habu**
This relief in the solar court at Medinet Habu shows a scene of sun worship. The king leads a procession of baboons, who were believed to worship the sun, in praise of the sun god Ra.

△ **Ceiling of Medinet Habu**
The decorated surfaces of most of the Theban temples have lost their former pigments, but a few exceptions, such as this ceiling at Medinet Habu, show how colorfully they were originally painted.

with the gods, and they had architecture to match. Both Hatshepsut's temple and that of Ramesses III—which was built 300 years later—had an enclosed suite of rooms dedicated to Osiris, an open sunlit court dedicated to the sun god Ra-Horakhty, and a side chapel that honored the dead king's father. However, the most important element of these temples, and all of the mortuary temples of the period, was a central chapel, or set of chapels, which was built at the very heart of them.

These chapels were designed to house the sacred barque of Amen-Ra and his family, who, in the form of statues, visited the royal mortuary temples during religious festivals. This ritual connected the chief gods of Thebes to the monarch, who was buried just across the river from Karnak in the Valley of the Kings.

▷ **Ramesses II crowned by Amen-Ra**
Mortuary-temple reliefs often depict an individual king's relationship with the gods. Here, Amen-Ra affirms Ramesses II's right to rule, blessing him with a long and fruitful reign.

▽ **The Papyrus of Ani**
One of the finest Books of
the Dead belonged to Ani,
a scribe at Thebes during the
19th Dynasty. This vignette
shows the "Weighing of the
Heart," in which Ani and his
wife face final judgment
before the gods.

The *ba* of Ani
watches the
proceedings

Anubis weighs the
heart against the
feather of *maat*

Thoth records
the result of
the test

Ammit, "Eater of the Dead"

The Book of the Dead

"Chapters of Coming Forth by Day"

In the New Kingdom, one of an Egyptian's main concerns was how to reach the Field of Reeds—the kingdom of Osiris—and be accepted there for eternity. The journey to this paradise was not easy. The hopeful dead had to pass through a series of doorways guarded by fierce demons who demanded to know the correct answers to a series of questions before letting them pass through on their way.

Luckily, for wealthy Egyptians, the solution to this problem, as was so often the case with religious problems involving the afterlife, was to make sure that they had the correct piece of funerary equipment. In this case, it was a guidebook to the afterlife, which was both a road map and a helpful prompt to the questions that the deceased might face.

This guidebook took the form of a papyrus document that was called the "Chapters of Coming Forth by Day." This name emphasizes the optimistic aspect of the book, but it is more commonly known today as the "Book of the Dead." Books of the Dead were divided into series of "chapters," each of which had hieroglyphic text written by a scribe, usually accompanied by an illustration of what the text described, often referred to as a vignette. The most important chapters of the Book of the Dead were not only found in these documents, but were also sometimes painted on the walls of the inner rooms of private tombs, especially during the Ramesside Period.

The Negative Confession

The dead needed to be innocent of the crimes and sins that would prevent them from being accepted into the afterlife. They did this by reciting another section of the Book of the Dead called the "Negative Confession," which was essentially a denial of any sort of wrongdoing. These wrongdoings fell within the broad categories of what could be described as criminal acts, blasphemy against the gods, and antisocial behavior. Whether or not the dead had in fact committed any of these wrongdoings seems to have been less important than their official denial.

Weighing the Heart

Books of the Dead varied in length and quality, but the most important episode common to all of them was the final judgment in the court of the gods. In this trial, the heart of the deceased was weighed against the feather of *maat* to assess whether they were suitable to join the ranks of the blessed dead.

If the heart failed in its test against the feather of *maat*, its owner would not be allowed into the kingdom of Osiris, but would be thrown to a ferocious creature called Ammit, "Eater of the Dead." However, as all Books of the Dead show their owner being greeted by Osiris after passing this test, it is safe to assume that the papyrus was not just a guidebook, but also a guarantee of a successful outcome.

Religious festivals

The gods meet the public

For most of the year, the great temples of the New Kingdom were not accessible to the public, but during religious festivals, their doors were opened and the gods left their houses to go on procession.

The wide, open courtyards of many New Kingdom temples look as if they were built to hold large, regular gatherings of worshippers, but this was not the case. Egyptian temples, especially the great royal temples at places such as Thebes, were not made for worshippers, but to provide houses for the deities who owned them. The gods, usually in the form of statues, were kept in the innermost part of the temple—the sanctuary—where they would be offered food and incense and washed and dressed, sometimes several times a day, by special priests.

Going on parade

Although an ordinary person could not worship in the major temples, there were ways in which they could engage with the great state gods such as Amen-Ra. One of these was to leave a statue of themselves in a suitable pose within the outer parts of the temple representing those occasions when they were allowed in, namely during the great festivals that took place annually. For kings, this was an occasion to follow royal theology by taking the god to visit other temples

in a boat-shaped shrine. For the public, though, this was when the god's image (or, at least, a shrine in which the god was kept, hidden from view) was paraded through the city for everyone to see, giving them the chance to shout out their praises and offer prayers to the passing deity. Pictures of these processions appear on the walls of temples that hosted them and show ranks of priests carrying the elaborately decorated boats of the gods on their shoulders with poles.

Egyptologists know most about the major religious festivals at Thebes—notably the Opet Festival and the "Beautiful Festival of the Western Valley." In the first, Amen-Ra would be carried from Karnak to the Luxor Temple. The route of the procession varied from one period to another but might include traveling by river or along a road that was lined with sphinxes in the Late Period. In the Western Valley Festival, the god would cross the Nile and visit some of the royal mortuary temples on the West Bank.

Festivals and processions were not, however, limited to the great state temples. Local people also held festivals in their villages and paraded images of their gods from small, local temples. Archaeologists know most about this from the artisans' village of Deir el-Medina, where religious holidays formed an important part of life for the villagers.

△ **Temple statue**
A typical temple statue might show the worshipper offering images of the gods of the temple. This statue of Amennakht from Karnak depicts the Theban divine family of Amen-Ra, Mut, and Khonsu.

Shrine containing the god's statue

◁ **A procession**
This vivid ink sketch of a procession on an ostracon from Deir el-Medina shows a god's shrine in its ceremonial boat. Priests are carrying the barque on their shoulders, supported by long poles.

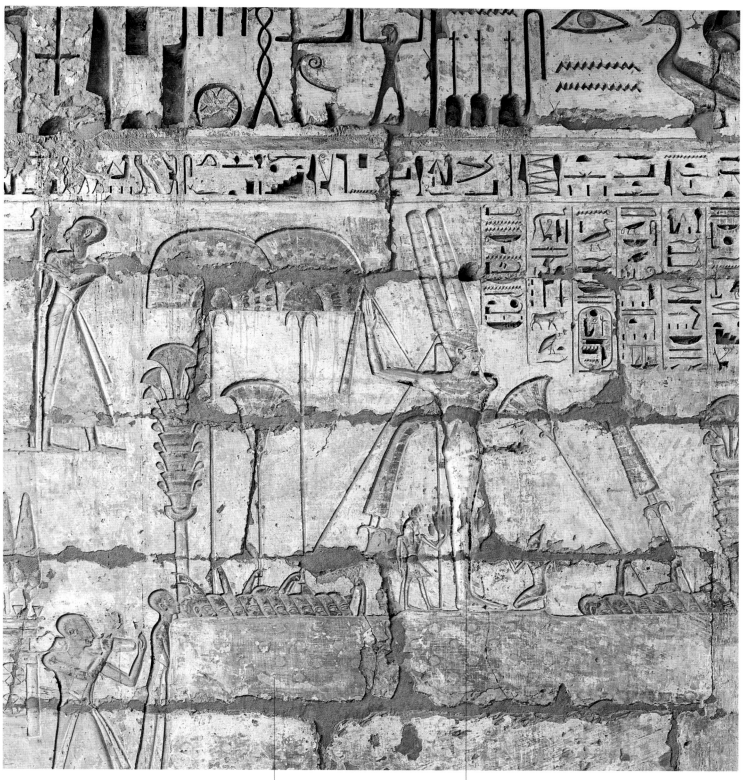

A canopy with gold rosettes covers the priests carrying the barque

The statue of the god Min appears without a shrine

△ **Min Festival at Medinet Habu**
Many mortuary temples were decorated with images of festivals held in and around them. This colorful relief of a procession of the god Min is from Ramesses III's temple at Medinet Habu.

Ramesses II

Egypt's greatest king

The wealth and power of Egypt during the 66-year reign of Ramesses II (1270–1213 BCE) enabled the long-lived and ambitious king to leave an unparalleled stamp on ancient Egypt that is still in evidence today.

△ **Ramesses II as a child**
Although this relief shows Ramesses II in a childlike pose—seated on a cushion, finger to mouth, hair in a sidelock—the presence of a royal cartouche indicates this was made after he became king as an adult.

The reign of Ramesses II was one of tradition and innovation. By emulating the kings of the past whom he admired, Ramesses hoped to create a royal dynasty that could rival the powerful 18th Dynasty.

Building on the past

To Ramesses II, Amenhotep lll was a hero. The king lists drawn up during the Ramesside Period exonerated Amenhotep III from the much-hated Amarna Period (see pp.178–179) and left out all of the kings who ruled between Amenhotep III and Horemheb. Ramesses II continued the work that his father had started, developing Amenhotep III's plans for some monuments and building significant additions for others. He showed his "respect" for Amenhotep III by adapting royal statues that had been carved during his reign and reusing them as his own. Ramesses' long reign gave

▷ **Divine being**
Ramesses II is often portrayed as a divine being. In this triad statue of a family group, he is depicted as a child sitting between his "father," the god Amen-Ra, and his "mother," the goddess Mut.

him the chance to develop many new projects. He rebuilt or added to virtually every significant temple in Egypt and built far more temples in Nubia than any previous king had. He also strengthened Egypt's borders by constructing fortress-towns along the edge of the Western Delta and the Mediterranean coast, anticipating the Libyan invasions of the late-19th and 20th Dynasties (see pp.240–241).

Pr-Ramesses

But Ramesses II's greatest achievement was a new royal city. The desire to enhance his hometown, the need for a military base closer to the threat from the Hittites, and possibly the simple desire for self-glorification inspired Ramesses II to found a new city near the old Hyksos capital of Avaris. It was called *Pr-Ramessu Aa-Nakhtu* (The House of Ramesses, Great of Victories) but is normally referred to as Pr-Ramesses. Very little of this city now remains above ground, but a combination of textual evidence and a series of excavations have made it clear that it was built on a massive scale, with temples, palaces, colossal statues, industrial areas, and military barracks.

1303 BCE Birth of Ramesses II

1274 BCE Battle of Kadesh

1255 BCE Abu Simbel inaugurated

1279 BCE Ramesses II becomes king

1259 BCE Peace treaty with the Hittites

1213 BCE Death of Ramesses II

△ Gold pectoral with cartouche
Most Ramesside jewelry that belonged to the king himself or were royal gifts to his advisers and family has been lost, but some rare examples have survived, such as this amulet bearing the king's name in a cartouche.

"He shall **direct this land**."

SETI I'S DECREE ABOUT
PRINCE RAMESSES

Heka scepter of
royal authority

▷ Strong king
This life-size statue of a youthful Ramesses II depicts him in a sophisticated style typical of the early part of his reign. Despite being made of hard granodiorite, the carving of Ramesses' muscular body beneath his finely pleated robe demonstrates the skill of the sculptor or sculptors.

Family and foes

Wives, children, and Hittites

In the first five years of his reign, Ramesses II tried to solve two of the problems faced by his predecessors. He needed to establish the succession by producing royal sons, and he had to face the Hittites, Egypt's most dangerous enemy.

Ramesses II is known to have fathered over 100 children, and to do that, he clearly needed more than one wife. Even before he came to the throne, he had been in a position to produce many sons and daughters. He refers to his father having "selected for me ... harim-women and female companions." These women were not equal in status though. The most important of them—those whose children formed the core of the royal family and would give the king an heir—were a small number of queens, including the Great Royal Wives.

Nefertari and Isetnofret

The first of these queens was Nefertari, who was not of royal birth herself, but quickly rose to prominence as Ramesses II's favored queen. Even before Seti I had died, she had produced Amenhirwenemef, Seti's grandson and her husband's first heir. She gave birth to five royal princes, but they all died before their father.

Nefertari had a special position at the royal court, similar to that of Queen Tiy during Amenhotep III's reign (see pp.176–177). She was worshipped as a form of the goddess Hathor and had her own Smaller Temple next to Ramesses II's Great Temple at Abu Simbel in Nubia. She was also given one of the most exquisitely decorated tombs in Egypt, in the Valley of the Queens, where she was buried after about 20 years of marriage.

During his marriage to Nefertari, Ramesses was also married to another important secondary queen named Isetnofret. Her children, like Nefertari's, appear in

processional scenes in Ramesses II's temples, which show a few of the most important royal children. Isetnofret was the mother of at least four children, including Khaemwese; Merenptah (Ramesses' eventual successor); and a daughter, Bintanath.

After the deaths of Isetnofret and Nefertari, their daughters Bintanath and Meritamen took on the roles of Great Royal Wives. In Year 34, they were joined by the Hittite princess Maathorneferura, whose marriage to Ramesses was part of a growing diplomatic understanding between Egypt and the Hittite state. Meritamen disappeared late in the reign of Ramesses II and was replaced by Princess Nebettawy, another of Nefertari's daughters.

The Hittites

The early years of Ramesses' reign were successful in terms of domestic affairs, but less so regarding foreign policy, and Egypt's empire in particular. Ramesses' father had succeeded in regaining parts of the Levantine Empire that Egypt had lost at the end of the 18th Dynasty, but by the time Ramesses acceded to the throne, the Hittites were threatening this territory.

The young Ramesses II may have seen this crisis with the Hittites as an opportunity for him to demonstrate his military prowess, but he was tactically naive. When he took a large Egyptian army into Syria in the 5th year of his reign, he failed

△ **Queen Nefertari**
In her tomb in the Valley of the Queens, Nefertari is depicted with her name written in a cartouche. She is described as the "Great Royal Wife, Lady of the Two Lands, Mistress of Upper and Lower Egypt."

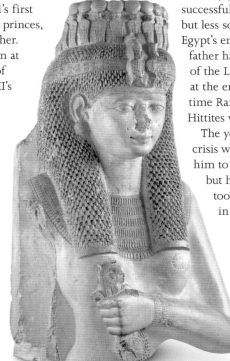

◁ **Princess Meritamen**
The daughter of Ramesses and Nefertari, Princess Meritamen, owned an extraordinary range of sculpture. This included colossal statues at Akhmim and Bubastis and this smaller statue once known as the "White Queen."

Elite Egyptian
chariot regiments

Egyptian infantry armed with
shields and battle-axes

to realize that a large Hittite army was waiting for him close to Kadesh and let the four divisions of his army lose contact with each other.

The Battle of Kadesh

When the Hittites launched a surprise attack, vast numbers of the Egyptian army were scattered and, according to Ramesses' own accounts of the battle, it was only his personal bravery that saved the day. The Hittites had missed their chance to crush the Egyptians and capture their king, but this was hardly an Egyptian victory. In the immediate aftermath of

the battle, as Ramesses' army retreated to Egypt, much of Canaan rose in revolt against them. It would take another 16 years of fighting before the Egyptians and the Hittites signed a peace treaty. When they did, they agreed on the borders between their realms and promised to cooperate with each other against their mutual enemies.

A suitably edited story of the Battle of Kadesh, highlighting Ramesses II's role as a mighty warrior leading his troops into the fray, became a major theme in the relief carvings with which Ramesses decorated the walls of his many temples.

△ **The Battle of Kadesh**
This relief from Ramesses II's cenotaph temple at Abydos shows the charioteers and infantry of the Egyptian army advancing into battle along the banks of the River Orontes.

"You are the **son of Amen**… you **devastate** the land of **Hatti** by **your valiant arm**."

RAMESSES II IS PRAISED BY HIS TROOPS AT KADESH

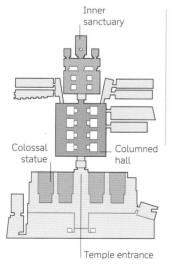

△ Abu Simbel Temple
One of the most spectacular temples ever built by an Egyptian king, both in terms of location and scale, Abu Simbel is dominated by four massive figures of Ramesses II at the entrance that are 66 ft (20 m) tall.

Ramesses in Nubia

A god builds his temples

At the beginning of his reign, Ramesses II launched a major program of temple building in Nubia to reinforce the idea of Egypt's imperial ownership and to convey the idea that the living king was himself divine.

By the time that Ramesses II took the throne, Nubia had been under the firm control of Egypt for 200 years. The administrative system that had been set up in the 18th Dynasty continued and Egyptians occupied the most important posts, especially that of head official, who was known as the "King's Son of Kush."

During the New Kingdom, the population of Nubia was largely made up of indigenous Nubians, but significant numbers of Egyptian colonists lived

Plan of Abu Simbel labels:
Inner sanctuary
Colossal statue
Columned hall
Temple entrance

◁ Plan of Abu Simbel
Although the rock-cut temple could not have the open-air court present in most New Kingdom temples, Abu Simbel followed their architectural lead in most other ways.

and worked in Nubia in their own towns. The remains of some of these towns have survived, so more is known about the Egyptians in Nubia than about the Nubians themselves.

Colonial towns
Towns such as Amara West were well-planned settlements laid out in Egyptian style. They had buildings that any Egyptian would recognize, such as a large temple built by Seti I. Nubia was governed at a local level from these towns, and their main purpose was to maximize income from Nubia for the Egyptian state, particularly from gold. Under Seti I, new regions of Nubia were explored for gold reserves, including the territory of Akuyta in the Eastern Desert.

Despite their differences, the lives of the Egyptian colonists and the Nubians were not totally separate. Egyptian objects are often found in Nubian graves, and there is archaeological evidence that the local Nubian rulers adopted some Egyptian customs. Several high-profile Nubian leaders, who were involved in the imperial administration, lived in a way that blended elements of both Nubian and Egyptian culture.

The best known of these Nubians is Hekanefer, prince of the Nubian territory of Miam. He built a rock-cut tomb for himself in Egyptian style and decorated in Egyptian fashion that was remarkably similar to the Theban tomb of his Egyptian contemporary, Amenhotep-Huy, "King's Son of Kush." Hekanefer is also depicted in Amenhotep-Huy's tomb as one of the leading Nubian tribute bearers, wearing a mixture of Egyptian and Nubian dress.

Abu Simbel

By the Ramesside Period, several important Egyptian temples had already been built in Nubia during the 18th Dynasty. The most significant were the two that Amenhotep III built for himself and his wife, Queen Tiy, at Soleb and Sedeinga. Ramesses II continued this tradition, but on a much grander scale. During his reign, he built temples throughout Lower Nubia.

One of the earliest temples to be started was also the most impressive—Abu Simbel. The Temple of Abu Simbel was a *speos* (cave) temple—one hewn directly

out of rock in the landscape. A few temples like this had already been built in Egypt, such as the Speos Artemidos of Hatshepsut and Seti I near Beni Hasan. The sandstone cliffs and mountains of Nubia were ideal materials for this type of temple, and Ramesses experimented with small examples, such as Beit el-Wali. But at Abu Simbel, he transformed an entire mountain into a temple and adapted features used in conventional temples of the period to suit the limitations of a cave temple.

The most striking features of Abu Simbel are the four colossal figures of Ramesses II at the entrance. They were based on free-standing statues at places such as Luxor Temple but made much larger. Abu Simbel seems to say that Egypt, during the reign of Ramesses II, had such strong ownership of Nubia that the king's presence was embedded in the landscape. The temple also conveyed a subtler message—that anyone who entered it and understood the texts and scenes on its walls would realize that the main god of the temple was, in effect, Ramesses himself.

In Year 38, a new "King's Son of Kush," Setau, built two more large temples, at Gerf Hussein and Wadi es-Sebua. Hastily built, they lacked quality and paled in significance in comparison to Abu Simbel.

△ **Nubian tribute bearers**
This painting from the tomb of Amenhotep-Huy shows Nubians, clad in a mixture of Nubian and Egyptian clothes and sporting Egyptian hairstyles, bearing gold. Their chariot, which is Egyptian, is being pulled by Nubian cattle.

▽ **The Small Temple at Abu Simbel**
Next to the temple of Abu Simbel stands a smaller one dedicated to Hathor and Ramesses II's wife, Nefertari. Here, the queen is shown as Hathor, flanked by statues of her husband.

"He has made a **temple, excavated** in the **mountain,** of **eternal workmanship.**"

RAMESSES II DESCRIBES HIS WORK AT ABU SIMBEL

Great Temple of Ramesses II
The exterior of the Great Temple of Ramesses II is justly
famous, but the interior is equally spectacular in its own
right. The vast halls of the temple were cut from the living
rock of the Nubian mountain into which it was excavated,
in an attempt to replicate the great open-air temples of the
period. The Great Hall is flanked by eight colossal statues
of Ramesses II in the guise of Osiris, the god of the afterlife
and resurrection. At the far end of the hall, a statue of the
deified Ramesses is shown seated with those of three other
gods: Ra-Horakhty, Amen-Ra, and Ptah.

Monuments at Thebes

Building in the domain of Amen-Ra

Adding to the collection of royal tombs and temples at Thebes was an important undertaking for the kings of the New Kingdom, and Ramesses II was one of the most enthusiastic contributors, erecting numerous monuments and temples.

Although Ramesses II's building program spanned the whole of Egypt, there are a few places where its impact is particularly apparent today. One of those places was Thebes, where Ramesses focused a great deal of his attention.

Karnak and Luxor

At Karnak, Ramesses II completed the hypostyle hall in the temple of Amen-Ra. He also added personal touches to the building, including a small temple at the eastern end, which was dedicated to "Ramesses-who-hears-prayers at the Upper Gateway of the Temple of Amen." This dedication hints at his interest in the new idea that the king himself was a god.

Ramesses also made additions to the Luxor Temple, which Amenhotep III had built on the site of an earlier building. It was planned to be a suitably impressive terminus for the procession of Amen-Ra and his family during the Opet festival. The final temple was the combined work of Amenhotep III and Ramesses II. Ramesses' most visible contribution was its pylon-fronted courtyard.

West bank

Ramesses II's tomb in the Valley of the Kings was not as big as his father's, but it was by no means small. Indeed, large tombs were an increasingly common feature of the Ramesside Period. However, Ramesses does seem to have been inventive in one respect. The

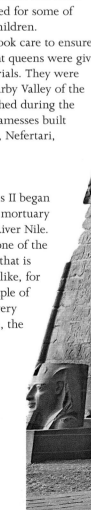

◁ **Colossal head**
This giant head of Ramesses II was found separated from its body in the Ramesseum. Large-scale statues of the king were a common feature of New Kingdom temples, and no ruler produced more of these than Ramesses.

tomb known as KV5, in the Valley of the Kings, is very unusual. It was not just for one individual, or even for a couple (like Yuya and Thuyu's tomb), but had more than 100 burial chambers that seem to have been reserved for some of Ramesses' many children.

Ramesses also took care to ensure that his important queens were given suitably royal burials. They were buried in the nearby Valley of the Queens, which had been established during the 18th Dynasty. It was there that Ramesses built a tomb for his most favored wife, Nefertari, and some of their children.

The Ramesseum

At the start of his reign, Ramesses II began a new project—to build his own mortuary temple on the west bank of the River Nile. Known as the Ramesseum, it is one of the few mortuary temples at Thebes that is still partially standing today—unlike, for example, the great mortuary temple of Amenhotep III. Although it was very different in terms of architecture, the

> ## "I am **Ozymandias**, **King of Kings**; look on **my Works** … and despair!"

PERCY BYSSHE SHELLEY, *OZYMANDIAS*

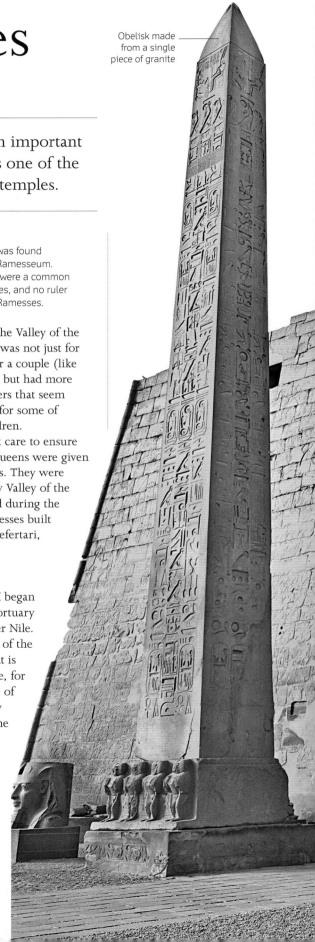

Obelisk made from a single piece of granite

Osiride pillars of the king
surround the courtyard

▽ **Luxor Temple**
Ramesses II added to Amenhotep III's temple at Luxor by building a great colonnaded courtyard fronted by this massive pylon gateway. He also added a pair of obelisks (the missing one is now in Paris) and colossal statues of himself to the front of the temple.

Statue of
the king

Ramesseum had similar functions to Hatshepsut's mortuary temple at Deir el-Bahri. It was where the gods of the afterlife could be honored; it provided a resting place for the barque of Amen during festival processions; and it was a place where the king's achievements (the Battle of Kadesh in the case of Ramesses II) could be displayed.

△ **The Ramesseum**
With its surviving columned interior halls and a colossal statue of the king that has collapsed, the Ramesseum is one of the most picturesque ruins of ancient Egypt.

Colossal statues

In art, the word "colossal" is often used to refer to any statue that is larger than life. Egyptian kings produced many statues that were bigger than the kings themselves, but some commissioned statues that were enormous. When building his own statues, Ramesses II looked to Amenhotep III for inspiration, especially the Colossi of Memnon statues built outside Amenhotep's mortuary temple at Kom el-Hetan.

Ramesses ordered colossal statues of himself to be erected in the major centers of the Nile Valley and Delta, especially at Pr-Ramesses (where none remains standing) and at Thebes. Part of their purpose was to serve as gods that ordinary people could worship, so many of them were placed where they could be seen by most of the Egyptian population, who did not have access to the interiors of temples.

One of the largest statues is a seated one of Ramesses in the Ramesseum. Now toppled over and broken, it was originally more than 62 ft (19 m) tall and weighed 1,000 tons (907 tonnes). Many scholars believe it was Shelley's inspiration for his poem *Ozymandias*.

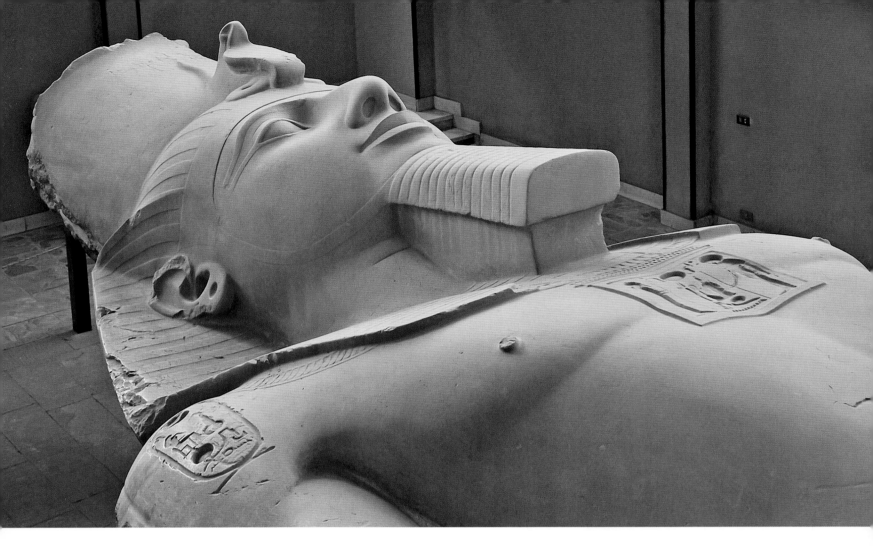

Memphis

The lost city

The foundation of Memphis as the capital of a newly united country was one of the defining moments of Egyptian history. For the next 3,000 years, it would remain one of the largest and most important cities in Egypt.

The ruins of Memphis lie on the western side of the Nile, not far from Cairo, in an area roughly 2 miles (4.5 km) from north to south and 1 mile (1.5 km) from east to west. They are located in agricultural land and a cluster of large mounds and depressions, such as Kom Rabia, Kom el-Qala, and Mit Rahina. These are the archaeological remains of the great metropolis that the historian Diodorus Siculus described as "the most famous city of Egypt ... the most favorable spot in the whole land," but they are not the remains of the earlier city, which was called

Ineb-Hedj, or "White Walls," and probably stood to the northwest of the current ruins. One of the problems with the archaeology of Memphis is that the location of the city gradually changed during the Dynastic

▷ **Hathor at Memphis**
Although the Temple of Ptah was the main building at Memphis, the kings also built minor temples to other deities, as seen in this capital of a column carved to look like Hathor.

RAMESSES II'S **GREAT WESTERN HALL**

The most visible archaeological remnant of the New Kingdom at Memphis is the great western hall that Ramesses II added to the Ptah Temple. Unlike Ramesses II's work at Luxor Temple, the Western Hall was not added to the front of the existing temple, but to the back (and possibly separate from it) and facing west rather than east. Maybe this orientation was planned so that the hall would look toward the pyramid-tombs of the Old and Middle Kingdom. Ramesses II also reused stone blocks from ancient buildings to build the western hall, suggesting that this might also have been part of a deliberate attempt to associate himself with past kings, especially at the time of his jubilee festival.

> "A **monument** for his father Ptah in excellent eternal work … its beauty was like the **horizon** of **heaven**."

AMENHOTEP III DESCRIBES THE TEMPLE HE BUILT AT MEMPHIS

little remains, and other important structures. These include the "Nebmaatra-United-with-Ptah" Temple, which was built by Amenhotep III as a "Mansion of Millions of Years." Although this temple no longer exists, its chief builder, Amenhotep, High Steward of Memphis, refers to its magnificence in his tomb autobiography. Under the Ramesside kings, more buildings were constructed in and around the enclosure, including smaller temples to Ptah and other deities. Seti I and Ramesses II were responsible for many of these, as was Merenptah, who built a palace there.

Beyond the temple enclosure, far less is known about what Memphis was like for the people who lived there, but a set of administrative documents from the reign of Seti I refers to the South District. This was a suburban area with a range of houses, including large villas like those excavated at Amarna.

Eventual decline

Memphis remained an important city even after Alexandria became the capital of Ptolemaic Egypt in 332 BCE. It was a significant commercial center and the Ptolemaic kings were crowned there, but its status declined during the Roman Period. The foundation of Fustat/Cairo after the Muslim invasion in the 7th century CE signaled the end of Memphis, and the city was finally abandoned.

Period, following the Nile as it moved east across its flood plain. Another problem is that the monuments of Memphis are poorly preserved compared to those of other sites, such as Thebes.

The name "Memphis" did not originally refer to the city, but was the Greek version of the name of the nearby pyramid of Pepi I, *Men-Nefer*. The name that was given to the temple of the city's main god, *Hwt-Ka-Ptah*, was also used to refer to the city as a whole, and when this was transcribed as *Aigyptos* by the Greeks, it became the name of the entire country.

Memphis in the New Kingdom

Thebes and Memphis were the two greatest cities in Egypt during the New Kingdom. Both received lavish royal patronage, and with good reason—Thebes was the domain of Amen and the place where the kings were buried, and Memphis was the administrative center of northern Egypt. Thebes is the better-known of the two cities today, but there is still enough archaeological evidence of some aspects of Memphis to create a sense of what it was like.

The heart of the city was the temple enclosure of the god *Hwt-ka-Ptah*, or Ptah. This enclosure contained both the Ptah temple itself, of which

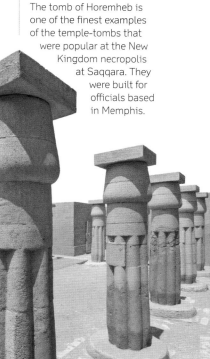

▽ **Horemheb's tomb**
The tomb of Horemheb is one of the finest examples of the temple-tombs that were popular at the New Kingdom necropolis at Saqqara. They were built for officials based in Memphis.

Sacred graffiti

Writing yourself onto history

In the New Kingdom, literate people were able to forge a link with the kings of the ancient past by visiting their monuments and inscribing their own personal record of their trip on them.

The Great Sphinx at Giza

△ **Visiting the sphinx**
This reconstruction of a New Kingdom stela shows two scribes visiting Old Kingdom monuments at Giza. Armed with writing implements, they are ready to inscribe graffiti wherever they chose.

During the New Kingdom, especially the Ramesside Period, educated people took an active interest in the past by visiting historic monuments. Although the sites were ancient to these New Kingdom "tourists," they did not seem strange, because they represented a culture and outlook very similar to their own. Most of these visitors had neither the resources nor authority to restore ancient buildings as Prince Khaemwese had done (see pp.226–227), but they were able to leave written evidence of their visits with graffiti.

Pilgrims at Memphis

Some officials from Memphis made a record of their trips to the greatest monuments of the distant past, the Old Kingdom royal pyramids. These monuments were nearby in the desert at sites such as Saqqara, where wealthy people from the New Kingdom were increasingly building their own tombs.

A good example of graffiti comes from the pyramid at Meidum. Within the small mortuary temple attached to the side of the pyramid is the following graffito: "Year 30 under the Majesty of [Amenhotep III] ... the scribe May came to see the very great pyramid of the Horus-King Snefru." May clearly knew what he was visiting, even though the pyramid had been built more than 1,000 years before he was born. Many other graffitists also knew which monuments from the Old Kingdom each king had built. In one graffito from Saqqara, the scribe Nashuyu

wrote that he "came to the district of the pyramid of Teti-beloved-of-Ptah and the pyramid of Djoser-discoverer-of-stoneworking." These graffiti were not intended to be disrespectful or damaging in any way, but to express respect for these ancient kings.

Tourism with benefits

As well as demonstrating respect, some graffiti make it quite clear that their writers expected to gain some benefits for themselves. This can be seen in a piece of graffiti from the 47th year of Ramesses II's reign that was found at the Djoser Step-Pyramid complex at Saqqara. The treasury official Hednakht wrote that he had come to "take a stroll and enjoy himself in the West of Memphis" with his brother, Panakht. But there was a more spiritual purpose to his trip than just an idle bit of weekend tourism. In his graffito, Hednakht addressed the gods and spirits associated with the Saqqara necropolis, asking them to give him a long, happy life and a good burial at the necropolis when his time came.

Not all graffiti were written on royal monuments, nor just at Memphis. A graffito from the Middle Kingdom tomb of the Vizier Intefiker at Thebes shows that scribes also visited private tombs. One graffiti writer expressed admiration for what he had been seen: "The scribe Bak <came> to see <this> tomb <of> the time of Sobekneferu. He found it like heaven in its interior."

The graffito begins with the date—Year 47

◁ **Hednakht's graffiti**
Most graffiti was written in black ink. This example from Djoser's Step Pyramid complex at Saqqara is written in the cursive script, hieratic, rather than in hieroglyphs.

△ **Graffiti on boulders at Sehel**

A different form of graffiti can be seen on the island of Sehel, on the First Cataract. Officials on quarrying missions left a memorial of their visit by chiseling their graffiti on the huge boulders of the island.

"Year 50 [of Ramesses II] ... **The coming of the scribe** Ptahemwia and his father Yupa **to see all the pyramids.**"

RECORD OF A VISIT TO MONUMENTS AT ABUSIR

Amenemopet, dressed in fashionable New Kingdom style

◁ **Detail on boulder**

The Overseer of Work, Amenemopet (right), left a graffito at Sehel showing him worshipping Anuket (left), one of the local deities of the First Cataract and Nubia.

Relief of Khaemwese
Khaemwese is shown here on a relief from Memphis or Saqqara. The sidelock of hair is not a sign of youth but, like the necklace he wears, part of the traditional dress of the High Priest of Ptah at Memphis.

Khaemwese

Restorer of Old and Middle Kingdom monuments

Mask made from a molded sheet of gold

Khaemwese, royal prince, son of Ramesses II, and High Priest of Ptah at Memphis, spent his life studying and restoring the ancient monuments of his ancestors. For this reason, he is sometimes described as the first Egyptologist.

Khaemwese was the fourth son of Ramesses II, born to the Great Royal Wife Isetnofret. Although he was behind his older brothers in the line of succession, he was a senior royal prince who briefly became heir to the throne toward the end of Ramesses II's reign.

High Priest

During the New Kingdom, the great temples of Egypt had become wealthy. They employed thousands of people and owned a large amount of land and other economic assets, such as mines and quarries. The High Priests of these temples were the chief executives of major corporations, as well as religious leaders. The most important of these temples were Amen-Ra at Thebes and Ptah at Memphis.

In the 16th year of his father's reign, Khaemwese became a Sm-Priest, or senior priest, of Ptah. He was in charge of the temple for 30 years before becoming the High Priest. Khaemwese carried out his duties diligently, knowing they were on behalf of his father. He oversaw the major expansion of temple building at Memphis (see pp.222–223) and organized jubilee festivities and building works throughout Egypt. But Khaemwese also had interests of his own.

Old and new tombs

During the Ramesside Period, Egyptians were fascinated by their history. For most people, a visit to an ancient site was all that was possible. But Khaemwese had the resources, the authority, and the imagination to go further. Living in Memphis, he was also close to the greatest monuments of the Old and Middle Kingdoms—some were even visible from the Ptah Temple in the city. Khaemwese ordered an extensive program of repair and restoration of the ancient monuments, which were in a poor condition. His method was to repair neglected stone buildings such as pyramids and sun temples and organize cults to perform offerings for the ancient kings who owned them. He then added an inscription to the repaired buildings telling the world what he had done.

Khaemwese also started new projects in the area around Memphis, notably a series of underground galleries at Saqqara—known as the Serapeum—for the burial of the sacred Apis bulls (see pp.272–273). It was in this complex that he probably planned to be buried.

△ **Gold funerary mask**
In 1851, Auguste Mariette began a destructive "excavation" of the Serapeum at Saqqara using dynamite. He recovered many burial goods, including this funerary mask.

◁ **Unas's pyramid**
Khaemwese's restoration work included two Old Kingdom pyramids: the Step Pyramid of Djoser (background) and the pyramid of Unas (foreground), where an inscription from the restoration is visible.

1282 BCE Khaemwese born during the reign of his grandfather, Seti I

1279 BCE Ramesses II becomes king

1265 BCE Khaemwese appointed Sm-Priest of Ptah at Memphis

1249 BCE Khaemwese organizes his father's 30-year jubilee

1235 BCE Khaemwese becomes High Priest of Ptah in Memphis

1230 BCE Khaemwese becomes crown prince

C.1224 BCE Death of Khaemwese

1213 BCE Death of Ramesses II

End of the 19th Dynasty

The successors of Ramesses II

The long reign of Ramesses II was followed by a period in which five kings ruled in just 27 years. It was a time of increasing instability, which ended with the collapse of the 19th Dynasty.

When Ramesses II died in 1213 BCE, most of the obvious candidates to inherit the throne had already died before him. It was his 13th son, Merenptah, whose mother had been Queen Isetnofret, who became king.

Merenptah

Already an old man when he took the throne, Merenptah ruled for a decade. He built the standard set of monuments, including a mortuary temple on the west bank of Thebes, next to the Temple of Amenhotep III, which he made full use of as a source of building material.

The most important events of Merenptah's reign involved Egypt's external enemies. He carried out a series of punitive military expeditions against troublesome vassals in the Levant and fought a defensive war against the Libyans, who had made serious incursions into Egyptian territory. This war took place in the fifth year of his reign and was recorded at Karnak on a victory stela that had once belonged to Amenhotep III. Although he won the war, his victory did not resolve the Libyan problem, which resurfaced during the reign of Ramesses III.

Merenptah's heirs

Merenptah's death in 1203 BCE triggered a succession crisis that dominated the remainder of the 19th Dynasty. Seti II, Merenptah's eldest son, was the legitimate heir, but his claim to the throne was challenged by Amenmesse, who may have been the son

▽ **Merenptah's tomb**
In this painted relief at the entrance to Merenptah's tomb in the Valley of the Kings, the sun god Ra-Horakhty welcomes the king to the afterlife.

◁ **Golden earring**
The Golden Tomb (KV56) in the Valley of the Kings contained a cache of gold jewelry dating to the end of the 19th Dynasty. It included this pair of earrings inscribed with the cartouche of Seti II.

of Seti II by a minor queen. The events of the next three years are unclear, partly because Seti II removed the royal cartouche of Amenmesse from his monuments, but it is possible that Amenmesse deposed Seti II for a short period or possibly only ruled in the south of Egypt. Whatever the case, Amenmesse died in around 1200 BCE, and Seti II himself only lived for another six years. This was just enough time for him to build temples at Karnak and Hermopolis Magna.

Siptah and Twosret

Seti II's successor was Siptah, who may have been the son of Seti II by a minor wife of Syrian origin, or even the son of Amenmesse. Siptah seems to have been too young to rule when he came to the throne, so the real power lay in the hands of Seti's senior queen, Twosret. The situation was similar to that of Hatshepsut and Tuthmosis III, but Siptah did not live to adulthood.

As regent, Twosret appears to have been supported by a man known as the "Chancellor of the Whole Land" Bay,

▷ **Statue of Seti II**
This fine quartzite statue of Seti II was found at Karnak. It shows the king seated with a ram's head, representing Amen-Ra, on his lap. The king's name is inscribed on his shoulders and on the base of the statue.

whose name suggests that he may not have been of Egyptian origin. Bay claimed that he "Established the King on his father's throne," an extraordinary boast for someone who was not royal, and which hints at the pivotal role that he played in the turbulent events of the period. Bay was executed in the fifth year of Siptah's reign, leaving Twosret as sole regent, and Siptah died the following year, 1188 BCE, after a nominal reign of just six years.

After Siptah's death, Twosret took the throne for herself, adopting the throne name Sitre-Meriamen. She ruled for only two years. Tomb KV14 in the Valley of the Kings, which had been started for Seti II and also possibly for Twosret, was extended during her regency with Siptah, and then again during her sole reign, but it was usurped by the man who succeeded her as king, Sethnakht, the founder of the 20th Dynasty. Twosret's final resting place is unknown.

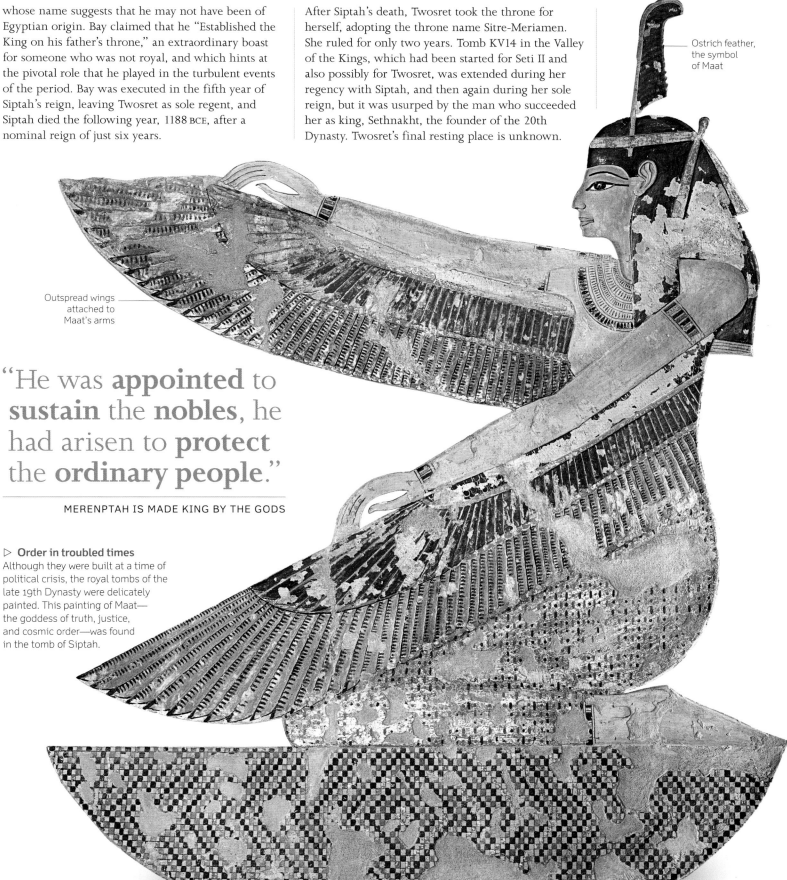

Ostrich feather, the symbol of Maat

Outspread wings attached to Maat's arms

> "He was **appointed** to **sustain** the **nobles**, he had arisen to **protect** the **ordinary people**."

MERENPTAH IS MADE KING BY THE GODS

▷ **Order in troubled times**
Although they were built at a time of political crisis, the royal tombs of the late 19th Dynasty were delicately painted. This painting of Maat—the goddess of truth, justice, and cosmic order—was found in the tomb of Siptah.

Life at Deir el-Medina

A community of royal tomb builders

The village of Deir el-Medina is one of Egypt's most important archaeological sites. Its treasures provide a unique insight into the daily lives of ordinary working people in ancient Egypt.

△ **Domestic help**
The villagers were given a team of support staff who supplied them with food and drink. These staff provided water, grain, and bread, as well as other types of food such as vegetables and fish.

When the New Kingdom kings decided to build a new royal necropolis near Thebes, they needed a skilled workforce. They did not require huge numbers of laborers to transport vast quantities of stone or mud brick as in the past, because the new royal tombs were not going to be pyramids, but would be built underground, in the sides of a steep valley in the desert. What this project needed, however, were skilled artisans who could carefully excavate the tombs and also, most importantly, decorate the internal walls.

A village of artisans

As these royal tombs were all in the same place, the Valley of the Kings, it made sense for the tomb builders and their families to live nearby, so a village was built to house them in the place that is known today as Deir el-Medina. The workers who lived there were part of a community that passed its skills down from father to son. The village was occupied for almost all of the New Kingdom—nearly 500 years— and the responsibility for creating the royal tombs was passed down through the generations. The tomb builders also created their own tombs, which were often highly decorated, close to the village (see pp.236–237).

The plan of Deir el-Medina changed over the years as new houses were added to accommodate more workers and their families. At its peak, there were around 70 houses in the village. The lives of the villagers were unusual, because they were working on a state project and so were directly supported by the government. Previous royal tombs had been broken into and robbed, so the remote Valley of the Kings was meant to be a secure place for royal burials.

Deir el-Medina was not meant to be secret, nor was it designed to keep its inhabitants prisoners, but it was built in a desert valley some distance from the main settlement at Thebes. Although villagers could walk down to the riverbank or the local market in an hour, this was rarely necessary, as the community was given

ATTENDANCE **REGISTER**

Several of the documents that have been found at Deir el-Medina record the attendance and absences of workers at the Valley of the Kings. It was clearly important to keep records, but the excuses that men gave either for not turning up for work at all or for turning up and then not working sometimes seem frivolous.

On this ostracon, which dates from the 40th year of Ramesses II's reign, the reasons that different workers give for not working include having to brew beer, drinking beer with friends, working on their own house improvements, and simply being too ill.

"**Year** 1, third **month** of winter, **day** 15. Giving clothes today to the **washermen**."

A LAUNDRY RECEIPT FROM DEIR EL-MEDINA

△ **Fuel for a fire**
Agricultural waste, such as animal dung, provided most of the fuel for fires in ancient Egypt. This bowl of dung was found in the tomb of the architect Kha at Deir el-Medina.

everything that it needed, including food and drink. Supplying the village with water alone must have been an enormous undertaking, and a train of donkeys carrying water jars to the village was probably a common sight. The village was situated at too high an altitude to sink a well: an attempt to do so was abandoned, leaving a huge, dry pit at the northern end of the village.

A village of scribes

When Deir el-Medina was excavated, the abandoned well yielded a very exciting find from ancient Egypt—a treasury of written documents, mainly on fragments of limestone called ostraca (see pp.246–247). These texts were written by the villagers, who were able to read and write because they had to write inscriptions on tombs. This was unusual for nonelite Egyptians.

Ranging from personal letters to receipts and records of court cases, the ostraca reveal a great deal about the everyday lives of the villagers. Along with remains of artifacts found in the village itself, which provide information about the villagers' religious practices (see pp.234–235), these texts have made it possible for archaeologists to find out more about Deir el-Medina than about any other community of the pre-Classical world.

▷ **Bust of an ancestor**
The villagers of Deir el-Medina worshipped both local and national gods, but they may also have revered their ancestors. Several busts found at the site appear to depict the deceased members of various households.

Open area (possibly for storage), part of the later expansion of the village

Main entrance to the village

Kitchen roofs made of loose matting to allow smoke to escape

▽ **Artisans' village**
Although the desert valley in which it was built had plenty of space, Deir el-Medina was deliberately made up of closely packed, terraced houses, with one narrow main street and an enclosure wall. The villagers seem to have preferred living in close contact with their neighbors to having space and privacy.

Donkey trains bringing water and other supplies to the village

Original external wall of the village, before it was expanded to house a larger workforce

Temporary shelters could be erected on the flat roofs of village houses

External wall surrounding the entire village

Deir el-Medina

The workmen's village

Deir el-Medina, which housed the workers who made the royal tombs in the Valley of the Kings, is the best-known settlement site from ancient Egypt. Thanks to the huge number of written texts that have survived from the village, a great deal is known about the lives of the people who lived there. These texts record everyday matters, from inventories and shopping lists to accusations of infidelity and theft; they even include jokes. Combined with this ancient written information, there are the physical remains of the village itself, the individual houses within it, and the objects that the owners left behind when the village was abandoned. This all provides a uniquely detailed insight into this ancient community.

▽ **Artisans' tools**
Evidence from Deir el-Medina indicates that although the workers who lived there were primarily employed on the state project of building royal tombs, they also did other work in their spare time, notably making funerary equipment for private customers.

Hand saw

Mortise chisel

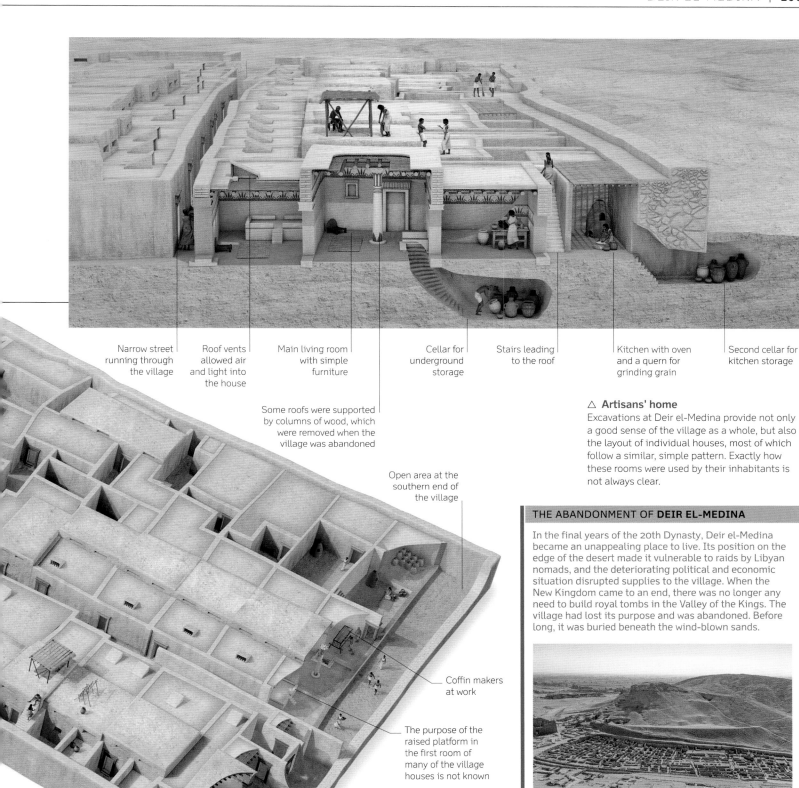

Narrow street running through the village

Roof vents allowed air and light into the house

Main living room with simple furniture

Some roofs were supported by columns of wood, which were removed when the village was abandoned

Cellar for underground storage

Stairs leading to the roof

Kitchen with oven and a quern for grinding grain

Second cellar for kitchen storage

Open area at the southern end of the village

Coffin makers at work

The purpose of the raised platform in the first room of many of the village houses is not known

One of the larger houses belonged to Sennedjem, whose tomb was just outside the village (see pp.236–237)

△ **Artisans' home**

Excavations at Deir el-Medina provide not only a good sense of the village as a whole, but also the layout of individual houses, most of which follow a similar, simple pattern. Exactly how these rooms were used by their inhabitants is not always clear.

THE ABANDONMENT OF **DEIR EL-MEDINA**

In the final years of the 20th Dynasty, Deir el-Medina became an unappealing place to live. Its position on the edge of the desert made it vulnerable to raids by Libyan nomads, and the deteriorating political and economic situation disrupted supplies to the village. When the New Kingdom came to an end, there was no longer any need to build royal tombs in the Valley of the Kings. The village had lost its purpose and was abandoned. Before long, it was buried beneath the wind-blown sands.

THE RUINS OF DEIR EL-MEDINA

Personal worship

Stelae in the New Kingdom

Some the most revealing pieces of evidence for the range of deities worshipped by the ancient Egyptians are stelae. Usually carved from limestone, these inscribed and painted stone slabs were used as reminders of the eternal devotion of people to their chosen gods.

△ **Nebethetepet hears Usersatet**
The ears on this stela show that the worshipper wants the deity to listen to their requests, especially the goddess Nebethetepet, "Who hears Prayer."

△ **Worshipping the moon god**
The text above is a long prayer to Thoth in his ibis form as the moon god Iah. He is being offered a wedjat-eye by a baboon, another animal associated with him.

△ **Baki worships "The Good Ram"**
The long text in the lower part of this stela is a hymn of praise by Baki to the god Amen-Ra in the form of his sacred animal, "The Good Ram."

△ **Two women worship Renenutet**
In this unusual stela with two parts, two women devote themselves to the snake goddess Renenutet, who had a protective role in the home.

"I will **make this stela** in your name and **establish this hymn** for you **in writing on its surface**."

NEBRE ADDRESSES THE GOD AMEN-RA

◁ **Foreign gods**
The Egyptians' acceptance of foreign gods is shown in this stela, on which the Egyptian god Min is joined by the Canaanite deities Qadesh (center) and Reshef (right).

Four snakes emerging from the mountain

The sun god Ra-Horakhy in his solar boat

△ **Amennakht worships the Peak**
On this stela, a scribe worships both the goddess Isis and "the Peak of the West," a Theban mountain associated with the snake goddess Meretseger.

△ **Mahu worships three deities**
This stela may be unfinished or was possibly intended just to be sketched in black paint. Mahu is seen worshipping, from left to right, the gods Meretseger, Mut, and Amen-Ra.

△ **Tripartite stela of Khabekhnet**
In the middle scene of this stela, Khabekhnet worships an unnamed prince and the cow goddess Hathor emerging from the Theban mountain.

△ **Mehytkhati worships Taweret**
The goddess Taweret is shown here in the form of a hippopotamus next to a table of offerings. Unusually, Mehytkhati is holding a bowl of burning incense.

△ **Amennakht praises Meretseger**
On this stela, a penitential Amennakht seeks forgiveness from the goddess Meretseger, believing she had punished him with temporary blindness.

△ **Huy and friends worship Hathor**
The lower part of this stela depicts the worshippers and the upper part a king (Ramesses II) acting as an intermediary between them and the goddess Hathor.

Tomb of Sennedjem

"Servant in the Place of Truth"

Although it is one of the smaller private tombs at Thebes, the tomb of Sennedjem at the workmens' village of Deir el-Medina is rightly famous. Its vivid paintings demonstrate the extraordinary skill of the craftsmen who lived at the site.

▽ **Interior of the tomb**
Every inch of Sennedjem's burial chamber is covered with paintings that show him and his wife meeting the gods in the afterlife. The paintings stretch up the walls and across the ceiling, over the space where the coffins were laid.

The villagers of Deir el-Medina were unlike most of the population of Egypt in several respects. One was that they could enjoy the benefit of well-constructed, well-equipped, and well-decorated tombs, because Deir el-Medina was a workmen's village, and the villagers built the tombs in the Valley of the Kings. This gave them the skills and maybe some of the raw materials to create such tombs for themselves. In the 18th Dynasty, most tombs were built to the east of the village, but in the Ramesside Period, they developed a new site on the desert slopes to the west.

A family tomb
Sennedjem lived at Deir el-Medina with his family during the reigns of Seti I and Ramesses II. His title, "Servant in the Place of Truth," identifies him as one of the workmen who were employed cutting and decorating royal tombs during the New Kingdom. Sennedjem's own tomb, one of the most important in the western cemetery at Deir el-Medina, was discovered with its contents intact in 1886. Unfortunately, the circumstances of the discovery meant that the objects recovered from the tomb

△ **Decorated jar**
This wine jar from Sennedjem's tomb is painted with garlands of flowers similar to those used in scenes of funeral feasts.

were not kept together and found their way into various collections and museums around the world, but the tomb itself remains a small jewel among Theban private tombs.

Sennedjem's tomb was shared by members of his family—his wife, Iynofret; his son and daughter-in-law, Khonsu and Tamaket; and Khonsu's daughter-in-law, Isis. Multiple burials seem to have been common at Deir el-Medina, where entire generations of families often shared the same tomb. Khabekhnet, another one of Sennedjem's sons, owned his own tomb, which contained a list of the people who would eventually come to use it. These include the Foreman Nekhemmut and his father Khonsu, who were descendants of Khabekhnet, but also the names of several workmen who may not even have been related to Khabekhnet's family.

Painting a tomb

Like other Deir el-Medina tombs of this period, Sennedjem's tomb had a simple building above ground—a tiny offering chapel topped with a small mud-brick pyramid. The underground rooms, however, although small, were covered with vividly painted scenes showing Sennedjem and Iynofret enjoying life after death and being accepted by the gods into the Field of Reeds—the fertile fields of the afterlife (see pp.22–23).

Sennedjem probably decorated the tomb himself, but workers sometimes paid more skilled colleagues to do the work for them rather than doing it themselves. A contract has been found, for example, in which a worker named Aanakht promises a colleague named Merysekhmet food and various items of clothing in return for painting the underground rooms of his tomb. This included the cost of the paint.

The tomb of a priest named Kynebu reveals how long it took to paint his tomb, a small rectangular room decorated with a standard set of tomb scenes depicting banquets, Kynebu worshipping Amenhotep I and Ahmose-

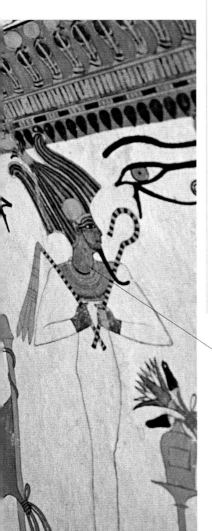

The god Osiris, king of the Field of Reeds

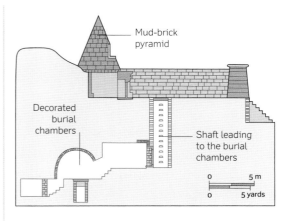

△ **Cross-section of the tomb**
Sennedjem's tomb is typical of those belonging to senior craftsmen of the Ramesside period at Deir el-Medina, with an exterior offering chapel and a painted burial chamber.

Nefertari (see pp.146–147), and an elaborate funeral procession. A graffito from this tomb records that it took three months and 19 days to paint.

Coffins

Among the burial goods recovered from Sennedjem's tomb is a fine set of coffins that belonged to his family. By the Ramesside Period, the exterior box coffins of earlier periods had been adapted, and the preferred style was now an outer and an inner coffin that were both shaped like a person. This shows that the skills of the Deir el-Medina workmen were not limited to tomb decorating—they were also excellent carpenters and could make coffins.

The price of a coffin depended on the quality of both the workmanship and the materials (wood, paint, varnish) that were used. Most coffins from the Ramesside Period cost between 20 and 40 deben. The most expensive ones recorded are a pair of inner and outer coffins costing 295 deben. At the time, a donkey cost from 25–40 deben, a pig 3–5 deben, and a bed 15–20 deben.

Large and elaborate floral collar

◁ **Mummy-board of Iynofret**
Iynofret's body was laid beneath a mummy-board inside an anthropoid coffin. The board was painted to show her as she was in life—in everyday linen clothes, including a floral collar, and wearing a wig.

Ramesses III

The last great king of the New Kingdom

Ramesses III had a long and eventful reign. He put an end to the political instability of the late 19th Dynasty and achieved a great deal as a builder and warrior, influenced by his role model, Ramesses II.

The origins of the 20th Dynasty are something of a mystery. The first king was Sethnakht, who came to the throne 27 years after the death of Ramesses II. The timing suggests that he may have been one of Ramesses II's grandsons by a lesser wife.

Sethnakht ruled for less than two years—maybe he was already an old man—and the throne then passed to his son, Ramesses III. The new king had a very obvious role model whom he wished to emulate—his famous namesake, Ramesses II. This emulation was made clear in three different areas: in his roles as a builder, a father, and as a warrior.

Medinet Habu

Ramesses III made significant additions to Karnak Temple and other minor buildings throughout Egypt, but his main architectural achievement was the last of the great mortuary temples at Thebes, Medinet Habu.

◁ **Tomb of Amenherkhepeshef**
The Valley of the Queens was an important cemetery for the tombs of Ramesside royal princes. Here, Prince Amenherkhepeshef stands behind his father, Ramesses III, as he meets the goddess Hathor.

Apart from Deir el-Bahri, this is the most complete mortuary temple in Egypt, mainly because no king after Ramesses III was able to build a monument on such an impressive scale or to plunder stone from the temple. Not only was the ground plan of Medinet Habu essentially the same as that of the Ramesseum built by Ramesses II, but the themes of the pictures on its walls were also remarkably similar (see pp.212–213).

One of these themes was the royal children. Like his namesake, Ramesses III commissioned scenes of the princes and princesses in royal procession. The children at the front of each procession are named and—in an extraordinary act of plagiarism—the names that they bear are the names of Ramesses II's own children. The procession of princes at Medinet Habu is a historically important document, as royal cartouches were later added to the princes who went on to become kings Ramesses IV, Ramesses VI, and Ramesses VIII.

Problems from abroad

Maybe the greatest historical importance of Medinet Habu was that it depicted and described Ramesses III's great military achievements. Like his predecessor, Ramesses had plenty of opportunities to prove himself as a powerful warrior king, but unlike Ramesses II, the wars that he had to wage were not in far-flung corners of the Egyptian empire, but on Egypt's very borders and within the country itself.

THE STELA OF BAKENKHONSU

Bakenkhonsu was High Priest of Amen in the early part of the 20th Dynasty. This stela commemorates the role that he played in restoring the royal statues at Karnak during the reign of Sethnakht. Bakenkhonsu describes the statues as "noble kings which had fallen into a state of destruction … some on their sides, others on their backs … by hands of the poor people." The stela proves that high officials were able to act on their own initiative in royal temples, but they did not always do so as a selfless act of piety. Bakenkhonsu also says that he "set up his (own) statue with them, through the wish that he might endure like them forever and ever in the Domain of Amen."

Bakenkhonsu is kneeling, with arms raised in praise of Amen-Ra

Ramesses III's greatest military achievement was to successfully repel three invasions: two by Libyans approaching from west of Egypt in the 5th and 11th years of his reign, and another by the Sea-Peoples from the east in the 8th year of his reign (see pp.240–241).

At a time when several of the major states in the Near East and eastern Mediterranean were being destroyed by similar invasions, Egypt under Ramesses III was able to stand firm and retain its sovereignty, even if its power was somewhat diminished in the process.

Crossed arms, typical of royal mummies of the period

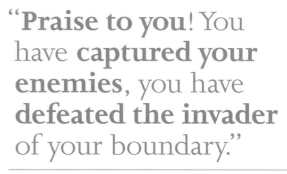

▷ **Ramesses III's sarcophagus**
The huge, 7.7-ton (7-tonne) granite lid of Ramesses III's sarcophagus shows the king modeled in high relief in the form of Osiris. He is flanked by the protective goddesses Isis and Nephthys.

Problems at home

Internal unrest began to cause problems toward the end of Ramesses III's reign. In his 29th year, the workmen at Deir el-Medina went on strike, because their wages had not been paid. This was an indication of the economic problems that lay ahead for later kings of the 20th Dynasty.

More seriously for the king himself, there was a plot to take his life within the royal court in Year 30 of his reign. One of the minor queens apparently conspired with other court officials to put her son, Pentaweret, on the throne instead of Prince Ramesses. The plot failed, the plotters were put to death, and Prince Ramesses later became king. Whether Ramesses III was actually murdered as a result of this plot is not known, but he died around this time and was succeeded by his chosen successor, Ramesses IV.

"**Praise to you**! You have **captured your enemies**, you have **defeated the invader** of your boundary."

AMEN-RA PRAISES RAMESSES III AT MEDINET HABU

RAMESSES III

◁ **Mummy of Ramesses III**
Ramesses III's mummy is one of the best-preserved royal bodies of the New Kingdom. It was one of several mummies that were removed from their tombs in the Valley of the Kings and secretly reburied in the Deir el-Bahri cache (see pp.244–245).

Threatening invaders

Sea-Peoples and Libyans

During the New Kingdom, the settled order of the civilizations in the eastern Mediterranean and the Near East was shattered by a series of violent mass migrations that Egypt only just managed to survive.

The greatest threat to Egypt during the New Kingdom did not come from any of the rival empires that had emerged in the Near East, such as the Mitanni or the Hittites. Nor did it come from Egypt's long-standing enemy, Nubia, but from two groups of peoples that the Egyptians had either failed to consider a threat or had not even heard of: the Libyans and the Sea-Peoples.

Libyans

Egyptologists use the term "Libyan" to refer to the seminomadic people who lived west of the Nile Valley and Delta. Most of them lived along the Mediterranean coast but traveled great distances over the Western Desert with their herds. The two main groups of Libyans were known to the Egyptians as Tjemeh and Tjehenu, and although they appear in

◁ **Libyan prisoner**
Like all foreigners, Libyans were stereotyped in Egyptian art, following established conventions. They were usually depicted with short, cropped hair with a sidelock; a short, pointed beard; and a long, open robe tied at the shoulder.

Egyptian records as early as the Unification Period (c.3000 BCE), they seem to have been of little interest to the Egyptians. They offered no potential for economic exploitation and, apart from the occasional raid on frontier settlements, they posed no military threat to Egypt. This situation changed drastically in the latter part of the 18th Dynasty, when new and much more powerful groups began to emerge.

The Meshwesh first appeared during the reign of Amenhotep III, and the Rebu/Libu during that of Ramesses II. They probably came from the uplands

▽ **Battle with the Sea-Peoples**
Ramesses III's battles with the Sea-Peoples on land and on water are depicted in great detail on the external walls of his Medinet Habu temple. On the left, an Egyptian boat attacks a Sea-Peoples vessel.

Egyptian troops armed with bows and spears

Distinctive Sea-People's helmet

△ Hands of the enemy
To ascertain how many of the enemy had been killed in battle, the Egyptians cut off parts of their enemy's bodies and gathered them to be counted. Here, a pile of hands is being collected.

▷ **The Israel stela**
This important stela describes Merenptah's war with the Libyans in detail. It also contains the first-known reference to a group of people called the Israelites, so it is popularly known as the Israel stela.

of Cyrenaica, in what is the modern state of Libya today. The problem for the Egyptians was that these new groups of Libyans had a long-term strategy of trying to enter Egypt in vast numbers, possibly to escape from the increasingly arid conditions on the Mediterranean coast. This was not a military invasion in the traditional sense, but a mass movement of entire communities of people who were prepared to fight for new territory.

Early indications of this problem can be seen in the war scenes depicted by Seti I at Karnak and the forts built by Ramesses II in the west, but the real crisis came during the reigns of Merenptah and Ramesses III. Between them, they had to contend with three serious Libyan invasions, each of which threatened the existence of Egypt. These wars ended in victories for the Egyptians, but they failed to solve the problem, which had major ramifications in the Third Intermediate Period.

Sea-Peoples

Sea-People armed with round shields and long swords

Ramesses III's wars against the Libyans took place in the 5th and 11th years of his reign. He also fought a major defensive war against the Sea-Peoples. Probably originating from the Ionian coast of Turkey, the Sea-Peoples first appeared as heavily armed pirates in the Mediterranean. One group, the Sherden, raided the Nile Delta early in Ramesses II's reign. A hundred years later, these people were no longer just a nuisance to the established coastal powers, but a powerful military force that crushed both the Mycenaean civilization of Greece and the Hittite empire.

The Sea-Peoples attacked Cyprus and rampaged through the Levant, sacking important cities, such as Ugarit. They upturned the status quo in the region and brought an end to the Late Bronze Age civilization that had

△ "Israel" detail
This hieroglyphic text is a close approximation of the word "Israel." It is not the name of a place, but of a group of people who may have been nomads.

flourished across the eastern Mediterranean and Near East. Only the Egyptians were able to stand against them. Ramesses III's victory in Year 8 of his reign saved Egypt from destruction, but the annihilation of its traditional partners forced it to face a new world order. This included a new threat to its empire in the Levant, where groups of Sea-Peoples, such as the Peleset (or Philistines), had settled.

Ramesses IV–XI

The end of the New Kingdom

The history of Egypt between the reigns of Ramesses IV and Ramesses XI was one of increasing instability. This affected both the authority of the king and the economic and political well-being of the country at large.

△ **Ramesses IV's tomb**
Although the later kings of the 20th Dynasty did not have the resources to build temples on a grand scale, they had suitably impressive tombs built for them in the Valley of the Kings.

One of the astonishing features of the period that followed the death of Ramesses III in 1153 BCE was the speed with which the crown changed hands among his sons and grandsons. He was succeeded by his son Ramesses IV (1153–1147 BCE), whose short reign put a second son, Ramesses V (1147–1143 BCE), on the throne. Ramesses V's early death without an heir meant that the next king was another of Ramesses III's sons—Ramesses VI (1143–1136 BCE)—who was followed in turn by the next son, Ramesses VII (1136–1129 BCE), who also died soon after. Ramesses VIII (1129–1126 BCE), another son of Ramesses III, stepped forward to be king, but he soon died, too, leaving the throne to Ramesses IX (1126–1108 BCE), whose relationship to the rest of this unfortunate

◁ **Shabti of Ramesses IV**
The royal tombs of the late 20th Dynasty had the same sets of burial goods as their predecessors, but relatively few objects of quality have survived from that time, apart from some royal shabti figures.

▷ Statue of Ramesses VI

This half-life-sized statue of Ramesses VI shows the king grasping the hair of a foreign captive. Ironically, it was during his reign that Egypt lost most of its empire, especially in the Levant.

family is not known. Ramesses X (1108–1099 BCE) might have been the son of Ramesses IX and the father of Ramesses XI (1099–1069 BCE). This rapid turnover of rulers may have been due to the relative ages and unlucky medical history of Ramesses III's descendants, but it reflected a more general sense of Egyptian decline during this period— a decline that was only going to get worse.

Royal tombs

After the death of Ramesses III, no major building projects went ahead for the rest of the New Kingdom—apart from creating royal tombs in the Valley of Kings. The workmen of Deir el-Medina were kept busy producing large tombs for Ramesses IV, Ramesses V, and Ramesses IX. They also built a small but serviceable tomb for Ramesses VII. Ramesses X's tomb has not been fully excavated, and that of Ramesses VIII has never been found. Although a tomb was completed for Ramesses XI, the last ruler of the New Kingdom, it is likely that it was never used and that he was buried at a location at Memphis that has yet to be discovered.

The end of the New Kingdom

Ramesses XI's reign may have been the longest since that of Ramesses III, but it was far less successful. In fact, his death hastened Egypt's decline, leading to the collapse of the New Kingdom, the end of royal authority, and the start of the Third Intermediate Period. It was a time of civil war and competing warlords, but also of great economic disruption. The failure of the central administration to address these problems is proved in documents found at Deir el-Medina. These describe both the increase in the price of grain due to inflation and the increasing number of tomb robberies at Thebes.

Priests and warlords

The short reigns of kings in this period meant that high officials had to maintain a sense of continuity in the country's government. Ramessesnakht, the High Priest of Amen, for example, remained in post from the first year of Ramesses IV's reign to some point during the reign of Ramesses IX. Some of these

"You shall double for me the long lifespan and the prolonged reign of Ramesses II."

RAMESSES IV MAKES AN UNSUCCESSFUL DEMAND OF OSIRIS

officials, however, became warlords. During the reign of Ramesses XI, Panehesy, the "King's Son of Kush," invaded southern Egypt, possibly in support of the king (based in Memphis) and to try and reinstate royal authority there. However, he was forced back into Nubia, which was lost to Egyptian control.

Other emerging warlords were descendants of Libyan prisoners of war who had settled in Egypt and risen to high military ranks. Foremost among these was a general called Herihor. When Panehesy was removed, Herihor became not only the real power in southern Egypt, but also the High Priest of Amen at Thebes. When he built monuments at Karnak, he did so in the name of Ramesses XI, but he showed his own royal ambitions by writing his name in a cartouche and depicting his children in procession, just as Ramesses III had done before him.

HERIHOR AND **NODJMET**

General and High Priest of Amen Herihor is shown below with his wife, Nodjmet, in a *Book of the Dead* that belonged to her. This document proves that the couple had royal pretensions, because Herihor is shown with a uraeus on his brow and Nodjmet is wearing the vulture crown of a queen. Herihor had 17 sons in total, and each one is described at the Khonsu Temple at Karnak as being the "King's Son of his Body." Despite the Egyptian names of their parents, some of these princes had names such as Masaharta, Masaqaharta, and Osorkon, which betray their Libyan origins.

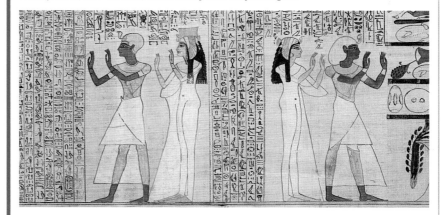

Tomb robberies

Thieves in the Valley of the Kings

The tombs in the Valley of the Kings, richly provided with valuable burial goods, were some of the most sacred sites in New Kingdom Egypt. But that did not prevent repeated attempts to steal from them.

The Egyptian approach to the afterlife meant that the graves and tombs of people of all classes had objects placed in them to help the deceased. The wealthy elite were often buried with extremely valuable items made of gold, silver, and semiprecious stones. This should not have been a problem, as the relationship between the living and the dead, according to tomb inscriptions, was one of respect. There were, however, always people willing to break taboos and risk the wrath of the gods by stealing from the dead, so in Egypt, there was a long history of robbing graves.

Stealing from royal tombs

Robbing a royal tomb was considered an especially serious crime, but it still happened, especially at times when law and order was breaking down. When the Old Kingdom pyramids were robbed in the First Intermediate Period, the state increased security at many of the Middle Kingdom pyramids, but to little effect. In the New Kingdom, royals were buried in

◁ **Impalement on a stake**
The Tomb Robbery Papyri refer to convicted criminals being "put to the wood." A hieroglyphic sign in this phrase leaves little doubt as to their grisly fate.

secret underground tombs in the Valley of the Kings to prevent further desecrations, but many of the tombs were not very secret at all and had large, obvious entrances. And so, when the authority of the New Kingdom kings began to collapse toward the end of the 20th Dynasty, little could be done to protect the Valley tombs. In fact, their semihidden location often worked in thieves' favor, as it enabled them to work without being disturbed by guards or passersby. By the end of the 20th Dynasty, even local officials were colluding in the robbery of tombs and temples.

The Tomb Robbery Papyri

A set of documents from the reigns of Ramesses IX and Ramesses XI, known as the Tomb Robbery Papyri, indicate that some of these robbers were brought to trial. The papyri describe tours of inspection of the royal tombs to discover which of them had been robbed, the questioning of suspects, and the sentencing of those found guilty.

The robbers' confessions make it clear that they were after the precious materials from which the stolen items were made rather than the actual items themselves. One group of robbers, who broke into the tomb of Sobekemsaf II, ended their pillaging spree by setting fire to the coffins they found, presumably to make it easier to remove the gold foil from them.

▽ **Bastinado in Mereruka**
This scene from the Old Kingdom tomb of Mereruka at Saqqara shows a group of criminals being interrogated. The process clearly involved physical violence.

▷ **Coffin of Ahmose-Meritamen**
The body of Ahmose-Meritamen was one of those found in the Deir el-Bahri cache. Stripped of any precious covering when it was removed from its original tomb, her coffin was painted yellow to replace the missing gold leaf.

"We took our copper tools and **forced** a way into the **pyramid** of this **king**."

CONFESSION OF A ROBBER FROM THE
LEOPOLD-AMHERST PAPYRUS

Although robbing royal tombs was clearly a lucrative business, the punishment for those caught was an extremely brutal death. It was described as being "put to the wood," which meant being impaled on a stake.

Caches of kings

One response by local authorities to the pillaging of the Valley of the Kings was to collect what was left in the semirobbed tombs and bury it in "caches" at more hidden locations, most notably the High Priest Pinudjem II, at Deir el-Bahri. In most cases, however, little more than the royal body itself was reinterred, in a much simpler coffin than the one in which it had originally been buried.

The Deir el-Bahri cache contained more than 50 bodies, including many of the New Kingdom kings, from Ahmose to Ramesses IX. The project seems, however, to have given Theban officials at the end of the New Kingdom a chance to enrich themselves with the precious materials stripped from the original tombs, claiming that they were acting in the best interests of the ancient kings. The main Deir el-Bahri cache was not discovered until the end of the 19th century.

▽ **Casket of Ramesses IX**
Most objects stolen from royal tombs were stripped of their precious metals and stones, but a few pieces survived and were reburied with the Deir el-Bahri cache. Among them was this gold and ivory casket inscribed for Ramesses IX.

Figured ostraca

Art in miniature

Ostraca are small fragments of pottery or, more commonly in ancient Egypt, flakes of limestone on which people wrote and did drawings. Deir el-Medina is the richest source of the most interesting and skillful of these informal works of art, produced by the craftsmen who painted the tombs in the Valley of the Kings.

A person climbs down the tomb shaft

▷ **Funeral scene**
This detailed line drawing of a funeral shows both mourners and the ceremony at the mouth of the tomb shaft, as well as the numerous underground burial chambers.

Coffins in the burial chamber

◁ **Woman nursing a child**
Detailed pictures of mothers nursing children are a common theme on ostraca at Deir el-Medina—maybe they were made to commemorate the arrival of a new child.

The tied-up hair of a woman who has just given birth

▷ **Building plan**
Some ostraca appear to have been working sketches for real building projects. This ostracon made of ceramic provides a plan for a shrine, including a set of measurements.

◁ **Domestic scene**
The artist has used a palette of several colors in this sketch of a mother with a child and a servant girl holding up a mirror.

The distinctive features of Akhenaten

The king wears, the blue crown

The *khepesh* sickle-shaped sword

The king smites his enemies

A fist holding horse reins

△ **Bearded king**
On this sample piece, the artist practiced drawing hands and arms. He has also drawn a royal head with some stubble, which may be a sign of mourning.

◁ **Amen gifts a sword**
This scene, found in many temples of the New Kingdom, shows Amen-Ra offering a sword to the king (Ramesses IX here) to defeat his enemies.

△ **Head of Akhenaten**
This practice piece depicting the head of Akhenaten shows the influence of the Amarna art style (see pp.178–179) in the modeling of the king's features.

△ Female acrobat
This is one of the most beautiful ostraca to survive from ancient Egypt. The artist probably created the colorful and detailed image of a female acrobat to be kept as a finished artwork.

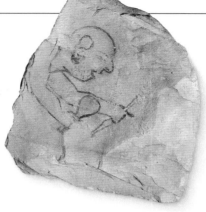

△ Worker with hammer and chisel
This simple but vivid sketch of an artisan working might be a portrait of the artist himself or one of his workmates.

△ Sketch of Senenmut
This image of Hatshepsut's adviser may have been a preparatory sketch for the almost identical images on the walls of his tomb at Thebes.

Ostrich-feather fan

An animal priest reads out the ritual

▷ Cat and mouse
The Egyptians were very amused by the idea of role reversal between humans and animals. This ostracon shows a cat serving an upper-class mouse.

△ A religious procession
In this parody of one of the religious festivals at Thebes, animals assume the roles of the god and the priests who are bearing him in procession.

▽ Meretseger
This large ostracon, 9 in (23 cm) across, was probably used as an object of devotion to the snake goddess of western Thebes, Meretseger. The text claims that it was made by the "Deputy of the Gang" at Deir el-Medina, Amenkhau.

This section reads "Meretseger, Lady of the West"

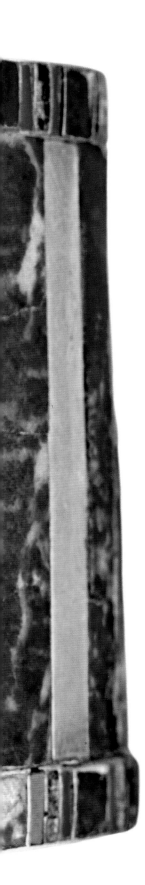

6

The Late
Period

c.1069–332 BCE

The Late Period

The death of Ramesses XI in 1069 BCE marked the beginning of a long period of political instability in Egypt. For the next 700 years, few Egyptian kings ever ruled the entire country. Historians have divided this period into two phases—the Third Intermediate Period (1069–664 BCE) and the Late Period (664–32 BCE)—each of which had its own distinctive characteristics. Not only was Egypt now divided—it no longer had an empire.

The Third Intermediate Period

After the collapse of the monarchy at the end of the New Kingdom, competing factions and individuals attempted to gain power in a weakened Egypt. In the south of the country, the High Priests of Amen were politically and economically powerful, while in the north, various local rulers based at Tanis in the eastern Delta claimed their right to the throne. The most dominant group of people during this period were not Egyptians, however, but the descendants of Libyans who had settled in Egypt after the great wars of the Late New Kingdom. These men had made careers for themselves as soldiers and were now powerful warlords. The names of these self-proclaimed kings indicate their Libyan origin; the 22nd Dynasty, for example, consists mainly of rulers named Sheshonq, Osorkon, and Takelot. They were ousted by the Nubian king Piankhy, who invaded Egypt and established the 25th Dynasty. However, the Nubians were then deposed after the Assyrians invaded Egypt.

◁ **Gold statuette of Amen**

The Late Period

The beginning of the Late Period can be dated to the accession of Psamtek I in 664 BCE. Initially a vassal of the Assyrians, Psamtek managed to wrest power from his overlords so that Egypt once again became unified under an Egyptian king, but this state of affairs did not last for long. One of the defining features of the Late Period was that Egypt came under Persian rule on two occasions. The first of these, from 525–404 BCE, was after Psamtek III was defeated by Cambyses, the first Persian ruler of Egypt. Persian rule was then broken by the 30th Dynasty, during which, from 380 BCE, Egypt was once again independent and united. However, the Persians returned in 343 BCE, only to be dislodged in 332 BCE by Alexander the Great, whom the Egyptians regarded as their liberator.

Art and culture

Although this long period was a time of political instability, and none of its rulers could equal the achievements of many of the Old, Middle, or New Kingdom kings, it was still a time of cultural innovation. The kings now built their tombs in temple precincts. Many of these tombs—those at Tanis in any case—remained intact, and their contents were not unearthed until the 20th century. Both the style of tombs and burial equipment changed during the period, but there was also a significant trend for archaism—looking back to the past for artistic inspiration. Although most of them are in poor condition, the monumental cityscapes of places such as Sais and Tanis show that the Late Period kings built innovative structures on a truly impressive scale.

1039 BCE Psusennes I becomes king. He is later buried at Tanis

874 BCE Osorkon II begins building works at Bubastis

727 BCE Invasion of Egypt by Piankhy. Egypt comes under rule of Nubian kings

1069 BCE Smendes becomes the first ruler of the 21st Dynasty

945 BCE Sheshonq I becomes the first, and most effective, king of the 22nd Dynasty

773 BCE Death of Sheshonq III. Political fragmentation in northern Egypt

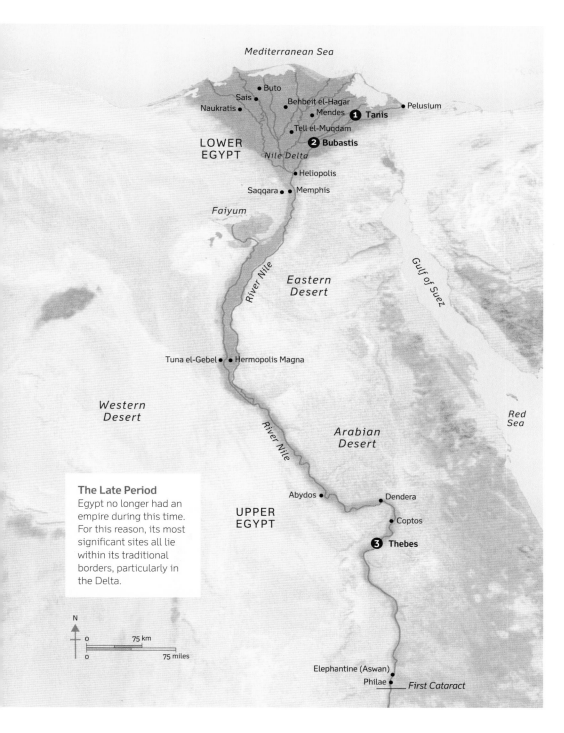

Mediterranean Sea

• Buto
Sais •
Naukratis •   Behbeit el-Hagar •
    Mendes •   **1** Tanis   • Pelusium
   • Tell el-Muqdam
LOWER EGYPT   **2** Bubastis
Nile Delta

   • Heliopolis
Saqqara •   • Memphis

Faiyum

Western Desert

Eastern Desert

River Nile

Gulf of Suez

Red Sea

Tuna el-Gebel •   • Hermopolis Magna

Arabian Desert

River Nile

The Late Period
Egypt no longer had an empire during this time. For this reason, its most significant sites all lie within its traditional borders, particularly in the Delta.

Abydos •   Dendera •

UPPER EGYPT   • Coptos

    3 Thebes

N

0   75 km
0   75 miles

Elephantine (Aswan) •
Philae • ——— *First Cataract*

1 Temple precincts, Tanis

2 Temple of Bastet, Bubastis

3 Tomb of Montuemhat, Thebes

664 BCE Psamtek I of Saïs becomes the first king of the 26th Dynasty

380 BCE Nectanebo I, the first king of the 30th Dynasty, begins major building works

332 BCE Alexander the Great takes Egypt from the Persians

671 BCE Assyrian invasions drive the Nubian kings out of Egypt

525 BCE Cambyses conquers Egypt. The first period of Persian rule begins

343 BCE Beginning of the second period of Persian rule

Third Intermediate Period
Dynasties 21–24

In the period following the collapse of the New Kingdom, Egypt was once again divided between local ruling families and powerful individuals, including high priests and Libyan warlords, who vied with each other for supremacy.

The death of Ramesses XI marked the end of the New Kingdom, but any real central authority had already been crumbling for many decades. The 21st Dynasty (1069–945 BCE) was made up of a series of men calling themselves kings, who were based in the northern city of Tanis, which had replaced Pr-Ramesses as the major city of the eastern Delta. The south of Egypt, meanwhile, was effectively ruled from Thebes by the High Priests of Amen.

North and south

This arrangement seems to have worked well, and the relations between the two regions was strengthened by the fact that people on both sides were often related to each other. For half a century, Psusennes I was king at Tanis, while his brother Menkheperre was High Priest at Thebes. In 984 BCE, Osorkon the Elder became king in the north, his name revealing the extent to which the ruling classes of Egypt had been infiltrated by families of Libyan origin. A precedent for this had already been established by the ascendancy of the General/High Priest Herihor at the end of the 20th Dynasty (see pp.242–243).

Sheshonq I, a "Great Chief of the Ma" (the Meshwesh Libyans) who was a nephew of Osorkon the Elder, founded the 22nd Dynasty (945–715 BCE).

Sheshonq's line of the family had been based in the eastern Delta, in the city of Bubastis. For the next 230 years, therefore, northern Egypt was ruled by kings with unashamedly Libyan names—Sheshonq, Osorkon, and Takelot—from their capital at Tanis.

Sheshonq's reign (945–924 BCE) was the most effective of the period. He installed his son, Iuput, as High Priest of Amen and built temples at Karnak. He also campaigned in what had once been Egypt's Levantine empire and even sacked Jerusalem. He was unable to unify Egypt, however, and after his death, the different regions began to pull apart once more.

Increasing fragmentation

During the reign of Sheshonq III (825–773 BCE), the challenge to royal authority began to make itself felt even in northern Egypt. The lists of kings in Manetho's 23rd and 24th Dynasties are an attempt to make sense of what had become an increasingly confusing situation, as Egypt broke down into a number of different regions competing with each other.

By the time Sheshonq V died in 730 BCE, local rulers had exerted their authority, and many of them were calling themselves king. The Delta was divided between rulers at Tanis, Bubastis, and Leontopolis in the east and several Great Chiefs of the Ma in the western Delta. There

The gods Horus (left) and Thoth (right)

Globular pot for offerings

▷ **Osorkon I**
Metal statues were one of the specialties of the craftsmen of the Third Intermediate Period. On this bronze statue of Osorkon I from the eastern Delta, the king's name and kilt are inlaid with gold.

▷ **Osirian triad**
This piece of temple treasure inscribed for Osorkon II shows Horus and Isis flanking the unusual crouching figure of Osiris. The finest materials were used for the triad: the figures are made of gold and the pillar is carved from lapis lazuli.

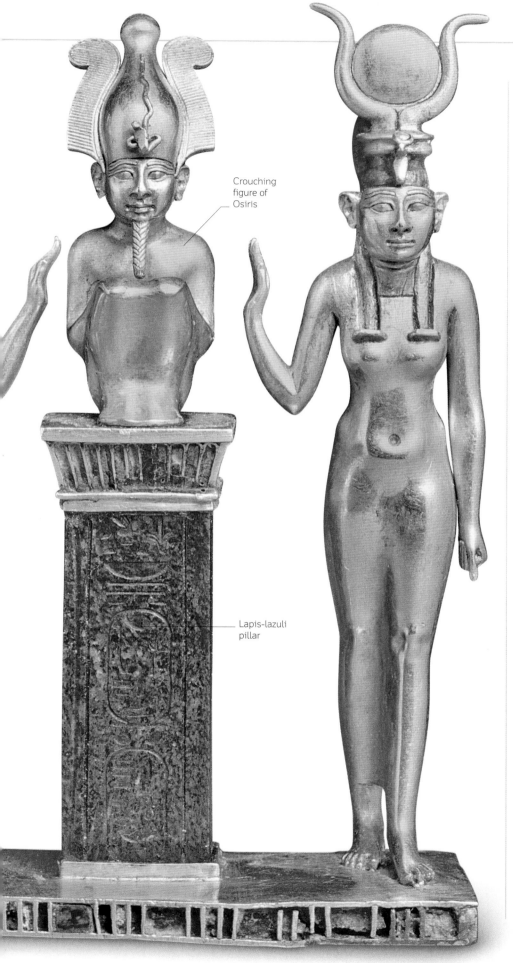

Crouching
figure of
Osiris

Lapis-lazuli
pillar

was also a Prince of the West named Tefnakht
(Manetho's 24th Dynasty), who was based at Sais.
In the Nile Valley of Middle Egypt, new local
rulers gained control of Herakleopolis Magna and
Hermopolis Magna, while the high priests of Amen
remained the dominant power in the south.

One positive result of this increasing fragmentation
was that the rival rulers of the different parts of Egypt
began to build temples, tombs, and monuments in the
various cities in which they were based rather than
concentrating on a few principal sites, such as Thebes.
The monuments built at this time were therefore
much more diverse in character than they had been
during previous periods.

These fragmentary sections of a divided Egypt were
never brought back together again by the Egyptians
themselves, nor by the Libyans. The reunification
of Egypt required the intervention of a strong
external power, and the Nubian 25th Dynasty
was to prove just such a power.

BUBASTIS

With a longer history than either Tanis or Pr-Ramesses,
Bubastis (modern Tell Basta) was one of the main urban
centers of the eastern Delta. Archaeological remains at
the site provide evidence of Old Kingdom *ka*-temples
built by Teti and Pepi I, a palace of the Middle Kingdom,
and extensive cemeteries for humans and sacred cats.
Ramesses II probably built there, but some of the
monuments at the site were originally erected at
Pr-Ramesses. The monumental center of Bubastis
was extended during the Third Intermediate Period,
especially under Osorkon I and Osorkon II, who built
a huge festival hall within the main temple complex.

THE CITY OF BUBASTIS

Tanis

The "Thebes of the North"

The most ambitious—and for archaeologists, the most exciting—project of the Third Intermediate Period was the development of the city of Tanis. It was built as a city fit to be a royal capital.

◁ **The temple enclosure at Tanis**
This view of Tanis shows the remains of the great Amen Temple in the background and the royal tombs in the foreground. The city was mostly built of stone that had been taken from Pr-Ramesses.

△ **Mask of Psusennes I**
The gold funerary mask of Psusennes I is the best known of the artifacts discovered at Tanis. It looks very similar to the mask found in the tomb of Tutankhamen.

They therefore removed much of the building material from Pr-Ramesses in particular—not just stone blocks, but also statues and obelisks—and reused it to suit their own purposes at Tanis. They built a great temple to Amen, as well as temples to Mut, Khonsu, and Horus.

The kings who were most actively involved in this construction work were Psusennes I and Sheshonq III. Some of the Ramesside monuments were reinscribed by the kings who moved them, but others were not. This caused considerable confusion among archaeologists when they began to excavate Tanis, and for many years, scholars believed that it was in fact the site of Pr-Ramesses. More recent work at Qantir finally proved that it was not.

By the end of the 20th Dynasty, the great Ramesside city of Pr-Ramesses had more or less been abandoned (see pp.220–221). A change in the direction of the branch of the Nile on which it stood had made the city useless as a river harbor, so it was replaced by a new city. This was built farther downstream on a large *gezira* (sand-island) alongside the Nile, at what became the site of Tanis (present-day San el-Hagar).

For the kings of the early Third Intermediate Period, the decision to build a new city represented a golden opportunity to create a metropolis that could rival Thebes as a great monumental center, dedicated to the god Amen. Tanis did in fact flourish for a short period of time, but it was then abandoned during the Roman Period.

Borrowed temples

In order to create this splendid "Thebes of the North" as quickly as possible and with few of the resources that had been available to the earlier kings of the New Kingdom—namely great wealth and the stone quarries of southern Egypt—the kings of the 21st and 22nd Dynasties had to plunder existing monuments.

Silver coffin embossed with figures of protective deities

Royal tombs

One of the most obvious ways in which Tanis was different from Thebes was that it had no desert valley nearby that could be used as a royal cemetery, as the Valley of the Kings had been. The kings of the Third Intermediate Period were also not wealthy enough to build huge, impressive royal tombs to rival those of the Old and Middle Kingdoms. They did not want to, however, because safety and secrecy were now vital. The Valley of the Kings had been plundered by thieves and the royal bodies had recently been moved to new locations (see pp.244–245), so the current rulers placed their tombs in the safest place they knew—within the enclosure walls of the main temple of their city. They also kept the tombs modest in size to aid discretion.

At Tanis, a corner of the Amen Temple Enclosure was set aside for a complex of small chambers, each just big enough to hold a sarcophagus and a few burial goods. Like the Enclosure itself, these were mainly built from stone taken from earlier structures.

Hidden splendor

This strategy of hiding tombs proved to be successful, and the small royal necropolis at Tanis remained undisturbed until it was rediscovered by archaeologists in 1939. It seems to have had an eventful history, however, because both the tombs and the burial goods and equipment were used and reused during the 21st and 22nd Dynasties. Four of the tombs may have been built for Psusennes I, Amenemope, Osorkon III, and Sheshonq III.

> "The temple **precincts** are still **impressive,** even **in their utter ruin.**"
>
> KEN KITCHEN, *THE THIRD INTERMEDIATE PERIOD IN EGYPT,* 1995

◁ **Scarab pectoral**
This rare pectoral shows a scarab with its wings spread for flight. Found in the tomb of Psusennes I, it bears the king's cartouche, which refers to him as "Beloved of Amen".

Sheshonq II and Takelot II were also buried there, and the other original occupants, or later interlopers possibly, may have included as many as eight more kings.

The burial equipment recovered from these tombs includes objects that were made for their owners, together with others that had been taken from previous tombs, especially from tombs built during the reign of Ramesses II. Although the number of funerary goods belonging to each king was relatively small, they included objects that were extraordinarily fine in quality. In fact, apart from the tomb of Tutankhamen, the Tanis necropolis is the most spectacular find of an Egyptian royal burial.

▽ **Coffin of Sheshonq II**
This silver coffin belonging to King Sheshonq II is one of the most remarkable objects found at the Tanis necropolis. The king has a falcon's head, which possibly associated him with the god Horus.

A flail, one of the symbols of kingship

The stomach was stored in a jar protected by the jackal-headed Duamutef

△ **Canopic jars**
By the New Kingdom, canopic jars, which were used to store body parts, were adorned with images of the Sons of Horus. These four deities were believed to guard the dead.

Mummification

Beneath the bandages

One of the most distinctive features of ancient Egyptian culture was the practice of preserving dead bodies. Known as "mummification," this custom played a key role in ensuring that when a person died, they had a successful afterlife.

The Egyptians believed that when a person died, their *ka* needed to be fed for eternity (see pp.50–51). For this to happen, the *ka* also required a physical host in which it could be nourished. Ideally, this was the body of the person who had died, so it became important to preserve the bodies of the dead. This idea may have been linked to the chance discovery that bodies buried in pits filled with sand had remained astonishingly well-preserved as a result of natural

dessication. This natural form of preservation no longer took place, however, when the Egyptians began to bury their dead in coffins. Something that started as a means of respecting the dead resulted in speeding up decomposition. To solve

◁ **Embalmers' cache**
The materials that were left over from preparing a body for mummification were often buried near the tomb of the deceased. This bag of natron was found close to the tomb of Tutankhamen.

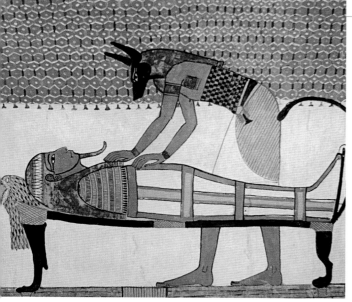

THE MUMMY OF YUYA

By the end of the 18th Dynasty, the Egyptians had finished developing their painstaking techniques for preserving the dead, but the results of these procedures were not always successful. The mummies of Yuya and Thuya, the parents of Queen Tiy, were given the best possible treatment before they were buried in their tomb in the Valley of the Kings. Even today, some 3,000 years later, their bodies still have a remarkably lifelike appearance. The body of Tutankhamen, however, which was buried at around the same time, was in a very poor state when it was discovered, owing to the botched efforts of his undertakers.

◁ **Anubis mummifies Sennedjem**
The Egyptians believed that the god Anubis guided the dead from this world to the next. He acted a divine undertaker, so he oversaw the mummification process.

this problem, rather than abandoning coffins and returning to desert burials, the Egyptians began to devise methods of artificially preserving bodies.

Wrapping the body

The first attempts at mummification were made during the Early Dynastic Period and the Old Kingdom and focused on maintaining the body's lifelike appearance. Linen bandages were bound tightly around it and were sometimes stiffened with plaster or resin that were shaped into features before they set. Although this failed to stop the flesh from decomposing inside the wrappings, it was often very effective in preserving the body's outer appearance.

Removing the organs

By the Middle Kingdom, the Egyptians had made considerable progress in solving the real problem, namely decomposition, which spread from the soft internal organs to the rest of the body. Their solution was to remove the internal organs and preserve them separately, in case the body required them in the afterlife. By the Third Intermediate Period, they had begun to extract not just the easily accessible organs of the abdomen and chest, but also the brain. This

was either drawn out through the nose or via the atlas vertebra at the base of the skull. Once the important organs had been removed, they were stored in jars called canopic jars—one each for the intestines, the liver, the lungs, and the stomach. Little attention was given to preserving the heart, which was often replaced by a more durable stone substitute, or the brain.

Drying the skin

After all of the internal organs had been extracted, the exterior of the body still had to be treated. The main method of doing this was to apply natron, a naturally occurring salt compound, to the skin. The embalmers used natron as a dry powder, which they heaped over the body, much as sand had been piled on top of bodies in desert burials.

According to Herodotus, this drying process took 70 days. In some cases, before a body was dried, the muscle tissue beneath its skin was removed and replaced by an inorganic substance, such as sand or linen. Finally, to enhance the appearance of the body, its toenails and fingernails were tied on to prevent them from dropping off. In some cases, false hair and false eyes were also added.

▽ **The mummy of Wah**
One of the most remarkable examples of a wrapped mummy is that of Wah, an "Overseer of the storehouse" from the Middle Kingdom. His body was wrapped in numerous sheets of linen.

▷ **Nest of coffins**
This view of all of the coffins belonging to Djeddjehutyefankh shows how they were carefully designed to fit inside each other. Together, they formed a multilayered sheath of physical and religious protection around Djeddjehutyefankh's body.

The coffins of Djeddjehutyefankh

Burial in the Late Period

▽ **The inner coffin**
Djeddjehutyefankh's innermost coffin is painted with images of protective deities. These include the four Sons of Horus and the sky goddess Nut, who spreads her wings over his chest.

From at least as early as the Middle Kingdom, Egyptians who could afford it chose to be buried in two coffins, one nested within the other. The inner coffin was anthropoid, or human-shaped, and the outer one was box-shaped. In the New Kingdom, this standard pair of coffins was gradually replaced by several different sizes of anthropoid coffins all nested inside each other. This style is best exemplified by the series of coffins (and stone sarcophagus) in which Tutankhamen was laid to rest (see pp.192–193).

In the Ramesside and Third Intermediate Periods, the external decoration of coffins became increasingly intricate, incorporating traditional religious texts and panels showing scenes of gods and goddesses. By the Late Period, this extensive elaborate decoration, along with the desire for multiple anthropoid coffins, led to the creation of some of the most complex coffin sets that were ever made.

Pedestal coffins

A good example of a coffin set from the 25th Dynasty is the one that belonged to Djeddjehutyefankh—one of a group of priests of the god of Montu who were buried at Deir el-Bahri, near Luxor. The innermost part of his coffin set is the wrapped and mummified body of Djeddjehutyefankh himself, which was covered with a netting of faience beads.

The anthropoid coffin in which the mummy was housed was typical of the period. It had a pedestal base, which may have been used to stand the coffin vertically on its end during the Opening of the Mouth ceremony that was often performed at funerals (see pp.260–261).

Djeddjehutyefankh's innermost coffin was decorated with funerary texts and images of funerary deities. The coffin in which it was nested was also highly decorated and was in turn contained by an outer coffin, the design of which was innovative for the period. This outer coffin had a vaulted lid and tall corner posts that were clearly designed to replicate the form of a chapel or shrine. The figure of either Anubis or Wepwawet—both of whom were jackal deities that guided the dead to the afterlife—was fixed to the lid, and each of its four posts held a wooden statue of the god Horus in the form of a falcon. As Horus was a sky god, the coffin lid itself probably represented the heavens.

The complexity of the coffins from this period was part of a more general trend, evident from the New Kingdom to the Late Period, of decorating coffins with scenes of gods and funerary texts rather than the walls of tombs. As the tomb walls became bare, the tombs themselves also became simpler. This marked a significant move away from the Old and Middle Kingdom traditions of building lavish tombs with elaborate offering chapels attached to them.

Anubis or Wepawet, jackal gods of the underworld

The boat of the sun god Ra is dragged across the sky

A false beard connects the deceased with Osiris

Falcons representing the sky god Horus

Hieroglyphic texts ask for the protection of the gods

Wrapped body covered with bead netting

Protective deities depicted within individual shrines

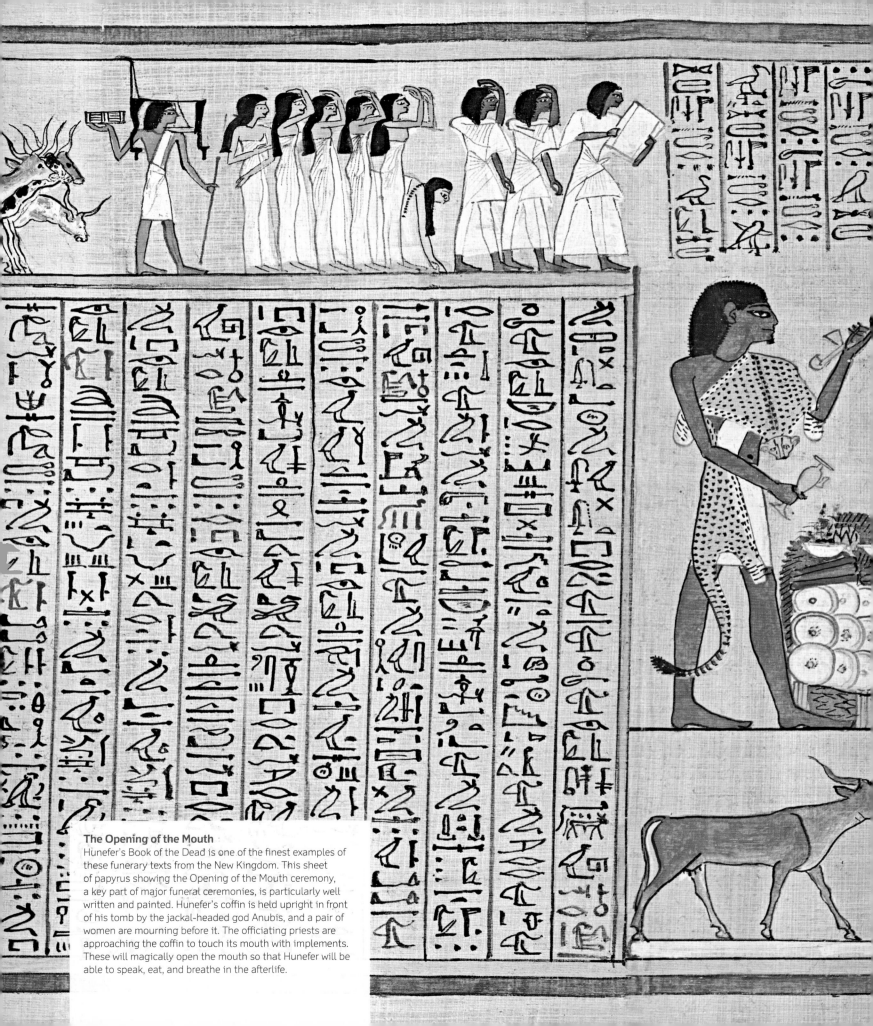

The Opening of the Mouth
Hunefer's Book of the Dead is one of the finest examples of these funerary texts from the New Kingdom. This sheet of papyrus showing the Opening of the Mouth ceremony, a key part of major funeral ceremonies, is particularly well written and painted. Hunefer's coffin is held upright in front of his tomb by the jackal-headed god Anubis, and a pair of women are mourning before it. The officiating priests are approaching the coffin to touch its mouth with implements. These will magically open the mouth so that Hunefer will be able to speak, eat, and breathe in the afterlife.

Shabtis

Servants for the afterlife

The Egyptians believed that when they died, they would have to work for Osiris in an afterlife known as the Field of Reeds. To avoid eternal physical labor, they were buried with shabtis—servant figurines that would magically do the work for them. They were shaped like mummies and equipped with tools.

Amenmose in everyday clothes

▷ **Painted shabti**
This shabti of the late New Kingdom clearly shows the head emerging from the white mummy wrappings and an agricultural tool in each hand. The lower part of the body has hieroglyphs on a yellow background.

Agricultural tool held by shabti

◁ **Stick shabti**
The most basic form of shabti was a crude piece of wood roughly carved to look like a mummy. It has an ink inscription that identifies the owner.

△ **Shabti of Amenmose**
A variation of the shabti was the small funerary figure representing the deceased. In this example, a faience figurine in everyday dress is contained within a box that resembles the owner's coffin.

Detachable lid for the shabti box

◁ **Shabti box**
Shabtis were usually produced as work gangs rather than single figures. Tomb owners stored large numbers (sometimes several hundreds) of their figures in boxes, which often had text to identify whom they belonged to.

Owner of the shabti box, Paramnekhu

▷ **Family shabtis**
These three shabtis from the tomb of the artisan Sennedjem at Deir el-Medina belonged to different members of his family. The female shabti belonged to his wife, the male "overseer" shabti was his son's, and the standard shabti belonged to Sennedjem.

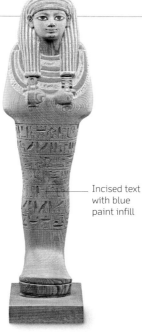

Incised text
with blue
paint infill

△ **Shabti of Yuya**
The finest shabtis were
works of art in their own
right, small statuettes carved
and painted with care, like
this example belonging to
Yuya, father of Queen Tiy.

△ **Shabti of Maya**
This large 16 in (41 cm)-
tall New Kingdom wooden
shabti has striking eyes and
eyebrows inlaid with stone
and glass, which give it a
vivid, lifelike appearance.

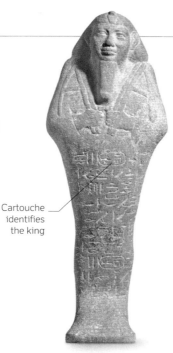

Cartouche
identifies
the king

△ **Shabti of Taharqa**
This shabti is part of a set
belonging to King Taharqa
of the 25th Dynasty. It is not
particularly well-modeled,
but it is made from granite,
making it extremely durable.

Incised text
wraps around
the body of
the shabti

△ **Shabti of a high priest**
Shabtis of the Late Period,
owned by the elite, are
better-modeled and larger
than those from earlier
periods. Like many coffins
of the same era, they are
mounted on pedestal bases.

△ **"Overseer" shabti**
"Overseer" shabtis took the
form of foremen who were in
charge of work gangs. The
Egyptians thought that like
real workers, large numbers
of shabtis needed managers
to oversee their tasks.

△ **Shabti of Ankhu**
Middle Kingdom tombs
contained fewer shabtis than
the tombs of the New Kingdom
and later periods. They were
sometimes made from very
hard materials, like this
example in granodiorite.

Colored
glaze
provides a
dramatic
effect

△ **Shabti of the lady Sati**
An example of the exquisite craftsmanship often
seen during the reign of Amenhotep III, this
faience shabti has a white glazed background
and hieroglyphs infilled with a blue glaze.

Nubian pharaohs

The 25th Dynasty in Egypt

△ **Shrine of Taharqa**
The shrine of Taharqa at Kawa, in Nubia, was primarily dedicated to Amen-Ra, who is depicted here in his ram-headed form. Taharqa is shown making offerings to the god, who sits beside the goddess Anuket.

The reunification of Egypt at the end of the Third Intermediate Period came in an unexpected way, when the Kushite kings of Nubia conquered their northern neighbor to create a short-lived joint kingdom.

By the end of the New Kingdom, the Egyptians had lost control of their Nubian empire, and they made no attempt to reconquer this territory during the Third Intermediate Period. Left to their own devices, and without any interference from Egypt for the next 300 years, the inevitable happened—the Nubians developed a strong state, much as they had previously during the Second Intermediate Period.

However, the Nubian rulers who emerged from the ruins of Egypt's empire were different from their predecessors in several respects. The most important power group of Nubians that emerged at this time came from farther upriver than Kerma and closer to the Fourth Cataract. By the end of the 8th century BCE,

they governed the whole of Nubia from their power base at Napata and buried their rulers at the site of el-Kurru. Their earliest tombs were round tumuli, similar to those that they had previously built at Kerma, but these tombs became increasingly Egyptian in appearance and eventually became small pyramids.

▷ **Piankhy's pyramid**
The tomb of Piankhy at el-Kurru is an early example of the way in which the Kushite kings took the basic form of an Egyptian pyramid and adapted it for their own use. The Nubian pyramids were much smaller than the earlier Egyptian ones and had steeper sides.

Another site that was very important to the Nubians was the ancient religious center at Gebel Barkal. This was dedicated to the god Amen, whom the Nubians had adopted as their own principal god.

Nubian conquest of Egypt

These Nubian rulers were ambitious to expand beyond Nubia's traditional frontiers, and they were able to take full advantage of Egypt's weakness. Their ruler, Kashta, started to refer to himself as the King of Upper and Lower Egypt—a claim that became more of a reality when his son, Piankhy, or Piye (747–716 BCE), began to take control of southern Egypt.

In the 21st year of his rule, Piankhy invaded northern Egypt in a campaign that was recorded on a great stela that the victorious king erected at Gebel Barkal. Piankhy's army then moved north down the Nile toward Memphis. He captured the city after a difficult siege, then returned to Nubia. It was still necessary, however, for Piankhy's successor, Shabaqo (716–702 BCE), to invade Egypt again early in his reign to bring the rulers of the Nile Delta firmly under Nubian control.

Nubian pharaohs

As rulers of a unified Nubian/Egyptian kingdom, the Kushite kings of the 25th Dynasty were very careful to present themselves in traditionally Egyptian ways, so they built or added to the temples of traditional Egyptian deities. As Amen was already its major deity, Thebes received particular royal favor, but the political capital of the Nubian kings was Memphis, possibly in deference to the earlier models of royal power established by the pyramid-

ESARHADDON'S VICTORY STELA

Esarhaddon became king of the Neo-Assyrian empire in 681 BCE, and ruled until his death in 669 BCE. Although his reign was fairly short and plagued by both illness and fighting within the royal family, it boasted one major achievement—the conquest of Egypt. Esarhaddon's initial attempt to invade Egypt in 674 BCE was beaten back by Taharqa, but the Assyrians returned in 671 BCE and moved into northern Egypt, defeating Taharqa's army and taking Memphis. Taharqa fled south, but his family was captured and sent to Assyria as hostages. Esarhaddon celebrated his victory on this stela, which shows him towering over two captives. The smaller prisoner, with a rope round his neck and wearing a uraeus, is either Taharqa or his son.

Esarhaddon

Egyptian captive

building kings of the Old Kingdom. Under Taharqa (690–664 BCE), extensive building works were carried out in both Egypt and Nubia.

The Assyrian invasion

Nubian control of Egypt was eventually ended by a series of Assyrian invasions that penetrated as far south as Thebes. Tantamani (664–656 BCE) attempted to recapture Egypt from the Assyrians, but he was defeated. This brought the 25th Dynasty to a close. The Assyrians did not aim to rule Egypt directly, so there is no Assyrian dynasty in Manetho's list of kings. Instead, they left control of the country in the hands of local rulers, who had sworn oaths of loyalty to the Assyrian king. This created a network of people who would compete for power when the Assyrian empire itself collapsed.

◁ **Lion pendant**
The gold base of this Nubian pendant shows clear Egyptian influence. It depicts a series of baboons with their hands raised to worship the sun god.

▷ **Sphinx of Taharqa**
The Kushite kings were keen to present themselves in traditional Egyptian ways. This included depicting the king in the form of a sphinx.

Double uraeus, representing both Egypt and Nubia

747 BCE Piankhy becomes ruler of Nubia

690 BCE Taharqa becomes king of Egypt

664 BCE Death of Taharqa

735 BCE Piankhy invades Egypt

671 BCE Esarhaddon invades Egypt

The Saite Period

The Egyptian kings of the 26th Dynasty

The Saite kings of the 26th Dynasty were the first native Egyptian rulers of a unified Egypt since Ramesses XI, but they had to cope with an increasing number of foreign enemies.

During the 26th Dynasty, Egypt became much more involved in the politics of the Near East and eastern Mediterranean and had to contend with the threats posed by various foreign powers, including Nubia, Assyria, Babylonia, Persia, and Greece.

The works of the Greek historians provide invaluable information about this period, especially those of Herodotus, who recorded all kinds of historical facts about the Egyptians, as well as unlikely gossip. These show that the Egyptians relied on both diplomacy and military measures to maintain its independence.

Psamtek I

One of Assyria's most important Egyptian vassals was Necho I of Sais (672–664 BCE), who was killed during Tantamani's attempt to reconquer Egypt in 664 BCE. Necho I's son, Psamtek I (664–610 BCE), succeeded his father as a vassal of the Assyrians and controlled the western Delta and Memphis. Early in his reign, he

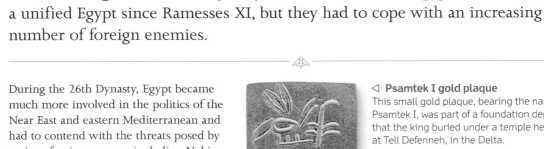

◁ **Psamtek I gold plaque**
This small gold plaque, bearing the name of Psamtek I, was part of a foundation deposit that the king buried under a temple he built at Tell Defenneh, in the Delta.

exploited Assyria's problems in other parts of its empire to extend his authority. He had taken control of the whole Delta by 660 BCE, and the rest of Egypt by 656 BCE. Without openly breaking with the Assyrians, he became the effective king of the whole of Egypt and the first native Egyptian to be so in 400 years.

Psamtek I built alliances with other local rulers, including the priesthood at Thebes, but he also created a powerful army that employed a large number of foreign mercenaries. He encouraged other foreigners to enter Egypt, especially Greek traders, for whom he developed the city of Naukratis in the western Delta and gave it a monopoly on receiving Greek trade into Egypt.

△ **Khonsirdis statue**
Temple donations in the Late Period often included bronze statues of a donor making a gift. This 16 in (40 cm) tall statue bears the name of Khonsirdis and dates from the reign of Psamtek I.

GOD'S **WIVES OF AMEN**

Originating in the 18th Dynasty, the title "God's Wife of Amen" was used to designate a royal woman who played an important role in the cult of Amen at Thebes. In the Third Intermediate Period, and especially during the 25th and 26th Dynasties, this role became increasingly important, as it was associated with the political and economic power of the Theban region. It became customary for the post to be held by a royal daughter and for the incumbent God's Wife to "adopt" her successor. The importance of these Wives is clear from the art of the period. Here, the God's Wife Shepenwepet II is depicted as a sphinx making an offering to the god Amen.

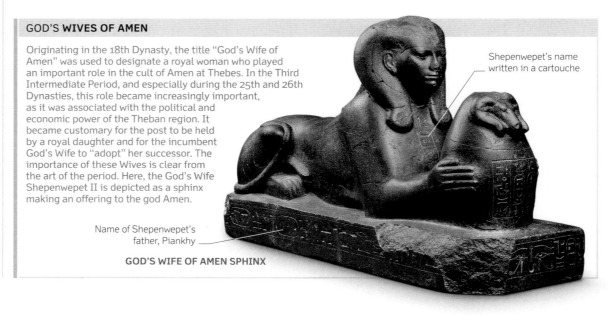

Shepenwepet's name written in a cartouche

Name of Shepenwepet's father, Piankhy

GOD'S WIFE OF AMEN SPHINX

> "It is **said** that **in the reign of Amasis**, Egypt attained to its **greatest prosperity**."
>
> HERODOTUS DESCRIBES THE REIGN OF AMASIS

The city of Sais

Although they ruled the whole of Egypt, the Saite kings, as their names suggests, were closely associated with the city of Sais in the western Delta. For this reason, Sais became a major monumental center under their rule. Building work centered on the temple of the goddess Neith, the patron deity of the 26th Dynasty. Following the practice of other Delta rulers, such as those of the 21st and 22nd Dynasties, the Saite kings also built their tombs in the city's temple enclosure, but sadly, these tombs and all of Sais's temples were thoroughly pillaged in later years.

Later kings of the 26th Dynasty

Psamtek I's long and successful reign brought a stability to Egypt that was rarely seen under the kings who succeeded him, but his son, Necho II (610–595 BCE), continued Psamtek I's policy of increasing Egypt's military strength. The army, with its large mercenary component, was vital in preventing an invasion of Egypt by the Chaldeans (Babylonians). It was also used by Necho's son, Psamtek II (595–589 BCE), in a campaign to neutralize a potential threat from Nubia. However, Apries (589–570 BCE), the son of Psamtek II, had a turbulent reign and was defeated in battle by the Babylonians in the Levant and the Greek colonists in Libya. This latter defeat was followed by a successful coup against Apries by the general Amasis, who became king (570–526 BCE).

Despite its inauspicious start, Amasis' reign was both long and prosperous, but his son, Psamtek III (526–525 BCE), had the misfortune of coming to the throne only a few months before the Persians, under King Cambyses, invaded Egypt. After Cambyses captured Memphis, Psamtek III was taken prisoner and was held in Persia, where he died.

▷ **Statue of Necho**
This bronze statue is a likeness of Necho, although it is not known which one. Kneeling with his hands open at his sides, the king is in the classic pose of making an offering to a god.

Inspired by the past

Archaism in art

During the 25th and 26 Dynasties, both kings and members of the nonroyal elite looked back to the artistic styles of Egypt's distant past for inspiration. This imitation of styles from ancient times is known as archaism.

Many Egyptians, both royal and elite, looked back at the long history of their country and the extraordinary number of monuments and works of art created by their forbears with great admiration. This respect for their cultural legacy is shown in the graffiti left behind in the New Kingdom and also by the many monuments that Khaemwese restored (see pp.226–227). This reverence also explains why the Egyptians sometimes revived styles of monuments that had been popular in ancient times, and built new royal pyramids at the beginning of the Middle Kingdom, for example.

Archaism in the Late Period

The desire to emulate the art of the past was especially strong during the Late Period, notably during the 25th and 26th Dynasties. For the Kushites (25th Dynasty), reviving ancient forms was one way to affirm that they were culturally Egyptian and thus fit to rule as kings of Egypt. The kings of the 26th Dynasty followed suit, possibly also wishing to stress their credentials as native Egyptian rulers and to imply that the great days of the past were returning. A good example of this tendency in

◁ **Relief from the tomb of Montuemhat**
These scenes of men gutting fish and women carrying baskets are reminiscent of the "scenes of daily life" depicted in Old Kingdom tombs in the area around Memphis.

the sphere of literature is the "Shabaqo Stone," which proclaimed itself a 25th Dynasty copy of an ancient text that the king had found on an ancient, worm-eaten papyrus.

Montuemhat

The best example of archaism is the tomb of a high official, Montuemhat, whose career encompassed the end of the 25th Dynasty, as well as the ascendancy of the Saites. His tomb, one of the largest at Thebes, was decorated with exceptionally fine reliefs copied in content and style from those of earlier monuments at Thebes—mainly from the New Kingdom, but also dating as far back as the Old Kingdom.

More than a dozen statues of Montuemhat have also survived, and these are an interesting blend of Late Period features (such as the hard, dark stone popular at the time) and ancient forms, including some that hark as far back as the Old Kingdom.

△ **Statue of Montuemhat**
This hardstone statue with its closely modeled face is clearly Late Period in style, but the form and dress of the figure are based on those of Old Kingdom private statues.

◁ **Montuemhat's tomb**
This tomb was built not far from Hatshepsut's mortuary temple at Deir el-Bahri. The mud-brick superstructure is just one part of a complex with extensive underground rooms and open courts.

This woman is described as the "Lady of the House"

Long halterneck robe of an elite male

△ **Archaic style**
The style of this finely carved relief in Montuemhat's tomb was modeled on reliefs in early 18th Dynasty tombs. There were many of these tombs at Thebes, and Montuemhat was probably familiar with them.

27th–31st Dynasties

Persians and Egyptians

For nearly 200 years, between 525 and 332 BCE, the native rulers of Egypt struggled, usually without success, to maintain their independence from the new regional superpower: the Persian Empire.

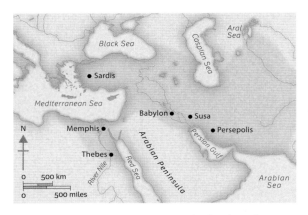

△ **The Persian Empire**
At its greatest extent, the Persian Empire stretched from Greece in the west to Pakistan in the east. Egypt formed its most southwesterly frontier.

Egypt's experience of falling under the control of a powerful empire from the east—the Assyrians—was repeated when the Persians invaded Egypt in 525 BCE. Psamtek III of Egypt was defeated by the Persian king, Cambyses, and Egypt duly became a satrapy (province) of the Persian Empire. Cambyses died just three years later, and the Egyptians mounted a brief revolt that was crushed by Cambyses' successor, Darius I (522–486 BCE).

The first Persian Period
Unlike the Assyrians, the Persians were keen to be seen as pharaonic-style rulers of Egypt, so they built temples in which they were depicted as Egyptian kings worshipping Egyptian gods. They were helped with this by a few key Egyptian officials who were willing to work for them, such as the

Chief Physician, Wadjhorresne. He carried out reconstruction work at Sais under Cambyses and Darius I, but not all of the Persian kings wanted to uphold Egyptian traditions in this way to display their kingship, notably Darius I's son Xerxes (486–465 BCE).

As Egypt was now a part of the Persian Empire, its most senior official, the satrap, was Persian, but much of the Egyptian administration was left as it was. The Persians intervened very little, as long as Egypt paid its taxes and contributed to Persia's military efforts, especially against the Greeks. There was also, though, little integration, cultural or otherwise, between the Egyptians and their new masters during Persian rule, and this fermented the minor revolts that local Egyptian leaders staged against the Persians.

The last native dynasties
The most serious of these revolts resulted in some local rulers, especially from the Delta, making claims on the throne itself. Although there is little detailed evidence from this period, it seems that after the death of Darius II in 405 BCE, a local ruler based at Sais, Amyrtaios (404–399 BCE), declared himself king of Egypt and became the sole ruler of the 28th Dynasty. Internal divisions within the Persian ruling family prevented a quick response to this revolt, but Amyrtaios' reign was cut short by another local ruler in the Nile Delta, Nepherites of Mendes, who founded the 29th Dynasty (399–380 BCE).

Water spout that was added later

Cartouche of Nectanebo II based on that of Senwosret I

◁ **Lion of Nectanebo II**
This is one of a pair of lions that Nectanebo II set up at the temple of Thoth in Hermopolis Parva. They were taken to Rome during Roman rule.

TOMB OF **PETOSIRIS**

The family of Petosiris held the important post of High Priest of the god Thoth at Hermopolis Magna for five generations, from the 30th Dynasty, through the second Persian Period, and into the reign of Alexander the Great. During this time, the priests carried out significant building works within the great temple enclosure, restoring damaged structures and building new ones. All of this is recorded in the autobiographical texts in Petosiris' tomb. In the form of a miniature temple, it is located at the nearby cemetery of Tuna el-Gebel.

Although the three kings of this dynasty had some authority over the whole of Egypt, they seem to have followed the example of other Delta rulers in choosing to be buried in their home city—in this case, Mendes.

The kings of the 30th Dynasty, who would be the last independent, native Egyptian rulers of Egypt for nearly 2,000 years, were more successful than their immediate predecessors. The two most important kings of this dynasty, which originated in the Delta city of Sebennytos, were its founder, Nectanebo I (380–362 BCE), and his grandson Nectanebo II (360–343 BCE). Both of these kings built temples on a grand scale that had not been seen in Egypt since the New Kingdom, notably in the Delta, but also in Upper Egypt.

The second Persian Period

In 343 BCE, the Persians, under Artaxerxes III, invaded Egypt again and defeated the forces of Nectanebo II, who fled south. Egypt became a Persian satrapy once more, and this time the Egyptians suffered greatly under the occupation. The Persians looted temples and imposed an oppressive imperial administration on the country. The Persians were so hated that when Alexander the Great invaded Egypt in 332 BCE, he was welcomed by the Egyptians as their liberator.

"All the **temples** were **without** their **servants** and the **priests** fled, not knowing what **was happening**."

PETOSIRIS DESCRIBES PERSIAN RULE IN EGYPT

▷ **Nectanebo II**
The kings of the 30th Dynasty were keen to be seen as traditional Egyptian pharaohs. This statue of Nectanebo II shows him being protected by the towering figure of the god Horus.

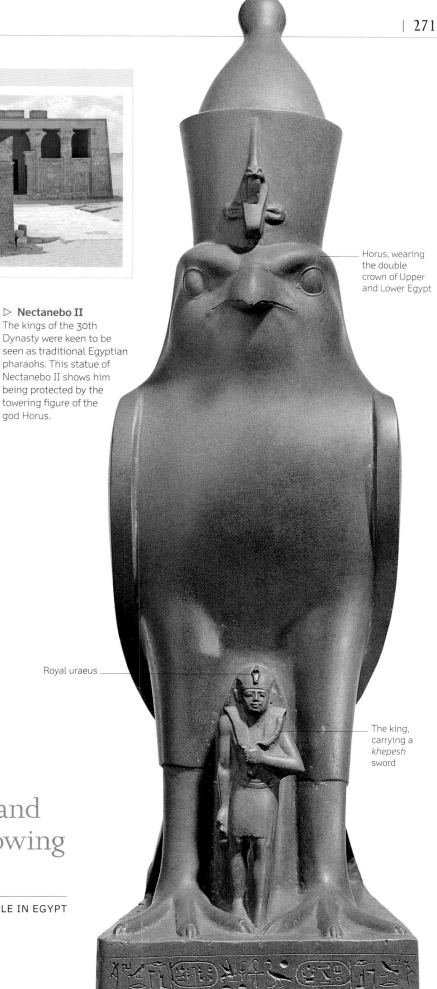

Horus, wearing the double crown of Upper and Lower Egypt

Royal uraeus

The king, carrying a *khepesh* sword

The goddess Isis accompanies the Apis bull

Horudja's title is "Doorkeeper" of the temple of Ptah

This stela is dated the 21st year of Psamtek I's reign

△ **Apis bull stela**
The site of the Apis bull burials, the Serapeum at Saqqara, became a place where devotees of the god left stelae recording their piety. In this stela, the worshipper, a man named Horudja, kneels before a statue of the god.

Animal cults

Sacred animals

There is a common misconception that the ancient Egyptians were obsessed with the worship of live animals. This was possibly closest to the truth during the Late Period, when animal cults became popular.

Even before the Late Period, Egypt had a long tradition of sacred animals. Many gods were given the appearance of a specific animal to identify them, and temple statues dedicated by nonroyals often show them offering a sacred animal (see p.169), but these offerings were only of images, not of actual animals. There were, however, a few real animals that the Egyptians believed to be the embodiments of actual gods. The most famous of these was the god Apis, who was worshipped at Memphis in the form of a living bull. When the bull died, it was buried with full honors (see p.227) and was then replaced by another living bull.

Sacred animals

This situation changed in the Late Period, however, when there was a huge surge of interest in sacred animals, and many of the animals that were associated with particular gods began to be treated as sacred in their own right.

The god Thoth, for example, was the main deity at the city of Hermopolis Magna, and his sacred animals were the ibis and the baboon. During the Late Period, ibises and baboons were kept in a sort of sacred zoo at Hermopolis, and pious pilgrims could pay for them to be buried in the underground tomb galleries that had been specially excavated for them at Tuna el-Gebel, the main desert necropolis for Hermopolis Magna. Payment for burial included the mummification and elaborate wrapping of the dead animals. The enterprise was presumably an important source of income for the temple of Thoth. The same thing also happened at other sites in Egypt, and many millions of creatures associated with local deities were mummified and buried in specially built mass graves. No animal was too small: near Esna, archaeologists have excavated preserved and wrapped fish that were associated with a local deity.

It is not clear why there was such an explosion of interest in animal cults at this time, other than the financial rewards for temples. One theory is that it might have been a cultural reaction to having to live under repeated foreign rule during the Late Period. For the native population, animal cults may have represented something distinctly Egyptian when they were facing domination, particularly by the Persians.

▷ **Figure of Bastet**
Donations to the goddess Bastet at Bubastis could include the gift of a mummified cat to the large cat cemetery there, but an alternative was a bronze figure of the goddess herself.

> "The practices of the **Egyptians** in their **worship of animals** are astonishing and **beyond belief**."

DIODORUS SICULUS, WRITING IN THE 1ST CENTURY BCE

Elaborate multi-colored bandaging

▷ **Ibis mummy**
The care taken with the external appearance of animal mummies did not always extend to the insides. When x-rayed, many of them have proved to be random collections of bones.

Pets

Dogs, cats, and monkeys

The Egyptians were not great pet owners in the sense that they grew personally attached to many different types of animals, but they were often especially fond of dogs and cats.

As an agricultural people, the ancient Egyptians lived alongside a wide variety of animals, both domesticated and wild. To them, animals were primarily a potential source of food, but they also provided a rich source of imagery when people wanted to represent the qualities and powers of the gods. Although lions, bulls, and crocodiles made excellent models for powerful deities, they were not suitable as domestic companions.

Appreciating animals

Pictures of animals in Egyptian tombs, especially New Kingdom tombs, suggest that artists were fascinated by the beauty of animals' fur, feathers, and colors. Given this appreciation of the beauty and entertaining behavior of some animals, it is not surprising to learn that many Egyptians, or upper-class Egyptians at any rate, had pets—domestic animals with little or no economic importance. Some of these animals were popular for aesthetic reasons—fish, for example, which were kept in garden ponds. The only two types of animals with which Egyptians seemed to form a personal bond were dogs and cats.

Dogs

The most popular pet throughout every period of ancient Egyptian history was the dog, depicted in art as both a companion or pet and a working animal. Numerous tomb scenes depict the tomb owner out hunting with dogs that had been specially bred for the purpose, such as the soluki, which was the dominant hunting dog during the New Kingdom. Other breeds included mastiffs and a short-legged dog that was similar to a dachshund.

▽ **"Green monkey"**
The space under a chair provided an ideal place to depict a pet. In this painting, a "green monkey" is shown eating fruit from a basket, but it is wisely tethered to the chair leg.

△ **Dogs in the tomb of Sirenput**
This relief of hunting dogs was carved on the exterior of the Middle Kingdom tomb of Sirenput at Qubbet el-Hawa. Many such images have been found on tombs, showing just how important dogs were to their upper-class owners.

Dogs were recorded or portrayed in the company of all kinds of people, including kings. Intef II, for example, had his pack of five Libyan hunting dogs depicted on the funerary stela of his tomb at Thebes, while a dog owned by a late Old Kingdom king was given its own tomb at Giza. Further down the social scale, humble agricultural workers were also shown in the company of a faithful canine companion (see p.23). The Egyptians rarely gave their animals personal names, but dogs were treated differently. Some of the names recorded are "Good Watcher,' "Brave One," and "Reliable One."

Cats

Egypt has often been claimed as the original home of the household cat. They were probably domesticated from the Middle Kingdom onward, as images of them do not appear in Old Kingdom tomb reliefs, but wild species are known from much earlier. The Egyptian word for cats, miw, is certainly derived from the sound that they make. During the New Kingdom, cats were often shown as pets in the tombs of the

▷ **The goddess Bastet**
This bronze statue from the Late Period shows Bastet in the form of a cat. As well as a gold nose-ring and earrings, she is adorned with religious symbols, including a silver pectoral with a protective wedjat-eye. The statue was probably presented to a temple as a gift.

Silver wedjat pectoral hung around the cat's neck

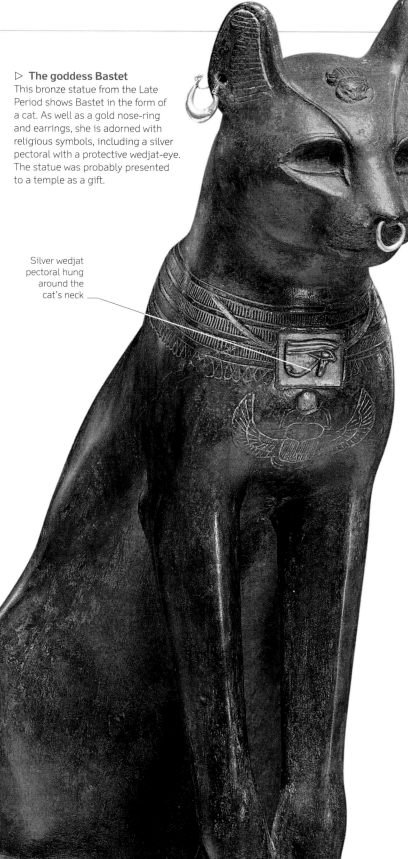

upper classes, especially with women. Unlike dogs, cats were rarely given personal names, but there were exceptions. One cat, known as "The Pleasant One," is depicted in the tomb of Puiemre, at Thebes. Another famous exception is "The She-Cat," who was buried in a stone coffin ordered specially for her by her owner, Prince Tuthmosis, son of Amenhotep III.

Unusual pets

Other animals apart from dogs and cats have been suggested as possible domestic pets in ancient Egypt. In New Kingdom art, monkeys, ducks, and geese are often shown in surprising domestic settings where pets might normally be—sitting beneath the chairs of their owners, for example (see far left).

These images might not, however, be realistic depictions of actual pets, but could symbolize the sexuality of the people shown alongside them. A good argument for this interpretation is the fact that so-called "green monkeys" are often shown in domestic settings, when in actual fact they were extremely dangerous and destructive.

▽ **Hunting cat**
This painting from Nebamun's tomb shows that dogs were not the only animals to accompany their owners on hunting expeditions. Cats were useful for catching fowl during boating trips in the marshes.

◁ **Mummy portrait**
This realistic Roman mummy portrait of a young woman was painted in the Classical style on a heavily decorated Egyptian-style coffin. There were many such examples of cultural crossover during the Greco-Roman Period.

7

The Greco-Roman Period

c.332 BCE–395 CE

The Greco-Roman Period

By 332 BCE, Egypt had become a passive corner of the part of the Mediterranean dominated first by the Greek states and then by the Romans. It is not surprising therefore that Egypt should be governed by rulers of Greek origin and then later absorbed into the Roman Empire.

The Ptolemies

After the break-up of Alexander the Great's empire that quickly followed his death in Babylon in 323 BCE, his general Ptolemy took control of Egypt. By 305 BCE, Ptolemy had declared himself king, and his dynasty went on to rule Egypt for the next three centuries.

The most striking feature of the Ptolemaic royal family was its internal power struggles, which it often resolved by means of murder or marriage. The rapid shifts of royal authority between individuals and couples within the dynasty are not easy to follow, especially when all of the men were called Ptolemy and most of the women either Arsinoe or Cleopatra. Meanwhile, alongside these deadly family conflicts, Ptolemaic Egypt was gradually becoming dependent on Rome as its protector and potential overlord.

Art and culture

Culturally, the Ptolemies' greatest achievement was the expansion and embellishment of Alexandria. This city, which Alexander the Great had founded, became one of the great maritime ports and centers of learning in the ancient world, filled with magnificent buildings displaying Ptolemaic power and culture. Beyond this Hellenistic city, the Ptolemies were also keen to stress their credentials as conventional kings of Egypt by building huge temples in traditional style. On the walls of these temples, they appeared in a manner that would have been recognized in the Old Kingdom. This trend continued in a more modest fashion under the Roman emperors. A blend of Classical and Egyptian styles can also be seen in many of the tombs and burial goods of nonroyal individuals.

Cleopatra VII and Rome

The end of the dynasty is entwined with the personal story of the Ptolemies' most famous queen—Cleopatra VII. Cleopatra's relationships with Julius Caesar and then Mark Antony can be seen as her attempt to hold on to her own power and to maintain Egyptian independence. After her defeat at the Battle of Actium in 31 BCE and her death the following year, Egypt was swiftly incorporated into the Roman Empire.

Few Roman emperors apart from Hadrian ever visited Egypt, but they were keen to present themselves as Egyptian kings on the walls of Egyptian temples. To the Romans, Egypt's main purpose was to supply grain. There were few revolts against Roman rule, as they were doomed to failure. The most significant development during this period was the arrival of Christianity, its adoption as the state religion, and the subsequent banning of pagan cults. This was the main reason why traditional Egyptian culture, which had lasted for more than 3,000 years, finally disappeared.

◁ **Statuette of Anubis**

305 BCE Ptolemy I becomes king and founds the Ptolemaic dynasty

196 BCE The Rosetta Stone is created

332 BCE Alexander the Great takes Egypt from the Persians

237 BCE Edfu Temple is founded

180 BCE Ptolemy VI becomes king. The Seleucids invade Egypt

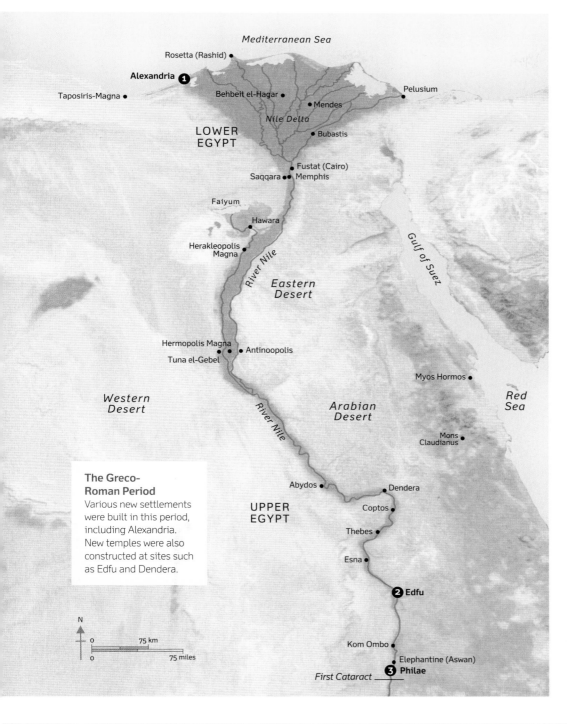

Mediterranean Sea

Rosetta (Rashid)

Alexandria ❶

Taposiris-Magna

Pelusium

Behbeit el-Hagar

Mendes

Nile Delta

LOWER EGYPT

Bubastis

Fustat (Cairo)

Saqqara Memphis

Faiyum

Hawara

Herakleopolis Magna

River Nile

Eastern Desert

Gulf of Suez

Hermopolis Magna

Antinoopolis

Tuna el-Gebel

Myos Hormos

Western Desert

River Nile

Arabian Desert

Red Sea

Mons Claudianus

The Greco-Roman Period
Various new settlements were built in this period, including Alexandria. New temples were also constructed at sites such as Edfu and Dendera.

Abydos

Dendera

UPPER EGYPT

Coptos

Thebes

Esna

N

0 — 75 km
0 — 75 miles

❷ **Edfu**

Kom Ombo

Elephantine (Aswan)

❸ **Philae**

First Cataract

❶ Catacombs, Alexandria

❷ Entrance pylon, Edfu Temple

❸ Kiosk of Trajan, Philae Temple

80 BCE Ptolemy XII becomes king

30 BCE Cleopatra dies and Egypt becomes a part of the Roman empire

298 CE Emperor Diocletian crushes a revolt in Egypt

379 CE Theodosius becomes emperor and bans pagan worship in Egypt

51 BCE Cleopatra VII becomes the joint ruler of Egypt

130 CE Emperor Hadrian visits Egypt

306 CE Constantine becomes emperor. He legalizes Christianity

Alexander the Great

The Macedonians arrive in Egypt

In 332 BCE, the Macedonian king Alexander the Great invaded Egypt and liberated the country from its Persian oppressors. In doing so, he paved the way for the ascendancy of Egypt's final royal dynasty: the Ptolemies.

In 336 BCE, King Philip II of Macedon (northern Greece) was assassinated, and the throne passed to his son, Alexander III, who is known today as Alexander the Great. Alexander inherited a kingdom that had risen to dominate Greece and the southern Balkans and was now ready to challenge the Persian Empire. Alexander accepted this challenge and was determined to replace the Persians as the dominant regional superpower.

In 334 BCE, Alexander crossed the Hellespont into Asia Minor and claimed his first major victory against the Persians at the Battle of Granicus. The following

◁ **Silver coin depicting Alexander**
Many of the coins produced after Alexander's death show him deified. As here, he is often depicted wearing a ram's horn, indicating that he is the son of Zeus-Amen (the ram was sacred to Amen).

year, he defeated Darius III, the Persian king, at the Battle of Issus. This left him free to take the cities that were still loyal to the Persians along the Levantine coast as far south as Gaza. He then marched his army south into Egypt, which was surrendered without a fight in 332 BCE. He seems to have been warmly welcomed by many

▽ **Alexander at war**
This mosaic, from the House of the Faun at Pompeii, is one of the most famous images of Alexander the Great. Probably based on an earlier painting, it shows Alexander's victory over the Persians at Issus.

Alexander leads his cavalry to attack the Persians

Alexander's famous horse, Bucephalus

Oxyathres, brother of Darius, tries to protect the king

Egyptians as a liberator from Persian rule. Alexander only stayed in Egypt for a short time, however, after which he pursued the Persians deep into their own territory, where he defeated them at the Battle of Gaugamela in 331 BCE.

Alexander in Egypt

Although brief, Alexander's stay in Egypt was eventful. He was careful to present himself as an Egyptian pharaoh, and duly had his name inscribed in a cartouche on monuments such as the sanctuary of Luxor Temple. His most significant physical legacy, however, was the foundation of Alexandria, the city named after him, which was to become one of the greatest urban and cultural centers in the Classical world (see pp.284–285).

Soon after his arrival in Egypt, Alexander set off on the long and arduous journey to the remote Siwa Oasis in Egypt's western desert to consult the famous oracle of Amen. He returned apparently satisfied with whatever the oracle told him, which may have been confirmation of his divine parentage. After this, he began to refer to himself as the son of Amen, just as Egyptian rulers such as Hatshepsut and Amenhotep III had done before him. Alexander, however, claimed his father was Zeus-Ammon, as the Greeks associated Zeus, the king of their gods, with Amen (known as Ammon in Greece), the most prominent Egyptian deity.

ORACLE **AT SIWA**

The isolation of the Siwa Oasis, deep in the remote Western Desert, meant that it was not considered to be part of Egypt until the Late Period. It became significant during the 26th Dynasty, when a temple dedicated to Amen was built there at a site known as el-Aghurmi. The temple stands on a hill surrounded by groves of lush date palms. It is thought to be the place where Alexander went to consult the oracle of Amen in 331 BCE. Alternatively, he may have visited him at the temple at Umm Ebeida, which was built by Nectanebo II.

The death of Alexander

Alexander died in Babylon in 323 BCE. The next rulers of Egypt were his half-brother, Philip Arrhidaeus, and Alexander IV, Alexander's son, who had not yet been born at the time of his death; however, these rulers were kings in name only. In reality, Alexander's empire was divided between his ambitious senior officers, the so-called Diadochi, or "successors." During the turbulent time of their rule, the general Ptolemy, son of Lagos, emerged as the custodian and then the king of Egypt. He was crowned Ptolemy I Soter ("the Savior") in 305 BCE.

Alexander in Alexandria

When Alexander died, his body became a precious item, and the problem arose of where it should be buried. Its travels are described in the works of various Greek and Roman historians. It was initially placed in a gold anthropoid coffin, which was then sent to Macedon for burial. Ptolemy I, however, realizing that owning the body would help legitimize his rule, hijacked the coffin on its way there and had it kept at Memphis.

His successor, Ptolemy II, then moved the body to Alexandria, where it remained in a tomb in the very center of the city. There, Alexander was not only remembered as the founder of the city, but was also worshipped as its patron god.

Under Ptolemy IX, Alexander's coffin was melted down to make gold coins and replaced with a glass coffin. This enabled visitors, such as Julius Caesar, Augustus, and even Emperor Caracalla in the 3rd century CE, to view Alexander's body. Records show that by 400 CE, the body had been removed from its tomb, but where it was taken remains a mystery.

Darius, in his chariot, panics at the sight of Alexander

▽ **Basalt water clock**
There are relatively few monuments naming Philip Arrhidaeus, Alexander's successor, as king of Egypt. This elaborate water clock, showing him with a variety of gods, is one exception.

Ptolemy I offers incense to the goddess Hathor

The early Ptolemies

Greeks on the throne of Egypt

Descended from the Macedonian general Ptolemy, the Ptolemaic dynasty was an intriguing mixture of Greek and Egyptian influences. This dual identity had a huge impact on Egyptian culture and foreign policy.

In 285 BCE, Ptolemy I appointed his son, Ptolemy II, as co-regent, following a long-established Egyptian tradition. This ensured a smooth transition of power when Ptolemy I died in 282 BCE, and the crown passed safely from the first king of the Ptolemaic dynasty to the second, but the history of the rest of the dynasty proved to be far less straightforward.

Thanks to the detailed accounts of Greek and Roman historians, it is clear that the following Ptolemies were constantly fighting with each other. Parents and children and brothers and sisters were all prepared to marry or murder each other whenever

Attachment for headdress

◁ **Statue of Arsinoe II**
Unusually, the queen is wearing a double uraeus on her brow. The main part of her headdress is missing, but it probably associated her with the goddess Hathor.

they saw fit, in their attempts to seize or hold onto power. Both the men and the women of this family were equally ambitious—and vicious.

Arsinoe II

A good example of a Ptolemaic woman swiftly rising to prominence was Arsinoe II. The daughter of Ptolemy I, she was first married to Lysimachus, ruler of Thrace, as part of a diplomatic alliance against the rival Seleucid dynasty, which was based mainly in Syria. After Lysimachus' death, she married her half-brother, Ptolemy Keraunos, and then her brother, Ptolemy II, after Keraunos murdered two of her sons.

Unusually, Arsinoe assumed the same titles as her brother/husband, and she appeared alongside him on coins that they minted (see p.284). Various towns were also named after her, and when she died, she

Cartouche containing Ptolemy's throne name, "Chosen of Ra, Beloved of Amen"

◁ **Relief of Ptolemy I**
This relief, from a now-destroyed temple at Kom Abu Billou, in the western Delta, shows Ptolemy I offering incense to Hathor. Depicted in a traditional Egyptian artistic style, Ptolemy is indistinguishable from a king of the Late Period.

Problems abroad

The most pressing foreign policy issue for the early Ptolemaic kings was the competition between Egypt and the other major powers in the Near East and eastern Mediterranean. All of these territories were ruled by Alexander the Great's successors. The Seleucid Empire, for example, was founded by Alexander's general, Seleucus, who became one of the Diadochi (see pp.280–281). These kings were part of a broader Hellenistic culture, and at different times over the next 300 years, they were both close allies and bitter rivals.

The high point of the Ptolemies' military success was during the reign of Ptolemy III (246–221 BCE), who captured Babylon from the Seleucids before being forced to return to Egypt. The low point was under Ptolemy V (205–180 BCE), when Egypt was defeated in the Sinai by Antiochus III, the Seleucid king. Antiochus invaded Egypt twice during the war of 170–168 BCE, and was even crowned king of Egypt in Memphis, but the intervention of the Romans forced the Seleucids to leave Egypt.

This retreat of the Seleucids signaled the end of Egypt as an independent Hellenistic state, but the country had not been destroyed. Instead, it had become a client state of the new superpower in the region—the Roman Republic.

△ **Mosaic of Berenike II**
This remarkable mosaic from Mendes is probably a portrait, in Hellenistic style, of Queen Berenike II. Her strange headdress, shaped like a ship's prow, may symbolize the Ptolemies' naval power.

was deified. Her cult persisted in Alexandria well into the Roman Period. In many ways, Arsinoe II became a role model for the later Ptolemaic queens.

Royal epithets

All of the male rulers of the Ptolemaic dynasty were called Ptolemy. At the time, they were not given regnal numbers (I, II, and so on), but epithets (descriptive phrases), to distinguish them from all the other kings with the same name. These epithets often sum up the kings and the close family bonds that they shared. Ptolemy I, for instance, was known as "Soter" (Savior), Ptolemy III was "Euergetes" (Benefactor), and Ptolemy IV was "Philopator" (Father-loving). Appropriately, Ptolemy II and Arsinoe II shared the epithet "Philadelphus" (Sibling-loving).

> "He brought back the **sacred images** of the **gods** which were found **within Asia**."

PTOLEMY I RESTORES THE THEFTS OF THE PERSIANS

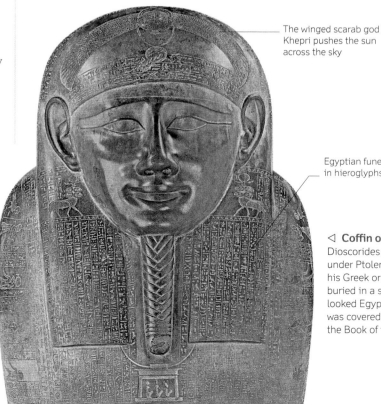

The winged scarab god Khepri pushes the sun across the sky

Egyptian funerary texts in hieroglyphs

◁ **Coffin of Dioscorides**
Dioscorides was a general under Ptolemy VI. Despite his Greek origins, he was buried in a stone coffin that looked Egyptian in style and was covered with texts from the Book of the Dead.

Alexandria

Queen of the Mediterranean

Alexandria was one of the greatest cities of the Mediterranean. The capital city of the Ptolemies, it was famed throughout the Classical world for its power, its wealth, and its stunning monuments.

The importance of maritime trade and naval power in the 3rd century BCE mean it is no surprise that Alexander founded his Egyptian capital on the Mediterranean coast. The site that he chose was the modest harbor town of Rhakotis, strategically positioned on a spit of land, with the sea to the north and Lake Mareotis to the south. It also had easy access by river to the Canopic branch of the Nile, which provided transport and communications links to the rest of Egypt.

Detailed descriptions of the city made by ancient Greek and Roman writers mean that a good deal is known about the layout of ancient Alexandria. However, very little of the city has been traced by archaeologists, and the most famous buildings there—the Pharos lighthouse, the tomb of Alexander,

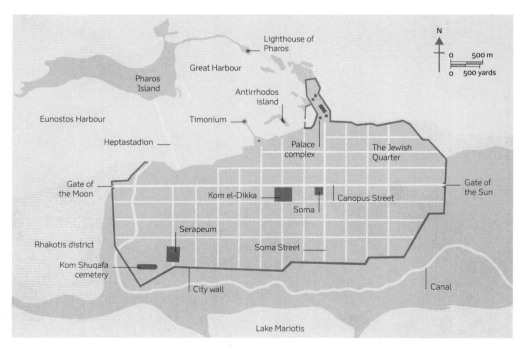

◁ **Coin of Ptolemy II and Arsinoe II**
The Alexandrian mint produced coins that were made of precious metals. This gold oktadrachm is stamped with the image of the joint rulers Ptolemy II and Arsinoe II.

and the royal palaces—have completely or largely disappeared. One hope for recovering more of the ancient city is the underwater archaeological exploration of the Great Harbor that is currently taking place, which has produced important evidence of palace complexes that sank into the sea as a result of a natural disaster.

A wonder of the world
As well as being the new capital of Egypt and the heart of Egypt's government, Alexandria was one of the most important trading centers in the Greco-Roman world. A great deal of wealth flowed into and through the city, and to accommodate the huge amount of goods that arrived in Alexandria, the Ptolemies built an artificial causeway between the mainland and Pharos Island. Known as the Heptastadion, this created two main harbors—the Great Harbor to the east and the smaller Eunostos Harbor to the west.

Alexandria also became the cultural center of Egypt—especially for the Ptolemies, who used it as an expression of *tryphe*, or conspicuous display. The Greek historian Strabo, who visited the city early in the Roman Period and left a detailed description of what he saw, noted that Alexandria "contains most beautiful public precincts and also the royal palaces which constitute one fourth or even one third of the whole circuit of the city."

▽ **Plan of Alexandria**
The street plan of Alexandria was based on a grid, which the Ptolemies adapted to suit the geography of the city. The Mediterranean lay to the north, and Lake Mareotis to the south.

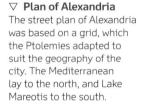

Lighthouse of Pharos

Great Harbour

Pharos Island

Antirrhodos island

Eunostos Harbour

Timonium

Heptastadion

Palace complex

The Jewish Quarter

Gate of the Moon

Kom el-Dikka

Soma

Canopus Street

Gate of the Sun

Serapeum

Rhakotis district

Soma Street

Kom Shuqafa cemetery

City wall

Canal

Lake Mariotis

N

0 ——— 500 m
0 ——— 500 yards

> "It contains 4,000 **palaces**; 4,000 **bathhouses**; 400 **theaters**; 12,000 **greengrocers**; and 12,000 tax-paying **Jews**."
>
> AMR IBN AL-AS DESCRIBES ALEXANDRIA IN 642 CE

◁ **Kom el-Dikka**
One of the few places in modern Alexandria where the ancient city can be seen is Kom el-Dikka. Built in the area of the Mouseion, it became a residential area in the Roman Period.

The most impressive of Alexandria's buildings by far was the lighthouse on the island of Pharos. One of the ancient Greeks' "Seven Wonders of the World," it stood on the outer rim of the great harbor and served as a major statement about the power and wealth of the kings who built it. Nothing remains of the ancient lighthouse today due to centuries of neglect and earthquakes.

Downtown

The main part of Alexandria was defined by two main roads—Canopus Street, which ran roughly west-east from the Gate of the Moon to the Gate of the Sun, and Soma Street, which ran roughly south-north. The point at which these two streets crossed was effectively the heart of the city, and it was there that the Ptolemies built the Soma. This was a burial complex containing the tombs of Alexander the Great and the Ptolemaic kings. Most of the city's other cemeteries were located outside the eastern or western gate of the main city. Consisting of underground tombs, these are the most impressive parts of ancient Alexandria that are still visible today.

The Mouseion and library

The Ptolemies were determined to make Alexandria the principal center of Greek learning, so they built and staffed an institute for teaching, learning, and research that was known as the Mouseion. An important part of it was the Library of Alexandria, which was a major attraction for scholars from all over the Greek-speaking world. At its height, this library contained more than 700,000 volumes. The Mouseion stood near the center of the city, possibly close to Kom el-Dikka, the ruins of which can still be seen today.

▷ **Pharos lighthouse**
The lighthouse on Pharos Island was not just impressive in size. It also required an extraordinary amount of resources to keep its beacon burning.

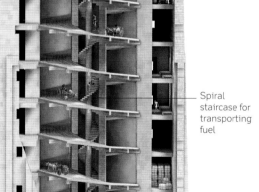

Statue of Poseidon (or Zeus)

Fire and reflecting mirror

Statue of Triton

Spiral staircase for transporting fuel

Egyptian Hellenism

Greek culture in Egypt

The arrival of the Greeks and Greek culture in Egypt during the Ptolemaic Period had a profound effect on the country and its people. This influence of Greek culture is known as Hellenism.

Alexander the Great's conquest of Egypt, and the foundation of the Ptolemaic dynasty that went on to rule for 300 years, had a much greater impact on Egypt than any of the previous foreign invasions. The Hyksos, the Assyrians, and the Persians had left few lasting marks on Egypt, while if anything, the Kushite kings revived traditional Egyptian culture. The Ptolemies, however, brought with them an entirely new culture. This culture was Greek, or Hellenistic, in nature, and it was taking root in all of the territories conquered by Alexander.

Greek culture

The continuing immigration of Greek settlers into Egypt, and the establishment of a Greek-speaking political elite around the Ptolemaic court, meant that Greek culture dominated Egypt. By controlling Egypt's political and economic institutions, the Ptolemies created a situation in which ambitious Egyptians had to adopt Greek customs to become part of the ruling elite. This rise of Hellenism had little impact on the lives of the average peasant farmer, but acceptance of a hybrid Egyptian/Greek culture became the norm among the upper classes.

Many of Egypt's new ruling class spoke both Egyptian and Greek, and many educated Egyptians took Greek names. For this reason, it is often difficult to determine who was Greek and who Egyptian in the written records. After a couple of generations, ethnic origins probably mattered little to elite Egyptians, and this included the royal family. The bilingual nature of the Egyptian court, and increasingly of Egypt at large, is reflected in the public documents of the time. These include the royal stelae that were set up in temples and often had trilingual inscriptions—the most famous of which is the Rosetta Stone (see pp.302–303).

Alexandria was the hub of this meeting of cultures, and its position as a major seaport exposed it to many influences from overseas apart from that of the Greeks. An important ingredient in this social and cultural mix came as the Jewish population of the city, and Egypt in general, increased during the 2nd century BCE.

Greek and Egyptian cities

Before the arrival of Alexander, Egypt already had a city that was predominantly Greek in character. This was the trading center of Naukratis, in the western Delta. The Ptolemies founded several similar new towns and cities, including Ptolemais in Upper Egypt. These were places in which the lives of Greek citizens were organized on both social and political levels in ways that would have been familiar in Greece itself.

△ **Funerary stela**
This stela from a tomb in Alexandria is entirely Greek in style. The central figure represents the deceased, clasping hands with the woman standing in front of him in a gesture of farewell.

Egyptian-style sphinx

"Pompey's Pillar," actually a triumphal column built by Diocletian

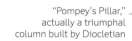

◁ **Ruins of the Serapeum**
This temple complex dedicated to the god Serapis (himself a Hellenistic invention) was a major center of Greco-Egyptian culture in Alexandria. The tall column is a later addition, erected by the Emperor Diocletian.

△ Underground tombs at Alexandria
The subterranean elite cemeteries are some of the best-preserved parts of ancient Alexandria. Their mixture of Greek and Egyptian features shows that in death as in life, their occupants regarded themselves as hybrid Greco-Egyptian.

Most of the well-established cities were now given new Greek names linking the Egyptian god most closely associated with the city with its nearest Greek equivalent. Many of those cities are still known by their Greek names today. The place that the Egyptians originally called Khemenu, for example, is now better known as Hermopolis Magna, because its principal god, Thoth, was considered to be on a par with the Greek god Hermes.

STATUE FROM **ANTIRRHODOS**

The island of Antirrhodos was part of a Ptolemaic palace complex located in what is now the eastern harbor of Alexandria. Like much of the seafront part of the ancient city, the island sank after an earthquake in around the 4th century CE. Ongoing underwater excavations have unearthed some very fine sculptures from the site. They include this statue of a priest, carved in a Hellenistic style very different from that of traditional Egyptian sculpture. The priest, who may have belonged to a cult of Isis, is clasping a vessel that may represent the god Osiris, the husband of Isis.

STATUE OF A PRIEST

"The Alexandrians **flocked** to the festival, filled with **enthusiasm**, and shouted **acclamations** in **Greek and Egyptian**, and some in **Hebrew**."

C. P. CAVAFY, "ALEXANDRIAN KINGS"

Traditional religion

Egyptian gods in Greco-Roman Egypt

The arrival of the Ptolemies did little to change the basic nature of Egyptian religion. People still worshipped a variety of different gods, but the merging of Greek and Egyptian culture introduced new gods and rituals.

Hellenism could have posed a threat to the way in which Egyptian religion was practiced, as the Ptolemies built new, Greek-style temples in which to worship the Greek gods that they brought with them. But although the educated Egyptian elite, who historically made up the priesthood for all the major temples in Egypt, may have had to adopt Greek customs in many aspects of their daily life, this was not the case with religion.

In fact, Egyptian Hellenism was a blend of Greek and Egyptian customs, and the Greeks seem to have been especially intrigued by Egyptian religion, as shown by some of their mortuary rituals. Building traditional-style Egyptian temples was an obvious way for the Ptolemaic kings to enhance their credentials as the legitimate rulers of Egypt, approved by the Egyptian gods. This was made obvious by the grand scale of their temple building, as it was to a lesser extent in the case of the Roman emperors.

Old gods, new gods

The range of gods worshipped did, however, change, and new forms of old gods became popular.

△ **Ptolemaic priest**
As in earlier periods, the Egyptians carved statues of priests to place within temples. The distinctive appearance of this statue is due to the combination of Egyptian and Greek styles of sculpture.

▷ **Statue of Tutu**
Son of the goddess Neith, Tutu was a deity who took the form of a royal sphinx. He first appeared in the Late Period and was popular in the Ptolemaic and Roman Periods.

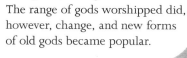

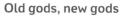

◁ **Bust of Serapis**
Although his figure looks much like a Greek god such as Zeus, it represents a new god, Serapis. He was created from a combination of the underworld deity Osiris and the living bull god Apis.

Gods associated with youthfulness came to the fore, including the child Horus in the Greco-Egyptian form of Harpocrates. New gods were also created to suit the spirit of Egyptian Hellenism. The most significant god added to the pantheon of Egyptian gods at this time was Serapis. Based on a combination of the Egyptian gods Apis and Osiris, Serapis did not look like either of them, but had a heavily bearded human head and looked very much like Zeus. This was a deity who could be worshipped by both Greeks and Egyptians.

The cult worship of divine statues within temples, which was not very different from Greek customs, continued, as did processions and festivals. In one of the most important festivals of the Ptolemaic Period, the "Beautiful Feast of Behdet," statues of Horus from Edfu and Hathor from Dendera were borne 105 miles (170 km) along the Nile to visit each other in their respective temples.

Egyptian gods outside Egypt

During the Roman Period, traditional Egyptian gods and Greco-Egyptian deities like Serapis continued to flourish among the educated elite in the major cities. Egyptian deities were also worshipped farther afield within the Roman Empire. Serapis and Isis were especially popular—a temple was built for Isis in London and one for Serapis in York.

▽ **The cult of Isis in Italy**
Isis was worshipped throughout the Roman Empire, including Italy. This wall painting from the city of Herculaneum shows a religious ceremony for the goddess, with several features imported from the Egyptian cult, such as sacred ibises.

Egyptian-style sphinx

Chief priest with cult image

Priest shakes a sistrum

Greco-Roman temples

Reviving traditions of kings from the past

The defining monuments of the Ptolemaic and Roman Periods are the many great temples that were built. In structure and style, these hark back to the temples of the New Kingdom, but they also had innovative features.

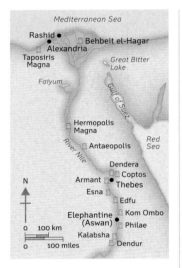

△ **Ptolemaic temples**
The Ptolemies built temples throughout most of Egypt. The best-preserved of them lie in the far south of the country and Nubia.

The Ptolemaic kings clearly thought it politically expedient to show that they were the rulers of Egypt in the time-honored way—by being portrayed as pharaohs on the walls of temples, following Egyptian artistic convention. They therefore built and maintained traditional Egyptian temples, adding to existing ones or building new ones of their own. In fact, their legacy in terms of monuments is not so much the classical architecture of Alexandria, the city that they created, but what is left of the temples that they built, most of which are in the south of Egypt and Nubia.

The subsequent Roman emperors were also keen to be seen as pharaohs, but as they stayed in Rome, they were less involved in building projects in Egypt than the Ptolemies.

Ptolemaic temples

As the Ptolemies had enormous resources at their disposal, they were able to build on a grand scale that had not been seen since the New Kingdom, bar a few

◁ **Horus at Edfu**
As in earlier periods, the temples of the Ptolemaic Period were embellished with statues depicting the gods of the temple. This black granite statue of Horus stands in the courtyard of his temple at Edfu.

exceptions. They did relatively little to alter the basic structure of the most important temples, such as those at Thebes and Memphis, but in many places they swept away the existing temples to build entirely new ones. Many of these are still standing today and represent what many people think of as a typical Egyptian temple.

The best of the major temples built by the Ptolemies are those dedicated to Hathor at Dendera, to Khnum at Esna, to Horus at Edfu, and to Horus and Sobek at Kom Ombo. They also undertook a massive redevelopment of the modest earlier temple buildings on the island of Philae (see pp.290–293).

Preserving tradition

Determined to uphold Egyptian tradition, the Ptolemies built temples in the style of their New Kingdom predecessors. At Edfu, for example, a massive pylon gateway opened onto an open, colonnaded court. Behind this, densely columned halls (now called the pronaos) hid the sanctuary (the naos) at the heart of the temple, where the god's statue was kept. At Dendera, the great pronaos with its Hathor-topped columns looks original, but it was in fact based on a similar but more modest style of

◁ **Kom Ombo**
The outer walls of the Kom Ombo temple are no longer standing, so its columned interior is open to the elements. It is similar in style to the architecture of the New Kingdom.

architecture of the New Kingdom. Likewise, the double-axis and parallel shrines of the temple at Kom Ombo look innovative, but they were based on existing architectural styles.

Change in emphasis

The decoration on the walls of temples did change in some ways. The basic repertoire of images showing kings making offerings to the gods, smiting enemies, and processing at festivals remained important, but now there was a new emphasis on showing scenes from mythology that were connected to the gods of the temple.

At Edfu, for example, there are extensive images of Horus, the god of kingship, fighting his uncle Seth for the throne of Egypt in a way that would have been considered inappropriate in the New Kingdom. Seth, in the form of a hippopotamus, is shown being hunted down and speared by Horus.

◁ **Column at Esna**
Column capitals carved to look like leaves and flowers had been popular in temples since the Old Kingdom. In Greco-Roman temples, they were made more complex and colorful.

The temple as cosmos

The Ptolemies' interest in mythology did not just influence temple decoration, but also extended to the temple itself. They regarded the building as a model of the cosmos and its innermost parts as the mythical island on which creation took place (see pp.134–135). This helps explain some of the new architectural features in Ptolemaic temples, including underground crypts to mimic the underworld and chapels on the roof of the temple to symbolize the sky, as at Dendera. The Ptolemies also included decorative features to represent marshland plants, illustrating the flora that might have grown on the Island of Creation.

▽ **Magnificent ceiling**
Every surface inside a Ptolemaic temple was completely covered in texts and pictures. On this ceiling in the temple at Dendera, images of gods are shown against a blue background representing the sky, as was appropriate for ceilings.

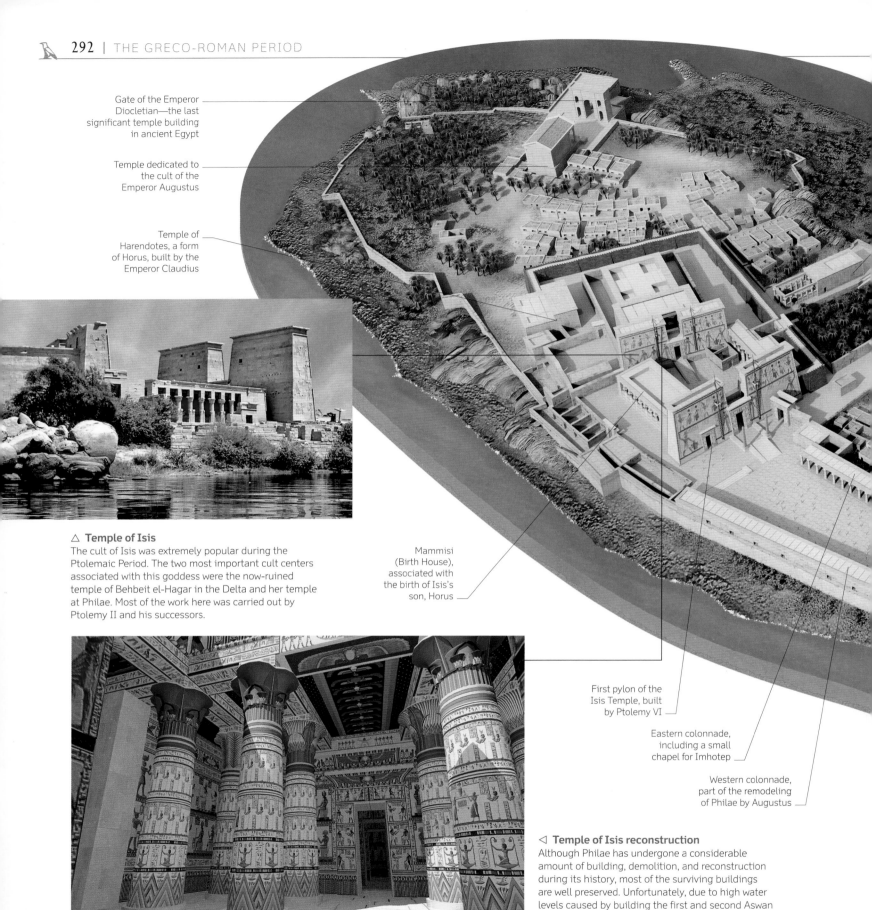

Gate of the Emperor Diocletian—the last significant temple building in ancient Egypt

Temple dedicated to the cult of the Emperor Augustus

Temple of Harendotes, a form of Horus, built by the Emperor Claudius

Mammisi (Birth House), associated with the birth of Isis's son, Horus

First pylon of the Isis Temple, built by Ptolemy VI

Eastern colonnade, including a small chapel for Imhotep

Western colonnade, part of the remodeling of Philae by Augustus

△ Temple of Isis

The cult of Isis was extremely popular during the Ptolemaic Period. The two most important cult centers associated with this goddess were the now-ruined temple of Behbeit el-Hagar in the Delta and her temple at Philae. Most of the work here was carried out by Ptolemy II and his successors.

◁ Temple of Isis reconstruction

Although Philae has undergone a considerable amount of building, demolition, and reconstruction during its history, most of the surviving buildings are well preserved. Unfortunately, due to high water levels caused by building the first and second Aswan Dams, the paintwork of the brightly colored walls, recreated here, has not survived as well.

Temple of Hathor, started by Ptolemy VI and completed by Augustus

◁ **Kiosk of Trajan**
One of the most striking buildings at Philae is the Kiosk of Trajan. It was partially decorated during Trajan's reign, but its construction may have been begun earlier in the Roman Period.

Granite boulders of the natural landscape

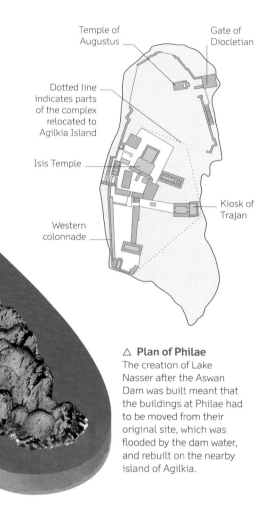

Temple of Augustus

Gate of Diocletian

Dotted line indicates parts of the complex relocated to Agilkia Island

Isis Temple

Kiosk of Trajan

Western colonnade

△ **Plan of Philae**
The creation of Lake Nasser after the Aswan Dam was built meant that the buildings at Philae had to be moved from their original site, which was flooded by the dam water, and rebuilt on the nearby island of Agilkia.

Temple of Arensnuphis, a Kushite god worshipped in Egyptian Nubia from the Ptolemaic Period

△ **Philae**
This digital reconstruction shows Philae Temple in its original setting, before the main buildings were moved to Agilkia island.

Kiosk of Nectanebo I of the 30th Dynasty

Philae Temple

The Pearl of the Nile

Philae is one of the best-preserved and most beautiful temple complexes from the Late and Greco-Roman Periods. South of modern Aswan, it is a series of sacred buildings built on an island in the Nile. It was dedicated mainly to the goddess Isis (a nearby island, Bigeh, was dedicated to Osiris), with ancillary temples for other deities, including Hathor, and Nubian deities such as Arensnuphis. Shrines to Isis were first erected in the 26th Dynasty, but the main building work began under kings of the 30th Dynasty and continued during the Ptolemaic and Roman Periods.

The later Ptolemies

The decline of dynastic Egypt

◇

During the reigns of the later Ptolemies, the political infighting within the royal dynasty reached its peak. At the same time, the Roman influence over the Ptolemies—and Egypt itself—was becoming an increasing problem.

Ptolemy V's marriage to the Seleucid princess Cleopatra I had been an astute diplomatic move, because it put an end for the time being to the rivalry between the Ptolemaic and Seleucid empires. The couple had three children: Ptolemy VI, Ptolemy VIII, and Cleopatra II, all of whom went on to rule Egypt.

After Ptolemy V was poisoned in 180 BCE, Cleopatra I acted as regent until her own death four years later. When she died, the control of Egypt passed into the hands of two powerful courtiers, Eulaeus and

Lenaeus, who decided that Ptolemy VI and Cleopatra II should marry and join with Ptolemy VIII to form a triumvirate of rulers. It was Eulaeus and Lenaeus who were responsible for the disastrous Sixth Syrian War (see pp.282–283), during which they fell from power. In the aftermath of the war, Ptolemy VI was briefly supported as a puppet king by the Seleucid king Antiochus IV, while the people of Alexandria supported Cleopatra II and Ptolemy VIII. But Ptolemy VIII was incompetent and dissolute, so the

△ **Co-regents**
This scene from the temple of Kom Ombo illustrates the Ptolemaic tradition of having several rulers on the throne at the same time. The god Horus is shown handing a sword to Ptolemy VIII, who is accompanied by his co-regents, Cleopatra II and Cleopatra III.

"All the kings after the **third Ptolemy** ... administered government **badly**."

STRABO, *GEOGRAPHY*

Alexandrians banished him from Egypt. To take his place, they invited Ptolemy VI to return from exile in Rome and to rule alongside Cleopatra II.

Ptolemy VIII

The death of Ptolemy VI in 145 BCE, from wounds incurred while fighting in Syria, encouraged Ptolemy VIII to return to Egypt, where he married Cleopatra II. Cleopatra II may have felt that this was necessary to protect her young son, Ptolemy VII, but he was murdered soon afterward anyway. Ptolemy VIII also married Cleopatra II's daughter, Cleopatra III. The king and the two queens ruled Egypt together for a while, but tensions within this uneasy group of three dominated Egyptian politics until the deaths of both Ptolemy VIII and Cleopatra II in 116 BCE.

Cleopatra III was left as regent for her two sons, Ptolemy IX and Ptolemy X. According to the terms of Ptolemy VIII's will, Cleopatra III was to choose which son should became king, but she did not do this, so the family descended into yet another round of feuding over the throne. During this turbulent time, Ptolemy IX was exiled in 107 BCE; Cleopatra III died in 101 BCE; Ptolemy X ruled on his own until 88 BCE; and Ptolemy IX returned from exile in 88 BCE, only to die just eight years later.

Ptolemy XII

Ptolemy XI had only been on the throne for a few days in 80 BCE when he was assassinated by an Alexandrian mob, who installed Ptolemy XII on the throne. This new Ptolemy, who called himself Neos Dionysos and was better known as Auletes (the flautist), was an illegitimate son of Ptolemy IX.

Ptolemy X's will had bequeathed Egypt to Rome, and this became a problem for Ptolemy XII. He began to bribe leading Roman politicians with huge sums of money that he raised by increasing taxes in Egypt and drawing loans from Roman creditors. Although he was confirmed on the throne by Julius Caesar in 59 BCE, Ptolemy was a lazy king and was forced into exile the following year. His attempts to restore himself to the throne with Roman backing bore fruit in 55 BCE, when he returned to Egypt with a Roman army led by Aulus Gabinius.

When Ptolemy XII died in 51 BCE, Rome acted as the executor of his will and his son, Ptolemy XIII, and his daughter, Cleopatra VII, were nominated joint rulers of Egypt. The real legacy that Ptolemy XII left to his children, however, was yet another dynastic feud, set against the background of an increasing Roman threat to Egyptian independence.

△ **Ptolemy XII**
Like other Ptolemaic rulers, Ptolemy XII saw himself as both a Greek ruler and an Egyptian pharaoh. In this Classical sculpture, the artist emphasized Ptolemy XII's Greek heritage.

◁ **Mosaic of soldiers**
Ptolemy XII relied heavily on support from abroad to control Egypt, mainly from Roman statesman, soldiers, and bankers. He was also backed by a mercenary army called the Gabiniani, which remained in Egypt when Ptolemy XII was restored to the throne in 55 BCE.

Roman mosaic of the Nile

This enormous mosaic measuring 19 x 14 ft (5.80 x 4.30 m) was found in a grotto in the ancient town of Praeneste (now known as Palestrina), not far from Rome. Created sometime between the 1st century BCE and the 1st century CE, it is a good illustration of the Romans' growing fascination with Egypt around the time that it became part of the Roman Empire. A blend of fact and fantasy, it depicts Egypt as a place of exotic wonders. The swirling Nile is crammed with islands that are home to all kinds of mysterious temples, towns, and strange, savage beasts, and boats of all kinds carry people across its waters.

◁ **Statue of Cleopatra**
There are few surviving statues that can confidently be identified as depicting Cleopatra VII. The triple uraeus on the brow of this royal head may indicate that it belongs to her, but this royal insignia has also been attributed to Cleopatra II and Cleopatra III.

Distinctive triple uraeus

Damage, possibly deliberate, to the statue's nose

Cleopatra VII

A queen of infinite variety

The view of Cleopatra as an exotic temptress, fostered by Shakespeare and Hollywood, owes much to the partial accounts of Roman authors. In reality, she was a skilled politician who tried to maintain Egypt's independence from Rome.

Caesar and Cleopatra

Cleopatra's first serious problem was not Rome but, as so often with the Ptolemies, her own family. Sharing the throne of Egypt with her brother, Ptolemy XIII, did not last, and the siblings soon found themselves at the heads of armies facing each other in the Delta.

Caesar's arrival in Egypt was fortuitous for Cleopatra, as he took her side against her brother, but the pair were besieged in Alexandria in the winter of 48/47 BCE until Roman reinforcements arrived and freed them. Ptolemy XIII fled and drowned in the Nile. Cleopatra then married her 11-year-old brother, Ptolemy XIV. She later gave birth to a son, Ptolemy XV Caesar (known as Caesarion), whose name indicated clearly who his father was.

◁ **Julius Caesar**
This statue of Caesar in Rome shows him in Roman armor. He dedicated a gold statue of Cleopatra in the temple of Venus Genetrix in Rome, the year before he was assassinated.

◁ **Coin of Mark Antony**
Coins issued by Mark Antony and Cleopatra show them both in profile as strong-featured individuals. Antony is depicted with a Roman nose and a very determined jaw.

Antony and Cleopatra

After the assassination of Caesar in 44 BCE, Cleopatra—now a widow again after the death of Ptolemy XIV—needed a new Roman protector. The two most powerful men to emerge from the crisis in Rome were colleagues, and later deadly rivals, Octavian and Mark Antony. By 40 BCE, Cleopatra had allied herself with Mark Antony and given birth to twins by him, Alexander Helios and Cleopatra Selene.

Together, Cleopatra and Antony planned an Egyptian-Roman alliance that would lead to Egypt regaining some of its former territories. They nominated Cleopatra's children as the future rulers of much of Rome's eastern empire and announced it in a public ceremony known as the "Donations of Alexandria." This was effectively a declaration of war against Octavian and the western empire. Octavian's victory over Antony and Cleopatra's forces at Actium in 31 BCE was decisive. By the end of 30 BCE, Cleopatra and Antony had committed suicide and Caesarion had been murdered. Egypt was then absorbed into the Roman Empire, ruled over by its first emperor, Octavian, soon to be known as Augustus.

△ **Caesarion at Dendera**
Cleopatra's son by Caesar, Ptolemy XV (Caesarion) is shown with his mother on the rear wall of the temple of Hathor at Dendera, making an offering to the goddess.

69 BCE Birth of Cleopatra, daughter of Ptolemy XII

48 BCE Caesar arrives in Egypt

44 BCE Death of Caesar

31 BCE Battle of Actium

51 BCE Death of Ptolemy XII. Cleopatra co-regent with Ptolemy XIII

47 BCE Birth of Caesarion

34 BCE Donations of Alexandria

30 BCE Death of Cleopatra

The end of ancient Egypt

The death of a civilization

The Roman Period was undoubtedly one of terminal decline for ancient Egyptian culture. By the 4th century CE, the Egyptians had not only lost their independence, many of them had also converted to Christianity.

△ **Head of Augustus**
The Roman emperors often portrayed themselves as traditional kings of Egypt. This bust of Augustus, which shows his curly hair beneath a nemes headcloth, is a mixture of Classical and Egyptian artistic styles.

Although the Ptolemies were Greek by origin, bred among themselves, and felt culturally Hellenistic, most of them had been born in Egypt, lived there, and had some idea of Egyptian cultural traditions, which they patronized by building temples and worshipping the Egyptian gods. By contrast, the Roman emperors who replaced the Ptolemaic kings as the effective rulers of Egypt had no connection with the country, did not live there, and saw Egypt as just one part of their wider empire. Egypt's primary importance to the Romans was economic. This was best demonstrated by the huge Roman cargo ships that were loaded with Egyptian grain in Alexandria and then sailed to the port of Ostia, in Italy, to feed the citizens of Rome.

Egypt under Roman rule

The Romans paid lip service to Egyptian culture, having themselves depicted as traditional kings of Egypt on temple walls, for example. Sometimes they even attempted to write their names or titles (*Kaisaros Autokrator*, Caesar the Ruler) in hieroglyphs, but few Roman emperors ever visited Egypt other than when they had to, as when Diocletian recaptured Alexandria after a local revolt in 298 CE.

A notable exception was Emperor Hadrian, who made a "grand tour" of the country during 10 months in 130–131 CE. This led to a fashion for building mock-Egyptian monuments in Rome, and Hadrian himself adapted his villa at Tivoli to incorporate Egyptian-style buildings and statues. In Egypt,

Hadrian also founded the city of Antinoopolis, which he named after his friend Antinous, who had died during Hadrian's Egyptian tour.

Coming of Christianity

The Ptolemaic Period, and the subsequent rule of the Romans in particular, effectively destroyed Egypt as a self-governing, independent country. Old cultural traditions such as building temples continued, and the pantheon of Egyptian gods was adapted to make room for newcomers, such as the god Serapis. Hieroglyphic texts were still written, but these became increasingly anachronistic—the ability to read and write the script must have been rare even among literate Egyptians. Documents, including those of an official nature, were written in Greek or Demotic, a cursive script used to transcribe the form of the Egyptian language that was spoken at the time.

The factor that was most responsible for the demise of Egyptian culture was the spread of Christianity. This made the pagan gods irrelevant, their temples useless, and hieroglyphic script pointless. This change did not happen overnight, but several key points stand out. The most important were the accession of the Christian-friendly Emperor Constantine (306–337 CE) and the Edict of Toleration, which put an end to the persecution of Christians

◁ **Defaced goddess**
The attempts of later monotheists to destroy or disfigure images of pagan gods were often crude. This image of the goddess Mut at Luxor Temple has been defaced but is otherwise intact.

"I added **Egypt** to the **empire** of the **Roman people**."

AUGUSTUS' OFFICIAL AUTOBIOGRAPHY, THE *RES GESTAE*

◁ **Coffin of Artemidorus**
This Roman Period coffin found at Hawara is one of the finest examples of a hybrid Egyptian-Classical work of art. Its body case is decorated with the Egyptian gods of the underworld, while the "mummy portrait" is Roman in style.

in the Roman Empire. This edict was issued by Constantine's previously anti-Christian co-Emperor, Galerius, in 311 CE. Christianity, which had been an underground cult until that time, rapidly increased its following after this official sanction. By the time of Constantine's death, more than half of the population of Egypt was probably Christian, and by the end of the 4th century CE, Christianity had become the dominant religion in the Roman Empire.

During the reign of Emperor Theodosius I (379–395 CE), the first of a series of official decrees banning pagan worship was issued. Also during the same reign, the last hieroglyphic text was written on a temple at Philae. Temples were gradually closed or converted into churches, and the images of the ancient Egyptian gods were vandalized. These acts of destruction were often organized by enthusiastic, anti-pagan monks, such as the famous Shenoute, who attacked many pagan monuments in Middle Egypt.

As new types of burial practice were introduced, elaborate painted tombs were no longer needed, nor were the paintings that had been used to decorate them. With the disappearance of her ancient kings, religion, art, architecture, and script, ancient Egypt had ceased to exist as a living culture.

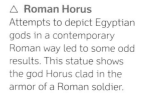

△ **Roman Horus**
Attempts to depict Egyptian gods in a contemporary Roman way led to some odd results. This statue shows the god Horus clad in the armor of a Roman soldier.

"Ptolemy" written in hieroglyphs within a royal cartouche

▽ **The three scripts**
The text of the Rosetta Stone is carved on the face of the stela three times—in hieroglyphs (top), Egyptian demotic (middle), and Greek (bottom).

△ **Hieroglyphic text**
The hieroglyphic text is an archaic script that would probably have been familiar to Egyptian scribes living 2,000 years before the Rosetta Stone was inscribed.

"Ptolemy" in Greek

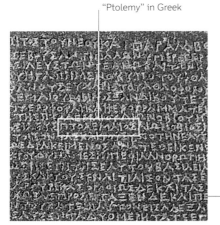

△ **Greek text**
This part of the text acknowledges the Greek (Macedonian) origins of the Ptolemaic rulers of Egypt, including Ptolemy V, who ordered the writing on the Rosetta Stone.

ΠΤΟΛΕΜΑΙΟΣ

△ **Royal names**
The key to understanding hieroglyphic text lay in recognizing that these two very different ways of writing the name Ptolemy, in Greek and hieroglyphs, should be pronounced the same way.

"*Je tiens l'affaire!*
(I have **the thing**.)"

The Rosetta Stone

Decoding Egyptian hieroglyphs

In 1799, during the Napoleonic occupation of Egypt, a group of French engineers was restoring a fortress of medieval origin at the town of el-Rashid (Rosetta) at one of the mouths of the Nile Delta. Among the stone rubble that had been used to build the fortress, they found blocks of stone that had been taken from ancient Egyptian monuments, including some from the western Delta city of Sais.

One of these stone blocks in particular caught their attention. It was a large fragment of dark granodiorite (a type of granite) 44 in (112 cm) tall, and the front of it was inscribed with horizontal lines of text that were clearly in three different scripts. This important artifact, now known as the Rosetta Stone, was handed over to the British as part of the terms of the French surrender in Egypt, and by 1802, it was in the British Museum. However, although the stone itself was in London, copies of the texts on it had been circulated among scholars who had been trying for some time to decipher Egyptian hieroglyphs.

Cracking the code

The text of the Rosetta Stone is not overwhelmingly important in the history of Egyptology. It was a decree announcing changes to the economic relationship between Ptolemy V and the priests of Egyptian temples. What is interesting about it is not what is said, but how it is said. It is written in three different forms of text and two different languages: Classical Greek, Demotic (the everyday cursive script of the Egyptians), and the traditional hieroglyphs used by priests, which were by then no longer in general use. Once scholars guessed that the Rosetta Stone, like some other monuments from roughly the same period, bore the same text written three times, they could use the text that they could read—Greek—as a key to deciphering the other two scripts. The language underlying these scripts was of course very different from Greek, but at least it gave them a starting point.

Signs and symbols

The most important discovery was that most of the hieroglyphs did not have some strange symbolic meaning, but represented sounds. This was most obvious in the name of the king, Ptolemy, which was easy to read in the Greek script. The fortunate guess that the text written within cartouches (ovals) was also a version of "Ptolemy" enabled scholars to start finding correlations between the Greek letters and the individual hieroglyphic signs.

Deciphering the hieroglyphs was a long, slow process, but the most important contribution was made by French scholar Jean-François Champollion. By 1822, he had effectively cracked the code, thereby enabling people to read and understand the ancient texts of dynastic Egypt once again.

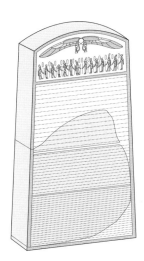

△ **Reconstructed stela**
Based on similar donation stelae from the Late and Ptolemaic Periods, the entire Rosetta Stone was probably about 71 in (180 cm) tall originally, and had images of the king and the gods running along the top.

Egyptian and world history

A timeline of dynasties, empires, and events

Egypt had one of the earliest civilizations, lasting thousands of years. The chart below shows how Egypt compares to some of the world's other great empires and includes a selection of key events and innovations that put the history of Egypt in the context of the wider world.

- **c.1777** BCE Sobekneferu, the first woman to rule in her own right as king of Egypt, begins her reign

- **c.2055** BCE Montuhotep II reunites Egypt

- **c.2667** BCE Djoser's reign begins; commissions the Step Pyramid at Saqqara

- **c.2181** BCE Pepi II dies; end of the Old Kingdom

- **c.1650–1550** BCE Hyksos rulers are in power alongside rulers in Thebes

- **c.3000** BCE First known use of papyrus

- **c.2375** BCE Unas becomes king; first Pyramid Text

- **c.3100** BCE Narmer unifies Egypt

- **c.2550** BCE The Great Pyramid of Giza is built

| c.2181–2055 BCE **First Intermediate Period** | 1650–1550 BCE **Second Intermediate Period** |

EGYPTIAN DYNASTIES

| c.3000–2686 BCE **Early Dynastic Period** | c.2686–2181 BCE **Old Kingdom** | 2055–1650 BCE **Middle Kingdom** |

| **3000** BCE | **2750** BCE | **2500** BCE | **2250** BCE | **2000** BCE | **1750** BCE |

WORLD EMPIRES AND KINGDOMS

Early Dynastic Sumer | Akkadian Empire | Ur III | Old Assyrian Empire

Indus civilization

Chinese civilization

Minoan civilization

Early Kerma, Nubia | Kerma kingdom, Nubia

Ancient Andean civilization

- **c.3200** BCE Newgrange passage tomb is built in Ireland

- **c.2600** BCE A stone circle is erected at Stonehenge in England

- **1790** BCE Hammurabi establishes a legal code for his Babylonian Empire

- **c.2340** BCE Sargon of Akkad's reign begins

- **1800** BCE Bronze is first used in central Europe

- **c.3500** BCE The Bronze Age begins in Mesopotamia

- **c.2600** BCE Planned cities in Indus Valley

- **c.2000** BCE The Minoan Palace of Knossos is built in Crete

• **c.1296** BCE Reign of Seti I begins

• **c.671** BCE Assyrians invade Egypt

• **51** BCE Cleopatra VII's reign begins

• **c.1279** BCE Ramesses II's reign begins; fights in the Battle of Kadesh

• **525** BCE Persian conquest of Egypt

• **c.726** BCE Nubian king Piankhy captures Egypt

c.1550 BCE Reign of hmose starts; continues expel the Hyksos

• **c.1126–1069** BCE Royal tomb robberies at Thebes

• **c.1352** BCE Akhenaten takes the throne; founds the city of Amarna

• **c.945** BCE Sheshonq I captures Jerusalem

• **c.305** BCE Ptolemy I's reign begins; starts construction of the Pharos lighthouse and Alexandria's library

• **1325** BCE Egyptian king Tutankhamen dies and is entombed

• **664** BCE Psamtek I develops Sais as a royal capital

• **332** BCE Alexander the Great captures Egypt from the Persians

• **c.1184** BCE Ramesses III becomes king; defeats the Libyans and the Sea-Peoples

• **c.31** BCE Egypt comes under Roman rule

1550–1295 BCE
Early New Kingdom

| **1295–1069** BCE **Late New Kingdom** | **1069–664** BCE **Third Intermediate Period** | **664–332** BCE **Late Period** | **332–395** BCE **Greco-Roman Period** |

1250 BCE   **1000** BCE   **750** BCE   **500** BCE   **250** BCE   **1** CE

edic civilization

Indian kingdoms

Ancient Rome

Mycenaean civilization

Classical Greece

Napatan kingdom, Nubia   **Meroitic kingdom, Nubia**

Olmec civilization in Mexico

• **1003** BCE Jewish king David unites Israel and Judah

• **c.508** BCE Democracy is established in Athens

• **c.146** BCE Romans destroy Carthage

• **c.600** BCE Coins used in Phoenicia

• **c.1046** BCE The Zhou Dynasty founded in China

• **c.200** BCE Paper invented in China

• **c.1400** BCE In Mesoamerica (Mexico and central America), rubber is used in games

• **c.750** BCE The Iron Age begins in central Europe

• **c.490** BCE The Battle of Marathon

• **c.4** BCE Jesus Christ is born

• **c.776** BCE First Olympic Games

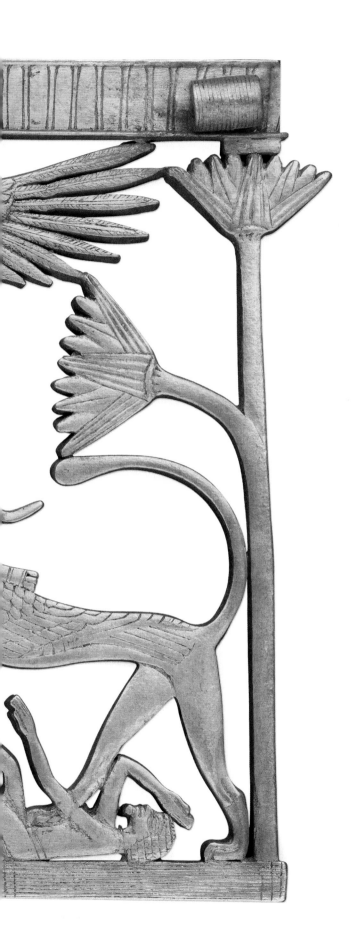

◁ **Pectoral of Mereret**
This large and exquisite gold pectoral belonged to Princess Mereret, a daughter of Amenemhat III. On either side of the king's cartouche, a pair of falcon-headed sphinxes crush the foreign enemies of Egypt.

Directory

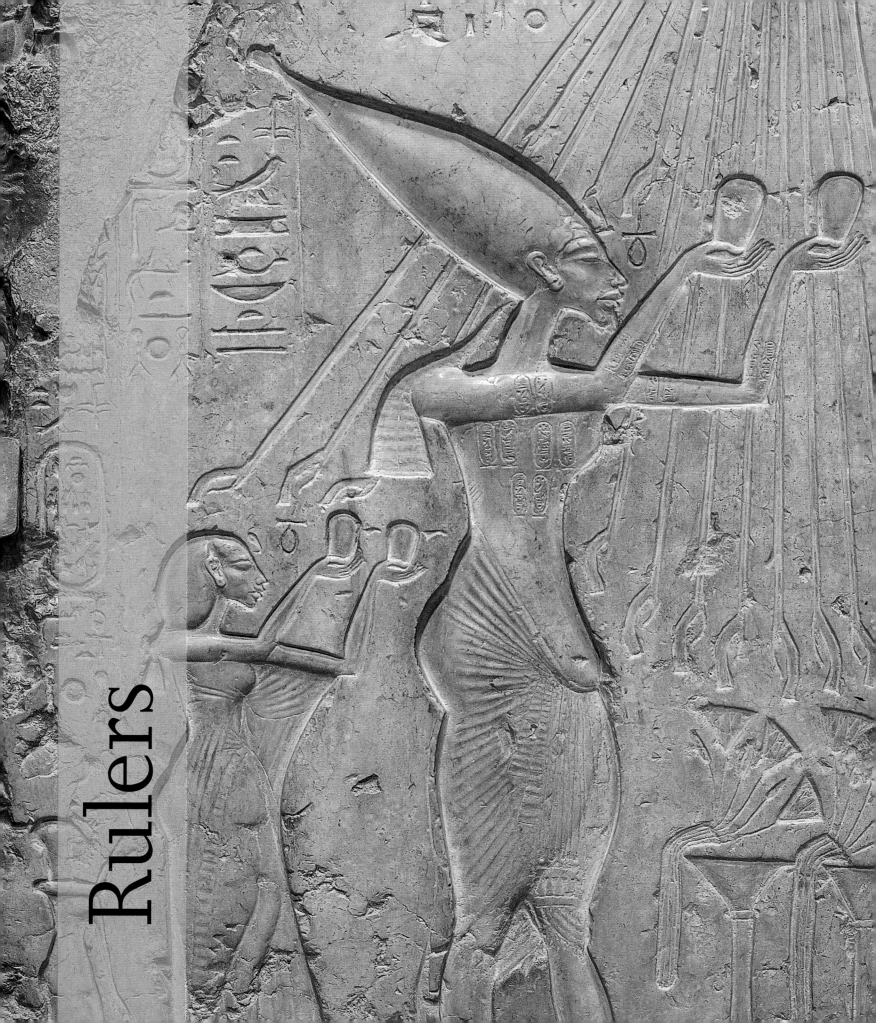

Rulers

The Early Dynastic Period (c. 3000–2686 BCE)

The origins of civilization in the Nile Valley remain a subject for debate, but it was around 3000 BCE that the first kings of Egypt emerged. From a capital at Abydos in Middle Egypt, these early kings molded two dynasties that would set the foundations for three millennia of pharaonic rule.

■ DYNASTY 0
(c. 3000 BCE)

Narmer

Narmer

Date unknown

The first named ruler of dynastic Egypt appears on an early artifact known as the Narmer Palette (see pp.44-45). Discovered at the site of Hierakonpolis (the former ancient city of Nekhen), north of Aswan, it dates from c.3000 BCE.

On one side the Palette shows the king wearing the white crown of Upper Egypt and on the other the red crown of Lower Egypt. From this, Narmer is usually credited with the unification of Egypt. Many Egyptologists believe that Narmer was the same person as Menes, who appears as the first king on the Abydos king list.

■ 1ST DYNASTY
(c. 3000–2890 BCE)

Aha
Djer
Djet
Den
Queen Merneith

Anedjib
Semerkhet
Qa'a

Djer

Date unknown

Djer enjoyed a lengthy reign of 41 years, according to the Palermo Stone, or 57 years, according to 300 BCE Egyptian priest Manetho. The priest describes Djer as a scholar and the author of a book on anatomy still in use in Greek times. An ivory tablet from Abydos records trips to the cities of Buto and Sais in the Nile Delta, and an inscription at Wadi Halfa, near the modern-day border of Sudan, documents Djer's military campaigns in Nubia.

He was buried at Abydos along with more than 300 retainers who either committed suicide or were killed before being buried alongside their king.

Queen Merneith

Date unknown

Djet's queen was his probable sister Merneith. After his death, she may have ruled as regent to their son, Den, before he was old enough to rule. This would make her the first female king and the earliest known queen in history. Evidence for her rule comes from a seal found in the tomb of Den, which includes Merneith's name among a list of 1st Dynasty kings, accompanied by the title "King's Mother."

■ 2ND DYNASTY
(2890–2686 BCE)

Hotepsekhemwy
Raneb
Nynetjer
Weneg
Sened
Peribsen
Khasekhemwy

Khasekhemwy

Date unknown

Khasekhemwy, whose name means "The two powers have appeared," came to power during a time of internal conflict in Egypt. An inscription on a stone vase records him "fighting the northern enemy within Nekheb." Nekheb was a city on the other side of the Nile, opposite of the southern capital of Nekhen. Khasekhemwy was victorious, and to seal the peace, he married a princess, Nemathap. His extensive tomb at Abydos was one of the largest that had been built up to that time.

△ Detail of the back of the Narmer Palette showing Egypt's first named king parading past his beheaded enemies

The Old Kingdom (2686–2181 BCE)

The four dynasties of the Old Kingdom saw the first great flourishing of Egyptian civilization. Ruling from the royal capital at Memphis, the newfound power of the kings was reflected in the funerary monuments they erected at Saqqara and Giza. These reached their apogee in the Great Pyramids.

△ Life-size statue of Djoser found in his Step Pyramid complex at Saqqara

■ 3RD DYNASTY (2686–2613 BCE)

Nebka 2686–2667 BCE
Djoser (Netjerikhet) 2667–2648 BCE
Sekhemkhet 2648–2640 BCE
Khaba 2640–2637 BCE
Sanakht
Huni 2637–2613 BCE

Djoser
Other name: Netjerikhet

2667–2648 BCE

Although he is now known as Djoser, the second king of the 3rd Dynasty was called Netjerikhet during his reign. There is evidence to suggest that he may have been the son of Khasekhemwy, the last king of the 2nd Dynasty, or the son (by a previous husband) of Nemathap, Khasekhemwy's queen.

During his 19-year reign (some scholars argue that it was 28), Djoser extended his rule as far south as Aswan and into Sinai, where his minions mined precious turquoise and copper. He also commissioned the construction of one of the most impressive monuments of the ancient world and the first building ever to be constructed entirely from stone, the Step Pyramid complex at Saqqara.

Sekhemkhet

2648–2640 BCE

Little is known about the third king of the 3rd Dynasty, who seems to have ruled only briefly. He is recorded in two rock inscriptions at Wadi Maghara in Sinai, suggesting that mines there were still active during his reign.

Excavations at Saqqara in the 1950s unearthed the remains of his pyramid complex at Saqqara, just southwest of that of Djoser. Only the first layer of the Step Pyramid was completed, but judging from the size of its base, it would have been larger than Djoser's pyramid, if it had been completed. The name Imhotep is inscribed in Sekhemkhet's complex, which suggests that the architect who planned Djoser's pyramid also worked for his successor.

■ 4TH DYNASTY (2613–2494 BCE)

Snefru 2613–2589 BCE
Khufu (Cheops) 2589–2566 BCE
Djedefre (Radjedef) 2566–2558 BCE
Khaefre (Chephren) 2558–2532 BCE
Menkaure (Mycerinus) 2532–2503 BCE
Shepseskaf 2503–2498 BCE

Snefru

2613–2589 BCE

Snefru's reign demonstrates the power wielded by Egypt's kings. Inscriptions record that Snefru commanded raids into Nubia to the south and Libya to the west. The three major pyramids that he left behind are proof of the centralization of government and its organizational abilities.

Snefru's earliest pyramid, at Meidum, was originally constructed as a step pyramid but later modified to become a true pyramid. The first of his pyramids at Dahshur was the first to be designed as a true pyramid, although builders were forced to reduce the angle of the sides halfway through construction, producing the "bent" appearance of the final structure. Later, Snefru successfully built a true pyramid at Dahshur, known today as the "Red Pyramid," which might be where he was buried.

Khufu
Other name: Cheops

2589–2566 BCE

Khufu followed the 24-year reign of his father, Snefru, with his own reign of 23 years. Little is known about him. Rock inscriptions in Wadi Maghara record the presence of his soldiers in Sinai, and an inscription on a boulder on Elephantine Island in Aswan

Khaefre
Other name: Chephren

2558–2532 BCE

Khaefre was the son of Khufu and the brother of his predecessor Djedefre. Not much is known about him. The Greek historian Herodotus described Khaefre as a cruel and tyrannical ruler (and said the same of Khufu), but he was writing 2,000 years after Khaefre's time, and modern historians consider this negative characterization of the king as untrustworthy. Egypt prospered under his reign, with evidence of trade with what are now Lebanon and Syria. Khaefre built the second-largest pyramid at Giza and is also usually credited with building the Sphinx, which appears to guard his pyramid.

Menkaure
Other name: Mycerinus

2532–2503 BCE

Menkaure was the son of Khaefre and grandson of Khufu and the builder of the third and smallest of the three main pyramids at Giza. Herodotus wrote that, unlike his father and grandfather, Menkaure was a benevolent ruler but that this displeased the gods, who had decreed that Egypt should suffer 150 years of tyranny. According to the Greek historian, Menkaure endured much misfortune, notably the early death of his only daughter. Menkaure's pyramid, unfinished on his death, was completed by his son, Shepseskaf.

indicates that his rule reached deep into the south of the country. His fame rests on the funerary monument that he built for himself, commonly known as the Great Pyramid of Giza.

△ Menkaure (right) with the goddess Hathor (center) and a nome god (left)

△ Ruins of the mortuary temple of Sahure, king of the 5th Dynasty, at Abusir

Unas

2375–2345 BCE

The last king of the 5th Dynasty is known largely because of his pyramid. He ruled during what historians believe was a period of economic decline. For reasons unknown, he broke with the tradition of the majority of his 5th-Dynasty predecessors and built his pyramid not at Abusir, but at Saqqara, near the southwest corner of the Step Pyramid of Djoser. He was not a particularly powerful king and his pyramid is the smallest of those from the Old Kingdom, but it is notable for being the first to be inscribed with Pyramid Texts.

■ 6TH DYNASTY
(2345–2181 BCE)

Teti 2345–2323 BCE
Userkara 2323–2321 BCE
Pepi I (Meryra) 2321–2287 BCE
Merenre 2287–2278 BCE
Pepi II (Neferkare)
  2278–2184 BCE
Nitiqret 2184–2181 BCE

Teti

2345–2323 BCE

The relationship between Teti and his predecessor, Unas, is uncertain. Unas appears to have died without any male heirs. Some historians suggest that Teti came to the throne through his marriage with Iput I, a daughter of Unas. Manetho records that Teti's rule came to an end when he was murdered by his palace guard. He was buried in the pyramid complex he built at Saqqara, in a chamber inscribed with Pyramid Texts. Evidence

■ 5TH DYNASTY
(2494–2345 BCE)

Userkaf 2494–2487 BCE
Sahure 2487–2475 BCE
Neferirkare 2475–2455 BCE
Shepseskare 2455–2448 BCE
Neferefre 2448–2445 BCE
Niuserre 2445–2421 BCE
Menkauhor 2421–2414 BCE
Djedkare Isesi 2414–2375 BCE
Unas 2375–2345 BCE

Userkaf

2494–2487 BCE

The parentage of Userkaf, the first king of the 5th Dynasty, is unknown. His reign was notable

for heralding the elevation of the sun god Ra to state deity. Userkaf introduced a new kind of monument to Egypt, a sun temple, which he built at Abu Gurob, a little way north of Saqqara. This took the form of an enclosure containing a sun altar in front of a stumpy obelisk, also known as a Benben stone.

Userkaf also constructed a pyramid complex near the enclosure wall of Djoser's Step Pyramid at Saqqara. A stone vessel, which was discovered on the Greek island of Kythira and bears Userkaf's name, is the earliest evidence of contact between ancient Egypt and the Aegean world.

Sahure

2487–2475 BCE

Evidence suggests that Sahure was the son of Userkaf. He was the first to build a pyramid complex at Abusir, close to his father's sun temple. Wall reliefs at the pyramid's mortuary temple depict many scenes of trade with other nations. One shows Egyptian ships bearing cedar trees from what is now Lebanon. The temple also records the first known expedition to the land of Punt, thought to have been in the Horn of Africa. Sahure is shown celebrating this venture, tending a myrrh tree in his palace garden.

suggests that during Teti's reign, he faced a challenge from the increasingly powerful nobles. His vizier, named Mereruka, left behind a funerary monument to rival that of the king in the form of a mastaba with 33 richly carved rooms.

Pepi I
Other name: Meryra

2321–2287 BCE

Pepi I was the son of Teti. Although he enjoyed a lengthy reign, it took place against the background of a continuing decline of royal power. He was also challenged on at least one, if not two occasions by internal conspiracies against him. Attempts to cement his authority resulted in an extensive building program, and temples and chapels were built all over Egypt during his reign.

There were also several military campaigns during his rule: into Nubia, Sinai, and the southern Levant. Pepi I built his funerary complex at Saqqara, along with at least another six pyramids for his wives. A copper statue of him that was found at Hierakonpolis is the earliest known example of a life-size metal sculpture.

Pepi II
Other name: Neferkara

2278–2184 BCE

Pepi II may have been the longest reigning of any Egyptian ruler. He was once thought to be the son of Pepi I, but it seems more likely that he was the son of his immediate predecessor, Merenre.

Pepi came to the throne as an infant—an alabaster statuette displayed in the Brooklyn Museum depicts the young Pepi II wearing the royal nemes headdress and a kilt, sitting on the lap of his mother, Ankhnesmeryre II. During his reign, royal power continued to wane, and this decline probably became more marked as the king grew older. Under Pepi II, more power was passed on to regional, high-ranking officials, especially in the south of Egypt, and this continued to draw central authority away from the royal capital of Memphis.

■ 7TH AND 8TH DYNASTIES
(2181–2160 BCE)

These were two little known dynasties of a short-lived line of kings reigning in rapid succession.

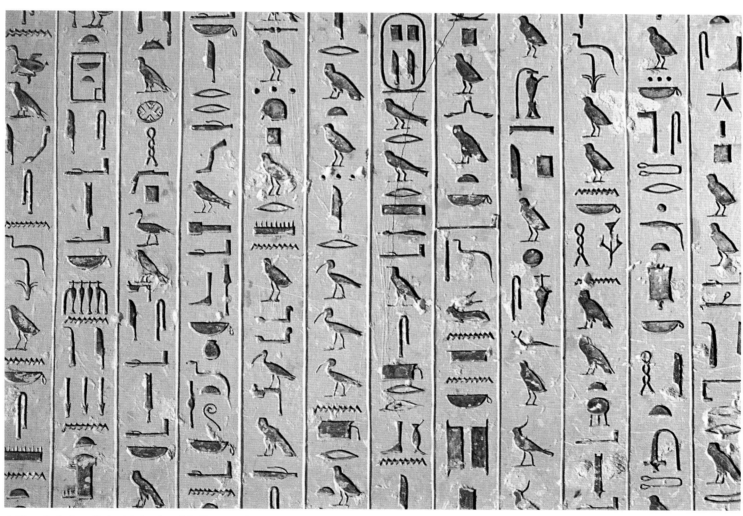

△ Hieroglyphs from the burial chamber of the Pyramid of Pepi I at Saqqara

First Intermediate Period (2181–2055 BCE)

Following the breakdown of the Old Kingdom, the rule of Egypt was divided between rival dynasties—those in Herakleopolis in northern Middle Egypt and Thebes in Upper Egypt. It was a time of disorder, during which no monuments were built.

■ 9TH AND 10TH DYNASTIES
(2160–2025 BCE)

Khety I (Meryibra)
Khety II (Nebkaura)
Khety III (Wahkara)
Merikare

■ 11TH DYNASTY (THEBES ONLY)
(2125–2055 BCE)

Montuhotep I (Tepy-a)
Intef I (Sehertawy)
   2125–2112 BCE
Intef II (Wahankh)
   2112–2063 BCE
Intef III (Nakhtnebtepnefer)
   2063–2055 BCE

Intef I
Other name: Sehertawy

2125–2112 BCE

Intef is thought to have been the son of Montuhotep I and Neferiu I and was the first of the 11th Dynasty to declare himself king, adopting the name Sehertawy, meaning "He who has brought calm to the Two Lands." In reality, he was the nomarch, or regional governor, of Thebes. He managed to extend his rule south to the First Cataract (modern Aswan), but the allied rival rulers of Hierakonpolis and Herakleopolis prevented him from extending his influence into Lower Egypt, so Intef did not succceed in reunifying the two regions of Egypt during his reign. When he died, he was buried in a rock-cut tomb on the West Bank, opposite Thebes, at a site known today as Saff el-Dawaba.

△ Relief from the mortuary temple of Mentuhotep II, the reunifying king

The Middle Kingdom (2055–1650 BCE)

Following Montuhotep II's reunification of Egypt, successive dynasties, ruling initially from Thebes and then later from Lisht in the Faiyum region, brought back strong central government. Egypt's territorial domain increased as the warrior king Senwosret III extended its borders into Nubia in the south. Advancements in art led to the quality of Egyptian statues reaching a peak.

■ 11TH DYNASTY CTD.
(2055–1985 BCE)

Montuhotep II (Nebhepetra)
   2055–2004 BCE
Montuhotep III (Sankhkara)
   2004–1992 BCE
Montuhotep IV (Nebtawyra)
   1992–1985 BCE

Montuhotep II
Other name: Nebhepetra

2055–2004 BCE

The fifth king of the 11th Dynasty is credited with reunifying Egypt after the turmoil of the First Intermediate Period and with beginning the Middle Kingdom.

In the 14th year of his reign, he sent an army to confront Herakleopolitan forces who had invaded Abydos. The exact date when reunification was achieved is not known, but it is thought that the conflict lasted for many years. The reunification led to a surge in trade and building. Montuhotep II removed all the nomarchs who had opposed him and promoted his authority through numerous building projects throughout Egypt, including his own mortuary temple at Deir el-Bahri, on the west bank at Thebes, which had become the national capital. This mortuary temple marked a radical break with the pyramids of his predecessors, taking the form of multiple terraces raised on colonnades.

■ 12TH DYNASTY
(1985–1773 BCE)

Amenemhat I
   (Sehetepibra)
   1985–1956 BCE
Senwosret I (Kheperkara)
   1956–1911 BCE
Amenemhat II
   (Nubkaura)
   1911–1877 BCE
Senwosret II (Khakheperra)
   1877–1870 BCE
Senwosret III (Khakaura)
   1870–1831 BCE
Amenemhat III (Nimaatra)
   1831–1786 BCE
Amenemhat IV
   (Maakherura)
   1786–1777 BCE
Sobekneferu (Sobekkara)
   1777–1773 BCE

Amenemhat I
Other name: Sehetepibra

1985–1956 BCE

Amenemhat I might have been the vizier of his predecessor, Montuhotep IV, and was of noble, not royal, lineage. Although he built and restored monuments at Thebes, he is best known for transferring the capital to a new town named Itj-Tawy, not far south of Memphis, in the region of the oasis of Faiyum.

Historians think that the move may have been a way of signaling a new beginning while dissolving the established power bases of his officials in Thebes. It may also have been militarily expedient, as it put the king and his army closer to the source of the ongoing Asiatic incursions from the north. From Itj-Tawy, Amenemhat I mounted expeditions against the Asiatics. He also still had to deal with challenges from the Nubians in

△ Pillar statue of Senwosret I portraying him as Osiris, god of the dead, holding the ankh, the "key of life"

the south. He was probably assassinated and was buried at his pyramid complex at Lisht.

Senwosret I
Other name: Kheperkara

1956–1911 BCE

When Senwosret became king on the death of Amenemhat I, his father, he already had 10 years' experience of ruling as co-regent. He continued his father's push into Nubia, establishing his authority as far south as the Second Cataract. He also sent expeditions into Egypt's Western Desert and established diplomatic relations along the coast of the eastern Mediterranean.

In Egypt, he promoted his rule by building temples. He erected two large granite obelisks at Heliopolis, one of which is still standing as the oldest obelisk in Egypt. Senwosret's reign was characterized by great wealth and prosperity and supreme craftsmanship in jewelry and sculpture, using materials such as amethyst, turquoise, copper, gneiss, and gold from Nubia. Senwosret was buried in his pyramid at Lisht, close to that of his father.

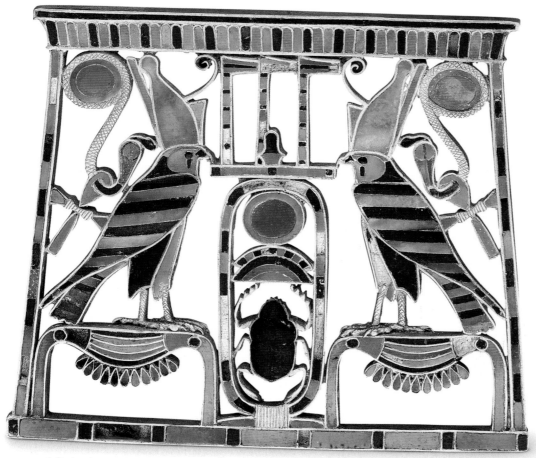

△ Pectoral composed around the throne name of Senwosret II, possibly belonging to the king's daughter

the Head of the South (Elephantine and Lower Nubia), which were governed by officials appointed by the king. Art became marked by greater realism and attention to detail, evident in the many surviving representations of the king, who is usually depicted with a somber expression and hooded eyelids. He commissioned numerous building projects, including expanding the Temple of Amen at Karnak and building his own pyramid complex at Dahshur and second tomb at Abydos. Senwosret III was one of the few Egyptian kings deified during their own lifetime.

Amenemhat III
Other name: Nimaatra

1831–1786 BCE

Senwosret III's son, Amenemhat III, reigned for 45 years, presiding over a period of great prosperity. He continued work begun by his father on a canal, known as the *Mer-Wer* (Great Canal), to link the Faiyum with the Nile. He built a large temple dedicated to Sobek at Kiman Faris, later known as Crocodilopolis by the Greeks, now buried beneath modern Faiyum City. He erected two pyramids: one in the Middle Kingdom necropolis at Dahshur and the other where he was buried, at Hawara in the Faiyum. Like his father, he left behind many statues notable for the realistic portrayal of his features.

Amenemhat IV
Other name: Maakherura

1786–1777 BCE

Amenemhat IV's relationship to his predecessor, Amenemhat III, remains unverified: he may have

Amenemhat II
Other name: Nubkaura

1911–1877 BCE

The stability and longevity of Senwosret's 45-year reign was replicated by that of his son, Amenemhat II, who ruled for about 34 years. Records show an expedition to the land of Punt during his reign, while jewelry bearing the king's cartouche found in royal tombs at Byblos in Lebanon is evidence of diplomatic relations. Toward the end of his life, Amenemhat II shared a brief co-regency with his successor and probable son, Senwosret II. Unlike his two predecessors who had built their pyramids at Lisht, Amenemhat II chose to build his mortuary complex at Dahshur.

Senwosret II
Other name: Khakheperra

1877–1870 BCE

The reign of Senwosret II, fourth king of the 12th Dynasty, may have lasted only seven or eight years, but he achieved much in that short time. He constructed an extensive irrigation system to develop agricultural land in the area around the Faiyum Oasis, 50 miles (80 km) southwest of Memphis. Middle Kingdom rulers established this region as an agricultural and religious center, and Sobek the crocodile god became a prominent deity. While Senwosret's direct predecessors were buried at Dahshur, he built his necropolis and pyramid at el-Lahun, on the edge of the Faiyum Oasis.

Senwosret III
Other name: Khakaura

1870–1831 BCE

The reign of Senwosret III, son of Senwosret II, marks a high point of the Middle Kingdom. He was a towering warrior king who led a series of campaigns into Nubia to secure Egypt's southern borders. He added to the forts there, from the northern fort at Buhen at the Second Nile Cataract to Semna.

To facilitate his fleet, he had a canal cut around the First Cataract in the Nile at Aswan. He also campaigned in what is now Syria. To consolidate royal power within Egypt, he got rid of most of the nomarchs, dividing the country into the three districts of Lower Egypt, Upper Egypt, and been his son or grandson. Their rules overlapped in a two-year co-regency. The *Mer-Wer* (Great Canal) was completed during Amenemhat IV's reign, channeling fresh water to the Faiyum Depression to fill ancient Lake Moeris. He features little in written records except in relation to expeditions to the turquoise mines of Serabit el-Khadim in the Sinai; to mine amethyst at Wadi el-Hudi in southern Egypt; and, farther afield, to the land of Punt. Amenemhat IV completed a shrine at the temple of Hathor in the Sinai, but his tomb has not been identified.

Sobekneferu
Other name: Sobekkara

1777–1773 BCE

Sobekneferu, whose name means the "Beauty of Sobek," is the first woman for whom there is confirmed proof that she reigned in her own right as a female king of Egypt. She was the daughter of Amenemhat III, who ascended to the throne when Amenemhat IV died prematurely without a male heir. Her name appears on multiple king lists, including Turin, indicating she reigned for three years and 10 months.

Three headless statues of the queen, discovered in the Faiyum, depict her wearing a costume that combines elements of male and female dress. Unfortunately, the only head identified as Sobekneferu, which was held at the Egyptian Museum in Berlin, was lost during World War II.

She is known to have made additions to her father's funerary complex at Hawara and to have built at Herakleopolis Magna. Her own burial place, however, is unknown.

■ 13TH DYNASTY
(1773–after 1650 BCE)

Wegaf (Khutawyra)
Sobekhotep II
 (Sekhemra-khutawy)
Iykhernefert Neferhotep
 (Sankhtawy-sekhemra)
Ameny-intef-Amanememhat
 (Sankhibra)

Hor (Awibra)
Khendjer (Userkara)
Sobekhotep III
 (Sekhemra-sewadjtawy)
Neferhotep I
 (Khasekhemra)
Sahthor
Sobekhotep IV (Khaneferra)
Sobekhotep V
Ay (Merneferra)

■ 14TH DYNASTY
(1773–1650 BCE)

The obscure 14th Dynasty of minor kings ruled from the eastern Delta, and the capital of the dynasty was probably Avaris. The 14th Dynasty was probably contemporary with the 13th or 15th Dynasties.

△ Statuette of Amenemhat III showing a youthful king, recognizable from other, similar portrayals

Second Intermediate Period (1650–1550 BCE)

Once again, central government broke down. Rule in the north of Egypt was assumed by a foreign power, the Hyksos from the eastern Mediterranean region, who established a capital at Avaris in the Nile Delta.

■ 15TH DYNASTY (HYKSOS)
(1650–1550 BCE)

Salitis (Sekerher)
Khyan (Seuserenra) c.1600 BCE
Apepi (Aauserra) c.1555 BCE
Khamudi

■ 16TH DYNASTY
(1650–1580 BCE)

This dynasty of kings ruled Upper Egypt from Thebes for 70 years and were contemporary with the 15th Dynasty, the Hyksos rulers based in Lower Egypt. The two dynasties warred with one another during this period of division betwen Upper and Lower Egypt.

■ 17TH DYNASTY
(c.1580–1550 BCE)

Rahotep
Sobekemsaf I
Intef VI (Sekhemra)
Intef VII (Nubkheperra)
Intef VIII
   (Sekhemraherhermaat)
Sobekemsaf II
Sekenenre Taa c.1560 BCE
Kamose (Wadjkheperra)
   1555–1550 BCE

Kamose
Other name: Wadjkheperra

1555–1550 BCE

Kamose was the king who brought to an end the political uncertainty of the Second Intermediate Period and ushered in the beginning of the New Kingdom. He took up the battle begun by his probable father, Sekenenre Taa, against the Hyksos, who ruled much of Egypt from their base in the Nile Delta. In Kamose's third year, he led a fleet from Thebes down the Nile attacking Hyksos garrisons throughout Middle Egypt. A detailed account of the campaign was left on two stele at Karnak. Kamose also led two campaigns into Nubia. However, the king's reign was short, lasting no more than five years. There is no record to indicate how he died, and he was buried in a simple coffin at Thebes.

△ Detail from sarcophagus showing the face of Kamose, last king of the 17th Dynasty

The New Kingdom (1550–1069 BCE)

This era, which spanned three dynasties of kings, marked the pinnacle of ancient Egyptian civilization. These rulers were godlike beings that commanded vast territories and left behind immense works.

■ 18TH DYNASTY

(1550–1295 BCE)

Ahmose (Nebpehtyra)
  1550–1525 BCE
Amenhotep I
  (Djeserkara)
  1525–1504 BCE
Tuthmosis I (Aakheperkara)
  1504–1492 BCE
Tuthmosis II
  (Aakhepererenra)
  1492–1479 BCE
Tuthmosis III (Menkheperra)
  1479–1425 BCE
Hatshepsut (Maatkara)
  1473–1458 BCE
Amenhotep II (Aakheperura)
  1427–1400 BCE
Tuthmosis IV
  (Menkheperura) 1400–1390 BCE
Amenhotep III (Nebmaatra)
  1390–1352 BCE
Akhenaten /Amenhotep IV
  1352–1336 BCE
Smenkhkare (Neferneferuaten)
  1338–1336 BCE
Tutankhamen (Nebkhepererura)
  1336–1327 BCE
Ay (Kheperkheperura)
  1327–1323 BCE
Horemheb (Djeserkheperura)
  1323–1295 BCE

▷ Anthropoid coffin inscribed for Ahmose showing the long, curved beard of divinity strapped to his chin

Ahmose
Other name: Nebpehtyra

1550–1525 BCE

Ahmose I ascended the throne at a young age following the death of his uncle, Kamose. Initially, his mother, Ahhotep, reigned as regent. About halfway through his own reign, the king resumed the conflict with the Hyksos, leading attacks on Memphis; Heliopolis; and Avaris, the northerners' capital in the eastern Nile Delta. Once Ahmose had completed the expulsion of the Hyksos from the Delta, Thebes became the national capital. It would become the political center, as well as the religious center, as the worship of its local god Amen grew in importance.

With reunification came the start of a revival of the arts and monumental constructions. He built a cenotaph complex at Abydos (with a small pyramid) but was buried at Thebes.

Amenhotep I
Other name: Djeserkara

1525–1504 BCE

Amenhotep I's 21-year reign was peaceful for the most part, although tomb texts indicate that he led campaigns into Nubia, at the very least.

Records also show that he executed a number of building projects, including a massive limestone gateway and a barque shrine at Karnak. Egyptologists believe that Amenhotep I probably founded the artisans' village at Deir el-Medina, because he and his mother were its patron deities. The Ebers Papyrus, which is the main source for information on ancient Egyptian medicine, probably dates from this time, and texts suggest that the first water clock was invented during Amenhotep I's reign.

He was the first king to have a tomb separate from his mortuary complex, setting a trend that would continue throughout the New Kingdom.

His temple was located at the north end of Deir el-Bahri, but it was demolished to make way for the Temple of Queen Hatshepsut; the location of Amenhotep I's tomb has not been definitively identified.

Tuthmosis I
Other name: Aakheperkara

1504–1492 BCE

Amenhotep I's reign was marked by a series of military campaigns. Tuthmosis I campaigned in Nubia, leading a fleet up the Nile, and subsequent expeditions extended Egyptian rule south to the Fourth Cataract. Additional military actions pushed Egyptian influence all the way to the Euphrates in modern Syria.

On a stela at Abydos, Tuthmosis I records, "I made the boundaries of Egypt as far as that which the sun encircles … I made Egypt the superior of every land." In the Egyptian capital of Thebes, he made significant expansions to the temple at Karnak.

Tuthmosis I was the first king known to be buried in the Valley of the Kings. His mortuary temple has not been found, possibly because it was demolished or incorporated into the Temple of Hatshepsut.

Tuthmosis II

Other name: Aakheperenra

1492–1479 BCE

After the two oldest sons of Tuthmosis I died prematurely, the throne passed to his third son, who would become Tuthmosis II. His mother was Mutnefret, a minor wife of the king, making him a lesser son, so he married his fully royal half-sister, Hatshepsut, daughter of Ahmose, the Great Royal Wife of Tuthmosis I. Records of his reign are few, possibly due to Hatshepsut's later attempts to erase and replace his name with her own. Some historians believe Hatshepsut was the real power during her husband's reign. No royal tomb or a mortuary temple for Tuthmosis II has ever been identified.

Tuthmosis III

Other name: Menkheperra

1479–1425 BCE

The reign of Tuthmosis III is considered a golden era, during which Tuthmosis both expanded Egypt's territory and accumulated wealth. As he was an infant when his father, Tuthmosis II, died, his aunt and stepmother, Queen Hatshepsut, assumed rule of the country. When Tuthmosis III came of age, he became co-regent, then sole ruler in the 20th or 21st year of Hatshepsut's reign. During his 32 years of sole rule, Tuthmosis campaigned in Nubia and stormed through the Levant, gathering the spoils of war in what are now Israel, Palestine, Syria, and Lebanon. The wealth he acquired was used to fund building projects throughout Egypt, most notably at Karnak, where he refashioned the great temple complex. Several walls at Karnak feature scenes depicting Tuthmosis in traditional kingly fashion, smiting his enemies and accompanied by inscribed lists of captured cities and booty. When he died, Tuthmosis III was buried in the Valley of the Kings.

Hatshepsut

Other name: Maatkara

1473–1458 BCE

Hapshetsut was only the second historically confirmed female king to have ruled in Egypt by this time. In order to emphasize her right to rule, she associated herself with her powerful father, Tuthmosis I, and also with the god Amen-Ra. A "Divine Birth" scene at her mortuary temple at Deir el-Bahri shows Amen-Ra present within the body of Tuthmosis I when he impregnated Hatshepsut's mother, Queen Ahmose. In statuary and royal monuments, she often had herself portrayed as a male king. Her many achievements included a trading expedition to Punt that returned bearing 31 live myrrh trees, commemorated in relief at Deir el-Bahri. In addition to her own striking mortuary temple, she built prolifically throughout Egypt. At Karnak, she raised twin

△ A statue of Queen Hatshepsut at her mortuary temple in Deir el-Bahri, Luxor, portrays her as a male king

△ The vast Colossi of Memnon at Luxor, which once stood at the entrance gate to the mortuary temple of Amenhotep III

obelisks, at the time the tallest in the world, one of which still stands. When she died, she was buried in the Valley of the Kings in the tomb of her father, which she adapted by adding a second burial chamber for herself. Toward the end of the reign of Tuthmosis III, Hatshepsut's name and cartouches were chiseled out of her monuments, her statues pulled down, and even her obelisks walled up in an attempt to erase her name from history. It is still unclear why this happened.

Amenhotep III
Other name: Nebmaatra

1390–1352 BCE

The long reign of Amenhotep III represented another prosperous age for Egypt. Amenhotep's father, Tuthmosis IV, bequeathed a settled and flourishing empire, which stretched from the Euphrates in modern Syria down to the Fourth Cataract in present-day Sudan. Amenhotep's reign is one of the best documented of any Egyptian king, partly thanks to more than 200 large inscribed soapstone scarabs extolling his accomplishments.

Although Amenhotep had a large harem, his chief wife Tiy was highly revered, portrayed in statuary and temple reliefs at the same size as her husband, symbolizing a relationship of equals. The pair commissioned great monuments, the most magnificent of which was a mortuary temple that was larger in size that any previous king's complex. The temple was quarried for stone by kings who followed, so very little remains of it today, apart from the two huge statues of the king, popularly called the Colossi of Memnon.

Akhenaten
Other name: Neferneferuaton

1352–1332 BCE

Amenhotep IV was the second son of Amenhotep III and Tiy; their elder son died prematurely. Amenhotep IV married Nefertiti, his Great Royal Wife, about the time he took the throne.

Early in his reign, he introduced a monotheistic cult of sun worship of the Aten, portrayed as a solar disk. He built a temple to the Aten at Karnak and, in the fifth year of his reign, changed his name to Akhenaten. About the same time, he decreed that a new capital be built halfway between Thebes and Memphis, called Akhetaten, better known today as Amarna.

Along with the new cult and new city came a new artistic style in which representations of people, animals, and plants are more naturalistic than the traditional art of ancient Egypt. The portrayals of Akhenaten are radically different from other kings: he is shown with an exaggeratedly long face; thick lips; a sagging belly; and broad, almost feminine hips. The reasons for this are not understood.

After his death, later kings sought to erase Akhenaten's heretical reign from history: his monuments were dismantled, his statues destroyed, and his name excluded from lists of rulers.

Tutankhamen

Other name: Nebkhepererura

1336–1327 BCE

While still a child, Tutankhaten (as he was first named), probable son of Akhenaten, ascended the throne at Amarna. He remained there for only a short time before he abandoned the city of his father and moved the royal court to Memphis, while Thebes reverted to being the religious center of the country. The religious shift was reflected in the king's change of name to Tutankhamen. These decisions were probably not taken by Tutankhamen himself but by his advisors, who included a general named Horemheb and the king's vizier and eventual successor, Ay. The actions are recorded in the so-called Restoration Stela, erected at Karnak, which outlines the damage done in the reign prior to Tutankhamen and the actions taken to restore the gods to their proper position. The king restored monuments defaced under Akhenaten and undertook new building work, including at the temples of Karnak and Luxor.

The cause of his death, while still a teenager, remains unconfirmed. As a young and possibly crippled and sickly king who spent a relatively short time on the throne and whose rule was massively overshadowed by the divisive legacy of his father, Tutankhamen's reign achieved little of note. His fame today rests on the fact that his tomb remained intact and full of treasures that were only discovered in the 20th century.

△ Detail of jeweled back of Tutankhamen's throne showing the queen offering the king a drink

Horemheb

Other name: Djeserkheperura

1323–1295 BCE

Horemheb was the commander-in-chief of Akhenaten's army and held the same role under Tutankhamen, as well as being a diplomatic envoy and advisor. He was also the designated crown prince, but on the death of the boy king, the elderly vizier Ay assumed control, possibly while Horemheb was away campaigning. Ay's reign was brief, and before he died, he named Nakhtmin, who was possibly his son or adopted son, as his successor. Horemheb was still, however, able to seize the throne. He undertook domestic reforms with the aim of further reasserting the power of Thebes and Memphis, actions that are recorded on a stela known as the Great Edict of Horemheb, erected at Karnak. He added three pylons to the temple complex at Karnak, using recycled talatat blocks from

△ Colorful reliefs on columns in the Osiris Suite of the Temple of Seti I at Abydos

Akhenaten's monuments. He had two tombs: one at Saqqara and the other in the Valley of the Kings, where he was buried.

■ 19TH DYNASTY

(1295–1186 BCE)

Ramesses I (Menpehtyra)
1295–1294 BCE
Seti I (Menmaatra)
1294–1279 BCE
Ramesses II (Usermaatra Setepenra) 1279–1213 BCE
Merenptah (Baenra)
1213–1203 BCE
Amenmesse (Menmira)
1203–1200 BCE
Seti II (Userkheperura Setepenra) 1200–1194 BCE

Siptah (Akehnrasetepenra)
1194–1188 BCE
Twosret (Sitrameritamun)
1188–1186 BCE

Ramesses I
Other name: Menpehtyra

1295–1294 BCE

The first king to carry the name Ramesses was previously vizier to his predecessor, Horemheb. He was not of royal blood—Horemheb seems to have died childless—and was a military officer from a family with its roots in the Nile Delta. It is thought that he was already old when he came to the throne, and his extremely brief reign gave

him almost no time to make his mark on history. He was buried in a small and hastily finished tomb in the Valley of the Kings.

Seti I
Other name: Menmaatra

1294–1279 BCE

In contrast to the almost negligible reign of his father Ramesses I, Seti I left an indelible mark on Egyptian history. He campaigned in Syria, where he fought the Hittites, and in the Western Desert, where he battled Libyan incursions into Egypt. These episodes were recorded on some of the magnificent building projects carried out during his

reign, notably the great Hypostyle Hall in the Temple of Amen at Karnak, where Seti I's reliefs cover the north side. These scenes are executed in a more realistic style than previously seen, showing the influence of Amarna art. However, when Seti built a temple to the god Osiris at Abydos and had it inscribed with a king list, this omitted the Amarna kings, skipping directly from Amenhotep III to Horemheb.

Seti constructed a mortuary temple on the west bank at Thebes and his own splendid tomb in the Valley of the Kings—the longest, deepest, and most finely decorated of any of the kings' tombs.

△ Vast head at the Temple of Luxor, all that remains of a statue of Ramesses II—one of the many statues he commissioned during his reign

Ramesses II
Other name: Usermaatra Setepenra

1279–1213 BCE

From an early age, the boy who would become Ramesses II campaigned with his father Seti I. Once on the throne, he acquired a self-promoted reputation as a great warrior king, with his exploits—notably the significant Battle of Kadesh, against the Hittite armies in Syria—typically celebrated in stone. As a base for these campaigns in the eastern Mediterranean, he established the new capital city of Pr-Ramesses in the Nile Delta, but it was in the south that he left his mark.

He built on a monumental scale, adding to existing great temples at Karnak and Luxor and inscribing his cartouche prominently, even on buildings that he did not construct. On the west bank, he raised the Ramesseum, while at Abu Simbel, he had workers carve out a temple fronted by four colossal seated figures of himself.

Rather than the shallow reliefs of traditional Egyptian art, Ramesses had his masons engrave deeply into the stone, making it much more difficult for them to be erased or usurped later. During his 66-year reign, he ensured his name would live on: he erected more statues of himself than any other king and fathered more than 100 children.

Merenptah
Other name: Baenra

1213–1203 BCE

Merenptah was the 13th son of Ramesses II, who only came to power because all his older brothers had died. By the time he succeeded his long-lived father,

△ Granite sarcophagus from the tomb of Merenptah

he was probably in his late sixties or early seventies. His reign is documented in three inscriptions on a wall at the Temple of Amen at Karnak and on two stelae. They document campaigns Merenptah undertook against the powerful Libyans and other groups, including the Israelites. Although his reign was a relatively brief 10 years, he managed to build a mortuary temple on the west bank at Thebes and a tomb in the Valley of the Kings.

Seti II
Other name: Userkheperura Setepenra

1200–1194 BCE

Seti II was the crown prince and nominated successor to his father Merenptah. He was usurped by Amenmesse, who may have been another son of Merenptah, or even a son of Ramesses II. Some Egyptologists argue that Amenmesse did not succeed Merenptah, but was a rival king who briefly usurped Seti in Upper Egypt sometime around the third year of his reign. What is clear is that once Seti II was in power, he destroyed all traces of his rival.

A papyrus dating from Seti II's rule relates the "Tale of Two Brothers," a story of family conflict following the death of the father, which may have been a satire on the real-life political struggle between Seti and Amenmesse. Due to his short reign, Seti was buried in an only partially completed tomb in the Valley of the Kings.

Twosret
Other name: Sitrameritamun

1188–1186 BCE

Seti II was succeeded by Siptah, whose lineage remains the subject of debate. He was only about 10 years old at the time, so his stepmother, Twosret, royal wife of Seti II, ruled as regent. When Siptah died after just six years as king, Twosret assumed the throne as king in her own right. Her reign was short—just long enough to construct a modest mortuary temple next to the Ramesseum on the west bank at Thebes. It ended in a civil war, recorded in the Elephantine stela of her successor Sethnakht, who possibly overthrew Twosret and became the founder of the 20th Dynasty. He usurped the tomb of Twosret in the Valley of the Kings and replaced all images of the queen with those of himself.

20TH DYNASTY

(1186–1069 BCE)

Sethnakht (Userkhaura
Meryamun) 1186–1184 BCE

**Ramesses III (Usermaatra
Meryamun) 1184–1153 BCE**

**Ramesses IV (Heqamaatra
Setepenamun) 1153–1147 BCE**

Ramesses V (Usermaatra
Sekheperenra) 1147–1143 BCE

**Ramesses VI (Nebmaatra
Meryamun) 1143–1136 BCE**

Ramesses VII (Usermaatra
Setepenra Meryamun)
1136–1129 BCE

Ramesses VIII (Usermaatra
Akhenamun) 1129–1126 BCE

**Ramesses IX (Neferkara
Setepenra) 1126–1108 BCE**

Ramesses X (Khepermaatra
Setepenra) 1108–1099 BCE

**Ramesses XI (Menmaatra
Setepenptah) 1099–1069 BCE**

Ramesses III

**Other name: Usermaatra
Meryamun**

1184–1153 BCE

Ramesses III is generally
considered to be the last of
the great kings to rule Egypt.
He spent much of his 31-year
reign defending Egypt from

△ Remains of the hypostyle hall of Medinet Habu, the mortuary temple of Ramesses III at Luxor

foreign invasion. The main threat
came from the Sea-Peoples, a
coalition of unidentified peoples
that had swept down the eastern
Mediterranean shore.

During the eighth year of his
reign, Ramesses met them in a
great land and sea battle from
which the Egyptians emerged
victorious. He was also forced
to confront at least two Libyan
invasions. At the same time, an

economic crisis in Egypt caused
food rationing and workers'
strikes. There were still funds to
build, however, and Ramesses III's
funerary temple at Medinet
Habu, complete with carved
scenes commemorating his
victories in battle, is one of the
largest built in Egypt.

Ramesses III was assassinated
as a result of the "harem
conspiracy," a plot that was

conducted with the complicity
of a secondary wife and a group
of his court officials.

Ramesses IV

**Other name: Heqamaatra
Setepenamun**

1153–1147 BCE

The first act of Ramesses IV
on assuming the throne was
to punish those who conspired
against and murdered his father,
Ramesses III. He had them tried
and executed. Like the majority
of New Kingdom kings, he
initiated a building program: a
stela at Wadi Hammamat in the
Eastern Desert records that on
one expedition, he sent 8,368
men to quarry stone for building.
He enlarged his father's Temple
of Khonsu at Karnak and began
to build a large, colonnaded
mortuary temple at Deir el-Bahri.
But after a reign of just six years,
he died and was buried in the
Valley of the Kings.

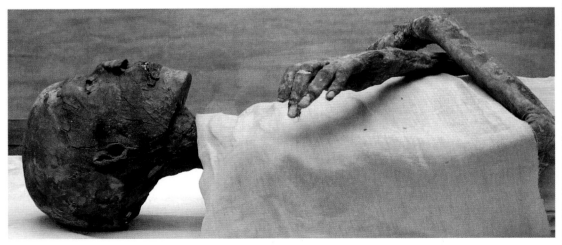

△ The mummy of Ramesses IV has remained intact for thousands of years

Ramesses VI

Other name: Nebmaatra Meryamun

1143–1136 BCE

Ramesses VI was a son of Ramesses III. He ruled in a period characterized by the waning power of the institution of the king and resided in Pr-Ramesses in Lower Egypt.

There were no means for the lavish building projects of old; instead, the king usurped the monuments of past rulers by engraving his cartouche over theirs. In the Valley of the Kings, Ramesses VI claimed a tomb created for his predecessor, Ramesses V, and had it extended and redecorated for himself. In doing so, his workmen covered up the entrance to the tomb of Tutankhamen, saving it from future tomb robbers.

Ramesses IX

Other name: Neferkara Setepenra

1126–1108 BCE

The reigns of both Ramesses VII and VIII were short and marred by instability across the whole of Egypt. Ramesses IX was able to restore a certain degree of order and enjoy some success in his attempts to restore Egypt's power and wealth during a reign that lasted for 18 years.

His building activities were largely centered on the sun-temple center of Heliopolis in Lower Egypt, although he would also leave his mark on the Temple of Amen-Ra at Karnak.

During his reign, tomb robbing in the Valley of the Kings became so common that an inspection of the royal tombs was carried out. As a result of the investigation, several thieves were arrested and subsequently tried.

△ One of many wall murals from the tomb of Ramesses VI in the Valley of the Kings

Ramesses XI

Other name: Menmaatra Setepenptah

1099–1069 BCE

Ramesses XI was the last king of the 20th Dynasty and the final king of the New Kingdom, bringing to a close the most glorious era of ancient Egyptian civilization. He ruled for 30 years, but Egypt was a seriously weakened country, periodically in the grip of famine thanks to poor harvests. He seemed to have spent much of his time in Memphis, and for much of his reign, his authority barely stretched beyond Lower Egypt.

The High Priest of Amen ruled the south from the religious center of Thebes, which itself was drawn into a violent internal power struggle during Ramesses XI's reign. While the king had a tomb prepared in the Valley of the Kings, it was unfinished at the time of his death, and it is not known where he was buried.

Third Intermediate Period (1069–664 BCE)

By the end of the Ramesside Period, strong centralized control had been replaced by the return of regional centers of power, and high priests and kings wrangled for control of the country. Where once kings had ruled over vast foreign territories, Egypt had now become inward-looking. A steady influx of non-Egyptians into the Nile Valley permeated society up to the highest level.

■ 21ST DYNASTY
(1069–945 BCE)

Smendes (Hedjkeperra
   Setepenra) 1069–1043 BCE
Amenemnisu (Neferkara)
   1043–1039 BCE
Psusennes I [Pasebakhaenniut]
   (Akheperra Setepenamun)
   1039–991 BCE
Amenemope (Usermaatra
   Setepenamun) 993–984 BCE
Osorkon the Elder (Akheperra
   Setepenra) 984–978 BCE
Siamun (Netjerkheperra
   Setepenamun) 978–959 BCE
Psusennes II [Pasebakhaenniut]
   (Titkheperura Setepenra)
   959–945 BCE

■ 22ND DYNASTY
(945–715 BCE)

Sheshonq (Hedjkheperra)
Osorkon I (Sekhemkheperra)
Sheshonq II (Heqakheperra)
Takelot I
Osorkon II (Usermaatra)
Takelot II (Hedjkheperra)
Sheshonq III (Usermaatra)
Pimay (Usermaatra)
Sheshonq V (Aakheperra)
Osorkon IV

Sheshonq
Other name: Hedjkheperra

Dates unknown

Sheshonq was of Libyan descent. His ancestors had settled in Egypt during the New Kingdom. Prior to taking the throne, he had served as commander of the Egyptian army and chief advisor to his predecessor, Psusennes II. Sheshonq's reign was a high point in the Third Intermediate Period: he brought the divided factions of Thebes and Tanis together into a loosely unified Egypt.

He cemented his control by making one son governor of Upper Egypt and High Priest of Amen, while another son became military commander at Herakleopolis. Stability at home allowed Sheshonq to pursue aggressive foreign policies, and he campaigned in the Levant, leaving monuments bearing his name at Byblos in what is now Lebanon and at Megiddo in Palestine.

■ 23RD DYNASTY
(818–715 BCE)

Pedubastis I (Usermaatra)
   818–793 BCE
Iuput I 800 BCE
Sheshonq IV 793–787 BCE

△ The ancient city of Tanis, capital of both the 21st and 22nd Dynasties

Osorkon III (Usermaatra)
   787–759 BCE
Takelot III (Usermaatra)
   764–757 BCE
Rudamon (Usermaatra)
   757–754 BCE
Peftjauawybast 740–725 BCE
Iuput II (Usermaatra) 754–712 BCE

■ 24TH DYNASTY
(727–715 BCE)

Tefnakht (Shepsesra)
   727–720 BCE
Bakenrenef (Bocchoris)
   720–715 BCE

■ 25TH DYNASTY
(747–656 BCE)

Piankhy (Menkheperra)
   747–716 BCE
Shabaqo (Neferkara) 716–702 BCE
Shabitqo (Djedkaura) 702–690 BCE
Taharqa (Khunefertemra)
   690–664 BCE
Tantamani (Bakara) 664–656 BCE

Taharqa
Other name: Khunefertemra

690–664 BCE

Taharqa was the fifth in the dynasty of Nubian (Kushite) kings. He was crowned in Memphis, and from Tanis in the Delta he ruled all Egypt, as well as his Nubian kingdom.

His reign was a time of great prosperity, and he built extensively throughout Egypt and Nubia. His army campaigned in the Levant, where it came into conflict with the Assyrian empire. Early victories were followed by later reversals, with the Assyrians capturing Memphis and advancing south as far as Thebes, forcing Taharqa to retreat into Nubia, where he died in 664 BCE.

Late Period (664–332 BCE)

Following rule by the Nubians of the 25th Dynasty, the Late Period was the last era of native Egyptian rule, squeezed between two periods of Persian occupation.

■ 26TH DYNASTY
(664–525 BCE)

Necho I 672–664 BCE
Psamtek I (Wahibra)
 664–610 BCE
Necho II (Wehemibra)
 610–595 BCE
Psamtek II (Neferibra)
 595–589 BCE
Apries (Haaibra) 589–570 BCE
Ahmose II [Amasis]
 (Khnemibra) 570–526 BCE
Psamtek III (Ankhkaenra)
 526–525 BCE

Psamtek I
Other name: Wahibra

664–610 BCE

Psamtek I's father, Necho I, ruled at Sais, in the Delta, when Egypt was occupied by the Assyrians. When Necho I died, the Assyrians recognized his son as king of Egypt, but his power extended no farther than the Delta. Via strategic alliances, he secured the support of Thebes and raised an army aided by Greek mercenaries to break the Assyrians' hold, becoming absolute ruler of Egypt by 656 BCE.

After consolidating Egypt, Psamtek made expeditions into northern Nubia to discourage any further ambitions of the Kushite kings. He would also ally with old enemies, the Assyrians, to confront the growing threat of the Babylonians.

■ 27TH DYNASTY (1ST PERSIAN PERIOD)
(525–404 BCE)

Cambyses 525–522 BCE
Darius I 522–486 BCE
Xerxes I 486–465 BCE
Artaxerxes I 465–424 BCE
Darius II 424–405 BCE
Artaxerxes II 405–359 BCE

■ 28TH DYNASTY
(404–399 BCE)

Amyrtaios 404–399 BCE

■ 29TH DYNASTY
(399–380 BCE)

Nepherites I [Nefaarud]
 399–393 BCE
Hakor [Achoris]
 [Khnemmaatra] 393–380 BCE
Nepherites II c.380 BCE

Nepherites I
Other name: Nefaarud

399–393 BCE

Amyrtaios, a native Egyptian, revolted against the Persians; with the assistance of Cretan mercenaries, he succeeded in expelling them from his country, at which point he proclaimed himself king. Little else is known about Amyrtaios except that five years into his reign, he was challenged by a general from the Delta city of Mendes. Amyrtaios was defeated in battle, and the victor went on to proclaim himself king under the name Nepherites I. The new king's reign was hardly any longer than that of his predecessor, but he did raise monuments across the country, and his name is mentioned in an inscription at the Serapeum at Saqqara in connection to the cult of the sacred Apis bull.

▷ Funerary figure or shabti bearing the name of Nepherites I, found in a tomb that may have belonged to the king

■ 30TH DYNASTY
(380–343 BCE)

Nectanebo I [Kheperkara]
380–362 BCE

Teos (Irma atenra) 362–360 BCE

Nectanebo II (Senedjemibra setepenanhur) 360–343 BCE

Nectanebo I
Other name: Kheperkara

380–362 BCE

Nectanebo was an army general. A stela found at Hermopolis suggests he came to power by overthrowing his predecessor, Nepherites II, the last king of the 29th Dynasty. Early in Nectanebo's reign, Egypt was invaded by a combined Persian and Greek army of over 200,000 troops; although the Egyptians suffered an initial defeat, they were able to make a successful counterattack and repel the invaders. After this, Nectanebo seems to have had a stable reign.

Another stela records how 10 percent of all taxes were to be used to fund temple building and support the priesthood. Nectanebo restored previously damaged or neglected monuments across the country; he also initiated many new buildings, including the Temple of Isis at Philae. Nectanebo was succeeded by his son, Teos.

Nectanebo II
Other name: Senedjemibra Setepenanhur

360–343 BCE

Nectanebo II was the last native ruler of ancient Egypt. It is probable that he seized power when his predecessor and uncle, Teos, was campaigning against the Persians in Palestine and

Syria. Nectanebo was able to do this by leveraging the support of the priests, who were unhappy at the heavy taxes imposed by Teos to fund his war. Nectanebo maintained the support of the priests by engaging in acts of piety—he began his reign by participating in the burial of a sacred Apis bull—and building many temples and religious sanctuaries, including those at Heliopolis, Athribis, and Bubastis. In about 351 BCE, the Persians invaded in an attempt to reclaim Egypt; after a year of fighting, in which Egypt was aided by its Greek allies, they were repelled. In 343 BCE, the Persians returned. This time, at the Battle of Pelusium, Nectanebo was defeated; he fled to Nubia and the Persians took control over Egypt for a second time.

■ 31ST DYNASTY (2ND PERSIAN PERIOD)
(343–332 BCE)

Artaxerxes III Ochus 343–338 BCE

Arses 338–336 BCE

Darius III Codoman 336–332 BCE

The Greco-Roman Period (332 BCE–395 CE)

The Greeks came to Egypt not as conquerors, but as liberators from Persian rule. During a roughly 300-year period of rule by kings largely named Ptolemy, Egypt became a fusion of Greek and Egyptian cultures. Toward the end of the period, a third culture was added to the mix: Roman.

■ MACEDONIAN DYNASTY
(332–310 BCE)

Alexander the Great
332–323 BCE

Philip Arrhidaeus 323–317 BCE

Alexander IV 317–310 BCE

Alexander the Great

332–323 BCE

After the assassination of Philip II of Macedonia in 336 BCE, his 20-year-old son Alexander took up his father's fight against the Persians. He defeated the army of Darius III at Issus in 333 BCE and entered Egypt the following year. At the oasis of Siwa, he consulted the oracle of Ammon and was hailed as the god's son and king. On the Mediterranean coast, he founded a city named for himself: Alexandria. He would not remain in Egypt long, but he initiated a rebuilding of monuments damaged by the Persians, and he appears in reliefs in the sanctuary at Luxor Temple. On leaving Egypt, he embarked on a series of campaigns that extended his empire all the way to the Indus River on the borders of India. He

△ Alexander the Great in a detail from a Roman mosaic depicting the Battle of Issus

died of fever in Babylon in 323 BCE. His funeral cortege, which was bound for Macedonia, was seized and redirected to Egypt, where his body was eventually laid to rest in Alexandria. The location of his tomb remains unknown.

■ PTOLEMAIC DYNASTY
(305–30 BCE)

Ptolemy I Soter I
305–285 BCE
Ptolemy II Philadelphus
285–246 BCE
Berenike II 246–221 BCE
Ptolemy III Euergetes I
246–221 BCE
Ptolemy IV Philopator
221–205 BCE
Ptolemy V Epiphanes
205–180 BCE
Ptolemy VI Philometor
180–145 BCE
Ptolemy VII Neos Philopator
145 BCE
Ptolemy VIII Euergetes II
170–116 BCE
Ptolemy IX Soter II
116–107 BCE
Ptolemy X Alexander I
107–88 BCE
Ptolemy IX Soter II (restored)
88–80 BCE
Ptolemy XI Alexander II 80 BCE
Ptolemy XII Neos Dionysos (Auletes) 80–51 BCE
Cleopatra VII Philopator
51–30 BCE
Ptolemy XIII 51–47 BCE
Ptolemy XIV 47–44 BCE
Ptolemy XV Caesarion 44–30 BCE

Ptolemy I Soter I

305–285 BCE

Ptolemy was a childhood friend of Alexander and one of his trusted generals. On Alexander's death, he hijacked the body and took it with him to Egypt as a means of legitimizing his rule in that country. Externally, much of his reign was spent warring with other former generals and would-be successors of Alexander to establish, maintain, and expand their kingdoms. Ptolemy married several times, notably into prominent Macedonian dynasties in order to cement valuable alliances. Within Egypt, he presented himself as a king and paid respect to the old gods and priesthood. He looked to consolidate the religions of the Egyptians and Greeks by promoting the worship of a new god named Serapis, who was a composite made up of both Egyptian and Greek gods. It was probably Ptolemy who began the construction of the Pharos lighthouse and the Mouseion, Alexandria's great library and center of learning.

△ Pharos of Alexandria, the lighthouse that may have been partially built by Ptolemy I Soter I

△ Bronze bust of Ptolemy II Philadelphus, during whose rule the city of Alexandria flourished

Ptolemy II Philadelphus

285–246 BCE

Ptolemy II was the son of Ptolemy I. Like many kings before him, he fought campaigns in Syria against the Seleucids, defended Egypt from Libyan incursions, and clashed with Nubia. Egypt was the dominant naval power in the eastern Mediterranean at the time, with a sphere of authority that extended all the way up into the northern Aegean.

Under Ptolemy II's rule, Alexandria reached new heights of technical and intellectual splendor as he completed the Pharos lighthouse and extended the Mouseion, the great library. He undertook building work throughout Egypt, including at Philae, and founded ports on the Red Sea, through which Egypt established trade links with India. Ptolemy II also commissioned an Egyptian priest, Manetho, to compile a history of this already ancient land.

Ptolemy III Euergetes I

246–221 BCE

Immediately on ascending to the throne on the death of his father, Ptolemy III was drawn into a war with the Seleucids. For the five years that he campaigned, he left his wife Berenike II to be the head of state in Egypt. She was the daughter of King Magas of Cyrene, a woman who possibly had her first husband assassinated for infidelity and who raced victorious chariot teams in games. According to a legend that arose much later, Berenike had vowed to sacrifice her long hair to the gods if Ptolemy III returned safely from battle; the shorn hair disappeared from the temple where it was placed, only to reappear in the heavens as the constellation of stars known as Coma Berenices (Latin for Berenike's Lock). Ptolemy III is credited with beginning the Temple of Horus at Edfu, but it wasn't completed until the time of Ptolemy XII.

Ptolemy XII Neos Dionysos

80–51 BCE

Ptolemy XII was the illegitimate son of Ptolemy IX who came to the throne after Ptolemy XI was lynched by the people when he murdered his popular queen after just 19 days of marriage. He wanted to legitimize his tenuous rule by gaining the approval of Rome. He spent heavily on bribing Roman officials to support him, using money gained by raising Egyptian taxes. This, and his subservience to Rome, made the Egyptian people rise up, and Ptolemy fled across the Mediterranean.

He was replaced on the Egyptian throne by his daughter Berenike IV. After three years, Ptolemy returned to Egypt with a Roman army, executed his daughter, and ruled until his death in 51 BCE. He was succeeded by a younger daughter, Cleopatra VII.

Cleopatra VII Philopator

51–30 BCE

Cleopatra became queen of Egypt at the age of 18. She possibly married her brother, Ptolemy XIII, but unquestionably refused to share the throne with him. The ensuing sibling conflict was resolved by the arrival of Roman general Julius Caesar in Alexandria, who settled in favor of the young queen. Cleopatra then married her younger brother, Ptolemy XIV, and also became Caesar's lover. After Caesar's death, Egypt became a pawn in the struggle for power between Octavian and Mark Antony, with Cleopatra supporting the latter.

When Octavian triumphed at the Battle of Actium and entered Egypt the following year, Cleopatra committed suicide. Although popular legend attributes her with great beauty, she was above all highly intelligent and a skilled politician. She was also said to be the only Ptolemaic ruler who could speak Egyptian.

△ Cleopatra VII and her son, Caeserion, presenting offerings to the gods in a relief on the Temple of Hathor at Dendera

Deities

Gods and goddesses of ancient Egypt

It is thought that the ancient Egyptians had around 1,500 gods and goddesses during the 3,000 years of their dynastic history. The deities are difficult to count, because some of them had multiple names, while others merged to create multiple personae. As time went by, many gods waned in importance and new, sometimes foreign deities joined the pantheon.

A

Aker

An ancient earth god who guarded the gate to the underworld. He allowed the king to enter it and protected him from demonic serpents. Aker dated back to the Early Dynastic Period and was described in the Pyramid Texts. The earliest depictions show him as a strip of land, with two heads representing the entrance and exit of the underworld. Later, he was shown as sphinx, with two heads facing away from each other.

Amaunet

The female counterpart and a consort of Amen, and one of the eight primeval deities known as the Ogdoad that were worshipped at Hermopolis Magna. Amaunet is usually shown in human form, wearing the red crown of Lower Egypt, even though she was not worshipped much beyond Thebes. A colossal statue of her that was erected in Tutankhamen's reign is still standing in the Record Hall of Tuthmosis III at Karnak.

Amen

Also written as Amun, Amen was one of the most important gods of ancient Egypt. He was first mentioned in the Pyramid Texts and was a member of the Hermopolitan Ogdoad—the eight primordial deities worshipped in Hermopolis. He appeared as a local god in the Theban region in the 12th Dynasty, when four kings all took the name Amenemhet, meaning "Amen is preeminent."

As the chief deity of Egypt, Amen was also worshipped beyond the Nile valley, within the Egyptian empire, including Nubia. He is usually depicted in human form wearing a short kilt and a double-plumed crown. He is also sometimes depicted as a ram.

Amen-Kamutef

As Amen-Kamutef, Amen was the first primeval god, who took the form of a snake to fertilize the first egg. Karnak Temple was said to occupy the site where Amen brought the world into being.

Amen-Min

From the 12th Dynasty, Amen was portrayed in an ithyphallic form as a fertility god and took on the identity of Min to become Amen-Min. An alternative name for this incarnation was Amen-Kamutef, meaning "Bull of his mother," a reference to his strength and potency.

Amen-Ra

As the cult of Amen grew, he was linked with the sun god Ra, the previous principal god of Egyptian kings. Eventually, he merged with Ra to become the all-powerful Amun-Ra.

△ Wall painting in Tuthmosis III's temple at Thebes showing him making an offering to Amen-Ra

△ Tomb painting depicting Anubis preparing the deceased for his journey to the afterlife

Ammit

Also spelled Ammut, Ammit was a composite creature made up of the most dangerous animals known to the ancient Egyptians: the head of a crocodile, the forelegs and body of a lion (or leopard), and the hindquarters of a hippopotamus.

Her name meant "Eater of the damned," and she supposedly devoured those who had led wicked lives and were not to be admitted into the afterlife. More demon than deity, she was feared rather than worshipped. She appears in funerary texts, such as the *Book of the Dead*.

Anath

Also spelled Anat, Anath was a deity introduced into Egypt from the Near East. She became popular in Egypt during the Middle Kingdom, notably during the Hyksos' period of rule. She was a fiercesome warrior goddess, and Ramesses II adopted her as his personal guardian in battle. She was also a goddess of fertility and sexuality and was regarded as the daughter of Ra and the wife of Seth. She was worshipped in Memphis and Tanis and was usually depicted as a human with a plumed crown and wielding a spear or battleaxe.

Andjety

An early minor god, Andjety was the local deity of the Lower Egyptian nome centered at Busiris in the Delta. In the Pyramid Texts, he is described as "Lord of the Dead" and as a god of rebirth. These roles were eventually usurped by Osiris, who also adopted some of the iconography that had previously been associated with Andjety, such as the crook and flail.

Anti

Also known as Nemty, Anti was a falcon-headed god whose cult center was at Tjebu (later known as Antaeopolis) in Middle Egypt. A ferryman who transported Ra and other gods, he was often depicted in a stylized boat that looked like a crescent moon.

Anubis

Also known as Anpu or Inpu, Anubis was the jackal-headed protector of graves and the dead as far back as the Early Dynastic Period. He was present at the Weighing of the Heart ceremony, which determined whether a soul would be allowed to enter the realm of the dead. He then admitted the innocent to the afterlife or abandoned the guilty to Ammit. He was also the god of embalming. His head was always black—rather than brown, as in real jackals—because black symbolized the regeneration made possible by the black, fertile soil of the Nile.

Anukis

The goddess Anukis (also known as Anuket) was worshipped in the area around the First Cataract, close to what is now Aswan, as well as farther south in Nubia. Along with Khnum and Satet, she was one of the triad of gods worshipped on Elephantine Island.

Every year, a Festival of Anukis was held when the Nile began to flood, during which people threw gifts into the river to please the goddess. She was usually depicted as a woman wearing a tall headdress made of ostrich plumes.

Apophis

Whereas Ra was the bringer of light, Apophis was a great serpent that represented darkness and nonexistence. According to mythic texts, just before dawn each day, Apophis attacked Ra as he emerged from the underworld in his solar barque, and the serpent had to be defeated.

Astarte

The Syro-Canaanite equivalent of the Babylonian goddess Ishtar, Astarte joined the pantheon of Egyptian gods during the 18th Dynasty. She was a goddess of love and fertility, but also of war, and she was worshipped in Egypt primarily as a warrior goddess. She was linked to the use of horses and chariots and was believed to protect the king's chariot during battles.

Aten

The Aten was the solar disk, or sun. By the middle of the New Kingdom, people worshipped the Aten as a sun god and he was depicted as a falcon-headed man, similar to Ra. During Amenhotep IV's reign, the Aten became the central god of the Egyptian state religion, and Amenhotep IV changed his name to Akhenaten, meaning "Effective for the Aten."

In Akhenaten's reign, the Aten was depicted as a solar disk with a uraeus (royal cobra) at its base. Its sun rays were like arms stretching to the Earth and each ray had a hand, often holding out an ankh, representing life.

△ Wall painting in the tomb of Ramesses I showing Atum fighting the serpent Apophis, the enemy of the sun

Atum

Atum was the first god, who arose at the beginning of time having created himself out of nothing. With his semen (or saliva), he also created two offspring, Shu and Tefnut, who in turn gave birth to the Earth (Geb) and the sky (Nut). As father of the gods, Atum was also the father of the kings.

Atum was a creator god. He was worshipped alongside Ra at Heliopolis, which means the "City of the Sun." Atum is usually depicted wearing the double crown of Upper and Lower Egypt. He is often shown sitting on a throne.

B

Babi

Dating back to the Old Kingdom, Babi was a baboon god and the guardian of the sky. He was aggressive and bloodthirsty and was said to live off the entrails of the dead. He was also considered to be a god of virility who ensured that the deceased were able to have sexual intercourse in the afterlife.

Banebdjedet

A ram god about whom very little is known, Banebdjedet (Banebdjed) had a cult center at Mendes, in the northeast Delta, during the Late Period.

He was known in the New Kingdom and is mentioned in reliefs at the temple of Ramesses III at Medinet Habu, where the god was claimed to be the king's father.

△ Bronze statuette of Bastet dating from the Late Ptolemaic Period

Bastet

In her earliest form, dating back to the Early Dynastic Period, Bastet was depicted as a woman with the head of a lioness. By the Middle Kingdom, she had become a cat-headed woman instead. Her character changed accordingly, from being a dangerous, warlike deity to one who was protective. Bastet's cult was based at Bubastis in the eastern Delta. Her priests kept cats in her temple, which were regarded as sacred and therefore mummified when they died.

Bastet was often depicted holding a sistrum (the sacred rattle of Hathor) and an ankh.

Bat

Bat (or Bata) was an early cow goddess and an important deity in the Predynastic Period. Her name is the feminine form of the word *ba*, the name of one of the major elements of the soul. She may have been the deity depicted on the Narmer Palette, but she was rarely shown otherwise.

Hathor and Bat may have been the same deity worshipped in different regions of Egypt. Bat was linked to the 7th Upper Egyptian nome, the area around modern Nag Hammadi in Middle Egypt. By the beginning of the New Kingdom, Bat had been superseded by Hathor.

Bes

A dwarflike demigod, Bes was not worshipped at temples and had no priests, but he was greatly valued as a protector of women and children, and he provided protection from snakes. He became a god of childbirth, able to scare off evil spirits, and often appeared in reliefs on the walls of mammisi (birth houses).

He was often depicted on household items, including bedheads, to protect those asleep, and on jewelry and amulets. He had a squat appearance, enlarged head, and masklike features, as well as a beard that curled into

△ Detail of a limestone relief of a ram-headed god from the Early Ptolemaic Period

spirals. His appearance might have been inspired by that of a male lion rearing up on its hind legs.

F

Four Sons of Horus

The Four Sons of Horus were four deities who personified the four canopic jars used during mummification and guarded the organs removed from the body. They were the human-headed Imseti (guardian of the liver), baboon-headed Hapi (lungs), the dog-headed Duamutef (stomach), and falcon-headed Qebehsenuef (guardian of the intestines).

G

Geb

One of the original gods, Geb was the son of Shu and Tefnut and the grandson of Atum, the self-created creator god. Geb personified the Earth. His worship began during the Predynastic Period, and his importance as one of the primeval gods is shown by the number of times that he is mentioned in the Pyramid Texts.

Geb was usually depicted as a man wearing the crown of Lower Egypt or as a man reclining on his side. He is sometimes green in color, with plants growing from his body, and he lies beneath the sky goddess Nut—who was his sister and his wife. He was occasionally portrayed as a goose—a bird that was often linked with creation— or as a man with a goose upon his head.

△ Wall painting from a tomb in the Valley of Kings depicting Horus (with a falcon head) and Geb

H

Hapi

The god Hapi (not the son of Horus, who had the same name) was the god of the inundation, the annual Nile flood that made the Nile Valley fertile. He was worshipped throughout Egypt but was particularly popular around Aswan and Gebel Silsila. Hapi is usually shown as a man with a swollen belly, drooping female breasts, and long hair. He often has blue skin and a clump of papyrus on his head. He was also depicted as the twin deities Hap-Reset (Upper Egypt) and Hap-Mehyt (Lower Egypt), shown either pouring water from a jug (representing the inundation) or tying together the symbolic plants of the two lands—the papyrus and lotus.

Harpocrates

In Ptolemaic Alexandria, Harpocrates was the infant son of Isis and Serapis. He was the Greek version of the Egyptian infant god Horus the Child, or *Har-pa-khered*, from which the name Harpocrates comes. In the Pyramid Texts, he is referred to as the "child with his finger in his mouth," which is how he was often depicted. The Greeks mistook this for a gesture of silence, so they made Harpocrates the god of secrets.

Hathor

One of ancient Egypt's greatest deities, Hathor was an ancient cow goddess closely connected to the sun god Ra and said to be his wife or daughter. Her name was written as a hieroglyph of a falcon within a walled building, *hwt hor*, meaning the "House of Horus," or mother of the falcon god. She had many roles, but, often described as the "Beautiful one," she was best known as the goddess of love, motherhood, and female sexuality.

Hathor worship was well established by the Old Kingdom, and her most important cult center was at Dendera. She was usually portrayed as a woman wearing a long wig, with a sun disk held between curved cow horns above her head, and often appears in a red sheath dress. She was also depicted as a woman with the head of a cow or as a cow with a face that was a blend of the human and the bovine.

Hatmehit

Her name means "She who is before the fishes," and Hatmehit was Egypt's only entirely piscine deity. She was worshipped in the Delta, particularly in Mendes, and was depicted as a fish or as a woman with a fish emblem on her head.

△ Tomb painting of the burial gods Kebehsenenuef, Hapi, and Imseti with the god Osiris (right)

△ Stone head of the goddess Hathor

Hauhet and Heh

Hauhet (female) and Heh (male) were two of the eight primeval deities, or Ogdoad, that were worshipped at Hermopolis Magna. They were the dual personifications of infinity. Heh is usually depicted kneeling with a notched palm branch in each hand—notched branches such as these were used for recording time in temples. In hieroglyphics, the figure of Heh was used to denote 1 million. Very little is known about the snake-headed goddess Hauhet.

Heka

Heka, whose name means "Using the *ka*," was the god of magic, or creative energy. He was believed to be the son of Khnum and Menhet, and the three formed the triad of Latopolis (Esna) in Upper Egypt.

Heka helped the sun god Ra on his daily journey across the sky by warding off evil spirits and demons. He was not served by a regular cult, but doctors were called "priests of Heka." He was usually depicted as a man, but in the Late Period, he was worshipped in the form of a child.

Heket

A frog midwife, Heket was a goddess of childbirth and fertility. She is mentioned as early as the Pyramid Texts. Pregnant women wore amulets depicting Heket for protection, and it is thought that her priestesses were trained midwives. She was depicted as a frog or as a woman with a frog's head. She appears beside Khnum, the creator god, in the birth colonnade at the mortuary temple of Hatshepsut. Khnum created each person on his potter's wheel and Heket breathed life into them.

Heryshef

The name of the ram god Heryshef means "He who is on his lake," which suggests that he was a god of creation who emerged from the waters of Nun. He was associated with Osiris and Ra and was known as the *ba* of these gods.

His cult dates as far back as the Early Period and was centered at Herakleopolis Magna. Ramesses II enlarged his temple there in the New Kingdom. Heryshef took the form of a king with the head of a long-horned ram. He wore the *atef* crown when associated with Osiris and the sun disk when linked with Ra.

△ Piece of a coffin depicting the god Heh kneeling and holding up two *renpet* (years) symbols

△ Wall painting from 1069–664 BCE depicting a harpist worshipping the god Ra-Horakhty, shown here with the head of a hawk

Hesat

Hesat was a cow goddess thought to be the earthly manifestation of Hathor. She was believed to provide humanity with milk (called "The beer of Hesat") and to suckle the king. She was connected with Mnevis, the living bull god worshipped at Heliopolis. Hesat was depicted as a divine white cow either with a sun disk between her horns or carrying a tray of food on her horns, and with milk flowing from her udders.

Horakhty

With a name meaning "Horus of the two horizons," Horakhty was an aspect of Horus specifically linked to the rising and setting sun. More specifically, he was the god of the east and the sunrise. He was eventually drawn into the sun-god cult of Heliopolis and fused with its solar god to become Ra-Horakhty.

Horakhty was usually depicted as a falcon or as a man with a falcon's head. He wore the solar disk and the double crown, or alternatively, the *atef* crown and the uraeus.

Horemakhet

As "Horus in the horizon," Horemakhet was another sun-god aspect of Horus. In this guise, he was often depicted as a sphinx with the head of a man, a lion, or a ram (the latter providing a link to the god Khepri, who represented the rising sun). The Sphinx at Giza may have been a representation of Horemakhet with the face of the 4th Dynasty king Khaefre.

Horus

Horus was one of the earliest Egyptian gods, first appearing in the Early Dynastic Period. The name Horus is Greek—in ancient Egyptian, the god was called Hr (or *Har* or *Hor*), which means "The distant one" or "The one on high." He was worshipped in many forms and assimilated many other gods, but his original form was as lord of the sky.

Horus was the son of Isis and Osiris. After Seth murdered Osiris (who was then the king of Egypt), Horus fought Seth for the throne. As the rightful heir, Horus was the god of kingship, and Egyptian kings were thought to be the living incarnation of him.

There were many sites associated with the worship of Horus, but he was closely associated with Nekhen, also known as Hierakonpolis, the "City of the Hawk." In the Delta region of Lower Egypt, he was worshipped at Khem (the Greek Letopolis), where he was known as Horus Khenty-khem, the "Foremost one of Khem."

I

Iah

Iah means "Moon," and he was a lunar god. He was an early deity, and he is mentioned in the Pyramid Texts, but later he was overshadowed by other, more prominent lunar gods, such as Khonsu and Thoth. He was depicted as a man wearing the symbols of the full and crescent moons.

Ihy

Ihy (or Ahy) was a child god associated with playing the sistrum (a sacred rattle). The sistrum was closely connected with the goddess Hathor, who was said to be Ihy's mother ("calf" is another meaning of Ihy). In the Coffin Texts and Book of the Dead, Ihy is referred to as the "Lord of bread" and "Master of brewing." He did not have any temples specifically dedicated to him but was worshipped at the Temple of Hathor at Dendera. He was depicted as a young boy wearing the sidelock of youth, with his finger held to his mouth and a sistrum in his right hand.

Imhotep

A real person, Imhotep was the vizier to the 3rd Dynasty king Djoser, for whom he oversaw the construction of the Step Pyramid complex at Saqqara. Among his other achievements, he may have been a skilled physician, because he was considered a demigod of healing after his death. Because of his scholarship, he was also linked with the cult of Thoth, the god of knowledge and writing.

The worship of Imhotep was particularly strong in the Greco-Roman Period, when his cult centers attracted the sick. He was usually depicted with a shaven head, wearing a long kilt, and with a papyrus roll on his lap.

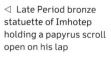

◁ Late Period bronze statuette of Imhotep holding a papyrus scroll open on his lap

Isis

The devoted sister-wife of Osiris and mother of Horus, Isis was Egypt's most powerful goddess. Her origins are unclear, but she appears many times in the 5th Dynasty Pyramid Texts. Over time, her importance grew, and she took on the attributes of many other goddesses. For much of ancient Egyptian history, she was not worshipped in her own temples but in those of other deities with whom she was associated. The first dedicated temples to Isis appeared in the 30th Dynasty, which was also when her most famous temple, at Philae, was begun. Isis worship subsequently spread around the eastern Mediterranean and throughout the Greek and Roman empires. She was usually depicted as a woman in a long sheath dress and crowned with the hieroglyphic throne symbol, or later, with the horns and solar disk appropriated from Hathor. She is also often shown kneeling with winged arms outstretched.

The image of Isis and the infant Horus was also popular in Egyptian art, and this may have influenced the iconography of Mary and the infant Jesus Christ in the early Christian Church.

K

Kauket and Kek

Kauket (female) and Kek (male) were two of the eight primeval deities, or Ogdoad, that were worshipped at Hermopolis Magna. They were the dual personifications of the chaotic darkness that existed before the

△ Detail of a wall painting in the Tomb of Horemheb showing Hathor facing the king

creation of the world. Kek was also associated with the dawn and given the epithet the "Bringer-in of the light," while Kauket was associated with the dusk and given the epithet "Bringer-in of the night."

Kek was depicted as a frog or as a man with a frog's head, and Kauket was depicted as a snake or a snake-headed woman.

Khentyamentiu

Meaning the "Foremost of the Westerners," this was the name of the original canine god of the necropolis at Abydos and patron of its Old Kingdom temple. "Westerners" was another name for the dead, because most of the Egyptian cemeteries were located on the western bank of the Nile, the symbolic direction of the setting sun and the underworld. In time, Khentyamentiu was superseded by Anubis.

Khepri

Khepri was a beetle god and represented the rising morning sun. He was undoubtedly inspired by the dung beetle, which rolls a ball of mud along the ground, suggesting the god pushing the solar disk across the sky. He was swallowed by the sky goddess Nut in the evening, then traveled through her body at night and was born again in the morning. As a result, Khepri was strongly associated with rebirth and resurrection, and scarab amulets were placed over the heart of the deceased during the mummification ritual.

Khepri did not have a cult of his own, but he was worshipped in many Egyptian temples. He was usually depicted as a scarab

△ The goddesses Isis and Nephthys sail in the solar boat with Khepri

beetle, sometimes pushing a solar disk, but he was occasionally also shown as a man with the head of a scarab beetle.

Khnum

Khnum was an important ram god, closely associated with the River Nile and the creation of life. One of the most ancient gods, he was worshipped as early as the Predynastic Period. Khnum was associated with the First Cataract of the Nile and was thought to control the annual inundation of the river from there. This deposited the fertile

black silt in which the Egyptians grew their crops. The silt also formed the clay from which the god molded all living things on his potter's wheel.

The cult of Khnum was based on Elephantine Island in what is now Aswan, near the First Cataract. He was worshipped there as head of a triad with his wife Satet and daughter Anukis. He was also worshipped at Esna. Khnum was depicted either as a ram or as a man with the head of a ram. He was sometimes shown with a potter's wheel or holding a jar with water flowing out of it, indicating his association with the source of the Nile.

Khonsu

Khonsu was a lunar god and a member of the all-powerful Theban triad, with Amen and Mut, venerated at their cult center at Thebes. As well as being associated with the moon, he was also a god of time and was believed to help women conceive children, livestock to breed, plants to grow, and fruit to ripen.

Khonsu is usually depicted as a young man in the pose of a mummy. He wears the sidelock of youth and a lunar disk resting in a crescent moon on his head. He often carries a crook and flail.

△ Detail of a 30th Dynasty mummy's cartonnage from Saqqara depicting winged Maat with a solar disk

M

Maat

The goddess Maat is the personification of the concept of *maat*, or cosmic order. She existed as early as the Old Kingdom and was mentioned in the Pyramid Texts. As well as combating chaos, she also played a role in the Weighing of the Heart ceremony—her feather was the measure that determined whether a soul could pass into the afterlife. She was depicted as a goddess wearing a tall ostrich feather on her head or was represented by the feather alone. Rulers were often depicted with emblems of Maat to emphasize their righteousness and their role in upholding justice.

Mehen

Mehen was a coiled serpent that protected Ra on his nightly journey through the underworld. The Coffin Texts describe the serpent god as being nine concentric rings that encircle the sun god.

Mehet-Weret

Her name means "Great flood," and Mehet-Weret was a cow goddess who was born from the waters of creation. Mehet-Weret was said to have given birth to the sun god Ra in the primeval marsh and then lifted him up into the sky between her horns. She represented the vast waterway of the sky upon which the sun god and the king sailed.

Menhyt

Menhyt (or Menhit, Menkhet) was a lesser-known lioness-headed goddess, possibly originating in Nubia. A war goddess who led the king's troops into battle, she was worshipped at Esna in Upper Egypt and in the Delta. Depictions show her wearing a solar disk and uraeus.

Meretseger

A goddess with a very specific role, Meretseger guarded the Theban necropolis. Her name appropriately meant "She who loves silence," but she was also known as Dehenet-Imentet, "Peak of the west," a reference to the pyramidal peak at the head of the Valley of the Kings. She was primarily worshipped by the workers at the necropolis, many of whom lived at Deir el-Medina, where numerous stelae devoted to the goddess have been found.

Meretseger was believed to punish those who committed crimes by blinding the offenders or inflicting poisonous snake or scorpion bites, so she was variously depicted as a cobra, a cobra with the head of a woman, or a snake with three heads (a woman, a cobra, and a vulture).

Meskhenet

A goddess of childbirth and a divine midwife, Meskhenet determined the destiny of the newborn, according to Egyptian mythology. She had no cult following, and there were no temples specifically dedicated to her, but she appeared on birthing bricks on which ancient Egyptian women squatted while giving birth. In ancient Egyptian iconography, she was represented by a birthing brick, sometimes with a human head. She was also shown as a woman wearing a columnar hat with two loops at the top representing a uterus.

Min

One of Egypt's most ancient deities, Min was an ithyphallic god of creation linked with male potency whose worship dated back to the Predynastic Period. Some of the earliest large-scale statues found in Egypt were images of Min. He was a god of the Eastern Desert and the protector of traveling caravans. He was also a god of fertility and sexuality. At the beginning of the harvest season, Min's statue was carried through the fields in a festival known as "The departure of Min." His cult center was Coptos (present-day Qift), the capital of the fifth nome of Upper Egypt.

Min was usually depicted as a mummiform human with an erect penis, wearing a crown with two large feathers. In his right hand, he held a flail up above his shoulder. His skin was black, like the fertile soil of the Nile. He was often shown standing in front of tables of Egyptian long-leaf lettuce. This was regarded as an aphrodisiac, because if you broke off a leaf, it oozed a milky substance that resembled semen.

◁ Limestone ostracon showing the workman Khnummose worshipping the snake goddess Meretseger

Mnevis bull

The Mnevis (known to Egyptians as *Mer-wer*) was the sacred bull of Heliopolis, regarded as the earthly manifestation of Ra. The bull was black all over, without any markings, and there would only be one Mnevis bull at any one time. When it died, it was honored with a burial in a special cemetery.

Montu

Montu was the falcon-headed warrior god who was the personification of the conquering spirit of kings. He was regarded as the Upper Egyptian counterpart of Ra of Heliopolis and was worshipped as the combined Montu-Ra, a god with the destructive power of the sun. Four rulers of the 11th Dynasty adopted the name Montuhotep, meaning "Montu is content."

Montu was mainly worshipped at Thebes, where his temple complex was part of the sacred precincts of Karnak. There was another temple dedicated to him, the earliest parts of which dated back to the Old Kingdom, at Medamud, northeast of Karnak. As Amen became more important at Thebes, Montu's prominence waned, but he continued to be popular with warrior kings such as Tuthmosis III and Ramesses II. Montu was often depicted in human form with a falcon's head, wearing a headdress of two long plumes, a solar disk, and the double uraeus. He sometimes carried a weapon to symbolize his warlike nature. Because of his links to bull cults, he was also depicted with the head of a bull.

Mut

Mut was the mother goddess of Thebes, the consort of Amen, and the mother of Khonsu. Together, they formed the all-powerful Theban triad of deities, who rose to prominence during the Middle Kingdom. Mut's origins are unknown, but she was probably a minor deity who replaced Amaunet, Amen's original wife, as time went by and became the god's new chief wife. When her husband merged with the sun god to become Amen-Ra, Mut inherited the title the "Eye of Ra."

She was associated with the lioness and was the southern counterpart of the northern lioness goddess Sekhmet. Mut was worshipped at her temple complex at Thebes, at Heliopolis and Tanis, and in the Western Desert oases of Dakhla and Kharga. She was sometimes

△ Detail of a wall relief showing the god Montu holding an ankh up to the face of Alexander the Great

depicted as a lioness-headed goddess or as a woman wearing a vulture headdress surmounted by either the white crown of Upper Egypt or the double crown of the combined Two Lands.

N

Naunet

Naunet was the feminine counterpart of Nun. Together, they were two of the eight primeval deities, or Ogdoad, that were worshipped at Hermopolis Magna.

Nebethetepet

A female counterpart of the creator god Atum, Nebethetepet was a minor Heliopolitan goddess. Her name meant "Lady of the offerings" or "Mistress of contentment."

Nefertem

The youthful god Nefertem was the personification of the blue lotus flower (*nymphaea cerulea*) that emerged from the primeval waters. Unsurprisingly, he was also the god of perfume. He was linked with Ra, the sun god, who also emerged from a lotus, and is referred to in the Pyramid Texts as "The lotus blossom that is before the nose of Ra."

At Memphis, Nefertem formed a triad with the god Ptah and his wife Sekhmet and was thought to be their son. He was usually portrayed as a beautiful young man wearing a lotus blossom on his head. He was sometimes shown as a lion-headed god (possibly in reference to his

△ Wall painting from the tomb of Horemheb at Thebes depicting Nefertem wearing a lotus headdress

mother, Sekhmet) or standing on the back of a lion. Egyptians often carried small statuettes of him as protective amulets, as they did with many other deities. A small, lifelike, carved wooden head of the young god emerging from a lotus was found in the tomb of Tutankhamen.

Nehebu-kau

The serpent god Nehebu-kau was a helpful, protective being whose name means "He who harnesses the spirits." He was associated with the afterlife and was thought to act on behalf of

deceased kings in many ways. He was also one of the 42 judges in the Court of Maat, which judged the deceased. Early depictions show the god as a great serpent, but he often appeared later as a man with the head and tail of a serpent or as a serpent with human arms or legs.

△ The vulture goddess Nekhbet protects the name of King Amenhotep III

Neith

Neith was one of Egypt's most ancient and powerful goddesses, worshipped as far back as the Predynastic Period. She was worshipped right up until the end of dynastic Egypt, and over the centuries, her mythology continued to develop.

In early times, she was seen as a warrior goddess, and her emblems were crossed arrows and bows. Another emblem was a weaving shuttle, a possible reference to a myth in which Neith wove the world into being. Texts at Esna refer to her as the creator of the world and the mother of the sun, Ra. By the New Kingdom, she was seen as the mother of all the gods and of humanity. She was also connected with Egyptian funerary rites. As the inventor of weaving, she was associated with the shrouds used in mummification. Neith was usually depicted as a woman, initially wearing two bows above her head, then later the red crown of Lower Egypt.

Nekhbet

Nekhbet was the vulture goddess of the city of Nekheb (present-day el-Kab) in Upper Egypt. She was strongly identified with the white crown of Upper Egypt and with the king. She appeared on the king's nemes headdress as a vulture or a snake and, from the 4th Dynasty, in a vulture headdress worn by the chief royal wife.

She was also a protector of royal children, and later of all young children and expectant mothers. Nekhbet was usually depicted as a vulture, often with the circular *shen* or "eternity" hieroglyph in her claws. She was also depicted in the form of a woman wearing the white crown of Upper Egypt or a vulture headdress.

Nephthys

The sister of Isis and Osiris and the sister-wife of Seth, Nephthys was a funerary goddess. Nephthys is the Greek form of her name, and the Egyptians knew her as *Nebet-hwt*, meaning "Mistress of the Mansion." The term "mansion" may have referred to the sky or to Egypt as a whole. She was one of the four deities at the core of the Osiris myth. When Osiris was murdered, she joined Isis in searching for the god, then reassembled and protected him when he was found.

This protection extended to the dead in general and, together with Isis, Nephthys became one of the four guardian deities of coffins and canopic jars. She was depicted as a female figure characterized only by the hieroglyphic symbols for her name above her head or occasionally as a kite. She often appeared at the ends or the corners of sarcophagi.

Nun

Nun was the personification of the primeval waters that existed at the time of creation, along with Naunet, the female form. He was more element than deity, and any body of water—including the Nile—could be called Nun. He was also depicted in human form, often shown supporting Ra's solar boat on his upraised arms.

Nut

Nut was the personification of the sky and the vault of the heavens. She was the daughter of Shu and Tefnut, the deities of air and moisture, and the granddaughter of the creator god Atum. The sun was believed to travel through her body each night to emerge again at the beginning of each new day. As a result, she was closely associated with the idea of resurrection.

The outstretched figure of Nut was often painted inside the lids of sarcophagi to protect the deceased. In other instances, she took the form of a naked woman painted with stars, with her body arching over the Earth below. Her arms and legs were the pillars of the sky, meeting the Earth at the horizon.

Onuris

Onuris is the Greek name for the Egyptian god of war and hunting, Anhur. He is usually shown as a standing man with a beard and a short wig topped with a uraeus and several tall plumes. In popular myth, he was the god sent by Ra to Nubia to bring back Mekhit, his lioness goddess daughter. The original cult center of Onuris was at Thinis, near Abydos. Later, during the 30th Dynasty, he was worshipped at the Delta city of Sebennytos.

△ Funerary stela showing Thoth introducing the deceased to Osiris and Isis beneath the arching body of the goddess Nut

△ Painting of the god Ptah sitting on a throne from the tomb of Irynefer at Deir el-Medina

Opet

Opet (or Ipet) was a hippopotamus goddess greatly venerated in the area around Thebes. A temple was built for her within the Karnak complex. In Theban theology, she was thought to be the mother of Osiris. She is mentioned in the Pyramid Texts in connection to offering kings nourishment at her breast. Opet was depicted as a female hippopotamus with sagging breasts and a big belly, standing upright on lionlike legs. Her back and tail were those of a crocodile.

Osiris

One of the most important deities in the ancient Egyptian pantheon, Osiris was the mythological ruler of Egypt who was viciously murdered and dismembered by his jealous brother, Seth. His scattered body parts were found by his sisters, Isis and Nephthys, and Osiris was brought back to a semblance of life to serve as lord of the dead. In this role, he presided over the judgment of dead souls.

To the Egyptians, he also symbolized renewed life, so he was regarded as a god of fertility, making the Nile flood and plants grow. The cult of Osiris was already well established by the 5th Dynasty, and the god's name appears frequently in the Pyramid Texts.

His main cult centers were Abydos in Middle Egypt and Busiris in the Delta. He was depicted as a green-skinned deity with a pharaoh's beard, partially wrapped like a mummy, wearing the *atef* crown, and holding a crook and flail.

P

Pakhet

With a name that means "She who scratches," Pakhet was a ferocious lioness goddess who hunted the desert by night. Her main cult area was around Beni Hasan in Middle Egypt, where there is a rock-cut chapel to the goddess that was created during the 18th Dynasty. Pakhet was portrayed as a feline-headed woman or as a large cat, often depicted killing snakes.

Ptah

Ptah was one of the earliest Egyptian gods, worshipped from the Early Dynastic Period onward. His center of worship was Memphis, where he formed part of a holy triad with his consort, the lioness goddess Sekhmet, and their son Nefertum.

He was presented by the priests of Memphis as a god of creation, known as the "Sculptor of the earth." Like the ram god Khnum, he formed everything, including the other gods. He was also a god of arts and crafts and the patron of sculptors, masons, carpenters, smiths, and other artisans.

Ptah was also widely celebrated as a god who listened to people's prayers. Egyptian temples often had shrines of the "hearing ear," where a worshipper's prayers were transmitted to the deity within the temple, and Ptah is often depicted on these shrines. He was usually depicted as a mummiform figure, with his hands emerging from his shroud to clasp a *was* scepter. He often wore a tight-fitting skullcap.

Ptah-Sokar-Osiris

From the end of the New Kingdom, Ptah also formed part of the triple deity Ptah-Sokar-Osiris. The union of creator god, god of the dead, and god of the afterlife represented the cycle of life. This composite god was depicted as a single mummiform figure with a headdress of a sun disk with twisted ram's horns and an atef crown. Statues of him often included a copy of spells from the Book of the Dead.

R

Ra

The sun god Ra (or Re) was one of Egypt's most important deities. He was considered to be the king of the gods and largely remained so throughout the long history of dynastic Egypt. Even when other gods rose to prominence, Ra was not superseded but became part of a composite deity, such as Amen-Ra, Atum-Ra, or Ra-Horakhty. There was an extensive mythology regarding Ra, who was variously the supreme creator, the king of the heavens, and the father of the king. From the 4th Dynasty onward, kings adopted the epithet "Son of Ra," and in the 5th Dynasty, several rulers built sun temples dedicated to Ra in the vicinity of their own mortuary complexes.

Ra enjoyed a renaissance in the New Kingdom, when the 18th Dynasty kings built several solar temples. This culminated in Akhenaten's attempts to establish the sun god, in the form of the Aten, as the one and only god. The Greeks associated Ra with Zeus, so he remained popular during the Ptolemaic Period. He was depicted in art in many forms, often as a fiery sun disk encircled by a cobra. He was also depicted as a man with a falcon's head or simply as a falcon, wearing the sun disk on his head in both cases.

△ Wooden figure of Ra, the ancient Egyptian sun god

△ Wall painting of the lioness-headed goddess Sekhmet at the Temple of Khnum in Esna

Renenutet

Despite taking the form of a snake, Renenutet was a benign goddess. Her name means "She who nourishes," and she was a divine nurse who suckled babies in general and the king in particular. She was also a goddess of the harvest, the serpent who protected crops and stored grain from being eaten by rats and mice. Her cult was particularly strong in the Faiyum and Delta, both important agricultural areas.

Shrines to Renenutet were often erected in the fields or granaries where the harvest was stored. She was usually depicted as an erect cobra wearing a solar disk and a double-plumed headdress. She was also portrayed as a woman with a snake's head.

Ruty

Ruty was not one but twin divine lion gods who guarded the eastern and western horizons. In the Book of the Dead, Ruty becomes the double lion over whose back the sun rises every day. The god was worshipped from early dynastic times and was linked with Heliopolis. Ruty was usually depicted as two lions positioned back to back with the solar disk between them.

S

Sah

Sah personified the constellation of Orion. He was the consort of Sothis, who represented Sirius. According to Egyptian mythology, Sah was swallowed by the underworld each dawn and then rose again every night. He was depicted as a human figure surrounded by stars and sailing across the sky in a skiff.

Satis

Satis was the goddess guardian of Egypt's southern borders. Because the route from the south was along the Nile, she was closely associated with both the river and the annual flood and with Elephantine Island in what is now Aswan. She was the consort of Khnum and the mother of Anukis. Satis was worshipped beyond Upper Egypt, because she also purified the dead with water from the underworld. In the Pyramid Texts, she is described performing this service for the king, and her name is inscribed on stone jars found at Saqqara dating back to the 3rd Dynasty.

Sekhmet

Sekhmet, whose name means "Powerful one," was the oldest, most important, and most fearsome of Egypt's various lioness-headed goddesses. She could breathe fire, and the hot desert winds were said to be her breath. She could also cause plagues and pestilence. However, she could avert plague and cure disease, too, so she was the patron of physicians and healers.

Sekhmet's main cult center was at Memphis, but when royal power shifted to Thebes in the New Kingdom, her attributes were added to those of Mut, who sometimes also took the form of a lioness. Amenhotep III had hundreds of statues of Sekhmet carved and set around the Temple of Mut at Karnak. She took the form of a lioness-headed woman wearing a long wig and had a solar disk on her head. She was often shown with the ankh of life in her hand.

Serapis

The Ptolemies invented Serapis as a hybrid of the Egyptian deities Osiris and Apis and several Greek deities, notably Zeus. Serapis was meant to form a link between the Greek and Egyptian populations when Greek Alexandria became Egypt's new capital.

Serapis was the personification of divine kingship, healing, fertility, and the afterlife. His consort was Isis. He was depicted as a man with a flowing beard, wearing Greek-style robes and often a cylindrical hat that looked like a woven basket.

Serket

The scorpion goddess Serket was a protective deity with strong healing powers, especially against poisonous bites. Together with Isis, Neith, and Nephthys, she was one of the four protective deities who guarded sarcophagi and canopic jars. She was also associated with motherhood. In the Pyramid Texts, she was said to nurse the king.

Serket also had a dark side and could use venomous scorpions and snakes against transgressors. She was usually depicted as a scorpion or a woman with a scorpion on her head.

Seshat

Seshat means "Female scribe," and she was the goddess of all forms of writing and record-keeping, including accounting. She was also the mistress of builders and was consulted about the planning of every temple. In particular, she was linked with the ritual known as *pedj shes* (stretching the cord) that was used to mark out the floor plan of a building's foundations.

Seshat was the king's scribe and duly recorded all of the royal achievements, including how many people had been killed or taken captive in battle. She was closely associated with the god Thoth and was variously said to be his consort, sister, or daughter.

In art, Seshat was depicted as a woman, often wearing a leopard skin, with an unusual headdress that looked like a seven-pronged star on a stick beneath a bowlike arc. She was often shown writing or marking notches on a palm rib to record the passage of time, possibly to record the length of the king's reign.

▽ Late Period bronze temple ornament of the scorpion goddess Serket

△ 19th Dynasty limestone stela of Aapehty from Deir el-Medina showing Aapehty worshipping the god Seth (left)

Seth

Seth (or Set) was one of the most ancient gods of Egypt. A desert deity, he represented chaos and confusion and was linked with terrifying events such as storms and earthquakes. He was worshipped in the Predynastic Period and was depicted on the famous Scorpion macehead.

Part of the Ennead of Heliopolis, Seth was the son of Geb and Nut and the brother of Osiris, Isis, and Nephthys. In one of the best-known Egyptian myths, he murders Osiris in a bid to become king, then loses his crown to his nephew, Horus.

Like many gods, Seth had a dual personality. He symbolized rage and was regarded as evil personified and the disruptor of *maat* (harmony), but he was also a god of great strength, and many warrior kings aligned themselves with him. In the Middle Kingdom, he was the god who stood at the front of the sun god Ra's barque to defend him against the serpent Apophis.

Seth was often worshipped in the eastern Delta and also in Upper Egypt, where one of his earliest cult centers was at Nubt, at the entrance to Wadi Hammamat. He was depicted as a man with a strange, curved, long-nosed animal's head and tall, erect, square-topped ears.

Shai

Shai personified fate or destiny and determined the length of a person's life. He was born with each person and remained with them until they faced their final judgment before Osiris, when he proffered a true and accurate account of their life.

△ Bronze crocodile on a shrine, representing the god Sobek

Shed

An aspect of Horus the Child, Shed protected people from the wild beasts of the desert and river. He was a minor god venerated mainly during the New Kingdom. He had no cult or temples of his own. He was depicted as a young boy wearing a kilt, usually grasping an animal in each hand and standing on the back of a crocodile.

Shu

One of the original Heliopolitan Ennead, Shu was the god of the air and sunlight. He created the atmosphere that enabled life to flourish and the winds that powered sailors' boats. Four pillars located at the cardinal points and known as the "Pillars of Shu" helped him keep the Earth and sky apart. He was usually depicted as a man wearing a tall ostrich feather on his head and carrying a *was*

scepter and an ankh. He was also sometimes shown standing on Geb (the Earth) with his arms raised to support Nut (the sky).

Sobek

Sobek was one of the oldest Egyptian gods and was by far the most powerful of several Egyptian gods that were associated with the crocodile. He was a god of the Nile who brought fertility to the land and acted as a symbol of kingly potency and might. In the Pyramid Texts, he was also referred to as the merciless one "who takes women from their husbands whenever he wishes."

The two main centers of Sobek worship were in the Faiyum, at what became known under the Ptolemies as Crocodilopolis, and at Kom Ombo in Upper Egypt. In the Late Period, Sobek's temples usually had pools containing sacred crocodiles, which were mummified when they died and then buried in necropolises. In

Egyptian art, Sobek was depicted as a crocodile or as a man with a crocodile's head. He often wore a plumed headdress with a horned sun disk or the atef crown.

Sokar

An ancient falcon god of Memphis, Sokar was associated with the afterlife. He was also the patron of the artisans who created the tombs and made the objects connected with burials and mummification.

Every year, Memphites celebrated a Sokar festival, during which a statue of the god was paraded on a henu barque (a boat with a high prow shaped like the horns of an oryx). By the New Kingdom, the festival had spread

to Thebes. Sokar was usually depicted in the form of a hawk- or a falcon-headed figure with a *was* scepter. He was also represented by a funerary mound topped by a falcon's head that was sometimes set in a boat.

Sothis

Also known as Soped, Sothis was the goddess who personified Sirius, or the Dog Star, the brightest star in the night sky. Her husband was Sah, god of the constellation of Orion. The importance of Sirius for the Egyptians was that its annual appearance on the eastern horizon heralded the arrival of the Nile flood and the start of the new agricultural year.

△ The god Ptah-Sokar-Osiris in the form of a falcon on a sacred barque

◁ 26th Dynasty graywacke statue of the hippopotamus goddess Taweret

T

Tatenen

The name Tatenen means "Risen land," and the god symbolized the rising of the primeval mound from the waters of original creation. He also represented the emergence of the black, fertile silt following the Nile's annual inundation. He was primarily worshipped in Memphis.

Taweret

Taweret was the most popular of the Egyptian hippopotamus goddesses and was believed to protect women and babies during childbirth. She had no formal cult temples but was often depicted on household goods, as well as on items relating to fertility and childbirth.

Expectant mothers often carried amulets depicting Taweret, in the hope that she would protect them. She was depicted with the head and body of a pregnant hippopotamus, the back of a crocodile, and the paws of a lion, with a woman's long hair. She often wore a short, cylindrical hat topped by two plumes, or horns and a solar disk.

Tefnut

Tefnut was the daughter of Atum and the sister-wife of Shu. She was the goddess of moisture and was also closely associated with both the sun and moon.

Thoth

The god Thoth (or Djehuty) was associated with knowledge and writing. He was one of the earliest gods, and his picture appeared on slate palettes of the Predynastic Period. He was said to have invented not only writing, but also medicine, magic, and even music. He was the keeper of secrets unknown to even the other gods, all of which were inscribed in the mysterious Book of Thoth. He was the scribe of the underworld who recorded the verdicts on the souls of the deceased, so he was known as "Master of the balance."

Thoth's enduring importance is shown by the insertion of his name in the names of New Kingdom rulers such as Tuthmosis (meaning "Thoth is born"). He was worshipped throughout the land, but his main cult center was at Hermopolis in Middle Egypt.

Depictions of Thoth often show him in the form of either an ibis or a baboon, but he was most commonly portrayed as a man with the head of an ibis.

W

Wadjet

The cobra goddess Wadjet was the patron deity of Lower Egypt, a counterpart to her sister, the vulture goddess Nekhbet of Upper Egypt. The two combined as the *nebty* (meaning "two ladies"), one of the names that the kings used to indicate their rule over both parts of Egypt. Wadjet was often described as an aggressive deity—she was sometimes called the

"Mistress of fear," as she could spit flames when defending the king.

Wadjet was usually depicted as an erect cobra with its hood extended in readiness to strike. It is in this form that Wadjet is depicted in the uraeus often shown attached to the solar disk.

Wepwawet

Wepwawet (or Upuaut) was an ancient jackal or wolf god who predated Anubis and all the other ancient Egyptian canine gods. Wepwawet is shown on one of the standards on the Narmer Palette. He was one of the earliest gods worshipped at Abydos, and his popularity spread throughout Egypt from there.

Wepwawet's name means "Opener of the ways" and is thought to refer to a number of things, one of them being the route into the underworld. In funerary texts, Wepwawet led the deceased through the underworld and guarded them during their perilous journey. He also led the king to ascension.

He was generally depicted as a wolf or jackal or a man with the head of a wolf or jackal. He was indistinguishable from Anubis and can often only be identified by the inclusion of his name or his attributes of a mace and bow. In animal form, however, Anubis was usually depicted as being black, while Wepwawet was gray.

Weret-Hekau

Weret-Hekau means "Great in magic" or "Great enchantress." The name was given to several goddesses, including Isis, Sekhmet, and Mut. In the Pyramid Texts, it was applied to

the uraeus and the crown of Lower Egypt as manifestations of the goddess Wadjet. Later, it is believed that Weret-Hekau took on an independent identity and became regarded as a goddess in her own right. A pendant found in the tomb of Tutankhamen depicts her as a snake-bodied figure with a plumed and horned headdress, suckling a standing figure of the boy king.

△ Wall painting in the Tomb of Khaemwese at Thebes depicting offerings being made to the god Thoth

Sites

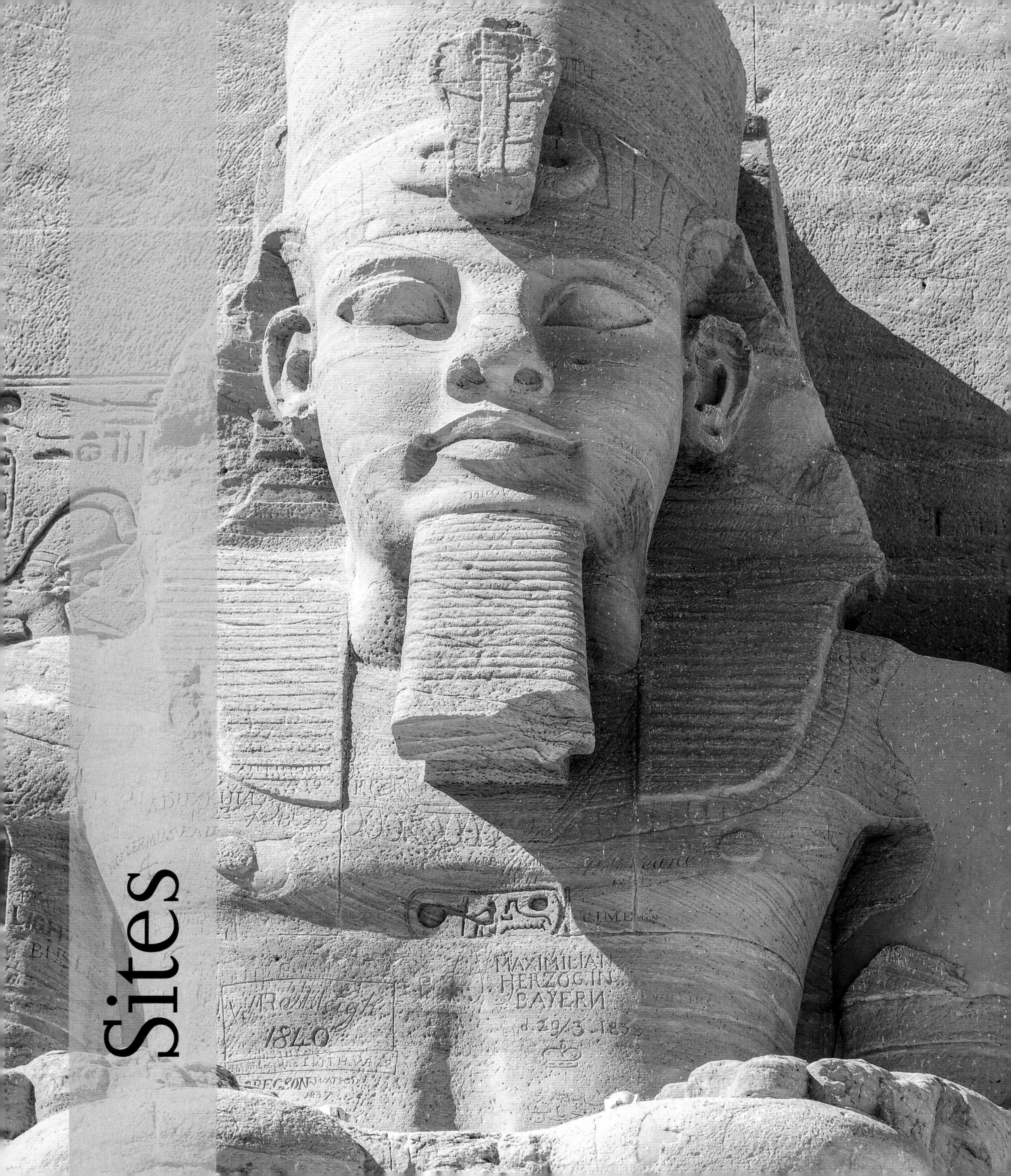

Alexandria and the Delta

The city of Alexander the Great only has a small number of mainly Roman ruins still visible. Few of the many ancient sites of the Delta have substantial remains today.

Greco-Roman Museum

5 El-Mathaf el-Rumani Street

Housed in a historic building with a neoclassical façade, this museum has a large and important collection relating to the Macedonian, Ptolemaic, and Roman Periods of ancient Egypt. The exhibits begin with busts of the city's founder, Alexander the Great. Other key items include statues of the god Serapis, in whom elements of both the Egyptian god Osiris and the Greek god Zeus were combined, and mosaics of Queen Berenike II. Cleopatra VII is depicted on a silver coin, and there are terracotta models of the Pharos of Alexandria, made when the lighthouse was still standing. A large Roman Period mosaic with a central panel of a Medusa's head offers a fine example of the blend of cultures that made up ancient Alexandria.

Alexandria National Museum

110 Horeyya Avenue

A villa that was once the United States consulate now serves as an introduction to ancient Egyptian history. Exhibits include alabaster statuary from Giza, a false door from Abydos, and a sandstone statue of Akhenaten. In the basement, a jackal-headed Anubis guards two Late Period painted sarcophagi.

Kom el-Dikka

El-Muhafza Street

At the southern end of the Soma, one of the two main streets of ancient Alexandria, Kom el-Dikka (Arabic for "mound of rubble") is an excavation of the Panion, or Park of Pan, a Greco-Roman pleasure garden. There is a small, well-preserved Roman theater and the remains of Roman baths and a villa, where large floor mosaics have been uncovered, including a design of nine panels, each of which depicts a different bird.

Kom el-Shuqafa

El-Nasseriya Street

One of the most fascinating places in Alexandria is this subterranean burial complex from 200 CE. Its three levels of tombs, hollowed out of solid rock, were probably for a wealthy family of nobles from the Roman Period. The decoration is a fusion of cultures, mixing elements of ancient Egyptian, Greek, and Roman iconography of the dead.

Bibliotheca Alexandrina

Al Azaritah WA

Inspired by the original great library of Alexandria, the new Bibliotheca opened in 2002. Its design is intended to represent a second sun rising, with letters and hieroglyphs carved on the external walls. It contains ancient manuscripts and books and houses a permanent exhibition.

Tanis

112 miles (180 km) northeast of Cairo

The ancient city of Tanis was one of the largest cities in the Delta for hundreds of years and a seat of power during the 21st and 22nd Dynasties. The site, which is only partly excavated, contains ruins of temples; numerous statues and carvings; and an important royal necropolis, where the tombs of three kings were discovered in 1939 with their burial goods still intact.

Bubastis

50 miles (80 km) northeast of Cairo

One of Egypt's oldest cities, Bubastis was once a royal residence, which reached the height of its power during the 22nd Dynasty. It was also a center of worship for the feline goddess Bastet, and many cats were mummified and buried here. The most visible remains at Bubastis today are the fallen blocks from the temples built in the New Kingdom and Third Intermediate Period.

△ The Roman theater at Kom el-Dikka, built during the 3rd century CE

Cairo and around

Cairo is a modern city, but it lies close to several major ancient sites. From the 7th century onward, the city developed around a Nile crossing that used to connect the Old Kingdom capital of Memphis, west of the river, to the sun temple center of Heliopolis, east of the river.

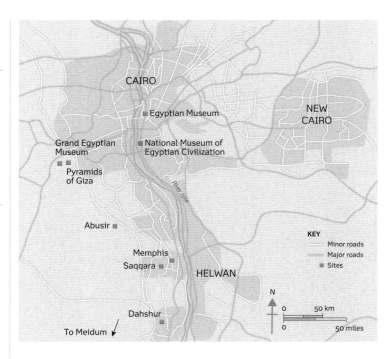

Egyptian Museum

Tahrir Square, central Cairo

This is the country's original museum of ancient Egyptian culture, built in Cairo in 1902. Until recently, it contained by far the world's greatest collection of artifacts from ancient Egypt.

Although many key exhibits have now been moved to the new Grand Egyptian Museum, the original museum remains a wonderful storehouse of Egyptian treasures. There is an immense number of statues from all periods, a wonderful collection of wooden models of daily life from the Middle Kingdom, and the painted mummy panels known as the Faiyum portraits. There are also royal mummies and the treasures of Tanis—gold funerary artifacts recovered from royal tombs in the Nile Delta.

National Museum of Egyptian Civilization

Fustat, southern Cairo

As part of its coverage of the entirety of Egyptian history, this new museum includes many artifacts from the Dynastic and Greco-Roman Periods. The highlight is a gallery displaying the mummified remains of 18 kings and four queens, including Ahmose I; Amenhotep I; Tuthmosis I, II, and III; Seti I; and Ramesses II and III. The room in which they are displayed is a recreation of a Theban tomb.

The Pyramids of Giza

Giza Plateau, 10 miles (16km) southwest of central Cairo

In the present age of towering skyscrapers and voyages to Mars, the pyramids have lost none of their capacity to evoke awe.

△ Interior of the main hall of the Egyptian Museum in Cairo

The Pyramid of Khufu is the sole survivor of the Seven Wonders of the Ancient World.

Inside the Great Pyramid, it is usually possible to access the main burial chamber along a series of inner passages. Back outside, the Solar Boat Museum on the south side of the Great Pyramid displays a reconstructed boat that was found in a pit beside the causeway that led to Khufu's mortuary temple.

Khafre's valley temple is in remarkably good condition but it is completely overshadowed by its neighbor, the enigmatic Great Sphinx.

The site also includes the Pyramid of Menkaure, three small queens' pyramids, and several Old Kingdom tombs with reliefs.

Grand Egyptian Museum

Giza Plateau, 10 miles (16 km) southwest of central Cairo

This new state-of-the-art glass-and-concrete museum is set into the side of the Giza Plateau and has views of the neighboring pyramids. A colossal statue of Ramesses II greets visitors in the main atrium from where a grand staircase lined with 87 statues of kings and gods leads up to the galleries. Exhibits cover all periods from Predynastic to Greco-Roman and are arranged chronologically.

The highlights are the galleries for Tutankhamen, displaying the contents of his tomb almost in their entirety, including his gold death mask and his coffins.

The museum has a replica of the boy king's small tomb, but the galleries used for the display are more than 60 times the size of the original burial space.

Saqqara

27 miles (44 km) south of central Cairo

Little visited in comparison to the Giza Plateau, Saqqara is one of the richest archaeological sites in Egypt. It is the desert necropolis built for several kings and many nobles of the Old Kingdom, who ruled from nearby Memphis.

The highlight is Djoser's Step Pyramid. This was the prototype for the structure that would reach its greatest glory at Giza. There are many points of interest in the enclosure surrounding the Step Pyramid, including a statue of Djoser in his stone serdab.

The nearby Pyramid of Teti boasts walls inscribed with Pyramid Texts, and the Tomb of Ankhma-Hor has painted scenes depicting surgical operations.

The Tomb of Mereruka has many lavish reliefs, including scenes of hunting from a boat among birds, fish, and hippopotamuses. Saqqara is also the home of the Serapeum, a series of catacombs created for the burial of sacred bulls, known as Apis bulls, complete with massive granite sarcophagi.

Abusir

17 miles (27 km) south of central Cairo

Lying between Giza and Saqqara, Abusir is a cluster of 5th Dynasty pyramids set among the sand dunes. They are all considerably smaller than even the smallest of the three Pyramids of Giza and are dilapidated, which means that few tourists ever visit.

Visitors may sometimes be able to access the northernmost of the group, the Pyramid of Sahure, to reach a small burial chamber. On the east side of the pyramid are the remains of Sahure's mortuary temple. The pyramid and complex of Neferirkare to the south was the site of a significant find in the late 19th century—illegal excavations uncovered documents, known as the Abusir Papyri, which revealed how mortuary temples were planned during the Old Kingdom. North of the pyramids is the site of Abu Gurob, which is known for its remains of two royal sun temples, one of which has a large limestone obelisk.

△ Djoser's Step Pyramid at Saqqara, with shrines representing temples in different parts of Egypt

△ The Sphinx of Memphis, thought to honor Hatshepsut

Dahshur

40 miles (64 km) south of central Cairo

There were originally as many as 10 pyramids at Dahshur, built during the 4th and 12th Dynasties. Still in evidence are three Middle Kingdom pyramids and two pyramids built for Snefru, the father of Khufu, builder of the Great Pyramid at Giza. The earlier of Snefru's two pyramids is known as the Bent Pyramid. It was built with a shallower slope partway up, making it look "bent". The other is the Red Pyramid.

Meidum

75 miles (120 km) south of central Cairo

This site contains several mud-brick mustabas and a large pyramid—Egypt's first straight-sided pyramid, probably built for Snefru of the 4th Dynasty. The structure was unsound, however, and the outer masonry appears to have collapsed over time to leave only the stepped core of the pyramid.

Kahun

78 miles (125 km) south of central Cairo

The most important surviving settlement of the Middle Kingdom, Kahun, was a town occupied by workers responsible for constructing the nearby pyramid that was built for Senwosret II. The town has been recovered with sand since its excavation from 1888–1890, but the pyramid remains. The fine limestone casing that once protected it was stripped away long ago and its mud-brick structure has been badly eroded by the elements.

Memphis

Mit Rahina, 24 miles (40 km) south of central Cairo

During the Old Kingdom, Memphis was the capital of Egypt and one of the greatest cities of the ancient world. Today, an open-air museum is built around a colossus of Ramesses II. The enormous statue is lying on its back, but if it were to stand upright, it would measure 40 ft (13 m) in height—it is the twin of the statue that greets visitors at the Grand Egyptian Museum in the Giza Plateau. Its prone position gives visitors the opportunity to examine the king up close. In the garden of the museum are more statues of Ramesses II, along with one of the largest alabaster sphinxes ever found.

Memphis lies on the road to Saqqara, and a visit there can be easily combined with a journey to the Step Pyramid of Djoser.

Middle to Upper Egypt

Ancient Egypt was divided into Lower and Upper Egypt. "Middle Egypt" was a 19th-century European term that included the region south of the Faiyum and north of Asyut. Its sites were well known to tourists on Nile steamers, but as visitors now fly to Luxor and Aswan, they are often passed over.

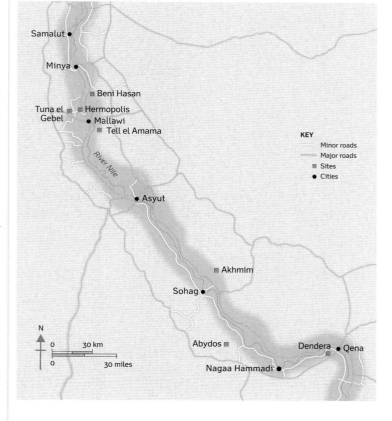

Beni Hasan

12 miles (20 km) south of Minya

Named after a local tribe that once inhabited the area, the Beni Hasan tombs date from the Middle Kingdom. There are 39 of them in total, all belonging to nobles and regional governors, but only four of them are open to the public.

All the tombs contain wall paintings of scenes of everyday life in ancient Egypt. The Tomb of Baqet has a wall depicting wrestlers, and the Tomb of Kheti has images of dancing, wine-making, and figures playing senet—a game that was similar to checkers. The Tomb of Amenemhat has beautiful scenes of hunting and farming, while the Tomb of Khnumhotep has figures hunting, fishing, and netting birds, among a menagerie of animals, including crocodiles, hippopotamuses, and big cats.

Hermopolis and Tuna el-Gebel

5 miles (8 km) northwest of Mallawi

From the Middle Kingdom, the city of Khemenu was a cult center for Thoth, the god of writing and wisdom. The city was later named Hermopolis Magna by the Ptolemaic kings, who associated Thoth with the Greek god Hermes.

The site's highlights include 24 huge columns from a Christian basilica from the 5th century CE and two colossal quartzite statues of Thoth in the form of a baboon.

Other ruins include a temple gateway from the Middle Kingdom and a pylon of Ramesses II.

There is more to be seen at nearby Tuna el-Gebel, which is the site of the ancient city's necropolis. Visitors can explore the catacombs, which were once filled with thousands of mummified ibises and fewer numbers of baboons, both animals that were considered sacred to Thoth.

Above ground are numerous mausoleums, including the Tomb of Petosiris, which was dedicated to a high priest of Thoth and designed to look like a temple. The decoration of the building combines elements of both Egyptian and Greek culture.

Nearby is the Tomb-chapel of Isadora, which displays the well-preserved mummy of Isadora. She was a wealthy woman who drowned in the Nile in around 150 CE. A cult subsequently grew up around her tomb.

△ An 18th Dynasty relief from Amarna depicting three cows grazing

Tell el-Amarna

7 miles (12 km) southwest of Mallawi

The remains of Akhetaten, the city built by the "heretic king" Akhenaten (Amenhotep IV), lie at a site known today as Tell el-Amarna. The ruins are widely spread over a site that stretches around 9 miles (15 km), north to south, on a desolate but atmospheric plain bounded by the River Nile on one side and a bay of cliffs on the other.

Amarna is the only ancient Egyptian city for which an almost complete ground plan exists. However, there are no standing structures left, and the many impressive finds from here have been moved to various museums. What remains for the visitor are two sets of rock-cut cliff tombs, one at each end of the former city. There are six Northern Tombs, which include the Tomb

△ The North Palace ruins at Tell el-Amarna

of Huya, a steward to Akhenaten's mother, Queen Tiy. A relief shows Tiy dining with her son and his family. The Tomb of Mery-Re I is decorated with a depiction of Akhenaten and his great temple that shows what the city looked like during its brief phase of glory. Part of the Southern Tombs, the Tomb of Ay is considered to be the finest tomb at Amarna: its wall paintings show Ay and his wife receiving ceremonial golden collars from Akhenaten and Nefertiti, watched by crowds of cheering onlookers.

About 4 miles (6.5 km) up a narrow wadi in the cliffs is the royal tomb that was intended for Akhenaten and his family. Unfortunately, its wall paintings have been virtually obliterated, with only a few scenes surviving.

Akhmim

1.8 miles (3 km) east of Sohag

On the outskirts of the city of Sohag, Akhmim is a large town traditionally known for textiles. It stands on the site of the ancient Egyptian settlement of Ipu. In 1982, excavations here uncovered a 33 ft (11 m) high statue of Meritamen, daughter and wife of Ramesses II. It is the largest statue of a queen found in Egypt. There is also a museum in Sohag with finds from the excavations of the Temple of Ramesses II at Akhmim.

Abydos

6 miles (10 km) southwest of El-Balyana

Abydos was the cult center of the god Osiris and the holiest town in ancient Egypt. It was the necropolis of 1st- and 2nd-Dynasty kings, and Senwosret III might have been buried there. The highlight for modern visitors

△ Painted relief from the Tomb of Seti I depicting Seti kneeling between the gods Khnum (left) and Amun (right)

is the Temple of Seti I, one of the most complete and beautiful temples in Egypt. It has a particularly fine inner hypostyle hall of 24 columns that resemble papyrus stems. The walls are inscribed with sunken reliefs, including a panel that shows Seti in front of Osiris. Many of the reliefs have retained their original colors. At the back of the hall is an unusual arrangement of seven shrines, each of which is devoted to a different god or goddess. A corridor known as the Gallery of the Kings contains a king list with the cartouches of 76 kings in more or less chronological order, ending with Seti.

Behind the temple is an unusual structure known as the Osireion, which is a cenotaph built by Seti I. Unfortunately, it is half-buried and filled with stagnant water. Northwest of Seti's temple, there is a smaller temple that was built by his son, Ramesses II.

Dendera

3 miles (5 km) southwest of Qena

Dendera was a cult center for the goddess Hathor from the Predynastic Period onward. The current temple dates from the Greco-Roman Period and is well preserved. Visitors walk straight into the Hypostyle Hall, which has columns topped with capitals carved to resemble the cow-eared goddess. It is possible to go up a staircase to the roof, where there are twin chapels. Inside one of the chapels is a plaster cast of the famous Dendera Zodiac—the original is now in the Louvre in Paris. Back on the ground, there are reliefs of Cleopatra and her son, Caesarion, on the exterior of the rear wall of the temple.

△ Interior of the Hypostyle Hall at Dendera Temple showing the columns topped with capitals of the goddess Hathor

Luxor

The present-day city of Luxor covers the site of Thebes, the religious center of the cult of Amen. Across the Nile, on the west bank, is the royal necropolis, the site of numerous mortuary temples and rock-cut tombs. Together, these sites make up a vast open-air museum.

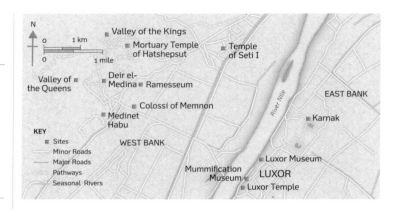

Temple of Luxor

Corniche el-Nil, east bank

Largely built by two of the greatest kings of the New Kingdom, Amenhotep III and Ramesses II, this temple sits alongside the Nile at the heart of present-day Luxor.

It is a perfect encapsulation of ancient Egyptian architecture and culture. The site has been remarkably well preserved, because it was buried beneath the sand for 2,000 years, until it was rediscovered in the 19th century.

The temple is approached by an avenue of sphinxes, which at one time stretched for 2 miles (3.2 km) to the great temple complex at Karnak. (This processional route has been under excavation for many years.) The great entrance pylon is the work of Ramesses II, and its reliefs show him slaying Hittites at the Battle of Kadesh.

△ Colossi in the Great Court of Ramesses II at the Temple of Luxor

The entrance is fronted by six colossal statues of the king and one obelisk—its missing twin now stands on the Place de la Concorde in Paris. Beyond the pylon is the Great Court of Ramesses II, leading to the Colonnade of Amenhotep III. This was the original entrance to the temple before the Ramesside additions. The walls here were decorated during the reign of Tutankhamen.

The highlight of the temple is the paved Sun Court of Amenhotep III, enclosed on three sides by towering columns that look like bundles of papyrus. Archaeologists discovered an impressive cache of statues in a pit beneath this court in 1989.

Parts of the temple's innermost chambers, which served as the cult sanctuary of Amen, were plastered over by the Romans between the 4th and 6th centuries CE and made into a shrine for their own gods.

The central sanctuary of the temple was rebuilt by Alexander the Great, with reliefs showing him as an Egyptian king.

During the Roman Period, the temple was converted into a fort for garrisoned troops. Visitors can find the remains of a Roman camp outlined in the earth to the east of the site, beside the approach to a 14th-century mosque that is still used for worship today.

Mummification Museum

Corniche el-Nil, east bank

This small museum is devoted to Egyptian burial practices, notably the art of mummification—the process of preserving a corpse. The exhibits concentrate on the implements and treatments that

△ Sandstone bust of Amenhotep IV (Akhenaten) at Luxor Museum

embalmers used to prepare a corpse for the afterlife. There are 19 display cases in the museum, spread across 11 topics. These include tools such as a spoon and metal spatula used to scrape the brain out of the skull, and embalming materials, such as samples of natron salts, bitumen, sawdust, and linen.

There are also examples of canopic jars used for storing internal organs, some beautiful painted coffin lids, and a statue of Anubis—the jackal-headed god of the dead who was closely associated with mummification

and embalming. There are numerous examples of animal mummies, but there is only one human mummy—that of Maserharti, who was a High Priest of Amen at Thebes during the 21st Dynasty.

Luxor Museum

Corniche el-Nil, east bank

This modern archaeological museum is largely devoted to finds made in and around Luxor. Its treasures are well lit and displayed, with informative

labeling in English and Arabic. Much of the collection dates from the New Kingdom, which is considered to be a golden age of Egyptian art. One of its greatest kings, Amenhotep III, appears in the museum in two very different representations. The first is a massive head, part of a colossus that belonged to the king's lost funerary temple on the west bank at Thebes. The second is a life-sized statue of the crocodile god Sobek, shown with his arm resting paternally around the young king's shoulders.

There are also some fine sculptures of Tuthmosis III, who shared part of his reign with his aunt and stepmother, Hatshepsut. On the upper floor, there are a few items from the tomb of Tutankhamen and exhibits relating to his father, Akhenaten, who is portrayed in three sandstone heads in the distinctive Amarna style.

There is also a wall of painted sandstone blocks (talatat), which come from one of the temples of Amenhotep IV, which he erected at Karnak before moving his capital north to Amarna and calling himself Akhenaten.

A wing dedicated to the glory of Thebes during the New Kingdom contains two royal mummies: those of Ahmose I, founder of the 18th Dynasty, and a mummy that is believed to be Ramesses I, founder of the 19th Dynasty.

A side gallery contains 16 mostly life-sized statues that were discovered by chance when archaeologists were collecting soil samples at Luxor Temple in 1989. The pride of the find was a 8 ft (2.5 m) tall red quartzite statue of one of the temple's main patrons, Amenhotep III.

△ Painting of the Precinct of Mut, part of the Karnak complex, Carl Friedrich Werner, 1867

Karnak

Sharia el-Karnak, east bank

Although much of it is now in ruins, Karnak is still one of the most spectacular sites in Egypt. At its heart lies the Temple of Amen. From modest beginnings in the 11th Dynasty, Karnak grew in size as one king after another amended the existing buildings and made their own additions, hoping to leave their mark on the country's most important religious center.

As well as being a place of worship, attended by a staff of professional priests, Karnak was also a center of administration, employing tens of thousands of workers. At its height, there were three main compounds: the main precinct, dedicated to Amen and dominated by the Great Temple of Amen; the precinct of Amen's consort Mut, linked to the main temple by an avenue of ram-headed sphinxes; and the precinct of the old Theban falcon god, Montu.

Most of the complex was the work of New Kingdom rulers, but the oldest parts date back to the Middle Kingdom. The Ptolemies, Romans, and even the early Christians all left their mark. Most of the site lay beneath the sand until excavation work began in the mid-19th century. Restoration is still in progress today.

Precinct of Amen

Amen was the local god of Karnak. During the New Kingdom, he was also the state god of Egypt. A canal once connected his temple complex to the River Nile. From the ancient canal's quay, a processional avenue of ram-headed sphinxes forms the approach to the first pylon, which serves as the grand precinct entrance. The pylon was a late addition, raised by the 30th Dynasty king Nectanebo I, and was never completed. Visitors pass through the entrance into the Great Court and through a second pylon, built by

Horemheb, an 18th Dynasty king, to arrive in the Great Hypostyle Hall. One of the most impressive ancient Egyptian structures, the hall is filled with 134 columns that are around 50 ft (15 m) tall except the center 12, which are 69 ft (21 m) high. The columns originally supported a roof, but this is long gone.

Another two pylons act as gateways to the earliest part of the temple, which is in a far more ruinous state. Huge granite obelisks were also erected by Tuthmosis I, Hatshepsut, and Tuthmosis III.

Deep within the complex is the Sanctuary of Amen, with a boxlike structure known as the Sacred Barque Shrine. This still contains the plinth on which the barque of Amen would have rested. This was a model boat that would be carried aloft on poles by the priests during festivals and processions.

South of the main temple is a large sacred lake, where the priests performed rituals involving washing.

Precinct of Mut

A second processional axis runs south from the Temple of Amen. It is marked by a series of four pylons and courts. Beyond the last of the pylons, an avenue of sphinxes leads to a partly excavated southern enclosure dedicated to Mut, the mother goddess of Thebes and consort of the god Amen.

Her temple was built during the reign of Amenhotep III. It contains the main Temple of Mut, as well as the remains of at least five minor temples and a U-shaped sacred lake.

More than 500 large, black granite statues of the lioness goddess Sekhmet, who was associated with Mut, have been discovered on the site. Some of them are still in place, but many are now in various museums around the world.

Precinct of Montu

North of the Temple of Amen, still within the Amen precinct enclosure, is an open-air museum that gathers together various archaeological finds from the site. This includes three shrines that were reconstructed from parts that were discovered elsewhere.

A gate in the northern wall of the precinct, beside a small Temple of Ptah, leads to the Montu Temple enclosure.

Falcon-headed Montu was one of the original deities of Thebes, and his temple dates back to the Middle Kingdom, predating most of the Temple of Amen. It was later rebuilt by Amenhotep III, among others, but is now in a very poor state. Its most notable feature is an ornate gateway, which dates from the reigns of Ptolemy III and Ptolemy IV.

△ Close-up of reliefs at the Great Hypostyle Hall at Karnak Temple

△ One of the two Colossi of Memnon on the west bank, Thebes

Colossi of Memnon

West bank

These two enormous statues of Amenhotep III, standing alone in a dusty clearing on the Theban plain, are almost all that is left of what may once have been Egypt's largest mortuary temple. The temple was built for the worship of Amenhotep III, but later kings plundered the site, which was also gradually destroyed by annual floods.

The two faceless colossi, each carved from a single block of stone, would have stood at the main entrance.

During the Hellenistic Period, the northernmost statue was famous for "singing" at sunrise, leading the Greeks to claim that the statues were of the legendary Ethiopian king Memnon. The Greeks thought that Memnon greeted his mother, the dawn goddess Eos, each morning.

Archaeologists think that the sound might have been caused by air passing through the stone when it was warmed by the first rays of the sun. It stopped after the statue was restored by the Roman emperor Septimius Severus. Excavation of the mortuary temple behind the statues is still in progress.

Medinet Habu

West bank

Although not as famous as the nearby temples of Hatshepsut or the Ramesseum, the often overlooked Medinet Habu is nevertheless one of the best preserved and most impressive temple complexes on the west bank. It is dominated by the huge mortuary temple of Ramesses III, the last of the great kings of the New Kingdom. At its height, Medinet Habu would have looked like a walled city with temples, palaces, chapels, and accommodation for the priests and officials.

The site is entered via the High Gate, which was inspired by Syrian architecture. Through the gate is the great court and the approach to the massive main temple. Ramesses III's many military campaigns are recorded in detail on the main pylon, including scenes of scribes tallying up the dead enemy by counting their severed hands and genitals. Reliefs on the second pylon show Ramesses III presenting his prisoners to the god Amen and his goddess wife, Mut. Some of the wall reliefs, ceilings, and columns have retained traces of their original colors, giving some idea of how dazzling these places must once have been.

Ramesseum

West bank

The most self-aggrandizing of kings, Ramesses II—whose four colossi tower over mere mortals at Abu Simbel—built his mortuary temple at Thebes as a further monument to his eternal greatness.

The huge complex took more than 20 years to build, but it has not survived the passage of time and is now in ruins, with just trenches, holes, and bases to indicate where the rest of the complex once stood. The first and second entrance pylons, which are covered in reliefs displaying Ramesses II's achievements and victories in battle, are also in a poor condition. All that remains to show the former glory of the main courts is a row of columns fronted by statues of Ramesses II as the god Osiris with his arms crossed, bearing the crook and flail. The link to Osiris—the lord of the afterlife—is not only a signal of the funerary nature of the temple, but was intended to honor him.

Nearby is the toppled and smashed head and shoulders of a colossus of Ramesses II. Estimated to have stood over six stories high, this was possibly the largest free-standing statue ever made in ancient Egypt. An image of the fallen statue inspired the poet Percy Bysshe Shelley to write his meditation on hubris and decay, the poem "Ozymandias."

Deir el-Medina

West bank

Excavations at this site have revealed a walled workers' village of more than 70 houses. This would have been home to many of the workmen and artisans who decorated the royal tombs cut into the surrounding cliffs and mountainsides, a settlement that lasted over 400 years. The ground floors of the individual homes are still clearly visible.

Beside the village is its small necropolis, with several tombs open to the public. The Tomb of Inherkhau, a foreman who lived during the reigns of Ramesses III

△ The artisans' village of Deir el-Medina, surrounded by a protective wall

and Ramesses IV, has a famous wall painting of a long-eared cat killing the serpent Apophis. The Tomb of Sennedjem displays scenes of the occupant and his

wife working in the Field of Reeds (the afterlife). The Tomb of Peshedu shows this 19th Dynasty servant praying beneath a palm tree beside a stream.

△ The Ramesseum, the mortuary temple of Ramesses II, with Osiride statues facing the second court

△ Falcon statue guarding the stairway leading to the Temple of Hatshepsut

Temple of Hatshepsut

Deir el-Bahri, west bank

The mortuary temple Hatshepsut had built for herself is prominent among the surviving monuments of ancient Egypt. The structure forgoes the usual arrangement of pylons and hypostyle halls and instead rises from the Theban plain in a series of broad terraces to meet the Theban mountains.

The innermost rooms are cut into the cliff face. The design may have been copied from that of the neighboring Temple of Montuhotep. Hatshepsut's temple has been extensively renovated and reconstructed to show quite clearly what it might once have looked like. The original garden that was full of exotic trees and plants no longer exists, and nor does the grand sphinx-lined procession, but some wonderful reliefs have survived.

Scenes on the walls of the temple's middle terrace depict Hatshepsut's divine birth and tell the story of an expedition that she sent to the distant land of Punt.

The highest level still has a few of the 24 colossal statues of Osiris that it once had. It also leads to the shrine to Amen-Ra, cut into the mountainside.

Valley of the Queens

West bank

At the far end of a wide wadi west of Deir el-Medina is Biban el-Harem, or the Valley of the Queens. This is where many of the royal brides, princesses, princes, and other members of the royal families of the 19th and 20th Dynasties were buried.

There are at least 75 tombs, and they include one of the most beautiful tombs in Egypt, that of Nefertari. She was the favorite wife of Ramesses II, builder of the Ramesseum and Abu Simbel, and her tomb reflects her status. Although modest in plan, with just an antechamber with an annexe and a main burial chamber, every surface is adorned with painted scenes of the queen wearing luxurious gowns while in the company of the gods. The ceiling of the burial chamber has a fantastic astronomical ceiling of gold stars on blue, representing the heavens. Extensive restoration has restored the artwork to its original glowing colors.

The other three tombs that can be visited are all fairly small, consisting of a short corridor that leads to one or two chambers, but they are richly decorated with colored reliefs.

The Tomb of Amenherkhepshef belonged to the appointed heir of the throne, who died young, before he could succeed his father, Ramesses III. Scenes on the walls show the prince and his father paying homage to the gods of the underworld.

The Tomb of Khaemwese belongs to another son of Ramesses III, and again, the pair are depicted in the company of various gods and goddesses.

The other tomb open to visitors is that of Queen Titi, who was married to one of the later Ramesside kings.

Tombs of the Nobles

Gurna, west bank

Less famous than the royal tombs in the Valley of the Kings are the more than 400 small tombs collectively known as the Tombs of the Nobles, which dot the hills behind the Ramesseum. They belong to nonroyals, such as governors, mayors, and scribes.

Because of the poor quality of the limestone here, there are few carved reliefs, but the tombs are extensively painted with scenes that provide an insight into everyday life in ancient Egypt.

Some of the finest tombs on the site are those belonging to Sennefer and Rekhmire. Sennefer was a mayor of Thebes and Overseer of the Granaries and Fields, Gardens, and Cattle of Amen. Reflecting this latter role, the ceiling of his tomb is covered with a tangle of painted vines, heavy with grapes.

Rekhmire was a vizier (chief advisor) during the reigns of Tuthmosis III and Amenhotep II, during which time the Egyptian empire was expanding. One wall of his tomb shows him accepting tribute from foreign countries, including gifts of animals: baboons, monkeys, and a giraffe from Nubia, as well as a bear from Syria. The Tomb of Nakht contains some of the best-known Egyptian tomb paintings, among them a group of three female musicians: one playing the lute, one a harp, and another a type of wind instrument.

△ The Tombs of the Nobles necropolis on the west bank, Thebes

Valley of the Kings

West bank

This isolated, arid valley in the steep-sided, rocky Theban Hills, dominated by the pyramid-shaped peak of El-Qurn (The Horn), was the burial site of choice for the kings of the New Kingdom.

Their tombs were designed to resemble the underworld, with a long, sloping corridor descending into either an antechamber or a series of pillared halls, ending in a burial chamber. No two tombs are exactly the same, although they share common features. Early tombs have a right-angled plan and later tombs one straight axis.

To assist them in the afterlife, kings decorated their tombs with symbolic depictions of the journey that they would take through the underworld and ritual paintings. In the earliest tombs, only the burial chamber was decorated, but later, the wall paintings were extended into the other rooms and corridors. Builders attempted to hide the entrances to the tombs but, despite their best efforts, tomb robbers still discovered them and looted almost all of them.

To date, 62 tombs have been discovered in the valley, but not all of them belong to kings. Each has been assigned a KV (Kings' Valley) number, reflecting the sequence in which it was found. Not all of the tombs are open to the public.

Tomb of Tutankhamen

This is the most visited tomb in the valley, as it is the only one that was discovered with all its contents intact. However, almost all of the treasures were taken to Cairo, where they can be seen at the Grand Egyptian Museum, along with a full-size replica of the tomb as it was when Howard Carter first cleared his way inside. What remains in the valley is a small and, for the most part, undecorated tomb—many scholars believe that it was originally built for a nonroyal. The quartzite sarcophagus can still be seen and the body is now displayed in a modern case in the tomb.

Other tombs

The longest, deepest, and most lavishly decorated tomb in the valley is the Tomb of Seti I [KV 17]. It burrows some 450 ft (137 m) down into the hillside through a series of steeply descending corridors and chambers. It contains well-preserved reliefs in all but two of its 11 chambers and side rooms. Wall paintings in the lower corridor depict the Opening of the Mouth ceremony, in which the king's soul was reawakened after death and his senses restored.

At the bottom of the passage is a six-pillared burial chamber with a vaulted ceiling showing the constellations and a line-up of the gods and goddesses.

A very long tunnel leads from this chamber deeper into the hillside, but it was never finished.

△ Stairs leading to the entrance of a royal tomb in the Valley of the Kings

△ The burial chamber of Tukankhamen's tomb, with its quartzite sarcophagus

The Tomb of Horemheb [KV 57] was the first to introduce bas-reliefs, in which the figures were carved out before being painted, as opposed to the earlier method of applying the paint straight to the wall.

Many of the figures remain unfinished—some were just roughly sketched out, while others were partly incised into the rock by a sculptor, ready for painting, which for some reason never took place.

The Tomb of Tuthmosis III [KV 34] predates those of Horemheb and Seti, and its decoration is far less elaborate: the figures adorning its walls are like stick figures. His tomb is hard to reach, as it has an entrance high above the valley floor designed to deter thieves, which it failed to do.

The Tomb of Amenhotep II [KV 35] is decorated in similar style to that of Tuthmosis III, but the complex is on a larger scale. In one of the small annexes off the unusual, split-level burial chamber, archaeologists found nine royal mummies.

Temple of Seti I

West bank

The grand mortuary temple of Seti I, which was completed by his son Ramesses II, was one of the major monuments of western Thebes. The temple's location, set away from the main tourist trail, means it receives relatively few visitors. Although the pylons and surrounding buildings are in ruins, the hypostyle hall, sanctuary, and antechambers at the heart of the temple are well preserved. There are also several reliefs that offer superb examples of New Kingdom art.

△ The Temple of Seti I on the west bank, with the Theban Hills beyond

Upper Egypt and Lower Nubia

The town of Aswan, beside the First Cataract, marked the southern border of ancient Egypt for much of its history. For long periods, however, Egyptian rule extended much farther.

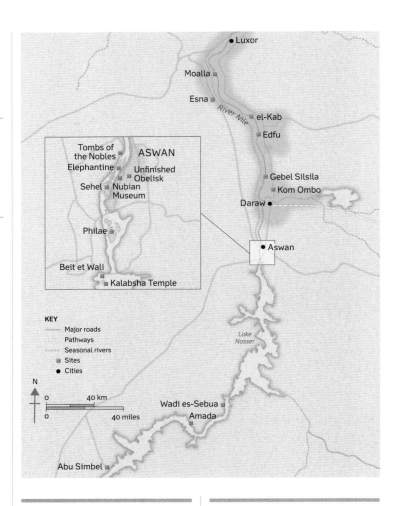

Moalla

21 miles (33 km) south of Luxor

The desert cemetery of Moalla contains the rock-cut tombs of the officials who were based at the town of Hefat during the First Intermediate Period. The largest and most famous of these is the decorated tomb of Ankhtify, who ruled much of southern Egypt at this time.

Esna

33 miles (54 km) south of Luxor

A busy market town on the west bank of the Nile, Esna is the site of the Greco-Roman Period Temple of Khnum. It was raised on the site of an earlier temple built by Tuthmosis III. Both of the temples were dedicated to the ram-headed god Khnum, who, according to one of the ancient Egyptian creation myths, molded humankind out of clay.

Over time, the temple was buried under silt that was deposited by the annual Nile floods, and the present-day town was built on top of it. Only the hypostyle hall, which was built during the reign of the Roman emperor Claudius (41–54 CE), has survived. Its roof is still intact and is at the same level as the foundations of the houses surrounding it. The ceiling of the hall displays astronomical scenes.

△ Painting of Edfu Temple, David Roberts, c.1847

el-Kab

50 miles (80 km) south of Luxor

This is the site of the former city of Nekheb, which stood across the river from the city of Hierakonpolis. Nekheb dates back to the Early Dynastic Period but rose to prominence in the New Kingdom. Its most notable feature today is the mudbrick city wall around it. Within the wall are the remains of a temple dedicated to Thoth, built by Ramesses II, and the Temple of Nekhbet, built during the Late Period. A nearby necropolis has some important New Kingdom tombs, including that of Ahmose, whose engagement in battles against the Hyksos are recorded in wall texts.

Edfu

71 miles (115 km) south of Luxor

Halfway between Luxor and Aswan, Edfu is the largest and best-preserved Greco-Roman temple in Egypt. With its succession of increasingly small spaces, culminating in the darkened, innermost Sanctuary of Horus, it gives visitors a good sense of how these ancient monuments might originally have been experienced. The temple was begun by Ptolemy III Euergetes I on the site of an earlier temple and completed by Ptolemy XII Neos Dionysos, the father of Cleopatra VII. It is entered by way of an almost intact great pylon, guarded by two great statues of Horus as a falcon. This leads to a large, colonnaded court and two hypostyle halls before reaching the inner sanctuaries, where there is a series of chapels with fine reliefs.

Gebel Silsila

43 miles (70 km) north of Aswan

South of Edfu, the Nile narrows as it forces its way between two sandstone cliffs. The rock here was quarried to provide the raw material for many of ancient Egypt's buildings.

The former quarries still bear clear masons' marks, as well as carved inscriptions. There are also several small chapels and shrines, including the Speos of Horemheb, a rock-cut chapel with a sanctuary containing seven statues, including those of Horemheb and the god Amen. The walls are covered in numerous reliefs.

Kom Ombo

25 miles (40 km) north of Aswan

Located on an arid bluff overlooking the River Nile, the temple at Kom Ombo has an unusual symmetrical layout— there are twin entrances, halls, and sanctuaries. This is because the temple was dedicated to two gods: the crocodile god Sobek and the falcon god Haroeris (Horus the Elder).

Ptolemy VI Philometor began work on the temple, and Ptolemy XII Neos Dionysos mostly completed it. Roman emperor Augustus added the entrance pylon. The Crocodile Museum nearby has a collection of around 40 mummified crocodiles, along with crocodile coffins and statues depicting Sobek. Many of the mummies came from the nearby necropolis of El-Shatb, south of the present-day town of Kom Ombo.

△ The entrance of Kom Ombo Temple, dedicated to the gods Sobek and Haroeris

△ Elephantine Island, with feluccas sailing nearby on the River Nile

Nearby is a rock-cut Nilometer, with stone stairs leading down to a small basin and walls calibrated to record the height of the annual flood, and so indicate the likely crop yield for the coming year.

Just north of the Nilometer is the Aswan Museum, which is home to a collection of artifacts found on digs in and around Aswan. These range from weapons and everyday utensils to statues, mummies, and sarcophagi.

Tombs of the Nobles

West bank of the River Nile at Aswan

The cliffs on the west bank of the River Nile, across from central Aswan, are pockmarked with the rock-cut Tombs of the Nobles. (In Arabic, the site is known as Qubbet el-Hawa.)

Dating from the Old and Middle Kingdoms, the tombs have a simple layout of an entrance hall, a pillared antechamber, and a corridor leading to a burial chamber. Many of the tombs are decorated with scenes of everyday life.

The largest and best preserved of these is the Tomb of Prince Sarenput II, governor of southern Egypt during the 12th Dynasty. A six-pillared entrance hall leads into the burial chamber, which is decorated with paintings of the prince and his son hunting and fishing.

The tombs of Mekhu, a noble from the 6th Dynasty who was murdered while on a military expedition in Nubia, and his son Sabni are crudely decorated with funeral and family scenes. The Tomb of Sarenput I, Guardian of the South during the 12th Dynasty and grandfather of Sarenput II, contains charming wall paintings that depict him with his family and dogs.

Elephantine Island

The River Nile at Aswan

Known as Abu or Yebu (elephant) in ancient times, this island on the River Nile is the oldest inhabited part of Aswan. Settlers arrived as far back as the Early Dynastic Period, when a fortress existed here guarding Egypt's southern border. The island was also the cult center of the ram-headed god Khnum, who was believed to control the flooding of the Nile. The ruins of the ancient settlement cover the southern tip of the island and include the partially reconstructed Temple of Khnum. The surviving structure dates from the Ptolemaic Period, but it stands on the site of much earlier temples—there are references to a Temple of Khnum on the island in the 3rd Dynasty. There are also the remains of a temple to Satet, Khnum's female counterpart, and a chapel of the local "saint" Heka-ib.

Nubian Museum

0.6 miles (1 km) south of central Aswan

This museum is dedicated to the history and culture of Nubia, the area between Aswan and Khartoum in present-day Sudan. Nubia was controlled by Egyptian kings. At the end of the Third Intermediate Period, Egypt was ruled by a Nubian dynasty.

The exhibits are displayed on three floors in a beautiful, purpose-built building that is inspired by traditional Nubian architecture. Highlights include statues from the 25th (Nubian) Dynasty and pottery bowls that date back 6,000 years. There are

△ The Nubian Museum at Aswan

also displays documenting the massive UNESCO rescue effort to move Nubia's monuments, notably the temple at Abu Simbel, away from the rising waters of Lake Nasser after the Aswan High Dam was built.

Unfinished obelisk

1 mile (1.5 km) south of central Aswan

Quarries in the vicinity of Aswan supplied some of the granite used to make ancient Egyptian statues, as well as adornments for temples, burial chambers, and other structures.

In one of these quarries lies an obelisk with three sides of its shaft almost completed. As the obelisk was being removed from the ground, the masons discovered a flaw in the rock, so they abandoned it, still partly attached to the surrounding rock. If it had been completed, it would have weighed a staggering 1,200 tons (1,090 tonnes) and stood 138 ft (42 m) high. This is nearly one-third larger than any other Egyptian obelisk ever erected. It is thought that the obelisk dates from the reign of Hatshepsut.

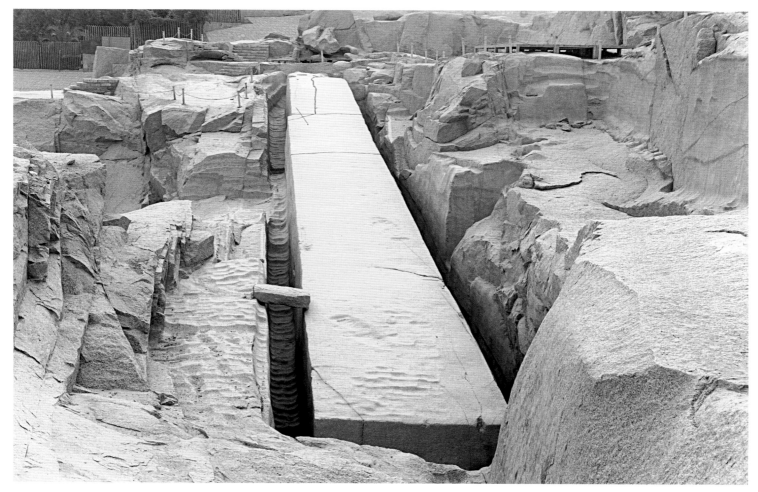

△ Partially quarried obelisk in an ancient Aswan quarry

△ Glimpse of the River Nile through a doorway at the Temple of Isis, Philae, on Agilika Island

Sehel Island

2 miles (3 km) south of Aswan

Sehel is a large island halfway between the town of Aswan and the old Aswan Dam. In ancient times, it was the site of a temple to Anukis (Anuket), the patron deity of the River Nile and consort of Khnum. The island was also used as a quarry for granite, and there are many inscriptions on boulders and cliffs at the southern end of it, mostly dating to the 18th and 19th Dynasties.

The most famous of the inscriptions is known as the Famine Stela. It records a seven-year period of drought and famine during the reign of Djoser in the Old Kingdom, but Egyptologists believe that the stela was actually inscribed about 2,500 years later, during the Ptolemaic Period.

Philae

Agilika Island, 4 miles (6 km) south of Aswan

Philae was the cult center of the goddess Isis, who, together with her husband Osiris, became one of the most important and widely worshipped Egyptian deities from the Late Period onward. Her temple on the island of Philae was one of the last ones built in traditional Egyptian style.

The earliest buildings on the site were probably constructed during the time of Taharqa of the 25th Dynasty, and the earliest surviving structures date from the reign of Nectanebo I of the 30th Dynasty. Most of what can be seen today, however, dates from the Ptolemaic Period, when the island became an important pilgrimage destination not

△ The relocated Temple of Kalabsha, built during the reign of Emperor Augustus

only for Egyptians, but for Isis worshippers from all around the Mediterranean.

When the High Dam was built in the 1960s, the rising waters of Lake Nasser threatened to submerge the island temple completely, so it was dismantled and moved to the higher ground of nearby Agilika Island. The UNESCO-led project took from 1972 to 1980 to complete, during which time Agilika was landscaped to look like Philae.

Boats drop visitors at the landing at the southern tip of the island, near the oldest building, the Kiosk of Nectanebo. From there, a long courtyard flanked by colonnades leads to the main Temple of Isis, built mainly in the late Ptolemaic and early Roman Periods.

The temple's Gate of Hadrian was inscribed in 394 CE with Egypt's last hieroglyphics. Other buildings on the island include the Temple of Hathor, which is decorated with reliefs of musicians, and the unfinished

columned pavilion by the water's edge known as the Kiosk of Trajan. The site also includes the remains of a church, which shows that Philae continued to be a significant center of Christian worship after people had ceased to worship the ancient Egyptian gods.

Kalabsha

West of the Aswan High Dam

Like nearby Philae, the Temple of Kalabsha is another Ptolemaic and Roman building that mimics earlier ancient Egyptian ones. The construction of the temple began in the late Ptolemaic Period and was completed during the reign of the Roman Emperor Augustus in the 1st century CE.

Dedicated to the Nubian fertility god Marul (Mandulis), the temple is approached by an imposing causeway leading up from the water's edge to the first pylon. Beyond is a colonnaded

court and a roofless hypostyle hall noted for its ornate column capitals and its reliefs, which show various kings and emperors in the presence of gods.

Close to the Temple of Kalabsha is the Temple of Beit el-Wali, which is dedicated to the god Amen. Built during the reign of Ramesses II, it is a small temple cut into the rock and fronted by a brick pylon and stone-floored forecourt. On the walls of the forecourt, Ramesses II is shown smiting his enemies, which include Nubians, Libyans, and Syrians. Inside the temple, there is simply an antechamber and a sanctuary. The latter contains a niche with a triad statue cut out of the rock that depicts Ramesses II between two deities.

Both Kalabsha and Beit el-Wali (along with the battered remains of the Roman Kiosk of Kertassi) were moved to this site near the Aswan High Dam in a German-funded rescue operation after the flooding of Nubia.

△ Entrance to the avenue of sphinxes at Wadi es-Sebua

including those found on the sanctuary's back wall, which depict Amenhotep II killing Syrian prisoners of war.

A short distance away is the rock-cut Temple of Derr, which was built during the time of Ramesses II. Its pylon and court are gone, but a ruined pillar hall remains, with reliefs depicting the Nubian campaigns of the warrior king. Also nearby is another rock-cut tomb, which belonged to Pennut, the viceroy of northern Nubia under Ramesses VI. The tomb is decorated with scenes of its owner's life.

Wadi es-Sebua

87 miles (140 km) south of the Aswan High Dam

The Temple of Ramesses II at Wadi es-Sebua is memorable for its striking location on the lonely desert shores of Lake Nasser. It is approached by an avenue of sphinxes that lend their name to the site: Wadi es-Sebua means "Valley of Lions."

Beyond an entrance pylon is a courtyard with 10 statues of Ramesses II, and, beyond that, a 12-pillared hall and a sanctuary that is partly carved into the rock. The sanctuary was later converted into a Christian church, and faint images of saints can be seen over the original reliefs.

A little farther north, in the 3rd century BCE, the Nubian king Arkamani began the Temple of Dakka, which was added to in the Ptolemaic and Roman Periods. It was dedicated to Thoth and has a large pylon, still in excellent condition, which can

be ascended for views of the surrounding landscape. Also in the vicinity is the small Temple of Maharraka, which dates from the Roman Period. It is dedicated to Isis and Serapis, the Alexandrian god. All that remains now is the hypostyle hall. The temples were originally located elsewhere and were moved here when Lake Nasser rose after the construction of the Aswan High Dam.

Amada

115 miles (185 km) south of the Aswan High Dam

Constructed during the reigns of Tuthmosis III and Amenhotep II, the Temple of Amada is the oldest surviving monument on Lake Nasser. It is dedicated to the gods Amen-Ra and Ra-Horakhty. The temple has some of the best-preserved reliefs in Nubia,

Abu Simbel

174 miles (280 km) south of Aswan

Carved out of a solid cliff in the 13th century BCE, the Great Temple of Ramesses II and the adjacent smaller Temple of Hathor are second possibly only to the Pyramids of Giza in terms of ancient Egyptian spectacle.

Although dedicated to Amen, Ptah, and Ra-Horakhty, the Great Temple is really all about Ramesses II, whose four colossal

△ The Temple of Amada, the oldest surviving temple in Nubia

enthroned statues—each 108 ft (33 m) high—proclaim the might of the king to anyone approaching from the south.

A doorway between the statues leads to a hypostyle hall with eight columns, each fronted by an Osiride statue of Ramesses II. Another antechamber with four columns is decorated with scenes of Ramesses II and his wife Nefertari making offerings to the gods. The innermost part of the temple is the sanctuary in which Ramesses II sits in the company of Amen, Ptah, and Ra-Horakhty. On two days every year, the sun penetrates the building and shines on these four statues that were once covered in gold.

Beside his Great Temple, Ramesses also had a smaller temple dedicated to the goddess Hathor carved out of the cliff face. The front of it is lined with six 30 ft (10 m) statues of Ramesses II and Nefertari.

△ Entrance to the Great Temple of Ramesses II and colossi at Abu Simbel

Glossary

A

aegis A protective necklace bearing the head of a deity.

Akhet The first season of the Egyptian calendar when the River Nile was flooded (*see* inundation).

Amarna The modern name for the city founded by Akhenaten. It also refers to aspects of culture during his reign.

Amarna Period (1352–1323 BCE) An era in the late-18th Dynasty when the capital of Egypt was moved to Akhetaten, a site now referred to as Amarna. The period is associated with a radical departure in religious and artistic ideas.

amulet A magical pendant with protective properties, worn by the living and the dead.

animal cult The worshipping of a deity through a representative animal.

ankh The hieroglyphic symbol for "life" in the shape of a looped cross.

antechamber A small room that leads to a larger room.

anthropoid In Egyptology, this refers to a coffin shaped to resemble a human.

Apis A sacred bull believed to be the living representative of the god Ptah.

apotropaic The magical ability to ward off harm and evil.

archaism A style of art, architecture, and writing that imitates older works. This became a cultural trend during the 25th and 26th Dynasties.

atef crown The feathered white crown of the god Osiris.

Aten The god promoted by King Akhenaten, depicted as solar disk emitting rays that end in hands.

B

ba The part of the soul believed to make an individual unique. In art, it was often represented by a human-headed bird.

barque A ceremonial boat used to transport statues of deities.

Book of the Dead A collection of spells intended to enable the soul of the deceased to navigate the afterlife.

C

calcite The crystalline form of limestone.

canopic jars Four containers used to store the internal organs (the stomach, lungs, liver, and intestines) during the mummification process (*see* mummification).

cartonnage A material made from layers of linen or papyrus covered with plaster.

cartouche An oval ring drawn around the name of a king or a queen.

Cataracts Six outcrops of rock that form rapids on the River Nile. The first one is at Aswan.

causeway A paved pathway, often linking a pyramid to a temple or a canal.

cenotaph A ceremonial tomb that is not built for burial.

Coffin Texts Magic spells that are inscribed into the interior of a coffin.

colossus (pl. colossi) A statue that is larger than life-size.

cult A system of religious worship or ritual.

cuneiform A script used across the ancient Near East, distinguished by its wedge-shaped symbols.

D

Delta The triangular-shaped area of fertile land between Cairo and the Mediterranean Sea.

demotic A cursive script based on hieratic that was quick to write.

Deshret The name for the red crown of Lower Egypt.

Duat The underworld, which the sun god Ra traveled through every night.

dynasty A succession of rulers from related families.

E

Early Dynastic Period (c.3000–2686 BCE) The period in Egyptian history immediately following the first unification of Upper and Lower Egypt.

embalming The preservation of a dead body from decay using chemicals, perfumes, salts, and ointments (*see* mummification).

epithet A descriptive word or a phrase that identifies a specific attribute of a person, place, or thing. For example, the epithet of Ptolemy I was "Soter" (Savior).

F

faience A ceramic material made mainly from quartz and usually glazed blue or green.

false door A magical, inscribed door found in tombs, which the spirit of the deceased (*ka*) can travel through to receive funerary offerings.

Field of Reeds The Egyptian afterlife where the god Osiris rules. Ancient Egyptians considered it to be heavenly paradise—an idealized version of Egypt.

flax A flowering plant used for its textile fibers. It was often spun into linen cloth.

funerary offerings Goods such as bread, beer, and wine provided by mourners or magically, through pictures and inscriptions.

G

gezira The Arabic word for "island," often used to refer to islands in the River Nile.

God's Wife The religious title held by some royal women, indicating a connection to the god Amen.

Greco-Roman Period (332 BCE–395 CE) An era in the history of ancient Egypt when the country was ruled by Macedonian and Roman leaders, starting with Alexander the Great.

H

Hedjet The name for the white crown of Upper Egypt.

Hellenism The culture and ideas of ancient Greece.

Hellenistic Period (332–30 BCE) *see* Ptolemaic Period.

hieratic A cursive script derived from hieroglyphs and typically used for correspondence.

hieroglyphs A script of pictorial signs typically used for official inscriptions.

Hittites The people of an ancient nation located in present-day Turkey.

Hyksos The Semitic people who ruled Egypt during the Second Intermediate Period (*see* Intermediate Period).

hypostyle hall A pillared temple hall.

I

Intermediate Period An unsettled period of time without a king in charge of the whole of Egypt.

inundation The annual flooding of the River Nile from August to November (*see* Akhet).

K

ka The life force of a person formed at birth. After the person's death, the *ka* lived in the tomb of the deceased, where it was provided funerary offerings to eat. It was represented in art as a double of the deceased.

Kemet The ancient Egyptian name for Egypt meaning "Black Land." It refers to the mud deposited from the River Nile during the annual flooding (*see* inundation).

king list An ordered record of the kings of Egypt since the first unification of Upper and Lower Egypt.

kohl A black powder often used as eyeliner.

Kush An area to the south of Egypt, in present-day northern Sudan.

L

lapis lazuli A dark-blue semiprecious stone, which the Egyptians imported from present-day Afghanistan.

Late Period (664-332 BCE) The era that immediately followed the Third Intermediate Period when Egypt was ruled by its last native Egyptian rulers, as well as Persian kings (*see* Intermediate Period).

lector priest A priest responsible for reciting ritual texts.

Levant The ancient name for a region on the eastern coast of the Mediterranean Sea, which included present-day Jordan, Lebanon, Syria, Palestine, Israel, and parts of southern Turkey.

Lower Egypt The northern area of Egypt at the end of the River Nile; the land around the Delta.

Luxor A city on the eastern bank of the River Nile, which includes the site of the Temple of Karnak.

M

maat The concepts of order, truth, and justice. They are represented by a goddess of the same name.

mastaba A bench-shaped tomb with a flat roof and an underground burial chamber.

Memphis For most of the Dynastic Period, this city south of the Delta was the administrative capital.

menat necklace A broad, beaded necklace with a counterpoise to redistribute the weight.

Menes The mythical first king of unified Egypt.

Middle Egypt An area that is roughly south of the Faiyum and north of Asyut. The term often refers to sites surrounding Amarna and Beni Hasan.

Mitanni The area of northern Mesopotamia between the Tigris and Euphrates Rivers.

mortuary cult A group of people who provided funerary offerings.

mortuary priest A person appointed to provide funerary offerings, usually on a daily basis.

mortuary temple A temple erected for funerary offerings and worship of a deceased royal person. Mortuary temples were usually constructed close to the deceased's tomb.

mummification The process of preserving a corpse.

mummiform To resemble, or be in the shape of, a wrapped mummy.

mummy The corpse of a human or animal that has been preserved by either natural or artificial means.

N

Naqada A village near Luxor with a predynastic cemetery. The word also refers to a predynastic Egyptian culture, which is divided into three phases known as Naqada I–III.

natron A natural salt used to dehydrate the body during the mummification process.

necropolis The term can refer to any ancient Egyptian cemetery.

nemes A striped headscarf worn by kings.

nomarch The governor or ruler of a nome (*see* nome).

nome An administrative area of Egypt, controlled by a nomarch (*see* nomarch).

Nubia The region south of Aswan, in present-day southern Egypt and northern Sudan.

O

obelisk A tall, square-based stone with a pyramidal top that symbolizes the sun's rays and was often erected at the entrance of a temple.

Opening of the Mouth A ritual performed on a mummy before burial. The priest releases the *ka* from the body, magically restoring its senses (*see* ka).

ostracon (pl. ostraca) A fragment of pottery or stone upon which people drew or wrote.

P

papyrus (pl. papyri) A writing material made from the stalks of a papyrus plant.

pectoral A jeweled ornament worn as a pendant around the neck.

Peret The second season in the Egyptian calendar when the crops were planted and grew.

peristyle court An open court with columns.

pharaoh The title of a king, meaning the "great house."

Predynastic Period (c.4400 BCE– c.3000 CE) The era before the unification of Egypt in 3000 BCE. It predated the dynasties of Egyptian kings.

Ptolemaic Period (332–30 BCE) An era during the Greco-Roman Period when Egypt was ruled by Macedonian kings, named after the 15 kings who took the name Ptolemy during this period (*see* Greco-Roman Period).

Punt The ancient Egyptian name for a land in eastern Africa. The Egyptians sent expeditions there to obtain goods such as incense, ebony, and animal skins.

pylon In Egyptology, this refers to the monumental entrance to a temple.

pyramid A tomb with a square base and four sloping sides, built to hold the mummified body of a king.

Pyramid Texts The magical spells inscribed on the interior walls of Old Kingdom pyramids.

pyramid town A village built for pyramid workers.

R

Ramesseum The mortuary temple of Ramesses II on the west bank of Thebes.

Ramesside Period (1295–1069 BCE) An era that lasted throughout the 19th and 20th Dynasties of ancient Egypt, named after the 11 kings who took the name Ramesses during this period.

registers In ancient Egyptian art, these are horizontal lines that separate the different scenes of an artwork and provide a "ground" for the figures.

relief A carving technique in which pictures are cut into a flat surface or raised out of a surface with the background cut away.

reserve head A stone carving of a head that was placed in the burial shaft of a deceased's tomb. There is no record of what its purpose was.

Roman Period (30 BCE–395 BCE) The era when Egypt was a province of the Roman Empire. It followed Octavian's victory over the forces of Mark Antony and Cleopatra VII at Actium in 30 BCE.

S

Saite Period (664–525 BCE) An era that lasted throughout the 26th Dynasty of ancient Egypt, when the capital of Egypt was moved to Sais.

sarcophagus A stone container for the coffin and/or mummy of the deceased.

scarab A dung beetle that the ancient Egyptians believed was sacred and associated with rebirth.

Sea-Peoples An alliance of seafaring tribes that invaded Egypt during the Ramesside Period.

Sed **festival** A royal jubilee or festival celebrating the king after 30 years of rule.

senet A popular board game from ancient Egypt, played on a board of 30 squares.

sepulchre A building or room, cut into rock, in which a dead person is buried.

serapeum A temple dedicated to the god Serapis. It is also the burial place for Apis bulls at Saqqara (*see* Apis).

serdab A walled-up chamber in a tomb made to contain a statue of the deceased.

serekh A rectangular panel containing the king's name, used in the Early Dynastic Period.

shabti A magical servant figurine believed to work on behalf of the deceased in the Field of Reeds.

Shemu The summer and third season in the Egyptian calendar, after the crops were harvested.

side-lock A distinctive hairstyle worn by children.

Sinai A peninsula in northeast Egypt, used by the Ancient Egyptians as a source for copper and turquoise and as a passage to the Levant.

sistrum A rattlelike instrument.

Sm-**priest** A senior priest who was responsible for reciting the Opening of the Mouth ritual.

solar boat The mythical boat in which the sun god Ra and his companions travel the sky, providing light to the world.

Sons of Horus The four deities (Imsety, Hapy, Duamutef, and Qebehsenuef) who protected the organs in the four canopic jars (*see* canopic jars).

soul house A miniature model dwelling placed in the tomb of its dead owner for use in the afterlife.

sphinx A creature with a lion's body and human head, often depicting a king.

stela (pl. stelae) An inscribed stone or wooden slab.

swnw The ancient Egyptian word for "doctor."

T

Thebes The religious capital of Egypt during the New Kingdom, located in present-day Luxor.

tomb model A wooden figure or set to be placed in a tomb as a funerary offering.

tumulus (pl. tumuli) An artificial mound built over a grave.

U

udjat eye (or wedjat eye) A protective symbol representing the eye of the god Horus.

unification In Egyptology, this refers to the merger of Upper and Lower Egypt into one kingdom, Egypt.

Unification Period (c.3000–2686 BCE) *see* Early Dynastic Period.

Upper Egypt The south of Egypt. The term sometimes includes Middle Egypt.

uraeus A depiction of a rearing cobra, worn on crowns or royal headdresses.

V

Valley of the Kings The burial site, used during the New Kingdom, that contained the royal tombs of the kings in Thebes.

Valley of the Queens The burial site of queens and royal children of the 19th and 20th Dynasties in Thebes.

vizier The highest official in ancient Egyptian government.

W

wadi A term for a dried-up river bed, often used to refer to a valley.

Ways of Horus An ancient road that lined Egypt with the Levant (*see* Levant).

Weighing of the Heart A ceremony in the *Duat* in which the deceased's heart was weighed against a single feather to see if they were worthy of entering the Field of Reeds.

Window of Appearances A covered balcony in a royal palace where the king and his family would appear before the public.

Index

Acknowledgments

DK would like to thank the following for their help with this book:
Rose Blackett-Ord for editorial assistance: Helen Peters for the index; Katie Cavanagh for design assistance; Daksheeta Pattni for secondary artworks; Peter Bull Art Studio for CGI artworks of Buhen Fortress, Khufu's pyramid, House of Ranefer, Tomb of Tutankhamen, and Deir el-Medina; Sonia Charbonnier for DTP assistance; Steve Crozier and Tom Morse for creative technical support; Simon Mumford for cartographic advice; Chhavi Nagpal, Devangana Ojha, and Tina Jindal for editorial assistance: Vikas Sachdeva for design assistance; DTP designer Anita Yadav; Picture Research Coordinator Sumita Khatwani; Jackets Editorial Coordinator Priyanka Sharma and Managing Jackets Editor Saloni Singh.

Museum. All rights reserved. **231** © **The Metropolitan Museum of Art:** Purchase, Fletcher Fund and The Guide Foundation Inc. Gift, 1966 (r). **Museo Egizio, Torino. 232-233** Peter Bull Art Studio. **232** © **The Trustees of the British Museum. All rights reserved. 233 Alamy Stock Photo:** Frederic Reglain (br). **Peter Bull Art Studio. 234 Museo Egizio, Torino:** Inv. Cat. 1592 / CC License (cl, ca, bc). **Steven Snape. 234-235 Getty Images:** De Agostini / DEA / G. Dagli Orti (c). **235** © **The Trustees of the British Museum. All rights reserved. Museo Egizio, Torino:** Inv. Cat. 1521 / CC License (br, ca, cla). **236 Getty Images:** De Agostini / DEA / G. Dagli Orti (b). © **The Metropolitan Museum of Art:** Funds from various donors, 1886 (tr). **237** © **The Metropolitan Museum of Art:** Funds from various donors, 1886 (b). **238 Archives scientifiques du CFEETK:** (bl). © **The Metropolitan Museum of Art:** Rogers Fund, 1933 (c). **239 Bridgeman Images:** Fitzwilliam Museum / Fitzwilliam Museum, University of Cambridge, UK (tr). **Sandro Vannini / Laboratoriorosso. 240** © **The Trustees of the British Museum. All rights reserved. 240-241 Getty Images:** De Agostini / DEA / ICAS94 (b). **241 Steven Snape. Sandro Vannini / Laboratoriorosso. 242 Photo Scala, Florence:** RMN-Grand Palais / Louvre / Georges Poncet (bc). **Sandro Vannini / Laboratoriorosso. 243** © **The Trustees of the British Museum. All rights reserved. Museo Egizio, Torino. 244 Sandro Vannini / Laboratoriorosso. 245 Sandro Vannini / Laboratoriorosso:** The Egyptian Museum, Cairo (l, br). **246 akg-images:** Erich Lessing (l). **Bridgeman Images:** Brooklyn Museum of Art / Gift of the Egyptian Exploration Society (br). © **The Trustees of the British Museum. All rights reserved. The University of Manchester:** (tr). **The Walters Art Museum, Baltimore:** (bl). **Sandro Vannini / Laboratoriorosso:** The Egyptian Museum, Cairo (bc). **247 Bridgeman Images:** Fitzwilliam Museum (tc). **Brooklyn Museum:** Charles Edwin Wilbour Fund, 37.51E / CC BY / Gavin Ashworth (c). © **The Metropolitan Museum of Art:** Anonymous Gift, 1931 (tr). **Museo Egizio, Torino:** Inv. Cat. 7052 / CC License (tl, cr, b). **248 Sandro Vannini / Laboratoriorosso:** The Egyptian Museum, Cairo. **250** © **The Metropolitan Museum of Art:** Purchase, Edward S. Harkness Gift, 1926 (bl). **251 Alamy Stock Photo:** Magica (br). **Sandro Vannini / Laboratoriorosso. 252 Bridgeman Images:** Brooklyn Museum of Art / Charles Edwin Wilbour Fund (bc). **252-253 Photo Scala, Florence:** RMN-Grand Palais / Louvre / Hervé Lewandowski (c). **253 Sandro Vannini / Laboratoriorosso. 254 Alamy Stock Photo:** agefotostock / J.D. Dallet (cla). **Sandro Vannini / Laboratoriorosso:** The Egyptian Museum, Cairo (tr). **254-255 Sandro Vannini / Laboratoriorosso:** The Egyptian Museum, Cairo (b). **255 Sandro Vannini / Laboratoriorosso:** The Egyptian Museum, Cairo (c). **256** © **The Metropolitan Museum of Art:** Gift of Joseph Veach Noble, 1988 (bc); Gift of Theodore M. Davis, 1910 (ftl); Theodore M. Davis Collection, Bequest of Theodore M. Davis, 1915 (tl); Theodore M. Davis Collection, Bequest of Theodore M. Davis, 1915 (tr); Gift of Theodore M. Davis, 1910 (ftr). **257 Getty Images:** Patrick Landmann / Cairo Museum (tr); Universal Images Group / Eye Ubiquitous / Jenny Pate (tl). © **The Metropolitan Museum of Art:** Rogers Fund and Edward S. Harkness Gift, 1940 (b). **258 Bridgeman Images:** Ashmolean Museum (bl). **259 Bridgeman Images:** Ashmolean Museum. **260-261** © **The Trustees of the British Museum. All rights reserved. 262** © **The Trustees of the British Museum. All rights reserved.** © **The Metropolitan Museum of Art:** Funds from various donors, 1886 (86.1.14, .18, .21, .28) (bl); Funds from various donors, 1886 (bc); Funds from various donors, 1886 (br); Funds from various donors, 1886 (fbr). **263** © **The Trustees of the British Museum. All rights reserved. Brooklyn Museum:** Gift of the Ernest Erickson Foundation, Inc, 86.226.21 / CC BY (tl, cr). © **The Metropolitan Museum of Art:** Gift of J. Pierpont Morgan, 1912 (fbl); Theodore M. Davis Collection, Bequest of Theodore M. Davis, 1915 (ftl); Rogers Fund, 1908 (bc). **264 Alamy Stock Photo:** Adam Eastland. **265** © **The Trustees of the British Museum. All rights reserved. The Cleveland Museum Of Art:** Purchase from the J. H. Wade Fund (bl). **Photo Scala, Florence:** bpk, Bildagentur fuer Kunst, Kultur und Geschichte, Berlin (tr). **266** © **The Trustees of the British Museum. All rights reserved. Photo Scala, Florence:** bpk, Bildagentur fuer Kunst, Kultur und Geschichte, Berlin / Jürgen Liepe (br). **267 Alamy Stock Photo:** agefotostock / Historical Views. **268 Alamy Stock Photo:** Magica (b). **Fine Arts Museums of San Francisco:** (c). **Photo Scala, Florence:** bpk, Bildagentur fuer Kunst, Kultur und Geschichte, Berlin / Juergen Liepe (tr). **269 The Cleveland Museum Of Art:** Gift of the Hanna Fund. **270 Getty Images:** iStock / membio (bl). **271 akg-images:** Erich Lessing (tc). © **The Metropolitan Museum of Art:** Rogers Fund, 1934 (r). **272 Photo Scala, Florence:** RMN-Grand Palais / Louvre / Hervé Lewandowski. **273** © **The Trustees of the British Museum. All rights reserved. Brooklyn Museum:** Gift of the Egypt Exploration Fund, 14.655a-b / CC BY (br). **274 Alamy Stock Photo:** Classic Image (bl). **Steven Snape. 275** © **The Trustees of the British Museum. All rights reserved. 276-277 Sandro Vannini / Laboratoriorosso:** The Egyptian Museum, Cairo. **278** © **The Metropolitan Museum of Art:** Gift of Mrs. Myron C. Taylor, 1938 (bl). **279 Alamy Stock Photo:** Images of Africa Photobank / David Keith Jones (tr); travelpixs (br). **Getty Images:** iStock / lbowmantravels (cr). **280** © **The Trustees of the British Museum. All rights reserved. Getty Images:** De Agostini / DEA / G. Nimatallah (b). **281** © **The Trustees of the British Museum. All rights reserved. Getty Images:** Hulton Archive / Heritage Images (tr). **282-283 Bridgeman Images:** Photograph © 2021 Museum of Fine Arts, Boston / Egypt Exploration Fund by subscription (t). **282** © **The Metropolitan Museum of Art:** Gift of Abby Aldrich Rockefeller, 1938 (bl). **283 akg-images:** Hervé Champollion (tr). **Photo Scala,**

Florence: RMN-Grand Palais / Louvre / Georges Poncet (bc). **284** © **The Trustees of the British Museum. All rights reserved. 285 Alamy Stock Photo:** eFesenko (cla). **286** © **The Metropolitan Museum of Art:** Gift of Darius Ogden Mills, 1904 (cl). **286-287 Getty Images:** iStock / Konstantin Aksenov (b). **287 Christoph Gerigk:** Franck Goddio / Hilti Foundation (br). **Getty Images:** De Agostini / DEA / G. Dagli Orti (t). **288 Getty Images:** De Agostini / DEA / G. Dagli Orti (cr). © **The Metropolitan Museum of Art:** Rogers Fund, 1965 (tl); Theodore M. Davis Collection, Bequest of Theodore M. Davis, 1915 (bl). **289 Alamy Stock Photo:** Album. **290 Alamy Stock Photo:** Jan Wlodarczyk (tr). **Getty Images:** Moment / skaman306 (bl). **291 Getty Images:** iStock / eleaner (tc); Moment / Nick Brundle Photography (b). **292-293 ALTAIR 4 MULTIMEDIA Srl. 292 123RF.com:** Jose Antonio Sanchez Romero (cl). **ALTAIR 4 MULTIMEDIA Srl. 293 Getty Images:** robertharding / Neale Clark (tc). **294 Alamy Stock Photo:** Mark Harmel (t). **295 Alamy Stock Photo:** www.BibleLandPictures.com (tr). **Getty Images:** De Agostini / DEA / A. De Gregorio (bl). **296-297 Sandro Vannini / Laboratoriorosso. 298 Getty Images:** De Agostini / DEA / S. Vannini. **299 Alamy Stock Photo:** A. Astes (bl). **Steven Snape. 300 Steven Snape. Yale University Art Gallery:** Lent by Yale Peabody Museum of Natural History, Barringer Collection, ANT.264259 (cla). **301** © **The Trustees of the British Museum. All rights reserved. 302** © **The Trustees of the British Museum. All rights reserved. 306 Sandro Vannini / Laboratoriorosso:** The Egyptian Museum, Cairo. **308 Sandro Vannini / Laboratoriorosso:** The Egyptian Museum, Cairo. **309 Getty Images:** De Agostini / DEA / G. Dagli Orti. **310 Steven Snape. 311 Bridgeman Images:** © Museum of Fine Arts, Boston / Harvard University / Boston Museum of Fine Arts Expedition. **312 Getty Images:** ullstein bild / Reinhard Dirscher. **313 Getty Images:** De Agostini / DEA / S. Vannini. **314** © **The Metropolitan Museum of Art:** Gift of Egypt Exploration Fund, 1907. **315 Alamy Stock Photo:** World History Archive. **316 Bridgeman Images:** Sandro Vannini. **317 Getty Images:** De Agostini / DEA / G. Dagli Orti. **318 Shutterstock. com:** Kharbine-Tapabor. **319 Sandro Vannini / Laboratoriorosso:** The Egyptian Museum, Cairo. **320 Getty Images:** iStock / mareandmare. **321 Getty Images:** Moment / Nick Brundle. **322 Sandro Vannini / Laboratoriorosso:** The Egyptian Museum, Cairo. **323 Getty Images:** Photodisc / Juergen Ritterbach (t). **324 akg-images:** Hervé Champollion. **325 Sandro Vannini / Laboratoriorosso. 326 Getty Images:** AFP (bl); Design Pics / Richard Maschmeyer (tr). **327 Sandro Vannini / Laboratoriorosso. 328 Getty Images:** Universal Images Group / MyLoupe. **329 Photo Scala, Florence:** Musee d'Archeologie Mediterraneenne, marseille / David Giancatarina. **330 Getty Images:** De Agostini / DEA / G. Nimatallah. **331 Getty Images:** Hulton Archive / The Print Collector. **332 Getty Images:** Universal Images Group / Leemage. **333 Steven Snape. 334 Sandro Vannini / Laboratoriorosso. 335 akg-images:** Andrea Jemolo. **336 Getty Images:** Universal Images Group / Universal History Archive. **337 Getty Images:** De Agostini / DEA / S.Vannini. **338** © **The Metropolitan Museum of Art:** Gift of Edward S. Harkness, 1918 (b); Purchase, Fletcher Fund and The Guide Foundation Inc. Gift, 1966 (tc). **339 akg-images:** François Guénet. **340** © **The Metropolitan Museum of Art:** Rogers Fund, 1930. **341 Alamy Stock Photo:** Peter Horree (tl); World History Archive (b). **342 Alamy Stock Photo:** www. BibleLandPictures.com. **343 Getty Images:** Hulton Fine Art Collection / Art Images (br). **344 Alamy Stock Photo:** Heritage Images / Werner Forman Archive / E. Strouhal. **345 Alamy Stock Photo:** Alain Guilleux. **346 Sandro Vannini / Laboratoriorosso. 347** © **The Trustees of the British Museum. All rights reserved. 348 Alamy Stock Photo:** Chris Deeney. **349 Bridgeman Images:** Mary Jelliffe. **350 Sandro Vannini / Laboratoriorosso. 351** © **The Metropolitan Museum of Art:** Gift of Egypt Exploration Fund, 1896. **352 Alamy Stock Photo:** Alain Guilleux. **353 Alamy Stock Photo:** Arpad Benedek. **354 Alamy Stock Photo:** Paul Vinten. **355 Alamy Stock Photo. 356** © **The Trustees of the British Museum. All rights reserved. 357 Bridgeman Images:** Ancient Art and Architecture Collection Ltd. (br). © **The Metropolitan Museum of Art:** Rogers Fund, 1958 (tl). **358 Alamy Stock Photo. 359 Getty Images:** De Agostini / DEA / G. Dagli Orti. **360 Getty Images:** Universal Images Group / Oneworld Picture / Stefan Lippmann. **361 Getty Images:** Universal Images Group / Werner Forman. **362 Getty Images:** AFP / Mohamed El-Shahed. **363 Alamy Stock Photo:** Reinhard Dirscherl. **364 Getty Images:** VCG / Corbis. **365 akg-images:** Erich Lessing. **366 Alamy Stock Photo:** Mike P Shepherd (t). **Getty Images:** De Agostini / DEA / G. Sioen (b). **367 Wallace Fung. 368 Alamy Stock Photo:** eFesenko. **369 Alamy Stock Photo:** World History Archive. **370 Getty Images:** Corbis / Fine Art Photographic Library. **371 Getty Images:** RooM / inigoarza. **372 123RF.com:** Mirko Kuzmanovic. **373 Alamy Stock Photo:** Peter Horree (b). **Getty Images:** Photodisc / Juergen Ritterbach (tr). **374 Alamy Stock Photo:** Design Pics Inc / Axiom Photographic. **375 Alamy Stock Photo:** Simon Evans. **376 Alamy Stock Photo:** Diego Fiore. **377 Getty Images:** Hulton Fine Art Collection / Art Images (t); Universal Images Group / Insights (br). **378 Getty Images:** Heritage Images / Historica Graphica Collection (bl). **379 Alamy Stock Photo:** Stig Alenäs. **380 Getty Images:** De Agostini / DEA / C. Sappa. **381 Alamy Stock Photo:** B. O'Kane (t). **Getty Images:** iStock / LuisPortugal (b). **382 Alamy Stock Photo:** eye35 stock. **383 Getty Images:** Jaroslav Frank. **384 akg-images:** Bildarchiv Steffens (b). **Getty Images:** De Agostini / DEA / A. Garozzo (t). **385 Getty Images:** iStock / PaulVinten

All other images © Dorling Kindersley

For further information see: www.dkimages.com